An Introduction To Philosophy: Ideas In Conflict

EDITED WITH INTRODUCTORY CHAPTERS
BY PETER Y. WINDT

West Publishing Company

St. Paul   New York   Los Angeles   San Francisco

Copy Editor: Ann Waters
Composition: Parkwood Composition Services, Inc.
Cover: © 1982 R. Hamilton Smith

Library of Congress Cataloging in Publication Data
Windt, Peter Y.
      An introduction to philosophy
      Text includes selections from Plato to the 20th century.
      Includes bibliographical references and index.
      1. Philosophy—Introduction—Addresses, essays, lectures.   I. Title.
BD21.W478   100   81-19649
ISBN 0-8299-0421-2   AACR2

FOR CAROLYN
AND FOR JETO

C O N T E N T S

CHAPTER 3

Analyzing Philosophical Discussion   49

CHAPTER 4

Freedom, Determinism, and Moral Responsibility   61

CHAPTER 5

Persons, Minds, and Bodies 159

CHAPTER 6

The Objectivity of Morals 217

CHAPTER 10

The Problem of Evil   451

CHAPTER 11

Perception and Knowledge of the Physical World   501

CHAPTER 12

The Rationality of Induction   555

APPENDIX I

Writing a Paper About Philosophy

APPENDIX II

Biographical Notes on the Authors

GLOSSARY

P R E F A C E

As is the case with many introductory texts, this book is based upon the gradual evolution over a number of years of materials employed in an introductory course in philosophy. I have tried to expand those materials to make them flexible enough to suit the interests and talents of a diverse group of instructors and the needs of a variety of students. The result is a text designed specifically for courses using a *problems approach* in what may be characterized loosely as the analytic tradition.

I take the fundamental aim of such a course to be acquainting the student with the character of philosophical puzzlement, and the character of the philosophical activity directed toward the resolution of that puzzlement. An important secondary aim is to prepare the student to read philosophical works independently, with at least a modicum of comprehension and critical consideration. The problems approach, as I conceive it, does not attempt to achieve these goals by *describing* philosophical activity to the student, but by inviting the student to *participate*. It is important to engage the student as much as possible to stir up genuine puzzlement about some philosophical issues, to promote empathy for a variety of viewpoints, and to encourage struggle with the difficulties encountered in developing and defending those viewpoints.

In such a course, the primary resource is the instructor, whose explanations, interpretations, critical comments, and dialogue with the students provides the model of what it is like to be engaged in philosophical work. The text serves as a collection of secondary resources which support the instructor's activity, rather than a self-sufficient discursive treatment of philosophical thought and method. It is this conception of the text as a collection of resources which has guided the formation of this book.

First, then, this text contains an anthology of readings, organized around nine major problems. It is somewhat, but not exactly, like several other available problems-oriented anthologies. I make no claim for completeness here. These are not *the* major problems of philosophy, nor do the individual selections represent all the important positions on each problem. I do claim that these problems are ones with which beginning students can become involved, and that they exhibit both the diversity and the interconnectedness typical of philosophical issues. To facilitate the student's engagement, each problem has been introduced in the form of a paradox—that is, as a set of mutually inconsistent statements, each of which is intuitively appealing and capable of a plausible defense. A brief afterword suggests some ways in which the problem may be significant for other theoretical or practical concerns the student may have.

My intention was to include substantially more than a one-semester or one-quarter course could employ. With the exception of the first problem (Chapter 4) the order in which problems appear in the text is not significant. Each has been presented as nearly as possible as an independent unit. One might follow the problem of freedom, determinism, and moral responsibility with a variety of combinations of issues. For example, chapters 4, 5, 11, 12, and 9 provide an emphasis on logic and epistemology. Ethical concerns are emphasized by choosing Chapters 4, 6, 7, 8 and 5 or 9. Methaphysical concerns dominate in the sequence of Chapters 4, 5, 6, 9, and 10. I prefer to use a diverse sampling of issues, typically Chapters 4, 12, 11, 9, and 10.

In addition to the anthology, a variety of materials have been included, all of them in response to interests or concerns which students frequently have expressed to me. These concerns include uncertainty about how to read and study the selections, unfamiliarity with the basics of critical reflection, and lack of a clear conception of the purposes served by student papers on philosophy. Consequently, I have included the following elements:

Chapter 1 presents a brief discussion of the philosophical enterprise. This is not a detailed or penetrating account of the nature of philosophy (I leave that task to the instructor who is inclined to take it up), but it should help students to acquire a rough idea of the sorts of things the authors of the selections and the instructor are trying to do and, thus, what the students themselves should be trying to do.

Chapter 2 makes several elementary observations about philosophical reasoning. It is *not* an introduction to logic, nor does it arm the student with all the critical tools necessary for the complete dissection and evaluation of the selections in the anthology. It is simply an attempt to give the student some conception of the character of organized standards of criticism and argument, as well as an attempt to reduce the number of elementary errors the student will commit in beginning interpretation and criticism.

In Chapter 3 a rather demanding method is sketched for reading and studying the selections. Students willing to make the effort usually find this method helpful.

Each of the first three selections in Chapter 4 is followed by a brief analysis which provides the student with a sample of the kinds of interpretive and critical thoughts which study of the selection might have suggested to a careful and critical reader. The purpose of these analyses is not to usurp or dictate the instructor's discussion of the selection but to help the student form a clearer notion of the goals at which study of the selections should aim. Review question at the end of each chapter provide a little further guidance of this kind.

An appendix has been included which offers some elementary suggestions about organizing a paper on a philosophical topic and then writing it. Hopefully, most instructors will not find it difficult to assign their favorite paper topics against the background of recommendations provided in this appendix.

Because students often express some curiosity about the authors of anthologized selections, brief biographical notes are included in a second appendix.

Finally, a glossary has been included in which several of the technical terms employed in philosophical literature are briefly explained.

Some may find conspicuous the omission of bibliographies for each of the chapters, as well as the minimal use of scholarly references. My experience suggests that students make little use of such features, and that they waste valuable space in an introductory text.

Comments will be received gratefully concerning the success or failure of any of these features, or additions or deletions which might improve the text.

There are many persons to whom I owe thanks. First, there are those thoughtful reviewers, all of whose comments (adverse or favorable) and suggestions about various drafts of the manuscript were illuminating and helpful: Professor Robert Brandom, University of Pittsburgh; Professor John H. Dreher, University of Southern California; Professor Ronald Epp, Memphis State University; Professor Tom Franks, Eastern Michigan University; Professor Sidney Gendin, Eastern Michigan University; Professor Jeffrie G. Murphy, University of Arizona; Professor Richard Richards, California State Polytechnic University; Professor Craig A. Staudenbaur, Michigan State University; Professor Bruce Vermazen, University of California; and Professor Mark B. Woodhouse, Georgia State University. Second, there is the congenial and helpful staff at West Publishing, without whose encouragement, suggestions, and incredible patience this book would never have reached production. And, third, I owe much to Florence Windt, who typed, proofread, and painstakingly untangled sentences to which no reader should have been subjected. Finally, I must acknowledge my debt to the many students whose questions, comments, and reactions have provided a testing ground for much of the material set forth here.

INTRODUCTION FOR STUDENTS

This book is designed for use in a beginning course in philosophy. But it does not attempt to survey the most important philosophical theories or the works of the best-known philosophers. Nor does it attempt to provide you with a mass of basic information about philosophy to commit to memory. In fact, except for the first two chapters, the book does not say much at all *about* philosophy.

Instead, the approach taken here is to *show* you what philosophy is like through the use of examples and through your own participation in philosophical activity. The readings in Chapters 4 through 12 are typical samples of work by philosophers on some of the issues which concern them. As you read and study these selections you should begin to form an idea of the sorts of problems which are philosophical ones, what philosophers try to achieve in dealing with these problems, and how they try to achieve it. And to help you "get the feel" of philosophical activity you will be encouraged to try your hand at working on the problems yourself, or at criticizing the views presented in some of the selections you read.

Of course, some guidance can make your reading and thinking more instructive. So, the first two chapters offer some remarks about philosophers, philosophy, philosophical problems, and the nature of philosophical reasoning. Chapter 3 suggests one way to organize your reading and study of the selections (something which gives many students trouble). Some review questions at the end of each chapter with selections have been provided to help you test your understanding of what you have read. And, finally, there is an appendix on writing papers about philosophical topics and a glossary of special terms which you will encounter in your reading. You should regard all these features as reference material to be consulted as you read and study the selections, or whenever else it might be helpful.

Philosophical thinking is hard work for most people, and that includes the trained philosophers who devote much of their lives to such thinking. Some of us find it enjoyable and rewarding hard work, others do not. But you will get through your beginning course more easily, find it less tiring, and learn more if you can develop some personal involvement with the problems you study. Ask yourself what stand you would take on each of the issues, and why you would take it. See if any of the readings clarify your position, or change it. With work and a little luck you may not only learn some of the things philosophers are trying to do and develop some useful critical skills, but you may develop and clarify some of your own ideas, too. If so, your work and experience with this material can be counted a success.

CHAPTER

1

About Philosophy and Philosophers

Throughout history, philosophy and philosophers have been regarded in a wide variety of ways by their contemporaries. In every age we find that some people have counted philosophers among the wisest and best human beings, while others have thought them to be foolish or wicked. Some have thought that philosophy provides the wisdom needed to guide one's life, while others have believed it to be impractical nonsense. Popular views of philosophy and philosophers are based on very slight contact with either, and such views usually amount to no more than hastily formed stereotypes. But even stereotypes are not *totally* disconnected from fact. Along with a substantial amount of misunderstanding, some of them contain a grain of truth.

Consider, for example, the following claims about philosophers:

1. Philosophers are impractical.

2. Philosophers are very intelligent.

3. Philosophers are all atheists.

4. Philosophers are all interested in religious belief.

5. Philosophers just like to argue.

6.   Philosophers are very good at dealing effectively with personal misfortune and adversity.

7.   Philosophers are interested in the meaning of life.

Most beginning philosophy students could add other popular stereotypes of philosophers to this list.

None of these stereotypes, however, is a better description of philosophers than of many other groups of people. For instance, some philosophers are, indeed, atheists, but others are agnostic, and still others believe in the existence of some deity. Or, again, for almost every kind of political position one can imagine, some philosopher can be found who is willing to defend that position. Some philosophers may have carefully worked out opinions about the significance of human life, but others have no interest at all in such things. In short, there is no special set of beliefs, opinions, or values which philosophers share. Neither is there a set of character traits which philosophers share. Some of them are extremely intelligent, some rather stupid. Some are athletic, or gifted artists, good mechanics, carpenters, successful in business; others are thoroughly inept at such things. A group of philosophers will exhibit the same kinds of weaknesses, strengths, interests, and other characteristics which any randomly selected group of people could be expected to show—*unless* they start to talk about philosophy. That is, the only special characteristic which philosophers have in common is their interest in philosophy. To know what makes one a philosopher, then, you must know what a philosopher does.

Popular stereotypes of philosophy itself also vary greatly. Some people think it is the study of the most basic truths about the universe and the human situation. Others consider philosophy as an attempt to formulate rules for the guidance of action. It is common, in this regard, to speak of one's philosophy of life—rules for the conduct of life—but we must not forget that people also talk of their philosophies of advertising, coaching, studying, or designing buildings. Indeed, whenever a little thought has gone into producing some principles for guiding some kind of activity, someone is likely to call that set of principles a philosophy. Still other stereotypes present philosophy as a kind of self-discipline, with which philosophers learn to confront their fate, and accept it without undue complaint or misery (this acceptance seems to be what many people mean by "being philosophical" about some unfortunate turn of events). The stereotypes mentioned so far are positive in character. To be called a philosopher or to have one's thoughts described as philosophical when these things are meant is to be given a compliment. But there are views of philosophy in which to be called a philosopher or to have one's thought described as philosophical is an insult. Some, for example, think of philosophy as pure speculation, in which one tries to imagine extravagant, wild theories; and some consider it mere quibbling over words and definitions.

Where are the grains of truth in all these stereotypes? This, of course, is to ask what philosophy really is, and that is the central question of this book. People think philosophically about a great number of things and with a variety of different goals in mind. We cannot expect a simple definition of such a complicated business. But we will present in this chapter a brief (and incomplete) description of some important features of philosophical thought, and in the following chapters you will find details, explanations, examples, and illustrations. Probably you will find that you have engaged in philosophical thought about philosophical problems without realizing it. And probably you will realize that some of what you had regarded as philosophical thinking really is not. With such realizations you will begin to develop a more accurate idea of the character of philosophical thought than the popular stereotypes.

THE RATIONAL PURSUIT OF UNDERSTANDING

Let us begin with this claim: *Philosophy is part of the rational pursuit of understanding*. As it stands, of course, the claim is quite vague. What is understanding, and how does one pursue it rationally? Which part of that pursuit is undertaken by philosophy? *What* is it that philosophy seeks to understand? Our portrait of philosophy will begin to emerge as we address these questions.

Rational Thinking

Thinking is involved in a great deal of what we do, including such things as composing music, making up a joke, naming a baby, daydreaming, designing a house, diagnosing a disease, making a mathematical calculation, and deciding what to have for lunch. Frequently, our thinking is directed toward a specific goal (as in designing a house, or diagnosing a disease), but sometimes (daydreaming) there may be no specific goal. If thinking is not directed toward some goal, then it makes no sense to say either that it has been successful or that it has been unsuccessful; but when it is directed toward a goal, we can measure the success of thinking in terms of whether the goal is achieved. For example, thought directed toward naming a baby succeeds if an acceptable name is produced and fails if no acceptable name is forthcoming. There can also be *degrees* of success in one's thinking. If thought is directed toward designing a house, and a merely adequate design results, then that thinking has been moderately successful, but not as successful as it would have been had a superior design resulted.

But not all *successful* goal-directed thinking is also *rational*—the two qualities are connected, but they are not the same. The rationality or irrationality of thinking is a matter of how it is done, rather than whether it happens to turn out successfully. Rational thought employs methods intended to protect the thinker from error, and to assure a sound basis for any conclusions drawn. Rational thought contrasts with such methods as guessing, using intuition, or depending upon superstition. If one's thinking were directed toward the diagnosis of a disease, for instance, it would be rational to consider all the facts about the patient's symptoms, what is known about the connections among such symptoms and various diseases, medical knowledge about the course of the diseases, and the chances that the patient has been exposed to them—that is, it is rational to consider evidence and be prepared to defend or prove the result of one's thought (the diagnosis). It would be irrational to decide what was wrong with the patient simply by guessing, flipping a coin (heads it's a cold, tails it's throat cancer) or deciding to believe what one hopes to be true. Nonetheless, sometimes it does happen that irrational thinking succeeds, or that rational thinking fails. We do sometimes make lucky guesses which are correct, even though irrational; and sometimes all the evidence we have is misleading, so that the best efforts we make to be rational lead us to the wrong conclusion.

Why, then, should we be concerned with rationality? There are two major reasons to consider here.   (1)   Those who believe that rational thought is superior to irrational thought are convinced that it offers a far more reliable approach than irrational methods. Although irrational methods may sometimes succeed, or rational methods may fail, the supporters of rationality maintain that in the long run rational thought will succeed far more frequently, and be much more reliable, than irrational thought.   (2)   Although irrational thought may, from time to time, succeed for some kinds of goals, there are some goals which never can be achieved with the use of irrational methods. For example, if one's goal is to give a *proof* of the truth of some belief, irrational methods could not succeed, even by accident. There can be no such thing as an *irrational proof.* Many of the goals of philosophical thinking are of this kind—they simply cannot be achieved, even accidentally, by irrational methods.

Knowing and Understanding

One goal of much philosophical thought is the acquisition of knowledge. This, by itself, would require the philosopher to be interested in rational methods of thought, for the difference between merely guessing something and *knowing* that it is so often amounts precisely to the difference between guessing and arriving at one's opinion rationally, through evidence and correct reasoning. But philosophers also are interested in a kind of understanding which involves more than simply acquiring knowledge, and rational thinking plays a central role in this kind of understanding.

To see what sort of understanding is meant here, consider this example: We may know that water boils at a lower temperature at high altitudes than it does at sea level, without *understanding* why it does. And there are various degrees of understanding possible. For instance, a person who knows that the air pressure is lower at high altitudes than at sea level, and that this accounts for the difference in boiling points at different altitudes, understands the phenomenon better than one who only knows that the boiling points are different. But such a person doesn't understand as well as one who can explain the importance of air pressure to boiling point in terms of the effects of heat on molecular motion in a liquid, the rate of molecular exchange between water and vapor in the air, and how that rate of exchange is affected by air pressure. And still better understanding might be possessed by a person who could explain the effects of heat on molecular motion in terms of molecular structure and energy transfer—and so on. In fact, it may well be that no one ever understands something *perfectly,* if that means that there is nothing left which could be explained further. Without seeking perfect understanding of this sort, however, we may find that in some cases we understand *well enough* for our purposes, while in other cases we do not.

How much understanding is enough? That question has no simple, general answer. It depends upon our reasons for wanting to understand. People who are motivated by their intellectual curiosity (e.g., theoretical scientists) sometimes seem to strive for the impossible—perfect, complete understanding. But where specific problems or projects are involved, less than perfect understanding may be adequate to meet the needs of the specific situation. The understanding of boiling points required for successful high-altitude cooking may be considerably less than that required for the design and construction of steam-powered electric generators, but in either case one might understand well enough to accomplish what was desired without understanding perfectly.

When the sort of understanding discussed here is the goal of one's thinking, rational methods of thinking are clearly preferable to irrational ones. Although guessing, playing hunches, or other irrational approaches might occasionally hit upon correct beliefs or workable policies, they could never produce this kind of understanding. Instead, for such understanding, we must rely upon evidence and explanation, the basic components of rational thought.

Thinking about Concepts

We have said that philosophy employs rational thought to seek knowledge and understanding. But we can make that claim about many enterprises. Physicists, physicians, economists, mathematicians, biologists, political scientists, and many others all seek the sort of understanding we have described. They differ from one another primarily because of what they seek to understand, and because of the special kinds of problems with which they deal. We may express one distinction between philosophy and other areas of rational thought this way: Philosophy seeks knowledge and understanding of our ideas or concepts, and attempts to solve problems which arise from failure to understand them well enough. (To say "ideas or concepts" is an abbreviated way of saying "our ways of thinking of things, our definitions, and our basic beliefs about the nature of things.") [1]

These terms and processes need clarification and explanation. How can we fail to understand our concepts? What kinds of problems could result from that? What could one do to gain clearer understanding, and how would one deal with the problems? Let us now consider two basic kinds of philosophical problems. As we describe each kind of problem and discuss examples, you will see how we may fail to understand concepts, and what steps we might take to improve our understanding and deal with problems which arise from the lack of it.

Problems in Conceptual Application

Many philosophical problems involve the question of whether a concept applies to certain kinds of situations. In order to understand this claim, we need to consider what it means to say that a concept *applies* to something. To *have* a concept of something is to be able to think about that kind of thing—to have an idea what that sort of thing is. If a person can think about trees, or about numbers, or about touchdowns, then that person has a concept of trees, and a concept of numbers, and a concept of touchdowns. Conversely, to say that one has no concept of something is to say that one has no idea of that sort of thing at all—that one is so unfamiliar with it that one cannot even entertain thoughts about it. A concept *applies* to the things of which it is the concept, and it does not apply to anything else. Thus, if something is a tree, then we can say that the concept "tree" applies to it. If something is a number,

---

1.   From now on we will use the term "concept" to refer to the basic ways in which we think about things. Some writers prefer "ideas," some prefer "predicates," some prefer to talk about the meanings of expressions, and some would prefer to find some entirely different way of making the points which follow. The differences are important, but they should not be forced on a reader just becoming acquainted with philosophy.

then the concept of number applies to it. And the concept of number does not apply to things which are not numbers, and so forth. It should be clear that there are concepts of everything we can think about, and thus we can talk about concepts of things, events, persons, places, times, and anything else which we can make the subject of our thought.

There are two basic ways in which questions can arise about whether a concept applies to something. Sometimes we cannot decide whether a concept applies to something because we don't have enough information about that thing. For example, suppose we wonder whether a man we know is a bachelor (that is, we wonder whether the concept "bachelor" applies to him). We wonder, because we don't know whether or not he is married, or ever has been married. In this case, we understand the concept itself well enough, but we don't know enough about him—the object to which the application of the concept is in question. On the other hand, sometimes we have all the information we need about something, but can't tell whether a concept applies because we are not clear enough about the concept itself. This, rather than the first kind of situation, is the sort of problem of conceptual application which is of philosophical interest. For clarification, let us consider an example.

We all can employ the concept of death—that is, we are able to think about and discuss death in a variety of situations. In ordinary circumstances a number of things commonly occur when that concept applies. For example, there is loss of consciousness, and bodily activity ceases. Circulation and respiration stop. Organs and tissues cease to function, and throughout the body a process of breakdown and decay begins. Further, these events are irreversible: consciousness, activity, circulation and respiration, organ and tissue function cannot be restored. When we observe such conditions all together we are sure that the concept of death applies—that is, that a death has occurred. When we observe an individual with none of these conditions—that is, one who is conscious, physically active, with all organs and systems functioning—we know that the concept does not apply to him. For such ordinary situations, we understand the concept of death well enough to recognize death when it occurs, and to deal with it in whatever ways seem appropriate to us.

With recent developments in medical technology, however, there are cases in which it is very difficult to decide whether the concept applies. It is now feasible to keep respiration and circulation going and most tissues and organs functioning for weeks, months, or even years after all possibility of further activity or consciousness has passed. In such cases there is disagreement about whether the concept of death applies or not. On one hand, the active, conscious existence of the person clearly is over. On the other hand, the body and many of its normal functions can be maintained, and the normal processes of breakdown and decay have not begun. In these cases, there is little more we could learn *about the patient* which could help us to decide whether to say death has occurred. What gives rise to the problem, and the debate over it, is that we do not understand the concept of death well enough to know how to use the information we have about such cases. And this is the sort of situation in which philosophy takes interest.

Some people might respond here by saying that while the problem is, perhaps, intellectually interesting, it really has no practical significance. After all, it is just a matter of definition—a mere dispute about words. In a sense, of course, this is a dispute about definition and the meaning of words, for the problem does involve disagreement about the definition of death, and the meanings of words like "death," "die," and also "life" and "alive." But this dispute does not trivialize the issue. For the problem also involves understanding what it is to be dead, or to be alive, and inadequate understanding of that can have a variety of serious practical effects. We are strongly committed to saving life, for example, and the medical technology which we employ to save it is expensive and demands a great deal of time and effort. Should we continue elaborate medical "life support" for patients of the sort described? It may be tempting to try to answer that question without worrying about whether such patients really are alive or dead, but that simply can't be done. A decision to continue medical treatment would make no sense unless we thought the patient was still alive. And if the decision is to discontinue treatment, the definition of death is very important. If we think the patient is already dead, then we need to understand clearly *why* we think so, in order to handle other cases correctly. For instance, would our decision lead to the conclusion that all severely retarded or brain-injured individuals are actually dead (and thus disposable)? If not, we need to understand why not. Or, if we think the patient alive, but that treatment should be discontinued anyway, then are we giving up our general commitment to the saving of life, and restricting it to the saving of only certain kinds of lives? Again, getting clear about just what kinds of lives need not be saved will be important. Death is important to us, and failing to understand it adequately means failing to understand exactly what we need to do when important decisions are to be made.

Some readers might object here that the concepts of life and death are so complex that no one ever will understand them completely. That agrees with the point made earlier that *perfect* understanding may be impossible. But the real issue here is the *adequacy* of our understanding. At present, our understanding of the concept of death is inadequate for us to deal confidently with several actual situations. We can certainly improve our understanding well enough to deal more confidently with these cases without insisting that our understanding be perfect. Our improved understanding might, of course, be confronted with new cases with which we would, again, be unable to cope. As long as understanding is imperfect, that is always a possibility. But even where perfection can't be achieved, some improvement is better than none.

If we grant the value of having improved understanding of at least some concepts, the question still remains, how is it to be acquired? One approach philosophers take to problems of conceptual application may be called *conceptual analysis*. The basic goal of this approach is to clarify to ourselves how we actually do think of the sorts of things whose concepts we are investigating. The principle of this approach is that we are confused, not because our concepts themselves are vague or inadequate, but because we are not precisely aware of what our own concepts really are. (This is not as strange as it may sound. We can run without knowing much about the ways in which our muscles move when we do so—might we not also be able to think about things without having a clear understanding of the concepts we employ when we do so?) An analytic approach to the problem of defining death would suppose that if we became clearer about how we really think and talk about death in a variety of cases, we would come to see the concept more clearly, and thus we would be able to decide whether it applies to the cases described. For example, if it turned out that we usually have in mind the end of conscious activity when we speak of death, then the patients in question might be regarded as having already died. On the other hand, if we discovered that our talk of death focused more on irreversible breakdown and functional failure of organs and tissues (when do we say that a plant or lower animal is dead?), we might be persuaded that the patients really are still alive.

Another approach is that of *conceptual reconstruction*. Reconstructionists are inclined to believe that our ordinary ways of thinking really are inadequate, confused, incomplete, or perhaps inconsistent. They may begin with analysis of the sort described above, but eventually they will advocate making some changes in our ways of thinking—actually modifying our concepts. A very moderate reconstructionist might say that our concept of death is incomplete at present, and that we need to decide how to extend it to cover the sorts of cases we have discussed. A more radical reconstructionist might claim that our way of thinking of death is actually confused—for example, that we sometimes appeal to the functional breakdown of organs and tissues, and sometimes to the cessation of conscious activity, and that we are inconsistent in doing so—and his solution will involve giving up a large part of our ordinary way of thinking about death, and replacing it with a new and improved way of thinking.

While some philosophers restrict themselves exclusively to analysis, and others are devoted almost entirely to radical reconstruction, it is not necessary to limit oneself to just one approach. Indeed, many philosophers employ both approaches, letting the details of the particular problem which interests them determine the way in which they attempt to improve their understanding.

Paradox

A second major kind of philosophical problem involves paradox. We have a paradox when we discover a group of our beliefs with this embarrassing combination of properties: (1) each belief in the group seems to be obviously true, and supportable with rational evidence and argument; and (2) reasoning which appears to be unquestionably correct shows us that not all the beliefs could be true simultaneously, that accepting some requires rejecting others. Paradox is uncomfortable and frustrating. We want (common sense and our best intuitions *demand* it) to hold every belief in the group, and we want just as strongly to adhere to the reasoning involved. If the reasoning is correct, however, some of the beliefs are incorrect; and if the beliefs are correct, then the reasoning is faulty. Somewhere, we will be forced to abandon something we have regarded as rationally acceptable.

For an example of paradox, consider this claim:

> (I)   Claim (I) in Chapter 1 of *An Introduction to Philosophy: Ideas in Conflict* is false.

Now try to decide whether the claim is true. At first glance it certainly seems that it should be either true or false. After all, it is not a question, or a command, or a wish, but an assertion which seems to say something definite—something which should be capable of being either correct or incorrect. But, of course, while we expect it to be true *or* false, we do not expect it to be *both*. One of the basic principles of rational thought is that no claim can be both true and false.

Yet, if we carefully consider what (I) says, difficulties arise, for (I) says, about itself, that it is fase. If what (I) says about itself were correct, then it would have to be false—because that *is* what it says. So, if (I) were true, it would have to be false, too. Since that isn't possible, it would seem that (I) must not be true. But if (I) were false, since that is *exactly* what it claims, it would have to be true. Again, we confront an impossibility. What has gone wrong?

The difficulty is that we seem to want to accept all of the following statements:

> (1)   Claim (I) does say something which must be either true or false.

> (2)   Claim (I) cannot be *both* true and false.

(3) If (I) were true, it would have to be false, also.

(4) If (I) were false, it would have to be true, also.

But if any three of statements (1)–(4) are correct, then the remaining one *must* be incorrect. Reason and common sense tell us that each of (1)–(4) is correct, but reason also tells us that they cannot all be correct together.

Notice that there is no comfortable way out of paradoxes like this one. All the beliefs making up the paradox seem reasonable, and so does the reasoning which shows us that they could not all be correct. To avoid inconsistency we must give up either the reasoning or at least one of the beliefs. But this means that we must give up something which seems reasonable— and to a person who is unaware of the paradox which leads us to give up something reasonable, we will seem to be silly, or to hold fantastic views when we do so. Here we see the grain of truth behind the stereotype of philosophy as a body of fantastic theories which reject common sense. When confronted with a paradox we must choose from among positions all of which seem to disagree with common sense. We can try to select the least unreasonable position from those available to us, but to a person who does not understand our reasons for the choice we still may seem irrational and silly.[2]

When we consider how philosophers decide which element of a paradox to reject, we find again that there is a difference between an analytic approach and a reconstructionist approach. The analytic approach presumes that we need to become much clearer in our understanding of the concepts of things involved in the paradox, and with sufficient clarity we will see that there really is a flaw in one (or more) of the beliefs, or in the reasoning. The reconstructionist, on the other hand, sees the paradox as proof of inconsistency in our ordinary ways of thinking, and will proceed to work out an improved set of ideas with which to think about the subjects involved in the paradox, ideas from which the inconsistencies of the paradox cannot be made to arise. As with the problem of conceptual application, we will find some philosophers using a combination of analytic and reconstructive methods.

Other Problems and Methods

So far, you have been given a brief description of two kinds of philosophical problems, and of two ways to approach such problems. Some philosophers would claim that there are no other significant kinds of philosophical prob-

---

2.   We do not claim that this sample paradox is of momentous importance. It is significant for philosophers who want to understand clearly what makes a claim true and what makes one false. The most popular approach to this paradox is to reject the first of statements (1)–(4), although it has not proved easy to explain precisely *why* (I) fails to make a claim which could be true or false.

lems or philosophical methods—that all significant philosophical issues turn on paradox or problems of conceptual application (or a combination of both), and that the analytic or reconstructive methods are the only legitimate ways of dealing with those issues. Many other philosophers would disagree. Some would claim that there are special kinds of knowledge about things other than concepts which philosophical reasoning can discover, and, perhaps, which cannot be discovered in any other way. Others would maintain that philosophy has the special task of drawing all human knowledge and experience together into a single coherent view of the universe and the significance of human existence in it. And other views of philosophical problems and methods for dealing with them have been proposed. A number of philosophers regard philosophical thought restricted to analytic or reconstructive approaches to paradox or problems in conceptual application as fragmentary and incomplete.

Since philosophers themselves disagree strongly about the nature of some of the kinds of problems with which they may deal, and about the methods they employ, it would be misleading for an introductory text such as this one to pretend to settle the issue. What is clear is that, whatever else philosophical thought may involve, struggling with the two kinds of problems described above is an important part of it. Coming to see clearly what such problems are like, and how philosophers attempt to deal with them, is an important step in understanding the philosophical enterprise.

The selections in Chapters 4–12 have been chosen primarily to illustrate philosophical thought about paradoxes and problems in conceptual application. But other issues do arise in several of them, and many of the authors go beyond purely analytical or reconstructive methods. As you encounter a variety of issues and techniques for dealing with them, you may begin to develop your own opinion about the scope of philosophical questions and the boundaries of the methods which legitimately may be employed to deal with them.

Philosophical Progress

People who have read a little philosophy sometimes are tempted to complain that philosophy makes no progress, that it solves no problems, that it has discussed the same questions for centuries without ever answering any of them. Enough has been said here to show that this objection is based on a misunderstanding of the nature of philosophy. The objection assumes that philosophy seeks simply to discover final answers to its questions, as if those answers could be listed somewhere for other people to look up when they needed them—just as one might look up the fact that the temperature at which water boils decreases as altitude increases. Philosophers, of course, do not provide authoritative answers of this kind, nor do they all agree about how to answer the questions in which they are interested. But that does not mean that there is no philosophical progress.

Recall that philosophy seeks *rational understanding,* rather than simple factual knowledge. The claim that a philosophical answer should be final, or authoritative, requires that answer to involve perfect understanding, in which no further improvement is possible. This kind of understanding may be impossible, but even if it were possible, we need not attain it to make some progress. To understand something better than it was understood previously is to make progress, even though the improved understanding still may be imperfect. And to improve one's understanding well enough to be able to deal with some situations which previously had seemed baffling is to make substantial progress, even if other situations remain baffling. Thus, the fact that philosophical answers are not final, and that philosophers continue to try to improve their understanding of what interests them, does not indicate that they have made no progress at all.

Because philosophy seeks understanding rather than mere information, it has a highly personal aspect. Individuals can measure their own philosophical progress in terms of the improvement of their own understanding of things. But one does not understand something merely by being told that it is so. Rational thought, argument, explanation, and debate are the tools philosophers use to obtain improved understanding. Philosophers cannot transfer their improved understanding to anyone else simply by saying what their conclusions are. Instead, philosophers must communicate their arguments and explanations as clearly as possible, and a person who wishes to benefit from their work must follow through those arguments and explanations, for it is the reasoning itself which produces the improved understanding. This is why it is more important to know *why* philosophers believe what they do than to know what their beliefs are. Simply to know what major conclusions some philosopher has reached is not even to begin really to *understand.* One's own philosophical progress always results from one's own careful, rational thought, whether retracing the thoughts of others or not. Indeed, many philosophers, improve their own understanding by following similar courses of thought to similar conclusions. In terms of their own progress, the repetition is not needless; and in terms of *our* progress, if one of them succeeds in presenting the case in a way which makes things clearer to us than did any previous presentations, the repetition is worth having.

DIVISIONS OF PHILOSOPHY

Since one of the goals of philosophy is the improvement of our understanding of ideas, philosophical thought may become concerned with any ideas about which improved understanding is worth seeking. There is no topic about which some philosophical discussion could not be produced, if it was worth the effort. But it is traditional to divide philosophical thought into a variety of categories, according to the sorts of ideas upon which it concentrates. Here are some of the most basic divisions.

Logic is the study of the rules and principles of rational thinking itself. Logicians deal with the nature of proof and inference, and the use of evidence in reasoning.

Epistemology studies the nature of knowledge, and the kinds of knowledge which it is humanly possible to acquire. One of the important aims of epistemologists is to understand clearly the difference between what we merely believe, and thus might be mistaken about, and what we know, and thus can rely upon.

Metaphysics deals with the basic concepts in terms of which we try to understand our universe. Among the things which metaphysicians try to understand are the nature of existence, space, time, matter, mind, change, and causation.

Ethics is concerned with rules of conduct and the concepts we employ in evaluating behavior and ways of life. A major concern of ethics is to clarify how such concepts as *good, bad, right, wrong,* and *duty* apply.

Aesthetics concentrates upon the concepts which we employ in judging the value and quality of art. Central concerns include the nature of beauty, ugliness, tragedy, metaphor, and humor.

Other special areas of philosophical thought frequently are recognized. Some of these are distinguished in terms of a special discipline, or area of study, whose basic concepts are the focal point of the philosophical work. For example, philosophers have developed such subjects as philosophy of history, philosophy of mathematics, and philosophy of science, which may be subdivided into such areas as philosophy of the social sciences, philosophy of biology, philosophy of psychology, philosophy of physics, etc. We can identify other areas of philosophical thought in terms of sets of practices or institutions whose concepts and rules are the object of the philosophical study. Examples of these are philosophy of law, philosophy of education, and political philosophy. Still other special areas of study are identified in terms of some central topic about which clearer understanding is sought, such as philosophy of language, philosophy of mind, philosophy of action, or philosophy of punishment. And, finally, there are areas such as philosophy of religion in which one studies a complex combination of related problems and draws from many of the areas already indicated.

All these areas of special concentration are not clearly separated. In fact, they overlap extensively, and it is common to find that in working on problems in one area one must become involved with issues which belong to other areas. For example, one of the central issues in philosophy of religion is how to respond rationally to the question whether a god or gods exist. This is a metaphysical question, but because a god would be a very special sort of being, one can argue that knowledge of the existence of such a being is itself of a very special sort, and this distinction introduces epistemological questions about the possibility and nature of such knowledge. But the epistemological discussion is likely to raise questions about the kinds of evidence and proof which might be employed in obtaining such knowledge, at which point deliberations about logic enter in. This interrelatedness of philosophical issues will be exemplified repeatedly in the selections making up Chapters 4–12.

Finally, you may wish to consider this question: If philosophical thought inspects the basic concepts and methods of other areas of investigation (such as the sciences or mathematics), then what kind of thought can investigate critically the concepts and methods employed by philosophy itself? There seems to be only one answer—that if such clarification of the basic concepts of philosophy is possible, it must be done philosophically. And, indeed, philosophical method is another of the subjects upon which philosophical thought concentrates. You have already been warned that there are several different opinions about which methods are more reliable and effective for dealing with philosophical problems, and that it would be inappropriate here simply to describe the "right" method without carefully examining all the alternatives. Nonetheless, there are several elementary ideas about rational thought which are widely accepted among philosophers. Familiarity with these ideas will make it easier for you to understand the selections in Chapters 4–12. Accordingly, several of these elementary ideas are presented in Chapter 2.

2

Elements of Philosophical Reasoning

Philosophers tend to respond to statements that interest them by asking, "How do you know that?" When this question is not asked sympathetically, it means, "I'll bet you *don't* know that, let's see you prove that you do." At other times it may be asked very sympathetically: "I'm glad you have that straight, now explain it to me so that I can know it too." In either case, the response to the question is likely to reveal far more than the statement itself does about the quality of the philosophical understanding upon which the statement is based. Most philosophers don't wait for someone to ask—they devote a major portion of their efforts to providing careful, detailed accounts of how they know whatever it is they claim to know.

Essential to these accounts are *arguments*—that is, attempts to prove to us that something is so, and *explanations* intended to show us why something is so or how it came about. Frequently these arguments and explanations involve *definitions* intended to clarify central concepts or establish important characteristics of whatever is being discussed. And, of course, all such accounts are based on some very fundamental attitudes and opinions about the *sources of knowledge*. There is serious disagreement among philosophers about how arguments, explanations, and definitions should be structured and what makes them acceptable. There is more disagreement about how we can come to know things. Still, there are many basic ideas which are employed so often that an understanding of them is assumed in most philosophical discussions. The four sections of this chapter will acquaint you with some of the most commonly encountered elementary ideas about arguments, explanations, definitions, and sources of knowledge.

ARGUMENT

When philosophers talk about an argument, they do not mean a kind of disagreement or dispute. For philosophical purposes, we define an argument as any attempt to establish the truth of some statement, claim, or belief by appealing to evidence or proof. If the attempt succeeds, we may say that the argument is a good one, or correct; and if the attempt fails, we can say that the argument is a bad one, or fallacious, or incorrect. Successful or not, every such attempt counts as an argument.

What are the elements of an argument? Suppose that someone argues this way:

Premise ——— (1) No person can be held morally responsible for behavior which is causally determined.

Premise ——— (2) Every bit of human behavior is causally determined.

Conclusion ———(3) Therefore, no person can be held morally responsible for any of his or her behavior.

In this simple example we can distinguish several basic elements. First, the statement (or claim, or belief) which the argument is intended to prove is called the *conclusion* of the argument. In our example, (3) is the conclusion. Second, the statements which the arguer accepts (believes to be true) and offers as evidence for the conclusion are called *premises* of the argument. The premises of our example are statements (1) and (2). Finally, since the arguer believes or expects us to believe statement (3) because of statements (1) and (2), we can say that the arguer *draws an inference from* (1) and (2) *to* (3), or, alternatively, that the arguer *infers* (3) *from* (1) and (2).

Now let us consider a more complex example:

(a) Let us assume that there are absolutely no limits to what God can do.

(b) Then God must be able to create an object which cannot be moved.

(c) And also, then, God must be able to move any object He creates.

(d) So, if our assumption is true, God must be able both to create an immovable object and to move it.

(e) But it is impossible for an object to be both immovable and movable by God.

(f) So, the assumption must be incorrect.

In this case, (a) is not a premise but an *assumption* or *hypothesis*.[1] When arguers request us to assume that some statement is true, for the purpose of argument, they are not claiming that the statement actually *is* true, but only asking us to pretend that it is for a while, in order to see what difference that would make. In argument, one uses such assumptions, sometimes along with premises, as the basis for inferences or chains of inference. The important point to remember in dealing with assumptions in argument is that, once an assumption has been introduced, no conclusion of an inference based on it can be regarded as *proved* by the argument. Whatever such arguments really prove must be expressed conditionally—that is, *if* the assumption(s) is (are) true, *then* the conclusion of an inference based upon the assumption(s) is true. In this example both (b) and (c) are hypothetical conclusions inferred from the assumption (a). And that is exactly what (d) says. On the other hand, (e) is not an assumption but a statement taken to be actually true. So, (f) is the conclusion of an inference from two premises, (d) and (e). Notice that in this case the conclusion of the whole argument, (f), is that the assumption made at the beginning of the argument is false. This is an example of a kind of argument called *reductio ad absurdum* (literally, "reduction to absurdity"), in which the strategy is to assume a statement in order to show that if it were true, some obviously false (absurd) statement would have to be true also— and thus the argument refutes the assumption.

Every argument must have at least one conclusion and involve at least one inference from one or more premises or assumptions. Arguments are generally more complex than our first, single-inference example. There may

---

1. Notice that this is a special, technical use of the term "assumption." In ordinary, nontechnical English an assumption is a belief taken for granted, without proof or evidence. Assumptions in the ordinary sense of the word *can* be premises in arguments, so it is important not to confuse the technical and the nontechnical uses of the word.

be more than one conclusion. The same conclusion may be inferred from different sets of premises or assumptions. Or an argument might consist of a complex chain of subarguments, in which the conclusion of one subargument functions as a premise in another subargument, and so on. And, frequently, some of the beliefs or claims involved in an argument may not be stated explicitly in words. Such claims may be taken for granted, or thought to be too obvious to need explicit statement—or they may be so fundamental to the arguer's way of thinking that the arguer fails to realize their role in the argument, and the need for stating them plainly. It can be a difficult challenge to discover and identify correctly the conclusions, premises, assumptions, and inferences in some arguments. But the first step to proper understanding of a philosophical argument (or any argument, for that matter) is to identify these elements as accurately as possible, and see how they are organized in the argument.

Correctness in Argument

Some arguments succeed, and show us that we could not be mistaken in believing their conclusions, while other arguments fail, and give us no good reason to accept their conclusions. Once you have identified the elements in an argument, you will be ready to try to decide whether it is successful or not.

There are two different considerations to make in evaluating the success of an argument. One consideration involves the truth or falsehood of the premises of the argument. Arguers should strive to employ only premises which are *true*—and if their arguments are to function successfully in providing understanding and conviction, they should employ only premises which we *know* to be true. Be sure to note, however, that it is not a requirement of a good argument that its *assumptions* be true.

The second consideration involves the quality of the inferences in the argument. The less likely it is that the conclusion of an argument could be false (if the premises or assumptions from which it is inferred were all true), the better the inference. Typically, philosophers recognize two different kinds of inferences. *Deductive* inferences are intended to provide such good evidence that it would be absolutely impossible for the conclusion of the inference to be false if all its premises or assumptions were true. *Inductive* inferences, on the other hand, succeed if the truth of their premises or assumptions would make it very unlikely, or improbable, that the conclusion could be false. But an inductive inference admits some possibility that the conclusion could be false even if all the premises or assumptions were true.

A deductive argument, then, attempts to employ only inferences for which it would be completely impossible for the conclusion to be false if the premises or assumptions upon which it is based were true. Such inferences are said to be *valid;* and if all the inferences in an argument are valid, we can say that the argument itself is valid. If it is possible, no matter how unlikely, for the conclusion of an inference to be false when all the premises or assumptions for the inference are true, then the inference is *invalid.* Inferences for which it is very unlikely, though possible, that the conclusion would be false when the premises or assumptions were true often are said to be *strong;* and where there is a good chance that the conclusion of an inference could be false when the premises or assumptions were true, the inference is said to be *weak.* Since strength and weakness are a measure of the degree of likelihood that a conclusion will be true when its premises are, we must be prepared to deal in degrees of strength and weakness. Some strong inferences may be stronger than others, and some weak inferences are weaker than others. There are, however, no degrees of validity. All weak inferences are invalid, and all strong inferences are invalid, also.[2]

If we combine our two basic considerations, we arrive at the following standards: (1) A purely deductive argument attempts to prove its conclusion by employing only valid inferences from only true premises. When such an argument succeeds (all the premises are true, and all the inferences

2. For illustration consider these simple inferences:

A. Everyone registered in this district may vote on the proposed bond issue. *Deductive valid*
   I am registered in this district.
   Therefore, I may vote on the proposed bond issue.

B. Anyone who drives while intoxicated breaks the law. *deductive invalid*
   My neighbor never drives while intoxicated.
   Therefore, my neighbor never breaks the law.

C. All but one of the thousands of lottery tickets are losers.
   My ticket is randomly selected from those thousands of lottery tickets. *inductive/strong*
   Therefore, my ticket is a loser.

D. My cousin is overweight.
   My cousin also is very lazy. *inductive/weak*
   Therefore, overweight people are lazy.

Inferences A and B are both *deductive*—that is, they are intended to establish their conclusions with certainty. Inferences C and D, on the other hand, are intended only to show that their conclusions are likely to be true, and thus they are *inductive* inferences.

It is not possible for the conclusion of A to be false if the premises are true, but it is possible for the conclusions of B, C, and D to be false while their premises are true. Thus, A is *valid,* while B, C, and D are *invalid.* If the premises of C were true, then the conclusion would be very likely to be true, so C is *strong.* But the premises of B and D offer very little evidence in support of their conclusions; they both are *weak* inferences.

valid), the argument is said to be *sound* or *cogent*. If one or more of the premises is false, or at least one of the inferences invalid, then the argument is flawed, or *unsound*.   (2)   An inductive argument attempts to support its conclusion by employing only true premises and only strong inductive inferences. In some cases, inductive arguments may employ a mixture of inductive and deductive inferences, and in those cases the deductive inferences all should be valid.   An inductive argument which meets these requirements may be said to *provide substantial support* for its conclusion. If an inductive argument involves one or more false premises, or at least one weak inference, then the argument is flawed.

The conclusion of a sound deductive argument, then, could not be false. And the conclusion of a successful inductive argument is very unlikely to be false. But what should we say about arguments which are flawed? First, it should be clear that discovering a flaw in an argument does not prove that the conclusion of the argument is false. An arguer could start with false premises, use weak inferences, and still wind up, by sheer luck, with a conclusion which happens to be true. Thus, if we want to establish that the conclusion of an argument is false, we shall have to construct an argument of our own which shows just that.

In addition, you should realize that some flaws may not seriously damage the effectiveness of the whole argument. For instance, suppose an argument involves two separate inferences which have the same conclusion. If one of these inferences is valid, and based on true premises, then that conclusion is proved, even if the other inference is weak and based upon false premises. Thus, the seriousness of a flaw depends upon the rest of the argument in which it occurs. Ultimately, the success or failure of a flawed argument rests upon the answer to this question: If all the flaws were stripped away from the argument, would what was left be adequate to prove or provide substantial support for the conclusion? If so, then the argument succeeds in spite of its flaws; if not, then it fails.

Now, how can we tell whether an inference really is correct? One major goal of the study of logic is to discover reliable and widely useful methods for determining whether inferences are valid or invalid, strong or weak. Much has been accomplished in the pursuit of this goal, and much more remains to be done. As you might imagine, a complete account of what is known about inferences would be very complex, and could not possibly be presented here.[3] But there is a simple approach to evaluating inferences which you may find useful as you read and evaluate the selections in following chapters.

That approach is this: if you want to evaluate an inference, try to think of some set of circumstances, whether real or fictitious, in which all the

3.   If you are interested in learning more about logic, several very good introductory texts are available; or you may want to consider taking a course in elementary logic.

premises (or assumptions) of the inference would be true but the conclusion would be false. If you *can* think of such a situation, and can give a good clear description of what it would be like, then you have shown that the inference *cannot be valid.* If you can think of many such situations, or if it is clear that such situations are likely actually to occur, then you have reason to suspect that the *strength* of the inference is not great, although this result is not as reliable or useful as the demonstration of invalidity.

There are obvious limitations on this approach. For one thing, an inference might be invalid, but you simply might fail to think of the right set of circumstances to show that it is. Failure to think of a situation which would show an inference invalid, then, cannot be taken as proof that it is valid. Or you may suspect that you have an appropriate set of circumstances in mind, but just cannot get a good clear description of them into words. In such a case it would be premature to claim that the inference is invalid—though it might be worthwhile to put some further effort into trying to work out the description. In spite of these limitations, this approach is a useful first step to take in appraising the correctness of any inference.

Other Standards of Evaluation

Besides truth of premises and correctness of inference, the success or failure of arguments depends upon several other factors. Here are a few of the most important such factors.

Vagueness and Ambiguity

A philosopher's choice of language, obviously, has a great deal to do with how well we will understand the point of view being presented. In some cases, an unfortunate choice of language may mislead us, or even the philosopher, into thinking that an important claim or argument has been presented, when in fact the language hides a mass of confusions. Foremost among the sources of such difficulties are vagueness and ambiguity.

To say that a statement is *vague* is to claim that it fails to be sufficiently clear and precise. Vagueness prevents us from understanding very accurately what the statement is intended to tell us. For example, consider this statement:

Historical forces determine everything that happens to us.

In the present context, this statement is quite vague. What sort of thing is an historical force? What is the difference between an event which is determined by an historical force, and one which is not? How would the world be different if what happens to us were not determined by historical forces? Our inability to answer these questions shows how very little the statement tells us.

In dealing with problems of vagueness, keep in mind three points: (1) Vagueness is a matter of degree. At one extreme, a statement may be so vague that we have no idea whatsoever what it might by trying to say. At the other extreme, a statement may be so precise that it leaves absolutely nothing which we could make any clearer. Very few statements achieve either of these extremes, and most statements do tell us something, and do leave some things open to further clarification.   (2) Vagueness is a function of context. That is, what a sentence tells us in one context may be much vaguer than what it tells us in another. For example, in the context of this chapter, the sentence about historical forces is very vague. But if it had appeared in the context of a lengthy discussion, in which it was explained what was meant by an historical force and how events could be determined by such forces, the degree of vagueness might have been considerably less.   (3) The amount of vagueness which can be tolerated is a function of context. The point here is that in different situations, we are interested in achieving different results. What is too vague to allow us to succeed with our aims in one discussion may be perfectly adequate for our aims in some other situation. For example, if a friend asks you to go hiking, and you say, "No, I don't feel well," what you have said about how you feel is not too vague to achieve its purpose, which is to explain why you have declined the invitation. Details about how you feel are not required for such an explanation to be effective. On the other hand, if you consult a physician about your health and respond to the question, "What's wrong?" by saying you don't feel well, what you say is much too vague to get a diagnosis under way. In that situation, you need to specify where you hurt, what the pain is like, under what circumstances it occurs, etc.

Vagueness presents a problem in argument anytime a statement employed is so vague that we can't tell whether any inferences in which it is involved are correct, or when we can't tell whether a conclusion we have reached really is relevant to the question it was intended to clarify. Vagueness can be an extremely serious problem in some arguments, but before you charge an argument with vagueness, be sure that you have properly assessed the degree of vagueness (sure that the context does not clarify the statement in question) and that it really does interfere with the purpose of the argument.

Ambiguity also involves difficulty in understanding what a statement tells us, but in this case the problem is not that there is lack of detail or precision in what is said, but that there are two or more (not especially vague) alternative claims which the ambiguous sentence might be making. For example, if the driver of a truck which hauls sections of tree trunks from the forest to the sawmill says that he keeps a log every day, we might wonder whether he meant that he was stealing part of his cargo each day, or that he kept a daily record of his trips—such as the mileage, destinations, and times of departure and arrival. Neither of these alternatives is particularly vague; the trouble is that we might not be sure which of them was the one the driver intended to convey.

Ambiguity is not a matter of degree. Either a sentence is ambiguous or it is not. If so, we can specify what the two or more claims are which it might be making. If not, then there is just a single claim it is making. But ambiguity is a function of context. A sentence which would be ambiguous in one situation may be perfectly clear in a different context. For example, if the driver's remark about keeping a log each day were made in response to a question about the pile of tree trunks in his backyard, we would not wonder if he might have been talking about his record keeping.

In ordinary conversation, ambiguity may cause us to misunderstand what is being said. But in argument a more complex difficulty can arise from ambiguity. Basically, this difficulty involves taking some word or expression to mean one thing while part of the argument is being presented, and then taking it to mean something else during the rest of the argument. To continue with the example we have been discussing, we might encounter this argument:

> Jones drives a truck for Clear-Cuts, Inc., and every day he writes down his departure and arrival times, the weight of his load, the mileage for each trip, and other details. So, he keeps a log each day. But the logs he hauls don't belong to him, and since he keeps what doesn't belong to him, he's really a thief.

In this example, of course, the ambiguity is so obvious that no one would fail to notice it, and thus no one would accept the argument. But similar transitions in meaning may occur in arguments in ways which are much harder to detect.[4]

4. Here is an example. Suppose that Jones, an enthusiastic amateur photographer who gets great pleasure from his cameras and darkroom, discovers that his granddaughter wants very much to own a certain sports car. To make her happy, he sells all his photographic equipment and buys her the car. Meanwhile, suppose that Smith sells his daughter's car (which she needs to get to and from her job, which makes it possible for her to support her sick husband and children) and he uses the money to buy a piece of jewelry for his mistress, in anticipation of the pleasure her gratitude will provide him. And now consider this argument:

Jones knew that the sports car would make his granddaughter very happy, and he takes great pleasure and satisfaction from her happiness. Since he wanted very much to make her happy, he really was satisfying a desire of his own and providing pleasure for himself when he sold his equipment and bought her the car. So, both Jones and Smith were acting in pursuit of their own desires and satisfaction. Each of them was selfish, therefore, and neither could be said to be significantly more or less selfish than the other.

Arguments of this kind often are used to provide a basis for the claim that all human action is selfish and that altruism and generosity are mythical. But there are two different notions of selfishness at work here. One notion holds that an action is selfish if it is done in pursuit of some goal of the agent. From that point

Where they do occur, they constitute a very serious flaw in the argument. For, in effect, such an argument really is divided into two segments, each dealing with one meaning of the ambiguous word or expression, and the two segments have little or nothing to do with each other. When this happens in an argument, the only remedy is to abandon all inferences in which the ambiguity has played a part, and try to replace them with new, correct inferences. Whether this remedy can be applied in actual cases depends upon whether such replacement inferences are available—usually, they are not.

Consistency

If all the statements in a group of two or more can be true simultaneously, those statements are said to be *consistent* with one another. If it is not possible for all the statements in a group to be true at the same time, then those statements are said to be *inconsistent* with one another. A successful argument must be consistent—that is, it must be at least possible for all the statements (premises and conclusions) in the argument to be true at the same time.[5] (In fact, in a good argument it is not only possible, but really the case.) If the statements in an argument are inconsistent, then at least one of them must be false. If you detect inconsistency in an argument, you should try to locate its source. Perhaps one of the premises is false. Perhaps a weak inference has been included in the argument. Perhaps, though this is unlikely, some strong inference from true premises has a false conclusion. Whatever the source of the trouble, unless the false statements, and any inferences based on them, are identified and struck from the argument, the whole argument must be regarded as unreliable. Once the false statements are removed, however, there may not be enough of the argument left to establish its conclusions adequately.

While consistency in an argument does not guarantee its correctness, we can be sure that an inconsistent argument has something wrong with it. For a simple example of inconsistency consider this argument:

of view, Jones and Smith do appear to be equally selfish—and, indeed, it is hard to imagine what an unselfish action would be like. But a second notion of selfishness depicts it as behavior in which one prefers one's own pleasure and gratification (no matter how trivial) to the wants, needs, and pleasures of others (no matter how important). And on this score, Jones and Smith are quite different. If the conclusion of the argument is that there is no moral difference between them, then the argument confuses evidence that Jones is as selfish as Smith, in the first sense of the word, with evidence that he is as selfish in the second sense of the word.

5.   Be sure to notice that neither assumptions nor the hypothetical conclusions based upon them are required to be consistent with the premises and conclusions in an argument. If you think carefully about the strategy of the reductio ad absurdum argument, you will see why it is important not to require consistency in assumptions and their hypothetical consequences.

The deliberate killing of one human being by another should never be permitted under any circumstances. Of course, it follows that murder should not be permitted and, since capital punishment has been shown to be the most effective means of preventing murder, it is clear that we should support capital punishment for murderers.

Since capital punishment does involve the deliberate killing of one human being by others, the conclusion of this argument is not consistent with its opening premise—they could not both be correct.

Circularity

Circularity occurs when a statement in an argument is made to depend upon itself. Simple circularity occurs when the conclusion of an inference also is employed as a premise in that inference. But circularity can arise in a variety of more complex forms. For example, a statement may appear as the conclusion of the last in a whole series of inferences but also turn out to be employed as a premise in one of the inferences in the series. Circular inferences and arguments also are said sometimes to *beg the question,* or to commit the fallacy of *petitio principii* (literally, "postulating the beginning").

Circular inferences or arguments cannot prove anything to us. The purpose of a proof is to provide us with some assurance or guarantee that if we believe the conclusion of the proof, we won't be mistaken. If we do not have such assurance about the premises of the proof, then it can't provide us with such assurance for its conclusion. In the case of circularity, however, if we have the required assurance about the premises, then we don't need the proof, because we already are assured of its conclusion (which is one of the premises). Thus, a circular argument is either unnecessary, or of no help. For example, consider this argument:

 (1) Attempted suicide always is irrational behavior. We know that because (2) people who attempt suicide all suffer from mental disorders, and (3) the behavior of those suffering from mental disorders is irrational. And (4) we can tell that those who attempt suicide suffer from mental disorders because of their irrational behavior, which is symptomatic of such disorders. (5) The irrational behavior which most frequently gives them away, of course, is the attempt at suicide itself.

The major conclusion of this argument is claim (1), that attempted suicide always is irrational. This claim is inferred validly from statements (2) and (3).

In turn, (2) is inferred from (4) and (5), but this inference completes the circle, for (5) depends upon the truth of (1), the very claim which it is supposed to support. If we already know that attempted suicide always is irrational, then this argument is unnecessary. If we do not already know that attempted suicide always is irrational, then we cannot be sure that having attempted suicide indicates either that such people were irrational in doing so or that they suffer from some "mental disorder."

Appeals to Emotion

Often it is possible to make statements which cause people to hope, wish, or desire that certain other statements be true. If people with such hopes and desires are careless, they may come to accept the statements they want to be true simply *because* they want them to be true, and with no other arguments or evidence. It is not unusual, for example, to hear people explain their belief in human immortality and personal survival after death in terms of their inability to accept the alternative—they find the prospect of final termination of their existence at death so fearsome that they simply cannot accept it. While such fear may cause them to believe in their own immortality, it does not provide any rational proof or evidence for the truth of that belief.

Many arguers do appeal to the emotions of their audience in the course of their arguments. They say things which give members of their audience feelings which may cause them to believe the conclusion of the argument. Appeals may be made to fear, pity, or sympathy; or members of the audience may be made to feel foolish if they disagree with the argument, or may be made to laugh at opposing views—the variety of possible appeals to emotion is great. But no matter how persuasive these appeals are, they cannot provide the kind of rational support for a conclusion which good argumentation requires.

In evaluating the role of emotions in an argument, we must distinguish between *appeals* to emotion and remarks which may merely *evoke* emotions. The difference is this: appeals to emotion are intended to get someone to accept a belief because of their emotional attitudes toward the subject of that belief; remarks which merely evoke emotions might produce emotional attitudes toward the subject of some beliefs, but they are not intended to employ those attitudes to cause anyone to accept or reject the beliefs. We can hardly discuss matters of importance without saying some things which will evoke emotions. The decisive logical issue is whether we intend to take advantage of such emotions to persuade others to accept some statements for which we have offered no evidence; or whether we do our best to ignore the evoked emotions and provide sound evidence in support of the statements we wish others to believe. The former procedure is not rationally acceptable, while the latter is. The conscientious pursuit of rational understanding, then, places an obligation upon an arguer to refrain from appealing to emotions, and an obligation upon readers and hearers of arguments to resist being swayed by their emotions.

Appeals to Authority

Appeals to authority are inferences in which one argues that a statement is true because someone, a purported authority, says so. Such an appeal to authority could rarely be valid. But there are many cases in which it might be strong, and many other cases in which it is weak. To accept expert opinion on some subject is to accept an appeal to authority—as is accepting a report of someone's own personal experience. In these cases, to accept such appeals is a part of rational behavior. But there are many situations in which it is a mistake to believe something simply because someone else has said it is so.

Deciding whether to accept an appeal to authority can be a complex procedure. These factors must be considered: (1) whether the supposed authority has the appropriate sort of expertise—is thoroughly familiar with the subject matter of the statement, has access to the relevant information, and so forth; (2) whether other recognized authorities agree with this authority's judgment; (3) whether there are any special influences which might distort the authority's judgment in this case, such as having a strong personal emotional or financial interest in having you believe the statement. We will not discuss details of methods for evaluating appeals to authority here, because such appeals very seldom are legitimate in philosophical debate. They may sometimes be appropriate to introduce facts of science, history, law, etc., which a philosopher may wish to employ as premises. But appeals to authority cannot be employed to justify any statements which would be part of the solution for a philosophical problem. One reason that appeals to authority cannot be so used is simply that there is no authoritative agreement about philosophical issues. If you recall the character of paradoxes, or philosophical problems about the application of concepts, you can see why you are likely to find very gifted and well-prepared philosophers who take opposing positions about all such issues. If everyone who had considered such an issue agreed about how to resolve it, the issue would have lost its status as a philosophical problem.

A second reason why appeals to authority should not be employed in philosophical argumentation involves the nature of philosophical progress. The aim of philosophical thought, remember, is to gain a clear understanding of, or perhaps to make revisions in, the concepts from which the philosophical problem is generated. Simply to accept someone's word about how to deal with a problem would not improve one's understanding of the issues or of the suggested solution. Once again, this means that philosophers who wish to help others to the solution of a philosophical problem must present their reasoning and arguments, and not just the conclusions of those arguments. And the student of philosophy who learns only the conclusions philosophers have reached, without being familiar with the reasoning which led them to those conclusions, is ignoring the most significant aspect of the philosopher's work.

Refutation by Counterexample

Our brief treatment of argument will conclude with this discussion of a very frequently employed device for *refuting* statements (that is, for proving them false). This device is the appeal to a counterexample. In order to explain how such appeals work we must first describe a kind of statement, called a *universal generalization,* and then proceed to our examination of counterexamples themselves.

A universal generalization is a statement which tells us something about the relationship between the members of some class of things and some property, quality, or characteristic. And what it tells us is either that *all* the members of the class have the property, quality, or characteristic, or else that *none* of them do. A few examples are:

All [persons] are *rational.*

No [animals] are *rational.*

Every[one] *always acts selfishly.*

Every[one in the lifeboat] was *over forty years old.*

In each example, the expression which indicates the class of things under consideration is in brackets, and the expression which indicates the property, quality, or characteristic is in italics.

Philosophers often use universal generalizations to express important parts of their views. And, just as often, critics of philosophical views try to show that some important universal generalization is false. The simplest way to do this is to produce a *counterexample.* A counterexample is a member of the relevant class of things which is *not* related to the property, quality, or characteristic in the way that the universal generalization claims it is. So, if you could point out a person who is not rational, or an animal which is, or a person who sometimes acts unselfishly, or someone in the lifeboat who is not over forty years old, you would be pointing out counterexamples to the universal generalizations given above as examples. If such counterexamples are genuine, then they show that the universal generalizations are false.

The strategy of refutation by counterexample is simple and straightforward. But putting it into practice can become a complex and difficult business. Here are some considerations which should be kept in mind when dealing with counterexamples.

1. There are other kinds of generalizations—statements which say, for example, that *most* members of some group have some property, or that a *few* of them do. These nonuniversal generalizations cannot be refuted by a single counterexample. (If someone says that *most* students are honest, we don't show him wrong by pointing out a single cheating student, but if he had said that *all* students are honest, then the single counterexample would have been enough to show him wrong.) So, before you attempt to argue by counterexample, be sure that the generalization to be refuted really is a universal one.

2. It is not unusual to encounter troublesome vagueness about the class or property with which the generalization deals. Suppose someone says:

Only people can have the right to life.

What kind of counterexample would refute this statement? First, notice that the statement does *not* say that *all* people have the right to life. So it would be a mistake to introduce a counterexample involving a person without the right to life. An appropriate counterexample would require an individual with a right to life, but which was not a member of the class of people. It is tempting to rephrase the generalization as

Everything with a right to life is a person.

or

No nonperson has the right to life.

Suppose, now, that someone asks us to imagine encountering an apelike animal which clearly is not a member of the species *homo sapiens,* but which can learn to speak English very well, do arithmetic, understand the importance of keeping promises—in short, a creature which exhibits very much the same needs and behavior as human beings do. And suppose we all agree that such a creature would have a right to life. Now, *if* the original generalization was claiming that no *possible* nonhuman being was a possible possessor of a right to life, then this imaginary case might count as a counterexample. On the other hand, if the claim was that no *actual,* existing nonhumans have a right to life, imaginary examples simply are not to the point.

Some people might respond to the imaginary counterexample by saying that such a creature clearly would have a right to life but that it also clearly was a person. At this point we might discover that the terms "person" and "people" were not being used to indicate members of the species *homo sapiens,* but members of some other, less clearly defined class.

The original generalization involves vagueness about the precise nature of both the class and the property which it tries to relate. In the face of such vagueness, it is not clear what would count as a real counterexample. But the search for a counterexample does expose such vagueness more quickly and effectively than would any other sort of study of the original generalization. To show that the generalization is not clear enough to respond to is not to refute it, but it is to point out a very serious difficulty with it.

3. You may encounter situations in which everyone agrees that if a description of a certain case were correct, that case would be a counterexample to an important universal generalization. But some people think that their arguments prove the generalization to be true, and argue that this shows that the description of the purported counterexample must be mistaken, while others are confident that the description of the counterexample is correct, and that it must show the generalization to be false. There is no simple way out of such a situation. Those who think they have found a counterexample will do well to look for arguments which would prove that their description of the case is correct. Both sides can look for flaws in the arguments of the other side. What is clear is that the appeal to counterexample by itself is not sufficiently convincing, and other arguments in its support are needed.

EXPLANATION

In evaluating explanations we must consider two factors. First, there is that which is to be explained—the *explanandum.* We may wish to explain facts, events, ideas, processes, or other things. When possible, it is helpful to formulate the explanandum as one or more statements which specify or describe whatever it is we want to explain. Second, there is the *explanans*—the statement, or collection of statements, which is to explain the explanandum to us. Thus, what we usually call an explanation of something is the explanans, for which that something is the explanandum. Some explanations may be very simple—even so simple that the explanans can be presented in a single statement. Other explanations involve enormous complexity, the explanandum involving a multiplicity of factors, and the explanans requiring the space of a whole book or more to present. And many explanations may include smaller explanations as parts, so that the explanandum of one subexplanation may be employed as part of the explanans of a larger explanation, and so forth.

Before we can decide how good an explanation is, we must become clear about the identity of the explanandum and explanans, so that we know just what is to be explained, and what is being offered as explanation. In addition, we must decide what kind of explanation is being offered. Some explanations are for *clarification* or *illustration.* In these cases, the statements in the explanans will be intended to remove vagueness or ambiguity, give illustrative examples, or in other ways make plain exactly what it is to which our attention is being directed. Other explanations are *purposive,* which means that they explain by pointing out motives, or reasons for the explanandum's being what it is. Still other explanations are *causal,* explaining something by pointing out the causes which led up to it. And, finally, there are *conceptual* explanations, which try to make clearer what sort of thing the explanandum really is, rather than how or why it came to be that way.

This list of kinds of explanations is not complete, nor are the divisions in it very sharp. There are explanations which do not fit any of these categories well, and there are other explanations which fit more than one of them. But anyone who gives an explanation, or who asks for one, should have a clear notion of the kind or kinds of explanation desired. Lack of clarity here is likely to result in an explanans which mixes up parts of several kinds of explanation without doing a really adequate job with any one part. In addition, before you can evaluate the success of an attempted explanation, you must be clear about the kinds of explanatory goals it has.

Correctness in Explanation

A good explanation makes it possible for us to understand something more clearly than we would without the explanation. But because of the variety in kinds of explanations, and in things to be explained, there is no simple set of characteristics which all good explanations share. To say anything substantial about what makes explanations succeed, then, we would need to divide them into groups whose members share similar approaches and similar goals, and then discuss in some detail the features which produce success in a certain kind of approach toward a certain kind of explanatory goal. Of course, such a discussion would be too complex and too long for inclusion here. On the other hand, there are some simple flaws which all explanations should avoid, and which can be presented briefly here.

Ambiguity and Vagueness

Both ambiguity and vagueness are undesirable in explanations. Ambiguity in an expression employed in either the explanans or explanandum will have the familiar result that the explanation really is divided into two portions, each one dealing with a different meaning of the ambiguous expression, and with no real connection between the two portions. Explanations with a flaw this serious usually have to be abandoned altogether.

What has been said about vagueness in argument applies in the case of explanation, too. How precise we must be is a function of the context and the goals of the explanation. In different situations, different degrees of imprecision may be tolerated. But to fail to be precise enough for the purposes of the explanation being undertaken is to introduce a flaw in the explanation, and if the vagueness is great enough, the attempt at explanation may turn out to have no value at all.

Consistency and Truth

It is generally agreed that all the statements in an explanation must be consistent with one another—it must be at least possible for all of them to be true simultaneously. There is less agreement among philosophers about whether all the statements in a good explanation must actually be true. Many would claim that if an explanation is to be satisfactory, then the statements in the explanans must be true. Others argue that there are reasons for accepting some explanations in which some of the major statements in the explanans may be false. One such reason might be this: The aim of many explanations is to make clear to us, in terms of what we already believe, how or why something takes place. An explanation might achieve that sort of clarity with outstanding success even if some of the familiar beliefs upon which it was based actually were false. From this point of view, the success of explanations is measured relative to the background of beliefs against which it is given, rather than against a standard of absolute truth. But it should be noted that in such a relativistic view, it is only undetected falsehood which might be acceptable in an explanation. An explanation in which an important part was played by a statement known or believed to be false would be rejected by nearly all philosophers.

The appeal to counterexample emerges here as a powerful critical device. Since explanations tend to include universal generalizations in their explanans, the appeal to counterexample may be employed to demonstrate the falsehood of some of those generalizations. It is particularly effective to find a case in which the statements in the explanans are not true of an instance of what was to be explained. For example, suppose someone offered an explanation of how a certain disease is contracted, in which it is claimed that the disease is transmitted from one person to another by direct physical contact. If we could find a case in which a person had acquired the disease without ever coming in contact with someone who already had it, we would have a counterexample which showed the attempt at explanation to be inadequate.

Circularity

Circularity in explanation arises whenever part or all of the understanding one is supposed to gain from the explanation is required in order to understand the explanans. The simplest kind of circularity involves actually using the explanandum in its own explanans, but there are many more complex ways in which explanations may be circular. Suppose, for example, that we wonder why a man wants very much to visit Spain, and we receive the "explanation" that he wants to visit Spain because he knows it would give him great pleasure to do so. But if we wonder why visiting Spain would give him such great pleasure, and we are told it is because he wants to do it very much, then the set of explanations has become circular. If the desire is to be explained in terms of anticipated pleasure, then the anticipation of pleasure must be explained without appealing to the desire. Successful explanations should not involve this or any other kind of circularity.

Regression of the Need for Explanation

Sometimes the explanans in an explanation will employ statements, or concepts, or principles which are as much or more in need of the same kind of explanation as was the original explanandum. In such cases we might say that the need for explanation regresses from the explanandum to the explanans. For example, some people, when considering the question, "Why is there a universe, instead of nothing at all?" reject the answer, "Because it just happened that way." They insist that we need more explanation than that. But some of them suggest that a satisfactory explanation of the existence of the universe is that God created it. Critics of this position have responded that this is not a satisfactory explanation because we are at least as much in need of an explanation for God's existence as we are for the existence of the universe. If the answers "It just happened" or "It's a mystery" are not satisfactory in the latter case, neither are they satisfactory in the former. According to such critics, the need for explanation regresses from the explanandum to the explanans; and where such regression occurs, no significant advance is made in our understanding of the explanandum.

The Scope of an Explanation

We generally believe that the more an explanation explains, the better it is; but an explanation must not be able to explain everything. Let us consider these two claims in order:

1. A thorough explanation frequently helps us to understand many things not directly involved in the original explanandum. For instance, a theory intended to explain the changes in shape and location of the continents over long periods of time may turn out also to explain aspects of earthquakes and volcanic activity. Such additional explanatory power offers evidence that the explanans is completely correct, or close to being so.

2. Some explanations could be used equally well no matter what the explanandum turned out to be. Such explanations lose their value because an important element of an explanation is that it tells us why *this* happened instead of something else. An explanans which could explain equally well every possible thing which *might* have happened really explains nothing, for it gives us no response to the question: Why this instead of that? When some personal disaster has occurred, for instance, people commonly ask why—why this illness, or accident, or death? And it is almost as common for them to receive the reply that it was fate, or destiny, or God's will. As explanations, such replies are worthless, because at any moment, for any person, no matter what is happening, we could say, "It is fate."[6] This point has nothing to do with whether we believe there are such forces as fate, destiny, karma, or divine will. If one received an explanation like this—"God has decided that the time has come to test your courage and endurance, and He knows that you are especially afraid of cancer, and that's why you have cancer now"— the objection could not be raised, because such an explanation does indicate why someone has cancer instead of, say, chicken pox.

Explanation as Proof

As you can see, there is no sharp division between explanation and argument. Sometimes an argument may explain nothing, and sometimes an explanation may prove nothing; but often it turns out that a proof of something also explains it, or that an explanation of something proves some things about it. Elements of both argument and explanation become entangled in complex ways when we are struggling for thorough understanding.

The best available explanation of something may include, in its explanans, some statements which we do not know to be true. But once we are sure that an explanation is the best one available, we may be able to employ that fact as evidence that *all* the statements in the explanans are true—whether we

---

6.   In most such cases, of course, to ask why is not to request an explanation but to lament, protest, call for sympathy, etc. And the proper response is not to give an explanation, but to extend compassion. Remarks such as "These things happen," or "It was fate," may have a legitimate *compassionate* use in such situations.

have any other evidence for some of them or not. In outline, the situation is this: We may determine that a certain explanation is free from detectable errors and that it fits with a substantial amount of our knowledge. We therefore accept it as the best available explanation for certain facts which we know to be true. Now, the explanans may include several statements for which we can give no deductive proof, offer no direct inductive evidence, and which we cannot confirm by simple observation. Because these statements are part of the best available explanation of something we know to be true, however, we have a strong reason to suppose that the statements themselves are true also. Thus, the power of the explanation serves as a kind of evidence for all the statements in the explanans.

Let us regard, without details, an example of this aspect of explanation. Consider how scientists came to believe that subatomic particles exist. They did not discover them by direct observation, as one might discover a new species of fish; nor are there any deductive or inductive arguments which show that such particles *must* exist if the physical world is to exist (there is more about that claim in Chapter 11). But the best explanation we can produce for what we observe in nature and in the laboratories of chemists and physicists includes statements to the effect that there are such particles. We believe the particles exist because their existence explains what we know from observation and inference. In some such cases, we will eventually acquire more direct evidence, but the strength of the explanation itself is the first ground for accepting some parts of the explanation.

DEFINITION

There is great variation in the purposes for which definitions may be employed, in the approaches which may be taken to forming them, and in the standards of correctness which may be applied to them. Many philosophers exhibit interest in definitions, but there is serious disagreement about the significance definitions have for philosophical thought. Some philosophers, especially those inclined toward conceptual analysis, think that philosophically interesting definitions should be accounts of the meanings of philosophically significant words or expressions. Those with reconstructionist inclinations see definition building as a means for assigning new, logically superior meanings to important expressions in order to provide us with both a more orderly and rational language and more precise concepts in which to do our speaking and thinking about difficult topics. Still other philosophers think that philosophically interesting definitions should aim at explaining the nature of things which words stand for, rather than the meanings of the words themselves.

And many philosophers have addressed themselves to philosophical problems and their solutions without discussing definitions at all.

In spite of such disagreement about what sort of thing should be defined (the *definiendum*) or what character the discussion which defines it (the *definiens*) should have, there is general agreement on some basic points which will seem familiar to you by now: The language in which definitions are framed should be free of vagueness and ambiguity. Definitions should be consistent. And definitions should avoid circularity, which in this case means employing the definiendum in the construction of the definiens—for example, using a word in a definition which is supposed to explain what that word itself means.

Many philosophical works involving definitions will presume some familiarity on the reader's part with the following topics.

Stipulative Definition

Sometimes we assign a special meaning to some word or expression. For instance, we might find it useful to do so if we want to concentrate our discussion or research on ideas which are not represented by any conveniently brief expressions in ordinary language. A definition which explains such a special assignment of meaning is called a *stipulative definition*. It is customary to allow a writer or speaker to stipulate a special meaning for any word or expression, as long as it is made clear precisely what meaning is being assigned to what expression, and in which contexts assignment is to apply. As long as such definitions accurately report the intentions of the stipulator, there can be no grounds for charging them with incorrectness—that is, to make an objection such as, "But that isn't what that word really means," would be to misunderstand the function of the stipulative definition. (Notice, this does not preclude us from objecting to some definitions if they interfere with, rather than promote, productive discussion.) In limited contexts, then, we can make words mean whatever we want them to mean, through the use of stipulative definitions.

Synonymy and Replacement

In many discussions, however, the purpose of a definition is not to assign a meaning to some expression, but to report accurately what that expression means when it is being employed normally. For example, a philosopher interested in the problems presented in Chapter 4 might try to construct a definition which reported precisely what people mean by "free" when they say that human beings have free will, or that some actions are free.

One widely accepted standard of success for such reportive definitions involves a replacement criterion: If the definiens provides us with a method for replacing the definiendum, wherever it occurs, with some other expression without significantly altering the meaning of what has been said, then the definition is correct.

One way to provide such a replacement, of course, is to find a synonymous expression. If, for example, we needed to explain some expressions in British English to someone familiar only with American English, we might offer definitions like this:

An elevator is called a lift.

A lorry is a truck.

These simple definitions by synonym pass the replacement requirement.

But we do not often find a simple synonym that will suit our needs. Consider the familiar word "door." If we think of the variety among doors, we see that a definiens of some complexity is required—for example, something along these lines:

A door is a piece of rigid material, mounted on hinges or designed to slide along a track, and located where it may be moved either to block off or to open up a passage into or out of a room, a building, or other enclosure such as a car or an airplane.

It seems bizarre to claim that this complex definiens, or something like it, has the same meaning as the simple word "door," but we still can make sense of the claim that, if we were to replace "door" in various sentences with "piece of rigid material ... airplane," the result (although terribly awkward) would say the same thing as the original sentence—make the same statement, ask the same question, give the same command, etc.

This approach to definition may succeed with many nouns, adjectives, verbs, or adverbs. But could we use it to explain the meaning of, for example, prepositions ("from," "to," "of") or articles ("a," "an," "the")? In these cases there seems to be no expression with which we could replace the word to be defined. Yet, a technique, called *definition in use,* does exist for formulating replacements for some such expressions.[7] For example, consider these statements:

The man who lives on Witchbane Hill is angry with us.

A man who lives on Witchbane Hill is angry with us.

7. This technique was introduced by Bertrand Russell.

If we tried to employ a synonymous definition to explain the difference between these two statements, we would be searching for different expressions to replace "the" and "a" in them without altering their meaning. But there are no such expressions. However, it is possible to give a procedure for restating such claims, so that the articles do not appear in the restatement, but the meaning is preserved. The first statement, for example, really tells us that there is something which is human, male, and lives on Witchbane Hill; that there is only one such thing, and that it (he) is angry with us. And the second statement tells us that there is at least one thing which is human, male, and living on Witchbane Hill; and that one such thing is angry with us. Schematically, "The F is G," can be replaced with

There is something which is F, and only one, and it is G.

And, "An F is G," can be replaced with

There is at least one F, and one F is G.

To show, in this way, how we could replace any statement containing a definite or indefinite article with another statement without the article, but having the same meaning, is one way of explaining what these articles contribute to the meaning of the original statements.

Is there any reliable way to tell that an original statement and its replacement really do have the same meaning? If we simply have to fall back on our intuitions at this point, the replacement criterion may not be worth much. Fortunately, we do not have to rely on our intuitions alone. If the statement and its replacement have the same meaning, they also must have the same truth-value—that is, if the original statement was true, its replacement must be true also, and if the original statement was false, its replacement must be false also. If one of the two statements could be true while the other was false, then there is some significant difference in their meanings, and the attempt at definition has gone wrong. To be sure, this is not all that is involved in preserving meaning while replacing one statement with another, but it gives us a widely used test for the success of a definition: A successful definition must give us a method for replacing any statement in which the definiendum occurs with some other statement not containing the definiendum, but without its being possible for the replacement to have a different truth-value than has the original statement.

Exact Definition

In some situations philosophers seek definitions which offer more than a synonymous replacement for the definiens. They seek definitions which explain the character of the *things* for which expressions stand, rather than merely reporting the meaning of the expressions. Such definitions often are expected to meet (or come very close to meeting) the requirements of an *exact definition*.

To understand properly the character of an exact definition, you must first understand what necessary conditions and sufficient conditions are. A *necessary condition* for something is a condition which must be satisfied if it is to be possible for that something to exist, or be the case. Thus, being a four-sided figure is a necessary condition for something's being a square. Being a mammal is a necessary condition for something's being a dog. But four-sided figures need not be squares, and mammals need not be dogs, so being a square is not a necessary condition for being four-sided, nor is being a dog a necessary condition for being a mammal. A *sufficient condition* for something is a condition the satisfaction of which guarantees that the something exists or is the case. Being red is a sufficient condition for being colored, and being in pain is a sufficient condition for being alive. But, since many colored things are not red, and many living things are not in pain, being colored is not a sufficient condition for being red, nor is being alive a sufficient condition for being in pain.

An exact definition is one in which the definiens consists of a list of necessary conditions for the definiendum, such that the sum of those necessary conditions, taken all together, is a sufficient condition for the definiendum. Let us consider a simple example, the definition of a bachelor:

> A bachelor is a human male, eligible for marriage, but who never has married.

If anything is a bachelor, it must be human and male. We do not count nonhumans or females of any kind as bachelors. These are two necessary conditions for something's being a bachelor. And, of course, a bachelor cannot be married, or ever have been married. This is a third necessary condition for something's being a bachelor. But unmarried male infants are not bachelors. A person must be of marriageable age to be a bachelor, and there we have a fourth necessary condition. No one of these necessary conditions is sufficient by itself. But if we take the sum of them, we do have a sufficient condition for something's being a bachelor. That is, anything which is human, male, eligible, and has never been married must be a bachelor. Thus, we have an exact definition of a bachelor.

Every statement of a necessary or a sufficient condition can be phrased as a universal generalization. All bachelors must be human, and all bachelors must be eligible, and so forth. Also, everything which is an eligible, never-married, human male is a bachelor. We can use this fact to test attempts at exact definition for their correctness—that is, we can look for counterex-amples. If we could find a bachelor who had been married at some time or who was not human, then we would have a counterexample to the claims that no bachelors have ever been married and that all bachelors are human. In that case, the definition of a bachelor given above would be said to be too *narrow,* since its definiens would exclude some of the cases which the definiendum includes. Or if we could find a never-married, eligible, human male who was not a bachelor, then we would have refuted the claim that all such individuals are bachelors. And in that case the given definition would be said to be too *broad,* since the definiens would include some cases not included by the definiendum. When such refutations by counterexample are found, they show us that it is a mistake to take certain conditions to be necessary or sufficient. On the other hand, if we find case after case in which whatever is described by the definiens also is described by the definiendum, and vice versa, we can become increasingly confident that the definition is correct.

Open Texture

One might think that the exact definition is the only really acceptable kind of definition to seek, so that if we fail to find an appropriate set of necessary and sufficient conditions, we must decide either that we still don't have a sound understanding of what we are trying to define, or else that what we are trying to define is so hopelessly vague and confused that it would be better to abandon it and invent new words and ideas with which to think more clearly. Several philosophers have resisted this view. They argue that many words and concepts which cannot be defined in terms of necessary and sufficient conditions are just as clear as they need to be to let us talk and think precisely about the situations with which they deal. For example, let us return to the definition of "door" which was offered a few pages ago. That definition told us of many features which doors commonly have, but how many of them really could be regarded as necessary or sufficient conditions for something's being a door? This is a way of asking whether we can think of any possible counterexample situation in which something is a door but fails to satisfy one of the conditions mentioned (showing that the condition is not *necessary*) or else that something satisfies all the conditions mentioned, but still is not a door (showing that the sum of the conditions is not *sufficient*). The way to approach the question is to think of as many different kinds of doors as you can, with as much variety as you can imagine, and see how well the proposed definition fits them. Here are some samples of this approach.   (1)   Must a door be made of rigid material? Many are, and there certainly is a difference between a door and a curtain. But some folding doors, and some doors for pets, are made of rather flexible materials. Could you make a screen door of insect netting, which just snapped or zipped into place, or would it have to have a rigid frame to really be a door? Do tents ever have doors, or are tent closures just flaps? (2) Must a door be mounted on hinges or a track? Doors can be dropped into place from above, or raised from below. Some doors have an iris diaphragm arrangement. A door could be mounted on a piston and rammed into place from a wall facing the doorway. In fact, our ways of opening and closing doors seem to be limited only by our imagination and ingenuity. It should be noted, too, that the mechanisms mentioned are also used for windows, gates, valves, lids, and other nondoors. (3) Is the function of every door to provide passage into or out of some enclosed space? The doors on kitchen cabinets and appliances don't provide for passage, but they do provide access to enclosed space. Doors in dollhouses or models often don't even provide access—does that mean they are not real doors? If you use a door for a desk or table, does that mean it really is no longer a door? And, again, windows, gates, vents, lids, and valves provide access to or even passage into and out of, many enclosed areas.

We could say considerably more about doors, but this is enough to show what kinds of considerations would lead some people to say that there can be no exact definition for the term. Yet, that does not seem to be a reason for inventing a new, more precise word. There are very few circumstances under which we have trouble recognizing a door when we encounter one, or making ourselves understood when we talk about doors. In spite of the lack of an exact definition, the concept and the word both seem to function effectively enough.

Concepts which cannot be given an exact definition, but still are not hopelessly confused, are said to be *open-textured*. Though we cannot give an exact definition of such concepts, we can explain them by another kind of definition which sometimes is called a *characterization*. In giving a characterization, we may describe some illustrative examples, and then point out common features which explain why the examples and many other cases like them are the sorts of things we are trying to define. We recognize that not all things that have these features will be what we are trying to define, and that some of the things we are trying to define will lack some of the features we mention. The point of the characterization is to set up a basis for comparisons. For example, if what we have said about doors makes clear what a lot of doors are like, then we are in a position to judge how *similar* new entities are to the doors with which we are familiar, and if the similarity is great enough, we will count the new entities as doors, too. If there are too many dissimilarities, we will decide that a newly encountered object is not a door, after all. And, we may encounter cases where the similarities and dissimilarities are so delicately balanced that we don't know how to decide. To sum up: the basic goal of exact definition is finding universal generalizations which describe features which *all* things of the kind being defined have in common; while the goal of characterization is to offer nonuniversal generalizations and examples which provide a basis for judgments of similarity.

As you might expect, the logic of characterizations is quite different from that of exact definitions. Since universal generalizations are not involved, appeals to counterexamples cannot be employed to show that a characterization is in error. In fact, there is considerable disagreement about how to defend or refute characterizations, and many excellent philosophers think that characterizations are not acceptable as definitions. In order to begin a study of philosophy you need not take sides on this issue—it is too complex and difficult to be a problem for beginning students. But you should be aware of the difference between a characterization and an exact definition, so that you can try to determine which of them is being provided in any discussion you read. To mistake one for the other is likely to cause you to misunderstand the arguments given for or against the attempt at definition or characterization.

SOURCES OF KNOWLEDGE

Throughout this chapter we have noted that serious disagreements exist among philosophers about which procedures in argument, explanation, or definition are acceptable, and which procedures involve a substantial risk of error. These disagreements are largely reflections of more fundamental disagreements about the kinds of knowledge which human beings can possess, and the sources from which human knowledge can be obtained. In this brief section, we will sketch a few of the issues involved in these fundamental disagreements.

A Priori and A Posteriori Knowledge

There is a long philosophical tradition that human knowledge has two basic sources. One of these is experience, which includes both the data provided for us by our physical senses and the data provided by our feelings and emotions. The other source is reason, which includes the capacity to draw inferences, and, according to some philosophers, any other source of belief which is not clearly an aspect of experience.

The distinction between the a priori and the a posteriori is based upon this distinction between experience and reason. Roughly speaking, what is *a priori* is available to us from the use of reason alone, without any appeal to experience; while what is *a posteriori* is available to us only through experience. One question, then, upon which philosophers have taken many different positions is, How much of human knowledge may be obtained a priori, and how much of it may be obtained a posteriori?

Concepts

The distinction between the a priori and the a posteriori bears upon our ability to acquire concepts or ideas. Some have maintained, at one extreme, that all our concepts are, or could be, acquired a priori, with no contribution from experience being necessary. In this view, the role played by experience is at most that of a convenient reminder which prompts reason to produce a concept which still could have been produced without the experience. At the other extreme, some hold that reason produces *no* concepts, except, perhaps, by combining ideas already acquired from experience into more complex ideas which may represent nothing yet encountered in experience. In this view, all our basic concepts are introduced by experience. And, finally, there are intermediate views holding that some concepts—for example, of simple observable properties such as redness or sweetness—could be acquired only by experiencing those properties; while other concepts—for example, "$\sqrt{-1}$"—require no prompting from experience but are produced solely by the activity of reason.

Knowledge

With respect to knowledge, the essential question is not whether we can know something without having had any experience at all (few philosophers would claim that we can), but whether we could know a particular fact without directly observing that it is true, or observing evidence of its truth. If such observational experience is a necessary condition of our knowing some fact, then that knowledge is a posteriori knowledge. If no supporting experience is required for us to know some fact, then we know it a priori.

Analytic and Synthetic Statements

Most of us would like to make some distinction between statements which are genuinely informative and those which, though true, seem to tell us nothing at all. The technical distinction between analytic and synthetic statements is significant in this regard. As it was introduced by Kant, the distinction is this: A statement is *analytic* if (a) the concept of the subject includes the concept of the predicate, and (b) the denial of the statement is a contradiction. Conversely, a statement is *synthetic* if (a') the concept of the predicate is *not* included in the concept of the subject, and (b') the denial of the statement is not a contradiction. Consider:

(1)   Bachelors are unmarried.

(2)   Ralph's car is green.

According to Kant's criteria, statement (1) would count as analytic, since the concept of a bachelor includes as a part (a necessary condition) the concept of being unmarried, and it would be inconsistent to claim that someone was a bachelor and also that he was married. But statement (2) would by synthetic, for the concept of being green is not a part of the concept of being Ralph's car, nor is it a contradiction to deny that Ralph's car is green.

But now consider:

(3)   Nothing can be totally red and totally green simultaneously.

While it would be inconsistent to claim that something is red and green at the same time, condition (a) does not seem to be satisfied by (3). Cases like this have led many philosophers to say, somewhat more vaguely than Kant, that analytic statements are those which are true "in virtue of the meanings of the words in the statement," thus counting (3) and statements like it as analytic.

Whether a synthetic statement is true depends upon what the world really is like. Statement (2), for instance, will be true if Ralph's car really is green, and false if the car is some other color. This feature of synthetic statements makes them informative for us. If we know that (2) is true, then we know something about the world. On the other hand, statements which are true only in virtue of the meanings of their words do not have this feature—they would be true no matter what the world was like. The truth of (1) does not tell us who is a bachelor, or even whether there are any bachelors. In fact, it tells us nothing about how things actually are.

It is clear that some analytic statements, while true, are useless. For example,

(4)   An unmarried man is not married.

is analytically true, and totally uninteresting. Sometimes such statements are said to be *trivially true,* or sometimes they are called *tautologies.* The important question about analytic statements is whether some of them are *more* than mere tautologies, or are nontrivially true—that is, worth knowing. Examples like (1), (3) and (4) do not offer much support for a positive answer to this question, but there are other cases to consider. For instance, a good case can be made for the claim that the theorems of algebra and geometry all are true in virtue of the meanings of the words in which they are expressed—that is, their truth follows from the definitions of such expressions as "integer," "sum," "parallel," "equal," etc. But it is implausible to claim that such theorems are uninformative, or merely trivially true.

Empiricism and Rationalism

A substantial number of philosophers have accepted the view that philosophy is an a priori enterprise. *Empirical* questions—that is, questions whose answers require observation or a posteriori appeals to experience—are thought to be the property of the sciences. From this point of view, the answer to the question, "What kinds of things can philosohy discover?" depends upon the answer to the question, "What can we know a priori?" There is especially important disagreement about whether we can learn synthetic truths through a priori methods. Those who think so often are identified as philosophical *rationalists.* Those who think that synthetic truths can be discovered only by a posteriori methods and that a priori methods can produce only analytic truth often are identified as *empiricists.* For an empiricist, of course, the question whether analytic statements can be nontrivial becomes the question whether philosophy itself can be nontrivial.

Intuition

Finally, we must consider the role of intuition in philosophical thought. Several philosophers have included intuition as a source of knowledge, and they generally agree about the following points: (a) intuition is not the same as experience—it does not involve the use of our physical senses, or our feelings or emotions; (b) intuition does not rely on argument or explanation—what we know by intuition is not a conclusion based on evidence, or the result of inference or other kinds of reasoning. Thus, intuition does not fit comfortably into either the a priori or the a posteriori category. Since it involves no reasoning, but is a simple, direct recognition that something is true, it seems to be a special kind of observation or experience—and so we might be tempted to count it as an a posteriori source of knowledge. But since we say that intuition does not involve any of the sources of experience we normally think of, we are tempted to treat it as an a priori source of knowledge. Is it, then, a special function of reason, a special kind of experience, or something different from either of these? Or is intuition not a source of knowledge at all?

CONCLUDING REMARK

In this chapter you have encountered many different views about how knowledge and understanding may be obtained. No attempt has been made to suggest which of these views is correct, which in error. There is much more which could be said about all the positions discussed, and there are many other important positions which might have been considered. Nothing has been settled here. But the aims of the chapter will be satisfied if this brief introduction to these issues and their special terminology leaves you better prepared to read, interpret, and critically evaluate the selections which follow.

3

Analyzing Philosophical Discussion

Philosophical discussion goes on both orally and in writing. In either form, it is often complex and difficult, and it demands all of one's attention and a lot of hard thought. Keeping the discussion clear, or even comprehensible, often requires very careful selection of words and ordering of statements. For all these reasons, most people find it easier to work with at least some of the discussion in writing, so that they can proceed at a comfortable pace, pause to consider some passages at length, go back to earlier parts of the discussion, and so on. This chapter will concentrate on providing an effective method for reading philosophical discussion and understanding it. Much of what is said here applies to listening with comprehension, also, but the demands on memory and concentration are greater in oral discussion.

THE BASIC APPROACH

Reading a philosophical discussion is not like reading a newspaper or light fiction. The kind of understanding at which philosophical writing is aimed demands more participation from a reader than is required for the passing on of information, or for entertainment. Thorough mastery of a philosophical work involves clearly understanding not only the issue and the author's position on it, but also the reasons the author has given for taking that position, some idea of alternative positions which have been rejected, and some opinion of the extent to which the author's position has been presented clearly and defended successfully. Such mastery will not be achieved with a single reading unless one is well-trained, talented, and already familiar with a substantial amount of philosophical literature. Even the most capable philosopher usually re-reads works which are to be mastered in fine detail. The method presented here involves multiple readings of the philosophical text. Fundamentally, there are three stages. First, skim the selection to get a sense of its direction and goals. Then read the whole selection carefully, noting how it is structured, where each major argument or explanation is, and how the major sections fit together. Finally, study the selection section by section, getting as clear as you can about the details of each argument and explanation, and formulating some critical opinion about the success of that particular section and its contribution to the aims of the whole work.

This program may sound tedious and difficult, especially if you have not done this sort of work before. In fact, it is difficult and time-consuming at first. But it involves skills which can be developed, and with practice most students can move through the various stages more quickly and efficiently than on their first few attempts. Some methodical approach like this is necessary if one is to grasp the nature of the problems being discussed, and the ways in which philosophers try to deal with them. The broader benefit in learning to read and study a selection in this way is that it is a sound method for approaching the critical study of any written work which presents and rationally defends a position on any topic.

COMPONENTS OF A PHILOSOPHICAL WORK

Before we consider the details of employing the method just outlined, let us distinguish a variety of the components which may be encountered in philosophical writing. Some of the selections will contain all of these components, while others will contain only some of them. There is no general way to decide whether the lack of some component counts as a defect in a work—what is required of each work depends entirely upon what the work sets out to accomplish, and each case must be judged independently.

Treatment of the Issues

Naturally, many portions of any philosophical work will be addressed directly to the philosophical issue the work is about. Among such portions are these components:

1. Statement of the problem. Sometimes the problem to be treated may be indicated with just a sentence or two, or perhaps just in the title of the work. Usually, however, the author devotes considerable space to describing the issues to be addressed. In some cases, if the author believes that the issue is especially complex or misunderstood by many people, you may find extensive discussion intended to explain and clarify the issue itself. There may be arguments intended to prove that the author's view of the problem is the proper one and that other views of it are mistaken. In fact, some very important papers have been devoted entirely to explaining more clearly what some philosophical problem was, without making any attempt to solve it.

2. Solution of the problem. Most philosophical works go beyond discussing the nature of some problem to suggest at least part of a solution to it. In such cases we must distinguish those parts of the work which state, explain, or illustrate the solution the author is proposing, and those parts in which arguments or explanations are presented in support of that proposed solution.

3. Discussion of alternative views. A really thorough discussion of a philosophical problem not only will present and defend a solution to the problem, but also will discuss alternative views. Such discussion could include a careful description of alternative views, explanations of why they might seem attractive to some people, and critical accounts indicating strengths and weaknesses—especially the weaknesses which make these alternatives inferior to the position the author defends. In most cases, these opposing views will have been presented and supported by other authors, but in many cases an author may want to develop alternatives to his own position which have not yet occurred to anyone else. To expose weaknesses in such alternatives serves both to forestall criticism of the author's own position and to support that position as the only acceptable one.

Structure-Indicating Components

Careful authors not only discuss the issues which concern them, but insert in their discussion various remarks which help us to understand how the discussion fits together. These remarks are not actually about the issues. Sometimes there are whole paragraphs which explain the aims of various parts of the work or explain how arguments or explanations are intended to support some claims made in the work. Or there may be warnings against supposing that certain statements or arguments are related in some way which the author doesn't intend. Sometimes the author may point out that there was gaps or incompleted portions in an argument or explanation, or that some statements are in need of support which the author cannot provide.

Not all structure-indicators appear in the form of descriptive paragraphs or sentences. There are numerous single words or short expressions which may be sprinkled throughout a discussion to indicate that some statements are premises, others conclusions, or that some statements are explained by others, and so forth. Expressions such as "thus," "therefore," "so," "hence," and "it follows that" follow premises and precede conclusions. Expressions such as "because," "since," "for the reason that," "is evidenced by," and "follows from the fact that" follow conclusions and indicate that premises are coming next. Other expressions (not hard to recognize if you are consciously looking for them) help a reader to see the structure of explanations, definitions, illustrations, and examples. These expressions are so common in ordinary speech and writing that we tend to use them without thinking about their real significance. But if you remember that they function to show us the structure of arguments, explanations, and other portions of complex discussions, and pay careful attention to them, they will help your understanding of what you read considerably.

Extraneous Material

It is not unusual for authors or lecturers to insert remarks, anecdotes, or even lengthy discussions about other topics into their discussions of philosophical issues. Sometimes these function as devices to keep the audience's attention, sometimes the author simply can't resist a chance to comment on some subject that has come up in or been suggested by the discussion, and sometimes the author simply loses the trail and wanders into irrelevant areas. However artful or entertaining these digressions may be, they contribute nothing to the discussion of the issues, and it is important to recognize them for what they are in order to dismiss them from further consideration.

THE METHOD IN DETAIL

Keeping the above preliminary remarks in mind, we can now proceed to a more detailed consideration of each of the three steps involved in the analysis of a philosophical discussion: (1) skimming the work, (2) reading it carefully, and (3) critical study of the work.

Skimming the Work

If when you start to read a complicated philosophical work you have trouble seeing the purpose of much of what you read, you can reduce this difficulty by having a rough idea of the aims of the work before beginning to read. The purpose of the preliminary skimming of the work is to provide that rough idea. Skimming is no substitude for careful reading. It cannot give a good grasp of the problems, arguments, or explanations. If it is done carefully, however, it can give some idea of the structure of the work. Do not spend too much time and effort on this initial skim of the material. The trick is to spend only a few minutes gathering your sketch of the work, without trying to understand details.

Skimming a work successfully should reveal (1) what major topics the author addresses, and where in the work they are discussed; (2) where the major claims or conclusions of the author appear, and, if more than one major topic is discussed, which of these claims is involved with which topic; (3) where any extensive arguments or explanations occur, and which topics or claims they are intended to clarify or support. If you keep such results in mind while you read, you will have some idea where the discussion is going and what it is trying to achieve. If you need any notes, they should amount to no more than a brief list of major topics, indicating what portions of the work are devoted to each topic. If you find yourself developing extensive notes or starting to underline passages, then you are picking out too much detail and starting to read, instead of skimming. Remember, the aim of skimming is only to gain a sense of direction as you give the work its first careful reading.

If a work is short (as the selections in this book are), you can skim by glancing at each page, or even at each paragraph. There are several things to look for. First, be sure to read the title of the selection, and all the headings and subheadings which occur in the text. These represent some effort on the part of the author to give the reader a sense of direction, and they can be very helpful. Then glance at the beginning and end of each paragraph. Typical paragraphs introduce their topics in the first or second sentence, and often the concluding sentence will suggest what the paragraph had to contribute, or what the next paragraph will be about. Look for words, expressions, or sentences which are italicized or emphasized in some other way. They are likely to reveal topics, important conclusions, or significant new concepts or terms. Try not to get involved in seeing what a paragraph actually says about things—just find out where various portions of the discussion occur.

Skimming short selections in this way may seem awkward or inefficient at first, but with practice you should be able to get a rough idea of most fifteen- to twenty-page works in four or five minutes. Familiarity with the subject matter helps. The more you know about philosophical problems and philosophical thinking, the more efficiently you will be able to determine the drift of a discussion by glancing quickly over the text.

It would be too tedious and slow to try to skim longer works in this way. Glancing at every paragraph, or every page in a book, for instance, would give you too much to remember and would take too much time. But books discuss topics in more detail than do shorter works, so that the number of topics, arguments, or explanations covered in one chapter of a book is likely to be smaller than one would find in an article or paper of similar length. To skim a book, start with the table of contents. If you are lucky, it will be an analytic table of contents—that is, titles of chapters will be followed with a brief description of the contents of that chapter. Sometimes one need look no further. On the other hand, some tables of contents give nothing more than the titles of the chapters. In this case, look for an index of subjects in the back of the book, in which you can see what some topics will be. You may need to skim through the individual chapters, looking for titles, headings, subheadings, and, especially, for summaries at the beginning or end of each chapter. Look for an introductory chapter, or a preface which outlines the plan of the book.

If none of these sources gives an idea of the plan of the book, then there will be little profit in trying to skim the whole work at once. Instead, skim the first chapter, read it carefully, then skim the second chapter, read it carefully, and so forth.

Reading the Work

Your first reading of a philosophical work should give a clear view of the problems the author is addressing, the positions being taken on those problems, and the location and character of the support offered for those positions. As much as possible, proceed straight through the work, without skipping sections, and without going back to reread, or stopping for extensive critical thought. You should have two major goals as you undertake this reading. One is to develop a substantial outline of the work. This outline will form the basis for the critical study you undertake later on. The second goal is to put yourself as sympathetically as possible, for the time being, into the author's viewpoint.

It is important to be sympathetic during a first reading. You cannot make an accurate critical evaluation of an author's position unless you understand that position thoroughly. If you know what the author has said, but it all seems totally implausible or silly, then you are in a weak position from which to begin criticism. Good criticism requires not only evaluating what an author *did* say, but also being able to project the author's viewpoint to take into account what the author *would* say in response to criticism. If you have no idea how the author's viewpoint could be appealing or tempting, you will be unable to make such projections. The point of critical strategy involved here is central. To show that a position on some issue is incorrect, your best procedure will be to make the very strongest case possible *for* that position, and then show that even that strongest case must fail. But it will be very difficult to develop the strongest case if you are unable to see how an author could have found his position plausible. This does not mean that you should try to believe or agree with what you read, but you should try hard to see how the claims, arguments, and explanations could seem correct to someone.

While reading, it will be important to take notes. We will discuss what these notes should contain below, but, first, consider the physical procedure for taking notes. Some readers leave the original text totally unmarked, and put all their notes on separate pages. Others rely on underlining and making marginal notes in the text. There are advantages and disadvantages for each procedure, which we can explain in terms of two features of notes taken on a first reading of a work. One is that they are not an independent record of your thoughts as you read, but merely personal reminders of those thoughts. The second feature is that as you study and reread the selection, you may decide that the initial notes were in error. Because they are merely reminders, the notes you take are of little or no value to anyone else. When you see what is underlined, or indicated with arrows, brackets, exclamation marks, etc., or when you read marginal notes, or a page of written remarks, you will recall what you were thinking when you made them. Such marks or notes almost always will be impossible for another person to interpret, and they could only distract and puzzle another reader. Because you may want to revise the notes as you study more carefully, it is important not to mark the text in ways that cannot be changed later. It is unwise, then, to make any notes or marks in the text in ink, or any other permanent medium. If you are working with a text others may want to use (a library book, or a book you intend to sell after reading), it ranges between vandalism and simple discourtesy to leave marginal notes and marks scattered through the text to distract other readers.

The major advantages of marking the text, or writing notes in its margins, are that it can be done quickly and easily and that your own notes are placed as close as possible to the text they concern. Writing notes on separate pages is more time-consuming, requires longer entries, and calls for some system for identifying the part of the text each note is about. On the other hand, longer comments are more easily entered on separate pages, and it is easier to revise and reorganize notes kept on separate pages. Perhaps the most efficient system is a combination of brief indications in the text and accompanying longer notes on separate pages.

Whatever method you use for note-taking, you should be discriminating in what you put down. Many students attempt to note every significant statement in a text. But carefully written texts may be very compact and contain no extraneous material, so that every statement is significant. At the end of the first reading, some students find that they have underlined, or even copied down in independent notes, almost every sentence in the text. Such a practice is useless for our purposes, since it makes no discrimination at all among the contents of the work and leaves one with no guide as a basis for further study. If you tend to make this mistake, you might try to take separate notes rather than underline. The extra effort involved in writing out notes will help you to be more selective and discriminating.

A final advantage of taking separate notes is that doing so may promote better understanding of the text. A common failing among students is that, although they can find important claims and arguments in the text, they do not really understand what they have located. If you understand a statement, then you should be able to put whatever it says into your own words. Merely underlining significant claims does locate them, but does not encourage you to become clear about what they say. If you force yourself to avoid quotation and keep separate notes in your own words, you will force yourself to grasp more clearly what you read and you will make it more difficult to pass over something without realizing that you don't understand what it means.

But, and this is important, do not get so wrapped up in taking notes that you destroy the continuity of your reading. Really detailed notes can be left for the third step in studying the text. What you should produce on the first careful reading is little more than a substantial outline of the discussion. If the work you are reading contains extraneous material, identify it so that you can leave it out of further consideration. The rest of the work should be broken up into its component parts, and your notes should indicate what is in each part and how it relates to the rest. What you need is to find a description of each issue being addressed, to locate each of the major claims the author wants to make on those issues, and to identify each explanation of, or argument supporting, each such claim. In one way or another, your notes should record the relationships among the various components of the work.

A useful way to regulate reading and note-taking may be this: as you complete each paragraph, ask yourself what its function was in the whole work. Did it present a problem, issue, or topic to be discussed? Did it present some major view of the author's? Was it part of some explanation or argument? Was it extraneous material? If you can identify the role of the paragraph in the whole work, then that role should be indicated in your notes. If you can't see the role of the paragraph, just make a note of that fact and go on. But if you find that several paragraphs in a row are mysterious, then you have lost the train of thought and need to go back and try to pick it up. Normally, reading notes should contain a remark for each paragraph, briefly indicating its role. Of course, if a single argument or explanation is several paragraphs long, you may need only a single entry to note the function of the whole group of paragraphs. And some paragraphs may contain several distinct items of importance and need to be noted in more detail. Be sure to watch for structure-indicating portions of the work, which will help show how various paragraphs are intended to be connected.

We have emphasized here that in reading and outlining a work for the first time, you should not try to pause and evaluate each portion. But do not interpret this emphasis as a strict prohibition of critical thinking. While you read, it may happen that certain questions, objections, additional evidence, or other relevant material will occur to you. In that case, jot them down in your notes, so that you can come back to them later.

Critical Study

When you have read the work and outlined its basic structure, you will be ready to begin a critical study in detail. Using your outline, select all the passages which are addressed to a common theme and organize them in their logical order. That is, decide which parts of the discussion are intended to support other parts, and which depend upon other parts. When you have organized a portion of the work in this way, you can begin a careful, very detailed study.

The first move in such a study is to get the structure of the discussion as clear as possible. For example, if it is an argument, locate all its inferences and identify their premises and conclusions. If it is an explanation, pick out exactly the explanandum and find all the ingredients of the explanans. Discard extraneous material. At this stage, try not to pass over a single sentence in the text without deciding what its function and significance are.

When the structure is as clear to you as possible, you can begin a critical examination of what you have organized. Is the discussion consistent? Is circularity avoided? Are the premises of inferences true? Are the inferences valid, or strong? Do the explanations measure up to the standards we have discussed? This is the point at which you will bring all the material presented in Chapter 2 into play. Ideally, one would examine every inference, definition, explanation, or statement which played a part in developing the major theme of the work. If you discover errors or incompleteness, then see if there are ways to correct them or to fill the gaps so that the major contentions of the discussion could still be defended. If the discussion fails to establish its major point, is it possible to devise a way to show that point to be mistaken?

Once you have worked through one section of the work in this critical way, take up another, and so on until all have been examined. Then review all the results to see what you think about the major contentions of the whole work. Are the statements upon which the author's views are based true, or are there some statements among them which can be shown to be false, or which are in doubt? Are the consequences of the author's views acceptable, or do they require us to adopt beliefs or courses of action which are absurd or just as paradoxical as the problem to which the views are a response? Are the author's views relatively complete, as a response to the questions which gave rise to them, or do they leave important questions unanswered, or puzzling statements unexplained or unsupported? And, finally, if you have discovered serious problems such as these in the work, are there ways in which those problems could be solved, in support of the author's views; or are there ways in which it could be shown that the problems involve errors which make the author's views indefensible?

Typically, you will not be able to complete this kind of critical evaluation. You will find statements about whose truth or falsity you are undecided, arguments or inferences which you are uncertain how to evaluate, gaps in the discussion about which you cannot tell whether they can be filled. Thus, you are unlikely to be in a position to decide that the work is totally successful or that it is simply a failure. Instead, you will have some idea of its strong or promising points and its weaknesses. Recalling the discussion in Chapter 1 about how one can make philosophical progress through improved under-standing, yet without understanding perfectly, you should be able to see that having reached a complex critical estimate of this sort about a philosophical work does represent genuine philosophical progress.

As it has been presented, this critical study of a philosophical work may seem too demanding to be reasonable. Do we really expect any beginning student to study this completely every aspect of a philosophical work? Of course not. In fact, accomplished philosophers must expend great effort and much time to give many works a really complete critical study—and even then, to say that a study is complete is not to say that all questions about the work have been answered. To expect a student to complete such an enterprise would not be reasonable at all.

But the skills required for this sort of work are skills which improve with training and practice. And they are skills upon which all good philosophical work depends. It is no more unreasonable to ask the beginner to *try* to develop such skills than it is to ask a beginning swimmer to try to swim, even though in either case we know that a beginner's performance will leave much to be desired. No amount of talking about how it is done can provide the kind of learning which results from trying it yourself.

So, as you read selections in the remaining chapters, make use of this method as best you can. Work with the review questions, which direct you to the major considerations you should have in mind. If you know others who are reading the same selections, discuss the issues with them. Be patient, and if you are diligent you should see that after some practice you have become more adept at this kind of reading and analysis, and that it is becoming less awkward. At that point, you will begin to see what the philosopher's job is like.

A sketch of a complex procedure like this one is incomplete without illustrations. In Chapter 4, three selections are followed by an extended discussion which points out some of what should be discovered in reading them and some of the considerations which should emerge in critical study. These extended discussions will not be complete—many interesting points could be added to them, and some of them you may think of yourself—but they will include enough critical work to give a clearer idea how such things are done.

4

Freedom, Determinism, and Moral Responsibility

For centuries philosophers have been puzzled by three seemingly incompatible tendencies in human thought. One is the tendency toward causal explanation. When we are confronted with any event, including the behavior of ourselves and other persons, we are inclined to believe that if we only knew enough we could explain how that event came to happen by pointing out its causes. That is, we tend to think that *every* event is the result of some set of causes. A second tendency which nearly all of us have is to treat persons as if they are morally responsible for some of their behavior. Thus, we praise or reward people for some of the things they do, and encourage them to behave similarly in the future. And we blame or punish people for other things they do, and warn them not to act that way again.

But, third, we also tend not to hold people responsible for *every* bit of their behavior. A little thought about the circumstances under which we do not praise or blame people for what they do reveals that we seem to withhold judgments of responsibility most readily when we are aware of a reasonably good causal explanation for the behavior in question. When we combine this tendency with the first two, we have the ingredients for a paradox, because it seems that we wish, simultaneously, to accept all three of the following claims:

(1) All human behavior is causally determined.

(2) Persons are morally responsible for some of their behavior.

(3) Persons are never morally responsible for behavior which is causally determined.

If any two of these claims are true, then the remaining one *must* be false (that can be established with deductively valid arguments). Yet, each of the claims seems plausible, and can be defended with impressive arguments. The selections in this chapter are addressed to the task of finding some satisfactory way to deal with this paradox.

One major theme in these selections is the disagreement between *causal determinism* and *indeterminism*. Causal determinism is the view that every event, no matter what kind of event it is, occurs and has the characteristics it has as a result of other events which are its causes. From this point of view, every event is an *effect*, and no event can occur by chance, spontaneously, or without cause. Causal determinists also hold that there is only one possible set of effects which can be produced by any set of causes. Thus, given the state of the world at one moment, there is only one possible condition in which it could be at any later moment. Causal determinism rejects the view that there ever are any real possible alternatives—at any time and in any place, the only way things possibly could have been is the way they actually are. A causal determinist, of course, would accept claim (1) and then choose between (2) and (3).

Indeterminism is simply the denial of determinism. The indeterminist claims that at least some events are not totally the result of a set of causes; that there are, at least sometimes, genuine alternative possibilities. Notice that indeterminists do not claim that *all* events are uncaused, but only that *some* are. Indeterminists may disagree among themselves as to how many uncaused events there are and what kinds of events they might be. For this reason we cannot say, generally, whether an indeterminist would accept or reject claim (1). This point is important, since many people have thought that they could appeal to modern physics to argue against (1). That is, many developments in physics suggest that events involving subatomic particles occur at random. If this were true, then it would support a kind of indeterminism and refute complete causal determinism. But human behavior does not occur at the subatomic level, and it might be that, although some subatomic events occur at random, all behavior by organisms still is causally determined. Thus, some indeterminists might agree with causal determinists that (1) is true.

There are indications that we do think deterministically about much of human behavior. When we try to explain what someone has done by appealing to that person's education, training, upbringing, or heredity or by considering the influences of disease, drugs, state of mind, or environmental irritations, we seem to be offering causal explanations. If we think a science of psychology is possible we are thereby committed to a deterministic view of much human behavior. Yet, many people who regard psychology as a genuine science, and who do give the kinds of explanations just indicated, would be reluctant to agree with (1). If we can clarify the extent to which we think human behavior is causally determined, we can take one step toward resolving this paradox.

A second step is to become clearer about the character of moral responsibility. Almost all of us do hold people responsible for some of what they do, for we do give credit or blame, do praise or rebuke, do hand out rewards or punishments. But what is the point of such practices? Do we engage in them because we think people might have (*could* have) acted differently, and we wish to commend their good choices and condemn their bad ones? Or is it simply that we want to influence (causally determine?) their future behavior by providing motives for increasing certain kinds of behavior and decreasing other kinds? Is the question whether a particular reward or punishment is appropriate a question about *justice* (is it deserved?) or about *efficiency* (will it produce the desired behavioral effects)? We frequently discuss rewards and punishments as if their function was to regulate the behavior of those to whom they are awarded. From that point of view, rewards and punishments are part of the system of causes which determine human behavior. Such considerations might incline us to accept (2) and reject (3). But, we often act as if we think people should not be held responsible for their behavior unless they *could* have acted in some other way. We tend to excuse from responsibility persons who can say, truly, "I couldn't help it," and we tend to accept causal explanations of actual behavior as evidence that no other behavior was possible. For example, the function of the insanity defense in law is not to show that the defendant did not do the deeds of which he is accused, but that they were effects of his abnormal condition. From this point of view it is tempting to accept (3) and then choose between (1) and (2).

It seems that we must reject at least one of the claims (1)–(3). But which one? One commonly defended position, often called *hard determinism*, accepts (1) and (3), thus rejecting (2). *Libertarianism*, on the other hand, accepts (2), agrees with the hard determinist in accepting (3) and disagrees in rejecting (1). Libertarians, then, all are indeterminists, although, as was pointed out above, not all indeterminists are libertarians. *Compatibilists* argue that claim (3) is mistaken, and thus that persons can be morally responsible for behavior which is causally determined. Typically, compatibilists accept claim (2), but they have no uniform position on (1). Some may reject (1), others may claim not to know whether or not (1) is true, and still others may accept (1), this last position often being called *soft determinism*.

While such labels have some use, we should not attach too much importance to them. There are other positions which people take, and, in any case, you should remember that the importance of any position is less a matter of the conclusions reached about claims (1)–(3) than of the arguments and explanations offered in support of those conclusions. Let us now turn to those arguments and explanations. (In the first three selections, each paragraph has been numbered to facilitate the discussion immediately following the selection.)

1

Of Man's Free Agency

BARON d'HOLBACH

[1]   Those who have pretended that the *soul* is distinguished from the body, is immaterial, draws its ideas from its own peculiar source, acts by its own energies, without the aid of any exterior object, have, by a consequence of their own system, enfranchised it from those physical laws according to which all beings of which we have a knowledge are obliged to act. They have believed that the soul is mistress of its own conduct, is able to regulate its own peculiar operations, has the faculty to determine its will by its own natural energy; in a word, they have pretended that man is a *free agent*.

[2]   It has been already sufficiently proved that the soul is nothing more than the body considered relatively to some of its functions more concealed than others: it has been shown that this soul, even when it shall be supposed immaterial, is continually modified conjointly with the body, is submitted to all its motion, and that without this it would remain inert and dead: that, consequently, it is subjected to the influence of those material and physical causes which give impulse to the body; of which the mode of existence, whether habitual or transitory, depends upon the material elements by which it is surrounded, that form its texture, constitute its temperament, enter into it by means of the aliments, and penetrate it by their subtility. The faculties which are called *intellectual*, and those qualities which are styled *moral*, have been explained in a manner purely physical and natural. In the last place it has been demonstrated that all the ideas, all the systems, all the affections, all the opinions, whether true or false, which man forms to himself, are to be at-

[From *The System of Nature*, chapter 11. Translated by H. D. Robinson (1868). First published in 1770.]

tributed to his physical and material senses. Thus man is a being purely physical; in whatever manner he is considered, he is connected to universal nature, and submitted to the necessary and immutable laws that she imposes on all the beings she contains, according to their peculiar essences or to the respective properties with which, without consulting them, she endows each particular species. Man's life is a line that nature commands him to describe upon the surface of the earth, without his ever being able to swerve from it, even for an instant. He is born without his own consent; his organization does in nowise depend upon himself; his ideas come to him involuntarily; his habits are in the power of those who cause him to contract them; he is unceasingly modified by causes, whether visible or concealed, over which he has no control, which necessarily regulate his mode of existence, give the hue to his way of thinking, and determine his manner of acting. He is good or bad, happy or miserable, wise or foolish, reasonable or irrational, without his will being for any thing in these various states. Nevertheless, in despite of the shackles by which he is bound, it is pretended he is a free agent, or that independent of the causes by which he is moved, he determines his own will, and regulates his own condition. . . .

[3]   The will, as we have elsewhere said, is a modification of the brain, by which it is disposed to action, or prepared to give play to the organs. This will is necessarily determined by the qualities, good or bad, agreeable or painful, of the object or the motive that acts upon his senses, or of which the idea remains with him, and is resuscitated by his memory. In consequence, he acts necessarily, his action is the result of the impulse he receives either from the motive, from the object, or from the idea which has modified his brain, or disposed his will. When he does not act according to this impulse, it is because there comes some new cause, some new motive, some new idea, which modifies his brain in a different manner, gives him a new impulse, determines his will in another way, by which the action of the former impulse is suspended: thus, the sight of an agreeable object, or its idea, determines his will to set him in action to procure it; but if a new object or a new idea more powerfully attracts him, it gives a new direction to his will, annihilates the effect of the former, and prevents the action by which it was to be procured. This is the mode in which reflection, experience, reason, necessarily arrests or suspends the action of man's will: without this he would of necessity have followed the anterior impulse which carried him towards a then desirable object. In all this he always acts according to necessary laws, from which he has no means of emancipating himself.

[4]   If when tormented with violent

thirst, he figures to himself in idea, or really perceives a fountain, whose limpid streams might cool his feverish want, is he sufficient master of himself to desire or not to desire the object competent to satisfy so lively a want? It will no doubt be conceded, that it is impossible he should not be desirous to satisfy it; but it will be said—if at this moment it is announced to him that the water he so ardently desires is poisoned, he will, notwithstanding his vehement thirst, abstain from drinking it: and it has, therefore, been falsely concluded that he is a free agent. The fact, however, is, that the motive in either case is exactly the same: his own conservation. The same necessity that determined him to drink before he knew the water was deleterious, upon this new discovery equally determines him not to drink; the desire of conserving himself either annihilates or suspends the former impulse; the second motive becomes stronger than the preceding, that is, the fear of death, or the desire of preserving himself, necessarily prevails over the painful sensation caused by his eagerness to drink: but, it will be said, if the thirst is very parching, an inconsiderate man without regarding the danger will risk swallowing the water. Nothing is gained by this remark: in this case, the anterior impulse only regains the ascendency; he is persuaded that life may possibly be longer preserved, or that he shall derive a greater good by drinking the poisoned water than by endur-

ing the torment, which, to his mind, threatens instant dissolution: thus the first becomes the strongest and necessarily urges him on to action. Nevertheless, in either case, whether he partakes of the water, or whether he does not, the two actions will be equally necessary; they will be the effect of that motive which finds itself most puissant; which consequently acts in the most coercive manner upon his will.

[5]   This example will serve to explain the whole phenomena of the human will. This will, or rather the brain, finds itself in the same situation as a bowl, which, although it has received an impulse that drives it forward in a straight line, is deranged in its course whenever a force superior to the first obliges it to change its direction. The man who drinks the poisoned water appears a madman; but the actions of fools are as necessary as those of the most prudent individuals. The motives that determine the voluptuary and the debauchee to risk their health, are as powerful, and their actions are as necessary, as those which decide the wise man to manage his. But, it will be insisted, the debauchee may be prevailed on to change his conduct: this does not imply that he is a free agent; but that motives may be found sufficiently powerful to annihilate the effect of those that previously acted upon him; then these new motives determine his will to the new mode of conduct he may

adopt as necessarily as the former did to the old mode.

[6]   Man is said to *deliberate*, when the action of the will is suspended; this happens when two opposite motives act alternately upon him. *To deliberate*, is to hate and to love in succession; it is to be alternately attracted and repelled; it is to be moved, sometimes by one motive, sometimes by another. Man only deliberates when he does not distinctly understand the quality of the objects from which he receives impulse, or when experience has not sufficiently apprised him of the effects, more or less remote, which his actions will produce. He would take the air, but the weather is uncertain; he deliberates in consequence; he weighs the various motives that urge his will to go out or to stay at home; he is at length determined by that motive which is most probable; this removes his indecision, which necessarily settles his will, either to remain within or to go abroad: this motive is always either the immediate or ultimate advantage he finds, or thinks he finds, in the action to which he is persuaded. . . .

[7]   The various powers, frequently very complicated, that act either successively or simultaneously upon the brain of man, which modify him so diversely in the different periods of his existence, are the true causes of that obscurity in morals, of that difficulty which is found, when it is desired to unravel the concealed springs of his enigmatical conduct. The heart of man is a labyrinth, only because it very rarely happens that we possess the necessary gift of judging it; from whence it will appear, that his circumstances, his indecision, his conduct, whether ridiculous or unexpected, are the necessary consequences of the changes operated in him; are nothing but the effect of motives that successively determine his will; which are dependent on the frequent variations experienced by his machine. According to these variations the same motives have not always the same influence over his will; the same objects no longer enjoy the faculty of pleasing him; his temperament has changed, either for the moment, or for ever: it follows as a consequence, that his taste, his desires, his passions, will change; there can be no kind of uniformity in his conduct; nor any certitude in the effects to be expected.

[8]   Choice by no means proves the free agency of man: he only deliberates when he does not yet know which to choose of the many objects that move him, he is then in an embarrassment, which does not terminate until his will is decided by the greater advantage he believes he shall find in the object he chooses, or the action he undertakes. From whence it may be seen, that choice is necessary, because he would not determine for an object, or for an

action, if he did not believe that he should find in it some direct advantage. That man should have free agency it were needful that he should be able to will or choose without motive, or that he could prevent motives coercing his will. Action always being the effect of his will once determined, and as his will cannot be determined but by a motive which is not in his own power, it follows that he is never the master of the determination of his own peculiar will; that consequently he never acts as a free agent. It has been believed that man was a free agent because he had a will with the power of choosing; but attention has not been paid to the fact that even his will is moved by causes independent of himself; is owing to that which is inherent in his own organization, or which belongs to the nature of the beings acting on him.[1] Is he the master of willing not to withdraw his hand from the fire when he fears it will be burnt? Or has he the power to take away from fire the property which makes him fear it? Is he the master of not choosing a dish of meat, which he knows to be agreeable, or analogous to his palate; of not preferring it to that which he knows to be disagreeable or dan-

gerous? It is always according to his sensations, to his own peculiar experience, or to his suppositions, that he judges of things, either well or ill; but whatever may be his judgment, it depends necessarily on his mode of feeling, whether habitual or accidental, and the qualities he finds in the causes that move him, which exist in despite of himself. . . .

[9]   Man's mode of thinking is necessarily determined by his manner of being; it must therefore depend on his natural organization, and the modification his system receives independently of his will. From this, we are obliged to conclude, that his thoughts, his reflections, his manner of viewing things, of feeling, of judging, of combining ideas, is neither voluntary nor free. In a word, that his soul is neither mistress of the motion excited in it, nor of representing to itself, when wanted, those images or ideas that are capable of counterbalancing the impulse it receives. This is the reason, why man, when in a passion, ceases to reason; at that moment reason is as impossible to be heard, as it is during an ecstacy, or in a fit of drunkenness. The wicked are never more than men who are either drunk or mad;

---

1.   Man passes a great portion of his life without even willing. His will depends on the motive by which he is determined. If he were to render an exact account of every thing he does in the course of each day—from rising in the morning to lying down at night—he would find that not one of his actions have been in the least voluntary; that they have been mechanical, habitual, determined by causes he was not able to forsee; to which he was either obliged to yield, or with which he was allured to acquiesce: he would discover, that all the motives of his labors, of his amusements, of his discourses, of his thoughts, have been necessary; that they have evidently either seduced him or drawn him along.

if they reason, it is not until tranquillity is re-established in their machine; then, and not till then, the tardy ideas that present themselves to their mind enable them to see the consequence of their actions, and give birth to ideas that bring on them that trouble, which is designated *shame, regret, remorse*.

[10] The errours of philosophers on the free agency of man, have arisen from their regarding his will as the *primum mobile*, the original motive of his actions; for want of recurring back, they have not perceived the multiplied, the complicated causes which, independently of him, give motion to the will itself; or which dispose and modify his brain, whilst he himself is purely passive in the motion he receives. Is he the master of desiring or not desiring an object that appears desirable to him? Without doubt it will be answered, no: but he is the master of resisting his desire, if he reflects on the consequences. But, I ask, is he capable of reflecting on these consequences, when his soul is hurried along by a very lively passion, which entirely depends upon his natural organization, and the causes by which he is modified? Is it in his power to add to these consequences all the weight necessary to counterbalance his desire? Is he the master of preventing the qualities which render an object desirable from residing in it? I shall be told: he ought to have learned to resist his passions; to contract a habit of putting a curb on his desires. I agree to it without any difficulty. But in reply, I again ask, is his nature susceptible of this modification? Does his boiling blood, his unruly imagination, the igneous fluid that circulates in his veins, permit him to make, enable him to apply true experience in the moment when it is wanted? And even when his temperament has capacitated him, has his education, the examples set before him, the ideas with which he has been inspired in early life, been suitable to make him contract this habit of repressing his desires? Have not all these things rather contributed to induce him to seek with avidity, to make him actually desire those objects which you say he ought to resist?

[11] The *ambitious man* cries out: you will have me resist my passion; but have they not unceasingly repeated to me that rank, honours, power, are the most desirable advantages in life? Have I not seen my fellow citizens envy them, the nobles of my country sacrifice every thing to obtain them? In the society in which I live, am I not obliged to feel, that if I am deprived of these advantages, I must expect to languish in contempt; to cringe under the rod of oppression?

[12] The *miser* says: you forbid me to love money, to seek after the means of acquiring it: alas! does not every thing tell me that, in this world,

money is the greatest blessing; that it is amply sufficient to render me happy? In the country I inhabit, do I not see all my fellow citizens covetous of riches? but do I not also witness that they are little scrupulous in the means of obtaining wealth? As soon as they are enriched by the means which you censure, are they not cherished, considered and respected? By what authority, then, do you defend me from amassing treasure? what right have you to prevent my using means, which, although you call them sordid and criminal, I see approved by the sovereign? Will you have me renounce my happiness?

[13] The *voluptuary* argues: you pretend that I should resist my desires; but was I the maker of my own temperament, which unceasingly invites me to pleasure? You call my pleasures disgraceful; but in the country in which I live, do I not witness the most dissipated men enjoying the most distinguished rank? Do I not behold that no one is ashamed of adultery but the husband it has outraged? do not I see men making trophies of their debaucheries, boasting of their libertinism, rewarded with applause?

[14] The *choleric man* vociferates: you advise me to put a curb on my passions, and to resist the desire of avenging myself: but can I conquer my nature? Can I alter the received opinions of the world? Shall I not be for ever disgraced, infallibly dishonoured in society, if I do not wash out in the blood of my fellow creature the injuries I have received?

[15] The *zealous enthusiast* exclaims: you recommend me mildness; you advise me to be tolerant; to be indulgent to the opinions of my fellow men; but is not my temperament violent? Do I not ardently love my God? Do they not assure me, that zeal is pleasing to him; that sanguinary inhuman persecutors have been his friends? As I wish to render myself acceptable in his sight, I therefore adopt the same means.

[16] In short, the actions of man are never free; they are always the necessary consequence of his temperament, of the received ideas, and of the notions, either true or false, which he has formed to himself of happiness; of his opinions, strengthened by example, by education, and by daily experience. So many crimes are witnessed on the earth only because every thing conspires to render man vicious and criminal; the religion he has adopted, his government, his education, the examples set before him, irresistibly drive him on to evil: under these circumstances, morality preaches virtue to him in vain. In those societies where vice is esteemed, where crime is crowned, where venality is constantly recompensed, where the most dreadful disorders are punished only in those who are too weak to enjoy

the privilege of committing them with impunity, the practice of virtue is considered nothing more than a painful sacrifice of happiness. Such societies chastise, in the lower orders, those excesses which they respect in the higher ranks; and frequently have the injustice to condemn those in the penalty of death, whom public prejudices, maintained by constant example, have rendered criminal.

[17] Man, then, is not a free agent in any one instant of his life; he is necessarily guided in each step by those advantages, whether real or fictitious, that he attaches to the objects by which his passions are roused: these passions themselves are necessary in a being who unceasingly tends towards his own happiness; their energy is necessary, since that depends on his temperament; his temperament is necessary, because it depends on the physical elements which enter into his composition; the modification of this temperament is necessary, as it is the infallible and inevitable consequence of the impulse he receives from the incessant action of moral and physical beings.

[18] In despite of these proofs of the want of free agency in man, so clear to unprejudiced minds, it will, perhaps, be insisted upon with no small feeling of triumph, that if it be proposed to any one, to move or not to move his hand, an action in the number of those called *indifferent,* he evidently appears to be the master of choosing; from which it is concluded that evidence has been offered of his free agency. The reply is, this example is perfectly simple; man in performing some action which he is resolved on doing, does not by any means prove his free agency: the very desire of displaying this quality, excited by the dispute, becomes a necessary motive, which decides his will either for the one or the other of these actions: what deludes him in this instance, or that which persuades him he is a free agent at this moment, is, that he does not discern the true motive which sets him in action, namely, the desire of convincing his opponent: if in the heat of the dispute he insists and asks, "Am I not the master of throwing myself out of the window?" I shall answer him, no; that whilst he preserves his reason there is no probability that the desire of proving his free agency, will become a motive sufficiently powerful to make him sacrifice his life to the attempt: if, notwithstanding this, to prove he is a free agent, he should actually precipitate himself from the window, it would not be a sufficient warranty to conclude he acted freely, but rather that it was the violence of his temperament which spurred him on to this folly. Madness is a state, that depends upon the heat of the blood, not upon the will. A fanatic

or a hero, braves death as necessarily as a more phlegmatic man or a coward flies from it.[2] . . .

[19] When it is said, that man is not a free agent, it is not pretended to compare him to a body moved by a simple impulsive cause: he contains within himself causes inherent to his existence; he is moved by an interior organ, which has its own peculiar laws, and is itself necessarily determined in consequence of ideas formed from perceptions resulting from sensations which it receives from exterior objects. As the mechanism of these sensations, of these perceptions, and the manner they engrave ideas on the brain of man, are not known to him; because he is unable to unravel all these motions; because he cannot perceive the chain of operations in his soul, or the motive principle that acts within him, he supposes himself a free agent; which, literally translated, signifies, that he moves himself by himself; that he determines himself without cause: when he rather ought to say, that he is ignorant how or for why he acts in the manner he does. It is true the soul enjoys an activity peculiar to itself: but it is equally certain that this activity would never be displayed, if some motive or some cause did not put it in a condition to exercise itself: at least it will not be pretended that the soul is able either to love or to hate without being moved, without knowing the objects, without having some idea of their qualities. Gunpowder has unquestionably a particular activity, but this activity will never display itself, unless fire be applied to it; this, however, immediately sets it in motion.

[20] It is the great complication of motion in man, it is the variety of his action, it is the multiplicity of causes that move him, whether simultaneously or in continual succession, that persuades him he is a free agent: if all his motions were simple, if the causes that move him did not confound themselves with each other, if they were distinct, if his machine were less complicated, he would perceive that all his actions were necessary, because he would be enabled to recur instantly to the cause that made him act. A man who should be always obliged to go towards the west, would always go on that side; but he would feel that, in so going, he was not a free agent: if he had another sense, as his actions or his motion, augmented by a sixth, would be still more varied and much more complicated, he would believe himself still more a free agent than he does with his five senses.

2.   There is, in point of fact, no difference between the man that is cast out of the window by another, and the man who throws himself out of it, except that the impulse in the first instance comes immediately from without, whilst that which determines the fall in the second case, springs from within his own peculiar machine, having its more remote cause also exterior. . . .

[21] It is, then, for want of recurring to the causes that move him; for want of being able to analyze, from not being competent to decompose the complicated motion of his machine, that man believes himself a free agent: it is only upon his own ignorance that he founds the profound yet deceitful notion he has of his free agency; that he builds those opinions which he brings forward as a striking proof of his pretended freedom of action. If, for a short time, each man was willing to examine his own peculiar actions, search out their true motives to discover their concatenation, he would remain convinced that the sentiment he has of his natural free agency, is a chimera that must speedily be destroyed by experience. . . .

[22] In despite of the gratuitous ideas which man has formed to himself on his pretended free agency; in defiance of the illusions of this supposed intimate sense, which, maugre his experience, persuades him that he is master of his will; all his institutions are really founded upon necessity: on this, as on a variety of other occasions, practice throws aside speculation. Indeed, if it was not believed that certain motives embraced the power requisite to determine the will of man, to arrest the progress of his passions; to direct them towards an end, to modify him, of what use would be the faculty of speech? What benefit could arise from education, from legislation, from morals, even from religion itself? What does education achieve, save give the first impulse to the human will; make man contract habits; oblige him to persist in them; furnish him with motives, whether true or false, to act after a given manner? When the father either menaces his son with punishment, or promises him a reward, is he not convinced these things will act upon his will? What does legislation attempt except it be to present to the citizens of a state those motives which are supposed necessary to determine them to perform some actions that are considered worthy; to abstain from committing others that are looked upon as unworthy? What is the object of morals, if it be not to show man that his interest exacts he should suppress the momentary ebullition of his passions, with a view to promote a more certain happiness, a more lasting well-being, than can possibly result from the gratification of his transitory desires? Does not the religion of all countries suppose the human race, together with the entire of nature, submitted to the irresistible will of a necessary being who regulates their condition after the eternal laws of immutable wisdom? Is not this God, which man adores, the absolute master of their destiny? Is it not this divine being who chooses and who rejects? The anathemas fulminated by religion, the promises it holds forth, are they not founded upon the idea of the effects these chimeras will necessar-

ily produce upon ignorant and timid people? Is not man brought into existence by this kind Divinity without his own knowledge? Is he not obliged to play a part against his will? Does not either his happiness or his misery depend on the part he plays?

[23] Education, then, is only necessity shown to children: legislation, is necessity shown to the members of the body politic: morals, is the necessity of the relations subsisting between men, shown to reasonable beings: in short, man grants necessity in every thing for which he believes he has certain unerring experience: that of which he does not comprehend the necessary connexion of causes with their effects he styles probability: he would not act as he does, if he was not convinced, or, at least, if he did not presume that certain effects will necessarily follow his actions. The moralist preaches reason, because he believes it necessary to man: the philosopher writes, because he believes truth must sooner or later prevail over falsehood: theologians and tyrants necessarily hate truth and despise reason, because they believe them prejudicial to their interests: the sovereign, who strives to terrify crime by the severity of his laws, but who, nevertheless, oftener renders it useful and even necessary to his purposes, presumes the motives he employs will be sufficient to keep his subjects within bounds. All reckon equally upon the power or upon the necessity of the motives they make use of, and each individual flatters himself, either with or without reason, that these motives will have an influence on the conduct of mankind. . . .

[24] All this proves the necessity of recurring to the primitive source of man's wanderings, if it be seriously intended to furnish him with suitable remedies. It is useless to dream of correcting his mistakes, until the true causes that move his will are unravelled, or until more real, more beneficial, more certain motives, are substituted for those which are found so inefficacious and so dangerous both to society and to himself. It is for those who guide the human will who regulate the condition of nations, to seek after these motives with which reason will readily furnish them; even a good book, by touching the heart of a great prince, may become a very powerful cause that shall necessarily have an influence over the conduct of a whole people; that shall decide upon the felicity of a portion of the human race.

[25] From all that has been advanced in this chapter, it results, that in no one moment of his existence is man a free agent. He is not the architect of his own conformation, which he holds from nature; he has no controul over his own ideas, or over the modification of his brain; these are due to causes, that, in despite of him, and without his own

knowledge, unceasingly act upon him; he is not the master of not loving or coveting that which he finds amiable or desirable; he is not capable of refusing to deliberate, when he is uncertain of the effects certain objects will produce upon him; he cannot avoid choosing that which he believes will be most advantageous to him; in the moment when his will is determined by his choice he is not competent to act otherwise than he does. In what instance, then, is he the master of his own actions? In what moment is he a free agent? . . .

ANALYSIS AND DISCUSSION

By skimming over this selection, you should have seen that d'Holbach defends determinism and rejects human free agency, and that he devotes a great deal of his discussion to offering causal explanations for human behavior. You should also have noticed that he says very little about moral responsibility. This is not much information, but it is all that skimming will reveal, and it is enough to give you a sense of direction as you begin to read the selection carefully.

THE READING OUTLINE

Your first reading of the selection should result in an outline showing the function of each paragraph. In this case, the selection has relatively little structure, and your outline would be little more than a list, like this:

[1] *Free agent* defined as a being which can originate action without being caused to do so.

[2] Argument: *soul* is just certain bodily functions whose workings are more concealed than others.

[3] *Will* defined as modification of the brain; argument: choice is causally determined.

[4] Example illustrating the argument—thirst.

[5] Choice determined by the strongest motive.

[6] *Deliberation* explained as being under the influence of conflicting motives.

[7] We don't realize this because of the complexity of the causes.

[8]–[9]   Choice does not prove freedom; it is merely the effect of deliberation as described above.

[10] Failing to perceive the complexity of the causes of our actions makes us think we are free. Argument: our actions are determined.

[11]–[15]   Examples illustrating the argument in [10].

[16]–[17]   Summary of argument in [10].

[18] Reply to a proposed counterexample.

[19]–[21]   Repeat: the complexity of the causes prevents us from understanding what they are. This makes us think we are free.

[22]–[23]   Our social institutions are founded on the concept of determinism, rather than free agency.

[24] These institutions can never be effective until we understand the real causes of human behavior.

[25] Summary of the position.

CRITICAL EVALUATION

At this point it is clear that d'Holbach would accept the claim that human behavior is causally determined, but still not clear how he might relate that claim to views about moral responsibility. Using the reading outline as a guide, you should now try to grasp the details of each argument, explanation, or set of claims, and see if each succeeds in its objectives.

Definitions of free agency, soul, will ([1]–[3])
In [1] d'Holbach defines a free agent as a being capable of originating action or refusing to act without being caused to do so. The view he wishes to refute is presented here as the view that human souls are free agents. But throughout the selection he alternates between rebutting the claim that souls are free agents and rebutting the claim that human will has free agency. A will is not the same thing as a soul, but do the differences matter as far as his arguments are concerned? Probably not.

In [2] d'Holbach says that he already has proved that the soul is merely the body, thought of in a certain way. If we recall his remarks about the complexity of deliberation (e.g., in [19]–[21]), we can see what this means. Certain bodily functions, for example, circulation of the blood, we understand reasonably well, and because we know many of the causes involved we find it easy to think of these as *purely mechanical* bodily functions. But other functions are "more concealed," that is, we don't understand the causal mechanisms at all. With respect to these, d'Holbach claims, because we know of no causes we suppose there are none, and instead attribute them to the *free agency* of a soul. Thus, what we regard as (merely) bodily functions, and what we regard as functions of soul, really is determined by the limits of our knowledge.

What of his claim that he has already *proved* that soul is really nothing but body performing those functions we don't understand? Here you confront one of the disadvantages of reading selections edited from long works. D'Holbach's arguments appear in the ten chapters preceding the one from which this selection was taken. To evaluate the arguments you would need to read the whole book. But some of their results are indicated briefly in [2]. We are told, for example, that without a body, soul could do nothing at all (there would be nothing to do it with) and that the soul is modified as the body is (e.g., if the body is blinded, the soul cannot see either). What this suggests is that appeals to free agency of the soul can explain nothing which could not be explained in terms of bodily mechansims. The concept of a soul *distinct* from body therefore contributes nothing to our understanding and can be dispensed with.

D'Holbach now begins to expound his deterministic position. If man is "a being purely physical," then man must be subject to physical laws, as is any physical being. Thus, the body and its characteristics result from external causes (e.g., heredity and the environmental circumstances controlling growth and nutrition). Habits of character and attitudes are caused by education and training (again, external causes). Sensory experience is externally caused. Desires, wishes, feelings, and beliefs all are effects of external causes acting upon the bodily mechanisms.

Now the stage is set for the critical claim that will is merely a special kind of modification of the brain which causes the body to act. The outline of d'Holbach's picture of humanity is complete. A human being is a complex mechanism which reacts in a variety of ways to its environment. External causes provide each person with a body and continually modify the condition of that body and its systems. Some of these modifications affect the brain to produce perceptions, feelings, beliefs, desires, etc. And some complex modifications of the brain set the body in motion—what we call action. Willing, then, is merely a kind of causally determined process in the brain.

Motivation, deliberation, and choice ([3]–[6], [8], [9])
Now, can we say anything about this willing mechanism? The last half of [3] suggests the following: to think of something—to have an idea of it—is to have one's brain in a certain condition. Some of our ideas are of agreeable

(attractive, desirable) things, others are of disagreeable things, and still other ideas are of things which are indifferent to us. The brain-state which is thinking of an agreeable thing also is a motivational state—that is, it causes the body to move in ways that promote the acquisition of the agreeable thing. The thought of something disagreeable also is motivational, causing the body to avoid that thing. Thoughts of indifferent things are not motivational—they are not causes of action at all.

At this point an objection should occur to us. The mechanism which d'Holbach suggests would seem to have us always simplemindedly pursuing things we find attractive and avoiding things unattractive. But it seems obvious that in fact we sometimes ignore attractive things or endure unattractive ones. Thus, the suggested account of willing seems not to agree with the facts. To respond to this kind of objection d'Holbach adds another factor—strength of motive. If we say that some motives are *stronger* than others, we can explain why we prefer one attractive thing to another, seek to avoid something undesirable at the cost of losing something desirable, ignore present goods for the sake of more attractive ones to come later, and so forth. Always, the strongest motive, or combination of motives, overrides weaker motives. This explanation begins in the last two-thirds of [3] and is illustrated by the example in [4]. It is then amplified in [5] and employed to explain deliberation ([6]) and choice ([8], [9]).

Let us pause, now, to examine this appeal to the strongest motive. Remember, the appeal arose because d'Holbach realized that we could find counterexamples to the universal generalizations that we always seek what we believe attractive or desirable and always avoid what we believe to be undesirable. So, he offers us instead the universal generalization that our actions always are caused by the *strongest* motive we have. But what, exactly, does this generalization mean? How are we to tell whether one motive actually is stronger than another? One thing d'Holbach should *not* do is to define or explain the stronger motive this way: Motive A can be known to be stronger than motive B if a person who was under the influence of both would be caused to pursue the goals involved in A rather than the goals involved in B. This explanation would be mistaken because it is circular. Recall, what was wanted was an explanation why, when people have conflicting motives, they follow one instead of another. D'Holbach's answer is: they follow the motive they do because it is stronger. But if being the stronger motive means only that the motive is the one people follow, d'Holbach's "explanation" amounts only to this: people follow one motive instead of another because it, rather than the other, is the one they follow—and that explains nothing at all.

What is needed, then, is some account (of what it is for a motive to be stronger than another) that does not appeal to the way we choose between conflicting motives. If you read [6] and [8] carefully, you will notice that d'Holbach claims that people always pursue what seems to them to be most to their advantage. Perhaps, then, we should say that the strongest motive is the one which is *thought to offer the greatest advantage* to the person whose motive it is. But does this help? You may think there are counterexamples—that we sometimes do not choose what we think is most to our advantage. Perhaps we think our *duty,* or the advantage of others, is more important in some cases. Or perhaps we are unwilling to take some risk for the sake of a great advantage. A major theme of Chapter 7 is the question whether people ever make choices they believe to be less advantageous than possible for themselves, so we will not pursue that question further here. But if the *most advantageous* choice were explained either as (a) the one stemming from the strongest motive, or (b) the one which would be preferred to all others, we would have circularity in the explanation again. It is not clear whether d'Holbach finally avoids circularity. (Notice, such circularity would not spoil *all* of his explanation of the causes of human behavior—it would mean only that he had no explanation of *choosing among alternatives.*)

Ignorance of causes ([7], [10], [19]–[21])
When we reject a belief held by many intelligent and thoughtful people, it is helpful to explain how they came to be mistaken about the belief—where their evidence was misleading, or how their reasoning went wrong. D'Holbach offers such an explanation at three different places in this selection; his reasoning is as follows:

1. Many of the causal mechanisms of the human organism are very complex. We cannot find simple laws saying that whenever a man is in such-and-such a situation he will react by doing so-and-so ([19]). Differences in physiology, past experience, and many other things determine how we react. Because of this complexity we still are ignorant of the real causes of most human behavior.

2. Those who believe in free agency infer that there are no causes from their ignorance of any causes. And this is their mistake. Of course, such a belief must involve the conviction that if there were causes we would know about them. D'Holbach rejects that conviction, blaming it on a failure to appreciate how complex and difficult to discover are the causes of our behavior.

Probably we should grant the first part of this explanation. *If* there are causal mechanisms for all human behavior, they are indeed complex and hard to discover. But the mistake mentioned in the second part of the explanation seems rather simpleminded for d'Holbach's more intelligent opponents to commit. In fact, many who believe in human free agency are as ignorant of the causes of cancer or the mechanisms of embryonic development as they are of causes of human behavior. But they do not believe, because of that ignorance, that cancer or embryonic development involve free agency. Instead, they think, as d'Holbach would, that the causes of these phenomena are very complex and hard to discover. Thus, we need to appeal to something besides ignorance of causes to explain belief in free agency in some situations and lack of that belief in others.

Argument that human actions are caused ([10]–[17])
The argument in this portion of the selection really amounts to a detailing of causes which influence human behavior. The major factors mentioned are summed up in [16]: one's temperament, received ideas (experience), notions about happiness, and opinions all play a part. One could act differently, *if* some of these characteristics were different, but we do not choose these characteristics ourselves. They are produced in us by external causes. In each of paragraphs [11]–[15], he chooses a type of defective character and outlines the kinds of external causes which would contribute to it—thus indicating that the kind of behavior resulting from that sort of character is not the result of free agency, but is caused by external factors.

This kind of argument is common in determinist writings. But how good is it? We might see, as a result of such arguments, that such factors *could* be causes of human behavior. But are they? Does he really provide evidence, for example, that the factors he mentions—rather than, say, chemical imbalances in the brain due to dietary deficiencies—account for a choleric character ([14])? It seems that d'Holbach would need to conduct the sorts of investigations which psychologists, physiologists, and other scientists employ to discover the real causes, if any, of human behavior. But he has not done so. Indeed, his appeal to our ignorance of the causes of behavior in [7], [10], and [19]–[21] *requires* that the present argument involve only speculation about possible causes. He cannot *consistently* claim both that we are generally ignorant of such causes *and* that he knows what they are.

A staunch determinist is likely to reply, at this point, "Well, it really doesn't matter whether he has the *right* causes here. What he does show is that there must be *some* causes, whatever they are." This tactic won't do at all. If we don't need to discover the actual causes in order to know that there are some causes, then aren't we supposing that we know already that behavior is caused? But this is what the argument was intended to prove, and the supposition would make it circular.

What this argument does, then, is to persuade us that there *could* be causes of human behavior. If an advocate of free agency has denied that a causal explanation might be possible, then d'Holbach's argument represents some progress. But it is not an adequate proof that human action actually is causally determined in the way that he suggests. (We will return to this point shortly.)

Reply to a counterexample ([18])

Indeterminists frequently try to propose a counterexample to deterministic claims by choosing some simple action and claiming that it is obvious that they can choose either to do it or not. Thus, they claim, no set of causes can be compelling this choice. D'Holbach's reply is that, in these cases, the desire to win the debate about determinism may turn out to be the strongest motive. Thus, if the determinist should predict that the indeterminist, say, will not leap out the window, the desire on the part of the indeterminist to falsify that prediction might actually *cause* him to make the leap. There is really nothing new in this reply, and once again we can say, "Yes, such motives *might* cause the behavior in question, but did they *actually* do so?"

A final argument—our social institutions ([22]–[24])

D'Holbach's final argument is based on the character of social institutions concerned with education, law, and the promotion of desirable behavior. The purpose of such institutions is to produce desirable behavior and to prevent undesirable behavior. But how could our laws, training, arguments, rewards, and punishments make any difference in the behavior of persons, unless they functioned as causes? Free agency, it seems, could not be affected at all by such institutions, and they could have no impact at all on a society of free persons. If we believe that such institutions matter, then, we are committed to a deterministic view of human nature.

Here, d'Holbach has raised a serious problem for libertarians. If human choices are truly uncaused, then how could education, information, rational thought, or deliberation have any impact on them? But if such things do not affect free choices, must not such choices be mere irrational accidents? Such accidents would hardly seem to be the kind of behavior for which we would award praise or blame. Thus, a dilemma arises for the libertarian: If actions are caused, we could not be responsible for them. But if they are mere chance events, we seem to have no moral responsibility for them either. Then, is there no moral responsibility no matter what we decide about determinism? D'Holbach does not develop this dilemma here, but you will encounter it again in the following selections.

About moral responsibility

In this selection we find no clear position on moral responsibility. D'Holbach clearly regards some behavior as good and some as bad. And he advocates using knowledge of the causes of behavior to promote a better society ([24]). But it does not emerge here whether he thinks we should continue to blame, praise, reward, punish, etc. He is a determinist, but it is not clear whether hard or soft.

A *summary remark*

We have claimed that d'Holbach says much to show that human behavior *might* be causally determined but little to prove that it *actually* is. Yet, many people find such discussions quite persuasive. Are we missing something in them, then? Perhaps so. Remember that some explanations can function as proof. What d'Holbach offers us here is a possible explanation of human behavior. *If* he is right, then we can undertand how people come to do what they do. Are there alternative indeterminist theories with as much explanatory power? Well, saying that an event occurs *by chance* seems to be saying there is *no* explanation for it. At first glance, this seems to put indeterminist theories at a marked disadvantage. But, so far, we have concentrated on *causal* explanations. Perhaps an indeterminist still can offer purposive explanations of behavior (she chose to do *this* because she wanted to achieve *that*), and some indeterminists will argue that purposive explanations make sense only where causal explanations do not apply. D'Holbach and other determinists would respond that purposive explanations *are* just causal explanations in disguise.

Of course, if scientific study showed that some human actions have no causes (as it may have done for some subatomic events), or discovered lots of causes of behavior, we would have factual evidence to support one or the other of these rival theories. But d'Holbach's discussion and this analysis of it certainly do not settle the issue. Have we made no progress then? On the contrary, we have isolated several questions which need to be answered before clear evidence for or against determinism can be produced—and that is a first step toward our understanding of the issue.

2

The Dilemma of Determinism

WILLIAM JAMES

[1]   A common opinion prevails that the juice has ages ago been pressed out of the free-will controversy, and that no new champion can do more than warm up stale arguments which every one has heard. This is a radical mistake. I know of no subject less worn out, or in which inventive genius has a better chance of breaking open new ground,—not, perhaps, of forcing a conclusion or of coercing assent, but of deepening our sense of what the issue between the two parties really is, of what the ideas of fate and of free-will imply. At our very side almost, in the past few years, we have seen falling in rapid succession from the press works that present the alternative in entirely novel lights. Not to speak of the English disciples of Hegel, such as Green and Bradley; not to speak of Hinton and Hodgson, nor of Hazard here,—we see in the writings of Renouvier, Fouillée, and Delboeuf how completely changed and refreshed is the form of all the old disputes. I cannot pretend to vie in originality with any of the masters I have named, and my ambition limits itself to just one little point. If I can make two of the necessarily implied corollaries of determinism clearer to you than they have been made before, I shall have made it possible for you to decide for or against that doctrine with a better understanding of what you are about. And if you prefer not to decide at all, but to remain doubters, you will at least see more plainly what the subject of your hesitation is. I thus disclaim

[From "The Dilemma of Determinism," an address to the Harvard Divinity Students. First published in 1884.]

openly on the threshold all pretension to prove to you that the freedom of the will is true. The most I hope is to induce some of you to follow my own example in assuming it true, and acting as if it were true. If it be true, it seems to me that this is involved in the strict logic of the case. Its truth ought not to be forced willy-nilly down our indifferent throats. It ought to be freely espoused by men who can equally well turn their backs upon it. In other words, our first act of freedom, if we are free, ought in all inward propriety to be to affirm that we are free. This should exclude, it seems to me, from the free-will side of the question all hope of a coercive demonstration,—a demonstration which I, for one, am perfectly contented to go without.

[2]   With thus much understood at the outset, we can advance. But not without one more point understood as well. The arguments I am about to urge all proceed on two suppositions: first, when we make theories about the world and discuss them with one another, we do so in order to attain a conception of things which shall give us subjective satisfaction; and, second, if there be two conceptions, and the one seems to us, on the whole, more rational than the other, we are entitled to suppose that the more rational one is the truer of the two. I hope that you are all willing to make these suppositions with me; for I am afraid that if

there be any of you here who are not, they will find little edification in the rest of what I have to say. I cannot stop to argue the point; but I myself believe that all the magnificent achievements of mathematical and physical science—our doctrines of evolution, of uniformity of law, and the rest—proceed from our indomitable desire to cast the world into a more rational shape in our minds than the shape into which it is thrown there by the crude order of our experience. The world has shown itself, to a great extent, plastic to this demand of ours for rationality. How much farther it will show itself plastic no one can say. Our only means of finding out is to try; and I, for one, feel as free to try conceptions of moral as of mechanical or of logical rationality. If a certain formula for expressing the nature of the world violates my moral demand, I shall feel as free to throw it overboard, or at least to doubt it, as if it disappointed my demand for uniformity of sequence, for example; the one demand being, so far as I can see, quite as subjective and emotional as the other is. The principle of causality, for example,—what is it but a postulate, an empty name covering simply a demand that the sequence of events shall some day manifest a deeper kind of belonging of one thing with another than the mere arbitrary juxtaposition which now phenomenally appears? It is as much an altar to an unknown god as the one that Saint Paul found at Athens.

All our scientific and philosophic ideals are altars to unknown gods. Uniformity is as much so as is free-will. If this be admitted, we can debate on even terms. But if any one pretends that while freedom and variety are, in the first instance, subjective demands, necessity and uniformity are something altogether different, I do not see how we can debate at all.

[3]   To begin, then, I must suppose you acquainted with all the usual arguments on the subject. I cannot stop to take up the old proofs from causation, from statistics, from the certainty with which we can foretell one another's conduct, from the fixity of character, and all the rest. But there are two *words* which usually encumber these classical arguments, and which we must immediately dispose of if we are to make any progress. One is the eulogistic word *freedom,* and the other is the opprobrious word *chance.* The word "chance" I wish to keep, but I wish to get rid of the word "freedom." Its eulogistic associations have so far overshadowed all the rest of its meaning that both parties claim the sole right to use it, and determinists to-day insist that they alone are freedom's champions. Old-fashioned determinism was what we may call *hard* determinism. It did not shrink from such words as fatality, bondage of the will, necessitation, and the like. Nowadays, we have a *soft* determinism which abhors harsh words, and,

repudiating fatality, necessity, and even predetermination, says that its real name is freedom; for freedom is only necessity understood, and bondage to the highest is identical with true freedom. Even a writer as little used to making capital out of soft words as Mr. Hodgson hesitates not to call himself a "free-will determinist."

[4]   Now, all this is a quagmire of evasion under which the real issue of fact has been entirely smothered. Freedom in all these senses presents simply no problem at all. No matter what the soft determinist mean by it,—whether he mean the acting without external constraint; whether he mean the acting rightly, or whether he mean the acquiescing in the law of the whole,—who cannot answer him that sometimes we are free and sometimes we are not? But there *is* a problem, an issue of fact and not of words, an issue of the most momentous importance, which is often decided without discussion in one sentence,—nay, in one clause of a sentence,—by those very writers who spin out whole chapters in their efforts to show what "true" freedom is; and that is the question of determinism, about which we are to talk to-night.

[5]   Fortunately, no ambiguities hang about this word or about its opposite, indeterminism. Both designate an outward way in which things may happen, and their cold

and mathematical sound has no sentimental associations that can bribe our partiality either way in advance. Now, evidence of an external kind to decide between determinism and indeterminism is, as I intimated a while back, strictly impossible to find. Let us look at the difference between them and see for ourselves. What does determinism profess?

[6]   It professes that those parts of the universe already laid down absolutely appoint and decree what the other parts shall be. The future has no ambiguous possibilities hidden in its womb: the part we call the present is compatible with only one totality. Any other future complement than the one fixed from eternity is impossible. The whole is in each and every part, and welds it with the rest into an absolute unity, an iron block, in which there can be no equivocation or shadow of turning.

With earth's first clay they did the
*   last man kneed,*
And there of the last harvest sowed
*   the seed.*
And the first morning of creation
*   wrote*
What the last dawn of reckoning
*   shall read.*

[7]   Indeterminism, on the contrary, says that the parts have a certain amount of loose play on one another, so that the laying down of one of them does not necessarily determine what the others shall be. It admits that possibilities may be in excess of actualities, and that things not yet revealed to our knowledge may really in themselves be ambiguous. Of two alternative futures which we conceive, both may now be really possible; and the one become impossible only at the very moment when the other excludes it by becoming real itself. Indeterminism thus denies the world to be one unbending unit of fact. It says there is a certain ultimate pluralism in it; and, so saying, it corroborates our ordinary unsophisticated view of things. To that view, actualities seem to float in a wider sea of possibilities from out of which they are chosen; and, *somewhere,* indeterminism says, such possibilities exist, and form a part of truth.

[8]   Determinism, on the contrary, says they exist *nowhere,* and that necessity on the one hand and impossibility on the other are the sole categories of the real. Possibilities that fail to get realized are, for determinism, pure illusions: they never were possibilities at all. There is nothing inchoate, it says, about this universe of ours, all that was or is or shall be actual in it having been from eternity virtually there. The cloud of alternatives our minds escort this mass of actuality withal is a cloud of sheer deceptions, to which "impossibilities" is the only name that rightfully belongs.

[9]   The issue, it will be seen, is a perfectly sharp one, which no eulogistic terminology can smear over or wipe out. The truth *must* lie with one side or the other, and its lying with one side makes the other false.

[10] The question relates solely to the existence of possibilities, in the strict sense of the term, as things that may, but need not, be. Both sides admit that a volition, for instance, has occurred. The indeterminists say another volition might have occurred in its place: the determinists swear that nothing could possibly have occurred in its place. Now, can science be called in to tell us which of these two point-blank contradicters of each other is right? Science professes to draw no conclusions but such as are based on matters of fact, things that have actually happened; but how can any amount of assurance that something actually happened give us the least grain of information as to whether another thing might or might not have happened in its place? Only facts can be proved by other facts. With things that are possibilities and not facts, facts have no concern. If we have no other evidence than the evidence of existing facts, the possibility-question must remain a mystery never to be cleared up.

[11] And the truth is that facts practically have hardly anything to do with making us either determinists or indeterminists. Sure enough, we make a flourish of quoting facts this way or that; and if we are determinists, we talk about the infallibility with which we can predict one another's conduct; while if we are indeterminists, we lay great stress on the fact that it is just because we cannot foretell one another's conduct, either in war or statecraft or in any of the great and small intrigues and businesses of men, that life is so intensely anxious and hazardous a game. But who does not see the wretched insufficiency of this so-called objective testimony on both sides? What fills up the gaps in our minds is something not objective, not external. What divides us into possibility men and anti-possibility men is different faiths or postulates,—postulates of rationality. To this man the world seems more rational with possibilities in it,—to that man more rational with possibilities excluded; and talk as we will about having to yield to evidence, what makes us monists or pluralists, determinists or indeterminists, is at bottom always some sentiment like this.

[12] The stronghold of the deterministic sentiment is the antipathy to the idea of chance. As soon as we begin to talk indeterminism to our friends, we find a number of them shaking their heads. This notion of alternative possibility, they say, this admission that any one of several things may come to pass, is, after all, only a roundabout name for chance;

and chance is something the notion of which no sane mind can for an instant tolerate in the world. What is it, they ask, but barefaced crazy unreason, the negation of intelligibility and law? And if the slightest particle of it exist anywhere, what is to prevent the whole fabric from falling together, the stars from going out, and chaos from recommencing her topsy-turvy reign?

[13] Remarks of this sort about chance will put an end to discussion as quickly as anything one can find. I have already told you that "chance" was a word I wished to keep and use. Let us then examine exactly what it means, and see whether it ought to be such a terrible bugbear to us. I fancy that squeezing the thistle boldly will rob it of its sting.

[14] The sting of the world "chance" seems to lie in the assumption that it means something positive, and that if anything happens by chance, it must needs be something of an intrinsically irrational and preposterous sort. Now, chance means nothing of the kind. It is a purely negative and relative term, giving us no information about that of which it is predicated, except that it happens to be disconnected with something else,—not controlled, secured, or necessitated by other things in advance of its own actual presence. As this point is the most subtile one of the whole lecture, and at the same time the point on which all the rest hinges, I beg you to pay particular attention to it. What I say is that it tells us nothing about what a thing may be in itself to call it "chance." It may be a bad thing, it may be a good thing. It may be lucidity, transparency, fitness incarnate, matching the whole system of other things, when it has once befallen, in an unimaginably perfect way. All you mean by calling it "chance" is that this is not guaranteed, that it may also fall out otherwise. For the system of other things has no positive hold on the chance-thing. Its origin is in a certain fashion negative: it escapes, and says, Hands off! coming, when it comes, as a free gift, or not at all.

[15] This negativeness, however, and this opacity of the chance-thing when thus considered *ab extra,* or from the point of view of previous things or distant things, do not preclude its having any amount of positiveness and luminosity from within, and at its own place and moment. All that its chance-character asserts about it is that there is something in it really of its own, something that is not the unconditional property of the whole. If the whole wants this property, the whole must wait till it can get it, if it be a matter of chance. That the universe may actually be a sort of joint-stock society of this sort, in which the sharers have both limited liabilities and limited powers, is of course a simple and conceivable notion.

[16] Nevertheless, many persons talk as if the minutest dose of disconnectedness of one part with another, the smallest modicum of independence, the faintest tremor of ambiguity about the future, for example, would ruin everything, and turn this goodly universe into a sort of insane sand-heap or nulliverse, no universe at all. Since future human volitions are as a matter of fact the only ambiguous things we are tempted to believe in, let us stop for a moment to make ourselves sure whether their independent and accidental character need be fraught with such direful consequences to the universe as these.

[17] What is meant by saying that my choice of which way to walk home after the lecture is ambiguous and matter of chance as far as the present moment is concerned? It means that both Divinity Avenue and Oxford Street are called; but that only one, and that one *either* one, shall be chosen. Now, I ask you seriously to suppose that this ambiguity of my choice is real; and then to make the impossible hypothesis that the choice is made twice over, and each time falls on a different street. In other words, imagine that I first walk through Divinity Avenue, and then imagine that the powers governing the universe annihilate ten minutes of time with all that it contained, and set me back at the door of this hall just as I was before the choice was made. Imagine then that, everything else being the same, I now make a different choice and traverse Oxford Street. You, as passive spectators, look on and see the two alternative universes,—one of them with me walking through Divinity Avenue in it, the other with the same me walking through Oxford Street. Now, if you are determinists you believe one of these universes to have been from eternity impossible: you believe it to have been impossible because of the intrinsic irrationality or accidentality somewhere involved in it. But looking outwardly at these universes, can you say which is the impossible and accidental one, and which the rational and necessary one? I doubt if the most ironclad determinist among you could have the slightest glimmer of light on this point. In other words, either universe *after the fact* and once there would, to our means of observation and understanding, appear just as rational as the other. There would be absolutely no criterion by which we might judge one necessary and the other matter of chance. Suppose now we relieve the gods of their hypothetical task and assume my choice, once made, to be made forever. I go through Divinity Avenue for good and all. If, as good determinists, you now begin to affirm, what all good determinists punctually do affirm, that in the nature of things I *couldn't* have gone through Oxford Street,—had I done so it would have been chance, irrationality, insanity, a horrid gap in nature,—I simply call your attention

to this, that your affirmation is what the Germans call a *Machtspruch,* a mere conception fulminated as a dogma and based on no insight into details. Before my choice, either street seemed as natural to you as to me. Had I happened to take Oxford Street, Divinity Avenue would have figured in your philosophy as the gap in nature; and you would have so proclaimed it with the best deterministic conscience in the world.

[18] But what a hollow outcry, then, is this against a chance which, if it were present to us, we could by no character whatever distinguish from a rational necessity! I have taken the most trivial of examples, but no possible example could lead to any different result. For what are the alternatives which, in point of fact, offer themselves to human volition? What are those futures that now seem matters of chance? Are they not one and all like the Divinity Avenue and Oxford Street of our example? Are they not all of them *kinds* of things already here and based in the existing frame of nature? Is any one ever tempted to produce an *absolute* accident, something utterly irrelevant to the rest of the world? Do not all the motives that assail us, all the fu-

tures that offer themselves to our choice, spring equally from the soil of the past; and would not either one of them, whether realized through chance or through necessity, the moment it was realized, seem to us to fit that past, and in the completest and most continuous manner to interdigitate with the phenomena already there?[1]

[19] The more one thinks of the matter, the more one wonders that so empty and gratuitous a hubbub as this outcry against chance should have found so great an echo in the hearts of men. It is a word which tells us absolutely nothing about what chances, or about the *modus operandi* of the chancing; and the use of it as a war-cry shows only a temper of intellectual absolutism, a demand that the world shall be a solid block, subject to one control,— which temper, which demand, the world may not be bound to gratify at all. In every outwardly verifiable and practical respect, a world in which the alternatives that now actually distract *your* choice were decided by pure chance would be by *me* absolutely undistinguished from the world in which I now live. I am, therefore, entirely willing to call it,

---

1.   A favorite argument against free-will is that if it be true, a man's murderer may as probably be his best friend as his worst enemy, a mother be as likely to strangle as to suckle her first-born, and all of us be as ready to jump from fourth-story windows as to go out of front doors, etc. Users of this argument should properly be excluded from debate till they learn what the real question is. "Free-will" does not say that everything that is physically conceivable is also morally possible. It merely says that of alternatives that really *tempt* our will more than one is really possible. Of course, the alternatives that do thus tempt us are vastly fewer than the physical possibilities we can coldly fancy. Persons really tempted often do murder their best friends, mothers do strangle their first-born, people do jump out of fourth-story windows, etc.

so far as your choices go, a world of chance for me. To *yourselves,* it is true, those very acts of choice, which to me are so blind, opaque, and external, are the opposites of this, for you are within them and effect them. To you they appear as decisions; and decisions, for him who makes them, are altogether peculiar psychic facts. Self-luminous and self-justifying at the living moment at which they occur, they appeal to no outside moment to put its stamp upon them or make them continuous with the rest of nature. Themselves it is rather who seem to make nature continuous; and in their strange and intense function of granting consent to one possibility and withholding it from another, to transform an equivocal and double future into an inalterable and simple past.

[20] But with the psychology of the matter we have no concern this evening. The quarrel which determinism has with chance fortunately has nothing to do with this or that psychological detail. It is a quarrel altogether metaphysical. Determinism denies the ambiguity of future volitions, because it affirms that nothing future can be ambiguous. But we have said enough to meet the issue. Indeterminate future volitions *do* mean chance. Let us not fear to shout it from the house-tops if need be; for we now know that the idea of chance is, at bottom, exactly the same thing as the idea of gift,—the one simply being a disparaging, and the other a eulogistic, name for anything on

which we have no effective *claim.* And whether the world be the better or the worse for having either chances or gifts in it will depend altogether on *what* these uncertain and unclaimable things turn out to be.

[21] And this at last brings us within sight of our subject. We have seen what determinism means: we have seen that indeterminism is rightly described as meaning chance; and we have seen that chance, the very name of which we are urged to shrink from as from a metaphysical pestilence, means only the negative fact that no part of the world, however big, can claim to control absolutely the destinies of the whole. But although, in discussing the word "chance," I may at moments have seemed to be arguing for its real existence, I have not meant to do so yet. We have not yet ascertained whether this be a world of chance or no; at most, we have agreed that it seems so. And I now repeat what I said at the outset, that, from any strict theoretical point of view, the question is insoluble. To deepen our theoretic sense of the *difference* between a world with chances in it and a deterministic world is the most I can hope to do; and this I may now at last begin upon, after all our tedious clearing of the way.

[22] I wish first of all to show you just what the notion that this is a deterministic world implies. The implications I call your attention to are all bound up with the fact that it is

a world in which we constantly have to make what I shall, with your permission, call judgments of regret. Hardly an hour passes in which we do not wish that something might be otherwise; and happy indeed are those of us whose hearts have never echoed the wish of Omar Khayam—

That we might clasp, ere closed, the
*   book of fate,*
And make the writer on a fairer
*   leaf*
Inscribe our names, or quite obliter-
*   ate.*

Ah! Love, could you and I with fate
*   conspire*
To mend this sorry scheme of things
*   entire,*
Would we not shatter it to bits, and
*   then*
Remould it nearer to the heart's
*   desire?*

[23] Now, it is undeniable that most of these regrets are foolish, and quite on a par in point of philosophic value with the criticisms on the universe of that friend of our infancy, the hero of the fable The Atheist and the Acorn,—

Fool! had that bough a pumpkin
*   bore,*
Thy whimsies would have worked no
*   more. . . .*

Even from the point of view of our own ends, we should probably make a botch of remodelling the universe.

How much more then from the point of view of ends we cannot see! Wise men therefore regret as little as they can. But still some regrets are pretty obstinate and hard to stifle,—regrets for acts of wanton cruelty or treachery, for example, whether performed by others or by ourselves. Hardly any one can remain *entirely* optimistic after reading the confession of the murderer at Brockton the other day: how, to get rid of the wife whose continued existence bored him, he inveigled her into a desert spot, shot her four times, and then, as she lay on the ground and said to him, "You didn't do it on purpose, did you, dear?" replied, "No, I didn't do it on purpose," as he raised a rock and smashed her skull. Such an occurrence, with the mild sentence and self-satisfaction of the prisoner, is a field for a crop of regrets, which one need not take up in detail. We feel that, although a perfect mechanical fit to the rest of the universe, it is a bad moral fit, and that something else would really have been better in its place.

[24] But for the deterministic philosophy the murder, the sentence, and the prisoner's optimism were all necessary from eternity; and nothing else for a moment had a ghost of a chance of being put into their place. To admit such a chance, the determinists tell us, would be to make a suicide of reason; so we must steel our hearts against the thought. And here our plot thickens, for we see

the first of those difficult implications of determinism and monism which it is my purpose to make you feel. If this Brockton murder was called for by the rest of the universe, if it had to come at its preappointed hour, and if nothing else would have been consistent with the sense of the whole, what are we to think of the universe? Are we stubbornly to stick to our judgment of regret, and say, though it *couldn't* be, yet it *would* have been a better universe with something different from this Brockton murder in it? That, of course, seems the natural and spontaneous thing for us to do; and yet it is nothing short of deliberately espousing a kind of pessimism. The judgment of regret calls the murder bad. Calling a thing bad means, if it mean anything at all, that the thing ought not to be, that something else ought to be in its stead. Determinism, in denying that anything else can be in its stead, virtually defines the universe as a place in which what ought to be is impossible,—in other words, as an organism whose constitution is afflicted with an incurable taint, an irremediable flaw. The pessimism of a Schopenhauer says no more than this,—that the murder is a symptom; and that it is a vicious symptom because it belongs to a vicious whole, which can express its nature no otherwise than by bringing forth just such a symptom as that at this particular spot. Regret for the murder must transform itself, if we are determinists and wise, into a larger re-

gret. It is absurd to regret the murder alone. Other things being what they are, *it* could not be different. What we should regret is that whole frame of things of which the murder is one member. I see no escape whatever from this pessimistic conclusion, if, being determinists, our judgment of regret is to be allowed to stand at all.

[25] The only deterministic escape from pessimism is everywhere to abandon the judgment of regret. That this can be done, history shows to be not impossible. The devil, *quoad existentiam,* may be good. That is, although he be a *principle* of evil, yet the universe, with such a principle in it, may practically be a better universe than it could have been without. On every hand, in a small way, we find that a certain amount of evil is a condition by which a higher form of good is bought. There is nothing to prevent anybody from generalizing this view, and trusting that if we could but see things in the largest of all ways, even such matters as this Brockton murder would appear to be paid for by the uses that follow in their train. An optimism *quand même,* a systematic and infatuated optimism like that ridiculed by Voltaire in his Candide, is one of the possible ideal ways in which a man may train himself to look on life. Bereft of dogmatic hardness and lit up with the expression of a tender and pathetic hope, such an optimism has been the grace of

some of the most religious characters that ever lived.

Throb thine with Nature's throbbing breast,
And all is clear from east to west.

[26] Even cruelty and treachery may be among the absolutely blessed fruits of time, and to quarrel with any of their details may be blasphemy. The only real blasphemy, in short, may be that pessimistic temper of the soul which lets it give way to such things as regrets, remorse, and grief.

[27] Thus, our deterministic pessimism may become a deterministic optimism at the price of extinguishing our judgments of regret.

[28] But does not this immediately bring us into a curious logical predicament? Our determinism leads us to call our judgments of regret wrong, because they are pessimistic in implying that what is impossible yet ought to be. But how then about the judgments of regret themselves? If they are wrong, other judgments, judgments of approval presumably, ought to be in their place. But as they are necessitated, nothing else *can* be in their place; and the universe is just what it was before,— namely, a place in which what ought to be appears impossible. We have got one foot out of the pessimistic bog, but the other one sinks all the deeper. We have rescued our actions from the bonds of evil, but our judgments are now held fast. When murders and treacheries cease to be sins, regrets are theoretic absurdities and errors. The theoretic and the active life thus play a kind of seesaw with each other on the ground of evil. The rise of either sends the other down. Murder and treachery cannot be good without regret being bad: regret cannot be good without treachery and murder being bad. Both, however, are supposed to have been foredoomed; so something must be fatally unreasonable, absurd, and wrong in the world. It must be a place of which either sin or error forms a necessary part. From this dilemma there seems at first sight no escape. Are we then so soon to fall back into the pessimism from which we thought we had emerged? And is there no possible way by which we may, with good intellectual consciences, call the cruelties and the treacheries, the reluctance and the regrets, *all* good together?

[29] Certainly there is such a way, and you are probably most of you ready to formulate it yourselves. But, before doing so, remark how inevitably the question of determinism and indeterminism slides us into the question of optimism and pessimism, or, as our fathers called it, "the question of evil." The theological form of all these disputes is the simplest and the deepest, the form from which there is the least es-

cape,—not because, as some have sarcastically said, remorse and regret are clung to with a morbid fondness by the theologians as spiritual luxuries, but because they are existing facts of the world, and as such must be taken into account in the deterministic interpretation of all that is fated to be. If they are fated to be error, does not the bat's wing of irrationality still cast its shadow over the world? . . .

[30] We have thus clearly revealed to our view what may be called the dilemma of determinism, so far as determinism pretends to think things out at all. A merely mechanical determinism, it is true, rather rejoices in not thinking them out. It is very sure that the universe must satisfy its postulate of a physical continuity and coherence, but it smiles at any one who comes forward with a postulate of moral coherence as well. I may suppose, however, that the number of purely mechanical or hard determinists among you this evening is small. The determinism to whose seductions you are most exposed is what I have called soft determinism,—the determinism which allows considerations of good and bad to mingle with those of cause and effect in deciding what sort of a universe this may rationally be held to be. The dilemma of this determinism is one whose left horn is pessimism and whose right horn is subjectivism. In other words, if determinism is to escape pessimism, determinism is to escape pessimism,

it must leave off looking at the goods and ills of life in a simple objective way, and regard them as materials, indifferent in themselves, for the production of consciousness, scientific and ethical, in us. . . .

[31] The only consistent way of representing a pluralism and a world whose parts may affect one another through their conduct being either good or bad is the indeterministic way. What interest, zest, or excitement can there be in achieving the right way, unless we are enabled to feel that the wrong way is also a possible and a natural way,—nay, more, a menacing and an imminent way? And what sense can there be in condemning ourselves for taking the wrong way, unless we need have done nothing of the sort, unless the right way was open to us as well? I cannot understand the willingness to act, no matter how we feel, without the belief that acts are really good and bad. I cannot understand the belief that an act is bad, without regret at its happening. I cannot understand regret without the admission of real, genuine possibilities in the world. Only *then* is it other than a mockery to feel, after we have failed to do our best, that an irreparable opportunity is gone from the universe, the loss of which it must forever after mourn.

[32] If you insist that this is all superstition, that possibility is in the eye of science and reason impossi-

bility, and that if I act badly 'tis that the universe was foredoomed to suffer this defect, you fall right back into the dilemma, the labyrinth, of pessimism and subjectivism, from out of whose toils we have just wound our way.

[33] Now, we are of course free to fall back, if we please. For my own part, though, whatever difficulties may beset the philosophy of objective right and wrong, and the indeterminism it seems to imply, determinism, with its alternative of pessimism or romanticism, contains difficulties that are greater still. But you will remember that I expressly repudiated awhile ago the pretension to offer any arguments which could be coercive in a so-called scientific fashion in this matter. And I consequently find myself, at the end of this long talk, obliged to state my conclusions in an altogether personal way. This personal method of appeal seems to be among the very conditions of the problem; and the most any one can do is to confess as candidly as he can the grounds for the faith that is in him, and leave his example to work on others as it may.

[34] Let me, then, without circumlocution say just this. The world is enigmatical enough in all conscience, whatever theory we may take up toward it. The indeterminism I defend, the free-will theory of popular sense based on the judgment of regret, represents that world as vulnerable, and liable to be injured by certain of its parts if they act wrong. And it represents their acting wrong as a matter of possibility or accident, neither inevitable nor yet to be infallibly warded off. In all this, it is a theory devoid either of transparency or of stability. It gives us a pluralistic, restless universe, in which no single point of view can ever take in the whole scene; and to a mind possessed of the love of unity at any cost, it will, no doubt, remain forever inacceptable. A friend with such a mind once told me that the thought of my universe made him sick, like the sight of the horrible motion of a mass of maggots in their carrion bed.

[35] But while I freely admit that the pluralism and the restlessness are repugnant and irrational in a certain way, I find that every alternative to them is irrational in a deeper way. The indeterminism with its maggots, if you please to speak so about it, offends only the native absolutism of my intellect,—an absolutism which, after all, perhaps, deserves to be snubbed and kept in check. But the determinism with its necessary carrion, to continue the figure of speech, and with no possible maggots to eat the latter up, violates my sense of moral reality through and through. When, for example, I imagine such carrion as the Brockton murder, I cannot conceive it as an act by which

the universe, as a whole, logically and necessarily expresses its nature without shrinking from complicity with such a whole. And I deliberately refuse to keep on terms of loyalty with the universe by saying blankly that the murder, since it does flow from the nature of the whole, is not carrion. There are *some* instinctive reactions which I, for one, will not tamper with. The only remaining alternative, the attitude of gnostical romanticism, wrenches my personal instincts in quite as violent a way. It falsifies the simple objectivity of their deliverance. It makes the goose-flesh the murder excites in me a sufficient reason for the perpetration of the crime. It transforms life from a tragic reality into an insincere melodramatic exhibition, as foul or as tawdry as any one's diseased curiosity pleases to carry it out. And with its consecration of the "roman naturaliste" state of mind, and its enthronement of the baser crew of Parisian *littérateurs* among the eternally indispensable organs by which the infinite spirit of things attains to that subjective illumination which is the task of its life, it leaves me in presence of a sort of subjective carrion considerably more noisome than the objective carrion I called it in to take away.

[36] No! better a thousand times, than such systematic corruption of our moral sanity, the plainest pessimism, so that it be straightforward; but better far than that the world of chance. Make as great an uproar about chance as you please, I know that chance means pluralism and nothing more. If some of the members of the pluralism are bad, the philosophy of pluralism, whatever broad views it may deny me, permits me, at least, to turn to the other members with a clean breast of affection and an unsophisticated moral sense. And if I still wish to think of the world as a totality, it lets me feel that a world with a *chance* in it of being altogether good, even if the chance never come to pass, is better than a world with no such chance at all. That "chance" whose very notion I am exhorted and conjured to banish from my view of the future as the suicide of reason concerning it, that "chance" is—what? Just this,—the chance that in moral respects the future may be other and better than the past has been. This is the only chance we have any motive for supposing to exist. Shame, rather, on its repudiation and its denial! For its presence is the vital air which lets the world live, the salt which keeps it sweet. . . .

ANALYSIS AND DISCUSSION

Skimming James's selection reveals that he is an indeterminist, and, if you are a good skimmer, that he is a libertarian. You should be able to spot much discussion of *chance*, and a complex argument toward the end which deals with determinism, pessimism, and chance. You should expect him to argue that chance events do occur and to defend human freedom on that basis. You also should be able to tell that the argument about pessimism is intended to count against determinism.

THE READING OUTLINE

This essay was delivered as a public lecture, and its style is designed to appeal to a late nineteenth-century audience. You should not let the rhetorical embellishments prevent you from finding the arguments and explanations. James organized his lectures and essays very carefully, and there is a definite structure to be discovered here.

I. The problem: determinism vs. indeterminism—[1]–[11].

  A. Indeterminism, soft determinism and freedom—[3], [4].

  B. Method for dealing with the problem—[2], [5], [9]–[11], [21].

  [1] James won't try to prove indeterminism, but will try to persuade us to accept it.

  [2] The best theory about the world is the one that provides most subjective satisfaction and that is most rational.

  [3]–[4] Soft determinism has confused the concept of freedom, so this discussion will concentrate only on the concept of chance.

  [5] The issue cannot be settled scientifically.

  [6], [8] Determinism claims that there are no real possibilities.

  [7] Indeterminism claims that there are real possibilities.

  [9] Either determinism or indeterminism must be true.

  [10], [11] Repeat: science can't prove either theory, and we can decide between them only on the basis of subjective satisfaction.

II. Chance—[12]–[21].

  A. Chance thought to be irrational by determinists—[12].

  B. Chance is only the absence of causation, and not irrational—[13]–[20].

  [12] Determinists believe any chance would threaten *all* rational explanation.

  [13]–[15] Chance is only the absence of cause, and need not be chaotic, irrational, or evil.

[16]–[18] Determinism really offers no better explanations of many events than does chance.

[19]–[20] Chance only means real alternatives, not irrationality.

[21] Repeat of theme in [10], [11].

III. The dilemma of determinism—[22]–[30].

   [22]–[23] We do regret some events, and seem justified in doing so.

   [24]–[25] Suppose determinism is true: then either we must regret the whole world, or believe that nothing is regrettable.

   [26]–[28] If nothing (else?) were regrettable, then our regrets would be regrettable, and the whole universe still would be regrettable.

   [29] This leads us into the problem of evil.

   [30] The only alternative to pessimism is to reject all values.

IV. Comparison of determinism and indeterminism—[31]–[36].

   [31] *Action* would have no point if determinism were true.

   [32] Universal pessimism is a consequence of rejecting indeterminism.

   [33] Repeat: we can't attain proof but must rely on subjective satisfaction.

   [34]–[36] Each view offers some subjective satisfaction, but indeterminism is most satisfactory when we consider values as well as mechanical causation.

CRITICAL EVALUATION

Since the four major segments of the discussion are interconnected, it is not surprising that James has scattered portions of some arguments throughout all four segments. Now it is time to collect all portions of each argument, and see what we can discover about their effectiveness.

Determinism vs. indeterminism ([1], [6]–[8])
The issue, James says, is whether determinism or indeterminism is correct. Determinism is characterized by him as the view that there are no "ambiguous possibilities" in the future—that every event is so completely determined by causes that from any past state of affairs only one course of development for the world is really possible. On the other hand, indeterminism holds that there are real alternative possibilities. James claims that he will not try to

prove one view is correct, but will show us certain consequences of the views which may persuade us to adopt indeterminism.

Indeterminism, soft determinism, and freedom ([3], [4])

James obviously is unhappy with the way in which soft determinists talk about freedom (you will see an example of soft determinism in the next selection). He accuses them of trying to take advantage of the favorable emotional connotations of the word to make determinism seem more attractive than it really is. Clearly, he would favor the claim that only uncaused actions can be free. But he proposes here to avoid debate about the definition of freedom, because the points he wishes to make all can be put in terms of *chance*.

When we consider the use he finally makes of the concept of chance ([31]–[36]), it becomes clear that James regards an event's occurring by chance as a necessary condition for its being an action for which there is moral responsibility (a free action). But perhaps it is not a sufficient condition. This point will be important when we consider his footnote to [18].

Method for dealing with the issue ([2], [5], [9]–[11], [21], [33])

The key to James's whole argument is found in [2] with the two suppositions he makes there: (*a*) the aim of theories about the world is to obtain subjective satisfaction; and (*b*) of two competing theories we are entitled to accept the one which is, on the whole, more rational.

The nature of subjective satisfaction is not explored thoroughly in this selection. If you carefully study the rest of the paragraphs associated with this theme, you should gather that James believes that theories about the basic nature of the world cannot be *proved* to be true; and that he takes the purpose of such theories to be to *make sense* out of the world. Our experience of the world presents us with an enormous variety of phenomena. James tells us that our theories result from trying to find principles which would explain why the phenomena occur as they do. But the theories are sweeping in their scope (the law of gravitation is about all bodies everywhere and everywhen; determinism is about all events), and while we can get confirming evidence for them, we can never hope to find enough factual evidence to prove them conclusively. What we must do then, according to James, is to seek those theories which have the greatest explanatory power. But this is a method of theory selection which is *subjective* in that the test of success is an appeal to the effects of the theory *on us*. The more the theory helps us to make sense of the world, render it intelligible, see organization and order in it, the more subjective satisfaction the theory gives, and the more rational it seems.

Thus, theories are evaluated not only on the basis of the facts of experience, but also on the basis of human psychology. They depend for their acceptability on the kinds of considerations which actually do give us a sense of understanding. And we are entitled to accept the theory which gives us the greatest overall sense of understanding.

James agrees that the belief that all events follow causal laws does give us a lot of subjective satisfaction—does help to make sense of what we observe. But he argues that events can succeed or fail to make *moral* sense, or *purposive* sense, as well as causal sense. So, to decide which of two competing theories makes the best sense overall, we need to consider all the ways in which theories can explain or fail to explain. In comparing determinism and indeterminism, then, we need to decide not only which theory makes the best mechanical sense, but also which one makes the best moral sense, the best purposive sense, and the best sense in any other category of explanation we might discover. It should be clear now that his strategy will be to concede that determinism makes more mechanical sense than does indeterminism, but claim that it makes so much less sense in other ways that, overall, it is the less rational of the two theories. This approach to the evaluation of rival theories is interesting and important, but much more needs to be said before we can be really clear about its significance and acceptability.

Chance ([12]–[15], [19], [20])

For James, to say that there are real alternative possibilities (indeterminism) is to say that some events occur *by chance*. So, it is important for him to investigate the nature of chance and its effects on subjective satisfaction. In [12] he claims determinists believe that if there is *any* chance in the universe *all* coherent explanation becomes impossible. And in several places James suggests that determinists find the idea of chance *offensive* (morally offensive? aesthetically offensive?). He wants to show that chance is not thoroughly bad. So, he points out that to say an event occurs by chance means *only* that until the event actually did occur there was no combination of causes which could guarantee that it, rather than something else, would occur. Chance events need not be evil, or ugly, or even unexpected. They are only events which *might not have happened*. And since he is not claiming that everything happens by chance, James sees no reason why causal explanations are not available for the majority of events which obviously do not occur by chance. Saying that some things happen by chance, then, does not cost much in terms of the subjective satisfaction provided by causal explanations.

The dilemma of determinism ([22]–[30])

On the other hand, the deterministic denial of chance does cost us a great deal in *moral* subjective satisfaction, according to James. Here is his argument:

First, we should note that, as a matter of fact, we do have feelings of regret ([22], [23]). That is, there are events which we wish had not happened, or think should not have happened. James makes it clear that he thinks some of these regrets are rational, but that is not part of the argument at this point.

Now, let us *assume* that determinism is correct—that is, we are going to do some hypothetical reasoning to see what some consequences of determinism are. The strategy is to construct the following dilemma:

(a) Either our regrets are rational or they are not.

(b) If they are, then the whole universe is regrettable.

(c) If they are not, then the whole universe is regrettable or else there are no values at all.

(d) Therefore, the whole universe is regrettable or else there are no values at all.

But since the assumption about determinism is involved in the proof of the dilemma's conclusion, the conclusion of the hypothetical reasoning will be that *if* determinism is true, then so is the claim (d). It is this conditional statement which James will employ in his final comparison of determinism and indeterminism. Now let us look at the dilemma in detail.

Statement (a) seems safe enough. But what about (b)? If some of our regrets are justified, why should we then regret the whole universe? It is because of the assumption that determinism is true. From the deterministic point of view an event could not be avoided unless its causes were avoided. And those causes could not be different than they are unless *their* causes were different, and so on. Additionally, different causes would produce differences in effects other than the one we wish to change. So, to wish that an event had not happened is to wish that its causes, and their causes—ultimately, the whole world—had been different than it is. Assuming that determinisim is true, then, if it is rational to regret any event in the world, it is rational to regret them all ([24]).

Then what if we claim that no events are rationally regrettable? James suggests ([25]) that this would be morally absurd, but that even if we accepted it there would be a problem. For, remember, we *do* regret things. If it is irrational to do so, then we *should not* do so. But then it would be rational to regret our irrational feelings of regret, and the argument used to support (b) comes into play again—we wind up regretting the whole world.

Here we are supposing still that it is rational to regret something. What if we claim that absolutely no regrets are rational, no matter what they are? Well, then we would not be required to regret the whole universe. But consider the cost of this alternative. We would have to claim that nothing which happens could have been replaceable by something better—and thus we give up all judgments of value.

So, if determinism is correct, we must either abandon our concepts of value, or pessimistically suppose that the whole world is regrettable. This is our conclusion (d).

Has James made any mistakes in this argument? There are two possibilities which may have occurred to you. The first is that it may be a mistake to think that we must regret the causes of all regrettable events. May we not simply welcome the good and regret the bad consequences of any situations, without supposing that the whole world should have been different? Probably James would respond that such "regretting" is too insipid to have any moral significance. The morally appropriate response to the murder he described is to *wish it had never happened*, and to a determinist that means wishing *this* world did not exist. And to *accept* the murder, simply because it is part of a world we find overall acceptable is to abandon our values, for we *should* wish such things would not occur. But such wishes seem not to be available to the determinist.

The second possible objection you may have considered is that we might try to construct a counterdilemma based on the fact that we do approve of some events. Could we then argue that we should approve of the whole world? Trying to formulate this argument can be very instructive and you might find it profitable to spend some time with it. But you will encounter at least two difficulties: (*a*) it will be hard to get an exact replica of the "regrets" argument, because we don't approve of irrational approval, but we do regret irrational regrets; (*b*) if you *do* work out the "approval" argument, James could respond by saying, "Well, now we have two conditional proofs showing that a determinist should both regret *and* approve the whole world. Then determinism turns out to be inconsistent, and even worse off than I claimed."

Comparison of determinism and indeterminism ([16]–[18], [31]–[36])
At last, James is ready to compare the two theories. We cannot accept them both ([9]), so we must choose according to which theory provides the greatest overall subjective satisfaction—that is, according to which theory makes the best sense of our experience to us.

With respect to mechanical explanation, James concedes that determinism provides somewhat more satisfaction. But we must be careful not to overrate its advantage. There are several considerations:

1. In [16]–[18] James discusses the (chance) selection of his route home after the lecture, and he suggests that determinism really offers no explanation of such choices. While the determinist will claim, *after the choice is made,* that certain causes rendered it inevitable, he cannot say what those causes were, nor could he predict, before the choice was

made, what it would be. This does not prove the determinist wrong, but it does show that he cannot give many of the explanations which he claims are possible. (This is a version of a criticism already raised against d'Holbach.)

2. James is prepared to accept causal explanations where they do not involve human choice and action, so his indeterminism does not give up *all* the benefits of causal explanation.

3. In the footnote to [18] James responds to the objection that if we act by chance we are apt to do *anything at all*. This makes understanding our behavior much more difficult. But, says James, chance selections are made only among the possibilities which *really tempt* us. So chance does not introduce as much irrationally as one might expect, when compared to causal explanation of action.

On the other hand, from a moral point of view, determinism renders action, decision, value, effort, sacrifice, dedication, conscience, and much else totally incoherent. Such things have a point only where there are real alternative possibilities. Indeterminism offers a vastly greater amount of subjective satisfaction than does determinism with respect to these things. On balance, then, James believes that indeterminism explains the world more satisfactorily than determinism.

Concluding critical remarks
Let us return to the footnote to [18]. It is full of trouble for James. For one thing, notice that he abandons the term "chance" here and returns to "free-will." The reason is obvious. As James says, we do not think that free actions can turn out in any old way at all. On the other hand, it is not so clear that where events occur by chance they might not actually turn out in any way that is remotely possible. Since James has gone back on his promise ([3], [4]) not to drag freedom into the discussion, he owes us an account of what else, besides chance, is involved in free action.

But his hints at that account introduce problems for his whole view. Our chance actions, he says, are selected only from those possibilities which *really tempt* us. What, exactly, is the difference between these possibilities and possibilities which are merely "physically conceivable"? Is James saying that causation restricts the real possibilities to just a few (those which really tempt us) and then we select from those tempting possibilities by chance? If so, can we really make sense of the concept of chance events which are, somehow, causally restricted? And do not difficult counterexamples begin to emerge? Consider, for example, a woman who, being much abused by her husband, is really tempted to kill him, but also really tempted to endure their relationship, say, for the sake of the children. Suppose she decides to endure, and we commend her for her strength, patience, and sense of duty. Would these commendations make sense if her choice between endurance and escape-by-murder were a matter of *chance*? Or suppose that someone is really tempted to do only one thing—something good or something horrible. Does James's view tell us that such a person has no *chance* to act otherwise, and thus is not morally responsible? Isn't there something wrong with a theory which tells us people who are not even tempted to do the wrong thing, or not even tempted to do the right thing, all are excused from moral responsibility?

James wants his indeterminism to be able to take advantage of causal explanations wherever they are not in conflict with moral understanding. But he may fail to understand the reservations determinists have about such combinations of causation and chance. Most determinists would say that causal laws must be stateable as *universal* generalizations, and that a single counterexample disproves the causal connection. In claiming that some of our actions occur by chance, James is claiming that it is common for complex biochemical mechanisms (our bodies) to behave in ways which do not exemplify any causal laws. Determinists would claim that this means that at the level of tissues, organs, cells, molecules, etc., this must mean that some simpler component structures of the body fail to obey what we take to be laws of chemistry and physics. But that would be to prove that there are no such laws. Thus, they suspect, chance cannot be introduced at the level of human behavior without undercutting most causal laws. It is this fear that chance will undermine the possibility of *any* causal explanation (and not some fussy desire for perfect order) which many determinists find disturbing, and they would find James's combination of chance and causation incoherent. If they are right, then James may have radically misevaluated the subjective satisfaction his view can supply. For his comparison of the two theories to succeed, he seems to need to appeal to causal laws which can be expressed with less-than-universal generalizations. Can we really accept such "laws" as the basis for rational explanation?

3

When Is a Man Responsible?

MORITZ SCHLICK

1. The Pseudo-Problem of Freedom of the Will

[1]   With hesitation and reluctance I prepare to add this chapter to the discussion of ethical problems. For in it I must speak of a matter which, even at present, is thought to be a fundamental ethical question, but which got into ethics and has become a much discussed problem only because of a misunderstanding. This is the so-called problem of the freedom of the will. Moreover, this pseudo-problem has long since been settled by the efforts of certain sensible persons; and, above all, the state of affairs just described has been often disclosed—with exceptional clarity by Hume. Hence it is really one of the greatest scandals of philosophy that again and again so much paper and printer's ink is de-

voted to this matter, to say nothing of the expenditure of thought, which could have been applied to more important problems (assuming that it would have sufficed for these). Thus I should truly be ashamed to write a chapter on "freedom." In the chapter heading, the word "responsible" indicates what concerns ethics, and designates the point at which misunderstanding arises. Therefore the concept of responsibility constitutes our theme, and if in the process of its clarification I also must speak of the concept of freedom I shall, of course, say only what others have already said better; consoling myself with the thought that in this way alone can anything be done to put an end at last to that scandal.

[2]   The main task of ethics (of which we convinced ourselves in

[From *Problems of Ethics* by Moritz Schlick (1930). English translation by David Rynin first published in 1939. Reprinted by permission of the translator and Dover Publications, Inc.]

Chapter I) is to explain moral behavior. To explain means to refer back to laws: every science, including psychology, is possible only in so far as there are such laws to which the events can be referred. Since the assumption that *all* events are subject to universal laws is called the principle of causality, one can also say, "Every science presupposes the principle of causality." Therefore every explanation of human behavior must also assume the validity of causal laws; in this case the existence of psychological laws. (If for example our law of motivation of Chapter II were incorrect, then human conduct would be quite unexplained.) All of our experience strengthens us in the belief that this presupposition is realized, at least to the extent required for all purposes of practical life in intercourse with nature and human beings, and also for the most precise demands of technique. Whether, indeed, the principle of causality holds universally, whether, that is, *determinism* is true, we do not know; no one knows. But we do know that it is impossible to settle the dispute between determinism and indeterminism by mere reflection and speculation, by the consideration of so many reasons for and so many reasons against (which collectively and individually are but pseudo-reasons). Such an attempt becomes especially ridiculous when one considers with what enormous expenditure of experimental and logical skill contemporary physics carefully approaches the question of whether causality can be maintained for the most minute intra-atomic events.

[3]   But the dispute concerning "freedom of the will" generally proceeds in such fashion that its advocates attempt to refute, and its opponents to prove, the validity of the causal principle, both using hackneyed arguments, and neither in the least abashed by the magnitude of the undertaking. (I can exclude only Bergson from this criticism, with whom, however, this whole question is not an ethical but a metaphysical problem. His ideas, which in my opinion will not stand epistemological analysis, are of no significance for us.) Others distinguish two realms, in one of which determinism holds, but not in the other. This line of thought (which was unfortunately taken by Kant) is, however, quite the most worthless (though Schopenhauer considered it to be Kant's most profound idea).

[4]   Fortunately, it is not necessary to lay claim to a final solution of the causal problem in order to say what is necessary in ethics concerning responsibility; there is required only an analysis of the concept, the careful determination of the meaning which is in fact joined to the words "responsibility" and "freedom" as these are actually used. If men had made clear to themselves the sense

of those propositions, which we use in everyday life, that pseudo-argument which lies at the root of the pseudo-problem, and which recurs thousands of times within and outside of philosophical books, would never have arisen.

[5]   The argument runs as follows: "If determinism is true, if, that is, all events obey immutable laws, then my will too is always determined, by my innate character and my motives. Hence my decisions are necessary, not free. But if so, then I am not responsible for my acts, for I would be accountable for them only if I could do something about the way my decisions went; but I can do nothing about it, since they proceed with necessity from my character and the motives. And I have made neither, and have no power over them: the motives come from without, and my character is the necessary product of the innate tendencies and the external influences which have been effective during my lifetime. Thus determinism and moral responsibility are incompatible. Moral responsibility presupposes freedom, that is, exemption from causality."

[6]   This process of reasoning rests upon a whole series of confusions, just as the links of a chain hang together. We must show these confusions to be such, and thus destroy them.

2. Two Meanings of the Word "Law"

[7]   It all begins with an erroneous interpretation of the meaning of "law." In practice this is understood as a rule by which the state prescribes certain behavior to its citizens. These rules often contradict the natural desires of the citizens (for if they did not do so, there would be no reason for making them), and are in fact not followed by many of them; while others obey, but under *compulsion*. The state does in fact compel its citizens by imposing certain sanctions (punishments) which serve to bring their desires into harmony with the prescribed laws.

[8]   In natural science, on the other hand, the word "law" means something quite different. The natural law is not a *pre*scription as to how something should behave, but a formula, a *de*scription of how something does in fact behave. The two forms of "laws" have only this in common: both tend to be expressed in *formulae*. Otherwise they have absolutely nothing to do with one another, and it is very blameworthy that the same word has been used for two such different things; but even more so that philosophers have allowed themselves to be led into serious errors by this usage. Since natural laws are only descriptions of what happens, there can be in regard to them no talk of "compulsion." The

laws of celestial mechanics do not prescribe to the planets how they have to move, as though the planets would actually like to move quite otherwise, and are only forced by these burdensome laws of Kepler to move in orderly paths; no, these laws do not in any way "compel" the planets, but express only what in fact planets actually do.

[9]   If we apply this to volition, we are enlightened at once, even before the other confusions are discovered. When we say that a man's will "obeys psychological laws," these are not civic laws, which compel him to make certain decisions, or dictate desires to him, which he would in fact prefer not to have. They are laws of nature, merely expressing which desires he *actually has* under given conditions; they describe the nature of the will in the same manner as the astronomical laws describe the nature of planets. "Compulsion" occurs where man is prevented from realizing his natural desires. How could the rule according to which these natural desires arise itself be considered as "compulsion"?

3. Compulsion and Necessity

[10] But this is the second confusion to which the first leads almost inevitably: after conceiving the laws of nature, anthropomorphically, as order imposed *nolens volens* upon the events, one adds to them the concept of "necessity." This word, derived from "need," also comes to us from practice, and is used there in the sense of inescapable compulsion. To apply the word with this meaning to natural laws is of course senseless, for the presupposition of an opposing desire is lacking; and it is then confused with something altogether different, which is actually an attribute of natural laws. That is, universality. It is of the essence of natural laws to be universally valid, for only when we have found a rule which holds of events without exception do we *call* the rule a law of nature. Thus when we say "a natural law holds necessarily" this has but one legitimate meaning: "It holds in *all* cases where it is applicable." It is again very deplorable that the word "necessary" has been applied to natural laws (or, what amounts to the same thing, with reference to causality), for it is quite superfluous, since the expression "universally valid" is available. Universal validity is something altogether different from "compulsion"; these concepts belong to spheres so remote from each other that once insight into the error has been gained one can no longer conceive the possibility of a confusion.

[11] The confusion of two concepts always carries with it the confusion of their contradictory opposites. The opposite of the universal validity of a formula, of the existence of a law, is the nonexistence of a law, indeterminism, a causality; while the op-

posite of compulsion is what in practice everyone calls "freedom." Here emerges the nonsense, trailing through centuries, that freedom means "exemption from the causal principle," or "not subject to the laws of nature." Hence it is believed necessary to vindicate indeterminism in order to save human freedom.

4. Freedom and Indeterminism

[12] This is quite mistaken. Ethics has, so to speak, no moral interest in the purely theoretical question of "determinism or indeterminism?," but only a theoretical interest, namely: in so far as it seeks the laws of conduct, and can find them only to the extent that causality holds. But the question of whether man is morally free (that is, has that freedom which, as we shall show, is the presupposition of moral responsibility) is altogether different from the problem of determinism. Hume was especially clear on this point. He indicated the inadmissible confusion of the concepts of "indeterminism" and "freedom"; but he retained, inappropriately, the word "freedom" for both, calling the one freedom of "the will," the other, genuine kind, "freedom of conduct." He showed that morality is interested only in the latter, and that such freedom, in general, is unquestionably to be attributed to mankind. And this is quite correct. Freedom means the opposite of compulsion; a man is *free* if he does not act under *compulsion*,

and he is compelled or unfree when he is hindered from without in the realization of his natural desires. Hence he is unfree when he is locked up, or chained, or when someone forces him at the point of a gun to do what otherwise he would not do. This is quite clear, and everyone will admit that the everyday or legal notion of the lack of freedom is thus correctly interpreted, and that a man will be considered quite free and responsible if no such external compulsion is exerted upon him. There are certain cases which lie between these clearly described ones, as, say, when someone acts under the influence of alcohol or a narcotic. In such cases we consider the man to be more or less unfree, and hold him less accountable, because we rightly view the influence of the drug as "external," even though it is found within the body; it prevents him from making decisions in the manner peculiar to his nature. If he takes the narcotic of his own will, we make him completely responsible for *this* act and transfer a part of the responsibility to the consequences, making, as it were, an average or mean condemnation of the whole. In the case also of a person who is mentally ill we do not consider him free with respect to those acts in which the disease expresses itself, because we view the illness as a disturbing factor which hinders the normal functioning of his natural tendencies. We make not him but his disease responsible.

5. The Nature of Responsibility

[13] But what does this really signify? What do we mean by this concept of responsibility which goes along with that of "freedom," and which plays such an important role in morality? It is easy to attain complete clarity in this matter; we need only carefully determine the manner in which the concept is used. What is the case in practice when we impute "responsibility" to a person? What is our aim in doing this? The judge has to discover who is responsible for a given act in order that he may *punish* him. We are inclined to be less concerned with the inquiry as to who deserves *reward* for an act, and we have no special officials for this; but of course the principle would be the same. But let us stick to punishment in order to make the idea clear. What is punishment, actually? The view still often expressed, that it is a natural *retaliation* for past wrong, ought no longer to be defended in cultivated society; for the opinion that an increase in sorrow can be "made good again" by further sorrow is altogether barbarous. Certainly the origin of punishment may lie in an impulse of retaliation or vengeance; but what is such an impulse except the instinctive desire to destroy the *cause* of the deed to be avenged, by the destruction of or injury to the malefactor? Punishment is concerned only with the institution of causes, of *motives* of conduct, and

this alone is its meaning. Punishment is an educative measure, and as such is a means to the formation of motives, which are in part to prevent the wrongdoer from repeating the act (reformation) and in part to prevent others from committing a similar act (intimidation). Analogously, in the case of reward we are concerned with an incentive.

[14] Hence the question regarding responsibility is the question: Who, in a given case, is to be punished? Who is to be considered the true wrongdoer? This problem is not identical with that regarding the original instigator of the act; for the great-grandparents of the man, from whom he inherited his character, might in the end be the cause, or the statesmen who are responsible for his social milieu, and so forth. But the "doer" is the one *upon whom the motive must have acted* in order, with certainty, to have prevented the act (or called it forth, as the case may be). Consideration of remote causes is of no help here, for in the first place their actual contribution cannot be determined, and in the second place they are generally out of reach. Rather, we must find the person in whom the decisive junction of causes lies. The question of who is responsible is the question concerning the *correct point of application of the motive*. And the important thing is that in this its meaning is completely exhausted; behind it there lurks no mysterious connec-

tion between transgression and requital, which is merely *indicated* by the described state of affairs. It is a matter only of knowing who is to be punished or rewarded, in order that punishment and reward function as such—be able to achieve their goal.

[15] Thus, all the facts connected with the concepts of responsibility and imputation are at once made intelligible. We do not charge an insane person with responsibility, for the very reason that he offers no unified point for the application of a motive. It would be pointless to try to affect him by means of promises or threats, when his confused soul fails to respond to such influence because its normal mechanism is out of order. We do not try to give him motives, but try to heal him (metaphorically, we make his sickness responsible, and try to remove its causes). When a man is forced by threats to commit certain acts we do not blame him, but the one who held the pistol at his breast. The reason is clear: the act would have been prevented had we been able to restrain the person who threatened him; and this person is the one whom we must influence in order to prevent similar acts in the future.

6. The Consciousness of Responsibility

[16] But much more important than the question of when a man is said to be responsible is that of when he

himself feels responsible. Our whole treatment would be untenable if it gave no explanation of this. It is, then, a welcome confirmation of the view here developed that the subjective feeling of responsibility coincides with the objective judgment. It is a fact of experience that, in general, the person blamed or condemned is conscious of the fact that he was "rightly" taken to account— of course, under the supposition that no error has been made, that the assumed state of affairs actually occurred. What is this consciousness of having been the true doer of the act, the actual instigator? Evidently not merely that it was he who took the steps required for its performance; but there must be added the awareness that he did it "independently," "of his own initiative," or however it be expressed. This feeling is simply the consciousness of *freedom*, which is merely the knowledge of having acted of one's *own* desires. And "one's own desires" are those which have their origin in the regularity of one's character in the given situation, and are not imposed by an external power, as explained above. The absence of the external power expresses itself in the well-known feeling (usually considered characteristic of the consciousness of freedom) *that one could also have acted otherwise*. How this indubitable experience ever came to be an argument in favor of indeterminism is incomprehensible to me. It is of course obvious that I should have acted differently had I *willed* something else; but the feeling never says that I could also have willed something else, even though this is true, if, that is, other motives had been present. And it says even less that under *exactly the same* inner and outer conditions I could also have willed something else. How could such a feeling inform me of anything regarding the purely theoretical question of whether the principle of causality holds or not? Of course, after what has been said on the subject, I do not undertake to demonstrate the principle, but I do deny that from any such fact of consciousness the least follows regarding the principle's validity. This feeling is not the consciousness of the absence of a cause, but of something altogether different, namely, of *freedom*, which consists in the fact that I can act as I desire.

[17] Thus the feeling of responsibility assumes that I acted freely, that my own desires impelled me; and if because of this feeling I willingly suffer blame for my behavior or reproach myself, and thereby admit that I might have acted otherwise, this means that other behavior was compatible with the laws of volition—of course, granted other motives. And I myself desire the existence of such motives and bear the pain (regret and sorrow) caused me by my behavior so that its repetition will be prevented. To blame oneself means just to apply motives of im-

provement to oneself, which is usually the task of the educator. But if, for example, one does something under the influence of torture, feelings of guilt and regret are absent, for one knows that according to the laws of volition no other behavior was possible—no matter what ideas, because of their feeling tones, might have functioned as motives. The important thing, always, is that the feeling of responsibility means the realization that one's self, one's own psychic processes constitute the point at which motives must be applied in order to govern the acts of one's body.

7. Causality as the Presupposition of Responsibility

[18] We can speak of motives only in a causal context; thus it becomes clear how very much the concept of responsibility rests upon that of causation, that is, upon the regularity of volitional decisions. In fact if we should conceive of a decision as utterly without any cause (this would in all strictness be the indeterministic presupposition) then the act would be entirely a matter of *chance*, for chance is identical with the absence of a cause; there is no other opposite of causality. Could we under such conditions make the agent responsible? Certainly not. Imagine a man, always calm, peaceful and blameless, who suddenly falls upon and begins to beat a stranger. He is

held and questioned regarding the motive of his action, to which he answers, in his opinion truthfully, as we assume: "There was no motive for my behavior. Try as I may I can discover no reason. My volition was without any cause—I desired to do so, and there is simply nothing else to be said about it." We should shake our heads and call him insane, because we have to believe that there was a cause, and lacking any other we must assume some mental disturbance as the only cause remaining; but certainly no one would hold him to be responsible. If decisions were causeless there would be no sense in trying to influence men; and we see at once that this is the reason why we could not bring such a man to account, but would always have only a shrug of the shoulders in answer to his behavior. One can easily determine that in practice we make an agent the more responsible the more motives we can find for his conduct. If a man guilty of an atrocity was an enemy of his victim, if previously he had shown violent tendencies, if some special circumstance angered him, then we impose severe punishment upon him; while the fewer the reasons to be found for an offense the less do we condemn the agent, but make "unlucky chance," a momentary aberration, or something of the sort, responsible. We do not find the causes of misconduct in his character, and therefore we do not try to influence it for the better: this and only this is the significance of the fact that we do not put the responsibility upon him. And he too feels this to be so, and says, "I cannot understand how such a thing could have happened to me."

[19] In general we know very well how to discover the causes of conduct in the characters of our fellow men; and how to use this knowledge in the prediction of their future behavior, often with as much certainty as that with which we know that a lion and a rabbit will behave quite differently in the same situation. From all this it is evident that in practice no one thinks of questioning the principle of causality, that, thus, the attitude of the practical man offers no excuse to the metaphysician for confusing freedom from compulsion with the absence of a cause. If one makes clear to himself that a causeless happening is identical with a chance happening, and that, consequently, an indetermined will would destroy all responsibility, then every desire will cease which might be father to an indeterministic thought. No one can prove determinism, but it is certain that we assume its validity in all of our practical life, and that in particular we can apply the concept of responsibility to human conduct only in so far as the causal principle holds of volitional processes.

[20] For a final clarification I bring together again a list of those concepts which tend, in the traditional

treatment of the "problem of free-dom," to be confused. In the place of the concepts on the left are put, mistakenly, those of the right, and those in the vertical order form a chain, so that sometimes the previous confusion is the cause of that which follows:

Natural Law.	Law of State.
Determinism (Causality).	Compulsion.
(Universal Validity).	(Necessity).
Indeterminism (Chance).	Freedom.
(No Cause).	(No Compulsion).

ANALYSIS AND DISCUSSION

The organization of this selection, along with the informative headings of the sections, make very instructive skimming possible. You should begin your first reading with the knowledge that Schlick thinks the whole debate about free agency is confused, that he thinks this confusion is based on misunderstanding of the character of natural laws, and that he will try to explain responsibility independently of assumptions about indeterminism.

THE READING OUTLINE

The style of this selection contrasts sharply with that of the previous two. Schlick keeps his writing compact, highly organized, and methodical. Your outline is sketched for you in the divisions of the selection.

I. The pseudo-problem of free will—[1]–[12].

    A. The traditional debate described—[1]–[6].

    B. Confusions in the traditional debate—[7]–[12].

        1. Ambiguity of "law"—[7]–[9].

        2. Distinction between compulsion and necessity—[10], [11].

        3. Distinction between freedom and indeterminism—[12].

   [1] The (un)importance of indeterminism for ethics was established long ago, but confusions about responsibility keep an irrelevant debate alive.

CRITICAL EVALUATION

Most students find it a relief to read Schlick's straightforward style after struggling with d'Holbach and James. But that style can be the cause of some misunderstanding. It is so smooth, and carries you along so easily, that you may tend to overlook difficulties as you read. It is important to ask at frequent intervals whether his claims are as clear as they seem, and whether objections might be raised which he has not considered.

The traditional problem of free agency ([1]–[6])

With respect to the debate about determinism and indeterminism, Schlick makes two points: (*a*) that the correct answer has not been established; (*b*) that the issue is not relevant to any questions of ethics. In support of the first claim, he calls our attention to the complexity of the scientific debate about the significance of some data in the literature of physics. The point, here, is that the proper way to discover whether events are caused is to investigate them scientifically, and discover either their causes or else that no causal regularities seem to apply. To do this for all kinds of events would nearly amount to completing science—and we are not even close to such a formidable objective. But, in any case, he also argues that if we understand more clearly what moral responsibility is, we will see that the truth of indeterminism is not a necessary condition of freedom or moral responsibility. Rather, he claims in [2], and will argue in [17]–[19], that we would not describe human actions as free or responsible unless we did think they resulted from certain kinds of causes. Thus, while Schlick and James agree about the lack of proof of either determinism or indeterminism, Schlick is convinced that to the extent that human behavior might occur by chance, in the way James suggests, it would be impossible to count anyone as responsible for that behavior.

In [5] Schlick offers a compact statement of the argument that caused behavior cannot be free or responsible. His sketch seems quite accurate. Since he intends to show that the argument depends upon confusions which he is going to clear up, we should return to this statement of the argument and see if we really can locate in it the confusions which he intends to discuss.

The confusions ([7]–[12])

First ([7]–[9]) we should distinguish two meanings of the word "law." Civic laws are kinds of commands, which tell us what we should do, and which provide various kinds of enforcement institutions to make us do it, whether we want to or not. Natural laws, on the other hand, are true universal generalizations which describe how things always happen. The important point to grasp is the difference between a command and a generalization. The command is neither true nor false, but it can be obeyed or disobeyed. The generalization can be true or false, but it demands nothing from us. If we think of the nature of counterexamples, this difference becomes clearer. To discover a single counterexample to a universal generalization is to prove the generalization false. Thus, if we think we have discovered a law of nature and then we find some counterexample to it, we learn that the statement we thought was a law is false and, thus, not a law (true description) after all. But if we act in a way a civic law forbids, we do not thereby prove the law wrong— we simply break it, and become subject to whatever penalties it may involve.

Now, if it has effective institutions for enforcement, a civic law may *compel* our obedience—that is, it may be backed up with various forces which intimidate us, or physically restrain us, or in other ways cause us to obey— whether or not we want to. But a true description does not *compel* anyone to do anything against one's wishes—it simply says, as a matter of fact, how things happen to come about.

Finally, [11], [12], we should notice that one who is not *compelled* to act against his wishes is *free* to act in accordance with them. One whose actions fit no universal generalizations about causes and effects is one who acts by *chance*. Freedom is the opposite of compulsion, but indeterminism is the opposite of universal describability.

The confusion Schlick sees in the argument in [5], then, is a huge fallacy of ambiguity. Because of the distinct meanings of "law" and "necessity," talking about natural laws in the argument produces serious misunderstanding. We are persuaded that such laws *compel* us to obey and thus interfere with our freedom. But natural laws—generalizations—cannot compel, or interfere with freedom. Thus, if we remove the confusion, we see that there is no conflict between causal laws and free, responsible action. To act freely is to act in accordance with one's own desires, wishes, inclinations, or other motives. Not to be free is to be caused by external events to act contrary to or in spite of such personal motives. In either case, there are causes. The important difference between free action and unfree behavior has to do with whether the causes are part of the agent's own character, or whether they are alien to the agent—external, compelling causes.

Many people find this account of Schlick's very persuasive. Certainly it seems absurd to suppose that a true description can compel any behavior. But you should consider these questions: (1) what is the difference between a causal law and other true universal generalizations? (2) Does this account really respond to James's concerns about real possiblities? The first question reminds us that not every universal generalization is a causal law. If we figure out what else is required for a generalization to be a causal law, could we find that something about the circumstances causal laws describe does compel, or otherwise interfere with free action? And the second question reminds us that if the system of causal laws exists—if there are true generalizations describing every event—then only one event would fit compatibly with all those descriptions in any given situation. And in that sense, there still would be only one real possiblity. Whether you think these considerations important will have to wait until you see what else Schlick has to say about responsibility.

Responsibility, punishment, and rewards ([13]–[15])

Schlick claims that we are responsible for our free actions—that is, for actions whose causes lie within ourselves, rather than outside. But there is an obvious objection to this. If determinism is true, then there are causes for all our motives, traits of character, etc., and eventually the train of causes can be traced to a variety of external situations. As d'Holbach emphasized, we do not choose our bodies, our brains, our education and experience—and they mold our personalities. So, what, exactly does this distinction between internal and external causes amount to?

The response is based on an analysis of the function of the concept of responsibility. To hold a person responsible, says Schlick, is to say that the person is one who could be appropriately punished or rewarded for the behavior in question. And since the purpose of rewards and punishments is to control future behavior, the real question about responsibility is whether we could act upon a person so as to improve behavior (the person's or someone else's) in an efficient way. We do not punish the parents of an adult misbehaver because it is too late for tinkering with the parental personalities to produce significant changes in their child's behavior. We do not punish the mentally ill because their illnesses prevent the punishment from changing behavior in the way desired. If Smith forces Jones to do something nasty, we punish Smith rather than Jones, because that is the most efficient point at which to make the desired modifications.

Feelings of responsibility ([16], [17])

Often, indeterminists argue that we all feel free, uncompelled, and responsible for much of what we do. This is taken as evidence that at least in those cases what we do is not causally determined. Schlick responds by agreeing that we have such feelings, but what they show is that no external forces prevent us from doing what our internal motives make attractive to us. We are *not* compelled, in such cases, and we are free. But far from proving indeterminism, all this does is to show that our own motives and characters can effectively cause our actions in these cases.

Responsibility and chance ([18]–[20])

Finally, Schlick argues that we could not be morally responsible for chance events. A truly chance event would be disconnected from all our traits of character, our training, our experience and beliefs, our deliberation—it would be as much a surprise to us as to anyone else. In a very real sense, it would not be our action at all, but merely something which has happened to us. For us to be responsible, our actions must in some way reflect our character, aims, desires, etc.

And, in fact, we do suppose that people's characters determine their actions. We believe that we know how our friends will react to many situations, who will be angry, who pleased, what they will say, and so forth. If human behavior really occurred by chance, there would be no point in believing in this sort of predictability. This point is especially important if we consider that we all think we know some people who are most predictable with respect to behavior for which they are held morally responsible—that is, we know people who we are confident will do their duty and pursue the good, and we know others who will certainly be selfish and cowardly in demanding circumstances.

Thus, Schlick argues, moral responsibility requires causation rather than chance, and a defense of indeterminism is either not relevant or actually damaging to claims about moral responsibility.

Concluding remarks

Schlick has presented us with a tidy and impressive package. If he is right we can save the scientific account of the world *and* ethics. And as we consider the theory in the abstract, it tends to be very attactive. But will it stand up to hard criticism? What is required here is to take each of the claims he has made and subject it to a thorough series of possible counterexamples. Do we always link our judgments of responsibility with punishments and rewards in the way he suggests? Is the purpose of punshment or of reward always what he claims? Do causal explanations excuse us from responsibility only when they point to external determinants of behavior?

You should put some effort into trying to find possible counterexamples to Schlick's claims, and then figuring out how he would respond to them. Several cases of the appropriate kind are introduced in the selection by Campbell in this chapter. But, to start you on your way, here are some issues to consider:

1. We think there are differences between punishment, education, medical treatment, and rational arguments. But all are methods for altering and controlling behavior, and we think all are to be employed at whatever point

will make them most effective. On Schlick's account, then, how can we explain the differences among them?

2. An alternative view of punishment and reward might be called *meritorian*. According to this view, whether a person should be punished or rewarded, and the extent of the punishment or reward, is to be decided according to what the person *deserves*. Schlick dismisses such a view as barbarous ([13]) but does that really dispose of it? Schlick's view seems to suggest that the appropriate punishment or reward is the one which is most effective in producing the desired kinds of behavior. If a sure cure for robbery was very pleasant to the robber, would we still regard it as the appropriate punishment? If the most effective treatment for parking violations was very painful, would we regard it as justified? Schlick should not be sold short here, for his view can be defended vigorously. (For instance, he might reply that an unduly painful punishment may cause so much fear of the law in the punishees that other aspects of their behavior will be worsened.) Still, you may find cases in which the only just assignment of punishments and rewards seems to require consideration of what a person deserves. And once we introduce such considerations, we might ask whether a person *deserves* any punishment or reward for behavior which, given the character and motives the person had, was the only *possible* behavior.

4

What Means This Freedom?

JOHN HOSPERS

... As a preparation for developing my own views on the subject, I want to mention a factor that I think is of enormous importance and relevance: namely, unconscious motivation. There are many actions—not those of an insane person (however the term "insane" be defined), nor of a person ignorant of the effects of his action, nor ignorant of some relevant fact about the situation, nor in any obvious way mentally deranged—for which human beings in general and the courts in particular are inclined to hold the doer responsible, and for which, I would say, he should not be held responsible. The deed may be planned, it may be carried out in cold calculation, it may spring from the agent's character and be continuous with the rest of his behavior, and it may be perfectly true that he could have done differently *if* he had wanted to; nonetheless his behavior was brought about by unconscious conflicts developed in infancy, over which he had no control and of which (without training in psychiatry) he does not even have knowledge. He may even *think* he knows why he acted as he did, he may *think* he has conscious control over his actions, he may even *think* he is fully responsible for them; but he is not. ...

Now, I am not saying that none of these persons should be in jails or asylums. Often society must be protected against them. Nor am I saying that people should cease the practices of blaming and praising, punishing and rewarding; in general these devices are justified by the results—although very often they have practically no effect; the deeds are done from inner compulsion, which is not lessened when the threat of punishment is great. I am only saying that frequently persons we think responsible are not properly to be called so; we mistakenly think them responsible because we assume they are like those in whom no unconscious drive (toward this type of behavior) is present, and that their behavior can be changed by reasoning, exhorting, or threatening.

I

I have said that these persons are not responsible. But what is the criterion for responsibility? Under precisely what conditions is a person to be held morally responsible for an action? Disregarding here those conditions that have to do with a person's *ignorance* of the situation or the effects of his action, let us concentrate on those having to do with his "inner state." There are several criteria that might be suggested:

1. The first idea that comes to mind is that responsibility is determined by the presence or absence of *premeditation*—the opposite of "premeditated" being, presumably, "unthinking" or "impulsive." But this will not do—both because some acts are not premeditated but responsible, and because some are premeditated and not responsible.

Many acts we call responsible can be as unthinking or impulsive as you please. If you rush across the street to help the victim of an automobile collision, you are (at least so we would ordinarily say) acting responsibly, but you did not do so out of premeditation; you saw the accident, you didn't think, you rushed to the scene without hesitation. It was like a reflex action. But you acted responsibly: unlike the knee jerk, the act was the result of past training and past thought about situations of this kind; that is why you ran to help instead of ignoring the incident or running away. When something done originally from conviction or training becomes habitual, it becomes *like* a reflex action. As Aristotle said, virtue should become second nature through habit: a virtuous act should be performed *as if* by instinct; this, far from detracting from its moral worth, testifies to one's mastery of the desired type of behavior; one does not have to make a moral effort each time it is repeated.

There are also premeditated acts for which, I would say, the person is not responsible. Premeditation, especially when it is so exaggerated as to issue in no action at all, can be the result of neurotic disturbance or what we sometimes call an emotional "block," which the person inherits from long-past situations. In Hamlet's revenge on his uncle (I use this example because it is familiar to all of us), there was no lack, but rather a surfeit, of premeditation; his actions were so exquisitely premeditated as to make Freud and Dr. Ernest Jones look more closely to find out what lay behind them. The very premeditation camouflaged unconscious motives of which Hamlet himself was not aware. I think this is an important point, since it seems that the courts often assume that premeditation is a criterion of responsibility. If failure to kill his uncle had been considered a crime, every court in the land would have convicted Hamlet. . . .

2. Shall we say, then, that a person is not responsible for his act unless he can *defend it with reasons*? I am afraid that this criterion is no better than the previous one. First, intellectuals are usually better at giving reasons than nonintellectuals, and according to this criterion would be more responsible than persons acting from moral conviction not implemented by reasoning; yet it is very doubtful whether we should want to say that the latter are the more responsible. Second, the giving of reasons itself may be suspect. The reasons may be rationalizations camouflaging unconscious motives of which the agent knows nothing. . . . One's intelligence and reasoning power do not enable one to escape from unconsciously motivated behavior; it only gives one greater facility in rationalizing that behavior; one's intelligence is simply used in the interests of the neurosis—it is pressed into service to justify with

reasons what one does quite independently of the reasons.

If these two criteria are inadequate, let us seek others.

3. Shall we say that a person is responsible for his action unless it is the *result of unconscious forces* of which he knows nothing? Many psychoanalysts would probably accept this criterion. If it is not largely reflected in the language of responsibility as ordinarily used, this may be due to ignorance of fact: most people do not know that there are such things as unconscious motives and unconscious conflicts causing human beings to act. But it may be that if they did, perhaps they would refrain from holding persons responsible for certain actions.

I do not wish here to quarrel with this criterion of responsibility. I only want to point out the fact that if this criterion is employed a far greater number of actions will be excluded from the domain of responsibility than we might at first suppose. Whether we are neat or untidy, whether we are selfish or unselfish, whether we provoke scenes or avoid them, even whether we can exert our powers of will to change our behavior—all these may, and often do, have their source in our unconscious life.

4. Shall we say that a person is responsible for his act unless it is *compelled*? Here we are reminded of Aristotle's assertion (*Nicomachean Ethics*, Book III) that a person is responsible for his act except for

reasons of either ignorance or compulsion. Ignorance is not part of our problem here (unless it is unconsciously induced ignorance of facts previously remembered and selectively forgotten—in which case the forgetting is again compulsive), but compulsion is. How will compulsion do as a criterion? The difficulty is to state just what it means. When we say an act is compelled in a psychological sense, our language is metaphorical—which is not to say that there is no point in it or that, properly interpreted, it is not true. Our actions are compelled in a literal sense if someone has us in chains or is controlling our bodily movements. When we say that the storm compelled us to jettison the cargo of the ship (Aristotle's example), we have a less literal sense of compulsion, for at least it is open to us to go down with the ship. When psychoanalysts say that a man was compelled by unconscious conflicts to wash his hands constantly, this is also not a literal use of "compel"; for nobody forced his hands under the tap. Still, it is a typical example of what psychologists call *compulsive* behavior: it has unconscious causes inaccessible to introspection, and moreover nothing can change it—it is as inevitable for him to do it as it would be if someone were forcing his hands under the tap. In this it is exactly like the action of a powerful external force; it is just as little within one's conscious control.

In its area of application this interpretation of responsibility comes to much the same as the previous one. And this area is very great indeed. For if we cannot be held responsible for the infantile situations (in which we were after all passive victims), then neither, it would seem, can we be held responsible for compulsive actions occurring in adulthood that are inevitable consequences of those infantile situations. And, psychiatrists and psychoanalysts tell us, actions fulfilling this description are characteristic of all people some of the time and some people most of the time. Their occurrence, once the infantile events have taken place, is inevitable, just as the explosion is inevitable once the fuse has been lighted; there is simply more "delayed action" in the psychological explosions than there is in the physical ones.

(I have not used the word "inevitable" here to mean "causally determined," for according to such a definition every event would be inevitable if one accepted the causal principle in some form or other; and probably nobody except certain philosophers uses "inevitable" in this sense. Rather, I use "inevitable" in its ordinary sense of "cannot be avoided." To the extent, therefore, that adult neurotic manifestations *can* be avoided, once the infantile patterns have become set, the assertion that they are inevitable is not true.)

5. There is still another criterion, which I prefer to the previous ones, by which a man's responsibility for an act can be measured: the degree to which that act can (or could have been) *changed by the use of reasons*. Suppose that the man who washes his hands constantly does so, he says, for hygienic reasons, believing that if he doesn't do so he will be poisoned by germs. We now convince him, on the best medical authority, that his belief is groundless. Now, the test of his responsibility is whether the changed belief will result in changed behavior. If it does not, as with the compulsive hand washer, he is not acting responsibly, but if it does, he is. It is not the *use* of reasons, but their *efficacy in changing behavior*, that is being made the criterion of responsibility. And clearly in neurotic cases no such change occurs; in fact, this is often made the defining characteristic of neurotic behavior: it is unchangeable by any rational considerations.

II

I have suggested these criteria to distinguish actions for which we can call the agent responsible from those for which we cannot. Even persons with extensive knowledge of psychiatry do not, I think, use any one of these criteria to the exclusion of the others; a conjunction of two or more may be used at once. But however they may be combined or selected in actual application, I believe we can make the distinction along some such lines as we have suggested.

But is there not still another possible meaning of "responsibility" that we have not yet mentioned? Even after we have made all the above distinctions, there remains a question in our minds whether we are, in the final analysis, *responsible for any of our actions at all*. The issue may be put this way: How can anyone be responsible for his actions, since they grow out of his character, which is shaped and molded and made what it is by influences—some hereditary, but most of them stemming from early parental environment—that were not of his own making or choosing? This question, I believe, still troubles many people who would agree to all the distinctions we have just made but still have the feeling that "this isn't all." They have the uneasy suspicion that there is a more ultimate sense, a "deeper" sense, in which we are *not* responsible for our actions, since we are not responsible for the character out of which those actions spring. . . .

Let us take as an example a criminal who, let us say, strangled several persons and is himself now condemned to die in the electric chair. Jury and public alike hold him fully responsible (at least they utter the words "he is responsible"), for the murders were planned down to the minutest detail, and the defendant tells the jury exactly how he planned them. But now we find out how it all came about; we learn of parents who rejected him from babyhood, of the childhood spent in one foster home after another, where it was always plain to him that he was not wanted; of the constantly frustrated early desire for affection, the hard shell of nonchalance and bitterness that he assumed to cover the painful and humiliating fact of being unwanted, and his subsequent attempts to heal these wounds to his shattered ego through defensive aggression.... The poor victim is not conscious of the inner forces that exact from him this ghastly toll; he battles, he schemes, he revels in pseudoaggression, he is miserable, but he does not know what works within him to produce these catastrophic acts of crime. His aggressive actions are the wriggling of a worm on a fisherman's hook. And if this is so, it seems difficult to say any longer, "He is responsible." Rather, we shall put him behind bars for the protection of society, but we shall no longer flatter our feeling of moral superiority by calling him personally responsible for what he did.

Let us suppose it were established that a man commits murder only if, sometime during the previous week, he has eaten a certain combination of foods—say, tuna fish salad at a meal also including peas, mushroom soup, and blueberry pie.

What if we were to track down the factors common to all murders committed in this country during the last twenty years and found this factor present in all of them, and only in them? The example is of course empirically absurd; but may it not be that there is *some* combination of factors that regularly leads to homicide? ...

When such specific factors are discovered, won't they make it clear that it is foolish and pointless, as well as immoral, to hold human beings responsible for crimes? Or, if one prefers biological to psychological factors, suppose a neurologist is called in to testify at a murder trial and produces X-ray pictures of the brain of the criminal; anyone can see, he argues, that the *cella turcica* was already calcified at the age of nineteen; it should be a flexible bone, growing, enabling the gland to grow. All the defendant's disorders might have resulted from this early calcification. Now, this particular explanation may be empirically false; but who can say that no such factors, far more complex, to be sure, exist?

When we know such things as these, we no longer feel so much tempted to say that the criminal is responsible for his crime; and we tend also (do we not?) to excuse him—not legally (we still confine him to prison) but morally; we no longer call him a monster or hold him personally responsible for what he did. Moreover, we do this in general, not merely in the case of crime: "You must excuse Grandmother for being irritable; she's really quite ill and is suffering some pain all the time." Or: "The dog always bites children after she's had a litter of pups; you can't blame her for it: she's not feeling well, and besides she naturally wants to defend them." Or: "She's nervous and jumpy, but do excuse her: she has a severe glandular disturbance."

Let us note that the more *thoroughly* and *in detail* we know the causal factors leading a person to behave as he does, the more we tend to exempt him from responsibility.

. . .

But one may still object that so far we have talked only about neurotic behavior. Isn't nonneurotic or normal or not unconsciously motivated (or whatever you want to call it) behavior still within the area of responsibility? There are reasons for answering "No" even here, for the normal person no more than the neurotic one has caused his own character, which makes him what he is. Granted that neurotics are not responsible for their behavior (that part of it which we call neurotic) because it stems from undigested infantile conflicts that they had no part in bringing about, and that are external to them just as surely as if their behavior had been forced on them by a malevolent deity (which is indeed one theory on the subject); but the so-called normal person is equally the product of causes in which his volition took no part. And if, unlike the neurotic's, his behavior is changeable by rational considerations, and if he has the will power to overcome the effects of an unfortunate early environment, this again is no credit to him; he is just lucky. If energy is available to him in a form in which it can be mobilized for constructive purposes, this is no credit to him, for this too is part of his psychic legacy. Those of us who can discipline ourselves and develop habits of concentration of purpose tend to blame those who cannot, and call them lazy and weak-willed; but what we fail to see is that they literally *cannot* do what we expect; if their psyches were structured like ours, they could, but as they are burdened with a tyrannical superego (to use psychoanalytic jargon for the moment), and a weak defenseless ego whose energies are constantly consumed in fighting endless charges of the superego, they simply cannot do it, and it is irrational to expect it of them. We cannot with justification blame them for their inability, any more than we can congratulate ourselves for our ability. This lesson is hard to learn, for we constantly and naïvely assume that other people are constructed as we ourselves are.

. . .

The position, then, is this: if we *can* overcome the effects of early environment, the ability to do so is itself a product of the early environment. We did not give ourselves this ability; and if we lack it we cannot be blamed for not having it. Sometimes, to be sure, moral exhortation brings out an ability that is there but not being used, and in this lies its *occasional* utility; but very often its use is pointless, because the ability is not there. The only thing that can overcome a desire, as Spinoza said, is a stronger contrary desire; and many times there simply is no wherewithal for producing a stronger contrary desire. Those of us who do have the wherewithal are lucky.

There is one possible practical advantage in remembering this. It may prevent us (unless we are compulsive blamers) from indulging in righteous indignation and committing the sin of spiritual pride, thanking God that we are not as this publican here. And it will protect from our useless moralizings those who are least equipped by nature for enduring them.

As with responsibility, so with deserts. Someone commits a crime and is punished by the state; "he deserved it," we say self-righteously—as if we were moral and he immoral, when in fact we are lucky and he is unlucky—forgetting that there, but for the grace of God and a fortunate early environment, go we. . . .

III

I want to make it quite clear that I have not been arguing for determinism. Though I find it difficult to give

any sense to the term "indeterminism," because I do not know what it would be like to come across an uncaused event, let us grant indeterminists everything they want, at least in words—influences that suggest but do not constrain, a measure of acausality in an otherwise rigidly causal order, and so on—whatever these phrases may mean. With all this granted, exactly the same situation faces the indeterminist and the determinist; all we have been saying would still hold true. "Are our powers innate or acquired?"

Suppose the powers are declared innate; then the villian may sensibly ask whether he is responsible for what he was born with. A negative reply is inevitable. Are they then acquired? Then the ability to acquire them—was that innate? or acquired? It is innate? Very well then. . . .[1]

The same fact remains—that we did not cause our characters, that the influences that made us what we are are influences over which we had no control and of whose very existence we had no knowledge at the time. This fact remains for "determinism" and "indeterminism" alike. And it is this fact to which I would appeal, not the specific tenets of traditional forms of "determinism," which seem to me, when analyzed, empirically empty.

1. W. I. Matson, "The Irrelevance of Free-will to Moral Responsibility," *Mind* LXV (October 1956); p. 495.

"But," it may be asked, "isn't it your view that nothing ultimately *could* be other than it is? And isn't this deterministic? And isn't it deterministic if you say that human beings could never act otherwise than they do, and that their desires and temperaments could not, when you consider their antecedent conditions, be other than they are?"

I reply that all these charges rest on confusions.

1. To say that nothing *could* be other than it is, is, taken literally, nonsense; and if taken as a way of saying something else, misleading and confusing. If you say, "I can't do it," this invites the question, "No? Not even if you want to?" "Can" and "could" are power words, used in the context of human action; when applied to nature they are merely anthropomorphic. "Could" has no application to nature—unless, of course, it is uttered in a theological context: one might say that God *could* have made things different. But with regard to inanimate nature "could" has no meaning. Or perhaps it is intended to mean that the order of nature is in some sense *necessary*. But in that case the sense of "necessary" must be specified. I know what "necessary" means when we are talking about propositions, but not when we are talking about the sequence of events in nature.

2. What of the charge that we could never have acted otherwise than we did? This, I submit, is simply not true. Here the exponents of Hume-Mill-Schlick-Ayer "soft determinism" are quite right. I could have gone to the opera today instead of coming here; that is, if certain conditions had been different, I should have gone. I could have done many other things instead of what I did, if some condition or other had been different, specifically if my desire had been different. I repeat that "could" is a power word, and "I could have done this" means approximately "I *should* have done this *if* I had wanted to." In this sense, all of us could often have done otherwise than we did. I would not want to say that I should have done differently even if *all* the conditions leading up to my action had been the same (this is generally not what we mean by "could" anyway); but to assert that I could have is empty, for if I *did* act differently from the time before, we would automatically say that one or more of the conditions were different, whether we had independent evidence for this or not, thus rendering the assertion immune to empirical refutation. (Once again, the vacuousness of "determinism.")

3. Well, then, could we ever have, not acted, but *desired* otherwise than we did desire? This gets us once again to the heart of the matter we were discussing in the previous section. Russell said, "We can do as we please but we can't please as we please." But I am persuaded that even this statement conceals a fatal mistake. Let us follow

the same analysis through. "I could have done X" means "I should have done X if I had wanted to." "I could have wanted X" by the same analysis would mean "I should have wanted X if I had wanted to"—which seems to make no sense at all. (What does Russell want? To please as he doesn't please?)

What does this show? It shows, I think, that the only meaningful context of "can" and "could have" is that of *action*. "Could have acted differently" makes sense; "could have desired differently," as we have just seen, does not. Because a word or phrase makes good sense in one context, let us not assume that it does so in another.

I conclude, then, with the following suggestion: that we operate on two levels of moral discourse, which we shouldn't confuse; one (let's call it the upper level) is that of actions; the other (the lower, or deeper, level) is that of the springs of action. Most moral talk occurs on the upper level. It is on this level that the Hume-Mill-Schlick-Ayer analysis of freedom fully applies. As we have just seen, "can" and "could" acquire their meaning on this level; so, I suspect, does "freedom." So does the distinction between compulsive and noncompulsive behavior, and among the senses of "responsibility," discussed in the first section of this paper, according to which we are responsible for some things and not for others. All these distinctions are perfectly valid on this level (or in

this dimension) of moral discourse; and it is, after all, the usual one—we are practical beings interested in changing the course of human behavior, so it is natural enough that 99 per cent of our moral talk occurs here.

But when we descend to what I have called the lower level of moral discourse, as we occasionally do in thoughtful moments when there is no immediate need for action, then we must admit that we are ultimately the kind of persons we are because of conditions occurring outside us, over which we had no control. But while this is true, we should beware of extending the moral terminology we used on the other level to this one also. "Could" and "can," as we have seen, no longer have meaning here. "Right" and "wrong," which apply only to actions, have no meaning here either. I suspect that the same is true of "responsibility," for now that we have recalled often forgotten facts about our being the product of outside forces, we must ask in all seriousness what would be added by saying that we are not *responsible* for our own characters and temperaments. What would it mean even? Has it a significant opposite? What would it be like to be responsible for one's own character? What possible situation is describable by this phrase? Instead of saying that it is *false* that we are responsible for our own characters, I should prefer to say that the utterance is meaningless—meaningless in the sense that it describes no possible situation, though it *seems* to because the word "responsible" is the same one we used on the upper level, where it marks a real distinction. If this is so, the result is that *moral* terms—at least the terms "could have" and "responsible"—simply drop out on the lower level. What remains, shorn now of moral terminology, is the point we tried to bring out in Part II: whether or not we have personality disturbances, whether or not we have the ability to overcome deficiencies of early environment, is like the answer to the question whether or not we shall be struck down by a dread disease: "it's all a matter of luck." It is important to keep this in mind, for people almost always forget it, with consequences in human intolerance and unnecessary suffering that are incalculable.

5

Of Liberty and Necessity

DAVID HUME

... It is universally allowed that matter, in all its operations, is actuated by a necessary force, and that every natural effect is so precisely determined by the energy of its cause that no other effect, in such particular circumstances, could possibly have resulted from it. The degree and direction of every motion is, by the laws of nature, prescribed with such exactness that a living creature may as soon arise from the shock of two bodies as motion in any other degree or direction than what is actually produced by it. Would we, therefore, form a just and precise idea of *necessity*, we must consider whence that idea arises when we apply it to the operation of bodies.

It seems evident that, if all the scenes of nature were continually shifted in such a manner that no two events bore any resemblance to each other, but every object was entirely new, without any similitude to whatever had been seen before, we should never, in that case, have attained the least idea of necessity, or of a connexion among these objects. We might say, upon such a supposition, that one object or event has followed another; not that one was produced by the other. The relation of cause and effect must be utterly unknown to mankind. Inference and reasoning concerning the operations of nature would, from that moment, be at an end; and the memory and senses remain the only canals, by which the knowledge of any real existence could possibly have access to the mind. Our idea, therefore, of necessity and causation arises entirely from the uniformity observable in the operations of nature, where similar objects are constantly conjoined together, and the mind is determined by custom to infer the

[From *An Enquiry Concerning Human Understanding*, Section VIII. First published in 1748.]

one from the appearance of the other. These two circumstances form the whole of that necessity, which we ascribe to matter. Beyond the constant *conjunction* of similar objects, and the consequent *inference* from one to the other, we have no notion of any necessity or connexion.

If it appear, therefore, that all mankind have ever allowed, without any doubt or hesitation, that these two circumstances take place in the voluntary actions of men, and in the operations of mind; it must follow, that all mankind have ever agreed in the doctrine of necessity, and that they have hitherto disputed, merely for not understanding each other.

As to the first circumstance, the constant and regular conjunction of similar events, we may possibly satisfy ourselves by the following considerations. It is universally acknowledged that there is a great uniformity among the actions of men, in all nations and ages, and that human nature remains still the same, in its principles and operations. The same motives always produce the same actions: The same events follow from the same causes. Ambition, avarice, self-love, vanity, friendship, generosity, public spirit: these passions, mixed in various degrees, and distributed through society, have been, from the beginning of the world, and still are, the source of all the actions and enterprises, which have ever been observed among mankind. Would you know the sentiments, inclinations, and course of life of the Greeks and Romans? Study well the temper and actions of the French and English: You cannot be much mistaken in transferring to the former *most* of the observations which you have made with regard to the latter. Mankind are so much the same, in all times and places, that history informs us of nothing new or strange in this particular. Its chief use is only to discover the constant and universal principles of human nature, by showing men in all varieties of circumstances and situations, and furnishing us with materials from which we may form our observations and become acquainted with the regular springs of human action and behaviour. These records of wars, intrigues, factions, and revolutions, are so many collections of experiments, by which the politician or moral philosopher fixes the principles of his science, in the same manner as the physician or natural philosopher becomes acquainted with the nature of plants, minerals, and other external objects, by the experiments which he forms concerning them. . . .

We must not, however, expect that this uniformity of human actions should be carried to such a length as that all men, in the same circumstances, will always act precisely in the same manner, without making any allowance for the diversity of characters, prejudices, and opinions. Such a uniformity in every particular, is found in no part of nature. On the contrary, from observing the variety of conduct in different men, we are enabled to form a greater variety of maxims, which still suppose a degree of uniformity and regularity.

Are the manners of men different in different ages and countries? We learn thence the great force of custom and education, which mould the human mind from its infancy and form it into a fixed and established character. Is the behaviour and conduct of the one sex very unlike that of the other? Is it thence we become acquainted with the different characters which nature has impressed upon the sexes, and which she preserves with constancy and regularity? Are the actions of the same person much diversified in the different periods of his life, from infancy to old age? This affords room for many general observations concerning the gradual change of our sentiments and inclinations, and the different maxims which prevail in the different ages of human creatures. Even the characters, which are peculiar to each individual, have a uniformity in their influence; otherwise our acquaintance with the persons and our observation of their conduct could never teach us their dispositions, or serve to direct our behaviour with regard to them.

I grant it possible to find some actions, which seem to have no regular connexion with any known motives, and are exceptions to all the measures of conduct which have ever been established for the gov-ernment of men. But if we would willingly know what judgement should be formed of such irregular and extraordinary actions, we may consider the sentiments commonly entertained with regard to those irregular events which appear in the course of nature, and the operations of external objects. All causes are not conjoined to their usual effects with like uniformity. An artificer, who handles only dead matter, may be disappointed of his aim, as well as the politician, who directs the conduct of sensible and intelligent agents.

The vulgar, who take things according to their first appearance, attribute the uncertainty of events to such an uncertainty in the causes as makes the latter often fail of their usual influence; though they meet with no impediment in their operation. But philosophers, observing that, almost in every part of nature, there is contained a vast variety of springs and principles, which are hid, by reason of their minuteness or remoteness, find, that it is at least possible the contrariety of events may not proceed from any contingency in the cause, but from the secret operation of contrary causes. This possibility is converted into certainty by farther observation, when they remark that, upon an exact scrutiny, a contrariety of effects always betrays a contrariety of causes, and proceeds from their mutual opposition. A peasant can give no better reason for the stopping of any clock or watch than to say it does not commonly go right: But an artist easily perceives that the same force in the spring or pendulum has always the same influence on the wheels; but fails of its usual effect, perhaps by reason of a grain of dust, which puts a stop to the whole movement. From the observation of several parallel instances, philosophers form a maxim that the connexion between all causes and effects is equally necessary, and that its seeming uncertainty in some instances proceeds from the secret opposition of contrary causes.

Thus, for instance, in the human body, when the usual symptoms of health or sickness disappoint our expectation; when medicines operate not with their wonted powers; when irregular events follow from any particular cause; the philosopher and physician are not surprised at the matter, nor are ever tempted to deny, in general, the necessity and uniformity of those principles by which the animal economy is conducted. They know that a human body is a mighty complicated machine: That many secret powers lurk in it, which are altogether beyond our comprehension: That to us it must often appear very uncertain in its operations: And that therefore the irregular events, which outwardly discover themselves, can be no proof that the laws of nature are not observed with the greatest regularity in its internal operations and government.

The philosopher, if he be consistent, must apply the same reasoning to the actions and volitions of intelligent agents. The most irregular and unexpected resolutions of men may frequently be accounted for by those who know every particular circumstance of their character and situation. A person of an obliging disposition gives a peevish answer: But he has the toothache, or has not dined. A stupid fellow discovers an uncommon alacrity in his carriage: But he has met with a sudden piece of good fortune. Or even when an action, as sometimes happens, cannot be particularly accounted for, either by the person himself or by others; we know, in general, that the characters of men are, to a certain degree, inconstant and irregular. This is, in a manner, the constant character of human nature; though it be applicable, in a more particular manner, to some persons who have no fixed rule for their conduct, but proceed in a continued course of caprice and inconstancy. The internal principles and motives may operate in a uniform manner, notwithstanding these seeming irregularities; in the same manner as the winds, rain, clouds, and other variations of the weather are supposed to be governed by steady principles; though not easily discoverable by human sagacity and enquiry.

Thus it appears, not only that the conjunction between motives and voluntary actions is as regular and uniform as that between the cause and effect in any part of nature;

but also that this regular conjunction has been universally acknowledged among mankind, and has never been the subject of dispute, either in philosophy or common life. . . .

And indeed, when we consider how aptly *natural* and *moral* evidence link together, and form only one chain of argument, we shall make no scruple to allow that they are of the same nature, and derived from the same principles. A prisoner who has neither money nor interest, discovers the impossibility of his escape, as well when he considers the obstinacy of the gaoler, as the walls and bars with which he is surrounded; and, in all attempts for his freedom, chooses rather to work upon the stone and iron of the one, than upon the inflexible nature of the other. The same prisoner, when conducted to the scaffold, foresees his death as certainly from the constancy and fidelity of his guards, as from the operation of the axe or wheel. His mind runs along a certain train of ideas: The refusal of the soldiers to consent to his escape; the action of the executioner; the separation of the head and body; bleeding, convulsive motions, and death. Here is a connected chain of natural causes and voluntary actions; but the mind feels no difference between them in passing from one link to another: Nor is less certain of the future event that if it were connected with the objects present to the memory or senses, by a train of causes, cemented together by what we are

pleased to call a *physical* necessity. The same experienced union has the same effect on the mind, whether the united objects be motives, volition, and actions; or figure and motion. We may change the name of things; but their nature and their operation on the understanding never change.

Were a man, whom I know to be honest and opulent, and with whom I live in intimate friendship, to come into my house, where I am surrounded with my servants, I rest assured that he is not to stab me before he leaves it in order to rob me of my silver standish; and I no more suspect this event than the falling of the house itself, which is new, and solidly built and founded.—*But he may have been seized with a sudden and unknown frenzy.*—So may a sudden earthquake arise, and shake and tumble my house about my ears. I shall therefore change the suppositions. I shall say that I know with certainty that he is not to put his hand into the fire and hold it there till it be consumed: And this event, I think I can foretell with the same assurance, as that, if he throw himself out at the window, and meet with no obstruction, he will not remain a moment suspended in the air. No suspicion of an unknown frenzy can give the least possibility to the former event, which is so contrary to all the known principles of human nature. A man who at noon leaves his purse full of gold on the pavement at Charing-Cross, may as well expect that it will fly away like a feather, as that he will find it untouched an hour after. Above one half of human reasonings contain inferences of a similar nature, attended with more or less degrees of certainty proportioned to our experience of the usual conduct of mankind in such particular situations.

I have frequently considered, what could possibly be the reason why all mankind, though they have ever, without hesitation, acknowledged the doctrine of necessity in their whole practice and reasoning, have yet discovered such a reluctance to acknowledge it in words, and have rather shown a propensity, in all ages, to profess the contrary opinion. The matter, I think, may be accounted for after the following manner. If we examine the operations of body, and the production of effects from their causes, we shall find that all our faculties can never carry us farther in our knowledge of this relation than barely to observe that particular objects are *constantly conjoined* together, and that the mind is carried, by a *customary transition*, from the appearance of one to the belief of the other. But though this conclusion concerning human ignorance be the result of the strictest scrutiny of this subject, men still entertain a strong propensity to believe that they penetrate farther into the powers of nature, and perceive something like a necessary connexion between the cause and the effect. When again they turn their reflections towards the operations of their own minds, and *feel* no such connexion of the motive and the action; they are thence apt to suppose, that there is a difference between the effects which result from material force, and those which arise from thought and intelligence. But being once convinced that we know nothing farther of causation of any kind than merely the *constant conjunction* of objects, and the consequent *inference* of the mind from one to another, and finding that these two circumstances are universally allowed to have place in voluntary actions; we may be more easily led to own the same necessity common to all causes. And though this reasoning may contradict the systems of many philosophers, in ascribing necessity to the determinations of the will, we shall find, upon reflection, that they dissent from it in words only, not in their real sentiment. Necessity, according to the sense in which it is here taken, has never yet been rejected, nor can ever, I think, be rejected by any philosopher. It may only, perhaps, be pretended that the mind can perceive, in the operations of matter, some farther connexion between the cause and effect; and connexion that has not place in voluntary actions of intelligent beings. Now whether it be so or not, can only appear upon examination; and it is incumbent on these philosophers to make good their assertion, by defining or describing that necessity, and pointing it out to us in the operations of material causes.

It would seem, indeed, that men begin at the wrong end of this question concerning liberty and necessity, when they enter upon it by examining the faculties of the soul, the influence of the understanding, and the operations of the will. Let them first discuss a more simple question, namely, the operations of body and of brute unintelligent matter; and try whether they can there form any idea of causation and necessity, except that of a constant conjunction of objects, and subsequent inference of the mind from one to another. If these circumstances form, in reality, the whole of that necessity, which we conceive in matter, and if these circumstances be also universally acknowledged to take place in the operations of the mind, the dispute is at an end; at least, must be owned to be thenceforth merely verbal. But as long as we will rashly suppose, that we have some farther idea of necessity and causation in the operations of external objects; at the same time, that we can find nothing farther in the voluntary actions of the mind; there is no possibility of bringing the question to any determinate issue, while we proceed upon so erroneous a supposition. The only method of undeceiving us is to mount up higher; to examine the narrow extent of science when applied to material causes; and to convince ourselves that all we know of them is the constant conjunction and inference above mentioned. We may, perhaps, find that it is with difficulty we are induced to fix such narrow limits to human understanding: But we can afterwards find no difficulty when we come to apply this doctrine to the actions of the will. For as it is evident that these have a regular conjunction with motives and circumstances and characters, and as we always draw inferences from one to the other, we must be obliged to acknowledge in words that necessity, which we have already avowed, in every deliberation of our lives, and in every step of our conduct and behaviour.

But to proceed in this reconciling project with regard to the question of liberty and necessity; the most contentious question of metaphysics, the most contentious science; it will not require many words to prove, that all mankind have ever agreed in the doctrine of liberty as well as in that of necessity, and that the whole dispute, in this respect also, has been hitherto merely verbal. For what is meant by liberty, when applied to voluntary actions? We cannot surely mean that actions have so little connexion with motives, inclinations, and circumstances, that one does not follow with a certain degree of uniformity from the other, and that one affords no inference by which we can conclude the existence of the other. For these are plain and acknowledged matters of fact. By liberty, then, we can only mean *a power of acting or not acting, according to the determinations of the will*; that is, if we choose to remain at rest, we may; if we choose to move, we also may. Now this hypothetical liberty is universally allowed to belong to every one who is not a prisoner and in chains. Here, then, is no subject of dispute.

Whatever definition we may give of liberty, we should be careful to observe two requisite circumstances; *first*, that it be consistent with plain matter of fact; *secondly*, that it be consistent with itself. If we observe these circumstances, and render our definition intelligible, I am persuaded that all mankind will be found of one opinion with regard to it.

It is universally allowed that nothing exists without a cause of its existence, and that chance, when strictly examined, is a mere negative word, and means not any real power which has anywhere a being in nature. But it is pretended that some causes are necessary, some not necessary. Here then is the advantage of definitions. Let any one *define* a cause, without comprehending, as a part of the definition, a *necessary connexion* with its effect; and let him show distinctly the origin of the idea, expressed by the definition; and I shall readily give up the whole controversy. But if the foregoing explication of the matter be received, this must be absolutely impracticable. Had not objects a regular conjunction with each other, we should never have entertained any notion of cause and effect; and this regular conjunction produces that inference of the understanding, which is the only connexion, that we can have any comprehension of. Whoever attempts a definition of cause, exclusive of these circumstances, will be obliged either to employ unintelligible terms or such as are synonymous to the terms which he endeavours to define. And if the definition above mentioned be admitted; liberty, when opposed to necessity, not to constraint, is the same thing with chance; which is universally allowed to have no existence.
. . .

Necessity may be defined two ways, conformably to the two definitions of *cause*, of which it makes an essential part. It consists either in the constant conjunction of like objects, or in the inference of the understanding from one object to another. Now necessity, in both these senses, (which, indeed, are at bottom the same) has universally, though tacitly, in the schools, in the pulpit, and in common life, been allowed to belong to the will of man; and no one has ever pretended to deny that we can draw inferences concerning human actions, and that those inferences are founded on the experienced union of like actions, with like motives, inclinations, and circumstances. The only particular in which any one can differ, is, that either, perhaps, he will refuse to give the name of necessity to this property of human actions: But as long as the meaning is understood, I hope the word can do no harm: Or that he will maintain it possible to discover something farther in the operations of matter. But this, it must be acknowledged, can be of no consequence to morality or religion, whatever it may be to natural philosophy or metaphysics. We may here be mistaken in asserting that there is no idea of any other necessity or connexion in the actions of body: But surely we ascribe nothing to the actions of the mind, but what everyone does, and must readily allow of. We change no circumstance in the received orthodox system with regard to the will, but only in that with regard to material objects and causes. Nothing, therefore, can be more innocent, at least, than this doctrine.

All laws being founded on rewards and punishments, it is supposed as a fundamental principle, that these motives have a regular and uniform influence on the mind, and both produce the good and prevent the evil actions. We may give to this influence what name we please; but, as it is usually conjoined with the action, it must be esteemed a *cause*, and be looked upon as an instance of that necessity, which we would here establish.

The only proper object of hatred or vengeance is a person or creature, endowed with thought and consciousness; and when any criminal or injurious actions excite that passion, it is only by their relation to the person, or connexion with him. Actions are, by their very nature, temporary and perishing; and where they proceed not from some *cause* in the character and disposition of the person who performed them, they can neither redound to his honour, if good; nor infamy, if evil. The actions themselves may be blameable; they may be contrary to all the rules of morality and religion: But the person is not answerable for them; and as they proceeded from nothing in him that is durable and constant, and leave nothing of that nature behind them, it is impossible he can, upon their account, become the object of punishment or vengeance. According to the principle, therefore, which denies necessity, and consequently causes, a man is as pure and untainted, after having committed the most horrid crime, as at the first moment of his birth, nor is his character anywise concerned in his actions, since they are not derived from it, and the wickedness of the one can never be used as a proof of the depravity of the other.

Men are not blamed for such actions as they perform ignorantly and casually, whatever may be the consequences. Why? but because the principles of these actions are only momentary, and terminate in them alone. Men are less blamed for such actions as they perform hastily and unpremeditately than for such as proceed from deliberation. For what reason? but because a hasty temper, though a constant cause or principle in the mind, operates only by intervals, and infects not the whole character. Again, repentance wipes off every crime, if attended with a reformation of life and manners. How is this to be accounted for? but by asserting that actions render a person criminal merely as they are proofs of criminal principles in the mind; and when, by an alteration of these principles, they cease to be just proofs, they likewise cease to be criminal. But, except upon the doctrine of necessity, they never were just proofs, and consequently never were criminal.

It will be equally easy to prove, and from the same arguments, that *liberty*, according to that definition above mentioned, in which all men agree, is also essential to morality, and that no human actions, where it is wanting, are susceptible of any moral qualities, or can be the objects either of approbation or dislike. For as actions are objects of our moral sentiment, so far only as they are indications of the internal character, passions, and affections; it is impossible that they can give rise either to praise or blame, where they proceed not from these principles, but are derived altogether from eternal violence. . . .

6

Is "Freewill" A Pseudo-Problem?

C. A. CAMPBELL

I

... Here ... is Schlick's theory. Let us now examine it.

In the first place, it is surely quite unplausible to suggest that the common assumption that moral freedom postulates some breach of causal continuity arises from a confusion of two different types of law. Schlick's distinction between descriptive and prescriptive law is, of course, sound. It was no doubt worth pointing out, too that descriptive laws cannot be said to "compel" human behavior in the same way as prescriptive laws do. But it seems to me evident that the usual reason why it is held that moral freedom implies some breach of causal continuity, is not a belief that causal laws "compel" as civil laws "compel," but simply the belief that the admission of unbroken causal continuity entails a *further* admission which is directly incompatible with moral responsibility; *viz.* the admission that no man could have acted otherwise than he in fact did. Now it may, of course, be an error thus to assume that a man is not morally responsible for an act, a fit subject for moral praise and blame in respect of it, unless he could have acted otherwise than he did. Or, if *this* is not an error, it may still be an error to assume that a man could not have acted otherwise than he did, in the sense of the phrase that is crucial for moral responsibility, without there occurring some breach of causal continuity. Into these matters we shall have to enter

[From *Mind*, Vol. 60 (1951), pp. 446–457. Reprinted by permission of *Mind*.]

very fully at a later stage. But the relevant point at the moment is that these (not *prima facie* absurd) assumptions about the conditions of moral responsibility have very commonly, indeed normally, been made, and that they are entirely adequate to explain why the problem of Free Will finds its usual formulation in terms of partial exemption from causal law. Schlick's distinction between prescriptive and descriptive laws has no bearing at all upon the truth or falsity of these assumptions. Yet if these assumptions are accepted, it is (I suggest) really inevitable that the Free Will problem should be formulated in the way to which Schlick takes exception. Recognition of the distinction upon which Schlick and his followers lay so much stress can make not a jot of difference.

As we have seen, however, Schlick does later proceed to the much more important business of disputing these common assumptions about the conditions of moral responsibility. He offers us an analysis of moral responsibility which flatly contradicts these assumptions; an analysis according to which the only freedom demanded by morality is a freedom which is compatible with Determinism. If this analysis can be sustained, there is certainly no problem of "Free Will" in the traditional sense.

But it seems a simple matter to show that Schlick's analysis is untenable. Let us test it by Schlick's own claim that it gives us what we mean by "moral responsibility" in ordinary linguistic usage.

We do not ordinarily consider the lower animals to be morally responsible. But *ought* we not to do so if Schlick is right about what we mean by moral responsibility? It is quite possible, by punishing the dog who absconds with the succulent chops designed for its master's luncheon, favourably to influence its motives in respect of its future behaviour in like circumstances. If moral responsibility is to be linked with punishment as Schlick links it, and punishment conceived as a form of education, we should surely hold the dog morally responsible? The plain fact, of course, is that we don't. We don't, because we suppose that the dog "couldn't help it": that its action (unlike what we usually believe to be true of human beings) was simply a link in a continuous chain of causes and effects. In other words, we do commonly demand the contra-causal sort of freedom as a condition of moral responsibility.

Again, we do ordinarily consider it proper, in certain circumstances, to speak of a person no longer living as morally responsible for some present situation. But *ought* we to do so if we accept Schlick's essentially "forward-looking" interpretation of punishment and responsibility? Clearly we cannot now favourably affect the dead man's motives. No doubt they could *at one time* have been favourably affected.

But that cannot be relevant to our judgment of responsibility if, as Schlick insists, the question of who is responsible "is a matter only of knowing who is to be punished or rewarded." Indeed he expressly tells us, as we saw earlier, that in asking this question we are not concerned with a "great-grand-parent" who may have been the "original instigator," because, for one reason, this "remote cause" is "out of reach." We cannot bring the appropriate educative influence to bear upon it. But the plain fact, of course, is that we do frequently assign moral responsibility for present situations to persons who have long been inaccessible to any punitive action on our part. And Schlick's position is still more paradoxical in respect of our apportionment of responsibility for occurrences in the distant past. Since in these cases there is no agent whatsoever whom we can favourably influence by punishment, the question of moral responsibility here should have no meaning for us. But of course it has. Historical writings are studded with examples.

Possibily the criticism just made may seem to some to result from taking Schlick's analysis too much *au pied de la lettre*. The absurd consequences deduced, it may be said, would not follow if we interpreted Schlick as meaning that a man is morally responsible where his motive is such as can *in principle* be favourably affected by reward or punishment—whether or not we

who pass the judgment are in a position to take such action. But with every desire to be fair to Schlick, I cannot see how he could accept this modification and still retain the essence of his theory. For the essence of his theory seems to be that moral responsibility has its whole meaning and importance for us in relation to our potential control of future conduct in the interests of society. (I agree that it is hard to believe that anybody *really* thinks this. But it is perhaps less hard to believe to-day than it has ever been before in the history of modern ethics.)

Again, we ordinarily consider that, in certain circumstances, the *degree* of a man's moral responsibility for an act is affected by considerations of his inherited nature, or of his environment, or of both. It is our normal habit to "make allowances" (as we say) when we have reason to believe that a malefactor had a vicious heredity, or was nurtured in his formative years in a harmful environment. We say in such cases "Poor chap, he is more to be pitied than blamed. We could scarcely expect him to behave like a decent citizen with *his* parentage or upbringing." But this extremely common sort of judgment has no point at all if we mean by moral responsibility what Schlick says that we mean. On *that* meaning the degree of a man's moral responsibility must presumably be dependent upon the degree to which we can favourably affect his future motives, which is quite another matter. Now there is no reason to believe that the motives of a man with a bad heredity or a bad upbringing are either less or more subject to educative influence than those of his more fortunate fellows. Yet it is plain matter of fact that we do commonly consider the degree of a man's moral responsibility to be affected by these two factors.

A final point. The extremity of paradox in Schlick's identification of the question "Who is morally blameworthy?" with the question "Who is to be punished?" is apt to be partially concealed from us just because it is our normal habit to include in the meaning of "punishment" an element of "requital for moral transgression" which Schlick expressly denies to it. On that account we commonly think of "punishment," in its strict sense, as implying moral blameworthiness in the person punished. But if we remember to mean by punishment what Schlick means by it, a purely "educative measure," with no retributive ingredients, his identification of the two questions loses such plausibility as it might otherwise have. For clearly we often think it proper to "punish" a person, in *Schlick's* sense, where we are not at all prepared to say that the person is morally blameworthy. We may even think him morally commendable. A case in point would be the unmistakably sincere but muddle-headed person who at the cost of great suffering to himself steadfastly pursues as his "duty" a

course which, in our judgment is fraught with danger to the common weal. We should most of us feel entitled, in the public interest, to bring such action to bear upon the man's motives as might induce him to refrain in future from his socially injurious behaviour: in other words, to inflict upon him what Schlick would call "punishment." But we should most of us feel perfectly clear that in so "punishing" this misguided citizen we are not proclaiming his moral blameworthiness for moral wickedness.

Adopting Schlick's own criterion, then, looking simply "to the manner in which the concept is used," we seem bound to admit that constantly people do assign moral responsibility where Schlick's theory says they shouldn't, don't assign moral responsibility where Schlick's theory says they should, and assign degrees of moral responsibility where on Schlick's theory there should be no difference in degree. I think we may reasonably conclude that Schlick's account of what we mean by moral responsibility breaks down.

The rebuttal of Schlick's arguments, however, will not suffice of itself to refute the pseudo-problem theory. The indebtedness to Schlick of most later advocates of the theory may be conceded; but certainly it does not comprehend all of significance that they have to say on the problem. There are recent analyses of the conditions of moral responsibility containing sufficient new matter, or sufficient old matter in a more precise and telling form, to require of us now something of a fresh start. In the section which follows I propose to consider some representative samples of these analyses—all of which, of course, are designed to show that the freedom which moral responsibility implies is not in fact a contra-causal type of freedom.

But before reopening the general question of the nature and conditions of moral responsibility there is a *caveat* which it seems to me worth while to enter. The difficulties in the way of a clear answer are not slight; but they are apt to seem a good deal more formidable than they really are because of a common tendency to consider in unduly close association two distinct questions: the question "Is a contra-causal type of freedom implied by moral responsibility?" and the question "Does a contra-causal type of freedom anywhere exist?". It seems to me that many philosophers (and I suspect that Moritz Schlick is among them) begin their enquiry with so firm a conviction that the contra-causal sort of freedom nowhere exists, that they find it hard to take very seriously the possibility that it is *this* sort of freedom that moral responsibility implies. For they are loth to abandon the commonsense belief that moral responsibility itself is something real. The implicit reasoning I take to be this. Moral responsibility is real. If moral responsiblity is real, the free-

dom implied in it must be a fact. But contra-causal freedom is not a fact. Therefore contra-causal freedom is not the freedom implied in moral responsibility. I think we should be on our guard against allowing this or some similar train of reasoning (whose premises, after all, are far from indubitable) to seduce us into distorting what we actually find when we set about a direct analysis of moral responsibility and its conditions.

II

The pseudo-problem theorists usually, and naturally, develop their analysis of moral responsibility by way of contrast with a view which, while it has enjoyed a good deal of philosophic support, I can perhaps best describe as the common view. It will be well to remind ourselves, therefore, of the main features of this view.

So far as the *meaning*, as distinct from the *conditions*, of moral responsibility is concerned, the common view is very simple. If we ask ourselves whether a certain person is morally responsible for a given act (or it may be just "in general"), what we are considering, it would be said, is whether or not that person is a fit subject upon whom to pass moral judgment; whether he can fittingly be deemed morally good or bad, morally praiseworthy or blameworthy. This does not take us any great way: but (*pace* Schlick) so far as it goes it does not seem to me seriously disputable. The really interesting and controversial question is about the *conditions* of moral responsibility, and in particular the question whether freedom of a contra-causal kind is among these conditions.

The answer of the common man to the latter question is that it most certainly *is* among the conditions. Why does he feel so sure about this? Not, I argued earlier, because the common man supposes that causal law exercises "compulsion" in the sense that prescriptive laws do, but simply because he does not see how a person can be deemed morally praiseworthy or blameworthy in respect of an act which he could not help performing. From the standpoint of moral praise and blame, he would say—though not necessarily from other stand-points—it is a matter of indifference whether it is by reason of some external constraint or by reason of his own given nature that the man could not help doing what he did. It is quite enough to make moral praise and blame futile that in either case there were no genuine alternatives, no open possibilities, before the man when he acted. He could not have acted otherwise than he did. And the common man might not unreasonably go on to stress the fact that we all, even if we are linguistic philosophers, do in our actual practice of moral judgment appear to accept the common

view. He might insist upon the point alluded to earlier in this paper, that we do all, in passing moral censure, "make allowances" for influences in a man's hereditary nature or environmental circumstances which we regard as having made it more than ordinarily difficult for him to act otherwise than he did: the implication being that if we supposed that the man's heredity and environment made it not merely very *difficult* but actually *impossible* for him to act otherwise than he did, we could not properly assign moral blame to him at all.

Let us put the argument implicit in the common view a little more sharply. The moral "ought" implies "can." If we say that *A* morally ought to have done *X*, we imply that in our opinion, he could have done *X*. But we assign moral blame to a man only for failing to do what we think he morally ought to have done. Hence if we morally blame *A* for not having done *X*, we imply that he could have done *X* even though in fact he did not. In other words, we imply that *A* could have acted otherwise than he did. And that means that we imply, as a necessary condition of a man's being morally blameworthy, that he enjoyed a freedom of a kind not compatible with unbroken causal continuity.

III

Now what is it that is supposed to be wrong with this simple piece of argument?—For, of course, it must be rejected by all these philosophers who tell us that the traditional problem of Free Will is a mere pseudo-problem. The argument looks as though it were doing little more than reading off necessary implications of the fundamental categories of our moral thinking. One's inclination is to ask "If one is to think morally at all, how else than this *can* we think?".

In point of fact, there is pretty general agreement among the contemporary critics as to what is wrong with the argument. Their answer in general terms is as follows. No doubt *A*'s moral responsibility does imply that he could have acted otherwise. But this expression "could have acted otherwise" stands in dire need of analysis. When we analyse it, we find that it is not, as is so often supposed, simple and unambiguous, and we find that in *some* at least of its possible meanings it implies *no* breach of causal continuity between character and conduct. Having got this clear, we can further discern that only in one of these *latter* meanings is there any compulsion upon our moral thinking to assert that if *A* is morally blameworthy for an act, *A* "could have acted otherwise than he did." It follows that, contrary to common belief, our moral thinking does *not* require us to posit a contra-causal freedom as a condition of moral responsibility.

So much of importance obviously turns upon the validity or otherwise of this line of criticism that

we must examine it in some detail and with express regard to the *ipsissima verba* of the critics.

In the course of a recent article in *Mind*, entitled "Free Will and Moral Responsiblity," Mr. Nowell-Smith (having earlier affirmed his belief that "the traditional problem has been solved") explains very concisely the nature of the confusion which, as he thinks, has led to the demand for a contra-causal freedom. He begins by frankly recognizing that "It is evident that one of the necessary conditions of moral action is that the agent 'could have acted otherwise' " and he adds "it is to this fact that the Libertarian is drawing attention." Then, after showing (unexceptionably, I think) how the relationship of "ought" to "can" warrants the proposition which he has accepted as evident, and how it induces the Libertarian to assert the existence of action that is "uncaused," he proceeds to point out, in a crucial passage, the nature of the Libertarian's error:

The fallacy in the argument (he contends) lies in supposing that when we say "A could have acted otherwise" we mean that A, being what he was and being placed in the circumstances in which he was placed, *could have done something other than what he did. But in fact we never do mean this.*

What then *do* we mean here by "*A* could have acted otherwise"? Mr.

Nowell-Smith does not tell us in so many words, but the passage I have quoted leaves little doubt how he would answer. What we really mean by the expression, he implies, is not a *categorical* but a *hypothetical* proposition. We mean "A could have acted otherwise, *if he did not happen to be what he in fact was,* or *if he were placed in circumstances other than those in which he was in fact placed.*" Now, *these* propositions, it is easy to see, are in no way incompatible with acceptance of the causal principle in its full rigour. Accordingly the claim that our fundamental moral thinking obliges us to assert a contra-causal freedom as a condition of moral responsibility is disproved.

Such is the "analytical solution" of our problem offered (with obvious confidence) by one able philosopher of to-day, and entirely representative of the views of many other able philosophers. Yet I make bold to say that its falsity stares one in the face. It seems perfectly plain that the hypothetical propositions which Mr. Nowell-Smith proposes to substitute for the categorical proposition cannot express "what we really mean" in this context by "A could have acted otherwise," for the simple reason that these hypothetical propositions have no bearing whatsoever upon the question of the moral responsibility of A. And it is A whose moral responsibility we are talking about—a definite person A with a definitive character and in a definitive set of circumstances. What conceivable significance could it have for our attitude to A's responsibility to know that someone with a *different* character (or A with a different character, if that collocation of words has any meaning), or A in a different set of circumstances from those in which A as we are concerned with him was in fact placed, "could have acted otherwise"? No doubt this suppositious being *could* have acted otherwise than the definitive person A acted. But the point is that where we are reflecting, as we are supposed in this context to be reflecting, upon the question of A's moral responsibility, our interest in this suppositious being is precisely *nil*.

The two hypothetical propositions suggested in Mr. Nowell-Smith's account of the matter do not, however, exhaust the speculations that have been made along these lines. Another very common suggestion by the analysts is that what we really mean by "A could have acted otherwise" is "A could have acted otherwise *if he had willed, or chosen, otherwise.*" This was among the suggestions offered by G. E. Moore in the well-known chapter on Free Will in his *Ethics*. It is, I think, the suggestion he most strongly favoured: though it is fair to add that neither about this nor about any other of his suggestions is Moore in the least dogmatic. He does claim, for, I think, convincing reasons, that "we *very often* mean by 'could' merely 'would, *if* so-and-so had chosen.'" And he concludes "I must confess that I cannot feel certain that this may not be all that we usually mean and understand by the assertion that we have Free Will."

This third hypothetical proposition appears to enjoy also the support of Mr. C. L. Stevenson. Mr. Stevenson begins the chapter of *Ethics and Language* entitled "Avoidability-Indeterminism" with the now familiar pronouncement of his School that "controversy about freedom and determinism of the will . . . presents no permanent difficulty to ethics, being largely a product of confusions." A major confusion (if I understand him rightly) he takes to lie in the meaning of the term "avoidable," when we say "*A*'s action was avoidable"—or, I presume, "*A* could have acted otherwise." He himself offers the following definition of "avoidable"—" '*A*'s action was avoidable' has the meaning of 'If *A* had made a certain choice, which in fact he did not make, his action would not have occurred.' " This I think we may regard as in substance identical with the suggestion that what we really mean by "*A* could have acted otherwise" is "*A* could have acted otherwise *if* he had chosen (or willed) otherwise." For clarity's sake we shall here keep to this earlier formulation. In either formulation the special significance of the third hypothetical proposition, as of the two hypothetical propositions already considered, is that it is compatible with strict determinism. If this be indeed all that we mean by the "freedom" that conditions moral responsibility, then those philosophers are certainly wrong who hold that moral freedom is of the contra-causal type.

Now this third hypothetical proposition does at least possess the merit, not shared by its predecessors, of having a real relevance to the question of moral responsiblity. If, *e.g.,* *A* had promised to meet us at 2 p.m., and he chanced to break his leg at 1 p.m., we should not blame him for his failure to discharge his promise. For we should be satisfied that he *could not* have acted otherwise, even if he had so chosen; or *could not*, at any rate, in a way which would have enabled him to meet us at 2 p.m. The freedom to translate one's choice into action, which we saw earlier is for Schlick the *only* freedom required for moral responsibility, is without doubt *one* of the conditions of moral responsibility.

But it seems easy to show that this third hypothetical proposition does not exhaust what we mean, and *some*times is not even *part* of what we mean, by the expression "could have acted otherwise" in its moral context. Thus it can hardly be even part of what we mean in the case of that class of wrong actions (and it is a large class) concerning which there is really no question whether the agent could have acted otherwise, *if* he had chosen otherwise. Take lying, for example. Only in some very abnormal situation could it occur to one to doubt whether *A*, whose power of speech was evinced by his telling a lie, was in a position to tell what he took to be the truth *if* he had so chosen. Of *course* he was. Yet it still makes good sense for one's moral thinking to ask whether *A*, when lying, "could have acted otherwise": and we still require an affirmative answer to this question if *A*'s moral blameworthiness is to be established. It seems apparent, therefore, that in this class of cases at any rate one does *not* mean by "*A* could have acted otherwise," "*A* could have acted otherwise *if* he had so chosen."

What then *does* one mean in this class of cases by "*A* could have acted otherwise"? I submit that the expression is taken in its simple, categorical meaning, without any suppressed "if" clause to qualify it. Or perhaps, in order to keep before us the important truth that it is only as expressions of *will* or *choice* that acts are of moral import, it might be better to say that a condition of *A*'s moral responsibility is that he could have *chosen* otherwise. We saw that there is no real question whether *A* who told a lie could have acted otherwise *if* he had chosen otherwise. But there is a very real question, at least for any person who approaches the question of moral responsibility at a tolerably advanced level of reflection, about whether *A* could have *chosen* otherwise. Such a person will doubtless be acquainted with the claims advanced in some quarters that causal law operates universally: or/and with the theories of some philosophies that the universe is throughout the expression of a single supreme principle; or/and with the doctrines of some theologians that the world is created, sustained and governed by an Omniscient and Omnipotent Being. Very understandably such world-views awaken in him doubts about the validity of his first, easy, instinctive assumption that there are genuinely open possibilities before a man at the moment of moral choice. It thus becomes for him a real question whether a man could have chosen otherwise than he actually did, and, in consequence, whether man's moral responsibility is really defensible. For how can a man be morally responsible, he asks himself, if his choices, like all other events in the universe, could not have been otherwise than they in fact were? It is precisely against the background of world-views such as these that for reflective people the problem of moral responsibility normally arises.

Furthermore, to the man who has attained this level of reflexion, it will in *no* class of cases be a sufficient condition of moral responsibility for an act that one could have acted otherwise *if* one had chosen otherwise—not even in these cases where there *was* some possibility of the operation of "external constraint." In these cases he will, indeed expressly recognize freedom from external constraint as a *necessary condition*, but not as a *sufficient* condition. For he will be aware that, even granted *this* freedom, it is still conceivable that the agent had no freedom to choose otherwise than he did, and he will therefore require that the latter sort of freedom be added if moral responsibility for the act is to be established.

I have been contending that, for persons at a *tolerably advanced level of reflexion*, "A could have acted otherwise," as a condition of *A*'s moral responsibility, means "*A* could have chosen otherwise." The qualification italicised is of some importance. The unreflective or unsophisticated person, the ordinary "man in the street," who does not know or much care what scientists and theologians and philosophers have said about the world, sees well enough that *A* is morally responsible only if he could have acted otherwise, but in his intellectual innocence he will, very probably, envisage nothing capable of preventing *A* from having acted otherwise except some material impediment—like the broken leg in the example above. Accordingly, for the unreflective person, "A could have acted otherwise," as a condition of moral responsibility, *is* apt to mean no more than "*A* could have acted otherwise *if* he had so chosen."

It would appear, then, that the view now favoured by many philosophers, that the freedom required for moral responsibility is merely freedom from external constraint, is a view which they share only with the less reflective type of layman. Yet it should be plain that on a matter of this sort the view of the unreflective person is of little value by comparison with the view of the reflective person. There are some contexts, no doubt, in which lack of sophistication is an asset. But this is not one of them. The question at issue here is as to the kind of impediments which might have prevented a man from acting otherwise than he in fact did: and on this question knowledge and reflexion are surely prerequisites of any answer that is worth listening to. It is simply on account of the limitations of his mental vision that the unreflective man interprets the expression "could have acted otherwise," in its context as a condition of moral responsibility, solely in terms of external constraint. He has failed (as yet) to reach the intellectual level at which one takes into account the implications for moral choices of the world-views of science, religion, and philosophy. If on a matter of this complexity the philosopher finds that his analysis accords with the utterances of the uneducated he has, I suggest, better cause for uneasiness than for self-congratulation. . . .

AFTERWORD

While working through the selections in this chapter you may have found that your sympathies lie with one particular approach to the issues. Before you leave the topic, it might be instructive for you to consider whether the approach which seems most promising to you is consistent with your behavior and the ways in which you tend to form your practical policies. For example, most of us know some persons whose behavior in certain kinds of situations is quite predictable. An example might be a person who we are sure would lie rather than admit to having made a mistake. Now, would you be inclined to think that there are causal factors which explain such predictable regularity in the behavior of these persons? If so, does that tend to lead you to *excuse* them from responsibility for their behavior (the lying)? Or would you regard such persons as even more blameworthy than people whose behavior is less predictable?

Or, again, how would you respond to the following?

1. To what extent do we want our legal system to accept causal explanations of behavior as excuses from legal responsibility for that behavior? Should *all* causally determined behavior be excused? *None* of it? Or should we specify some kinds of causes which do provide legitimate excuses, while excluding others? (For instance, if the causes of behavior are *illness* or *personality derangement*, might we excuse a person for behavior we would find blameworthy in a healthy individual?)

2. Some prominent psychologists have proposed that behavioral technology should be used to train (condition) people to act morally. If this means using the technology to *cause* people to act in desirable ways, could we regard such people as responsible for their own goodness? Or would the technology limit their freedom in an undesirable way, stripping from them whole areas of choice and possible action?

3. Suppose it becomes possible, eventually, to predict some kinds of wrongdoing with great accuracy. Would it be a good idea to use such prediction as the basis for measures intended to prevent the wrongdoing? If we were certain that a person would commit a crime unless prevented by punishment (being imprisoned, for instance), would it be all right to punish before the crime is committed, in order to prevent the crime? If not, *why* must we wait until the damage is done before we institute the punishment?

4. If we do have wills which are not causally determined, then how is it possible for education, training, or law to make any difference at all? To the extent that they do work, don't they just *cause* us to behave in certain ways, and thereby reduce our freedom and responsiblity? And if they don't cause

us to behave in certain ways, then why should we think they make any difference at all? Should the libertarian oppose such institutions because they must be either ineffective or immoral?

Your answers to these questions, and others like them, may show that your actions and choices in practical situations agree with the philosophical theory you prefer. On the other hand, you may find that your practices and your theoretical preferences do not agree. In that case, you will confront the perplexing problem whether to adjust your theoretical views to agree with your practices, or to adjust your practices to conform to theory.

REVIEW QUESTIONS

Selection 1

1. Does d'Holbach deny that we can consider alternative courses of action, select one of them, or change our minds later on? What does he deny we can do?

2. According to d'Holbach, is human nature determined primarily by heredity or by environment, or both?

3. How could d'Holbach distinguish between insane or irrational behavior and rational behavior?

4. Why is it so important for d'Holbach to show us that the causes of human behavior are very *complex*?

Selection 2

5. Is James trying to refute determinism or not? Explain.

6. James says that the facts have hardly anything to do with making us determinists or indeterminists. What does he mean?

7. Why does James regard it as important to establsh that "*chance*" is a purely negative term? What does he mean by that?

8. How does James try to prove that if determinism were true we would have to regret the whole universe?

Selection 3

9. Is Schlick a determinist or not?

10. What are the two meanings of the word "law" which Schlick distinguishes? Why is this distinction so important to his position?

11. According to Schlick, how do we determine when persons are morally responsible for their actions?

12. Schlick says we are often right in feeling that we could have chosen or acted in some other way than we in fact did—but that this fact doesn't count against determinism. Explain.

13. Why does Schlick say we couldn't be responsible for chance events, if there were any?

Selection 4

14. According to Hospers, are there circumstances in which it is correct to hold persons responsible for their actions? Explain.

15. Hospers suggests that sometimes it is all right to hold legally responsible a person who is not morally responsible. Why?

16. Hospers says we employ two levels of moral discourse, which we should not confuse. What does he mean, and how does the distinction between the two levels help us to understand when people are responsible for what they do?

Selection 5

17. Explain as precisely as you can Hume's definitions of *necessity* and *liberty*. What is the importance of these definitions for his argument?

18. What reasons does Hume give us for believing that our moral behavior is causally determined?

19. What considerations does Hume offer in favor of the view that human liberty belongs to almost every person? Under what circumstances would a person fail to possess human liberty?

20. Hume says that men frequently "begin at the wrong end of this question concerning liberty and necessity." What does he mean? What is involved in beginning at the right end, and what difference does the right beginning make?

Selection 6

21. Why does Campbell think the distinction between natural and civil law is not relevant to the question of moral responsibility?

22. What is the purpose of the cases involving animals, dead persons, etc., in Part I? What does Campbell intend them to show?

23. What is Campbell's account of what we mean when we say a person "could have done otherwise"? How does this differ from Schlick's or Hume's account? What is the importance of the difference?

24. Is Campbell an indeterminist or a determinist? How can you tell?

C H A P T E R

5

Persons, Minds, and Bodies

It is customary to think of human beings as possessors of both a body and a mind—creatures whose activities could not be explained without appealing to both physical and mental characteristics. It seems obvious that we act upon, and react to, our physical surroundings in a variety of physical and physiological ways for which having a body is a necessary condition. It seems equally obvious that our thoughts and feelings are very different in character from such physical happenings, and that having a mind is a necessary condition for such thinking and feeling. And, finally, it seems clear that there must be plenty of *interaction* between our minds and our bodies, and that we could not begin to understand our own nature without appealing to various ways in which our thoughts and feelings are affected by what happens to our bodies, and to ways in which our bodily behavior is influenced by various thoughts and feelings (such as our desires, fears, intentions).

If we try to describe the distinction between the mental and the physical, we are likely to come up with something like this: Events or things which are physical have a definite spatial location, and can be at rest or in motion from one place to another. They have a size and a shape, and such properties as mass, density, or hardness. On the other hand, mental events or things definitely do not have mass, density, size, or shape. In fact, not even spatial location seems assignable to things like thoughts, desires, or ideas.

But if we develop this distinction between the mental and the physical, a problem begins to emerge. For, how can there possibly be any interaction between things as different as the mental and the physical? How can something with no physical properties at all cause motion or change to occur in something with mass, shape, and spatial location? Or how can something physical cause changes to occur in something which has no location, or mass, or boundaries, etc.? There is, so to speak, no way for one kind of thing to get a grip on a thing of the other kind. If the mental and the physical are as different from one another as our description of the distinction suggests, then it seems that interaction between them would be impossible.

The problem can be posed in the form of a paradox, for what has been said suggests that we have reasons for accepting all of these statements:

(1) Individual human nature involves possession of both mind and body, and considerable interaction between them as well.

(2) Mind and body belong to distinct metaphysical categories. (That is, they exist in totally different ways, and have completely different kinds of properties.)

(3) Things belonging to distinct metaphysical categories cannot interact.

But it is not possible for all these statements to be true simultaneously.

Some approaches to this paradox are based upon metaphysical *monism*—the belief that there is only one basic kind of stuff in the world. Some monists claim that all reality is physical, others claim that all reality is mental. And a few monists have claimed that it is neither physical nor mental, but something else.

Now, the monist might attack the problem by rejecting (1)—that is, by denying that human beings have minds or mental attributes at all, or by denying that they have bodies or physical attributes. But it is more common for the monist to accept (1) and reject (2). Such a monist will agree that we have both mental and physical attributes, but deny that there is any fundamental difference in kind between the physical and the mental. Typically, this denial involves some kind of *reductionism*, in which it is argued either (*a*) that the attributes we call mental really are special kinds of physical events or processes, such as conditions of the brain and nervous system; or (*b*) that the attributes we call physical really are special kinds of mental events. The advantage of monistic approaches to the problem is that they relieve us of the need to explain how interaction between radically different kinds of things is possible, for such approaches deny that there are radical differences between the physical and the mental. But this denial has its own problems, since it is no easy task to explain the apparent differences between the physical and the mental without admitting some fundamental real differences.

Other approaches to the paradox are based upon metaphysical *dualism*, which acknowledges the existence of two fundamentally different kinds of being—the physical and the mental—and agrees that human nature involves aspects of both. The dualist thus accepts statement (2), and looks for error in (1) or (3). *Interactionist* dualists disagree with (3), arguing that interaction between mind and body is possible. Interactionists may disagree about the extent of interaction possible. Some of them will defend the view that physical events can cause a variety of mental events, *and* that mental events can cause a variety of physical events. Other interactionists, the *epiphenomenalists*, accept the claim that physical events can produce mental events, but reject any kind of causation in the other direction. In either case, the major challenge for the interactionist is to explain to us how interaction is possible—to make sense of it for us—and to give us some reason to believe that it actually does take place.

Finally, there are dualists who reject the claim that there is any interaction between mind and body—thereby rejecting the part of (1) which declares that such interaction occurs. This approach has the advantage of accepting the commonsense view that we are both mental and physical beings, while avoiding the necessity of explaining how mind-body interaction is possible. But it must confront the difficult task of explaining, without any appeal to interaction, why the mental and physical aspects of our existence are so intricately coordinated.

Thus, several different issues are involved in this problem. One of these issues concerns finding the correct account of the makeup of a person—are persons simply certain kinds of bodies, or are they minds, or are they combinations of both—and if the last, with or without interaction? A second issue is whether or not the mental and the physical are radically different, or whether they can be shown to be variant forms of some single more basic kind of being. And, finally, there is the question how, if at all, mind and body can interact. As you read the following selections, try to discover how each author connects these issues together, and which ones are seen as most important, or most difficult, in the attempt to arrive at a satisfactory solution to the problem.

7

The Dual Nature of Man

RENÉ DESCARTES

I Am a Thinking Thing

... I will now consider anew what I formerly believed myself to be, before I entered on the present train of thought; and of my previous opinion I will retrench all that can in the least be invalidated by the grounds of doubt I have adduced, in order that there may at length remain nothing but what is certain and indubitable. What then did I formerly think I was? Undoubtedly I judged that I was a man. But what is a man? Shall I say a rational animal? Assuredly not; for it would be necessary forthwith to inquire into what is meant by animal, and what by rational, and thus, from a single question, I should insensibly glide into others, and these more difficult than the first; nor do I now possess enough of leisure to warrant me in wasting my time amid subtleties of this sort. I prefer here to attend to the thoughts that sprung up of themselves in my mind, and were inspired by my own nature alone, when I applied myself to the consideration of what I was. In the first place, then, I thought that I possessed a countenance, hands, arms, and all the fabric of members that appears in a corpse, and which I called by the name of body. It further occurred to me that I was nourished, that I walked, perceived, and thought, and all those actions I referred to the soul; but what the soul itself was I either did not stay to consider, or, if I did, I imagined that it was something extremely rare and subtile, like wind, or flame, or ether, spread through my grosser parts. As regarded the body, I did not even doubt of its nature, but thought I distinctly knew it, and if I had wished to describe it according to the notions I then entertained, I should

[From *Meditations on First Philosophy* (1641), Meditations II, VI, and *The Principles of Philsophy* (1644). Translated by John Veitch (1853).]

have explained myself in this manner: By body I understand all that can be terminated by a certain figure; that can be comprised in a certain place, and so fill a certain space as therefrom to exclude every other body; that can be perceived either by touch, sight, hearing, taste, or smell; that can be moved in different ways, not indeed of itself, but by something foreign to it by which it is touched [and from which it receives the impression]; for the power of self-motion, as likewise that of perceiving and thinking, I held as by no means pertaining to the nature of body; on the contrary, I was somewhat astonished to find such faculties existing in some bodies.

But [as to myself, what can I now say that I am], since I suppose there exists an extremely powerful, and, if I may so speak, malignant being, whose whole endeavours are directed towards deceiving me? Can I affirm that I possess any one of all those attributes of which I have lately spoken as belonging to the nature of body? After attentively considering them in my own mind, I find none of them that can properly be said to belong to myself. To recount them were idle and tedious. Let us pass, then, to the attributes of the soul. The first mentioned were the powers of nutrition and walking; but, if it be true that I have no body, it is true likewise that I am capable neither of walking nor of being nourished. Perception is another attribute of the soul; but perception

too is impossible without the body: besides, I have frequently, during sleep, believed that I perceived objects which I afterwards observed I did not in reality perceive. Thinking is another attribute of the soul; and here I discover what properly belongs to myself. This alone is inseparable from me. I am—I exist: this is certain; but how often? As often as I think; for perhaps it would even happen, if I should wholly cease to think, that I should at the same time altogether cease to be. I now admit nothing that is not necessarily true: I am therefore, precisely speaking, only a thinking thing, that is, a mind (*mens sive animus*), understanding, or reason,—terms whose signification was before unknown to me. I am, however, a real thing, and really existent; but what thing? The answer was, a thinking thing. The question now arises, am I aught besides? I will stimulate my imagination with a view to discover whether I am not still something more than a thinking being. Now it is plain I am not the assemblage of members called the human body; I am not a thin and penetrating air diffused through all these members, or wind, or flame, or vapour, or breath, or any of all the things I can imagine; for I supposed that all these were not, and, without changing the supposition, I find that I still feel assured of my existence.

But it is true, perhaps, that those very things which I suppose to be non-existent, because they are unknown to me, are not in truth different from myself whom I know. This is a point I cannot determine, and do not now enter into any dispute regarding it. I can only judge of things that are known to me: I am conscious that I exist, and I who know that I exist inquire into what I am. It is, however, perfectly certain that the knowledge of my existence, thus precisely taken, is not dependent on things, the existence of which is as yet unknown to me: and consequently it is not dependent on any of the things I can feign in imagination. Moreover, the phrase itself, I frame an image (*effingo*), reminds me of my error; for I should in truth frame one if I were to imagine myself to be anything, since to imagine is nothing more than to contemplate the figure or image of a corporeal thing; but I already know that I exist, and that it is possible at the same time that all those images, and in general all that relates to the nature of body, are merely dreams [or chimeras]. From this I discover that it is not more reasonable to say, I will excite my imagination that I may know more distinctly what I am, than to express myself as follows: I am now awake, and perceive something real; but because my perception is not sufficiently clear, I will of express purpose go to sleep that my dreams may represent to me the object of my perception with more truth and clearness. And, therefore, I know that nothing of all that I can embrace in imagination belongs to

the knowledge which I have of myself, and that there is need to recall with the utmost care the mind from this mode of thinking, that it may be able to know its own nature with perfect distinctness.

But what, then, am I? A thinking thing, it has been said. But what is a thinking thing? It is a thing that doubts, understands [conceives], affirms, denies, wills, refuses, that imagines also, and perceives. Assuredly it is not little, if all these properties belong to my nature. But why should they not belong to it? Am I not that very being who now doubts of almost everything; who, for all that, understands and conceives certain things, who affirms one alone as true, and denies the others; who desires to know more of them, and does not wish to be deceived; who imagines many things, sometimes even despite his will; and is likewise percipient of many, as if through the medium of the senses. Is there nothing of all this as true as that I am, even although I should be always dreaming, and although he who gave me being employed all his ingenuity to deceive me? Is there also any one of these attributes that can be properly distinguished from my thought, or that can be said to be separate from myself? For it is of itself so evident that it is I who doubt, I who understand, and I who desire, that it is here unnecessary to add anything by way of rendering it more clear. And I am as certainly the same being who imagines; for, although it may be (as I before supposed) that nothing I imagine is true, still the power of imagination does not cease really to exist in me and to form part of my thoughts. In fine, I am the same being who perceives, that is, who apprehends certain objects as by the organs of sense, since, in truth, I see light, hear a noise, and feel heat. But it will be said that these presentations are false, and that I am dreaming. Let it be so. At all events it is certain that I seem to see light, hear a noise, and feel heat; this cannot be false, and this is what in me is properly called perceiving (sentire), which is nothing else than thinking. From this I begin to know what I am with somewhat greater clearness and distinctness than heretofore. ... *Back to 509*

The Difference between Mind and Body

... It cannot be doubted that in each of the dictates of nature there is some truth: for by nature, considered in general, I now understand nothing more than God himself, or the order and disposition established by God in created things; and by my nature in particular I understand the assemblage of all that God has given me.

But there is nothing which that nature teaches me more expressly [or more sensibly] than that I have a body which is ill affected when I feel pain, and stands in need of food and drink when I experience the sensations of hunger and thirst, etc. And therefore I ought not to doubt but that there is some truth in these informations.

Nature likewise teaches me by these sensations of pain, hunger, thirst, etc., that I am not only lodged in my body as a pilot in a vessel, but that I am besides so intimately conjoined, and as it were intermixed with it, that my mind and body compose a certain unity. For if this were not the case, I should not feel pain when my body is hurt, seeing I am merely a thinking thing, but should perceive the wound by the understanding alone, just as a pilot perceives by sight when any part of his vessel is damaged; and when my body has need of food or drink, I should have a clear knowledge of this, and not be made aware of it by the confused sensations of hunger and thirst: for, in truth, all these sensations of hunger, thirst, pain, etc., are nothing more than certain confused modes of thinking, arising from the union and apparent fusion of mind and body. ...

... I here remark, in the first place, that there is a vast difference between mind and body, in respect that body, from its nature, is always divisible, and that mind is entirely indivisible. For in truth, when I consider the mind, that is, when I consider myself in so far only as I am a thinking thing, I can distinguish in myself no parts, but I very clearly discern that I am somewhat absolutely one and entire; and although the whole mind seems to be united to the whole body, yet, when a foot, an arm, or any other part is cut off, I am conscious that nothing has been taken from my mind; nor can the faculties of willing, perceiving, conceiving, etc., properly be called its parts, for it is the same mind that is exercised [all entire] in willing, in perceiving, and in conceiving, etc. But quite the opposite holds in corporeal or extended things; for I cannot imagine any one of them [how small soever it may be], which I cannot easily sunder in thought, and which, therefore, I do not know to be divisible. This would be sufficient to teach me that the mind or soul of man is entirely different from the body, if I had not already been apprised of it on other grounds.

I remark, in the next place, that the mind does not immediately receive the impression from all the parts of the body, but only from the brain, or perhaps even from one small part of it, viz., that in which the common sense *(sensus communis)* is said to be, which as often as it is affected in the same way, gives rise to the same perception in the mind, although meanwhile the other parts of the body may be diversely disposed, as is proved by innumerable experiments, which it is unnecessary here to enumerate.

I remark, besides, that the nature of body is such that none of its parts can be moved by another part a little removed from the other, which cannot likewise be moved in the same way by any one of the parts that lie between those two, although the most remote part does not act at all. As, for example, in the cord *A, B, C, D* [which is in tension], if its last part *D* be pulled, the first part *A* will not be moved in a different way than it would be were one of the intermediate parts *B* or *C* to be pulled, and the last part *D* meanwhile to remain fixed. And in the same way, when I feel pain in the foot, the science of physics teaches me that this sensation is experienced by means of the nerves dispersed over the foot, which, extending like cords from it to the brain, when they are contracted in the foot, contract at the same time the inmost parts of the brain in which they have their origin, and excite in these parts a certain motion appointed by nature to cause in the mind a sensation of pain, as if existing in the foot: but as these nerves must pass through the tibia, the leg, the loins, the back, and neck, in order to reach the brain, it may happen that although their extremities in the foot are not affected, but only certain of their parts that pass through the loins or neck, the same movements, nevertheless, are excited in the brain by this motion as would have been caused there by a hurt received in the foot, and hence the mind will necessarily feel pain in the foot, just as if it had been hurt; and the same is true of all the other perceptions of our senses.

I remark, finally, that as each of the movements that are made in the part of the brain by which the mind is immediately affected, impresses it with but a single sensation, the most likely supposition in the circumstances is, that this movement causes the mind to experience, among all the sensations which it is capable of impressing upon it, that one which is the best fitted, and generally the most useful for the preservation of the human body when it is in full health. But experience shows us that all the perceptions which nature has given us are of such a kind as I have mentioned; and accordingly, there is nothing found in them that does not manifest the power and goodness of God. Thus, for example, when the nerves of the foot are violently or more than usually shaken, the motion passing through the medulla of the spine to the innermost parts of the brain affords a sign to the mind on which it experiences a sensation, viz., of pain, as if it were in the foot, by which the mind is admonished and excited to do its utmost to remove the cause of it as dangerous and hurtful to the foot. It is true that God could have so constituted the nature of man as that the same motion in the brain would have informed the mind of something altogether different: the motion might, for example, have been the occasion on which the mind became conscious of itself, in so far as it is in the brain, or in so far as it is in some place intermediate between the foot and the brain, or, finally, the occasion on which it perceived some other object quite different, whatever that might be; but nothing of all this would have so well contributed to the preservation of the body as that which the mind actually feels. In the same way, when we stand in need of drink, there arises from this want a certain parchedness in the throat that moves its nerves, and by means of them the internal parts of the brain, and this movement affects the mind with the sensation of thirst, because there is nothing on that occasion which is more useful for us than to be made aware that we have need of drink for the preservation of our health; and so in other instances. . . .

Of Perception

. . . Although the human soul is united to the whole body, it has, nevertheless, its principal seat in the brain, where alone it not only understands and imagines, but also perceives; and this by the medium of the nerves, which are extended like threads from the brain to all the other members, with which they are so connected that we can hardly touch any one of them without moving the extremities of some of the nerves spread over it; and this motion passes to the other extremities of those nerves which are collected in the brain round the seat of the soul, as I have already explained with sufficient minuteness in the fourth chapter of the Dioptrics. But the movements which are thus excited in the brain by the nerves, variously affect the soul or mind, which is intimately conjoined with the brain, according to the diversity of the motions themselves. And the diverse affections of the mind or thoughts that immediately arise from these motions, are called perceptions of the senses *(sensuum perceptiones),* or, as we commonly speak, sensations *(sensus).* ...

It is clearly established, however, that the soul does not perceive in so far as it is in each member of the body, but only in so far as it is in the brain, where the nerves by their movements convey to it the diverse actions of the external objects that touch the parts of the body in which they are inserted. For, in the first place, there are various maladies, which, though they affect the brain alone, yet bring disorder upon, or deprive us altogether of the use of, our senses, just as sleep, which affects the brain only, and yet takes from us daily during a great part of our time the faculty of perception, which afterwards in our waking state is restored to us. The second proof is, that though there be no disease in the brain [or in the members in which the organs of the external senses are], it is nevertheless sufficient to take away sensation from the part of the body where the nerves terminate, if only the movement of one of the nerves that extend from the brain to these members be obstructed in any part of the distance that is between the two. And the last proof is, that we sometimes feel pain as if in certain of our members, the cause of which, however, is not in these members where it is felt, but somewhere nearer the brain, through which the nerves pass that give to the mind the sensation of it. I could establish this fact by innumerable experiments; I will here, however, merely refer to one of them. A girl suffering from a bad ulcer in the hand, had her eyes bandaged whenever the surgeon came to visit her, not being able to bear the sight of the dressing of the sore; and, the gangrene having spread, after the expiry of a few days the arm was amputated from the elbow [without the girl's knowledge]; linen cloths tied one above the other were substituted in place of the part amputated, so that she remained for some time without knowing that the operation had been performed, and meanwhile she complained of feeling various pains, sometimes in one finger of the hand that was cut off, and sometimes in another. The only explanation of this is, that the nerves which before stretched downwards from the brain to the hand, and then terminated in the arm close to the elbow, were there moved in the same way as they required to be moved before in the hand for the purpose of impressing on the mind residing in the brain the sensation of pain in this or that finger. [And this clearly shows that the pain of the hand is not felt by the mind in so far as it is in the hand, but in so far as it is in the brain.] . . .

In the next place, it can be proved that our mind is of such a nature that the motions of the body alone are sufficient to excite in it all sorts of thoughts, without it being necessary that these should in any way resemble the motions which give rise to them, and especially that these motions can excite in it those confused thoughts called sensations *(sensus, sensationes)*. For we see that words, whether uttered by the voice or merely written, excite in our minds all kinds of thoughts and emotions. On the same paper, with the same pen and ink, by merely moving the point of the pen over the paper in a particular way, we can trace letters that will raise in the minds of our readers the thoughts of combats, tempests, or the furies, and the passions of indignation and sorrow; in place of which, if the pen be moved in another way hardly different from the former, this slight change will cause thoughts widely different from the above, such as those of repose, peace, pleasantness, and the quite opposite passions of love and joy. Some one will perhaps object that writing and speech do not immediately excite in the mind any passions, or imaginations of things different from the letters and sounds, but afford simply the knowledge of these, on occasion of which the mind, understanding the significa-tion of the words, afterwards excites in itself the imaginations and pas-sions that correspond to the words. But what will be said of the sensa-tions of pain and titillation? The mo-tion merely of a sword cutting a part of our skin causes pain [but does not on that account make us aware of the motion or figure of the sword]. And it is certain that this sensation of pain is not less different from the motion that causes it, or from that of the part of our body which the sword cuts, than are the sensations we have of colour, sound, odour, or taste. On this ground we may con-clude that our mind is of such a na-ture that the motions alone of certain bodies can also easily excite in it all the other sensations, as the motion of a sword excites in it the sensation of pain. . . .

8

Of Personal Identity

DAVID HUME

There are some philosophers, who imagine we are every moment intimately conscious of what we call our Self; that we feel its existence and its continuance in existence; and are certain, beyond the evidence of a demonstration, both of its perfect identity and simplicity. The strongest sensation, the most violent passion, say they, instead of distracting us from this view, only fix it the more intensely, and make us consider their influence on *self* either by their pain or pleasure. To attempt a farther proof of this were to weaken its evidence; since no proof can be deriv'd from any fact, of which we are so intimately conscious; nor is there any thing, of which we can be certain, if we doubt of this.

Unluckily all these positive assertions are contrary to that very experience, which is pleaded for them, nor have we any idea of *self,* after the manner it is here explain'd. For from what impression cou'd this idea be deriv'd? This question 'tis impossible to answer without a manifest contradiction and absurdity; and yet 'tis a question, which must necessarily be answer'd, if we wou'd have the idea of self pass for clear and intelligible. It must be some one impression, that gives rise to every real idea. But self or person is not any one impression, but that to which our several impressions and ideas are suppos'd to have a reference. If any impression gives rise to the idea of self, that impression must continue invariably the same, thro' the whole course of our lives; since self is suppos'd to exist after that manner. But there is no impression constant and invariable. Pain and pleasure, grief and joy, passions and sensations succeed each other, and never all exist at the same time. It cannot, therefore, be from any of these impressions, or from any other,

[From *A Treatise of Human Nature,* Book I, Part IV, section VI. First published in 1739.]

that the idea of self is deriv'd; and consequently there is no such idea.

But farther, what must become of all our particular perceptions upon this hypothesis? All these are different, and distinguishable, and separable from each other, and may be separately consider'd, and may exist separately, and have no need of any thing to support their existence. After what manner, therefore, do they belong to self; and how are they connected with it? For my part, when I enter most intimately into what I call *myself,* I always stumble on some particular perception or other, of heat or cold, light or shade, love or hatred, pain or pleasure. I never can catch *myself* at any time without a perception, and never can observe any thing but the perception. When my perceptions are remov'd for any time, as by sound sleep; so long am I insensible of *myself,* and may truly be said not to exist. And were all my perceptions remov'd by death, and cou'd I neither think, nor feel, nor see, nor love, nor hate after the dissolution of my body, I shou'd be entirely annihilated, nor do I conceive what is farther requisite to make me a perfect non-entity. If any one upon serious and unprejudic'd reflexion, thinks he has a different notion of *himself,* I must confess I can reason no longer with him. All I can allow him is, that he may be in the right as well as I, and that we are essentially different in this particular. He may, perhaps, perceive something simple and continu'd, which he calls *himself;* tho' I am certain there is no such principle in me.

But setting aside some metaphysicians of this kind, I may venture to affirm of the rest of mankind, that they are nothing but a bundle or collection of different perceptions, which succeed each other with an inconceivable rapidity, and are in a perpetual flux and movement. Our eyes cannot turn in their sockets without varying our perceptions. Our thought is still more variable than our sight; and all our other senses and faculties contribute to this change; nor is there any single power of the soul, which remains unalterably the same, perhaps for one moment. The mind is a kind of theatre, where several perceptions successively make their appearance; pass, re-pass, glide away, and mingle in an infinite variety of postures and situations. There is properly no *simplicity* in it at one time, nor *identity* in different; whatever natural propension we may have to imagine that simplicity and identity. The comparison of the theatre must not mislead us. They are the successive perceptions only, that constitute the mind; nor have we the most distant notion of the place, where these scenes are represented, or of the materials, of which it is compos'd.

What then gives us so great a propension to ascribe an identity to these successive perceptions, and to suppose ourselves possest of an invariable and uninterrupted existence thro' the whole course of our lives? In order to answer this question, we must distinguish betwixt personal identity, as it regards our thought or imagination, and as it regards our passions or the concern we take in ourselves. The first is our present subject; and to explain it perfectly we must take the matter pretty deep, and account for that identity, which we attribute to plants and animals; there being a great analogy betwixt it, and the identity of a self or person.

We have a distinct idea of an object, that remains invariable and uninterrupted thro' a suppos'd variation of time; and this idea we call that of *identity* or *sameness*. We have also a distinct idea of several different objects existing in succession, and connected together by a close relation; and this to an accurate view affords as perfect a notion of *diversity,* as if there was no manner of relation among the objects. But tho' these two ideas of identity, and a succession of related objects be in themselves perfectly distinct, and even contrary, yet 'tis certain, that in our common way of thinking they are generally confounded with each other. That action of the imagination, by which we consider the uninterrupted and invariable object, and that by which we reflect on the succession of related objects, are almost the same to the feeling, nor is there much more effort of thought requir'd in the latter case than in the former. The relation facilitates the transition of the mind from one object to another, and renders its passage as smooth as if it contemplated one continu'd object. This resemblance is the cause of the confusion and mistake, and makes us substitute the notion of identity, instead of that of related objects. However at one instant we may consider the related succession as variable or interrupted, we are sure the next to ascribe to it a perfect identity, and regard it as invariable and uninterrupted. Our propensity to this mistake is so great from the resemblance above-mention'd, that we fall into it before we are aware; and tho' we incessantly correct ourselves by reflexion, and return to a more accurate method of thinking, yet we cannot long sustain our philosophy, or take off this biass from the imagination. Our last resource is to yield to it, and boldly assert that these different related objects are in effect the same, however interrupted and variable. In order to justify to ourselves this absurdity, we often feign some new and unintelligible principle, that connects the objects together, and prevents their interruption or variation. Thus we feign the continu'd existence of the perceptions of our senses, to remove the interruption; and run into the notion of a *soul,* and *self,* and *substance,* to disguise the variation. But we may farther observe, that where we do not give rise to such a fiction, our propension to confound identity with relation is so great, that we are apt to imagine something unknown and mysterious, connecting the parts, beside their relation; and this I take to be the case with regard to the identity we ascribe to plants and vegetables. And even when this does not take place, we still feel a propensity to confound these ideas, tho' we are not able fully to satisfy ourselves in that particular, nor find any thing invariable and uninterrupted to justify our notion of identity.

Thus the controversy concerning identity is not merely a dispute of words. For when we attribute identity, in an improper sense, to variable or interrupted objects, our mistake is not confin'd to the expression, but is commonly attended with a fiction, either of something invariable and uninterrupted, or of something mysterious and inexplicable, or at least with a propensity to such fictions. What will suffice to prove this hypothesis to the satisfaction of every fair enquirer, is to shew from daily experience and observation, that the objects, which are variable or interrupted, and yet are suppos'd to continue the same, are such only as consist of a succession of parts, connected together by resemblance, contiguity, or causation. For as such a succession answers evidently to our notion of diversity, it can only be by mistake we ascribe to it an identity; and as the relation of parts, which leads us into this mistake, is really nothing but a quality, which produces an association of ideas, and an easy transition of the imagi-

nation from one to another, it can only be from the resemblance, which this act of the mind bears to that, by which we contemplate one continu'd object, that the error arises. Our chief business, then, must be to prove, that all objects, to which we ascribe identity, without observing their invariableness and uninterruptedness, are such as consist of a succession of related objects.

In order to this, suppose any mass of matter, of which the parts are contiguous and connected, to be plac'd before us; 'tis plain we must attribute a perfect identity to this mass, provided all the parts continue uninterruptedly and invariably the same, whatever motion or change of place we may observe either in the whole or in any of the parts. But supposing some very *small* or *inconsiderable* part to be added to the mass, or substracted from it; tho' this absolutely destroys the identity of the whole, strictly speaking; yet as we seldom think so accurately, we scruple not to pronounce a mass of matter the same, where we find so trivial an alteration. The passage of the thought from the object before the change to the object after it, is so smooth and easy, that we scarce perceive the transition, and are apt to imagine, that 'tis nothing but a continu'd survey of the same object.

There is a very remarkable circumstance, that attends this experiment; which is, that tho' the change of any considerable part in a mass of matter destroys the identity of the whole, yet we must measure the greatness of the part, not absolutely, but by its *proportion* to the whole. The addition or diminution of a mountain wou'd not be sufficient to produce a diversity in a planet; tho' the change of a very few inches wou'd be able to destroy the identity of some bodies. 'Twill be impossible to account for this, but by reflecting that objects operate upon the mind, and break or interrupt the continuity of its actions not according to their real greatness, but according to their proportion to each other: And therefore, since this interruption makes an object cease to appear the same, it must be the uninterrupted progress of the thought, which constitutes the imperfect identity.

This may be confirm'd by another phænomenon. A change in any considerable part of a body destroys its identity; but 'tis remarkable, that where the change is produc'd *gradually* and *insensibly* we are less apt to ascribe to it the same effect. The reason can plainly be no other, than that the mind, in following the successive changes of the body, feels an easy passage from the surveying its condition in one moment to the viewing of it in another, and at no particular time perceives any interruption in its actions. From which continu'd perception, it ascribes a continu'd existence and identity to the object.

But whatever precaution we may use in introducing the changes gradually, and making them proportionable to the whole, 'tis certain, that where the changes are at last observ'd to become considerable, we make a scruple of ascribing identity to such different objects. There is, however, another artifice, by which we may induce the imagination to advance a step farther; and that is, by producing a reference of the parts to each other, and a combination to some *common end* or purpose. A ship, of which a considerable part has been chang'd by frequent reparations, is still consider'd as the same; nor does the difference of the materials hinder us from ascribing an identity to it. The common end, in which the parts conspire, is the same under all their variations, and affords an easy transition of the imagination from one situation of the body to another.

But this is still more remarkable, when we add a *sympathy* of parts to their *common end,* and suppose that they bear to each other, the reciprocal relation of cause and effect in all their actions and operations. This is the case with all animals and vegetables; where not only the several parts have a reference to some general purpose, but also a mutual dependance on, and connexion with each other. The effect of so strong a relation is, that tho' every one must allow, that in a very few years both vegetables and animals endure a *total* change, yet we still attribute identity to them, while their form, size, and substance are entirely alter'd. An oak, that grows from a small plant

to a large tree, is still the same oak; tho' there be not one particle of matter, or figure of its parts the same. An infant becomes a man, and is sometimes fat, sometimes lean, without any change in his identity.
. . .

We now proceed to explain the nature of *personal identity,* which has become so great a question in philosophy, especially of late years in *England,* where all the abstruser sciences are study'd with a peculiar ardour and application. And here 'tis evident, the same method of reasoning must be continu'd, which has so successfully explain'd the identity of plants, and animals, and ships, and houses, and of all the compounded and changeable productions either of art or nature. The identity, which we ascribe to the mind of man, is only a fictitious one, and of a like kind with that which we ascribe to vegetables and animal bodies. It cannot, therefore, have a different origin, but must proceed from a like operation of the imagination upon like objects.

But lest this argument shou'd not convince the reader; tho' in my opinion perfectly decisive; let him weigh the following reasoning, which is still closer and more immediate. 'Tis evident, that the identity, which we attribute to the human mind, however perfect we may imagine it to be, is not able to run the several different perceptions into one, and make them lose their characters of distinction and difference, which are

essential to them. 'Tis still true, that every distinct perception, which enters into the composition of the mind, is a distinct existence, and is different, and distinguishable, and separable from every other perception, either contemporary or sucessive. But, as, notwithstanding this distinction and separability, we suppose the whole train of perceptions to be united by identity, a question naturally arises concerning this relation of identity; whether it be something that really binds our several perceptions together, or only associates their ideas in the imagination. That is, in other words, whether in pronouncing concerning the identity of a person, we observe some real bond among his perceptions, or only feel one among the ideas we form of them. This question we might easily decide, if we wou'd recollect what has been already prov'd at large, that the understanding never observes any real connexion among objects, and that even the union of cause and effect, when strictly examin'd, resolves itself into a customary association of ideas. For from thence it evidently follows, that identity is nothing really belonging to these different perceptions, and uniting them together; but is merely a quality, which we attribute to them, because of the union of their ideas in the imagination, when we reflect upon them. Now the only qualities, which can give ideas an union in the imagination, are these three relations above-mention'd. These are the uniting principles in the ideal world, and without them every distinct object is separable by the mind, and may be separately consider'd, and appears not to have any more connexion with any other object, than if disjoin'd by the greatest difference and remoteness. 'Tis, therefore, on some of these three relations of resemblance, contiguity and causation, that identity depends; and as the very essence of these relations consists in their producing an easy transition of ideas; it follows, that our notions of personal identity, proceed entirely from the smooth and uninterrupted progress of the thought along a train of connected ideas, according to the principles above-explain'd.

The only question, therefore, which remains, is, by what relations this uninterrupted progress of our thought is produc'd, when we consider the successive existence of a mind or thinking person. And here 'tis evident we must confine ourselves to resembalance and causation, and must drop contiguity, which has little or no influence in the present case.

To begin with *resemblance;* suppose we cou'd see clearly into the breast of another, and observe that succession of perceptions, which constitutes his mind or thinking principle, and suppose that he always preserves the memory of a considerable part of past perceptions; 'tis evident that nothing cou'd more contribute to the bestowing a rela-

tion on this succession amidst all its variations. For what is the memory but a faculty, by which we raise up the images of past perceptions? And as an image necessarily resembles its object, must not the frequent placing of these resembling perceptions in the chain of thought, convey the imagination more easily from one link to another, and make the whole seem like the continuance of one object? In this particular, then, the memory not only discovers the identity, but also contributes to its production, by producing the relation of resemblance among the perceptions. The case is the same whether we consider ourselves or others.

As to *causation;* we may observe, that the true idea of the human mind, is to consider it as a system of different perceptions or different existences, which are link'd together by the relation of cause and effect, and mutually produce, destroy, influence, and modify each other. Our impressions give rise to their correspondent ideas; and these ideas in their turn produce other impressions. One thought chaces another, and draws after it a third, by which it is expell'd in its turn. In this respect, I cannot compare the soul more properly to anything than to a republic or commonwealth, in which the several members are united by the reciprocal ties of government and subordination, and give rise to other persons, who propagate the same republic in the incessant changes of its parts. And as the same individual republic may not only change its members, but also its laws and constitutions; in like manner the same person may vary his character and disposition, as well as his impressions and ideas, without losing his identity. Whatever changes he endures, his several parts are still connected by the relation of causation. And in this view our identity with regard to the passions serves to corroborate that with regard to the imagination, by the making our distant perceptions influence each other, and by giving us a present concern for our past or future pains or pleasures. . . .

9

The Pre-established Harmony of Body and Soul

GOTTFRIED WILHELM LEIBNIZ

Having settled these things, I thought I had gained my haven, but when I set myself to meditate upon the union of soul and body I was as it was driven back into the deep sea. For I found no way of explaining how the body transmits anything to the soul or *vice versa,* nor how one substance can communicate with another created substance. So far as can be gathered from his writings, M. Descartes gave this up; but his disciples, seeing that the common opinion is inconceivable, held that we are aware of the qualities of bodies, because God makes thoughts arise in the soul on occasion of the motions of matter; and, on the other hand, when our soul wishes to move the body, they hold that it is God who moves the body for it. And as

communication of motions also appeared to them inconceivable, they were of opinion that God gives motion to a body on occasion of the motion of another body. This is what is called the *system of occasional causes,* which has been brought into wide repute by the excellent reflexions of the author of the *Recherche de la Vérité* [Malebranche—Ed.'s note].

It must be admitted that they have gone far into the difficulty in telling us what cannot take place; but they do not appear to have removed it by their explanation of what actually does happen. It is quite true that one created substance has, in the strict metaphysical sense, no real influence upon another, and that all things and all their reality are continually produced by the power

[From *New System of the Nature of Substances* (1695), sections 12–16; and *Third Explanation of the New System* (1696). Translated by Robert Latta (1898).]

[*vertu*] of God. But to solve problems it is not enough to make use of a general cause and to introduce what is called *Deus ex machina*. For to do this, without offering any other explanation which can be derived from the order of secondary causes, is just to have recourse to miracle. In philosophy we must endeavour to give a reason for things by showing how they are carried out by the Divine wisdom in conformity with the notion of the matter we are dealing with.

Accordingly, being obliged to admit that it is impossible the soul or any other real substance should receive anything from outside, unless through the Divine omnipotence, I was insensibly led to an opinion which surprised me, but which seems inevitable and which, in fact, has very great advantages and very considerable beauties. It is this, that God at first so created the soul, or any other real unity, that everything must arise in it from its own inner nature with a perfect *spontaneity* as regards itself and yet with a perfect *conformity* to things outside of it. And thus our inner feelings (that is to say, those which are in the soul itself and not in the brain or in the finer parts of the body), being only connected phenomena of external things or rather genuine appearances and, as it were, well-ordered dreams, these internal perceptions in the soul itself must come to it from its original constitution, that is to say from the representative nature (capable of expressing beings outside of it in relation to its organs) which was given to it at creation and which constitutes its individual character. And accordingly, since each of these substances accurately represents the whole universe in its own way and from a certain point of view, and the perceptions or expressions of external things come into the soul at their appropriate time, in virtue of its own laws, as in a world by itself and as if there existed nothing but God and the soul, ... there will be a perfect agreement between all these substances, which will have the same result as would be observed if they had communication with one another by a transmission of species or of qualities, such as the mass of ordinary philosophers suppose. Further, as the organized mass, in which is the point of view of the soul, is more nearly expressed by the soul and, conversely, is ready of itself to act, according to the laws of the corporeal mechanism, at the moment the soul desires it, without either of them interfering with the laws of the other—the animal spirits and the blood having exactly at that moment the right motions to correspond to the passions and perceptions of the soul—this mutual relationship, prearranged in each substance in the universe, produces what we call their *communication* and alone constitutes *the union of soul and body*. And in this way we can understand how the soul has its seat in the body through an immediate presence, which is as near as possible, since the soul is in the body as the unit is in the multiplicity which is the resultant of units.

This hypothesis is very possible. For why might not God in the beginning give to substance an inner nature or force which could regularly produce in it—as in an *automaton* that is *spiritual or endowed with a living principle, but free* in the case of a substance which partakes of reason—everything that will happen to it, that is to say, all the appearances or expressions it will have, and that without the help of any created thing? This is the more likely since the nature of substance necessarily requires and essentially involves a progress or change, without which it would have no force to act. And as the nature of the soul is to represent the universe in a very exact way (though with greater or less distinctness), the succession of representations which the soul produces for itself will correspond naturally to the succession of changes in the universe itself: while, on the other hand, the body has also been adapted to the soul to fit the circumstances in which the soul is conceived as acting outwardly. This adaptation of the body to the soul is the more reasonable inasmuch as bodies are made only for spirits, which alone are capable of entering into fellowship with God and celebrating His glory. Thus as soon as we see that this *hypothesis of agree-ments* is possible, we see also that it is the most reasonable hypothesis and that it gives a wonderful idea of the harmony of the universe and the perfection of the works of God.

There is also this great advantage in our hypothesis, that instead of saying that we are free only apparently and enough for practical purposes, as several clever people have held, we must rather say that we are only apparently constrained, and that, to use strict metaphysical language, we possess a perfect independence as regards the influence of all other created things. This also throws a wonderful light upon the immortality of our soul and the ever unbroken preservation of our individuality, which is perfectly well-ordered by its own nature and independent of all external contingencies, whatever appearance there may be to the contrary. Never has any system more completely shown our high calling. Every spirit being like a world apart, sufficient to itself, independent of every other created thing, involving the infinite, expressing the universe, is as lasting, as continuous in its existence and as absolute as the very universe of created things. Thus we should hold that each spirit should always play its part in the universe in the way that is most fitted to contribute to the perfection of the society of all spirits, which constitutes their moral union in the City of God. There is also here a new and surprisingly clear proof of the existence of God. For this perfect agreement of so many substances which have no communication with one another can come only from their common cause. . . .

Some learned and acute friends of mine having considered my new hypothesis on the great question of *the union of soul and body*, and having found it of value, have asked me to give some explanations regarding the objections which have been brought against it and which arose from its not having been rightly understood. I think the matter may be made intelligible to minds of every kind by the following illustration.

Suppose two clocks or two watches which perfectly keep time together. Now that may happen *in three ways*. The first way consists in the mutual influence of each clock upon the other; the second, in the care of a man who looks after them; the third, in their own accuracy. *The first way*, that of influence, was ascertained on trial by the late M. Huygens, to his great astonishment. He attached two large pendulums to the same piece of wood. The continual swinging of these pendulums imparted similar vibrations to the particles of the wood; but as these different vibrations could not continue in their proper order, without interfering with one another, unless the pendulums kept time together, it happened, by a kind of wonder, that even when their swinging was deliberately disturbed they soon came to swing together again, somewhat like

two stretched strings that are in unison.

The second way of making two clocks (even though they be bad ones) constantly keep time together would be to put them in charge of a skilled workman who should keep them together from moment to moment. I call this the way of assistance.

Finally, *the third way* will be to make the two clocks at first with such skill and accuracy that we can be sure that they will always afterwards keep time together. This is the way of pre-established agreement.

Now put the soul and the body in place of the two clocks. Their agreement or sympathy will also arise in one of these three ways. *The way of influence* is that of the common philosophy; but as we cannot conceive material particles or immaterial species or qualities which can pass from one of these substances into the other, we are obliged to give up this opinion. *The way of assistance* is that of the system of occasional causes; but I hold that this is to introduce *Deus ex machina* in a natural and ordinary matter, in which it is reasonable that God should intervene only in the way in which He supports all the other things of nature. Thus there remains only my hypothesis, that is to say, *the way of the harmony pre-established* by a contrivance of the Divine foresight, which has from the beginning formed each of these substances in so perfect, so regular and accurate a manner that by merely following its own laws which were given to it when it came into being, each substance is yet in harmony with the other, just as if there were a mutual influence between them, or as if God were continually putting His hand upon them, in addition to His general support.

I do not think that I need offer any further proof unless I should be required to prove that God is in a position to make use of this contrivance of foresight, of which we have instances even among men, in proportion to the skill they have. And supposing that God is able to make use of this means, it is very evident that this is the best way and the most worthy of Him. It is true that I have also other proofs of it, but they are deeper and it is unnecessary to adduce them here.

10

On the Hypothesis That Animals Are Automata

THOMAS H. HUXLEY

In the seventeenth century, the idea that the physical processes of life are capable of being explained in the same way as other physical phenomena, and, therefore, that the living body is a mechanism, was proved to be true for certain classes of vital actions; and, having thus taken firm root in irrefragable fact, this conception has not only successfully repelled every assault which has been made upon it, but has steadily grown in force and extent of application, until it is now the expressed or implied fundamental proposition of the whole doctrine of scientific Physiology. ... But there remains a doctrine to which Descartes attached great weight, so that full acceptance of it became a sort of note of a thoroughgoing Cartesian, but which, nevertheless, is so opposed to ordinary prepossessions that it attained more general notoriety, and gave rise to more discussion, than almost any other Cartesian hypothesis. It is the doctrine that brute animals are mere machines or automata, devoid not only of reason, but of any kind of consciousness.
. . .

Descartes' line of argument is perfectly clear. He starts from reflex action in man, from the unquestionable fact that, in ourselves, co-ordinate, purposive, actions may take place, without the intervention of consciousness or volition, or even contrary to the latter. As actions of a certain degree of complexity are brought about by mere mechanism, why may not actions of still greater

[From "On the Hypothesis That Animals Are Automata, and Its History," first published in 1874 and reprinted in Huxley's *Methods and Results*.]

complexity be the result of a more refined mechanism? What proof is there that brutes are other than a superior race of marionettes, which eat without pleasure, cry without pain, desire nothing, know nothing, and only simulate intelligence as a bee simulates a mathematician? . . .

It must be premised, that it is wholly impossible absolutely to prove the presence or absence of consciousness in anything but one's own brain, though, by analogy, we are justified in assuming its existence in other men. Now if, by some accident, a man's spinal cord is divided, his limbs are paralysed, so far as his volition is concerned, below the point of injury; and he is incapable of experiencing all those states of consciousness which, in his uninjured state, would be excited by irritation of those nerves which come off below the injury. If the spinal cord is divided in the middle of the back, for example, the skin of the feet may be cut, or pinched, or burned, or wetted with vitriol, without any sensation of touch, or of pain, arising in consciousness. So far as the man is concerned, therefore, the part of the central nervous system which lies beyond the injury is cut off from consciousness. It must indeed be admitted, that, if any one think fit to maintain that the spinal cord below the injury is conscious, but that it is cut off from any means of making its consciousness known to the other consciousness in the brain, there is no means of driving

him from his position by logic. But assuredly there is no way of proving it. . . .

However near the brain the spinal cord is injured, consciousness remains intact, except that the irritation of parts below the injury is no longer represented by sensation. On the other hand, pressure upon the anterior division of the brain, or extensive injuries to it, abolish consciousness. Hence, it is a highly probable conclusion, that consciousness in man depends upon the integrity of the anterior division of the brain, while the middle and hinder divisions of the brain, and the rest of the nervous centres, have nothing to do with it. And it is further highly probable, that what is true for man is true for other vertebrated animals.

We may assume, then, that in a living vertebrated animal, any segment of the cerebro-spinal axis (or spinal cord and brain) separated from that anterior division of the brain which is the organ of consciousness, is as completely incapable of giving rise to consciousness as we know it to be incapable of carrying out volitions. Nevertheless, this separated segment of the spinal cord is not passive and inert. On the contrary, it is the seat of extremely remarkable powers. In our imaginary case of injury, the man would, as we have seen, be devoid of sensation in his legs, and would have not the least power of moving them. But, if the soles of his feet were tickled, the legs would be drawn up just as vigorously as they would have been before the injury. We know exactly what happens when the soles of the feet are tickled; a molecular change takes place in the sensory nerves of the skin, and is propagated along them and through the posterior roots of the spinal nerves, which are constituted by them, to the grey matter of the spinal cord. Through that grey matter the molecular motion is reflected into the anterior roots of the same nerves, constituted by the filaments which supply the muscles of the legs, and, travelling along these motor filaments, reaches the muscles, which at once contract, and cause the limbs to be drawn up.

In order to move the legs in this way, a definite co-ordination of muscular contractions is necessary; the muscles must contract in a certain order and with duly proportioned force; and moreover, as the feet are drawn away from the source of irritation, it may be said that the action has a final cause, or is purposive.

Thus it follows, that the grey matter of the segment of the man's spinal cord, though it is devoid of consciousness, nevertheless responds to a simple stimulus by giving rise to a complex set of muscular contractions, co-ordinated towards a definite end, and serving an obvious purpose.

If the spinal cord of a frog is cut across, so as to provide us with a segment separated from the brain, we shall have a subject parallel to the injured man, on which experiments can be made without remorse; as we have a right to conclude that a frog's spinal cord is not likely to be conscious, when a man's is not.

Now the frog behaves just as the man did. The legs are utterly paralysed, so far as voluntary movement is concerned; but they are vigorously drawn up to the body when any irritant is applied to the foot. But let us study our frog a little farther. Touch the skin of the side of the body with a little acetic acid, which gives rise to all the signs of great pain in an uninjured frog. In this case, there can be no pain, because the application is made to a part of the skin supplied with nerves which come off from the cord below the point of section; nevertheless, the frog lifts up the limb of the same side, and applies the foot to rub off the acetic acid; and, what is still more remarkable, if the limb be held so that the frog cannot use it, it will, by and by, move the limb of the other side, turn it across the body, and use it for the same rubbing process. It is impossible that the frog, if it were in its entirety and could reason, should perform actions more purposive than these: and yet we have most complete assurance that, in this case, the frog is not acting from purpose, has no consciousness, and is a mere insensible machine.

But now suppose that, instead of making a section of the cord in the middle of the body, it had been made in such a manner as to separate the hindermost division of the brain from the rest of the organ, and suppose the foremost two-thirds of the brain entirely taken away. The frog is then absolutely devoid of any spontaneity; it sits upright in the attitude which a frog habitually assumes; and it will not stir unless it is touched; but it differs from the frog which I have just described in this, that, if it be thrown into the water, it begins to swim, and swims just as well as the perfect frog does. But swimming requires the combination and successive co-ordination of a great number of muscular actions. And we are forced to conclude, that the impression made upon the sensory nerves of the skin of the frog by the contact with the water into which it is thrown, causes the transmission to the central nervous apparatus of an impulse which sets going a certain machinery by which all the muscles of swimming are brought into play in due co-ordination. If the frog be stimulated by some irritating body, it jumps or walks as well as the complete frog can do. The simple sensory impression, acting through the machinery of the cord, gives rise to these complex combined movements.

It is possible to go a step farther. Suppose that only the anterior division of the brain—so much of it as lies in front of the "optic lobes"—is removed. If that operation is performed quickly and skil-fully, the frog may be kept in a state of full bodily vigour for months, or it may be for years; but it will sit unmoved. It sees nothing: it hears nothing. It will starve sooner than feed itself, although food put into its mouth is swallowed. On irritation, it jumps or walks; if thrown into the water it swims. If it be put on the hand, it sits there, crouched, perfectly quiet, and would sit there for ever. If the hand be inclined very gently and slowly, so that the frog would naturally tend to slip off, the creature's fore paws are shifted on to the edge of the hand, until he can just prevent himself from falling. If the turning of the hand be slowly continued, he mounts up with great care and deliberation, putting first one leg forward and then another, until he balances himself with perfect precision upon the edge; and if the turning of the hand is continued, he goes through the needful set of muscular operations, until he comes to be seated in security, upon the back of the hand. The doing of all this requires a delicacy of co-ordination, and a precision of adjustment of the muscular apparatus of the body, which are only comparable to those of a rope-dancer. To the ordinary influences of light, the frog, deprived of its cerebral hemispheres, appears to be blind. Nevertheless, if the animal be put upon a table, with a book at some little distance between it and the light, and the skin of the hinder part of its body is then irritated, it will jump forward, avoiding the book by passing to the right or left of it. Therefore, although the frog appears to have no sensation of light, visible objects act through its brain upon the motor mechanism of its body.

It is obvious, that had Descartes been acquainted with these remarkable results of modern research, they would have furnished him with far more powerful arguments than he possessed in favour of his view of the automatism of brutes. The habits of a frog, leading its natural life, involve such simple adaptations to surrounding conditions, that the machinery which is competent to do so much without the intervention of consciousness, might well do all. And this argument is vastly strengthened by what has been learned in recent times of the marvellously complex operations which are performed mechanically, and to all appearance without consciousness, by men, when, in consequence of injury or disease, they are reduced to a condition more or less comparable to that of a frog, in which the anterior part of the brain has been removed. A case has recently been published by an eminent French physician, Dr. Mesnet, which illustrates this condition so remarkably, that I make no apology for dwelling upon it at considerable length.

A sergeant of the French army, F——, twenty-seven years of age, was wounded during the battle of Bazeilles, by a ball which fractured his left parietal bone. He ran his bayonet through the Prussian soldier who wounded him, but almost immediately his right arm became paralysed; after walking about two hundred yards, his right leg became similarly affected, and he lost his senses. When he recovered them, three weeks afterwards, in hospital at Mayence, the right half of the body was completely paralysed, and remained in this condition for a year. At present, the only trace of the paralysis which remains is a slight weakness of the right half of the body. Three or four months after the wound was inflicted, periodical disturbances of the functions of the brain made their appearance, and have continued ever since. The disturbances last from fifteen to thirty hours; the intervals at which they occur being from fifteen to thirty days.

For four years, therefore, the life of this man has been divided into alternating phases—short abnormal states intervening between long normal states.

In the periods of normal life, the ex-sergeant's health is perfect; he is intelligent and kindly, and performs, satisfactorily, the duties of a hospital attendant. The commencement of the abnormal state is ushered in by uneasiness and a sense of weight about the forehead, which the patient compares to the constriction of a circle of iron; and, after its termination, he complains, for some hours, of dulness and heaviness of the head. But the transition from the normal to the abnormal state takes place in a few minutes, without convulsions or cries, and without anything to indicate the change to a bystander. His movements remain free and his expression calm, except for a contraction of the brow, an incessant movement of the eyeballs, and a chewing motion of the jaws. The eyes are wide open, and their pupils dilated. If the man happens to be in a place to which he is accustomed, he walks about as usual; but, if he is in a new place, or if obstacles are intentionally placed in his way, he stumbles gently against them, stops, and then, feeling over the objects with his hands, passes on one side of them. He offers no resistance to any change of direction which may be impressed upon him, or to the forcible acceleration or retardation of his movements. He eats, drinks, smokes, walks about, dresses and undresses himself, rises and goes to bed at the accustomed hours. Nevertheless, pins may be run into his body, or strong electric shocks sent through it, without causing the least indication of pain; no odorous substance, pleasant or unpleasant, makes the least impression; he eats and drinks with avidity whatever is offered, and takes asafœtida, or vinegar, or quinine, as readily as water; no noise affects him; and light influences him only under certain conditions. Dr. Mesnet remarks, that the sense of touch alone seems to persist, and indeed to be more acute and delicate than in the normal state:

and it is by means of the nerves of touch, almost exclusively, that his organism is brought into relation with the external world. Here a difficulty arises. It is clear from the facts detailed, that the nervous apparatus by which, in the normal state, sensations of touch are excited, is that by which external influences determine the movements of the body, in the abnormal state. But does the state of consciousness, which we term a tactile sensation, accompany the operation of this nervous apparatus in the abnormal state? or is consciousness utterly absent, the man being reduced to an insensible mechanism? . . .

As I have pointed out, it is impossible to prove that F____ is absolutely unconscious in his abnormal state, but it is no less impossible to prove the contrary; and the case of the frog goes a long way to justify the assumption that, in the abnormal state, the man is a mere insensible machine.

If such facts as these had come under the knowledge of Descartes, would they not have formed an apt commentary upon that remarkable passage in the "Traité de l'Homme," which I have quoted elsewhere, but which is worth repetition?—

All the functions which I have attributed to this machine (the body), as the digestion of food, the pulsation of the heart and of the arteries; the nutrition and the growth of the limbs; respiration, wakefulness, and sleep; the reception of light, sounds, odours, flavours, heat, and such like qualities, in the organs of the external senses; the impression of the ideas of these in the organ of common sensation and in the imagination; the retention or the impression of these ideas on the memory; the internal movements of the appetites and the passions; and lastly the external movements of all the limbs, which follow so aptly, as well the action of the objects which are presented to the senses, as the impressions which meet in the memory, that they imitate as nearly as possible those of a real man; I desire, I say, that you should consider that these functions in the machine naturally proceed from the mere arrangement of its organs, neither more nor less than do the movements of a clock, or other automaton, from that of its weights and its wheels; so that, so far as these are concerned, it is not necessary to conceive any other vegetative or sensitive soul, nor any other principle of motion or of life, than the blood and the spirits agitated by the fire which burns continually in the heart, and which is no wise essentially different from all the fires which exist in inanimate bodies.

And would Descartes not have been justified in asking why we need deny that animals are machines, when men, in a state of unconsciousness, perform, mechanically, actions as complicated and as seemingly rational as those of any animals?

But though I do not think that Descartes' hypothesis can be positively refuted, I am not disposed to accept it. The doctrine of continuity is too well established for it to be permissible to me to suppose that any complex natural phenomenon comes into existence suddenly, and without being preceded by simpler modifications; and very strong arguments would be needed to prove that such complex phenomena as those of consciousness, first make their appearance in man. We know, that, in the individual man, consciousness grows from a dim glimmer to its full light, whether we consider the infant advancing in years, or the adult emerging from slumber and swoon. We know, further, that the lower animals possess, though less developed, that part of the brain which we have every reason to believe to be the organ of consciousness in man; and as, in other cases, function and organ are proportional, so we have a right to conclude it is with the brain; and that the brutes, though they may not possess our intensity of consciousness, and though, from the absence of language, they can have no trains of thoughts, but only trains of feelings, yet have a consciousness which, more or less distinctly, foreshadows our own.

I confess that, in view of the struggle for existence which goes on in the animal world, and of the frightful quantity of pain with which it must be accompanied, I should be glad if the probabilities were in favour of Descartes' hypothesis; but, on the other hand, considering the terrible practical consequences to domestic animals which might ensue from any error on our part, it is as well to err on the right side, if we err at all, and deal with them as weaker brethren, who are bound, like the rest of us, to pay their toll for living, and suffer what is needful for the general good. . . .

But though we may see reason to disagree with Descartes' hypothesis that brutes are unconscious machines, it does not follow that he was wrong in regarding them as automata. They may be more or less conscious, sensitive, automata; and the view that they are such conscious machines is that which is implicitly, or explicitly, adopted by most persons. When we speak of the actions of the lower animals being guided by instinct and not by reason, what we really mean is that, though they feel as we do, yet their actions are the results of their physical organisation. We believe, in short, that they are machines, one part of which (the nervous system) not only sets the rest in motion, and co-ordinates its movements in relation with changes in surrounding bodies, but is provided with special apparatus, the function of which is the calling into existence of those states of consciousness which are termed sensations, emotions, and ideas. I believe that this generally accepted view is the best expression of the facts at present known.

It is experimentally demonstrable—any one who cares to run a pin into himself may perform a sufficient demonstration of the fact—that a mode of motion of the nervous system is the immediate antecedent of a state of consciousness. All but the adherents of "Occasionalism," or of the doctrine of "Pre-established Harmony" (if any such now exist), must admit that we have as much reason for regarding the mode of motion of the nervous system as the cause of the state of consciousness, as we have for regarding any event as the cause of another. How the one phenomenon causes the other we know, as much or as little, as in any other case of causation; but we have as much right to believe that the sensation is an effect of the molecular change, as we have to believe that motion is an effect of impact; and there is as much propriety in saying that the brain evolves sensation, as there is in saying that an iron rod, when hammered, evolves heat.

As I have endeavoured to show, we are justified in supposing that something analogous to what happens in ourselves takes place in the brutes, and that the affections of their sensory nerves give rise to molecular changes in the brain, which again give rise to, or evolve, the corresponding states of consciousness. Nor can there be any reasonable doubt that the emotions of brutes, and such ideas as they possess, are similarly dependent upon molecular brain changes. Each sensory impression leaves behind a record in the structure of the brain—an "ideagenous" molecule, so to speak, which is competent, under certain conditions, to reproduce, in a fainter condition, the state of consciousness which corresponds with that sensory impression; and it is these "ideagenous molecules" which are the physical basis of memory.

It may be assumed, then, that molecular changes in the brain are the causes of all the states of consciousness of brutes. Is there any evidence that these states of consciousness may, conversely, cause those molecular changes which give rise to muscular motion? I see no such evidence. The frog walks, hops, swims, and goes through his gymnastic performances quite as well without consciousness, and consequently without volition, as with it; and, if a frog, in his natural state, possesses anything corresponding with what we call volition, there is no reason to think that it is anything but a concomitant of the molecular changes in the brain which form part of the series involved in the production of motion.

The consciousness of brutes would appear to be related to the mechanism of their body simply as a collateral product of its working, and to be as completely without any power of modifying that working as the steam-whistle which accompanies the work of a locomotive engine is without influence upon its machinery. Their volition, if they have

any, is an emotion indicative of physical changes, not a cause of such changes.

This conception of the relations of states of consciousness with molecular changes in the brain—of *psychoses* with *neuroses*—does not prevent us from ascribing free will to brutes. For an agent is free when there is nothing to prevent him from doing that which he desires to do. If a greyhound chases a hare, he is a free agent, because his action is in entire accordance with his strong desire to catch the hare; while so long as he is held back by the leash he is not free, being prevented by external force from following his inclination. And the ascription of freedom to the greyhound under the former circumstances is by no means inconsistent with the other aspect of the facts of the case—that he is a machine impelled to the chase, and caused, at the same time, to have the desire to catch the game by the impression which the rays of light proceeding from the hare make upon his eyes, and through them upon his brain.

Much ingenious argument has at various times been bestowed upon the question: How is it possible to imagine that volition, which is a state of consciousness, and, as such, has not the slightest community of nature with matter in motion, can act upon the moving matter of which the body is composed, as it is assumed to do in voluntary acts? But if, as is here suggested, the voluntary acts of brutes—or, in other words, the acts which they desire to perform—are as purely mechanical as the rest of their actions, and are simply accompanied by the state of consciousness called volition, the inquiry, so far as they are concerned, becomes superfluous. Their volitions do not enter into the chain of causation of their actions at all.

The hypothesis that brutes are conscious automata is perfectly consistent with any view that may be held respecting the often discussed and curious question whether they have souls or not; and, if they have souls, whether those souls are immortal or not. It is obviously harmonious with the most literal adherence to the text of Scripture concerning "the beast that perisheth"; but it is not inconsistent with the amiable conviction ascribed by Pope to his "untutored savage," that when he passes to the happy hunting-grounds in the sky, "his faithful dog shall bear him company." If the brutes have consciousness and no souls, then it is clear that, in them, consciousness is a direct function of material changes; while, if they possess immaterial subjects of consciousness, or souls, then, as consciousness is brought into existence only as the consequence of molecular motion of the brain, it follows that it is an indirect product of material changes. The soul stands related to the body as the bell of a clock to the works, and consciousness answers to the sound which the bell gives out when it is struck. . . .

It is quite true that, to the best of my judgment, the argumentation which applies to brutes holds equally good of men; and, therefore, that all states of consciousness in us, as in them, are immediately caused by molecular changes of the brain-substance. It seems to me that in men, as in brutes, there is no proof that any state of consciousness is the cause of change in the motion of the matter of the organism. If these positions are well based, it follows that our mental conditions are simply the symbols in consciousness of the changes which takes place automatically in the organism; and that, to take an extreme illustration, the feeling we call volition is not the cause of a voluntary act, but the symbol of that state of the brain which is the immediate cause of that act. We are conscious automata, endowed with free will in the only intelligible sense of that much-abused term—inasmuch as in many respects we are able to do as we like—but none the less parts of the great series of causes and effects which, in unbroken continuity, composes that which is, and has been, and shall be—the sum of existence. . . .

11

Sensations and Brain Processes

J. J. C. SMART

Suppose that I report that I have at this moment a roundish, blurry-edged after-image which is yellowish towards its edge and is orange towards its centre. What is it that I am reporting?[1] One answer to this question might be that I am not reporting anything, that when I say that it looks to me as though there is a roundish yellow orange patch of light on the wall I am expressing some sort of *temptation*, the temptation to say that there *is* a roundish yellow orange patch on the wall (though I may know that there is not such a patch on the wall). This is perhaps Wittgenstein's view in the *Philosophical Investigations* (see paragraphs 367, 370). Similarly, when I "report" a pain, I am not really reporting anything (or, if you like, I am reporting in a queer sense of "reporting"), but am doing a sophisticated sort of wince. (See paragraph 244: "The verbal expression of pain replaces crying and does not describe it." Nor does it describe anything else?) I prefer most of the time to discuss an after-image rather than a pain, because the word "pain" brings in something which is irrelevant to my purpose: the notion of "distress." I think that

[From *The Philosophical Review*, Vol. 68 (1959), pp. 141–156. Reprinted by permission of *The Philosophical Review* and J. J. C. Smart.]

1. This paper takes its departure from arguments to be found in U. T. Place's "Is Consciousness a Brain Process?" (*British Journal of Psychology*, XLVII, 1956, 44–50). I have had the benefit of discussing Place's thesis in a good many universities in the United States and Australia, and I hope that the present paper answers objections to his thesis which Place has not considered, and presents his thesis in a nearly more unobjectionable form. This paper is meant also to supplement "The 'Mental' and the 'Physical'," by H. Feigl (in *Minnesota Studies of the Philosophy of Science*, II, 370–497), which argues for much the same thesis as Place's.

"he is in pain" entails "he is in distress," that is, that he is in a certain agitation-condition. Similarly, to say "I am in pain" may be to do more than "replace pain behavior": it may be partly to report something, though this something is quite nonmysterious, being an agitation-condition, and so susceptible of behavioristic analysis. The suggestion I wish if possible to avoid is a different one, namely that "I am in pain" is a genuine report, and that what it reports is an irreducibly psychical something. And similarly the suggestion I wish to resist is also that to say "I have a yellowish orange after-image" is to report something irreducibly psychical.

Why do I wish to resist this suggestion? Mainly because of Occam's razor. It seems to me that science is increasingly giving us a viewpoint whereby organisms are able to be seen as physico-chemical mechanisms: it seems that even the behavior of man himself will one day be explicable in mechanistic terms. There does seem to be, so far as science is concerned, nothing in the world but increasingly complex arrangements of physical constituents. All except for one place: in consciousness. That is, for a full description of what is going on in a man you would have to mention not only the physical processes in his tissue, glands, nervous system, and so forth, but also his states of consciousness: his visual, auditory, and tactual sensations, his aches and pains. That these should be *correlated* with brain processes does not help, for to say that they are *correlated* is to say that they are something "over and above." You cannot correlate something with itself. You correlate footprints with burglars, but not Bill Sikes the burglar with Bill Sikes the burglar. So sensations, states of consciousness, do seem to be the one sort of thing left outside the physicalist picture, and for various reasons I just cannot believe that this can be so. That everything should be explicable in terms of physics (together of course with descriptions of the ways in which the parts are put together—roughly, biology is to physics as radio-engineering is to electro-magnetism) except the occurrence of sensations seems to me to be frankly unbelievable. Such sensations would be "nomological danglers," to use Feigl's expression.[2] It is not often realized how odd would be the laws whereby these nomological danglers would dangle. It is sometimes asked, "Why can't there be psycho-physical laws which are of a novel sort, just as the laws of electricity and magnetism were novelties from the standpoint of Newtonian mechanics?" Certainly we are pretty sure in the future to come across new ultimate laws of a novel type, but I expect them to relate simple constituents: for example, whatever ultimate particles are then in vogue. I cannot believe that ultimate

2. Feigl, *op. cit.,* p. 428.

laws of nature could relate simple constituents to configurations consisting of perhaps billions of neurons (and goodness knows how many billion billions of ultimate particles) all put together for all the world as though their main purpose in life was to be a negative feedback mechanism of a complicated sort. Such ultimate laws would be like nothing so far known in science. They have a queer "smell" to them. I am just unable to believe in the nomological danglers themselves, or in the laws whereby they would dangle. If any philosophical arguments seemed to compel us to believe in such things, I would suspect a catch in the argument. In any case it is the object of this paper to show that there are no philosophical arguments which compel us to be dualists.

The above is largely a confession of faith, but it explains why I find Wittgenstein's position (as I construe it) so congenial. For on this view there are, in a sense, no sensations. A man is a vast arrangement of physical particles, but there are not, over and above this, sensations or states of consciousness. There are just behavioral facts about this vast mechanism, such as that it expresses a temptation (behavior disposition) to say "there is a yellowish-red patch on the wall" or that it goes through a sophisticated sort of wince, that is, says "I am in pain." Admittedly Wittgenstein says that though the sensation "is not a something," it is nevertheless "not a nothing either"

(paragraph 304), but this need only mean that the word "ache" has a use. An ache is a thing, but only in the innocuous sense in which the plain man, in the first paragraph of Frege's *Foundations of Arithmetic*, answers the question "what is the number one?" by "a thing." It should be noted that when I assert that to say "I have a yellowish-orange after-image" is to express a temptation to assert the physical-object statement "there is a yellowish-orange patch on the wall," I mean that saying "I have a yellowish-orange after-image" is (partly) the exercise of the disposition which is the temptation. It is not to *report* that I have the temptation, any more than is "I love you" normally a report that I love someone. Saying "I love you" is just part of the behavior which is the exercise of the disposition of loving someone.

Though, for the reasons given above, I am very receptive to the above "expressive" account of sensation statements, I do not feel that it will quite do the trick. Maybe this is because I have not thought it out sufficiently, but it does seem to me as though, when a person says "I have an after-image," he *is* making a genuine report, and that when he says "I have a pain," he *is* doing more than "replace pain-behavior," and that "this more" is not just to say that he is in distress. I am not so sure, however, that to admit this is to admit that there are nonphysical correlates of brain processes. Why should not sensations just be brain processes of a certain sort? There are, of course, well-known (as well as lesser-known) philosophical objections to the view that reports of sensations are reports of brain-processes, but I shall try to argue that these arguments are by no means as cogent as is commonly thought to be the case.

Let me first try to state more accurately the thesis that sensations are brain processes. It is not the thesis that, for example, "after-image" or "ache" means the same as "brain process of sort X" (where "X" is replaced by a description of a certain sort of brain process). It is that, in so far as "after-image" or "ache" is a report of a process, it is a report of a process that *happens to be* a brain process. It follows that the thesis does not claim that sensation statements can be *translated* into statements about brain processes.[3] Nor does it claim that the logic of a sensation statement is the same as that of a brain-process statement. All it claims is that in so far as a sensation statement is a report of something, that something is in fact a brain process. Sensations are nothing over and above brain processes. Nations are nothing "over and above" citizens, but this does not prevent the logic of nation statements being very different from the logic of citizen statements, nor does it insure the translatability of nation statements into citizen statements. (I do not, however, wish to assert that the relation of sensation statements to brain-process statements is very like that of nation statements to citizen statements. Nations do not just *happen to be* nothing over and above citizens, for example. I bring in the "nations" example merely to make a negative point: that the fact that the logic of A-statements is different from that of B-statements does not insure that A's are anything over and above B's.)

Remarks on identity. When I say that a sensation is a brain process or that lightning is an electric discharge, I am using "is" in the sense of strict identity. (Just as in the—in this case necessary—proposition "7 is identical with the smallest prime number greater than 5.") When I say that a sensation is a brain process or that lightning is an electric discharge I do not mean just that the sensation is somehow spatially or temporally continuous with the brain process or that the lightning is just spatially or temporally continuous with the discharge. When on the other hand I say that the successful general is the same person as the small boy who stole the apples I mean only that the successful general I see before me is a time slice of the same four-dimensional object of which the small boy stealing apples is an earlier time slice. However, the four-dimensional object which has the general-I-see-before-me for its late

3. See Place, *op. cit.,* p. 45, near top, and Feigl, *op. cit.,* p. 390, near top.

time slice is identical in the strict sense with the four-dimensional object which has the small-boy-stealing-apples for an early time slice. I distinguish these two senses of "is identical with" because I wish to make it clear that the brain-process doctrine asserts identity in the *strict* sense.

I shall now discuss various possible objections to the view that the processes reported in sensation statements are in fact processes in the brain. Most of us have met some of these objections in our first year as philosophy students. All the more reason to take a good look at them. Others of the objections will be more recondite and subtle.

Objection 1. Any illiterate peasant can talk perfectly well about his after-images, or how things look or feel to him, or about his aches and pains, and yet he may know nothing whatever about neurophysiology. A man may, like Aristotle, believe that the brain is an organ for cooling the body without any impairment of his ability to make true statements about his sensations. Hence the things we are talking about when we describe our sensations cannot be processes in the brain.

Reply. You might as well say that a nation of slug-abeds, who never saw the morning star or knew of its existence, or who had never thought of the expression "the Morning Star," but who used the expression "the Evening Star" perfectly well, could not use this expression to refer to the same entity as we refer to (and describe as) "the Morning Star." [4]

You may object that the Morning Star is in a sense not the very same thing as the Evening Star, but only something spatiotemporally continuous with it. . . .

There is, however, a more plausible example. Consider lightning.[5] Modern physical science tells us that lightning is a certain kind of electrical discharge due to ionization of clouds of water-vapor in the atmosphere. This, it is now believed, is what the true nature of lightning is. Note that there are not two things: a flash of lightning and an electrical discharge. There is one thing, a flash of lightning, which is described scientifically as an electrical discharge to the earth from a cloud of ionized water-molecules. The case is not at all like that of explaining a footprint by reference to a burglar. We say that what lightning really is, what its true nature as revealed by science is, is an electric discharge. (It is not the true nature of a footprint to be a burglar.)

To forestall irrelevant objections, I should like to make it clear that by "lightning" I mean the publicly observable physical object, lightning, not a visual sense-datum of lightning. I say that the publicly

4. Cf. Feigl, *op. cit.,* p. 439.
5. See Place, *op. cit.,* p. 47; also Feigl, *op. cit.,* p. 438.

observable physical object lightning is in fact the electric discharge, not just a correlate of it. The sense-datum, or at least the having of the sense-datum, the "look" of lightning, may well in my view be a correlate of the electric discharge. For in my view it is a brain state *caused* by the lightning. But we should no more confuse sensations of lightning with lightning than we confuse sensations of a table with the table.

In short, the reply to Objection 1 is that there can be contingent statements of the form "A is identical with B," and a person may well know that something is an A without knowing that it is a B. An illiterate peasant might well be able to talk about his sensations without knowing about his brain processes, just as he can talk about lightning though he knows nothing of electricity.

Objection 2. It is only a contingent fact (if it is a fact) that when we have a certain kind of sensation there is a certain kind of process in our brain. Indeed it is possible, though perhaps in the highest degree unlikely, that our present physiological theories will be as out of date as the ancient theory connecting mental processes with goings on in the heart. It follows that when we report a sensation we are not reporting a brain-process.

Reply. The objection certainly proves that when we say "I have an after-image" we cannot *mean* something of the form "I have such and such a brain-process." But this does not show that what we report (having an after-image) is not *in fact* a brain process. "I see lightning" does not *mean* "I see an electric discharge." Indeed, it is logically possible (though highly unlikely) that the electrical discharge account of lightning might one day be given up. Again, "I see the Evening Star" does not *mean* the same as "I see the Morning Star," and yet "the Evening Star and the Morning Star are one and the same thing" is a contingent proposition. Possibly Objection 2 derives some of its apparent strength from a "Fido"—Fido theory of meaning. If the meaning of an expression were what the expression named, then of course it *would* follow from the fact that "sensation" and "brain-process" have different meanings that they cannot name one and the same thing.

Objection 3.[6] Even if Objections 1 and 2 do not prove that sensations are something over and above brain-processes, they do prove that the qualities of sensations are something over and above the qualities of brain-processes. That is, it may be possible to get out of asserting the existence of irreducibly psychic processes, but not out of asserting the existence of irreducibly psychic *properties*. For suppose we identify the Morning Star with the Evening Star. Then there must be some prop-

---

6. I think this objection was first put to me by Professor Max Black. I think it is the most subtle of any of those I have considered, and the one which I am least confident of having satisfactorily met.

erties which logically imply that of being the Morning Star, and quite distinct properties which entail that of being the Evening Star. Again, there must be some properties (for example, that of being a yellow flash) which are logically distinct from those in the physicalist story.

Indeed, it might be thought that the objection succeeds at one jump. For consider the property of "being a yellow flash." It might seem that this property lies inevitably outside the physicalist framework within which I am trying to work (either by "yellow" being an objective emergent property of physical objects, or else by being a power to produce yellow sense-data, where "yellow," in this second instantiation of the word, refers to a purely phenomenal or introspectible quality). I must therefore digress for a moment and indicate how I deal with secondary qualities. I shall concentrate on color.

First of all, let me introduce the concept of a normal percipient. One person is more a normal percipient than another if he can make color discriminations that the other cannot. For example, if A can pick a lettuce leaf out of a heap of cabbage leaves, whereas B cannot though he can pick a lettuce leaf out of a heap of beetroot leaves, then A is more normal than B. (I am assuming that A and B are not given time to distinguish the leaves by their slight difference in shape, and so forth.) From the concept of "more normal than" it is easy to see how we can intro-

duce the concept of "normal." Of course, Eskimos may make the finest discriminations at the blue end of the spectrum, Hottentots at the red end. In this case the concept of a normal percipient is a slightly idealized one, rather like that of "the mean sun" in astronomical chronology. There is no need to go into such subtleties now. I say that "This is red" means something roughly like "A normal percipient would not easily pick this out of a clump of geranium petals though he would pick it out of a clump of lettuce leaves." Of course it does not exactly mean this: a person might know the meaning of "red" without knowing anything about geraniums, or even about normal percipients. But the point is that a person can be *trained* to say "This is red" of objects which would not easily be picked out of geranium petals by a normal percipient, and so on. (Note that even a color-blind person can reasonably assert that something is red, though of course he needs to use another human being, not just himself, as his "color meter.") This account of secondary qualities explains their unimportance in physics. For obviously the discriminations and lack of discriminations made by a very complex neurophysiological mechanism are hardly likely to correspond to simple and nonarbitrary distinctions in nature.

I therefore elucidate colors as powers, in Locke's sense, to evoke certain sorts of discriminatory responses in human beings. They are also, of course, powers to cause sensations in human beings (an account still near Locke's). But these sensations, I am arguing, are identifiable with brain processes.

Now how do I get over the objection that a sensation can be identified with a brain process only if it has some phenomenal property, not possessed by brain processes, whereby one-half of the identification may be, so to speak, pinned down?

My suggestion is as follows. When a person says, "I see a yellowish-orange after-image," he is saying something like this: *"There is something going on which is like what is going on when* I have my eyes open, am awake, and there is an orange illuminated in good light in front of me, that is, when I really see an orange." (And there is no reason why a person should not say the same thing when he is having a veridical sense-datum, so long as we construe "like" in the last sentence in such a sense that something can be like itself.) Notice that the italicized words, namely "there is something going on which is like what is going on when," are all quasi-logical or topic-neutral words. This explains why the ancient Greek peasant's reports about his sensations can be neutral between dualistic metaphysics or my materialistic metaphysics. It explains how sensations can be brain-processes and yet how those who report them need know nothing about

brain-processes. For he reports them only very abstractly as "something going on which is like what is going on when . . ." Similarly, a person may say "someone is in the room," thus reporting truly that the doctor is in the room, even though he has never heard of doctors. (There are not two people in the room: "someone" *and* the doctor.) This account of sensation statements also explains the singular elusiveness of "raw feels"— why no one seems to be able to pin any properties on them. Raw feels, in my view, are colorless for the very same reason that *something* is colorless. This does not mean that sensations do not have properties, for if they are brain-processes they certainly have properties. It only means that in speaking of them as being like or unlike one another we need not know or mention these properties.

This, then, is how I would reply to Objection 3. The strength of my reply depends on the possibility of our being able to report that one thing is like another without being able to state the respect in which it is like. I am not sure whether this is so or not, and that is why I regard Objection 3 as the strongest with which I have to deal.

Objection 4. The after-image is not in physical space. The brain-process is. So the after-image is not a brain-process.

Reply. This is an *ignoratio elenchi*. I am not arguing that the after-image is a brain-process, but that the experience of having an after-image is a brain-process. It is the *experience* which is reported in the introspective report. Similarly, if it is objected that the after-image is yellowy-orange but that a surgeon looking into your brain would see nothing yellowy-orange, my reply is that it is the experience of seeing yellowy-orange that is being described, and this experience is not a yellowy-orange something. So to say that a brain-process cannot be yellowy-orange is not to say that a brain-process cannot in fact be the experience of having a yellowy-orange after-image. There is, in a sense, no such thing as an after-image or a sense-datum, though there is such a thing as the experience of having an image, and this experience is described indirectly in material object language, not in phenomenal language, for there is no such thing. We describe the experience by saying, in effect, that it is like the experience we have when, for example, we really see a yellowy-orange patch on the wall. Trees and wallpaper can be green, but not the experience of seeing or imagining a tree or wallpaper. (Or if they are described as green or yellow this can only be in a derived sense.)

Objection 5. It would make sense to say of a molecular movement in the brain that it is swift or slow, straight or circular, but it makes no sense to say this of the experience of seeing something yellow.

Reply. So far we have not given sense to talk of experiences as swift or slow, straight or circular. But I am not claiming that "experience" and "brain-process" mean the same or even that they have the same logic. "Somebody" and "the doctor" do not have the same logic, but this does not lead us to suppose that talking about somebody telephoning is talking about someone over and above, say, the doctor. The ordinary man when he reports an experience is reporting that something is going on, but he leaves it open as to what sort of thing is going on, whether in a material solid medium, or perhaps in some sort of gaseous medium, or even perhaps in some sort of nonspatial medium (if this makes sense). All that I am saying is that "experience" and "brain-process" may in fact refer to the same thing, and if so we may easily adopt a convention (which is not a change in our present rules for the use of experience words but an addition to them) whereby it would make sense to talk of an experience in terms appropriate to physical processes.

Objection 6. Sensations are private, brain processes are *public*. If I sincerely say, "I see a yellowish-orange after-image" and I am not making a verbal mistake, then I cannot be wrong. But I can be wrong about a brain-process. The scientist looking into my brain might be having an illusion. Moreover, it makes sense to say that two or more people are observing the same brain-process but not that two or more people are reporting the same inner experience.

Reply. This shows that the language of introspective reports has a different logic from the language of material processes. It is obvious that until the brain-process theory is much improved and widely accepted there will be no *criteria* for saying "Smith has an experience of such-and-such a sort" *except* Smith's introspective reports. So we have adopted a rule of language that (normally) what Smith says goes.

Objection 7. I can imagine myself turned to stone and yet having images, aches, pains, and so on.

Reply. I can imagine that the electrical theory of lightning is false, that lightning is some sort of purely optical phenomenon. I can imagine that lightning is not an electrical discharge. I can imagine that the Evening Star is not the Morning Star. But it is. All the objection shows is that "experience" and "brain-process" do not have the same meaning. It does not show that an experience is not in fact a brain process.

This objection is perhaps much the same as one which can be summed up by the slogan: "What can be composed of nothing cannot be composed of anything."[7] The argument goes as follows: on the brain-process thesis the identity between the brain-process and the experi-

ence is a contingent one. So it is logically possible that there should be no brain-process, and no process of any other sort, either (no heart process, no kidney process, no liver process). There would be the experience but no "corresponding" physiological process with which we might be able to identify it empirically.

I suspect that the objector is thinking of the experience as a ghostly entity. So it is composed of something, not of nothing, after all. On his view it is composed of ghost stuff, and on mine it is composed of brain stuff. Perhaps the counter-reply will be[8] that the experience is simple and uncompounded, and so it is not composed of anything after all. This seems to be a quibble, for, if it were taken seriously, the remark "What can be composed of nothing cannot be composed of anything" could be recast as an a priori argument against Democritus and atomism and for Descartes and infinite divisibility. And it seems odd that a question of this sort could be settled a priori. We must therefore construe the word "composed" in a very weak sense, which would allow us to say that even an indivisible atom is composed of something (namely, itself). The dualist cannot really say that an experience can be composed of nothing. For he holds that experiences are something over and above

---

7. I owe this objection to Mr. C. B. Martin. I gather that he no longer wishes to maintain this objection, at any rate in its present form.

8. Martin did not make this reply, but one of his students did.

material processes, that is, that they are a sort of ghost stuff. (Or perhaps ripples in an underlying ghost stuff.) I say that the dualist's hypothesis is a perfectly intelligible one. But I say that experiences are not to be identified with ghost stuff but with brain stuff. This is another hypothesis, and in my view a very plausible one. The present argument cannot knock it down a priori.

Objection 8. The "beetle in the box" objection (see Wittgenstein, *Philosophical Investigations*, paragraph 293). How could descriptions of experiences, if these are genuine reports, get a foothold in language? For any rule of language must have public criteria for its correct application.

Reply. The change from describing how things are to describing how we feel is just a change from uninhibitedly saying "this is so" to saying "this looks so." That is, when the naive person might be tempted to say, "There is a patch of light on the wall which moves whenever I move my eyes" or "A pin is being stuck into me," we have learned how to resist this temptation and say "It *looks as though* there is a patch of light on the wallpaper" or "It *feels as though* someone were sticking a pin into me." The introspective account tells us about the individual's state of consciousness in the same way as does "I see a patch of light" or "I feel a pin being stuck into me": it differs from the corresponding perception statement in so far as (a) in the perception statement the individual "goes beyond the evidence of his senses" in describing his environment and (b) in the introspective report he withholds descriptive epithets he is inclined to ascribe to the environment, perhaps because he suspects that they may not be appropriate to the actual state of affairs. Psychologically speaking, the change from talking about the environment to talking about one's state of consciousness is simply a matter of inhibiting descriptive reactions not justified by appearances alone, and of disinhibiting descriptive reactions which are normally inhibited because the individual has learned that they are unlikely to provide a reliable guide to the state of the environment in the prevailing circumstances.[9] To say that something looks green to me is to say that my experience is like the experience I get when I see something that really is green. In my reply to Objection 3, I pointed out the extreme openness or generality of statements which report experiences. This explains why there is no language of private qualities. (Just as "someone," unlike "the doctor," is a colorless word.) . . .

I have now considered a number of objections to the brain-process thesis. I wish now to conclude by some remarks on the logical status of the thesis itself. U. T. Place seems to hold that it is a straight-out scientific hypothesis. If so, he is

9. I owe this point to Place, in correspondence.

partly right and partly wrong. If the issue is between (say) a brain-process thesis and a heart thesis, or a liver thesis, or a kidney thesis, then the issue is a purely empirical one, and the verdict is overwhelmingly in favor of the brain. The right sorts of things don't go on in the heart, liver, or kidney, nor do these organs possess the right sort of complexity of structure. On the other hand, if the issue is betwen a brain-or-heart-or-liver-or-kidney thesis (that is, some form of materialism) on the one hand and epiphenomenalism on the other hand, then the issue is not an empirical one. For there is no conceivable experiment which could decide between materialism and epiphenomenalism. This latter issue is not like the average straight-out empirical issue in science, but like the issue between the nineteenth-century English naturalist Philip Gosse and the orthodox geologists and paleontologists of his day. According to Gosse, the earth was created about 4000 B.C. exactly as described in *Genesis*, with twisted rock strata, "evidence" of erosion, and so forth, and all sorts of fossils, all in their appropriate strata, just as if the usual evolutionist story had been true. Clearly this theory is in a sense irrefutable: no evidence can possibly tell against it. Let us ignore the theological setting in which Philip Gosse's hypothesis had been placed, thus ruling out objections of a theological kind, such as "what a queer God who would go to such elaborate lengths to deceive us." Let us suppose that it is held that the universe just *began* in 4004 B.C. with the initial conditions just everywhere as they were in 4004 B.C., and in particular that our own planet began with sediment in the rivers, eroded cliffs, fossils in the rocks, and so on. No scientist would ever entertain this as a serious hypothesis, consistent though it is with all possible evidence. The hypothesis offends against the principles of parsimony and simplicity. There would be far too many brute and inexplicable facts. Why are pterodactyl bones just as they are? No explanation in terms of the evolution of pterodactyls from earlier forms of life would any longer be possible. We would have millions of facts about the world as it was in 4004 B.C. that just have to be *accepted*.

The issue between the brain-process theory and epiphenomenalism seems to be of the above sort. (Assuming that a behavioristic reduction of introspective reports is not possible.) If it be agreed that there are no cogent philosophical arguments which force us into accepting dualism, and if the brain process theory and dualism are equally consistent with the facts, then the principles of parsimony and simplicity seem to me to decide overwhelmingly in favor of the brain-process theory. As I pointed out earlier, dualism involves a large number of irreducible psychophysical laws (whereby the "nomological danglers" dangle) of a queer sort, that just have to be taken on trust, and are just as difficult to swallow as the irreducible facts about the paleontology of the earth with which we are faced on Philip Gosse's theory.

12

Scientific Materialism and the Identity Theory

NORMAN MALCOLM

I

My main topic will be, roughly speaking, the claim that mental events or conscious experiences or inner experiences are brain processes. I hasten to say, however, that I am not going to talk about "mental events" or "conscious experiences" or "inner experiences." These expressions are almost exclusively philosophers' terms, and I am not sure that I have got the hang of any of them. Philosophers are not in agreement in their use of these terms. One philosopher will say, for example, that a pain in the foot is a mental event, whereas another will say that a pain *in the foot* certainly is not a *mental* event.

I will avoid these expressions, and concentrate on the particular example of *sudden thoughts*. Sud-denly remembering an engagement would be an example of suddenly thinking of something. Suddenly realizing, in a chess game, that moving this pawn would endanger one's queen, would be another example of a sudden thought. Professor Smart says that he wishes to "elucidate thought as an inner process," and he adds that he wants to identify "such inner processes with brain processes." He surely holds, therefore, that thinking and thoughts, including sudden thoughts, are brain processes. He holds also that conscious experiences, illusions, and aches and pains are brain processes, and that love is a brain state. I will restrict my discussion, however, to sudden thoughts.

My first inclination, when I began to think on this topic, was to

[From *Dialogue,* Vol. 3 (1964), pp. 115–124. Reprinted by permission of *Dialogue,* the Canadian Philosophical Association, and Norman Malcolm.]

believe that Smart's view is false—that a sudden thought certainly is not a brain process. But now I think that I do not know what it *means* to say that a sudden thought is a brain process. In saying this I imply, of course, that the proponents of this view also do not know what it means. This implication is risky for it might turn out, to my surprise and gratification, that Smart will explain his view with great clarity.

In trying to show that there is real difficulty in seeing what his view means, I will turn to Smart's article "Sensations and Brain Processes." He says there that in holding that a sensation is a brain process he is "using 'is' in the sense of strict identity." "I wish to make it clear," he says, "that the brain process doctrine asserts identity in the *strict* sense." I assume that he wishes to say the same about the claimed identity of a thought with a brain process. Unfortunately he does not attempt to define this "strict sense of identity," and so we have to study his examples.

One of his examples of a "strict identity" is this: 7 is identical with the smallest prime number greater than 5. We must remember, however, that one feature of "the identity theory," as I shall call it, is that the alleged identity between thoughts, sensations, etc., and brain processes, is held to be *contingent*. Since the identity of 7 with the smallest prime greater than 5 is *a priori* and relates to timeless objects, it does not provide me with any clue as to how I

am to apply the notion of "strict identity" to temporal events that are *contingently* related. The example is unsatisfactory, therefore, for the purpose of helping me to deal with the question of whether thoughts are or are not "strictly identical" with certain brain processes.

Let us move to another example. Smart tells us that the sense in which the small boy who stole apples is the same person as the victorious general, is *not* the "strict" sense of "identity." He thinks there is a mere spatio-temporal continuity between the apple-stealing boy and the general who won the war. From this *non*-example of "strict identity" I think I obtain a clue as to what he means by it. Consider the following two sentences: "General De Gaulle is the tallest Frenchman"; "The victorious general is the small boy who stole apples." Each of these sentences might be said to express an identity: yet we can see a difference between the two cases. Even though the victorious general *is* the small boy who stole apples, it is possible for the victorious general to be in this room at a time when there is *no* small boy here. In contrast, if General De Gaulle *is* the tallest Frenchman, then General De Gaulle is not in this room unless the tallest Frenchman is here. It would be quite natural to say that this latter identity (if it holds) is a *strict* identity, and that the other one is not. I believe that Smart would say this. This suggests to me the following rule for his "strict identity": If something, *x*, is in a certain place at a certain time, then something, y, is strictly identical with x only if y is in the same place at that same time.

If we assume that Smart's use of the expression "strict identity" is governed by the necessary condition I have stated, we can possibly understand why he is somewhat hesitant about whether to say that the Morning Star is strictly identical with the Evening Star. Smart says to an imaginary opponent: "You may object that the Morning Star is in a sense not the very same thing as the Evening Star, but only something spatio-temporally continuous with it. That is, you may say that the Morning Star is not the Evening Star in the strict sense of 'identity' that I distinguished earlier." Instead of rebutting this objection, Smart moves on to what he calls "a more plausible example" of strict identity. This suggests to me that Smart is not entirely happy with the case of the Stars as an example of strict identity. Why not? Perhaps he has some inclination to feel that the planet that is both the Morning and Evening Star, is not the Morning Star *at the same time* it is the Evening Star. If this were so, the suggested necessary condition for "strict identity" would not be satisfied. Smart's hesitation is thus a further indication that he wants his use of the expression "strict identity" to be governed by the rule I have stated.

Let us turn to what Smart calls his "more plausible" example of strict identity. It is this: Lightning is an electric discharge. Smart avows that this is truly a strict identity. This example provides additional evidence that he wants to follow the stated rule. If an electrical discharge occurred in one region of the sky and a flash of lightning occurred simultaneously in a different region of the sky, Smart would have no inclination to assert (I think) that the lightning was strictly identical with the electric discharge. Or if electrical discharges and corresponding lightning flashes occurred in the same region of the sky, but not at the same time, there normally being a perceptible interval of time between a discharge and a flash, then Smart (I believe) would not wish to hold that there was anything more strict than a systematic correlation (perhaps causal) between electric discharges and lightning.

I proceed now to take up Smart's claim that a sudden thought is strictly identical with some brain process. It is clear that a brain process has spatial location. A brain process would be a mechanical, chemical or electrical process in the brain substance, or an electric discharge from the brain mass, or something of the sort. As Smart puts it, brain processes take place "inside our skulls."

Let us consider an example of a sudden thought. Suppose that when I am in my house I hear the sound of a truck coming up the driveway and it suddenly occurs to me that I have not put out the milk bottles.

Now is this sudden thought (which is also a sudden memory) literally inside my skull? I think that in our ordinary use of the terms "thought" and "thinking", we attach no meaning to the notion of determining the bodily location of a thought. We do not seriously debate whether someone's sudden thought occurred in his heart, or his throat, or his brain. Indeed, we should not know what the question meant. We should have no idea what to look for to settle this "question." We do say such a thing as "He can't get the thought out of his head"; but this is not taken as giving the location of a thought, any more than the remark "He still has that girl on the brain," is taken as giving the location of a girl.

It might be replied that *as things are* the bodily location of thoughts is not a meaningful notion; but if massive correlations were discovered between thoughts and brain processes then we might *begin* to locate thoughts in the head. To this I must answer that our philosophical problem *is* about how things are. It is a question about our *present* concepts of thinking and thought, not about some conjectured future concepts.

The difficulty I have in understanding Smart's identity theory is the following. Smart wants to use a concept of "strict identity." Since there are a multitude of uses of the word "is," from the mere fact that he tells us that he means "is" in the sense of "strict identity," it does not

follow that he has explained which use of "is" he intends. From his examples and non-examples, I surmise that his so-called "strict identity" is governed by the necessary condition that if x occurs in a certain place at a certain time, then y is strictly identical with x only if y occurs in the same place at the same time. But if x is a brain process and y is a sudden thought, then this condition for strict identity is not (and cannot be) satisfied. Indeed, it does not even make sense to set up a test for it. Suppose we had determined, by means of some instrument, that a certain process occurred inside my skull at the exact moment I had the sudden thought about the milk bottles. How do we make the further test of whether my *thought* occurred inside my skull? For it would have to be a *further* test: it would have to be logically independent of the test for the presence of the brain process, because Smart's thesis is that the identity is *contingent*. But no one has any notion of what it would mean to test for the occurrence of the thought inside my skull *independently* of testing for a brain process. The idea of such a test is not intelligible. Smart's thesis, as I understand it, requires this unintelligible idea. For he is not satisfied with holding that there is a systematic correlation between sudden thoughts and certain brain processes. He wants to take the additional step of holding that there is a "strict identity." Now his concept of strict identity either embodies the necessary condition I stated previously, or it does not. If it does not, then I do not know what he means by "strict identity," over and above systematic correlation. If his concept of strict identity does embody that necessary condition, then his concept of strict identity cannot be meaningfully applied to the relationship between sudden thoughts and brain processes. My conclusion is what I said in the beginning: the identity theory has no clear meaning.

II

I turn now to a different consideration. A thought requires circumstances or, in Wittgenstein's word, "surroundings" (Umgebung). Putting a crown on a man's head is a coronation, only in certain circumstances. The behavior of exclaiming, "Oh, I have not put out the milk bottles," or the behavior of suddenly jumping up, rushing to the kitchen, collecting the bottles and carrying them outside—such behavior expresses the thought that one has not put out the milk bottles, *only in certain circumstances*.

The circumstances necessary for this simple thought are complex. They include the existence of an organized community, of a practice of collecting and distributing milk, of a rule that empty bottles will not be collected unless placed outside the door, and so on. These practices, arrangements and rules could exist only if there was a common language; and this in turn would presuppose shared activities and agreement in the use of language. The thought about the milk bottles requires a background of mutual purpose, activity and understanding.

I assume that if a certain brain process were strictly identical with a certain thought, then the occurrence of that brain process would be an absolutely sufficient condition for the occurrence of that thought. If this assumption is incorrect, then my understanding of what Smart means by "strict identity" is even *less* than I have believed. In support of this assumption I will point out that Smart has never stated his identity theory in the following way: *In certain circumstances* a particular brain process is identical with a particular thought. His thesis has not carried such a qualification. I believe his thesis is the following: A particular brain process is, *without qualification*, strictly identical with a particular thought. If this thesis were true it would appear to follow that the occurrence of that brain process would be an absolutely sufficient condition for the occurrence of that thought.

I have remarked that a necessary condition for the occurrence of my sudden thought about the milk bottles is the previous existence of various practices, rules and agreements. If the identity theory were true, then the surroundings that are necessary for the existence of my sudden thought would also be necessary for the existence of the brain process with which it is identical.[1] That brain process would not have occurred unless, for example, there was or had been a practice of delivering milk.

This consequence creates a difficulty for those philosophers who, like Smart, hold both to the identity theory and also to the viewpoint that I shall call "scientific materialism." According to the latter viewpoint, the furniture of the world "in the last resort" consists of "the ultimate entities of physics." Smart holds that everything in the world is "explicable in terms of physics." It does not seem to me that this can be true. My sudden thought about the milk bottles was an occurrence in the world. That thought required a background of common practices, purposes and agreements. But a reference to a practice of (*e.g.*) delivering milk could not appear in a proposition of physics. The word "electron" is a term of physics, but the phrase "a practice of delivering milk" is not. There could not be an explanation of the occurrence of my thought (an explanation taking account of all the necessary circumstances) which was stated solely in terms of the entities and laws of physics.

My sudden thought about the milk bottles is not unique in requiring surroundings. The same holds for any other thought. No thought would be explicable wholly in the terms of physics (and/or biology) because the circumstances that form the "stage-setting" for a thought cannot be described in the terms of physics.

Now if I am right on this point, and if the identity theory were true, it would follow that none of those *brain processes* that are identical with thoughts could be given a purely physical explanation. A philosopher who holds both to the identity theory and to scientific materialism is forced, I think, into the self-defeating position of conceding that many brain processes are not explicable solely in terms of physics. The position is self-defeating because such a philosopher regards a brain process as a *paradigm* of something wholly explicable in terms of physics.

A defender of these two positions might try to avoid this outcome by claiming that the circumstances required for the occurrence of a thought, do themselves consist of configurations of ultimate particles (or of their statistical properties, or something of the sort). I doubt, however, that anyone knows what it would mean to say, for example, that the *rule* that milk bottles will not be

---

1.   It is easy to commit a fallacy here. The circumstances that I have mentioned are *conceptually* necessary for the occurrence of my thought. If the identity theory were true it would not follow that they were *conceptually* necessary for the occurrence of the brain process that is identical with that thought. But it would follow that those circumstances were necessary for the occurrence of the brain process *in the sense* that the brain process *would not* have occurred in the absence of those circumstances.

collected unless placed outside the door, is a configuration of ultimate particles. At the very least, this defence would have to assume a heavy burden of explanation.

III

There is a further point connected with the one just stated. At the foundation of Smart's monism there is, I believe, the desire for a homogeneous system of explanation. Everything in the world, he feels, should be capable of the same *kind* of explanation, namely, one in terms of the entities and laws of physics. He thinks we advance toward this goal when we see that sensations, thoughts, etc., are identical with brain processes.

Smart has rendered a service to the profession by warning us against a special type of fallacy. An illustration of this fallacy would be to argue that a sensation is not a brain process because a person can be talking about a sensation and yet not be talking about a brain process. The verb "to talk about" might be called an "intentional" verb, and this fallacy committed with it might be called "the intentional fallacy." Other intentional verbs would be "to mean," "to intend," "to know," "to predict," "to describe," "to notice," and so on.

It is easy to commit the intentional fallacy, and I suspect that Smart himself has done so. The verb "to explain" is also an intentional verb and one must beware of using it to produce a fallacy. Suppose that the Prime Minister of Ireland is the ugliest Irishman. A man might argue that this cannot be so, because someone might be explaining the presence of the Irish Prime Minister in New York and yet not be explaining the presence in New York of the ugliest Irishman. It would be equally fallacious to argue that since the Irish Prime Minister and the ugliest Irishman *are* one and the same person, therefore, to explain the presence of the Prime Minster *is* to explain the presence of the ugliest Irishman.

I wonder if Smart has not reasoned fallaciously, somewhat as follows: If a sudden thought *is* a certain brain process, then to *explain* the occurrence of the brain process *is* to explain the occurrence of the thought. Thus there will be just one kind of explanation for both thoughts and brain processes.

The intentional fallacy here is transparent. If a thought is identical with a brain process, it does not follow that to explain the occurrence of the brain process is to explain the occurrence of the thought. And in fact, an explanation of the one differs in *kind* from an explanation of the other. The explanation of why someone *thought* such and such, involves different assumptions and principles and is guided by different interests than is an explanation of why this or that process occurred in his brain. These explanations belong to different *systems* of explanation.

I conclude that even if Smart were right in holding that thoughts are strictly identical with brain processes (a claim that I do not yet find intelligible) he would not have established that there is one and the same explanation for the occurrence of the thoughts and for the occurrence of the brain processes. If he were to appreciate this fact then, I suspect, he would no longer have any *motive* for espousing the identity theory. For this theory, even if true, would not advance us one whit toward the single, homogenous system of explanation that is the goal of Smart's materialism. . . .

AFTERWORD

In reflecting on the significance of the preceding selections, you may find it useful to consider two questions. One question is: How do the discussions you have read about persons, minds, and bodies relate to the issues raised about determinism, freedom, and moral responsibility in Chapter 4? Are some of the views about minds, bodies, and interaction inconsistent with hard determinism, or with soft determinism, or with libertarianism? Are certain views about persons, minds, and bodies necessary conditions for some positions on the nature of free action and moral responsibility? Trying to work out some of the ways in which these two sets of issues are related can lead to a better understanding of all the issues involved.

A second question to consider is this: What importance do different theories about persons, minds, and bodies have for our views about the possibility of continuing human existence after death? For example, it seems that physical monism is not likely to provide us with grounds for believing in the possibility of survival after death. If all of human nature is physical, our empirical evidence strongly favors the view that personality, thought, and awareness all are irretrievably lost with death. Nor does the epiphenomenalist seem to offer us much hope for personal survival. Spiritual monism, on the other hand, as well as many varieties of dualism, may seem to leave more room for the possibility of some kind of personal survival after death—simply because these theories regard the mental aspects of our existence as not completely dependent upon our physical nature. But these are only first impressions. Could clever physical monists or epiphenomenalists work out a way in which some possibility of survival after death might be consistent with their views? Or, if dualistic interactionists regard the interaction between mind and body as fundamental to human nature, will it turn out to be very difficult to make a case for the survival of a "mental personality" when all interaction with the physical has ceased? Once more, working out the ways in which the selections you have read come to bear on the question of survival after death should enhance your understanding of those selections.

REVIEW QUESTIONS

Selection 7

1. What reasons does Descartes give for identifying himself as a thinking being, rather than a physical being?

2. In what ways does Descartes characterize the differences between mind and body?

3. Descartes claims that the brain plays an especially important role in mind-body interaction. What kinds of evidence does he offer for this claim?

4. Do you think Descartes' discussion explains how mind-body interaction is possible? Why, or why not?

Selection 8

5. What arguments does Hume use to show that we never perceive ourselves? What does he think this shows about our ideas of ourselves? Why?

6. What is a person, according to Hume? A mind? A body? Something else? Explain.

7. Hume distinguishes carefully between *identity* and a *succession of related objects*. What important mistake does he think results from confusing these two things?

8. If Hume is right about the nature of persons, is there still a problem about interaction between mind and body? Explain.

Selection 9

9. Suppose you step on a sharp stone with your bare feet, and respond to the pain by jumping back. How would Leibniz account for this apparent interaction between body and mind?

10. Does Leibniz seem to require a deterministic or an indeterministic view of human action? Explain.

11. Leibniz seems to concede the impossibility of interaction between minds and bodies. But he appeals to God's ability to act upon both mind and body. Does this raise the problem of interaction in another form? Why, or why not?

Selection 10

12. Huxley says that Descartes could have used the information about the frog to support his views that animals are automata. Explain.

13. Precisely what does the case of Sergeant F ____illustrate? If the abnormal condition became permanent would you be inclined to say that Sergeant F ____had *died*? Why or why not?

14. What arguments does Huxley give to show that animals do have some conscious experience?

15. Would you say Huxley was an indeterminist, a hard determinist, or a soft determinist? Why?

Selection 11

16. Why does Smart reject the idea that psychical phenomena might be correlated with brain states? What does he mean when he calls psychical phenomena "nomological danglers"?

17. In his reply to Objection 3, Smart discusses the nature of secondary properties. How does that discussion support his reply? Why does he regard Objection 3 as the strongest objection with which he must deal?

18. What does Smart think is wrong with epiphenomenalist views such as Huxley's? In what ways does he think epiphenomenalism resembles Gosse's view?

Selection 12

19. Malcolm raises several difficulties for Smart's treatment of *strict identity*. What are they? Has Smart indicated any way of dealing with such difficulties? Explain.

20. Why does Malcolm suggest that Smart would have to claim that a sudden thought is literally in one's head? Do you think Malcolm's position on the nature of sudden thoughts would be regarded by Smart as involving a commitment to the existence of nomological danglers?

21. Why does Malcolm regard a background of practices, purposes, and agreements important in explaining the occurrence of a sudden thought? Do you think this is the same *kind* of explanation that Smart is attempting to provide by appealing to the laws of physics? Explain.

22. What is the *intentional fallacy*? In what way does Malcolm think that Smart has committed it?

6

The Objectivity of Morals

To say that moral judgments are *objective* is to say that they can be correct or incorrect, true or false. Now, while many people are inclined to *say* that moral judgments are not really objective, nearly everyone, in the course of ordinary life, seems to *act* as if they are. For most of us, hardly a day passes in which we do not say of some action that it was right or wrong, good or bad, within the agent's rights or not, a violation of someone else's rights or not, a successful or an unsuccessful way of meeting the agent's duties and obligations. And we say of persons or groups that they are good, or wicked, or kind, or cruel, and so on. Further, it is not unusual to find that other people disagree with us about such things—and to become engaged in debate about whose opinion is correct, with each person offering various facts and theories as evidence in support of some of the competing judgments and against others. In these situations, we appear to act as if we were dealing with objective matters of fact, which can be supported by appeal to evidence and argument.

If moral judgments are objective, and if we know what we are talking about when we make them, then we should be able to say what kinds of factual situations they are about. For example, if we say that actions or persons are *good*, we should be able to explain what characteristics of those actions or persons make them good. If we say that someone has a right to behave in a certain way, then we ought to be able to explain which facts in the situation provide such a right. This characteristic also holds for the other kinds of moral judgments we make. In short, we should be able to say what goodness, badness, right, wrong, and other moral properties really are, and we should be able to give an account of the sorts of facts which count as evidence for or against judgments involving such properties.

But the disagreement about the nature of morality is notorious. Attempt after attempt to define the moral properties has fallen victim to well-selected counterexamples. What seems to be conclusive evidence to some seems irrelevant to others. The problem is not that we fail to find agreement in detail about questions of morals. We seem unable even to begin to agree about fundamental points upon which to build a theory of morals. Because of this confusion it is tempting to suppose that, after all, rational argument and matters of fact simply are not relevant to moral judgments.

Thus, we find it tempting to accept all three of these statements:

(1) Moral judgments are objective, i.e., true or false.

(2) The correctness or incorrectness of objective judgments is a matter of fact, to be discovered through observation and the use of reason.

(3) Moral judgments do not refer to, or depend upon, matters of fact.

But, of course, these statements form an inconsistent set, and all three of them cannot be true at once. So, the beliefs which we might be naturally inclined to hold about the status of moral judgments are paradoxical in character. How should we alter them to avoid inconsistency?

Objectivist theories in ethics accept statements (1) and (2), and attempt to refute (3) by providing an explanation of the manner in which moral judgments do refer to or depend upon the facts. Such objectivist theories can be separated into *naturalistic* and *non-naturalistic* ethical theories. Naturalistic theories attempt to explain how moral judgments can be based upon the kinds of facts we are accustomed to observe in nature or society. For example, some naturalistic theories try to explain goodness and duty in terms of selfish desires (egoism), others appeal to the goal of maximizing pleasure (utilitarianism), and still others define values in terms of accepted practices in a given society (cultural relativism). Other naturalistic theories appeal to several other kinds of facts. The principal challenge for all such theories is to provide a method for basing value judgments on fact without becoming vulnerable to attack by counterexample. This challenge has proved very difficult to meet.

Non-naturalists have responded to the challenge by suggesting that there are very special moral properties and facts which are quite unlike the ordinary facts of nature. They take these facts to be the subject of moral judgments. In many cases, it is supposed that we must possess a special moral sense, different from all our other senses, with which we recognize these facts. It is much more difficult to think of obvious counterexamples to such non-naturalistic theories, but that may be because it is very difficult to understand what the theories really tell us. What is the nature of these very special kinds of facts, and how could we tell whether our special moral sense was correct or in error?

The difficulties with naturalistic and non-naturalistic theories have persuaded many philosophers that objectivism must be given up. Accordingly, they reject (1) and accept (2) and (3). This kind of approach to the problem has the advantage of not requiring a theory which defines or explains the nature of moral facts and moral properties. But a new difficulty arises, for if our moral judgments are not objective and do not make claims which could be true or false, then what *is* their function? What do we accomplish, or try to accomplish, when we make such judgments, debate about them, use them as a guide for action, etc.? Non-objectivist ethical theories need to make clear to us what the real non-objective function of moral judgments is. Some such theories claim that moral judgments are expressions of our preferences and feelings. Others compare moral judgments to commands or recommendations for action. The principal challenge for these theories is to make sense of our extensive use of debate and argument about moral judgments—after all, one does not try to prove or give evidence for a command, or a simple expression of feeling.

As you read the following selections, then, one goal you should have in mind is to discover the author's position on the function of moral judgments, Are they held to be objective or not? If not, what function do they serve? If so, what kinds of facts are they thought to report? A second goal should be to find an account of the role of reason and argument in making moral judgments. How would the author explain our practice of appealing to non-moral facts to support our moral judgments?

13

Ethical Relativism

RICHARD B. BRANDT

A Greek philosopher who lived in the fifth century B.C., named Protagoras, seems to have believed two things: first, that moral principles cannot be shown to be valid for everybody; and second, that people ought to follow the conventions of their own group. Something like this combination of propositions probably had been thought of before his time. Primitive people are well aware that different social groups have different standards, and at least sometimes doubt whether one set of standards can really be shown to be superior to others. Moreover, probably in many groups it has been thought that a person who conforms conscientiously to the standards of his own group deserves respect.

Views roughly similar to those of Protagoras may be classified as forms of *ethical relativism*. The term "ethical relativism," however, is used in different senses, and one should be wary when one comes across it. Sometimes one is said to be a relativist if he thinks that an action that is wrong in one place might not be in another, so that one is declared a relativist if he thinks it wrong for a group of Eskimos to strip a man of his clothing twenty miles from home on January 1, but not wrong for a tribe at the equator. If "relativism" is used in this sense, then practically everyone is a relativist, for practically everyone believes that particular circumstances make a difference to the morality of an act—that, for instance, it is right to lie in some circumstances but wrong in others. Again, one is sometimes said to be a relativist if he asserts a pair of causal propositions: that different social groups sometimes have different values (ethical opinions) as a result of historical developments;

[Richard B. Brandt, *Ethical Theory*, 1959, chapter 11 (Prentice-Hall). Reprinted by permission of the author.]

and that an individual's values are near-replicas of the tradition of his group, however strongly he may feel that they are "his own" or that they are "valid" and can be supported by convincing reasons. We shall not use "ethical relativism" for either of these views, but reserve it for a theory at least fairly close to that of Protagoras.[1]

The Question: "Are Conflicting Ethical Opinions Equally Valid?"

The position of Protagoras, however, is somewhat vague, and if we are to assess it, we must sharpen it. It is also convenient to deal separately with its two parts. We shall begin with a restatement of the first part of his theory, and then assess it at some length; only then shall we consider the second half of his position. As we go on, we shall see that the first part of his theory is theoretically more interesting and important than the second. For this reason, we shall apply the term "ethical relativism" to any theory that agrees with our sharpened form of Protagoras' first point, irrespective of its attitude toward the second.

It is clarifying to substitute, in place of our initial statement of Protagoras' view, the following, as a brief formulation of the relativist thesis in ethics: *"There are conflicting ethical opinions that are equally valid."* But this formulation requires discussion in order to be clear.

The first thing to notice—although the fact will not be obvious until we have explained the phrase "equally valid"—is that the statement is *about* ethical opinions or statements, but is not an ethical statement itself. It is not like saying, "Nothing is right or wrong!" or "Some things are both right and wrong!" It is a metaethical theory.

Next, the statement is cautious. It does not say that no ethical opinions are valid for everybody. It says only that some ethical opinions are not more valid than some other ethical opinions that conflict with them.

Third, our relativist thesis is not merely the claim that different individuals sometimes in fact have conflicting ethical opinions. It does assert this, but it goes further. It holds that the conflicting ethical opinions are *equally valid.* We do not establish this merely by showing that people disagree. Nor do we establish it by showing that individuals'

---

1. It is useful to compare Protagoras' relativism with the special theory of relativity in physics. One implication of this theory is that measurements of certain physical quantities, like the temporal distance between two events, will come out differently for different frames of reference (one "frame of reference" being the set of observers having the same relative rectilinear motion). All the careful observations in *one* frame will give the *same* result; and in this sense there is a "right" answer for this frame. But different frames will have different "right" answers, and there is in principle no way of showing that one of these is the "really right" answer. However, certain quantities (like the spatio-temporal distance between two events) are absolutes, in the sense that careful measurements will give one right answer for everybody.

ethical opinions are at least to some extent dependent on the cultural stream within which they stand. Everyone must agree to this—although everyone must also admit that somehow societies often spawn their own moral critics. Nor do we establish it by showing that the standards of a given society have their causes. Of course they do; and so do the scientific opinions in a given society, although we hardly think this necessarily impugns their universal validity.

Fourth, what do we mean by "conflicting ethical opinions"? We mean, of course, by an "opinion" the readiness to make a sincere statement. Thus, a person has an "ethical opinion" to the effect that a particular thing is right or wrong if he could, when asked, make without deception an ethical statement to the effect that that thing is right or wrong. (We explained how to identify an "ethical" statement in Chapter 1.) Now, suppose Mr. A makes an ethical statement, and Mr. B makes a different ethical statement. How shall we tell whether the two statements "conflict"? A sufficient condition of conflict is this: that both statements are about the *same subject* (we explain this in a moment), and the one applies to this subject an ethical predicate *P,* and the other applies to it the same ethical predicate prefaced by the English "not" or something that means or entails the same. For instance, one may say "is morally right" and the other may

say "is not morally right," of the very same subject. But now, when do two ethical statements have the *same subject?* This is a more awkward question. We cannot test this just by observing the verbal forms. For instance, Thomas Jefferson said, approximately, "A revolution every few years is a fine thing." But suppose Karl Marx also said, "A revolution every few years is a fine thing." Could we assume that these two men were necessarily saying the same thing? Of course not. Or again, suppose Mr. A, a resident of the South Pacific, says it is right to bury one's father alive on his sixtieth birthday, irrespective of his state of health; and suppose I say this is not right. Are we talking about the same thing? Not necessarily. The kind of situation Mr. A has in mind is likely to be very different from the kind of situation I have in mind. Perhaps he is assuming that the body one will have in the next world will be exactly like the kind one has just before departing this life (and hence, may think it advisable to depart before feebleness sets in); whereas I may think one has no further existence at all after one's earthly demise. He is talking about burying alive a father who will exist in the next world in a certain kind of body; and I am not. In this situation, it is only confusing to say that our ethical opinions "conflict." Let us say that two people are *talking about the same subject* only in the following situation. Let us suppose A and B make conflicting ethical predications about something or some kind of thing, ostensibly the same for both. But suppose further there is some property P that A more or less consciously believes this thing or kind of thing has, whereas B does *not* believe this. Further, let us suppose that if A *ceased* to believe this, he would cease to have the same ethical opinion about it but agree with B; and let us suppose that if B *began* to believe this (other things being equal), he would change his ethical opinion and agree with A. In this case, let us say that A and B are *not* appraising the same subject. But if there is no more-or-less conscious belief having the status described, then we shall say that they *are* talking about the same subject, and that their ethical opinions are conflicting.

But now, finally, what is the meaning of the phrase "equally valid"? In order to clarify this, let us draw a parallel with language we use in appraising scientific theories. Suppose we have two conflicting theories about natural phenomena. Each of these theories might explain a large part of the known facts, but not all of them, at least not very well. We might then say, "In the light of presently known facts, the two theories are equally plausible." On the other hand, we might make a more radical supposition. Suppose, when thinking about these theories, we make the daring forecast about future evidence, that when scientific investigation has been indefinitely prolonged and all possible experimental data are in, both of these theories will explain all the facts, and there will be no ground for a rational preference of one to the other, although parts of the two theories do contradict each other. In this case, we might say, although this sounds startling, "Although these theories are mutually contradictory in some respects, they are both *valid*." What a person who made such a statement would be saying is that the use of a refined inductive logic, on a complete set of experimental data, would support as strongly confirmed *both* of two conflicting theories. We need not argue whether in fact this case ever does or even could arise, but we can understand the possibility, and the important thing is the parallel with ethics. Now, the ethical relativist is not merely making the uninteresting claim, when he says two conflicting ethical statements are equally valid, that the two statements are equally plausible in the light of the facts known at present. He is saying something much more radical, about what would happen if one were testing these statements by the best possible ethical methodology, and in the light of a complete system of factual or nonethical knowledge. In other words, he is saying that the application of a "rational" method in ethics would support, equally, two conflicting ethical statements even if there were available a complete system of factual knowledge—or else that there is no "rational" method in ethics comparable to an ideal inductive method for empirical science.

I have used the phrase "rational method in ethics" as designating something roughly parallel in ethics to inductive logic in empirical science. This idea will be familiar to us from the preceding chapter, where we argued that the Qualified Attitude Method has this status.

We can now explain exactly what it means to say that two conflicting ethical statements are "equally valid." What it means to say this, is that *either* there is *no* unique rational or justified method in ethics, *or* that the use of the unique rational method in ethics, in the presence of an ideally complete system of factual knowledge, would still not enable us to make a distinction between the ethical statements being considered.

The ethical relativist asserts that there are at least *some* instances of conflicting ethical opinions that are equally valid in this sense.

There are more, and less, radical relativists. The more radical kind of relativist asserts that there are conflicting ethical opinions and that there is *no unique rational method in ethics.* To mark this, let us call him a "methodological relativist" or an "ethical skeptic." The less radical relativist does not say there is no unique rational method, but says that there are still some instances of conflicting ethical opinions that are equally valid. Let us call him a "non-methodological relativist." We must look at the logic of, and the evidence

supporting, these two kinds of relativism separately. . . .

. . . Ethical relativism may be true, in the sense that there are *some* cases of conflicting ethical judgments that are equally valid; but it would be a mistake to take it as a truth with pervasive scope. Relativism as an emphasis is misleading, because it draws our attention away from the central identities, from widespread agreement on the items we care most about. Furthermore, the actual agreement on the central things suggests the possibiity that, with better understanding of the facts, the scope of agreement would be much wider.

A Special Brand of Ethics for Relativists?

So much, then, for the truth and scope of the relativist principle: "There are conflicting ethical opinions that are equally valid."

Acceptance of this principle, we have said, by our definition makes one an "ethical relativist." But we noted at the beginning of this chapter that relativists often espouse some further thesis—a particular ethical commitment, which they may regard as being implied by the foregoing principle of relativism. Protagoras, we saw, urged that people *should* follow the conventions of their group. An executive committee of the American Anthropological Association, in a published statement on human rights, included the remark that "*respect* for differences between cultures is *validated* by the scientific fact that no technique of qualitatively evaluating cultures has been discovered."[2] Also, Ruth Benedict closed her *Patterns of Culture* with these words:

The recognition of cultural relativity carries with it its own values, which need not be those of the absolutist philosophies. It challenges customary opinions. . . . It rouses pessimism because it throws old formulae into confusion. . . . As soon as the new opinion is embraced as customary belief, it will be another trusted bulwark of the good life. We shall arrive then at a more realistic social faith, accepting as grounds of hope and as new bases for tolerance the co-existing and equally valid patterns of life which mankind has created for itself from the raw materials of existence.[3]

This same theme of tolerance was sounded by Professor Melville Herskovits, who wrote in an influential book: "The relativist point of view brings into relief the *validity* of every set of norms *for* the people whose lives are guided by them."[4]

Other inferences from the relativist view are different. As the writer has heard some students put it, "If all moral codes are equally valid, why should one not change to a code that is somewhat *less demanding* on the individual?"

Are there really any such *ethical consequences* of the relativist thesis we have been discussing? Or, irrespective of whether these views are implied by relativism, are they defensible on their own merits as part of an ethical creed for relativists? To try to answer these questions is to engage in a discussion of *normative* ethics as distinct from critical ethics. But let us do this. Let us look at *tolerance* as an ideal for ethical relativists.

The first question we must ask is whether the advocate of tolerance as a creed for relativists is saying that tolerance is only one among "equally valid" conflicting ethical opinions. Does he, that is, say that *intolerance* is equally as valid as tolerance, or not? He could be saying this: "We relativists, for our part, espouse the value of tolerance. But, as scientists, we recognize that intolerance is equally valid." Is relativism with its plea for tolerance only a "point of view," like another culture? Or is tolerance a value securely founded on the methods of science?

Perhaps we do best to answer these questions by considering what relativists can *consistently* say, not

2. *American Anthropologist* XLIX (1947); 539–43; italics mine.

3. Ruth Benedict, *Patterns of Culture* (Boston: Houghton Mifflin Company, 1934), p. 278.

4. *Man and His Words* (New York: Alfred A. Knopf, Inc., 1948), p. 76. Professor Asher Moore, in "Emotivism: Theory and Practice," *Journal of Philosophy* LV (1958), 375–82, contends that the relativist thesis teaches the normative ideal of charity toward the ethical views of others.

what they actually do say. (We must remember that anthropologists are not familiar with the terminology of philosophers, and we should not read too much into the use of words like "valid" and "validated." Furthermore, very possibly the writers we have quoted had not considered their words carefully.)

Suppose one is a methodological relativist, a skeptic. Suppose he holds the emotive theory about the meaning and function of ethical language, and believes that there is no unique rational method for criticizing ethical opinions. In this case, he will have no use for the phrase "is a valid view" in ethics (except as a mode of expressing his own ethical views, tantamount to "That is right"), although he may say that various conflicting views are "equally valid," as a way of stating his metaethical theory that there is no unique rational method in ethics. Now, according to this view, the value of intolerance is as justified (or unjustified) as that of tolerance. So why should he advocate it? Certainly there can be no reason in the sense that the correctness of such a position follows from the facts of science; indeed, according to this theory *no* ethical thesis has this status. One who is a relativist might easily as well say, "Since no system is more valid than any other, let each of us advance his own!" So, *intolerance* could be the outcome of relativism. Nevertheless, there may be something about the relativist doctrine that tends to *incline the attitudes* of its advocates toward tolerance, not only in the sense of not condemning any moral systems, but in the sense of active advocacy of a policy of encouraging, say, members of primitive groups to retain their distinctive and traditional moral patterns. It may be that Ruth Benedict meant no more than this when she wrote that "recognition" of relativity "carries with it its own values." If there is this causal influence of the doctrine of relativism on the values of its advocates, we must simply recognize it. There is no inconsistency between relativism and praising tolerance (and so forth)—as there is no inconsistency between relativism and praising anything you please. It is consistent, then, (1) to be a relativist, (2) to be influenced causally by one's convictions in the direction of tolerance, and (3) to give expression to one's favorable attitudes to tolerance by praising tolerance. It is *not* consistent for a methodological relativist to claim that tolerance has a status of "greater validity" (in the sense we gave this term) than intolerance, though he may condemn intolerance, in moral language, to his heart's content. Further, it is *not* consistent for a methodological relativist to say that the correctness of the ideal of tolerance "follows" from the facts of science, or from the theoretical position of methodological relativism, or from any other fact.

But suppose one is less radical a relativist—a relativist of the nonmethodological variety. What then? In this case, one does not necessarily say that *all* moral judgments are only as valid as conflicting ones. At least, one is committed by the definition of "relativism" only to saying that some are so. One is, of course, also not committed by the definition to saying that *only* some moral judgments have this status. A nonmethodological relativist may be, as we suggested, a one hundred per cent relativist or only a one per cent relativist. The point is that he does think there is a "unique rational method" that in principle might identify some moral judgments as unacceptable; this leaves much room for difference of opinion about whether a few, or many, ethical judgments are only as valid as some competing ones. Now, the consequence is that a relativist *can* consistently say that *tolerance is justified*—that this matter is one about which it is not true that conflicting opinions are equally valid. He *can* hold this—although he *cannot* reasonably say that the relativistic thesis *logically entails* such a view; obviously it entails no such thing.

One may ask such a relativist, however, how he can justify *wholesale* tolerance, including tolerance for social practices about which there are *not* two conflicting and equally justified moral opinions— assuming he thinks that there are some points about which only one moral opinion is justified. Can he, for instance, justify tolerance for intolerance?

Our question, however, needs to be clarified. Indeed, one source of confusion about the present issue has been a failure to distinguish two quite different issues, and two corresponding senses of "tolerance." In one sense of "tolerance," we may speak of tolerating a man and his opinions, in the sense of feeling and showing respect for him and his opinions. But one can have respect for a man and his convictions, and nevertheless believe his views happen to be mistaken; one can respect a man and yet be motivated to try to change his views, or even, if the matter is serious, take action to place legal restrictions on his ability to put his opinions into practice. We may respect the conscientious objector in wartime; but we may find it necessary to make it a crime to preach his doctrine.

Tolerance in the first sense is a firmly entrenched part of the Anglo-American moral system, among relativists and absolutists alike. It is traditional to have respect for the sincere moral opinions of others even when we differ with them. We do not blame sincere conscientious objectors, even if we think them mistaken and confused. There are limits to such respect, however. If a man commits a hideous crime, and defends himself on the ground that his conscience told him to do it, we do not excuse him, but think so much the worse of his conscience for having advised him as it did. We regard him as a bad man, no better for what he chooses to call the advice of conscience. In other words, we think there is a certain range within which decent people can have differences of opinion; when a person goes beyond this range, we accuse him of rationalizing or insensitivity. Things are somewhat different when a person with whom we disagree comes from another culture. In such cases, we stretch the range of tolerance; we feel there is, on account of cultural background, an excuse for moral opinions or actions we should not tolerate from a member of our cultural tradition. Even here, however, the stretch is possibly not indefinite. For instance, if a headhunter took the life of a child with no mercy or qualms, what should we think? It is hard to say. At any rate, the point is that we do not *blame* people for their actions insofar as they are consonant with their own moral convictions—within certain limits.

Now, is it tolerance only in this sense that some relativists wish to advocate? If so, no one need quarrel with them—unless they say that the morality of tolerance is entailed by the thesis of relativism, or that it is the special preserve of relativists, which it certainly is not. But sometimes they seem to go further. When they say that a given people's standards are *valid* for them, they seem to be saying that we should *advise* or at least *not discourage* people from conforming to their traditional moral doctrines; that groups like the United Nations should *take no steps to interfere* with local practices like slavery or racial discrimination, no matter how horrible they may be. In other words, some relativists seem to advocate, *wholesale, condoning* the accepted practices of other peoples.

How can the relativist justify this? Let us repeat that no such moral statement is logically entailed by the thesis of methodological relativism. We may concede, of course, that there is perhaps a tendency for a relativist to develop favorable attitudes toward the distinctive practices of individual groups, and to be inclined to urge conformity to these practices (no matter how devastating to the welfare of the natives). We also agree that there is no inconsistency in this. But nonmethodological relativism leaves open the possibility that there are *not* two conflicting but equally valid opinions about slavery, or putting people to death on the basis of witchcraft accusations, or denying a person civil and political rights because of his color. Then, if there are not two equally valid opinions on these matters, how can the relativist advocate that we condone such practices, wholesale? If the relativist view on these matters is to be justified, he has no alternative but to argue each issue on its merits, on the basis of evaluated moral principles, and unless conflicting opinions are equally valid on *every* issue, the relativist is not justified in advocating wholesale tolerance for everything, in this second sense of "tolerance," unless there is some general moral argument for condoning the accepted practices of other groups.

Some relativists do offer such

a general moral argument for tolerance in this sense. Let us look at it. Briefly, it is that every working set of institutions is better for its practitioners than chaos, for every such set of institutions serves important functions, else the group would not have managed to survive. Now, it is argued, one should avoid interfering with such systems, because interference may destroy.

This reasoning, however, is unimpressive. It takes for granted a monolithic cohesion and inflexibility of institutional systems that is unproved. Why will a whole way of life collapse if we forbid headhunting, abolish slavery, forbid death penalties for conviction on witchcraft charges? Why must any interference be crippling to a way of life? It is far from obvious why there should not be interference to root out an institution that produces slavery.

Methodological relativism, then, may lead (psychologically, not logically) to advocating tolerance; but it is inconsistent for such a relativist to claim that tolerance has any objective superiority to intolerance. *Nonmethodological* relativism *permits* saying that tolerance is valid and intolerance not. But equally it leaves open the possibility of determining the one and only one justified opinion on many ethical issues. Therefore, it is not easy to see how a relativist is justified in a wholesale advocacy of tolerance in the sense of condoning unjustifiable behavior unless he produces some reasons that have as yet not been produced.

Let us consider the question, "If all moral codes are equally valid, why should one not change to a code that is somewhat *less demanding* on the individual?" In reply to this, two comments are pertinent. In the first place, we have already noticed (Chapter 4) that the ethical convictions of our social group are by no means necessarily correct. If we have doubts about a given standard, we can review it, apply the "rational" methods of ethical reflection to it; and if it does not stand up, then it would seem that normally the thing to do is to admit it and to start practicing the standard that can be justified (although whether we should raises a further moral issue). If a standard is repressive and makes no sense, it needs review; and we do not have to go afield and find a society with different standards, to have reason to question the prevailing convictions of our group. But there is a second point. Suppose we have reviewed some issue, and have applied the "standard" method, and have come to the conclusion that people *should* do a certain thing. However, as it happens, we *prefer* to do something else. Further, suppose we find another society with a valid standard that permits us to do what we want to do. Does relativism justify our doing what we wish to do? It is not obvious that it does, for, if we have reviewed the problem with the "standard" method and have come to a certain conclusion, there is certainly question whether the code of this other society *is* "equally valid."

It is not impossible that there could be reason to think it so; and it is puzzling whether, if this situation did arise, there would be an obligation to follow one's own assessment of the situation. Perhaps there is a moral principle: "Each person is obligated to follow the judgment arrived at by his own application of the standard method." Whether there is, perhaps we can decide later.

As a result of all this discussion, what do we conclude theoretically, in our critical ethics? First, we reject methodological relativism, on the ground that in the preceding chapter we showed that there is a "standard" method for evaluating moral statements, and that there are good and sufficient reasons for using this method. But second, we decided that nonmethodological relativism is not inconsistent with our having a "standard" method—although to decide this we had to discuss further what the standard method is. Moreover, we decided that, although the issue is a fine one, the evidence rather supports the view that different persons could apply the standard method properly and come out with conflicting answers to *some* ethical questions. To this extent, we agree with the view of the nonmethodological relativist. However, to say this, is not to say that there can be two conflicting but equally valid opinions on all, or many, or even important ethical issues. The serious question is: On what ethical issues can we show that one and only one opinion is correct? But this question is the question of normative ethics. . . .

14

What Utilitarianism Is

JOHN STUART MILL

... The creed which accepts as the foundation of morals, Utility, or the Greatest Happiness Principle, holds that actions are right in proportion as they tend to promote happiness, wrong as they tend to produce the reverse of happiness. By happiness is intended pleasure, and the absence of pain; by unhappiness, pain, and the privation of pleasure. To give a clear view of the moral standard set up by the theory, much more requires to be said; in particular, what things it includes in the ideas of pain and pleasure; and to what extent this is left an open question. But these supplementary explanations do not affect the theory of life on which this theory of morality is grounded—namely, that pleasure, and freedom from pain, are the only things desirable as ends; and that all desirable things (which are as numerous in the utilitarian as in any other scheme) are desirable either for the pleasure inherent in themselves, or as means to the promotion of pleasure and the prevention of pain.

Now, such a theory of life excites in many minds, and among them in some of the most estimable in feeling and purpose, inveterate dislike. To suppose that life has (as they express it) no higher end than pleasure—no better and nobler object of desire and pursuit—they designate as utterly mean and grovelling; as a doctrine worthy only of swine, to whom the followers of Epicurus were, at a very early period, contemptuously likened; and modern holders of the doctrine are occasionally made the subject of equally polite comparisons by its German, French, and English assailants.

When thus attacked, the Epicureans have always answered, that it is not they, but their accusers, who represent human nature in a de-

[From *Utilitarianism,* chapter 2, 4th edition (1871). First published in 1861.]

grading light; since the accusation supposes human beings to be capable of no pleasures except those of which swine are capable. If this supposition were true, the charge could not be gainsaid, but would then be no longer an imputation; for if the sources of pleasure were precisely the same to human beings and to swine, the rule of life which is good enough for the one would be good enough for the other. The comparison of the Epicurean life to that of beasts is felt as degrading, precisely because a beast's pleasures do not satisfy a human being's conceptions of happiness. Human beings have faculties more elevated than the animal appetites, and when once made conscious of them, do not regard anything as happiness which does not include their gratification. I do not, indeed, consider the Epicureans to have been by any means faultless in drawing out their scheme of consequences from the utilitarian principle. To do this in any sufficient manner, many Stoic, as well as Christian elements require to be included. But there is no known Epicurean theory of life which does not assign to the pleasures of the intellect, of the feelings and imagination, and of the moral sentiments, a much higher value as pleasures than to those of mere sensation. It must be admitted, however, that utilitarian writers in general have placed the superiority of mental over bodily pleasures chiefly in the greater permanency, safety, uncostliness, etc., of the former—that is, in their circumstantial advantages rather than in their intrinsic nature. And on all these points utilitarians have fully proved their case; but they might have taken the other, and, as it may be called, higher ground, with entire consistency. It is quite compatible with the principle of utility to recognise the fact, that some *kinds* of pleasure are more desirable and more valuable than others. It would be absurd that while, in estimating all other things, quality is considered as well as quantity, the estimation of pleasures should be supposed to depend on quantity alone.

If I am asked, what I mean by difference of quality in pleasures, or what makes one pleasure more valuable than another, merely as a pleasure, except its being greater in amount, there is but one possible answer. Of two pleasures, if there be one to which all or almost all who have experience of both give a decided preference, irrespective of any feeling of moral obligation to prefer it, that is the more desirable pleasure. If one of the two is, by those who are competently acquainted with both, placed so far above the other that they prefer it, even though knowing it to be attended with a greater amount of discontent, and would not resign it for any quantity of the other pleasure which their nature is capable of, we are justified in ascribing to the preferred enjoyment a superiority in quality, so far outweighing quantity as to render it, in comparison, of small account.

Now it is an unquestionable fact that those who are equally acquainted with, and equally capable of appreciating and enjoying, both, do give a most marked preference to the manner of existence which employs their higher faculties. Few human creatures would consent to be changed into any of the lower animals, for a promise of the fullest allowance of a beast's pleasures; no intelligent human being would consent to be a fool, no instructed person would be an ignoramus, no person of feeling and conscience would be selfish and base, even though they should be persuaded that the fool, the dunce, or the rascal is better satisfied with his lot than they are with theirs. They would not resign what they possess more than he, for the most complete satisfaction of all the desires which they have in common with him. If they ever fancy they would, it is only in cases of unhappiness so extreme, that to escape from it they would exchange their lot for almost any other, however undesirable in their own eyes. A being of higher faculties requires more to make him happy, is capable probably of more acute suffering, and is certainly accessible to it at more points, than one of an inferior type; but in spite of these liabilities, he can never really wish to sink into what he feels to be a lower grade of existence. We may give what explanation we please to this unwillingness; we may attribute it to pride, a name which is given indiscriminately to some of the most and to some of the least estimable feelings of which mankind are capable; we may refer it to the love of liberty and personal independence, an appeal to which was with the Stoics one of the most effective means for the inculcation of it; to the love of power, or to the love of excitement, both of which do really enter into and contribute to it: but its most appropriate appellation is a sense of dignity, which all human beings possess in one form or other, and in some, though by no means in exact, proportion to their higher faculties, and which is so essential a part of the happiness of those in whom it is strong, that nothing which conflicts with it could be, otherwise than momentarily, an object of desire to them. Whoever supposes that this preference takes place at a sacrifice of happiness—that the superior being, in anything like equal circumstances, is not happier than the inferior—confounds the two very different ideas, of happiness, and content. It is indisputable that the being whose capacities of enjoyment are low, has the greatest chance of having them fully satisfied; and a highly-endowed being will always feel that any happiness which he can look for, as the world is constituted, is imperfect. But he can learn to bear its imperfections, if they are at all bearable; and they will not make him envy the being who is indeed unconscious of the imperfections, but only because he feels not at all the good which those imperfections qualify. It is better to be a human being dissatisfied than a pig satisfied; better to be Socrates dissatisfied than a fool satisfied. And if the fool, or the pig, is of a different opinion, it is because they only know their own side of the question. The other party to the comparison knows both sides.

It may be objected, that many who are capable of the higher pleasures, occasionally, under the influence of temptation, postpone them to the lower. But this is quite compatible with a full appreciation of the intrinsic superiority of the higher. Men often, from infirmity of character, make their election for the nearer good, though they know it to be the less valuable; and this no less when the choice is between two bodily pleasures, than when it is between bodily and mental. They pursue sensual indulgences to the injury of health, though perfectly aware that health is the greater good. It may be further objected, that many who begin with youthful enthusiasm for everything noble, as they advance in years sink into indolence and selfishness. But I do not believe that those who undergo this very common change, voluntarily choose the lower description of pleasures in preference to the higher. I believe

that before they devote themselves exclusively to the one, they have already become incapable of the other. Capacity for the nobler feelings is in most natures a very tender plant, easily killed, not only by hostile influences, but by mere want of sustenance; and in the majority of young persons it speedily dies away if the occupations to which their position in life has devoted them, and the society into which it has thrown them, are not favourable to keeping that higher capacity in exercise. Men lose their high aspirations as they lose their intellectual tastes, because they have not time or opportunity for indulging them; and they addict themselves to inferior pleasures, not because they deliberately prefer them, but because they are either the only ones to which they have access, or the only ones which they are any longer capable of enjoying. It may be questioned whether any one who has remained equally susceptible to both classes of pleasures, ever knowingly and calmly preferred the lower; though many, in all ages, have broken down in an ineffectual attempt to combine both.

From this verdict of the only competent judges, I apprehend there can be no appeal. On a question which is the best worth having of two pleasures, or which of two modes of existence is the most grateful to the feelings, apart from its moral attributes and from its consequences, the judgment of those who are qualified by knowledge of both, or, if they differ, that of the majority among them, must be admitted as final. And there needs be the less hesitation to accept this judgment respecting the quality of pleasures, since there is no other tribunal to be referred to even on the question of quantity. What means are there of determining which is the acutest of two pains, or the intensest of two pleasurable sensations, except the general suffrage of those who are familiar with both? Neither pains nor pleasures are homogeneous, and pain is always heterogeneous with pleasure. What is there to decide whether a particular pleasure is worth purchasing at the cost of a particular pain, except the feelings and judgment of the experienced? When, therefore, those feelings and judgment declare the pleasures derived from the higher faculties to be preferable *in kind,* apart from the question of intensity, to those of which the animal nature, disjoined from the higher faculties, is susceptible, they are entitled on this subject to the same regard.

I have dwelt on this point, as being a necessary part of a perfectly just conception of Utility or Happiness, considered as the directive rule of human conduct. But it is by no means an indispensable condition to the acceptance of the utilitarian standard; for that standard is not the agent's own greatest happiness, but the greatest amount of happiness altogether; and if it may possibly be doubted whether a noble character is always the happier for its nobleness, there can be no doubt that it makes other people happier, and that the world in general is immensely a gainer by it. Utilitarianism, therefore, could only attain its end by the general cultivation of nobleness of character, even if each individual were only benefited by the nobleness of others, and his own, so far as happiness is concerned, were a sheer deduction from the benefit. But the bare enunciation of such an absurdity as this last, renders refutation superfluous.

According to the Greatest Happiness Principle, as above explained, the ultimate end, with reference to and for the sake of which all other things are desirable (whether we are considering our own good or that of other people), is an existence exempt as far as possible from pain, and as rich as possible in enjoyments, both in point of quantity and quality; the test of quality, and the rule for measuring it against quantity, being the preference felt by those who, in their opportunities of experience, to which must be added their habits of self-consciousness and self-observation, are best furnished with the means of comparison. This, being, according to the utilitarian opinion, the end of human action, is necessarily also the standard of morality; which may accordingly be defined, the rules and precepts for human conduct, by the observance of which an existence such as has been described might be, to the greatest extent possible, secured to all mankind; and not to them only, but, so far as the nature of things admits, to the whole sentient creation. . . .

. . . The main constituents of a satisfied life appear to be two, either of which by itself is often found sufficient for the purpose: tranquillity, and excitement. With much tranquillity, many find that they can be content with very little pleasure: with much excitement, many can reconcile themselves to a considerable quantity of pain. There is assuredly no inherent impossibility in enabling even the mass of mankind to unite both; since the two are so far from being incompatible that they are in natural alliance, the prolongation of either being a preparation for, and exciting a wish for, the other. It is only those in whom indolence amounts to a vice, that do not desire excitement after an interval of repose; it is only those in whom the need of excitement is a disease, that feel the tranquillity which follows excitement dull and insipid, instead of pleasurable in direct proportion to the excitement which preceded it. When people who are tolerably fortunate in their outward lot do not find in life sufficient enjoyment to make it valuable to them, the cause generally is, caring for nobody but themselves. To those who have neither public nor private affections, the excitements of life are much curtailed, and in any case dwindle in value as the time

approaches when all selfish interests must be terminated by death: while those who leave after them objects of personal affection, and especially those who have also cultivated a fellow-feeling with the collective interests of mankind, retain as lively an interest in life on the eve of death as in the vigour of youth and health. Next to selfishness, the principal cause which makes life unsatisfactory, is want of mental cultivation. A cultivated mind—I do not mean that of a philosopher, but any mind to which the fountains of knowledge have been opened, and which has been taught, in any tolerable degree, to exercise its faculties—finds sources of inexhaustible interest in all that surrounds it; in the objects of nature, the achievements of art, the imaginations of poetry, the incidents of history, the ways of mankind past and present, and their prospects in the future. It is possible, indeed, to become indifferent to all this, and that too without having exhausted a thousandth part of it; but only when one has had from the beginning no moral or human interest in these things, and has sought in them only the gratification of curiosity. . . .

And this leads to the true estimation of what is said by the objectors concerning the possibility, and the obligation, of learning to do without happiness. Unquestionably it is possible to do without happiness; it is done involuntarily by nineteen-twentieths of mankind, even in those parts of our present world which are least deep in barbarism; and it often has to be done voluntarily by the hero or the martyr, for the sake of something which he prizes more than his individual happiness. But this something, what is it, unless the happiness of others, or some of the requisites of happiness? It is noble to be capable of resigning entirely one's own portion of happiness, or chances of it: but, after all, this self-sacrifice must be for some end; it is not its own end; and if we are told that its end is not happiness, but virtue, which is better than happiness, I ask, would the sacrifice be made if the hero or martyr did not believe that it would earn for others immunity from similar sacrifices? Would it be made, if he thought that his renunciation of happiness for himself would produce no fruit for any of his fellow creatures, but to make their lot like his, and place them also in the condition of persons who have renounced happiness? All honour to those who can abnegate for themselves the personal enjoyment of life, when by such renunciation they contribute worthily to increase the amount of happiness in the world; but he who does it, or professes to do it, for any other purpose, is no more deserving of admiration than the ascetic mounted on his pillar. He may be an inspiriting proof of what men *can* do, but assuredly not an example of what they *should*.

Though it is only in a very imperfect state of the world's arrangements that any one can best serve the happiness of others by the absolute sacrifice of his own, yet so long as the world is in that imperfect state, I fully acknowledge that the readiness to make such a sacrifice is the highest virtue which can be found in man. I will add, that in this condition of the world, paradoxical as the assertion may be, the conscious ability to do without happiness gives the best prospect of realizing such happiness as is attainable. For nothing except that consciousness can raise a person above the chances of life, by making him feel that, let fate and fortune do their worst, they have not power to subdue him: which, once felt, frees him from excess of anxiety concerning the evils of life, and enables him, like many a Stoic in the worst times of the Roman Empire, to cultivate in tranquillity the sources of satisfaction accessible to him, without concerning himself about the uncertainty of their duration, any more than about their inevitable end.

Meanwhile, let utilitarians never cease to claim the morality of self-devotion as a possession which belongs by as good a right to them, as either to the Stoic or to the Transcendentalist. The utilitarian morality does recognise in human beings the power of sacrificing their own greatest good for the good of others. It only refuses to admit that the sacrifice is itself a good. A sacrifice which does not increase, or tend to increase, the sum total of happiness, it considers as wasted. The only self-renunciation which it applauds, is devotion to the happiness, or to some of the means of happiness, of others; either of mankind collectively, or of individuals within the limits imposed by the collective interests of mankind. . . .

Again, defenders of utility often find themselves called upon to reply to such objections as this—that there is not time, previous to action, for calculating and weighing the effects of any line of conduct on the general happiness. This is exactly as if any one were to say that it is impossible to guide our conduct by Christianity, because there is not time, on every occasion on which anything has to be done, to read through the Old and New Testaments. The answer to the objection is, that there has been ample time, namely, the whole past duration of the human species. During all that time mankind have been learning by experience the tendencies of actions; on which experience all the prudence, as well as all the morality of life, is dependent. People talk as if the commencement of this course of experience had hitherto been put off, and as if, at the moment when some man feels tempted to meddle with the property or life of another, he had to begin considering for the first time whether murder and theft are injurious to human happiness. Even then I do not think that he would find the question very puzzling; but, at all events, the matter is now done to his hand. It is truly a whimsical supposition that if mankind were agreed in considering utility to be the test of morality, they would remain without any agreement as to what *is* useful, and would take no measures for having their notions on the subject taught to the young, and enforced by law and opinion. There is no difficulty in proving any ethical standard whatever to work ill, if we suppose universal idiocy to be conjoined with it; but on any hypothesis short of that, mankind must by this time have acquired positive beliefs as to the effects of some actions on their happiness; and the beliefs which have thus come down are the rules of morality for the multitude, and for the philosopher until he has succeeded in finding better. That philosophers might easily do this, even now, on many subjects; that the received code of ethics is by no means of divine right; and that mankind have still much to learn as to the effects of actions on the general happiness, I admit, or rather, earnestly maintain. The corollaries from the principle of utility, like the precepts of every practical art, admit of indefinite improvement, and, in a progressive state of the human mind, their improvement is perpetually going on. But to consider the rules of morality as improvable, is one thing; to pass over the intermediate generalizations entirely, and endeavour to test each individual action directly by the first principle, is another. It is a strange notion that the acknowledgement of a first principle is inconsistent with the admission of secondary ones. To inform a traveller respecting the place of his ultimate destination, is not to forbid the use of landmarks and direction-posts on the way. The proposition that happiness is the end and aim of morality, does not mean that no road ought to be laid down to that goal, or that persons going thither should not be advised to take one direction rather than another. Men really ought to leave off talking a kind of nonsense on this subject, which they would neither talk nor listen to on other matters of practical concernment. Nobody argues that the art of navigation is not founded on astronomy, because sailors cannot wait to calculate the Nautical Almanack. Being rational creatures, they go to sea with it ready calculated; and all rational creatures go out upon the sea of life with their minds made up on the common questions of right and wrong, as well as on many of the far more difficult questions of wise and foolish. And this, as long as foresight is a human quality, it is to be presumed they will continue to do. Whatever we adopt as the fundamental principle of morality, we require subordinate principles to apply it by: the impossibility of doing without them, being common to all systems, can afford no argument against any one in particular: but gravely to argue as if no such secondary principles could be had, and as if mankind had remained till now,

and always must remain, without drawing any general conclusions from the experience of human life, is as high a pitch, I think, as absurdity has ever reached in philosophical controversy. . . .

. . . It is not the fault of any creed, but of the complicated nature of human affairs, that rules of conduct cannot be so framed as to require no exceptions, and that hardly any kind of action can safely be laid down as either always obligatory or always condemnable. There is no ethical creed which does not temper the rigidity of its laws, by giving a certain latitude, under the moral responsibility of the agent, for accommodation to peculiarities of circumstances; and under every creed, at the opening thus made, self-deception and dishonest casuistry get in. There exists no moral system under which there do not arise unequivocal cases of conflicting obligation. These are the real difficulties, the knotty points both in the theory of ethics, and in the conscientious guidance of personal conduct. They are overcome practically with greater or with less success according to the intellect and virtue of the individual; but it can hardly be pretended that any one will be the less qualified for dealing with them, from possessing an ultimate standard to which conflicting rights and duties can be referred. If utility is the ultimate source of moral obligations, utility may be invoked to decide between them when their demands are incompatible. Though the application of the standard may be difficult, it is better than none at all: while in other systems, the moral laws all claiming independent authority, there is no common umpire entitled to interfere between them; their claims to precedence one over another rest on little better than sophistry, and unless determined, as they generally are, by the unacknowledged influence of considerations of utility, afford a free scope for the action of personal desires and partialities. We must remember that only in these cases of conflict between secondary principles is it requisite that first principles should be appealed to. There is no case of moral obligation in which some secondary principle is not involved; and if only one, there can seldom be any real doubt which one it is, in the mind of any person by whom the principle itself is recognised.

15

Morality and the Good Will

IMMANUEL KANT

The Good Will

Nothing in the whole world, or even outside of the world, can possibly be regarded as good without limitation except a *good will*. No doubt it is a good and desirable thing to have intelligence, sagacity, judgment, and other intellectual gifts, by whatever name they may be called; it is also good and desirable in many respects to possess by nature such qualities as courage, resolution, and perseverance; but all these gifts of nature may be in the highest degree pernicious and hurtful, if the will which directs them, or what is called the *character,* is not itself good. The same thing applies to *gifts of fortune.* Power, wealth, honour, even good health, and that general well-being and contentment with one's lot which we call *happiness,* give rise to pride and not infrequently to insolence, if a man's will is not good; nor can a reflective and impartial spectator ever look with satisfaction upon the unbroken prosperity of a man who is destitute of the ornament of a pure and good will. A good will would therefore seem to be the indispensable condition without which no one is even worthy to be happy.

A man's will is good, not because the consequences which flow from it are good, nor because it is capable of attaining the end which it seeks, but it is good in itself, or because it wills the good. By a good will is not meant mere well-wishing; it consists in a resolute employment of all the means within one's reach, and its intrinsic value is in no way increased by success or lessened by failure.

This idea of the absolute value of mere will seems so extraordinary that, although it is endorsed even by

[From *The Metaphysics of Morality* (1785), sections I, II. Translated by John Watson (1888).]

the popular judgment, we must subject it to careful scrutiny.

If nature had meant to provide simply for the maintenance, the well-being, in a word the happiness, of beings which have reason and will, it must be confessed that, in making use of their reason, it has hit upon a very poor way of attaining its end. As a matter of fact the very worst way a man of refinement and culture can take to secure enjoyment and happiness is to make use of his reason for that purpose. Hence there is apt to arise in his mind a certain degree of *misology,* or hatred of reason. Finding that the arts which minister to luxury, and even the sciences, instead of bringing him happiness, only lay a heavier yoke on his neck, he at length comes to envy, rather than to despise, men of less refinement, who follow more closely the promptings of their natural impulses, and pay little heed to what reason tells them to do or to leave undone. It must at least be admitted, that one may deny reason to have much or indeed any value in the production of happiness and contentment, without taking a morose or ungrateful view of the goodness with which the world is governed. Such a judgment really means that life has another and a much nobler end than happiness, and that the true vocation of reason is to secure that end.

The true object of reason then, in so far as it is practical, or capable of influencing the will, must be to produce a will which is *good in itself,* and not merely good *as a means* to something else. This will is not the only or the whole good, but it is the highest good, and the condition of all other good, even of the desire for happiness itself. It is therefore not inconsistent with the wisdom of nature that the cultivation of reason which is essential to the furtherance of its first and unconditioned object, the production of a good will, should, in this life at least, in many ways limit, or even make impossible, the attainment of happiness, which is its second and conditioned object.

To bring to clear consciousness the conception of a will which is good in itself, a conception already familiar to the popular mind, let us examine the conception of *duty,* which involves the idea of a good will as manifested under certain subjective limitations and hindrances.

I pass over actions which are admittedly violations of duty, for these, however useful they may be in the attainment of this or that end, manifestly do not proceed *from* duty. I set aside also those actions which are not actually inconsistent with duty, but which yet are done under the impulse of some natural inclination, although *not a direct inclination* to do these particular actions; for in these it is easy to determine whether the action that is consistent with duty, is done *from duty* or with some selfish object in view. It is more difficult to make a clear distinction of motives when there is a *direct* inclination to do a certain action, which is itself in conformity with duty. The preservation of one's own life, for instance, is a duty; but, as everyone has a natural inclination to preserve his life, the anxious care which most men usually devote to this object, has no intrinsic value, nor the maxim from which they act any moral import. They preserve their life *in accordance with* duty, but not *because of* duty. But, suppose adversity and hopeless sorrow to have taken away all desire for life; suppose that the wretched man would welcome death as a release, and yet takes means to prolong his life simply from a sense of duty; then his maxim has a genuine moral import.

But, secondly, an action that is done from duty gets its moral value, *not from the object* which it is intended to secure, but from the maxim by which it is determined. Accordingly, the action has the same moral value whether the object is attained or not, if only the *principle* by which the will is determined to act is independent of every object of sensuous desire. What was said above makes it clear, that it is not the object aimed at, or, in other words, the consequences which flow from an action when these are made the end and motive of the will, that can give to the action an unconditioned and moral value. In what, then, can the moral value of an action consist, if it does not lie in the will itself, as

directed to the attainment of a certain object? It can lie only in the principle of the will, no matter whether the object sought can be attained by the action or not. For the will stands as it were at the parting of the ways, between its *a priori* principle, which is formal, and its *a posteriori* material motive. As so standing it must be determined by something, and, as no action which is done from duty can be determined by a material principle, it can be determined only by the formal principle of all volition.

From the two propositions just set forth a third directly follows, which may be thus stated: *Duty is the obligation to act from reverence for law*. Now, I may have a natural *inclination* for the object that I expect to follow from my action, but I can never have *reverence* for that which is not a spontaneous activity of my will, but merely an effect of it; neither can I have reverence for any natural inclination, whether it is my own or another's. If it is my own, I can at most only approve of it; if it is manifested by another, I may regard it as conducive to my own interest, and hence I may in certain cases even be said to have a love for it. But the only thing which I can reverence or which can lay me under an obligation to act, is the law which is connected with my will, not as a consequence, but as a principle; a principle which is not dependent upon natural inclination, but overmasters it, or at least allows it to have no influence whatever in determining my course of action. Now if an action which is done out of regard for duty sets entirely aside the influence of natural inclination and along with it every object of the will, nothing else is left by which the will can be determined but objectively the *law* itself, and subjectively *pure reverence* for the law as a principle of action. Thus there arises the maxim, to obey the moral law even at the sacrifice of all my natural inclinations.

The supreme good which we call moral can therefore be nothing but the *idea of the law* in itself, in so far as it is this idea which determines the will, and not any consequences that are expected to follow. Only a *rational* being can have such an idea, and hence a man who acts from the idea of the law is already morally good, no matter whether the consequences which he expects from his action follow or not.

Now what must be the nature of a law, the idea of which is to determine the will, even apart from the effects expected to follow, and which is therefore itself entitled to be called good absolutely and without qualification? As the will must not be moved to act from any desire for the results expected to follow from obedience to a certain law, the only principle of the will which remains is that of the conformity of actions to universal law. In all cases I must act in such a way *that I can at the same time will that my maxim should become a universal law*. This is what

is meant by conformity to law pure and simple; and this is the principle which serves, and must serve, to determine the will, if the idea of duty is not to be regarded as empty and chimerical. As a matter of fact the judgments which we are wont to pass upon conduct perfectly agree with this principle, and in making them we always have it before our eyes.

May I, for instance, under the pressure of circumstances, make a promise which I have no intention of keeping? The question is not, whether it is prudent to make a false promise, but whether it is morally right. To enable me to answer this question shortly and conclusively, the best way is for me to ask myself whether it would satisfy me that the maxim to extricate myself from embarrassment by giving a false promise should have the force of a universal law, applying to others as well as to myself. And I see at once, that, while I can certainly will the lie, I cannot will that lying should be a universal law. If lying were universal, there would, properly speaking, be no promises whatever. I might say that I intended to do a certain thing at some future time, but nobody would believe me, or if he did at the moment trust to my promise, he would afterwards pay me back in my own coin. My maxim thus proves itself to be self-destructive, so soon as it is taken as a universal law.

Duty, then, consists in the obligation to act from *pure* reverence for the moral law. To this motive all others must give way, for it is the condition of a will which is good *in itself*, and which has a value with which nothing else is comparable. . . .

Hypothetical and Categorical Imperatives

Everything in nature acts in conformity with law. Only a rational being has the faculty of acting in conformity with the *idea* of law, or from principles; only a rational being, in other words, has a will. And as without reason actions cannot proceed from laws, will is simply practical reason. If the will is infallibly determined by reason, the actions of a rational being are subjectively as well as objectively necessary; that is, will must be regarded as a faculty of choosing *that only* which reason, independently of natural inclination, declares to be practically necessary or good. On the other hand, if the will is not invariably determined by reason alone, but is subject to certain subjective conditions or motives, which are not always in harmony with the objective conditions; if the will, as actually is the case with man, is not in perfect conformity with reason; actions which are recognized to be objectively necessary, are subjectively contingent. The determination of such a will according to objective laws is therefore called *obligation*. That is to say, if the will of a rational being is not absolutely good, we conceive of it as capable of being determined by objective laws of rea-

son, but not as by its very nature necessarily obeying them.

The idea that a certain principle is objective, and binding upon the will, is a command of reason, and the statement of the command in a formula is an *imperative*.

All imperatives are expressed by the word *ought*, to indicate that the will upon which they are binding is not by its subjective constitution necessarily determined in conformity with the objective law of reason. An imperative says, that the doing, or leaving undone of a certain thing would be good, but it addresses a will which does not always do a thing simply because it is good. Now, that is practically *good* which determines the will by ideas of reason, in other words, that which determines it, not by subjective influences, but by principles which are objective, or apply to all rational beings as such. *Good* and *pleasure* are quite distinct. Pleasure results from the influence of purely subjective causes upon the will of the subject, and these vary with the susceptibility of this or that individual, while a principle of reason is valid for all.

A perfectly good will would, like the will of man, stand under objective laws, laws of the good, but it could not be said to be under an *obligation* to act in conformity with those laws. Such a will by its subjective constitution could be determined only by the idea of the good. In reference to the Divine will, or any other holy will, imperatives have no meaning; for here the will is by its very nature necessarily in harmony with the law, and therefore *ought* has no application to it. Imperatives are formulæ, which express merely the relation of objective laws of volition in general to the imperfect will of this or that rational being, as for instance, the will of man.

Now, all imperatives command either *hypothetically* or *categorically*. A hypothetical imperative states that a certain thing must be done, if something else which is willed, or at least might be willed, is to be attained. The categorical imperative declares that an act is in itself or objectively necessary, without any reference to another end.

Every practical law represents a possible action as good, and therefore as obligatory for a subject that is capable of being determined to act by reason. Hence all imperatives are formulæ for the determination of an action which is obligatory according to the principle of a will that is in some sense good. If the action is good only because it is a means to *something else*, the imperative is *hypothetical*; if the action is conceived to be good *in itself*, the imperative, as the necessary principle of a will that in itself conforms to reason, is *categorical*.

An imperative, then, states what possible action of mine would be good. It supplies the practical rule for a will which does not at once do an act simply because it is good, either because the subject does not know it to be good, or because, knowing it to be good, he is influenced by maxims which are opposed to the objective principles of a practical reason.

The hypothetical imperative says only that an action is good relatively to a certain *possible* end or to a certain *actual* end. In the former case it is *problematic*, in the latter case *assertoric*. The categorical imperative, which affirms that an action is in itself or objectively necessary without regard to an end, that is, without regard to any other end than itself, is an *apodictic* practical principle.

Whatever is within the power of a rational being may be conceived to be capable of being willed by some rational being, and hence the principles which determine what actions are necessary in the attainment of certain possible ends, are infinite in number.

Yet there is one thing which we may assume that all finite rational beings actually make their end, and there is therefore one object which may safely be regarded, not simply as something that they *may* seek, but as something that by a necessity of their nature they actually *do* seek. This object is *happiness*. The hypothetical imperative, which affirms the practical necessity of an action as the means of attaining happiness, is *assertoric*. We must not think of happiness as simply a possible and problematic end, but as an end that we may with confidence presuppose *a priori* to be sought by everyone, belonging as it does to the very nature of man. Now skill in the choice of means to his own greatest well-being may be called *prudence*, taking the word in its more restricted sense. An imperative, therefore, which relates merely to the choice of means to one's own happiness, that is, a maxim of prudence, must be hypothetical; it commands an action, not absolutely, but only as a means to another end.

Lastly, there is an imperative which directly commands an action, without presupposing as its condition that some other end is to be attained by means of that action. This imperative is *categorical*. It has to do, not with the matter of an action and the result expected to follow from it, but simply with the form and principle from which the action itself proceeds. The action is essentially good if the motive of the agent is good, let the consequences be what they may. This imperative may be called the imperative of *morality*.

How are all these imperatives possible? The question is not, How is an action which an imperative commands actually realized? but, How can we think of the will as placed under obligation by each of those imperatives? Very little need be said to show how an imperative of skill is possible. He who wills the end, wills also the means in his power which are indispensable to the attainment of the end. Looking simply at the act of will, we must say

that this proposition is analytic. If a certain object is to follow as an effect from my volition, my causality must be conceived as active in the production of the effect, or as employing the means by which the effect will take place. The imperative, therefore, simply states that in the conception of the willing of this end there is directly implied the conception of actions necessary to this end. No doubt certain synthetic propositions are required to determine the particular means by which a given end may be attained, but these have nothing to do with the principle or act of the will, but merely state how the object may actually be realized.

Were it as easy to give a definite conception of happiness as of a particular end, the imperatives of prudence would be of exactly the same nature as the imperatives of skill, and would therefore be analytic. For, we should be able to say, that he who wills the end wills also the only means in his power for the attainment of the end. But, unfortunately, the conception of happiness is so indefinite, that, although every man desires to obtain it, he is unable to give a definite and self-consistent statement of what he actually desires and wills. . . .

The Categorical Imperative

If I take the mere conception of a hypothetical imperative, I cannot tell what it may contain until the condition under which it applies is presented to me. But I can tell at once from the very conception of a categorical imperative what it must contain. Viewed apart from the law, the imperative simply affirms that the maxim, or subjective principle of action, must conform to the objective principle or law. Now the law contains no condition to which it is restricted, and hence nothing remains but the statement, that the maxim ought to conform to the universality of the law as such. It is only this conformity to law that the imperative can be said to represent as necessary.

There is therefore but one categorical imperative, which may be thus stated: *Act in conformity with that maxim, and that maxim only, which you can at the same time will to be a universal law.*

Now, if from this single imperative, as from their principle, all imperatives of duty can be derived, we shall at least be able to indicate what we mean by the categorical imperative and what the conception of it implies, although we shall not be able to say whether the conception of duty may not itself be empty.

The universality of the law which governs the succession of events, is what we mean by *nature*, in the most general sense, that is, the existence of things, in so far as their existence is determined in conformity with universal laws. The universal imperative of duty might therefore be put in this way: *Act as if the maxim from which you act were to become through your will a universal law of nature.*

If we attend to what goes on in ourselves in every transgression of a duty, we find, that we do not will that our maxim should become a universal law. We find it in fact impossible to do so, and we really will that the opposite of our maxim should remain a universal law, at the same time that we assume the liberty of making an exception in favour of natural inclination in our own case, or perhaps only for this particular occasion. Hence, if we looked at all cases from the same point of view, that is, from the point of view of reason, we should see that there was here a contradiction in our will. The contradiction is, that a certain principle is admitted to be necessary objectively or as a universal law, and yet is held not to be universal subjectively, but to admit of exceptions. What we do is, to consider our action at one time from the point of view of a will that is in perfect conformity with reason, and at another time from the point of view of a will that is under the influence of natural inclination. There is, therefore, here no real contradiction, but merely an antagonism of inclination to the command of reason. The universality of the principle is changed into a mere generality, in order that the practical principle of reason may meet the maxim half way. Not only is this limitation condemned by our own impartial judgment, but it proves that we actually recognize the validity of the categorical imperative, and merely allow ourselves to make a few exceptions in our own favour which we try to consider as of no importance, or as a necessary concession to circumstances. . . .

The Kingdom of Ends

Now, I say, that man, and indeed every rational being as such, *exists* as an end in himself, *not merely as a means* to be made use of by this or that will, and therefore man in all his actions, whether these are directed towards himself or towards other rational beings, must always be regarded as an end. No object of natural desire has more than a conditioned value; for if the natural desires, and the wants to which they give rise, did not exist, the object to which they are directed would have no value at all. . . . Rational beings, on the other hand, are called *persons*, because their very nature shows them to be ends in themselves, that is, something which cannot be made use of simply as a means. A person being thus an object of respect, a certain limit is placed upon arbitrary will. Persons are not purely subjective ends, whose existence has a value *for us* as the effect of our actions, but they are *objective ends*, or beings whose existence is an end in itself, for which no other end can be substituted. If all value were conditioned, and therefore contingent, it would be impossible to show that there is any supreme practical principle whatever.

If, then, there is a supreme practical principle, a principle which in relation to the human will is a categorical imperative, it must be an *objective* principle of the will, and must be able to serve as a universal practical law. For, such a principle must be derived from the idea of that which is necessarily an end for every one because it is an *end in itself*. Its foundation is this, that *rational nature exists as an end in itself*. Man necessarily conceives of his own existence in this way, and so far this is a *subjective* principle of human action. But in this way also every other rational being conceives of his own existence, and for the very same reason; hence the principle is also *objective*, and from it, as the highest practical ground, all laws of the will must be capable of being derived. The practical imperative will therefore be this: *Act so as to use humanity, whether in your own person or in the person of another, always as an end, never as merely a means. . . .*

The conception that every rational being in all the maxims of his will must regard himself as prescribing universal laws, by reference to which himself and all his actions are to be judged, leads to a cognate and very fruitful conception, that of a *kingdom of ends*.

By *kingdom*, I mean the systematic combination of different rational beings through the medium of common laws. Now, laws determine certain ends as universal, and hence, if abstraction is made from the individual differences of rational beings, and from all that is peculiar to their private ends, we get the idea of a complete totality of ends combined in a system; in other words, we are able to conceive of a kingdom of ends, which conforms to the principles formulated above.

All rational beings stand under the law, that each should treat himself and others, *never simply as means*, but always as *at the same time ends in themselves*. Thus there arises a systematic combination of rational beings through the medium of common objective laws. This may well be called a kingdom of ends, because the object of tnose laws is just to relate all rational beings to one another as ends and means. Of course this kingdom of ends is merely an ideal.

Morality, then, consists in the relation of all action to the system of laws which alone makes possible a kingdom of ends. These laws must belong to the nature of every rational being, and must proceed from his own will. The principle of the will, therefore, is, that no action should be done from any other maxim than one which is consistent with a universal law. This may be expressed in the formula: *Act so that the will may regard itself as in its maxims laying down universal laws*. Now, if the maxims of rational beings are not by their very nature in harmony with this objective principle, the principle of a universal system of laws, the necessity of acting in conformity with that principle is called practical obligation or *duty*. No doubt duty does not apply to the sovereign will in the kingdom of ends, but it applies to every member of it, and to all in equal measure. *Autonomy* is thus the foundation of the moral value of man and of every other rational being.

The three ways in which the principle of morality has been formulated are at bottom simply different statements of the same law, and each implies the other two.

An absolutely good will, then, the principle of which must be a categorical imperative, will be undetermined as regards all objects, and will contain merely the *form of volition* in general, a form which rests upon the *autonomy* of the will. The one law which the will of every rational being imposes upon itself, and imposes without reference to any natural impulse or any interest, is, that the maxims of every good will must be capable of being made a universal law. . . .

16

Good Cannot Be Defined

G. E. MOORE

What, then, is good? How is good to be defined? Now, it may be thought that this is a verbal question. A definition does indeed often mean the expressing of one word's meaning in other words. But this is not the sort of definition I am asking for. Such a definition can never be of ultimate importance in any study except lexicography. If I wanted that kind of definition I should have to consider in the first place how people generally used the word "good"; but my business is not with its proper usage, as established by custom. I should, indeed, be foolish, if I tried to use it for something which it did not usually denote: if, for instance, I were to announce that, whenever I used the word "good," I must be understood to be thinking of that object which is usually denoted by the word "table." I shall, therefore, use the word in the sense in which I think it is ordinarily used; but at the same time I am not anxious to discuss whether I am right in thinking that it is so used. My business is solely with that object or idea, which I hold, rightly or wrongly, that the word is generally used to stand for. What I want to discover is the nature of that object or idea, and about this I am extremely anxious to arrive at an agreement.

But, if we understand the question in this sense, my answer to it may seem a very disappointing one. If I am asked "What is good?" my answer is that good is good, and that is the end of the matter. Or if I am asked "How is good to be defined?" my answer is that it cannot be defined, and that is all I have to say about it. But disappointing as these answers may appear, they are of the very last importance. To readers who are familiar with philosophic terminology, I can express their importance by saying that they amount

[From *Principia Ethica* (Cambridge University Press), chapter I. First published in 1903.]

to this: That propositions about the good are all of them synthetic and never analytic; and that is plainly no trivial matter. And the same thing may be expressed more popularly, by saying that, if I am right, then nobody can foist upon us such an axiom as that "Pleasure is the only good" or that "The good is the desired" on the pretence that this is "the very meaning of the word."

Let us, then, consider this position. My point is that "good" is a simple notion, just as "yellow" is a simple notion; that, just as you cannot, by any manner of means, explain to any one who does not already know it, what yellow is, so you cannot explain what good is. Definitions of the kind that I was asking for, definitions which describe the real nature of the object or notion denoted by a word, and which do not merely tell us what the word is used to mean, are only possible when the object or notion in question is something complex. You can give a definition of a horse, because a horse has many different properties and qualities, all of which you can enumerate. But when you have enumerated them all, when you have reduced a horse to his simplest terms, then you can no longer define those terms. They are simply something which you think of or perceive, and to any one who cannot think of or perceive them, you can never, by any definition, make their nature known. It may perhaps be objected to this that we are able to describe to others, objects which they have never seen or thought of. We can, for instance, make a man understand what a chimaera is, although he has never heard of one or seen one. You can tell him that it is an animal with a lioness's head and body, with a goat's head growing from the middle of its back, and with a snake in place of a tail. But here the object which you are describing is a complex object; it is entirely composed of parts, with which we are all perfectly familiar—a snake, a goat, a lioness; and we know, too, the manner in which those parts are to be put together, because we know what is meant by the middle of a lioness's back, and where her tail is wont to grow. And so it is with all objects, not previously known, which we are able to define: they are all complex; all composed of parts, which may themselves, in the first instance, be capable of similar definition, but which must in the end be reducible to simplest parts, which can no longer be defined. But yellow and good, we say, are not complex: they are notions of that simple kind, out of which definitions are composed and with which the power of further defining ceases.

When we say, as Webster says, "The definition of horse is 'A hoofed quadruped of the genus Equus,'" we may, in fact, mean three different things. (1) We may mean merely: "When I say 'horse,' you are to understand that I am talking about a hoofed quadruped of the genus

Equus." This might be called the arbitrary verbal definition: and I do not mean that good is indefinable in that sense. (2) We may mean, as Webster ought to mean: "When most English people say 'horse,' they mean a hoofed quadruped of the genus Equus." This may be called the verbal definition proper, and I do not say that good is indefinable in this sense either; for it is certainly possible to discover how people use a word: otherwise, we could never have known that "good" may be translated by "gut" in German and by "bon" in French. But (3) we may, when we define horse, mean something much more important. We may mean that a certain object, which we all of us know, is composed in a certain manner: that it has four legs, a head, a heart, a liver, etc., etc., all of them arranged in definite relations to one another. It is in this sense that I deny good to be definable. I say that it is not composed of any parts, which we can substitute for it in our minds when we are thinking of it. We might think just as clearly and correctly about a horse, if we thought of all its parts and their arrangement instead of thinking of the whole: we could, I say, think how a horse differed from a donkey just as well, just as truly, in this way, as now we do, only not so easily; but there is nothing whatsoever which we could so substitute for good; and that is what I mean, when I say that good is indefinable.

But I am afraid I have still not removed the chief difficulty which may prevent acceptance of the proposition that good is indefinable. I do not mean to say that *the* good, that which is good, is thus indefinable; if I did think so, I should not be writing on Ethics, for my main object is to help towards discovering that definition. It is just because I think there will be less risk of error in our search for a definition of "the good," that I am now insisting that *good* is indefinable. I must try to explain the difference between these two. I suppose it may be granted that "good" is an adjective. Well "the good," "that which is good," must therefore be the substantive to which the adjective "good" will apply: it must be the whole of that to which the adjective will apply, and the adjective must *always* truly apply to it. But if it is that to which the adjective will apply, it must be something different from that adjective itself; and the whole of that something different, whatever it is, will be our definition of *the* good. Now it may be that this something will have other adjectives, beside "good," that will apply to it. It may be full of pleasure, for example; it may be intelligent: and if these two adjectives are really part of its definition, then it will certainly be true, that pleasure and intelligence are good. And many people appear to think that, if we say "Pleasure and intelligence are good," or if we say "Only pleasure and intelligence are good," we are defining "good." Well, I cannot deny that propositions of this nature may sometimes be called definitions; I do not know well enough how the word is generally used to decide upon this point. I only wish it to be understood that that is not what I mean when I say there is no possible definition of good, and that I shall not mean this if I use the word again. I do most fully believe that some true proposition of the form "Intelligence is good and intelligence alone is good" can be found; if none could be found, our definition of *the* good would be impossible. As it is, I believe *the* good to be definable; and yet I still say that good itself is indefinable.

"Good," then, if we mean by it that quality which we assert to belong to a thing, when we say that the thing is good, is incapable of any definition, in the most important sense of that word. The most important sense of "definition" is that in which a definition states what are the parts which invariably compose a certain whole; and in this sense "good" has no definition because it is simple and has no parts. It is one of those innumerable objects of thought which are themselves incapable of definition, because they are the ultimate terms by reference to which whatever *is* capable of definition must be defined. That there must be an indefinite number of such terms is obvious, on reflection; since we cannot define anything except by an analysis, which, when carried as far as it will go, refers us to

something, which is simply different from anything else, and which by that ultimate difference explains the peculiarity of the whole which we are defining: for every whole contains some parts which are common to other wholes also. There is, therefore, no intrinsic difficulty in the contention that "good" denotes a simple and indefinable quality. There are many other instances of such qualities.

Consider yellow, for example. We may try to define it, by describing its physical equivalent; we may state what kind of light-vibrations must stimulate the normal eye, in order that we may perceive it. But a moment's reflection is sufficient to shew that those light-vibrations are not themselves what we mean by yellow. *They* are not what we perceive. Indeed we should never have been able to discover their existence, unless we had first been struck by the patent difference of quality between the different colours. The most we can be entitled to say of those vibrations is that they are what corresponds in space to the yellow which we actually perceive.

Yet a mistake of this simple kind has commonly been made about "good." It may be true that all things which are good are *also* something else, just as it is true that all things which are yellow produce a certain kind of vibration in the light. And it is a fact, that Ethics aims at discovering what are those other properties belonging to all things which are good. But far too many philosophers have thought that when they named those other properties they were actually defining good; that these properties, in fact, were simply not "other," but absolutely and entirely the same with goodness. This view I propose to call the "naturalistic fallacy" and of it I shall now endeavour to dispose. . . .

Suppose a man says "I am pleased"; and suppose that is not a lie or a mistake but the truth. Well, if it is true, what does that mean? It means that his mind, a certain definite mind, distinguished by certain definite marks from all others, has at this moment a certain definite feeling called pleasure. "Pleased" *means* nothing but having pleasure, and though we may be more pleased or less pleased, and even, we may admit for the present, have one or another kind of pleasure; yet in so far as it is pleasure we have, whether there be more or less of it, and whether it be of one kind or another, what we have is one definite thing, absolutely indefinable, some one thing that is the same in all the various degrees and in all the various kinds of it that there may be. We may be able to say how it is related to other things: that, for example, it is in the mind, that it causes desire, that we are conscious of it, etc., etc. We can, I say, describe its relations to other things, but define it we can *not*. And if anybody tried to define pleasure for us as being any other natural object; if anybody were to

say, for instance, that pleasure *means* the sensation of red, and were to proceed to deduce from that that pleasure is a colour, we should be entitled to laugh at him and to distrust his future statements about pleasure. Well, that would be the same fallacy which I have called the naturalistic fallacy. That "pleased" does not mean "having the sensation of red," or anything else whatever, does not prevent us from understanding what it does mean. It is enough for us to know that "pleased" does mean "having the sensation of pleasure," and though pleasure is absolutely indefinable, though pleasure is pleasure and nothing else whatever, yet we feel no difficulty in saying that we are pleased. The reason is, of course, that when I say "I am pleased," I do *not* mean that "I" am the same thing as "having pleasure." And similarly no difficulty need be found in my saying that "pleasure is good" and yet not meaning that "pleasure" is the same thing as "good," that pleasure *means* good, and that good *means* pleasure. If I were to imagine that when I said "I am pleased," I meant that I was exactly the same thing as "pleased," I should not indeed call that a naturalistic fallacy, although it would be the same fallacy as I have called naturalistic with reference to Ethics. The reason of this is obvious enough. When a man confuses two natural objects with one another, defining the one by the other, if for instance, he confuses himself, who is one natural object, with "pleased" or with "pleasure" which are others, then there is no reason to call the fallacy naturalistic. But if he confuses "good," which is not in the same sense a natural object, with any natural object whatever, then there is a reason for calling that a naturalistic fallacy; its being made with regard to "good" marks it as something quite specific, and this specific mistake deserves a name because it is so common. As for the reasons why good is not to be considered a natural object, they may be reserved for discussion in another place. But, for the present, it is sufficient to notice this: Even if it were a natural object, that would not alter the nature of the fallacy nor diminish its importance one whit. All that I have said about it would remain quite equally true: only the name which I have called it would not be so appropriate as I think it is. And I do not care about the name: what I do care about is the fallacy. It does not matter what we call it, provided we recognise it when we meet with it. It is to be met with in almost every book on Ethics; and yet it is not recognised: and that is why it is necessary to multiply illustrations of it, and convenient to give it a name. It is a very simple fallacy indeed. When we say that an orange is yellow, we do not think our statement binds us to hold that "orange" means nothing else than "yellow," or that nothing can be yellow but an orange. Supposing the orange is also sweet! Does that bind us to say that "sweet" is exactly the same thing as "yellow," that "sweet" must be defined as "yellow"? And supposing it be recognised that "yellow" just means "yellow" and nothing else whatever, does that make it any more difficult to hold that oranges are yellow? Most certainly it does not: on the contrary, it would be absolutely meaningless to say that oranges were yellow unless yellow did in the end mean just "yellow" and nothing else whatever—unless it was absolutely indefinable. We should not get any very clear notion about things, which are yellow—we should not get very far with our science, if we were bound to hold that everything which was yellow, *meant* exactly the same thing as yellow. We should find we had to hold that an orange was exactly the same thing as a stool, a piece of paper, a lemon, anything you like. We could prove any number of absurdities; but should we be the nearer to the truth? Why, then, should it be different with "good"? Why, if good is good and indefinable, should I be held to deny that pleasure is good? Is there any difficulty in holding both to be true at once? On the contrary, there is no meaning in saying that pleasure is good, unless good is something different from pleasure. It is absolutely useless, so far as Ethics is concerned, to prove, as Mr. Spencer tries to do, that increase of pleasure coincides with increase of life, unless good *means* something different from either life or pleasure. He might just as well try to prove that an orange is yellow by shewing that it always is wrapped up in paper.

In fact, if it is not the case that "good" denotes something simple and indefinable, only two alternatives are possible: either it is a complex, a given whole, about the correct analysis of which there may be disagreement; or else it means nothing at all, and there is no such subject as Ethics. In general, however, ethical philosophers have attempted to define good, without recognising what such an attempt must mean. . . .

. . . It is very natural to make the mistake of supposing that what is universally true is of such a nature that its negation would be self-contradictory: the importance which has been assigned to analytic propositions in the history of philosophy shews how easy such a mistake is. And thus it is very easy to conclude that what seems to be a universal ethical principle is in fact an identical proposition; that, if, for example, whatever is called "good" seems to be pleasant, the proposition "Pleasure is the good" does not assert a connection between two different notions, but involves only one, that of pleasure, which is easily recognised as a distinct entity. But whoever will attentively consider with himself what is actually before his mind when he asks the question "Is plea-sure (or whatever it may be) after all good?" can easily satisfy himself that he is not merely wondering whether pleasure is pleasant. And if he will try this experiment with each suggested definition in succession, he may become expert enough to recognise that in every case he has before his mind a unique object, with regard to the connection of which with any other object, a distinct question may be asked. Every one does in fact understand the question "Is this good?" When he thinks of it, his state of mind is different from what it would be, were he asked "Is this pleasant, or desired, or approved?" It has a distinct meaning for him, even though he may not recognise in what respect it is distinct. Whenever he thinks of "intrinsic value," or "intrinsic worth," or says that a thing "ought to exist," he has before his mind the unique object—the unique property of things—which I mean by "good." Everybody is constantly aware of this notion, although he may never become aware at all that it is different from other notions of which he is also aware. But, for correct ethical reasoning, it is extremely important that he should become aware of this fact; and, as soon as the nature of the problem is clearly understood, there should be little difficulty in advancing so far in analysis. . . .

17

Commending and Choosing

R. M. HARE

The Primary Function
of the Word "Good"

I have said that the primary function of the word "good" is to commend. We have, therefore, to inquire what commending is. When we commend or condemn anything, it is always in order, at least indirectly, to guide choices, our own or other people's, now or in the future. Suppose that I say "The South Bank Exhibition is very good." In what context should I appropriately say this, and what would be my purpose in so doing? It would be natural for me to say it to someone who was wondering whether to go to London to see the Exhibition, or, if he was in London, whether to pay it a visit. It would, however, be too much to say that the reference to choices is always as direct as this. An American returning from London to New York, and speaking to some people who had

no intention of going to London in the near future, might still make the same remark. In order, therefore, to show that critical value-judgements are all ultimately related to choices, and would not be made if they were not so related, we require to ask, for what purpose we have standards.

It has been pointed out by Mr. Urmson that we do not speak generally of "good" wireworms. This is because we never have any occasion for choosing between wireworms, and therefore require no guidance in so doing. We therefore need to have no standards for wireworms. But it is easy to imagine circumstances in which this situation might alter. Suppose that wireworms came into use as a special kind of bait for fishermen. Then we might speak of having dug up a very good wireworm (one, for example, that was exceptionally fat and attractive to fish), just as now, no doubt, sea-fish-

[From *The Language of Morals* by R. M. Hare (1952), pp. 127–146. Reprinted by permission of Oxford University Press.]

ermen might talk of having dug up a very good lug-worm. We only have standards for a class of objects, we only talk of the virtues of one specimen as against another, we only use value-words about them, when occasions are known to exist, or are conceivable, in which we, or someone else, would have to choose between specimens. We should not call pictures good or bad if no one ever had the choice of seeing them or not seeing them (or of studying them or not studying them in the way that art students study pictures, or of buying them or not buying them). Lest, by the way, I should seem to have introduced a certain vagueness by specifying so many alternative kinds of choices, it must be pointed out that the matter can, if desired, be made as precise as we require; for we can specify, when we have called a picture a good one, within what class we have called it good; for example, we can say "I meant a good picture to study, but not to buy."

Some further examples may be given. We should not speak of good sunsets, unless sometimes the decision had to be made, whether to go to the window to look at the sunset; we should not speak of good billiard-cues, unless sometimes we had to choose one billiard-cue in preference to another; we should not speak of good men unless we had the choice, what sort of men to try to become. Leibniz, when he spoke of "the best of all possible worlds," had in mind a creator choosing between the possibilities. The choice that is envisaged need not ever occur, nor even be expected ever to occur; it is enough for it to be envisaged as occurring, in order that we should be able to make a value-judgement with reference to it. It must be admitted, however, that the most useful value-judgements are those which have reference to choices that we might very likely have to make.

It should be pointed out that even judgements about past choices do not refer merely to the past. As we shall see, all value-judgements are covertly universal in character, which is the same as to say that they refer to, and express acceptance of, a standard which has an application to other similar instances. If I censure someone for having done something, I envisage the possibility of him, or someone else, or myself, having to make a similar choice again; otherwise there would be no point in censuring him. Thus, if I say to a man whom I am teaching to drive "You did that manoeuvre badly" this is a very typical piece of driving-instruction; and driving-instruction consists in teaching a man to drive not in the past but in the future; to this end we censure or commend past pieces of driving, in order to impart to him the standard which is to guide him in his subsequent conduct.

When we commend an object, our judgement is not solely about that particular object, but is inescapably about objects like it. Thus, if I say that a certain motor-car is a good one, I am not merely saying something about that particular motor-car. To say something about that particular car, merely, would not be to commend. To commend, as we have seen, is to guide choices. Now for guiding a particular choice we have a linguistic instrument which is not that of commendation, namely, the singular imperative. If I wish merely to tell someone to choose a particular car, with no thought of the kind of car to which it belongs, I can say "Take that one." If instead of this I say "That is a good one," I am saying something more. I am implying that if any motor-car were just like that one, it would be a good one too; whereas by saying "Take that one," I do not imply that, if my hearer sees another car just like that one, he is to take it too. But further, the implication of the judgement "That is a good motor-car" does not extend merely to motor-cars *exactly* like that one. If this were so, the implication would be for practical purposes useless; for nothing is exactly like anything else. It extends to every motor-car that is like that one in the *relevant* particulars; and the relevant particulars are its virtues—those of its characteristics for which I was commending it, or which I was calling good about it. Whenever we commend, we have in mind something about the object commended which is the reason for our commendation. It therefore always makes

sense, after someone has said "That is a good motor-car," to ask "What is good about it?" or "Why do you call it good?" or "What features of it are you commending?" It may not always be easy to answer this question precisely, but it is always a legitimate question. If we did not understand why it was always a legitimate question, we should not understand the way in which the word "good" functions.

We may illustrate this point by comparing two dialogues . . . :

(1) X. Jones' motor-car is a good one.

> *Y. What makes you call it good?*
> *X. Oh, just that it's good.*
> *Y. But there must be some reason for your calling it good, I mean some property that it has in virtue of which you call it good.*
> *X. No; the property in virtue of which I call it good is just its goodness and nothing else.*
> *Y. But do you mean that its shape, speed, weight, manœuvrability etc., are irrelevant to whether you call it good or not?*
> *X. Yes, quite irrelevant; the only relevant property is that of goodness, just as, if I called it yellow, the only relevant property would be that of yellowness.*

(2) The same dialogue, only with "yellow" substituted for "good"

The reason why X's position in the first dialogue is eccentric is that since, as we have already remarked, "good" is a "supervenient" or "consequential" epithet, one may always legitimately be asked when one has called something a good something, "What is good about it?" Now to answer this question is to give the properties in virtue of which we call it good. Thus, if I have said, "That is a good motor-car" and someone asks "Why? What is good about it?" and I reply "Its high speed combined with its stability on the road," I indicate that I call it good in virtue of its having these properties or virtues. Now to do this is *eo ipso* to say something about other motor-cars which have these properties. If any motor-car whatever had these properties, I should have, if I were not to be inconsistent, to agree that it was, *pro tanto*, a good motor-car; though of course it might, although it had these properties in its favour, have other countervailing disadvantages, and so be, taken all in all, not a good motor-car.

This last difficulty can always be got over by specifying in detail why I called the first motor-car a good one. Suppose that a second motor-car were like the first one in speed and stability, but gave its passengers no protection from the rain, and

proved difficult to get into and out of. I should not then call it a good motor-car, although it had those characteristics which led me to call the first one good. This shows that I should not have called the first one good either if it too had had the bad characteristics of the second one; and so in specifying what was good about the first one, I ought to have added ". . . and the protection it gives to the passengers and the ease with which one can get into and out of it." This process could be repeated indefinitely until I had given a complete list of the characteristics of the first motor-car which were required to make me allow it to be a good one. This, in itself, would not be saying all that there was to be said about my standards for judging motor-cars—for there might be other motor-cars which, although falling short to a certain extent in these characteristics, had other countervailing good characteristics; for example, soft upholstery, large accommodation, or small consumption of petrol. But it would be at any rate some help to my hearer in building up an idea of my standards in motor-cars; and in this lies the importance of such questions and answers, and the importance of recognizing their relevance, whenever a value-judgement has been made. For one of the purposes of making such judgements is to make known the standard.

When I commend a motor-car I am guiding the choices of my hearer not merely in relation to that particular motor-car but in relation to motor-cars in general. What I have said to him will be of assistance to him whenever in the future he has to choose a motor-car or advise anyone else on the choice of a motor-car or even design a motor-car (choose what sort of motor-car to have made) or write a general treatise on the design of motor-cars (which involves choosing what sort of motor-cars to advise other people to have made). The method whereby I give him this assistance is by making known to him a standard for judging motor-cars.

This process has, as we have noticed, certain features in common with the process of defining (making known the meaning or application of) a descriptive word, though there are important differences. We have now to notice a further resemblance between showing the usage of a word and showing how to choose between motor-cars. In neither case can the instruction be done successfully unless the instructor is consistent in his teaching. If I use "red" for objects of a wide variety of colours, my hearer will never learn from me a consistent usage of the word. Similarly, if I commend motor-cars with widely different or even contrary characteristics, what I say to him will not be of assistance to him in choosing motor-cars subsequently, because I am not teaching him any consistent standard—or any standard at all, for a standard is by definition consistent. He will say, "I don't see

by what standards you are judging these motor-cars; please explain to me why you call them all good, although they are so different." Of course, I might be able to give a satisfactory explanation. I might say, "There are different sorts of motor-cars, each good in its way; there are sports cars, whose prime requisites are speed and manœuvrability; and family cars, which ought rather to be capacious and economical; and taxis, and so on. So when I say a car is good which is fast and manœuvrable, although it is neither capacious nor economical, you must understand that I am commending it as a sports car, not as a family car." But suppose that I did not recognize the relevance of his question; suppose that I was just doling out the predicate "good" entirely haphazard, as the whim took me. It is clear that in this case I should teach him no standard at all.

We thus have to distinguish two questions that can always be asked in elucidation of a judgement containing the word "good." Suppose that someone says "That is a good one." We can then always ask (1) "Good what—sports car or family car or taxi or example to quote in a logic-book?" Or we can ask (2) "What makes you call it good?" To ask the first question is to ask for the class within which evaluative comparisons are being made. Let us call it the class of comparison. To ask the second question is to ask for the virtues or "good-making characteristics." These two questions are, however, not independent; for what distinguishes the class of comparison "sports car" from the class "family car" is the set of virtues which are to be looked for in the respective classes. This is so in all cases where the class of comparison is defined by means of a functional word—for obviously "sports car," "family car," and "taxi" are functional to a very much higher degree than plain "motor-car." Sometimes, however, a class of comparison may be further specified without making it more functional; for example, in explaining the phrase "good wine" we might say "I mean good wine for this district, not good wine compared with all the wines that there are."

Now since it is the purpose of the word "good" and other value-words to be used for teaching standards, their logic is in accord with this purpose. We are therefore in a position at last to explain the feature of the word "good" which I pointed out at the beginning of this investigation. The reason why I cannot apply the word "good" to one picture, if I refuse to apply it to another picture which I agree to be in all other respects exactly similar, is that by doing this I should be defeating the purpose for which the word is designed. I should be commending one object, and so purporting to teach my hearers one standard, while in the same breath refusing to commend a similar object, and so undoing the lesson just imparted. By

seeking to impart two inconsistent standards, I should be imparting no standard at all. The effect of such an utterance is similar to that of a contradiction; for in a contradiction, I say two inconsistent things, and so the effect is that the hearer does not know what I am trying to say. . . .

"Good" in Moral Contexts

It is time now to ask whether "good," as used in moral contexts, has any of the features to which I have drawn attention in non-moral ones. It will no doubt be thought by some readers that all that I have said hitherto is entirely irrelevant to ethics. To think this is to miss the enlightenment of some very interesting parallels; but I have no right on my part to assume that "good" behaves in at all the fashion that I have described when it is used in morals. To this problem we must now address ourselves. . . .

We get stirred up about the goodness of men because we are men. This means that the acceptance of a judgement, that such and such a man's act is good in circumstances of a certain sort, involves the acceptance of the judgement that it would be good, were we ourselves placed in similar circumstances, to do likewise. And since we might *be* placed in similar circumstances, we feel deeply about the question. We feel less deeply, it must be admitted, about the question, whether it was a bad act of Agamemnon to sacrifice Iphigenia, than about the question, whether it was a bad act of Mrs. Smith to travel on the railway without paying her fare; for we are not likely to be in Agamemnon's position, but most of us travel on railways. Acceptance of a moral judgement about Mrs. Smith's act is likely to have a closer bearing upon our future conduct than acceptance of one about Agamemnon's. But we never envisage ourselves turning into chronometers.

These observations are to a certain extent confirmed by the behaviour of technicians and artists. As Hesiod pointed out, these people do get stirred up about their respective non-moral goodnesses, in the way that ordinary people get stirred up about moral questions: "Potters get angry with potters, and carpenters with carpenters, and beggars with beggars, and poets with poets." Commercial competition is not the only reason—for it is possible to compete without malice. When an architect, for example, says of another architect's house, with feeling, "That is a thoroughly badly designed house," the reason for the feeling is that if he were to admit that the house was well designed, he would be admitting that in avoiding in his own work features like those of the design in question, he had been wrong; and this might mean altering his whole way of designing houses, which would be painful.

Further, we cannot get out of being men, as we can get out of being architects or out of making or using chronometers. Since this is so, there is no avoiding the (often painful) consequences of abiding by the moral judgements that we make. The architect who was forced to admit that a rival's house was better than anything he had ever produced or could produce, might be upset; but in the last resort he could become a barman instead. But if I admit that the life of St. Francis was morally better than mine, and really mean this as an evaluation, there is nothing for it but to try to be more like St. Francis, which is arduous. That is why most of our "moral judgements" about the saints are merely conventional—we never intend them to be a guide in determining our own conduct.

Moreover, in the case of differences about morals it is very difficult, and, in cases where the effect on our own life is profound, impossible, to say "It's all a matter of taste; let's agree to differ"; for to agree to differ is only possible when we can be sure that we shall not be forced to make choices which will radically affect the choices of other people. This is especially true where choices have to be made cooperatively; it must be pointed out, however, that though most moral choices are of this kind, this sort of situation is not peculiar to morals. The members of the Kontiki expedition could not have agreed to differ about how to build their raft, and families sharing a kitchen cannot agree to differ about its organization. But although we can usually get out of building rafts or sharing kitchens, we cannot easily get out of living in societies with other people. Perhaps men living in complete isolation could agree to differ about morals. It would at any rate seem that communities not in close contact with one another could agree to differ about some moral questions without actual inconvenience. To say this, of course, is not necessarily to maintain any kind of moral relativism, for communities could agree to differ about whether the earth was round. To agree to differ is to say, in effect, "We will differ about this question, but let us not be angry or fight about it"; it is not to say "we will differ, but let us not differ"; for the latter would be a logical impossibility. And so if two communities agreed to differ about, say, the moral desirability of legalized gambling in their respective territories, what would happen would be this; they would say "We will continue to hold, one of us that it is wrong to legalize gambling, and the other that it is not wrong; but we will not get angry about each other's laws, or seek to interfere in each other's administration of them." And the same thing might be done about other matters than gambling, provided that what each community did had slight effect outside its own borders. Such agreements will not work, however, if one community holds it to be a moral duty to prevent certain practices taking place wherever they occur.

Such a case is worth considering in order to contrast with it the more usual state of affairs; normally the moral judgements that we make, and hold to, deeply affect the lives of our neighbours; and this in itself is enough to explain the peculiar place that we assign to them. If we add to this the logical point, already mentioned, that moral judgements always have a possible bearing on our own conduct, in that we cannot in the fullest sense accept them without conforming to them . . . , then no further explanation is needed of the special status of morals. This special status does not require a special logic to back it up; it results from the fact that we are using the ordinary apparatus of value-language in order to commend or condemn the most intimate actions of ourselves and those like us. We may add that the "emotivity" of much moral utterance, which some have thought to be of the essence of evaluative language, is only a symptom—and a most unreliable one—of an evaluative use of words. Moral language is frequently emotive, simply because the situations in which it is typically used are situations about which we often feel deeply. One of the chief uses of the comparison which I have been drawing between moral and non-moral value-language is to make it clear that the essential logical features of value-words can be present where the emotions are not markedly involved.

It might be objected that my account of the matter gives no means of distinguishing prudential judgements like "It is never a good thing to volunteer for anything in the Army" from properly moral judgements like "It is not good to break one's promises." But the considerations given earlier enable us to distinguish satisfactorily between these two classes of judgement. It is clear from the context that in the second case we are commending within a different class of comparison, and requiring a different set of virtues. Sometimes we commend an act within the class of acts having an effect upon the agent's future happiness; sometimes we commend an act within the class of acts indicative of his moral character, that is to say, those acts which show whether or not he is a good man—and the class of comparison "man" in this context is the class "man to try to become like." Which of these we are doing is always clear from the context, and there is nearly always a further verbal difference too, as in the example quoted. It must be admitted, however, that a great deal of research has still to be done on the different classes of comparison within which we commend people and acts.

When we use the word "good" in order to commend morally, we are always directly or indirectly commending *people*. Even when we use the expression "good act" or others like it, the reference is indirectly to human characters. This, as has often been pointed out, constitutes a difference between the words "good" and "right." In speaking, therefore, of moral goodness, I shall speak only of the expression "good man" and similar expressions. We have to consider whether in fact this expression has the same logical features as the non-moral uses of "good" which we have been discussing, remembering that clearly "man" in "good man" is not normally a functional word, and never so when moral commendation is being given.

First, let us take that characteristic of "good" which has been called its supervenience. Suppose that we say "St. Francis was a good man." It is logically impossible to say this and to maintain at the same time that there might have been another man placed in precisely the same circumstances as St. Francis, and who behaved in them in exactly the same way, but who differed from St. Francis in this respect only, that he was not a good man. I am supposing, of course, that the judgement is made in both cases upon the whole life of the subject, "inner" and overt. . . .

Next, the explanation of this logical impossibility does not lie in any form of naturalism; it is not the case that there is any conjunction C of descriptive characteristics such that to say that a man has C entails that he is morally good. For, if this were the case, we should be unable to commend any man for having those characteristics; we should only be able to say that he had them. Nevertheless, the judgement that a man is morally good is not logically independent of the judgement that he has certain other characteristics which we may call virtues or good-making characteristics; there is a relation between them, although it is not one of entailment or of identity of meaning.

Our previous discussion of non-moral goodness helps us to understand what the relation is. It is that a statement of the characteristics of the man (the minor or factual premiss) *together with* a specification of a standard for judging men morally (the major premiss), entails a moral judgement upon him. And moral standards have many of the features that we have found in other value-standards. "Good," as used in morals, has a descriptive and an evaluative meaning, and the latter is primary. To know the descriptive meaning is to know by what standards the speaker is judging. . . .

18

A Refutation of Morals

JOHN MACKIE

We all have moral feelings: all of us find that there are human actions and states of affairs of which we approve and disapprove, and which we therefore try to encourage and develop or to oppose. (This emotion of approval is different from liking, one difference being that its object is more general. If someone stands me a pint, I like it: if someone stands an enemy of mine a pint, I dislike it: but I should approve of a state of society which provided free beer all round. So if I hear of someone whom I have never met and to whom I am personally indifferent being stood a pint, I should not say that I like it, for I am not directly affected, but I may well approve of it, because it is an instance of the sort of thing I want to see everywhere. A thorough distinction of approval from liking and other relations would require further

discussion, but perhaps this will serve to indicate a contrast between classes with which we are all in fact acquainted. I shall suggest later a possible source of these generalised emotions.) But most of us do not merely admit that we have such *feelings*, we think we can also *judge* that actions and states are right and good, just as we judge about other matters of fact, that these judgements are either true or false, and that the qualities with which they deal exist objectively. This view, which almost everyone holds, may be crudely called "believing in morals." A few sceptics, however, think that there are only feelings of approval, no objective moral facts. (Of course the existence of a feeling is an objective fact, but not what is commonly called a moral fact.) One of their main arguments is that moral facts would be "queer," in that unlike other facts

[From *Australasian Journal of Philosophy*, Vol. 24, No. 1 (1946), pp. 77–86. Reprinted by permission of *Australasian Journal of Philosophy*.]

they cannot be explained in terms of arrangements of matter, or logical constructions out of sense-data, or whatever the particular theorist takes to be the general form of real things. This argument is not in itself very strong, or even very plausible, for unless we have good *a priori* grounds for whatever is taken as the basic principle of criticism, the criterion of reality, the mere fact that we seem to observe moral qualities and facts would be a reason for modifying that principle. Their other main argument, which is both older and more convincing, though not logically conclusive, is that although at any one time, in a particular social group, there is fairly complete agreement about what is right, in other classes, other countries, and above all in other periods of history and other cultures, the actual moral judgements or feelings are almost completely different, though perhaps there are a few feelings so natural to man that they are found everywhere. Now feelings may well change with changing conditions, but a judgement about objective fact should be everywhere the same: if we have a faculty of moral perception, it must be an extremely faulty one, liable not only to temporary illusions, as sight is, but to great and lasting error. Of course it may be that every society except our own is mistaken, that savages are morally backward because they lack our illuminating experience of the long-term effects of various kinds of action, and so on. But

this complacent view (not indeed very popular now) is shaken by the observation that the variations in moral feelings can be explained much more plausibly not as being due to mistakes, but as reflections of social habits. This moral relatively would be less alarming if we could say that the varying judgements were not ultimate, but were applications to different circumstances of a single principle or a small number of principles, which were everywhere recognised—for example, that whatever produces pleasure is good, that whatever society commands is right, or, at the very least, that we should always do what we believe to be right. But these principles are not commonly laid down first, and the particular judgements deduced from them: rather the particular judgements are made by ordinary people, whereas the principles are later invented by philosophers and manipulated in order to explain them. In any case there is just as little agreement about principles as about particular judgements.

We find on further enquiry that most, perhaps all, actual moral judgements are fairly closely correlated with what we may call social demands: any society or social group has regular ways of working, and, in order to maintain these, requires that its members should act in certain ways: the members—from whatever motive, perhaps mainly habit, which has compelled them to adapt their desires to the established customs—obey these requirements themselves and force their fellows to do so, or at least feel obliged to obey and approve of others obeying. They call "right" and "good" whatever accords with these ways of working. Moreover as the science of social history develops, it is more and more strongly suggested that ways of working and institutions have their own laws of growth, and that the desires or moral views of individuals do not so much control the history of society as arise out of it.

Belief in the objectivity of moral qualities is further undermined when we remark that whenever anyone calls an action or activity or state of affairs right or good (unless he is speaking in an ironical tone or puts these words in inverted commas) he himself either has a feeling of approval, or desires that the action should be done or the activity pursued or the state of affairs come into existence. (Only one of these alternatives is necessary, but they are often found together.)

None of these considerations is conclusive, but each has a certain weight: together they move the moral sceptic (who is often of a scientific and inductive turn of mind, and less devoted than some others to the clear light of intuition or the authority of reason) to conclude that in all probability we do not recognise moral facts, but merely have feelings of approval and disapproval, which arise in general from social demands and therefore vary from one society to another. This view I intend to examine and re-state, and to advance what I regard as decisive arguments for one of its more important aspects.

The simplest formulation of this view is that when someone says "this act is right" he means merely "I approve of this act." The well-known reply simply leaps into the reader's mind: when one person says that an act is right, another that the same act is wrong, they would not on this theory be disagreeing, whereas in fact they think they are. It will not do to say, with Stevenson,[1] that there is a disagreement in attitude, but not in belief: they think, at any rate, that they disagree in belief. Nor does one mean that "society approves of this act," since we frequently meet people who say "I know society approves of this, but it is wrong all the same." But there is no need for argument: direct introspection shows that when we use the terms "right," "good," and the rest, we never intend merely to state that there are feelings of approval. An improved formulation of the sceptical view is that in saying "this is right," and so on, we are not *stating* any approval, but only *expressing* one, that words like "right" and "wrong," "good" and "bad" are to be compared not with "red" and

---

1. *Ethics and Language,* Chapter I.

"square" but with exclamations or ejaculations like "ow!", "boo!", and "hurray!" This is certainly nearer the truth, and avoids the previous difficulties, but is, in another way, just as unplausible. For we do not think that we are merely ejaculating when we talk in moral terms. If we did, and if someone disagreed with us, we should merely disapprove of his approvals, and either try to coax him into a different emotional attitude, or if he proved obstinate, knock him down. In fact we reason with him. These facts, and the logical tangles that we get into when we try to restate fairly complex moral situations in the "boo-hurray" language, prove that we think, at least, that we are not merely expressing our emotions but are describing objective facts, and therefore that the meaning of moral terms is not parallel with that of ejaculations. Many refutations of the "boo-hurray" theory have been worked out, but they all depend upon and illustrate the fact that we *think* that we are doing things of quite different sorts when we say "right" and when we say "ow!" Now if philosophy could do no more than elucidate the meaning of the terms of common speech, remove confusions and rationalise the thought of ordinary men, there would be nothing more to be said. Moral terms do mean objective qualities, and everyone who uses them does so because he believes in objective moral facts. But if the very terms of common speech may include errors and con-

fusions within themselves, so that they cannot be used at all without falsity, if, we may add, philosophy may be permitted to enquire into these errors by observing a few facts for itself and founding inductive conclusions on them, the moral sceptic need not be so soon disheartened.

But he must modify his view again, and say that in using moral terms we are as it were objectifying our own feelings, thinking them into qualities existing independently of us. For example, we may see a plant, say a fungus, that fills us with disgust, but instead of stating that we have this feeling, or merely expressing and relieving it by an exclamation, we may ascribe to the fungus a semi-moral quality of foulness, over and above all the qualities that a physical scientist could find in it. Of course, in objectifying our feelings we are also turning them inside out: our feeling about the fungus is one of being disgusted, while the foulness we ascribe to the fungus means that it is disgusting. The supposed objective quality is not simply the feeling itself transferred to an external object, but is something that would inevitably arouse that feeling. (No one would say, "That fungus is foul, but I feel no disgust at it.") The feeling and the supposed quality are related as a seal or stamp and its impression.

This process of objectification is, I think, well known to psychologists and is not new in philosophy.

I believe that it resembles what Hume says we do when we manufacture the idea of necessary connection out of our feeling of being compelled, by the association of ideas, to pass from cause to effect, though here the process of turning inside out does not occur.

There are strong influences which might lead us thus to objectify moral feelings. As I have mentioned, our moral judgements seem to arise from approvals borrowed from society, or from some social group, and these are felt by the individual as external to himself. It is for this reason that they are universal in form, applying equally to himself and to others. They are thus formally capable of being objective laws, in contrast to the "selfish" desires of the individual. This generality or universality, which I mentioned as characteristic of the emotion of approval, is reflected in Rousseau's doctrine that the general will and therefore law must be general in their object, and in Kant's criterion of the possibility of universalisation of a moral law. Since we inevitably tend to encourage what we approve of, and to impose it upon others, we want everyone to adopt our approvals, and this will surely come about if they have only to perceive a genuinely existing objective fact, for what we feel is in general private, what we perceive may be common to all. Suppose that we approve of hard work: then if as well as a feeling of approval in our own minds there were an objective fact like "hard work is good," such that everyone could observe the fact and such that the mere observation would arouse in him a like feeling of approval, and even perhaps stimulate him to work, we should eventually get what we want done: people would work hard. And since what we want does not exist in fact, we naturally construct it in imagination: we objectify our feelings so thoroughly that we completely deceive ourselves. I imagine that this is the reason why our belief in moral objectivity is so firm: we much more readily admit that the foulness of a fungus is an objectification than that the depravity of people who break our windows is. If moral predicates were admitted to be what the moral sceptic says they are, we should never be able to extol a state of affairs as good in any sense which would induce people to bring it about, unless they already wanted it, though we might point out that this state had features which in fact they did desire, though they had not realised this: we should never be able to recommend any course of action, except in such terms as "if you want to be rich, be economical;" nor could we give commands by any moral authority, though we might again advise "if you don't want a bullet through your brains, come quietly;" and we should never be able to lecture anyone on his wickedness—an alarming prospect. The temptations to objectify feelings of approval, and to retain our belief in morals, are clearly strong ones.

This process of objectifying our feelings is, then, neither impossible nor improbable: there is also abundant evidence that it is just what has occurred. It is commonly believed by moralists that good means desirable in a sense such that the mere recognition that a thing is good makes us desire it, and similarly the conclusion of the practical syllogism is both "this is right" and the performance of the action. This is what we should expect if "right" were the objectification of a tendency to compel or command the kind of act so described, and "good" of desire and approval. This is again indicated by the use of the term "value" which is clearly borrowed from spheres like economics where value is created by demand—in fact a quality manufactured in imagination out of the relation of being demanded by someone, the abstraction being the easier because the demand is not essentially that of a single buyer, but of an indeterminate crowd of potential buyers: the analogy with the objectification of moral feelings, aided by their generality, is very plain. Anderson has pointed out (in "The Meaning of Good," published in the Journal for September, 1942) that whenever anyone argues "Y is good, X is a means to Y, therefore X is good" he must be using "good" in an economic sense, as relative to

some demand: now this is one of the commonest forms of argument in ordinary moral thought. There is nothing inconsistent in saying that "good" is the objectification of both desire and approval: its meaning is not quite fixed, and approval both is a development from liking and desiring, and attains its end when its object is generally desired. Further evidence is given by the categorical imperative, which looks very much like an abstraction from the commonplace hypothetical imperative, "if you want this, do that," and which may be described as the making objective and so absolute of advice which is properly relative to the condition of the presence of the desire. "Naturalistic" theories of ethics, which seem so absurd to a logician like G. E. Moore, who insists on the objective-quality aspect of moral terms, represent as it were partially successful attempts at objectification. "The good is the desired" and suchlike statements, which recur with remarkable persistence in philosophic history, plainly betray the emotional origin of moral terms. But there is no need to multiply examples: almost every moral term and style of moral thought may be seen to be borrowed from less lofty spheres, and in the course of the transfer objective qualities have appeared where only emotions were previously recognised.

In attempting to give an account of the origin of moral terms in this process of objectification, I do not, of course, claim that it is complete or precise in all respects. It is still open to discussion and correction on empirical grounds. We might go on to consider this process as a psychological process, investigating its causes, its similarities and contrasts with other mental processes, and the steps of which it is made up. We might ask whether "objectification" or some other name is really the most suitable, and also what are the precise motives objectified: we might consider, for example, Westermarck's argument[2] that "ought" normally expresses a conation, is sometimes but not necessarily or essentially imperative, and has its origin in disapproval rather than approval.

My discussion in this paper is intended to open the way for such discussions, not to settle them once and for all. What I am concerned to establish is simply the logical status of moral terms, not the psychological details of their origin; in effect I am asserting only that there are no facts of the form "this is right," that when we use such words the only fact is the existence of some feelings in ourselves or in others or in both, but that in using these terms we are falsely postulating or asserting something of the simple, objective form "this is right."

I am not, of course, disagreeing with the point mentioned several times by Anderson (for example in "The Meaning of Good," p. 120) that "I like this," "I approve of this," "this society approves of this," are all statements of objective fact and would in any particular case be true or false. But they are all of a different form from statements like "this is right," the latter attributing a predicate to a subject, the former asserting a relation between two or more things. When I say that we objectify, I mean that we believe in the truth of statements of the subject-predicate form.

This re-statement does away with the logical difficulties previously encountered by moral scepticism. Nor are there, I think, any non-logical difficulties in the way of our accepting this view, except the persistence of the belief that moral facts are objective. It might be claimed that this firm belief is based on an intuition, but it has no further arguments to support it, and we have indicated social and psychological causes which would produce such a belief even if it had no foundation. However firm the belief may be, therefore, it is not valid evidence for the existence of moral facts. But the true moralist will not be deterred by lack of evidence: he will perhaps be compelled to admit that moral judgements are evolved, historically, by objectification of feelings. But none the less, he will maintain, when evolved they *are* valid. But now we remind him of their variability, their correlation with social demands. Ac-

2. *The Origin and Development of the Moral Ideas,* Chapter VI.

tual moral judgements, en masse, cannot be valid, since they are mutually contradictory: in fact all the evidence suggests that not only are moral judgements derived from feelings, but there are no objective moral facts: the feelings are *all* that exists. . . .

AFTERWORD

Some theories of ethics point out one or more fundamental values and then argue that our actions and character should be judged in terms of their efficiency in promoting those values. Such theories, often called *teleological* ethical theories, attempt to base all moral judgments on the concept of a final purpose which our moral action should strive to pursue. Mill's utilitarianism is one example of such a theory. Other theories concentrate on the development of certain principles of action which ought to be followed whether or not they promote certain goals effectively. Such theories, often referred to as *deontological* ethical theories, tend to emphasize duties which we should try to carry out, or rights of persons which we should not violate. Kant's ethical theory is an example of a deontological theory.

Now, at the practical level, we seem to subscribe to both teleological and deontological values. That is, we tend to speak of certain things, such as health, longevity, or, especially, happiness, as if they provided the fundamental reasons for all we do. But we also speak of certain rights (such as the right to self-determination, or the right to life) and certain duties (such as the duty not to harm others) as if they should be respected regardless of consequences. Many serious practical moral problems reflect our ambivalence toward these two kinds of value, for those problems are difficult to manage precisely because we find that in them very important rights and duties clash with very important goals. For instance, we count it as a very important kind of (deontological?) wrong-doing to deceive people about important matters, or force them to do what they do not want to do. But we also regard it as a very important (teleological?) goal to protect the lives and health of persons. But suppose a physician has a patient who will refuse health-restoring treatment if the facts about the disease and the treatment are made known. Should the physician deceive the patient, or take legal steps to force the treatment on the patient, in order to save life and health? Or should life, health, and happiness be risked in order to respect the patient's right to know the facts about his own case and to decide about his own treatment?

Other examples of this kind of clash of values abound: Should people be forced involuntarily into military service to protect the political system which promotes their happiness and well-being? Should there be laws prohibiting persons from behaving in ways dangerous to themselves? Should children be provided with important information and training against their parents' wishes? You may find it helpful, in reviewing the preceding selections, to try to decide what each author would say about these cases in which rights, duties and goals seem to be in conflict. In addition, trying to decide how you yourself think such cases should be handled may help you to become clearer about the kind of position on the objectivity of moral judgments which seems most plausible to you.

REVIEW QUESTIONS

Selection 13

1. Precisely how does Brandt characterize the theory of *ethical relativism?* What views does he warn us not to confuse with this theory?

2. What are the details of Brandt's account of *conflicting ethical opinions?* Why is this important for the critical evaluation of the theory of ethical relativism?

3. Why does Brandt think it is inconsistent for a radical ethical relativist to claim that we have a moral obligation to be tolerant?

4. According to Brandt, would ethical relativism permit us to adopt whatever moral code we preferred? Explain.

Selection 14

5. How does Mill distinguish between pleasures of different quality? Why is this important?

6. Explain as clearly as you can the Greatest Happiness Principle.

7. According to Mill, can the Greatest Happiness Principle *require* us to sacrifice our happiness to achieve other goals? Explain.

8. How does Mill deal with the objection that we often do not have time to decide what the Greatest Happiness Principle requires?

Selection 15

9. How does Kant attempt to prove that reason is not intended to provide us with happiness?

10. What is Kant's distinction between acting *in accordance with* duty and acting *from* duty? What use does he make of this distinction?

11. Explain the difference between hypothetical and categorical imperatives. Why does Kant think that moral principles must not be hypothetical?

12. Use an example of Kant's, or make up one of your own, to explain how an appeal to the Categorical Imperative determines our duty.

13. How does Kant try to show that we should treat all persons equally?

Selection 16

14. When Moore says that good is *simple,* rather than complex, what does he mean?

15. According to Moore, what is the difference between *good* and *the good?*

16. What is the naturalistic fallacy? Moore would say that Mill has committed this fallacy. Explain why.

Selection 17

17. According to Hare, what is the principle function of the judgment that something is good?

18. How do appeals to facts serve as the basis for commendation, on Hare's view?

19. Why, according to Hare, do moral judgments about other people commit the makers of the judgments to certain kinds of behavior? How does this claim contribute to his theory?

20. Is Hare's theory an objectivist one or not? Explain.

Selection 18.

21. What are the initial considerations Mackie mentions which favor the view that moral judgments are not objective?

22. Mackie says, "in using moral terms we are ... objectifying our own feelings." What does he mean?

23. What practical advantages does Mackie see in allowing ourselves to objectify our feelings?

24. If Mackie's view is correct, what is the function of argument and appeals to evidence in support of our moral judgments? Explain.

7

Motives and Duty

We commonly accept that unselfishness is an admirable trait of character, and that if we are to act morally, we must sometimes act unselfishly. We expect ourselves to sacrifice our own interests, at least in minor ways, when doing so can be of great service to others; and we are taught to admire those who can make great sacrifices for the sake of others.

But on close inspection the very idea of unselfish action becomes suspect. The problem is not whether it is appropriate at times, but how it could be possible at all. For it is tempting to think this way: What we are concerned with, when we discuss moral behavior, is not what happens to us by accident, or what we do by reflex when there is no time to think, but what we deliberately choose to do, after at least a little consideration. And deliberate choice does not take place unless one has some motive or reason for making the choice. But must not every such motive involve some kind of interest or desire on the part of the person making the choice? And, surely, action intended to satisfy the desires or interests of the agent is *selfish* action. We understand quite well how a person can be motivated by his own interests and desires. What is hard to understand is how a person could be motivated to act without any such interests or desires, or, even more puzzling, to act *in spite of them.*

Finally, it is almost universally agreed that principles of moral behavior cannot require us to do the impossible. However we finally come to understand the statement (recall Chapter 4), it is true in some important sense that one cannot be morally responsible unless one could have acted otherwise. So, if unselfishness really is not possible, then it could not be a requirement in any reasonable system of moral principles.

Thus, we have reasons for accepting all three of these statements:

(1) Acting morally sometimes requires unselfish behavior.

(2) Unselfish behavior is impossible.

(3) What is impossible cannot be morally required.

But since all three statements form an inconsistent set, at least one of them must be rejected, or modified in some way.

Those who have been concerned with this issue have had little interest in rejecting (3) and arguing that reasonable moral principles can require the impossible. Thus, the real controversy has centered on the question whether unselfish behavior is possible, or whether adequate systems of moral principles must not require it. To understand the issues involved, it is important to distinguish two kinds of theories about selfish action.

The first kind of theory, called *psychological egoism,* holds that it is psychologically impossible for anyone to act without having some sort of personal (selfish) interest or desire which they believe will be served by the action. Notice that this is not a theory about what people *ought* to do, but about the limits placed by human nature on what it is possible for them to do. Notice, too, that the theory does not say that people always *do* serve their own interests when they act, but only that, in some way, they *think* they will. Since we all make mistakes, it is entirely compatible with this theory for us to think that we are serving some interest of our own, when actually we are acting against our own interests—and perhaps accidentally in the interests of others. Significant opposition to this theory, then, will involve the claim that people can *knowingly* act in ways which fail to serve, or may even hinder, their own interests.

The second kind of theory, called *ethical egoism,* is about what we ought to do, rather than about the ways in which we actually do act. It holds that the basis of morality is self-interest, and that all the principles of moral behavior must be grounded in an enlightened understanding of how each of us may best serve his own needs and desires. Ethical egoists, then, maintain that morality does not require altruism; and opposition to ethical egoism must involve the claim that at least some unselfish actions are morally required.

It is important to keep the distinction between the two kinds of egoism in mind, because different arguments and evidence apply to them. But, of course, the two theories are closely connected. Almost without exception, ethical egoists also are psychological egoists. In fact, most ethical egoists seem to arrive at their position by affirming psychological egoism (thus accepting statement (2)), recognizing that morality cannot require the impossible (thus accepting (3)), and then arguing that this proves that morality cannot require altruism (thus rejecting (1)). But you should notice that one *could* be an ethical egoist without believing psychological egoism. That is, one could believe that unselfish action is possible, but argue that morality never requires it. It is possible, too, for one to be a psychological egoist without subscribing to ethical egoism. But if one accepts statement (3), this would be possible only if one rejected morality altogether—that is, if one believed that morality has no legitimate status, and hence can require nothing at all of us. From one point of view, then, ethical egoism seems to be the position to which the psychological egoist is driven, if he wants to avoid disclaiming morality altogether.

The following selections deal with two major issues. The first of these is the issue of psychological egoism, and the kinds of motives it is possible for us to have for our actions. The second issue is whether an adequate set of moral principles can be found if we assume that psychological egoism is true. With respect to both issues you should pay particular attention to the ways in which different authors think of selfishness, for there may well be substantial confusion about what selfishness really is, and what should be counted as a selfish motive.

19

Self-Interest as the Basis of Morality

THOMAS HOBBES

Human Equality and the State of Nature

Nature hath made men so equal, in the faculties of the body, and mind; as that though there be found one man sometimes manifestly stronger in body, or of quicker mind than another; yet when all is reckoned together, the difference between man, and man, is not so considerable, as that one man can thereupon claim to himself any benefit, to which another may not pretend, as well as he. For as to the strength of body, the weakest has strength enough to kill the strongest, either by secret machination, or by confederacy with others, that are in the same danger with himself.

And as to the faculties of the mind, setting aside the arts grounded upon words, and especially that skill of proceeding upon general, and infallible rules, called science; which very few have, and but in few things; as being not a native faculty, born with us; nor attained, as prudence, while we look after somewhat else, I find yet a greater equality amongst men, than that of strength. For prudence, is but experience; which equal time, equally bestows on all men, in those things they equally apply themselves unto. That which may perhaps make such equality incredible, is but a vain conceit of one's own wisdom, which almost all men think they have in a greater degree, than the vulgar; that is, than all men but themselves, and a few others, whom by fame, or for concurring with themselves, they approve. For such is the nature of men, that

[From *Leviathan,* chapters 13, 14, 15. First published in 1651.]

howsoever they may acknowledge many others to be more witty, or more eloquent, or more learned; yet they will hardly believe there be many so wise as themselves; for they see their own wit at hand, and other men's at a distance. But this proveth rather that men are in that point equal, than unequal. For there is not ordinarily a greater sign of the equal distribution of any thing, than that every man is contented with his share.

From this equality of ability, ariseth equality of hope in the attaining of our ends. And therefore if any two men desire the same thing, which nevertheless they cannot both enjoy, they become enemies; and in the way to their end, which is principally their own conservation, and sometimes their delectation only, endeavour to destroy, or subdue one another. And from hence it comes to pass, that where an invader hath no more to fear, than another man's single power; if one plant, sow, build, or possess a convenient seat, others may probably be expected to come prepared with forces united, to dispossess, and deprive him, not only of the fruit of his labour, but also of his life, or liberty. And the invader again is in the like danger of another.

And from this diffidence of one another, there is no way for any man to secure himself, so reasonable, as anticipation; that is, by force, or wiles, to master the persons of all men he can, so long, till he see no other power great enough to endanger him: and this is no more than his own conservation requireth, and is generally allowed. Also because there be some, that taking pleasure in contemplating their own power in the acts of conquest, which they pursue farther than their security requires; if others, that otherwise would be glad to be at ease within modest bounds, should not by invasion increase their power, they would not be able, long time, by standing only on their defence, to subsist. And by consequence, such augmentation of dominion over men being necessary to a man's conservation, it ought to be allowed him.

Again, men have no pleasure, but on the contrary a great deal of grief, in keeping company, where there is no power able to over-awe them all. For every man looketh that his companion should value him, at the same rate he sets upon himself: and upon all signs of contempt, or undervaluing, naturally endeavours, as far as he dares, (which amongst them that have no common power to keep them in quiet, is far enough to make them destroy each other), to extort a greater value from his contemners, by damage; and from others, by the example.

So that in the nature of man, we find three principal causes of quarrel. First, competition; secondly, diffidence; thirdly, glory.

The first, maketh men invade for gain; the second, for safety; and the third, for reputation. The first use violence, to make themselves masters of other men's persons, wives, children, and cattle; the second, to defend them; the third, for trifles, as a word, a smile, a different opinion, and any other sign of undervalue, either direct in their persons, or by reflection in their kindred, their friends, their nation, their profession, or their name.

Hereby it is manifest, that during the time men live without a common power to keep them all in awe, they are in that condition which is called war; and such a war, as is of every man, against every man. For WAR, consisteth not in battle only, or the act of fighting; but in a tract of time, wherein the will to contend by battle is sufficiently known: and therefore the notion of *time,* is to be considered in the nature of war; as it is in the nature of weather. For as the nature of foul weather, lieth not in a shower or two of rain; but in an inclination thereto of many days together: so the nature of war, consisteth not in actual fighting; but in the known disposition thereto, during all the time there is no assurance to the contrary. All other time is PEACE.

Whatsoever therefore is consequent to a time of war, where every man is enemy to every man; the same is consequent to the time, wherein men live without other security, than what their own strength, and their own invention shall furnish them withal. In such condition, there is no place for industry; because the fruit thereof is uncertain:

and consequently no culture of the earth; no navigation, nor use of the commodities that may be imported by sea; no commodious building; no instruments of moving, and removing, such things as require much force; no knowledge of the face of the earth; no account of time; no arts; no letters; no society; and which is worst of all, continual fear, and danger of violent death; and the life of man, solitary, poor, nasty, brutish, and short. . . .

It may peradventure be thought, there was never such a time, nor condition of war as this; and I believe it was never generally so, over all the world.

. . . Howsoever, it may be perceived what manner of life there would be, where there were no common power to fear, by the manner of life, which men that have formerly lived under a peaceful government, use to degenerate into, in a civil war. . . .

To this war of every man, against every man, this also is consequent; that nothing can be unjust. The notions of right and wrong, justice and injustice have there no place. Where there is no common power, there is no law: where no law, no injustice. Force, and fraud, are in war the two cardinal virtues. Justice, and injustice are none of the faculties neither of the body, nor mind. If they were, they might be in a man that were alone in the world, as well as his senses, and passions. They are qualities, that relate to men in society, not in solitude. It is consequent also to the same condition, that there be no propriety, no dominion, no *mine* and *thine* distinct; but only that to be every man's, that he can get; and for so long, as he can keep it. And thus much for the ill condition, which man by mere nature is actually placed in; though with a possibility to come out of it, consisting partly in the passions, partly in his reason.

The passions that incline men to peace, are fear of death; desire of such things as are necessary to commodious living; and a hope by their industry to obtain them. And reason suggesteth convenient articles of peace, upon which men may be drawn to agreement. These articles, are they, which otherwise are called the Laws of Nature: whereof I shall speak more particularly, in the two following chapters.

Natural Laws and Contracts

The right of nature, which writers commonly call *jus naturale,* is the liberty each man hath, to use his own power, as he will himself, for the preservation of his own nature; that is to say, of his own life; and consequently, of doing any thing, which in his own judgment, and reason, he shall conceive to be the aptest means thereunto.

By LIBERTY, is understood, according to the proper signification of the word, the absence of external impediments: which impediments, may oft take away part of a man's power to do what he would; but cannot hinder him from using the power left him, according as his judgment, and reason shall dictate to him.

A LAW OF NATURE, *lex naturalis,* is a precept or general rule, found out by reason, by which a man is forbidden to do that, which is destructive of his life, or taketh away the means of preserving the same; and to omit that, by which he thinketh it may be best preserved. For though they that speak of this subject, use to confound *jus,* and *lex, right* and *law:* yet they ought to be distinguished; because RIGHT, consisteth in liberty to do, or to forbear; whereas LAW, determineth, and bindeth to one of them: so that law, and right, differ as much, as obligation, and liberty; which in one and the same matter are inconsistent.

And because the condition of man, as hath been declared in the precedent chapter, is a condition of war of every one against every one; in which case every one is governed by his own reason; and there is nothing he can make use of, that may not be a help unto him, in preserving his life against his enemies; it followeth, that in such a condition, every man has a right to every thing; even to one another's body. And therefore, as long as this natural right of every man to every thing endureth, there can be no security to any man, how strong or wise soever he be, of living out the time, which nature ordinarily alloweth men to live. And consequently it is a precept, or general rule of reason, *that every man, ought to endeavour peace, as far as he has hope of obtaining it; and when he cannot obtain it, that he may seek, and use, all helps, and advantages of war.* The first branch of which rule, containeth the first, and fundamental law of nature; which is, *to seek peace, and follow it.* The second, the sum of the right of nature; which is, *by all means we can, to defend ourselves.*

From this fundamental law of nature, by which men are commanded to endeavour peace, is derived this second law; *that a man be willing, when others are so too, as far-forth, as for peace, and defence of himself he shall think it necessary, to lay down this right to all things; and be contented with so much liberty against other men, as he would allow other men against himself.* For as long as every man holdeth this right, of doing any thing he liketh; so long are all men in the condition of war. But if other men will not lay down their right, as well as he; then there is no reason for any one, to divest himself of his: for that were to expose himself to prey, which no man is bound to, rather than to dispose himself to peace. This is that law of the Gospel; *whatsoever you require that others should do to you, that do ye to them.* And that law of all men, *quod tibi fieri non vis, alteri ne feceris.*[1]

To *lay down* a man's *right* to any thing, is to *divest* himself of the *liberty,* of hindering another of the benefit of his own right to the same. For he that renounceth, or passeth away his right, giveth not to any other man a right which he had not before; because there is nothing to which every man had not right by nature: but only standeth out of his way, that he may enjoy his own original right, without hindrance from him; not without hindrance from another. So that the effect which redoundeth to one man, by another man's defect of right, is but so much diminution of impediments to the use of his own right original.

Right is laid aside, either by simply renouncing it; or by transferring it to another. By *simply* RENOUNCING; when he cares not to whom the benefit thereof redoundeth. By TRANSFERRING; when he intendeth the benefit thereof to some certain person, or persons. And when a man hath in either manner abandoned, or granted away his right; then is he said to be OBLIGED, or BOUND, not to hinder those, to whom such right is granted, or abandoned, from the benefit of it: and that he *ought,* and it is his DUTY, not to make void that voluntary act of his own: and that such hindrance is INJUSTICE, and INJURY, as being *sine jure;*[2] the right being before renounced, or transferred. So that *injury,* or *injustice,* in the controver-

1. ["Do not do to others what you do not want done to you."—Ed. note.]

2. [i.e., without right.—Ed. note.]

sies of the world, is somewhat like to that, which in the disputations of scholars is called *absurdity*. For as it is there called an absurdity, to contradict what one maintained in the beginning: so in the world, it is called injustice, and injury, voluntarily to undo that, which from the beginning he had voluntarily done. The way by which a man either simply renounceth, or transferreth his right, is a declaration, or signification, by some voluntary and sufficient sign, or signs, that he doth so renounce, or transfer; or hath so renounced, or transferred the same, to him that accepteth it. And these signs are either words only, or actions only; or, as it happeneth most often, both words, and actions. And the same are the BONDS, by which men are bound, and obliged: bonds, that have their strength, not from their own nature, for nothing is more easily broken than a man's word, but from fear of some evil consequence upon the rupture.

Whensoever a man transferreth his right, or renounceth it; it is either in consideration of some right reciprocally transferred to himself; or for some other good he hopeth for thereby. For it is a voluntary act: and of the voluntary acts of every man, the object is some *good to himself*. And therefore there be some rights, which no man can be understood by any words, or other signs, to have abandoned, or transferred. As first a man cannot lay down the right of resisting them, that assault him by force, to take away his life; because he cannot be understood to aim thereby, at any good to himself. The same may be said of wounds, and chains, and imprisonment; both because there is no benefit consequent to such patience; as there is to the patience of suffering another to be wounded, or imprisoned: as also because a man cannot tell, when he seeth men proceed against him by violence, whether they intend his death or not. And lastly the motive, and end for which this renouncing, and transferring of right is introduced, is nothing else but the security of a man's person, in his life, and in the means of so preserving life, as not to be weary of it. And therefore if a man by words, or other signs, seem to despoil himself of the end, for which those signs were intended; he is not to be understood as if he meant it, or that it was his will; but that he was ignorant of how such words and actions were to be interpreted.

The mutual transferring of right, is that which men call CONTRACT. . . .

If a covenant be made, wherein neither of the parties perform presently, but trust one another; in the condition of mere nature, which is a condition of war of every man against every man, upon any reasonable suspicion, it is void: but if there be a common power set over them both, with right and force sufficient to compel performance, it is not void. For he that performeth first, has no assurance the other will perform after; because the bonds of words are too weak to bridle men's ambition, avarice, anger, and other passions, without the fear of some coercive power; which in the condition of mere nature, where all men are equal, and judges of the justness of their own fears, cannot possibly be supposed. And therefore he which performeth first, does but betray himself to his enemy; contrary to the right, he can never abandon, of defending his life, and means of living.

But in a civil estate, where there is a power set up to constrain those that would otherwise violate their faith, that fear is no more reasonable: and for that cause, he which by the covenant is to perform first, is obliged so to do. . . .

Origins of Justice and Morality

From that law of nature, by which we are obliged to transfer to another, such rights, as being retained, hinder the peace of mankind, there followeth a third; which is this, *that men perform their covenants made:* without which, covenants are in vain, and but empty words; and the right of all men to all things remaining, we are still in the condition of war.

And in this law of nature, consisteth the fountain and original of JUSTICE. For where no covenant hath preceded, there hath no right been transferred, and every man has right to every thing; and consequently, no

action can be unjust. But when a covenant is made, then to break it is *unjust:* and the definition of INJUSTICE, is no other than *the not performance of covenant.* And whatsoever is not unjust, is *just.*

But because covenants of mutual trust, where there is a fear of not performance on either part, as hath been said in the former chapter, are invalid; though the original of justice be the making of covenants; yet injustice actually there can be none, till the cause of such fear be taken away; which while men are in the natural condition of war, cannot be done. Therefore before the names of just, and unjust can have place, there must be some coercive power, to compel men equally to the performance of their covenants, by the terror of some punishment, greater than the benefit they expect by the breach of their covenant; and to make good that propriety, which by mutual contract men acquire, in recompense of the universal right they abandon: and such power there is none before the erection of a commonwealth. And this is also to be gathered out of the ordinary definition of justice in the Schools: for they say, that *justice is the constant will of giving to every man his own.* And therefore where there is no *own,* that is, no propriety, there is no injustice; and where there is no coercive power erected, that is, where there is no commonwealth, there is no propriety; all men having right to all things: therefore where there is no commonwealth, there nothing is unjust. So that the nature of justice, consisteth in keeping of valid covenants: but the validity of covenants begins not but with the constitution of a civil power, sufficient to compel men to keep them: and then it is also that propriety begins. . . .

These are the laws of nature, dictating peace, for a means of the conservation of men in multitudes; and which only concern the doctrine of civil society. There be other things tending to the destruction of particular men; as drunkenness, and all other parts of intemperance; which may therefore also be reckoned amongst those things which the law of nature hath forbidden; but are not necessary to be mentioned, nor are pertinent enough to this place.

And though this may seem too subtle a deduction of the laws of nature, to be taken notice of by all men; whereof the most part are too busy in getting food, and the rest too negligent to understand; yet to leave all men inexcusable, they have been contracted into one easy sum, intelligible even to the meanest capacity; and that is, *Do not that to another, which thou wouldest not have done to thyself;* which sheweth him, that he has no more to do in learning the laws of nature, but, when weighing the actions of other men with his own, they seem too heavy, to put them into the other part of the balance, and his own into their place, that his own passions, and self-love, may add nothing to the weight; and

then there is none of these laws of nature that will not appear unto him very reasonable. . . .

The laws of nature are immutable and eternal; for injustice, ingratitude, arrogance, pride, iniquity, acception of persons, and the rest, can never be made lawful. For it can never be that war shall preserve life, and peace destroy it.

The same laws, because they oblige only to a desire, and endeavour, I mean an unfeigned and constant endeavour, are easy to be observed. For in that they require nothing but endeavour, he that endeavoureth their performance, fulfilleth them; and he that fulfilleth the law, is just.

And the science of them, is the true and only moral philosophy. For moral philosophy is nothing else but the science of what is *good,* and *evil,* in the conversation, and society of mankind. *Good,* and *evil,* are names that signify our appetites, and aversions; which in different tempers, customs, and doctrines of men, are different: and divers men, differ not only in their judgment, on the senses of what is pleasant, and unpleasant to the taste, smell, hearing, touch, and sight; but also of what is conformable, or disagreeable to reason, in the actions of common life. Nay, the same man, in divers times, differs from himself; and one time praiseth, that is, calleth good, what another time he dispraiseth, and calleth evil: from whence arise disputes, controversies, and at last war. And therefore so long as a man is in the condition of mere nature, which is a condition of war, as private appetite is the measure of good, and evil: and consequently all men agree on this, that peace is good, and therefore also the way, or means of peace, which, as I have shewed before, are *justice, gratitude, modesty, equity, mercy,* and the rest of the laws of nature, are good; that is to say; *moral virtues;* and their contrary *vices,* evil. Now the science of virtue and vice, is moral philosophy; and therefore the true doctrine of the laws of nature, is the true moral philosophy. But the writers of moral philosophy, though they acknowledge the same virtues and vices; yet not seeing wherein consisted their goodness; nor that they come to be praised, as the means of peaceable, sociable, and comfortable living, place them in a mediocrity of passions: as if not the cause, but the degree of daring, made fortitude; or not the cause, but the quantity of a gift, made liberality. . . .

20

Motives and the Principle of Utility

JOHN STUART MILL

Ultimate Sanction of the Principle of Utility

The question is often asked, and properly so, in regard to any supposed moral standard—What is its sanction? what are the motives to obey it? or more specifically, what is the source of its obligation? whence does it derive its binding force? It is a necessary part of moral philosophy to provide the answer to this question; which, though frequently assuming the shape of an objection to the utilitarian morality, as if it had some special applicability to that above others, really arises in regard to all standards. It arises, in fact, whenever a person is called on to *adopt* a standard, or refer morality to any basis on which he has not been accustomed to rest it. For the customary morality, that which education and opinion have consecrated, is the only one which presents itself to the mind with the feeling of being *in itself* obligatory; and when a person is asked to believe that this morality *derives* its obligation from some general principle round which custom has not thrown the same halo, the assertion is to him a paradox; the supposed corollaries seem to have a more binding force than the original theorem; the superstructure seems to stand better without, than with, what is represented as its foundation. He says to himself, I feel that I am bound not to rob or murder, betray or deceive; but why am I bound to promote the general happiness? If my own happiness lies in something else, why may I not give that the preference?

[From *Utilitarianism,* chapters 3, 4, 4th edition (1871). First published in 1861.]

If the view adopted by the utilitarian philosophy of the nature of the moral sense be correct, this difficulty will always present itself, until the influences which form moral character have taken the same hold of the principle which they have taken of some of the consequences—until, by the improvement of education, the feeling of unity with our fellow creatures shall be (what it cannot be doubted that Christ intended it to be) as deeply rooted in our character, and to our own consciousness as completely a part of our nature, as the horror of crime is in an ordinarily well-brought up young person. In the mean time, however, the difficulty has no peculiar application to the doctrine of utility, but is inherent in every attempt to analyse morality and reduce it to principles; which, unless the principle is already in men's minds invested with as much sacredness as any of its applications, always seems to divest them of a part of their sanctity.

The principle of utility either has, or there is no reason why it might not have, all the sanctions which belong to any other system of morals. Those sanctions are either external or internal. Of the external sanctions it is not necessary to speak at any length. They are, the hope of favour and the fear of displeasure from our fellow creatures or from the Ruler of the Universe, along with whatever we may have of sympathy or affection for them, or of love and awe of Him, inclining us to do his will independently of selfish consequences. There is evidently no reason why all these motives for observance should not attach themselves to the utilitarian morality, as completely and as powerfully as to any other. Indeed, those of them which refer to our fellow creatures are sure to do so, in proportion to the amount of general intelligence; for whether there be any other ground of moral obligation than the general happiness or not, men do desire happiness; and however imperfect may be their own practice, they desire and commend all conduct in others towards themselves, by which they think their happiness is promoted. With regard to the religious motive, if men believe, as most profess to do, in the goodness of God, those who think that conduciveness to the general happiness is the essence, or even only the criterion, of good, must necessarily believe that it is also that which God approves. The whole force therefore of external reward and punishment, whether physical or moral, and whether proceeding from God or from our fellow men, together with all that the capacities of human nature admit, of disinterested devotion to either, become available to enforce the utilitarian morality, in proportion as that morality is recognised; and the more powerfully, the more the appliances of education and general cultivation are bent to the purpose.

So far as to external sanctions. The internal sanction of duty, whatever our standard of duty may be, is one and the same—a feeling in our own mind; a pain, more or less intense, attendant on violation of duty, which in properly-cultivated moral natures rises, in the more serious cases, into shrinking from it as an impossibility. This feeling, when disinterested, and connecting itself with the pure idea of duty, and not with some particular form of it, or with any of the merely accessory circumstances, is the essence of Conscience; though in that complex phenomenon as it actually exists, the simple fact is in general all encrusted over with collateral associations, derived from sympathy, from love, and still more from fear; from all the forms of religious feeling; from the recollections of childhood and of all our past life; from self-esteem, desire of the esteem of others, and occasionally even self-abasement. This extreme complication is, I apprehend, the origin of the sort of mystical character which, by a tendency of the human mind of which there are many other examples, is apt to be attributed to the idea of moral obligation, and which leads people to believe that the idea cannot possibly attach itself to any other objects than those which, by a supposed mysterious law, are found in our present experience to excite it. Its binding force, however, consists in the existence of a mass of feeling which must be broken through in order to do what violates our standard of right, and which, if we do

nevertheless violate that standard, will probably have to be encountered afterwards in the form of remorse. Whatever theory we have of the nature or origin of conscience, this is what essentially constitutes it.

The ultimate sanction, therefore, of all morality (external motives apart) being a subjective feeling in our own minds, I see nothing embarrassing to those whose standard is utility, in the question, what is the sanction of that particular standard? We may answer, the same as of all other moral standards—the conscientious feelings of mankind. Undoubtedly this sanction has no binding efficacy on those who do not possess the feelings it appeals to; but neither will these persons be more obedient to any other moral principle than to the utilitarian one. On them morality of any kind has no hold but through the external sanctions. Meanwhile the feelings exist, a fact in human nature, the reality of which, and the great power with which they are capable of acting on those in whom they have been duly cultivated, are proved by experience. No reason has ever been shown why they may not be cultivated to as great intensity in connexion with the utilitarian, as with any other rule of morals. . . .

It is not necessary, for the present purpose, to decide whether the feeling of duty is innate or implanted. Assuming it to be innate, it is an open question to what objects it naturally attaches itself; for the philosophic supporters of that theory are now agreed that the intuitive perception is of principles of morality, and not of the details. If there be anything innate in the matter, I see no reason why the feeling which is innate should not be that of regard to the pleasures and pains of others. If there is any principle of morals which is intuitively obligatory, I should say it must be that. If so, the intuitive ethics would coincide with the utilitarian, and there would be no further quarrel between them. Even as it is, the intuitive moralists, though they believe that there are other intuitive moral obligations, do already believe this to be one; for they unanimously hold that a large *portion* of morality turns upon the consideration due to the interests of our fellow creatures. Therefore, if the belief in the transcendental origin of moral obligation gives any additional efficacy to the internal sanction, it appears to me that the utilitarian principle has already the benefit of it.

On the other hand, if, as is my own belief, the moral feelings are not innate, but acquired, they are not for that reason the less natural. It is natural to man to speak, to reason, to build cities, to cultivate the ground, though these are acquired faculties. The moral feelings are not indeed a part of our nature, in the sense of being in any perceptible degree present in all of us; but this, unhappily, is a fact admitted by those who believe the most strenuously in their transcendental origin. Like the other acquired capacities above referred to, the moral faculty, if not a part of our nature, is a natural outgrowth from it; capable, like them, in a certain small degree, of springing up spontaneously; and susceptible of being brought by cultivation to a high degree of development. Unhappily it is also susceptible, by a sufficient use of the external sanctions and of the force of early impressions, of being cultivated in almost any direction: so that there is hardly anything so absurd or so mischievous that it may not, by means of these influences, be made to act on the human mind with all the authority of conscience. To doubt that the same potency might be given by the same means to the principle of utility, even if it had no foundation in human nature, would be flying in the face of all experience.

But moral associations which are wholly of artificial creation, when intellectual culture goes on, yield by degrees to the dissolving force of analysis: and if the feeling of duty, when associated with utility, would appear equally arbitrary; if there were no leading department of our nature, no powerful class of sentiments, with which that association would harmonize, which would make us feel it congenial, and incline us not only to foster it in others (for which we have abundant interested motives), but also to cherish it in ourselves; if there were not, in short, a natural basis of sentiment for utilitarian morality, it might well happen that this association also, even after it had been implanted by education, might be analysed away.

But there *is* this basis of powerful natural sentiment; and this it is which, when once the general happiness is recognised as the ethical standard, will constitute the strength of the utilitarian morality. This firm foundation is that of the social feelings of mankind; the desire to be in unity with our fellow creatures, which is already a powerful principle in human nature, and happily one of those which tend to become stronger, even without express inculcation, from the influences of advancing civilization. The social state is at once so natural, so necessary, and so habitual to man, that, except in some unusual circumstances or by an effort of voluntary abstraction, he never conceives himself otherwise than as a member of a body; and this association is riveted more and more, as mankind are further removed from the state of savage independence. Any condition, therefore, which is essential to a state of society, becomes more and more an inseparable part of every person's conception of the state of things which he is born into, and which is the destiny of a human being. Now, society between human beings, except in the relation of master and slave, is manifestly impossible on any other footing than that the interests of all are to be consulted. Society between equals can only exist on the understanding that the interests of all are to be regarded equally. And since in all states of civilization, every person, except an absolute monarch, has equals, every one is obliged to live on these terms with somebody; and in every age some advance is made towards a state in which it will be impossible to live permanently on other terms with anybody. In this way people grow up unable to conceive as possible to them a state of total disregard of other people's interests. They are under a necessity of conceiving themselves as at least abstaining from all the grosser injuries, and (if only for their own protection) living in a state of constant protest against them. They are also familiar with the fact of co-operating with others, and proposing to themselves a collective, not an individual, interest, as the aim (at least for the time being) of their actions. So long as they are co-operating, their ends are identified with those of others; there is at least a temporary feeling that the interests of others are their own interests. Not only does all strengthening of social ties, and all healthy growth of society, give to each individual a stronger personal interest in practically consulting the welfare of others; it also leads him to identify his *feelings* more and more with their good, or at least with an ever greater degree of practical consideration for it. He comes, as though instinctively, to be conscious of himself as a being who *of course* pays regard to others. The good of others becomes to him a thing naturally and necessarily to be attended to, like any of the physical conditions of our existence. Now, whatever amount of this feeling a person has, he is urged by the strongest motives both of interest and of sympathy to demonstrate it, and to the utmost of his power encourage it in others; and even if he has none of it himself, he is as greatly interested as any one else that others should have it. Consequently, the smallest germs of the feeling are laid hold of and nourished by the contagion of sympathy and the influences of education; and a complete web of corroborative association is woven round it, by the powerful agency of the external sanctions. This mode of conceiving ourselves and human life, as civilization goes on, is felt to be more and more natural. Every step in political improvement renders it more so, by removing the sources of opposition of interest, and levelling those inequalities of legal privilege between individuals or classes, owing to which there are large portions of mankind whose happiness it is still practicable to disregard. In an improving state of the human mind, the influences are constantly on the increase, which tend to generate in each individual a feeling of unity with all the rest; which feeling, if perfect, would make him never think of, or desire, any beneficial condition for himself, in the benefits of which they are not included. . . .

Proof of the Principle of Utility

It has already been remarked, that questions of ultimate ends do not admit of proof, in the ordinary acceptation of the term. To be incapable of proof by reasoning is common to all first principles; to the first premises of our knowledge, as well as to those of our conduct. But the former, being matters of fact, may be the subject of a direct appeal to the faculties which judge of fact—namely, our senses, and our internal consciousness. Can an appeal be made to the same faculties on questions of practical ends? Or by what other faculty is cognizance taken of them?

Questions about ends are, in other words, questions what things are desirable. The utilitarian doctrine is, that happiness is desirable, and the only thing desirable, as an end; all other things being only desirable as means to that end. What ought to be required of this doctrine—what conditions is it requisite that the doctrine should fulfil —to make good its claim to be believed?

The only proof capable of being given that an object is visible, is that people actually see it. The only proof that a sound is audible, is that people hear it: and so of the other sources of our experience. In like manner, I apprehend, the sole evidence it is possible to produce that anything is desirable, is that people do actually desire it. If the end which the utilitarian doctrine proposes to itself were not, in theory and in practice, acknowledged to be an end, nothing could ever convince any person that it was so. No reason can be given why the general happiness is desirable, except that each person, so far as he believes it to be attainable, desires his own happiness. This, however, being a fact, we have not only all the proof which the case admits of, but all which it is possible to require, that happiness is a good: that each person's happiness is a good to that person, and the general happiness, therefore, a good to the aggregate of all persons. Happiness has made out its title as *one* of the ends of conduct, and consequently one of the criteria of morality.

But it has not, by this alone, proved itself to be the sole criterion. To do that, it would seem, by the same rule, necessary to show, not only that people desire happiness, but that they never desire anything else. Now it is palpable that they do desire things which, in common language, are decidedly distinguished from happiness. They desire, for example, virtue, and the absence of vice, no less really than pleasure and the absence of pain. The desire of virtue is not as universal, but it is as authentic a fact, as the desire of happiness. And hence the opponents of the utilitarian standard deem that they have a right to infer that there are other ends of human action besides happiness, and that happiness

is not the standard of approbation and disapprobation.

But does the utilitarian doctrine deny that people desire virtue, or maintain that virtue is not a thing to be desired? The very reverse. It maintains not only that virtue is to be desired, but that it is to be desired disinterestedly, for itself. Whatever may be the opinion of utilitarian moralists as to the original conditions by which virtue is made virtue; however they may believe (as they do) that actions and dispositions are only virtuous because they promote another end than virtue; yet this being granted, and it having been decided, from considerations of this description, what *is* virtuous, they not only place virtue at the very head of the things which are good as means to the ultimate end, but they also recognise as a psychological fact the possibility of its being, to the individual, a good in itself, without looking to any end beyond it; and hold, that the mind is not in a right state, not in a state conformable to Utility, not in the state most conducive to the general happiness, unless it does love virtue in this manner— as a thing desirable in itself, even although, in the individual instance, it should not produce those other desirable consequences which it tends to produce, and on account of which it is held to be virtue. This opinion is not, in the smallest degree, a departure from the Happiness principle. The ingredients of happiness are very various, and each of them is desirable in itself, and not merely when considered as swelling an aggregate. The principle of utility does not mean that any given pleasure, as music, for instance, or any given exemption from pain, as for example health, are to be looked upon as means to a collective something termed happiness, and to be desired on that account. They are desired and desirable in and for themselves; besides being means, they are a part of the end. Virtue, according to the utilitarian doctrine, is not naturally and originally part of the end, but it is capable of becoming so; and in those who love it disinterestedly it has become so, and is desired and cherished, not as a means to happiness, but as a part of their happiness.

To illustrate this farther, we may remember that virtue is not the only thing, originally a means, and which if it were not a means to anything else, would be and remain indifferent, but which by association with what it is a means to, comes to be desired for itself, and that too with the utmost intensity. What, for example, shall we say of the love of money? There is nothing originally more desirable about money than about any heap of glittering pebbles. Its worth is solely that of the things which it will buy; the desires for other things than itself, which it is a means of gratifying. Yet the love of money is not only one of the strongest moving forces of human life, but money is, in many cases, desired in and for itself; the desire to possess it is often stronger than the desire to use it, and goes on increasing when all the desires which point to ends beyond it, to be compassed by it, are falling off. It may be then said truly, that money is desired not for the sake of an end, but as part of the end. From being a means to happiness, it has come to be itself a principal ingredient of the individual's conception of happiness. The same may be said of the majority of the great objects of human life—power, for example, or fame; except that to each of these there is a certain amount of immediate pleasure annexed, which has at least the semblance of being naturally inherent in them; a thing which cannot be said of money. Still, however, the strongest natural attraction, both of power and of fame, is the immense aid they give to the attainment of our other wishes; and it is the strong association thus generated between them and all our objects of desire, which gives to the direct desire of them the intensity it often assumes, so as in some characters to surpass in strength all other desires. In these cases the means have become a part of the end, and a more important part of it than any of the things which they are means to. What was once desired as an instrument for the attainment of happiness, has come to be desired for its own sake. In being desired for its own sake it is, however, desired as *part of* happiness. The person is made, or thinks he would be made, happy by its mere possession; and is made unhappy by failure to obtain it. The desire of it is not a different thing from the desire of happiness, any more than the love of music, or the desire of health. They are included in happiness. They are some of the elements of which the desire of happiness is made up. Happiness is not an abstract idea, but a concrete whole; and these are some of its parts. And the utilitarian standard sanctions and approves their being so. Life would be a poor thing, very ill provided with sources of happiness, if there were not this provision of nature, by which things originally indifferent, but conducive to, or otherwise associated with, the satisfaction of our primitive desires, become in themselves sources of pleasure more valuable than the primitive pleasures, both in permanency, in the space of human existence that they are capable of covering, and even in intensity.

Virtue, according to the utilitarian conception, is a good of this description. There was no original desire of it, or motive to it, save its conduciveness to pleasure, and especially to protection from pain. But through the association thus formed, it may be felt a good in itself, and desired as such with as great intensity as any other good; and with this difference between it and the love of money, of power, or of fame, that all of these may, and often do, render the individual noxious to the other members of the society to which he belongs, whereas there is nothing which makes him so much a blessing to them as the cultivation of the disinterested love of virtue. And consequently, the utilitarian standard, while it tolerates and approves those other acquired desires, up to the point beyond which they would be more injurious to the general happiness than promotive of it, enjoins and requires the cultivation of the love of virtue up to the greatest strength possible, as being above all things important to the general happiness.

It results from the preceding considerations, that there is in reality nothing desired except happiness. Whatever is desired otherwise than as a means to some end beyond itself, and ultimately to happiness, is desired as itself a part of happiness, and is not desired for itself until it has become so. Those who desire virtue for its own sake, desire it either because the consciousness of it is a pleasure, or because the consciousness of being without it is a pain, or for both reasons united; as in truth the pleasure and pain seldom exist separately, but almost always together, the same person feeling pleasure in the degree of virtue attained, and pain in not having attained more. If one of these gave him no pleasure, and the other no pain, he would not love or desire virtue, or would desire it only for the other benefits which it might produce to himself or to persons whom he cared for.

We have now, then, an answer to the question, of what sort of proof the principle of utility is susceptible. If the opinion which I have now stated is psychologically true—if human nature is so constituted as to desire nothing which is not either a part of happiness or a means of happiness, we can have no other proof, and we require no other, that these are the only things desirable. If so, happiness is the sole end of human action, and the promotion of it the test by which to judge of all human conduct; from whence it necessarily follows that it must be the criterion of morality, since a part is included in the whole.

And now to decide whether this is really so; whether mankind do desire nothing for itself but that which is a pleasure to them, or of which the absence is a pain; we have evidently arrived at a question of fact and experience, dependent, like all similar questions, upon evidence. It can only be determined by practised self-consciousness and self-observation, assisted by observation of others. I believe that these sources of evidence, impartially consulted, will declare that desiring a thing and finding it pleasant, aversion to it and thinking of it as painful, are phenomena entirely inseparable, or rather two parts of the same phenomenon; in strictness of language, two different modes of naming the same psychological fact: that to think of an object as desirable (unless for the sake of its consequences), and to think of it as pleasant, are one and the same thing; and that to desire anything, except in proportion as the idea of it is pleasant, is a physical and metaphysical impossibility. . . .

21

Upon the Love of Our Neighbour

JOSEPH BUTLER

Self-Love and Particular Affections

Every man hath a general desire of his own happiness; and likewise a variety of particular affections, passions, and appetites to particular external objects. The former proceeds from, or is self-love; and seems inseparable from all sensible creatures, who can reflect upon themselves and their own interest or happiness, so as to have that interest an object to their minds: what is to be said of the latter is, that they proceed from, or together make up that particular nature, according to which man is made. The object the former pursues is somewhat internal, our own happiness, enjoyment, satisfaction; whether we have, or have not, a distinct particular perception what

it is, or wherein it consists: the objects of the latter are this or that particular external thing, which the affections tend towards, and of which it hath always a particular idea or perception. The principle we call self-love never seeks any thing external for the sake of the thing, but only as a means of happiness or good: particular affections rest in the external things themselves. One belongs to man as a reasonable creature reflecting upon his own interest or happiness. The other, though quite distinct from reason, are as much a part of human nature.

That all particular appetites and passions are towards *external things themselves,* distinct from the *pleasure arising from them,* is manifested from hence; that there could

[From *Fifteen Sermons,* first published in 1726. This selection is drawn from Sermon XI.]

not be this pleasure, were it not for that prior suitableness between the object and the passion: there could be no enjoyment or delight from one thing more than another, from eating food more than from swallowing a stone, if there were not an affection or appetite to one thing more than another.

Every particular affection, even the love of our neighbour, is as really our own affection, as self-love; and the pleasure arising from its gratification is as much my own pleasure, as the pleasure self-love would have, from knowing I myself should be happy some time hence, would be my own pleasure. And if, because every particular affection is a man's own, and the pleasure arising from its gratification his own pleasure, or pleasure to himself, such particular affection must be called self-love; according to this way of speaking, no creature whatever can possibly act but merely from self-love; and every action and every affection whatever is to be resolved up into this one principle. But then this is not the language of mankind: or if it were, we should want words to express the difference, between the principle of an action, proceeding from cool consideration that it will be to my own advantage; and an action, suppose of revenge, or of friendship, by which a man runs upon certain ruin, to do evil or good to another. It is manifest the principles of these actions are totally different, and so want different words

to be distinguished by: all that they agree in is, that they both proceed from, and are done to gratify an inclination in a man's self. But the principle or inclination in one case is self-love; in the other, hatred or love of another. There is then a distinction between the cool principle of self-love, or general desire of our own happiness, as one part of our nature, and one principle of action; and the particular affections towards particular external objects, as another part of our nature, and another principle of action. How much soever therefore is to be allowed for self-love, yet it cannot be allowed to be the whole of our inward constitution; because, you see, there are other parts or principles which come into it.

Further, private happiness or good is all which self-love can make us desire, or be concerned about: in having this consists its gratification: it is an affection to ourselves; a regard to our own interest, happiness, and private good: and in the proportion a man hath this, he is interested, or a lover of himself. Let this be kept in mind; because there is commonly, as I shall presently have occasion to observe, another sense put upon these words. On the other hand, particular affections tend towards particular external things: these are their objects; having these is their end: in this consists their gratification: no matter whether it be, or be not, upon the whole, our interest or happiness. An action done from the former of these principles is called an interested action. An action proceeding from any of the latter has its denomination of passionate, ambitious, friendly, revengeful, or any other, from the particular appetite or affection from which it proceeds. Thus self-love as one part of human nature, and the several particular principles as the other part, are, themselves, their objects and ends, stated and shown.

Happiness and Self-Love

From hence it will be easy to see, how far, and in what ways, each of these can contribute and be subservient to the private good of the individual. Happiness does not consist in self-love. The desire of happiness is no more the thing itself, than the desire of riches is the possession or enjoyment of them. People may love themselves with the most entire and unbounded affection, and yet be extremely miserable. Neither can self-love any way help them out, but by setting them on work to get rid of the causes of their misery, to gain or make use of those objects which are by nature adapted to afford satisfaction. Happiness or satisfaction consists only in the enjoyment of those objects, which are by nature suited to our several particular appetites, passions, and affections. So that if self-love wholly engrosses us, and leaves no room for any other principle, there can be absolutely no

such thing at all as happiness, or enjoyment of any kind whatever; since happiness consists in the gratification of particular passions, which supposes the having of them. Self-love then does not constitute *this* or *that* to be our interest or good; but, our interest or good being constituted by nature and supposed, self-love only puts us upon obtaining and securing it.

Therefore, if it be possible, that self-love may prevail and exert itself in a degree or manner which is not subservient to this end; then it will not follow, that our interest will be promoted in proportion to the degree in which that principle engrosses us, and prevails over others. Nay further, the private and contracted affection, when it is not subservient to this end, private good, may, for any thing that appears, have a direct contrary tendency and effect. And if we will consider the matter, we shall see that it often really has. *Disengagement* is absolutely necessary to enjoyment: and a person may have so steady and fixed an eye upon his own interest, whatever he places it in, as may hinder him from *attending* to many gratifications within his reach, which others have their minds *free* and *open* to. Over-fondness for a child is not generally thought to be for its advantage: and, if there be any guess to be made from appearances, surely that character we call selfish is not the most promising for happiness. Such a temper may plainly be, and exert itself in a degree and manner which may give unnecessary and useless solicitude and anxiety, in a degree and manner which may prevent obtaining the means and materials of enjoyment, as well as the making use of them. Immoderate self-love does very ill consult its own interest: and, how much soever a paradox it may appear, it is certainly true, that even from self-love we should endeavour to get over all inordinate regard to, and consideration of ourselves. Every one of our passions and affections hath its natural stint and bound, which may easily be exceeded; whereas our enjoyments can possibly be but in a determinate measure and degree. Therefore such excess of the affection, since it cannot procure any enjoyment, must in all cases be useless; but is generally attended with inconveniences, and often is downright pain and misery. This holds as much with regard to self-love as to all other affections. The natural degree of it, so far as it sets us on work to gain and make use of the materials of satisfaction, may be to our real advantage; but beyond or besides this, it is in several respects an inconvenience and disadvantage. Thus it appears, that private interest is so far from being likely to be promoted in proportion to the degree in which self-love engrosses us, and prevails over all other principles; that *the contracted affection may be so prevalent as to disappoint itself, and even contradict its own end, private good.*

Self-Love and Benevolence

"But who, except the most sordidly covetous, ever thought there was any rivalship between the love of greatness, honour, power, or between sensual appetites, and self-love? No, there is a perfect harmony between them. It is by means of these particular appetites and affections that self-love is gratified in enjoyment, happiness, and satisfaction. The competition and rivalship is between self-love and the love of our neighbour: that affection which leads us out of ourselves, makes us regardless of our own interest, and substitute that of another in its stead." Whether then there be any peculiar competition and contrariety in this case, shall now be considered.

Self-love and interestedness was stated to consist in or be an affection to ourselves, a regard to our own private good: it is therefore distinct from benevolence, which is an affection to the good of our fellow-creatures. But that benevolence is distinct from, that is, not the same thing with self-love, is no reason for its being looked upon with any peculiar suspicion; because every principle whatever, by means of which self-love is gratified, is distinct from it: and all things which are distinct from each other are equally so. A man has an affection or aversion to another: that one of these tends to, and is gratified by doing good, that the other tends to, and is gratified by doing harm, does not in the least alter the respect which either one or the other of these inward feelings has to self-love. We use the word *property* so as to exclude any other persons having an interest in that of which we say a particular man has the property. And we often use the word *selfish* so as to exclude in the same manner all regards to the good of others. But the cases are not parallel: for though that exclusion is really part of the idea of property; yet such positive exclusion, or bringing this peculiar disregard to the good of others into the idea of self-love, is in reality adding to the idea, or changing it from what it was before stated to consist in, namely, in an affection to ourselves. This being the whole idea of self-love, it can no otherwise exclude good-will or love of others, than merely by not including it, no otherwise, than it excludes love of arts or reputation, or of any thing else. Neither on the other hand does benevolence, any more than love of arts or of reputation, exclude self-love. Love of our neighbour then has just the same respect to, is no more distant from, self-love, than hatred of our neighbour, or than love or hatred of any thing else.

Thus the principles, from which men rush upon certain ruin for the destruction of an enemy, and for the preservation of a friend, have the same respect to the private affection, and are equally interested, or equally disinterested: and it is of no avail, whether they are said to be one or the other. Therefore to those who are shocked to hear virtue spoken of as disinterested, it may be allowed that it is indeed absurd to speak thus of it; unless hatred, several particular instances of vice, and all the common affections and aversions in mankind, are acknowledged to be disinterested too. Is there any less inconsistence, between the love of inanimate things, or of creatures merely sensitive, and self-love; than between self-love and the love of our neighbour? Is desire of and delight in the happiness of another any more a diminution of self-love, than desire of and delight in the esteem of another? They are both equally desire of and delight in somewhat external to ourselves: either both or neither are so. The object of self-love is expressed in the term *self:* and every appetite of sense, and every particular affection of the heart, are equally interested or disinterested, because the objects of them all are equally self or somewhat else. Whatever ridicule therefore the mention of a disinterested principle or action may be supposed to lie open to, must, upon the matter being thus stated, relate to ambition, and every appetite and particular affection, as much as to benevolence. And indeed all the ridicule, and all the grave perplexity, of which this subject hath had its full share, is merely from words. The most intelligible way of speaking of it seems to be this: that self-love and the actions done in consequence of it (for these will presently appear to be the same as to this question) are interested; that particular affections towards external objects, and the actions done in consequence of those affections, are not so. But every one is at liberty to use words as he pleases. All that is here insisted upon is, that ambition, revenge, benevolence, all particular passions whatever, and the actions they produce, are equally interested or disinterested.

Thus it appears that there is no peculiar contrariety between self-love and benevolence; no greater competition between these, than between any other particular affections and self-love. This relates to the affections themselves. Let us now see whether there be any peculiar contrariety between the respective courses of life which these affections lead to; whether there be any greater competition between the pursuit of private and of public good, than between any other particular pursuits and that of private good.

Benevolence and Happiness

There seems no other reason to suspect that there is any such peculiar contrariety, but only that the course of action which benevolence leads to, has a more direct tendency to promote the good of others, than that course of action which love of reputation, suppose, or any other particular affection leads to. But that any affection tends to the happiness of another, does not hinder its tending to one's own happiness too. That others enjoy the benefit of the air and the light of the sun, does not hinder but that these are as much one's own private advantage now, as they would be if we had the property of them exclusive of all others. So a pursuit which tends to promote the good of another, yet may have as great tendency to promote private interest, as a pursuit which does not tend to the good of another at all, or which is mischievous to him. All particular affections whatever, resentment, benevolence, love of arts, equally lead to a course of action for their own gratification, i.e. the gratification of ourselves; and the gratification of each gives delight: so far then it is manifest they have all the same respect to private interest. Now take into consideration further, concerning these three pursuits, that the end of the first is the harm, of the second, the good of another, of the last, somewhat indifferent; and is there any necessity, that these additional considerations should alter the respect, which we before saw these three pursuits had to private interest; or render any one of them less conducive to it, than any other? Thus one man's affection is to honour as his end; in order to obtain which he thinks no pains too great. Suppose another, with such a singularity of mind, as to have the same affection to public good as his end, which he endeavours with the same labour to obtain. In case of success, surely the man of benevolence hath as great enjoyment as the man of ambition; they both equally having the end their affections, in the same degree, tended to: but in case of disappointment, the benevolent man has clearly the advantage; since endeavouring to do good considered as a virtuous pursuit, is gratified by its own consciousness, i.e. is in a degree its own reward. . . .

The short of the matter is no more than this. Happiness consists in the gratification of certain affections, appetites, passions, with objects which are by nature adapted to them. Self-love may indeed set us on work to gratify these: but happiness or enjoyment has no immediate connection with self-love, but arises from such gratification alone. Love of our neighbour is one of those affections. This, considered as a *virtuous principle*, is gratified by a consciousness of *endeavouring* to promote the good of others; but considered as a natural affection, its gratification consists in the actual accomplishment of this endeavour. Now indulgence or gratification of this affection, whether in that consciousness, or this accomplishment, has the same respect to interest, as indulgence of any other affection; they equally proceed from or do not proceed from self-love, they equally include or equally exclude this principle. Thus it appears, that *benevo-*

lence and the pursuit of public good hath at least as great respect to self-love and the pursuit of private good, as any other particular passions, and their respective pursuits. . . .

There is indeed frequently an inconsistence or interfering between self-love or private interest, and the several particular appetites, passions, affections, or the pursuits they lead to. But this competition or interfering is merely accidental; and happens much oftener between pride, revenge, sensual gratifications, and private interest, than between private interest and benevolence. For nothing is more common, than to see men give themselves up to a passion or an affection to their known prejudice and ruin, and in direct contradiction to manifest and real interest, and the loudest calls of self-love: whereas the seeming competitions and interfering, between benevolence and private interest, relate much more to the materials or means of enjoyment, than to enjoyment itself. There is often an interfering in the former, when there is none in the latter. . . .

This, I say, might be taken for granted, whilst it was not attended to, that the object of every particular affection is equally somewhat external to ourselves; and whether it be the good of another person, or whether it be any other external thing, makes no alteration with regard to its being one's own affection, and the gratification of it one's own private enjoyment. And so far as it is taken for granted, that barely having the means and materials of enjoyment is what constitutes interest and happiness; that our interest or good consists in possessions themselves, in having the property of riches, houses, lands, gardens, not in the enjoyment of them; so far it will even more strongly be taken for granted, in the way already explained, that an affection's conducing to the good of another, must even necessarily occasion it to conduce less to private good, if not to be positively detrimental to it. For, if property and happiness are one and the same thing, as by increasing the property of another, you lessen your own property, so by promoting the happiness of another, you must lessen your own happiness. But whatever occasioned the mistake, I hope it has been fully proved to be one; as it has been proved, that there is no peculiar rivalship or competition between self-love and benevolence: that as there may be a competition between these two, so there may also between any particular affection whatever and self-love; that every particular affection, benevolence among the rest, is subservient to self-love by being the instrument of private enjoyment; and that in one respect benevolence contributes more to private interest, i.e. enjoyment or satisfaction, than any other of the particular common affections, as it is in a degree its own gratification.

And to all these things may be added, that religion, from whence arises our strongest obligation to benevolence, is so far from disowning the principle of self-love, that it often addresses itself to that very principle, and always to the mind in that state when reason presides; and there can no access be had to the understanding, but by convincing men, that the course of life we would persuade them to is not contrary to their interest. It may be allowed, without any prejudice to the cause of virtue and religion, that our ideas of happiness and misery are of all our ideas the nearest and most important to us; that they will, nay, if you please, that they ought to prevail over those of order, and beauty, and harmony, and proportion, if there should ever be, as it is impossible there ever should be, any inconsistence between them: though these last too, as expressing the fitness of actions, are real as truth itself. Let it be allowed, though virtue or moral rectitude does indeed consist in affection to and pursuit of what is right and good, as such; yet, that when we sit down in a cool hour, we can neither justify to ourselves this or any other pursuit, till we are convinced that it will be for our happiness, or at least not contrary to it.

22

Ultimate Principles and Ethical Egoism

BRIAN MEDLIN

I believe that it is now pretty generally accepted by professional philosophers that ultimate ethical principles must be arbitrary. One cannot derive conclusions about what should be merely from accounts of what is the case; one cannot decide how people ought to behave merely from one's knowledge of how they do behave. To arrive at a conclusion in ethics one must have at least one ethical premiss. This premiss, if it be in turn a conclusion, must be the conclusion of an argument containing at least one ethical premiss. And so we can go back, indefinitely but not for ever. Sooner or later, we must come to at least one ethical premiss which is not deduced but baldly asserted. Here we must be a-rational; neither rational nor irra-

tional, for here there is no room for reason even to go wrong.

But the triumph of Hume in ethics has been a limited one. What appears quite natural to a handful of specialists appears quite monstrous to the majority of decent intelligent men. At any rate, it has been my experience that people who are normally rational resist the above account of the logic of moral language, not by argument—for that can't be done—but by tooth and nail. And they resist from the best motives. They see the philosopher wantonly unravelling the whole fabric of morality. If our ultimate principles are arbitrary, they say, if those principles came out of thin air, then anyone can hold any principle he pleases. Unless moral assertions are state-

[From *Australasian Journal of Philosophy*, Vol. 35, No. 2 (1957), pp. 111–118. Reprinted by permission of the *Australasian Journal of Philosophy*.]

ments of fact about the world and either true or false, we can't claim that any man is wrong, whatever his principles may be, whatever his behaviour. We have to surrender the luxury of calling one another scoundrels. That this anxiety flourishes because its roots are in confusion is evident when we consider that we don't call people scoundrels, anyhow, for being mistaken about their facts. Fools, perhaps, but that's another matter. Nevertheless, it doesn't become us to be high-up. The layman's uneasiness, however irrational it may be, is very natural and he must be reassured.

People cling to objectivist theories of morality from moral motives. It's a very queer thing that by doing so they often thwart their own purposes. There are evil opinions abroad, as anyone who walks abroad knows. The one we meet with most often, whether in pub or parlour, is the doctrine that everyone should look after himself. However refreshing he may find it after the high-minded pomposities of this morning's editorial, the good fellow knows this doctrine is wrong and he wants to knock it down. But while he believes that moral language is used to make statements either true or false, the best he can do is to claim that what the egoist says is false. Unfortunately, the egoist can claim that it's true. And since the supposed fact in question between them is not a publicly ascertainable one, their disagreement can never be resolved.

And it is here that even good fellows waver, when they find they have no refutation available. The egoist's word seems as reliable as their own. Some begin half to believe that perhaps it is possible to supply an egoistic basis for conventional morality, some that it may be impossible to supply any other basis. I'm not going to try to prop up our conventional morality, which I fear to be a task beyond my strength, but in what follows I do want to refute the doctrine of ethical egoism. I want to resolve this disagreement by showing that what the egoist says is inconsistent. It is true that there are moral disagreements which can never be resolved, but this isn't one of them. The proper objection to the man who says "Everyone should look after his own interests regardless of the interests of others" is not that he isn't speaking the truth, but simply that he isn't speaking.

We should first make two distinctions. This done, ethical egoism will lose much of its plausibility.

1. Universal and Individual Egoism

Universal egoism maintains that everyone (including the speaker) ought to look after his own interests and to disregard those of other people except in so far as their interests contribute towards his own.

Individual egoism is the attitude that the egoist is going to look after himself and no one else. The egoist cannot promulgate that he is going to look after himself. He can't even preach that he *should* look after himself and preach this alone. When he tries to convince me that he should look after himself, he is attempting so to dispose me that I shall approve when he drinks my beer and steals Tom's wife. I cannot approve of his looking after himself and himself alone without so far approving of his achieving his happiness, regardless of the happiness of myself and others. So that when he sets out to persuade me that he should look after himself regardless of others, he must also set out to persuade me that I should look after him regardless of myself and others. Very small chance he has! And if the individual egoist cannot promulgate his doctrine without enlarging it, what he has is no doctrine at all.

A person enjoying such an attitude may believe that other people are fools not to look after themselves. Yet he himself would be a fool to tell them so. If he did tell them, though, he wouldn't consider that he was giving them *moral* advice. Persuasion to the effect that one should ignore the claims of morality because morality doesn't pay, to the effect that one has insufficient selfish motive and, therefore, insufficient motive for moral behaviour is not moral persuasion. For this reason I doubt that we should call the individual egoist's attitude an ethical one. And I don't doubt this in the

way someone may doubt whether to call the ethical standards of Satan "ethical" standards. A malign morality is none the less a morality for being malign. But the attitude we're considering is one of mere contempt for all moral considerations whatsoever. An indifference to morals may be wicked, but it is not a perverse morality. So far as I am aware, most egoists imagine that they are putting forward a doctrine in ethics, though there may be a few who are prepared to proclaim themselves individual egoists. If the good fellow wants to know how he should justify conventional morality to an individual egoist, the answer is that he shouldn't and can't. Buy your car elsewhere, blackguard him whenever you meet, and let it go at that.

2. Categorical and Hypothetical Egoism

Categorical egoism is the doctrine that we all ought to observe our own interests, *because that is what we ought to do*. For the categorical egoist the egoistic dogma is the ultimate principle in ethics.

The hypothetical egoist, on the other hand, maintains that we all ought to observe our own interests, because .... If we want such and such an end, we must do so and so (look after ourselves). The hypothetical egoist is not a real egoist at all. He is very likely an unwitting utilitarian who believes mistakenly that the general happiness will be increased if each man looks wisely to his own. Of course, a man may believe that egoism is enjoined on us by God and he may therefore promulgate the doctrine and observe it in his conduct, not in the hope of achieving thereby a remote end, but simply in order to obey God. But neither is *he* a real egoist. He believes, ultimately, that we should obey God, even should God command us to altruism.

An ethical egoist will have to maintain the doctrine in both its universal and categorical forms. Should he retreat to hypothetical egoism he is no longer an egoist. Should he retreat to individual egoism his doctrine, while logically impregnable, is no longer ethical, no longer even a doctrine. He may wish to quarrel with this and if so, I submit peacefully. Let him call himself what he will, it makes no difference. I'm a philosopher, not a rat-catcher, and I don't see it as my job to dig vermin out of such burrows as individual egoism.

Obviously something strange goes on as soon as the ethical egoist tries to promulgate his doctrine. What is he doing when he urges upon his audience that they should each observe his own interests and those interests alone? Is he not acting contrary to the egoistic principle? It cannot be to his advantage to convince them, for seizing always their own advantage they will impair his. Surely if he does believe what he says, he should try to persuade them otherwise. Not perhaps that they should devote themselves to his interests, for they'd hardly swallow that; but that everyone should devote himself to the service of others. But is not to believe that someone should act in a certain way to try to persuade him to do so? Of course, we don't always try to persuade people to act as we think they should act. We may be lazy, for instance. But in so far as we believe that Tom should do so and so, we have a tendency to induce him to do so and so. Does it make sense to say: "Of course you should do this, but for goodness' sake don't"? Only where we mean: "You should do this for certain reasons, but here are even more persuasive reasons for not doing it." If the egoist believes ultimately that others should mind themselves alone, then, he must persuade them accordingly. If he doesn't persuade them, he is no universal egoist. It certainly makes sense to say: "I know very well that Tom should act in such and such a way. But I know also that it's not to my advantage that he should so act. So I'd better dissuade him from it." And this is just what the egoist must say, if he is to consider his own advantage and disregard everyone else's. That is, he must behave as an individual egoist, if he is to be an egoist at all.

He may want to make two kinds of objection here:

1. That it will not be to his disadvantage to promulgate the doctrine,

provided that his audience fully understand what is to their ultimate advantage. This objection can be developed in a number of ways, but I think that it will always be possible to push the egoist into either individual or hypothetical egoism.

2. That it is to the egoist's advantage to preach the doctrine if the pleasure he gets out of doing this more than pays for the injuries he must endure at the hands of his converts. It is hard to believe that many people would be satisfied with a doctrine which they could only consistently promulgate in very special circumstances. Besides, this looks suspiciously like individual egoism in disguise.

I shall say no more on these two points because I want to advance a further criticism which seems to me at once fatal and irrefutable.

Now it is time to show the anxious layman that we have means of dealing with ethical egoism which are denied him; and denied him by just that objectivism which he thinks essential to morality. For the very fact that our ultimate principles must be arbitrary means they can't be anything we please. Just because they come out of thin air they can't come out of hot air. Because these principles are not propositions about matters of fact and cannot be deduced from propositions about matters of fact, they must be the fruit of our own attitudes. We assert them largely to modify the attitudes of our fellows but by asserting them we

express our own desires and purposes. This means that we cannot use moral language cavalierly. Evidently, we cannot say something like "All human desires and purposes are bad." This would be to express our own desires and purposes, thereby committing a kind of absurdity. Nor, I shall argue, can we say "Everyone should observe his own interests regardless of the interests of others."

Remembering that the principle is meant to be both universal and categorical, let us ask what kind of attitude the egoist is expressing. Wouldn't that attitude be equally well expressed by the conjunction of an infinite number of avowals . . . [see Figure 1, p. 314]?—

From this analysis it is obvious that the principle expressing such an attitude must be inconsistent.

But now the egoist may claim that he hasn't been properly understood. When he says "Everyone should look after himself and himself alone," he means "Let each man do what he wants regardless of what anyone else wants." The egoist may claim that what he values is merely that he and Tom and Dick and Harry should each do what he wants and not care about what anyone else may want and that this doesn't involve his principle in any inconsistency. Nor need it. But even if it doesn't, he's no better off. Just what does he value? Is it the well-being of himself, Tom, Dick and Harry or merely their going on in a certain way regardless of whether or not this is going to promote their well-being? When he

---

Figure 1

I want myself to come out on top	and	I don't care about Tom, Dick, Harry . . .
and		and
I want Tom to come out on top	and	I don't care about myself, Dick, Harry . . .
and		and
I want Dick to come out on top	and	I don't care about myself, Tom, Harry . . .
and		and
I want Harry to come out on top	and	I don't care about myself, Dick, Tom . . .
etc.		etc.

---

urges Tom, say, to do what he wants, is he appealing to Tom's self-interest? If so, his attitude can be expressed . . . [as in Figure 2].

We need go no further to see that the principle expressing such an attitude must be inconsistent. I have made this kind of move already. What concerns me now is the alternative position the egoist must take up to be safe from it. If the egoist values merely that people should go on in a certain way, regardless of whether or not this is going to promote their well-being, then he is not appealing to the self-interest of his audience when he urges them to regard their own interests. If Tom has any regard for himself at all, the egoist's blandishments will leave him cold. Further, the egoist doesn't even have his own interest in mind when he says that, like everyone else, he should look after himself. A funny kind of egoism this turns out to be.

Perhaps now, claiming that he is indeed appealing to the self-interest of his audience, the egoist may

---

Figure 2

I want myself to be happy		I want myself not to care about Tom, Dick, Harry . . .
and	and	
I want Tom to be happy		

---

attempt to counter the objection of the previous paragraph. He may move into "Let each man do what he wants and let each man disregard what others want when their desires clash with his own." Now his attitude may be expressed . . . [as in Figure 3].

interested in the reply to it. For now we don't even need to tell him that the world isn't in fact like that. (What it's like makes no difference.) Now we can point out to him that he is arguing not as an egoist but as a utilitarian. He has slipped into hypothetical egoism to save his prin-

---

Figure 3

I want everyone to be happy	and	I want everyone to disregard the happiness of others when their happiness clashes with his own.

The egoist may claim justly that a man can have such an attitude and also that in a certain kind of world such a man could get what he wanted. Our objection to the egoist has been that his desires are incompatible. And this is still so. If he and Tom and Dick and Harry did go on as he recommends by saying "Let each man disregard the happiness of others, when their happiness conflicts with his own," then assuredly they'd all be completely miserable. Yet he wants them to be happy. He is attempting to counter this by saying that it is merely a fact about the world that they'd make one another miserable by going on as he recommends. The world could conceivably have been different. For this reason, he says, this principle is not inconsistent. This argument may not seem very compelling, but I advance it on the egoist's behalf because I'm

ciple from inconsistency. If the world were such that we always made ourselves and others happy by doing one another down, then we could find good utilitarian reasons for urging that we should do one another down.

If, then, he is to save his principle, the egoist must do one of two things. He must give up the claim that he is appealing to the self-interest of his audience, that he has even his own interest in mind. Or he must admit that, in . . . [Figure 3], although "I want everyone to be happy" refers to ends, nevertheless "I want everyone to disregard the happiness of others when their happiness conflicts with his own" can refer only to means. That is, his so-called ultimate principle is really compounded of a principle and a moral rule subordinate to that principle. That is, he is really a utilitarian who is urging everyone to go on in a certain way so that everyone may be happy. A utilitarian, what's more, who is ludicrously mistaken about the nature of the world. Things being as they are, his moral rule is a very bad one. Things being as they are, it can only be deduced from his principle by means of an empirical premiss which is manifestly false. Good fellows don't need to fear him. They may rest easy that the world is and must be on their side and the best thing they can do is be good.

It may be worth pointing out that objections similar to those I have brought against the egoist can be made to the altruist. The man who holds that the principle "Let everyone observe the interests of others" is both universal and categorical can be compelled to choose between two alternatives, equally repugnant. He must give up the claim that he is concerned for the wellbeing of himself and others. Or he must admit that, though "I want everyone to be happy" refers to ends, nevertheless, "I want everyone to disregard his own happiness when it conflicts with the happiness of others" can refer only to means.

I have said from time to time that the egoistic principle is inconsistent. I have not said it is contradictory. This for the reason that we can, without contradiction, express inconsistent desires and purposes. To do so is not to say anything like "Goliath was ten feet tall and not ten feet tall." Don't we all want to eat our cake and have it too? And when we say we do we aren't asserting a contradiction. We are not asserting a contradiction whether we be making an avowal of our attitudes or stating a fact about them. We all have conflicting motives. As a utilitarian exuding benevolence I want the man who mows my landlord's grass to be happy, but as a slug-a-bed I should like to see him scourged. None of this, however, can do the egoist any good. For we assert our ultimate principles not only to express our own attitudes but also to induce similar attitudes in others, to dispose them to conduct themselves as we wish. In so far as their desires conflict, people don't know what to do. And, therefore, no expression of incompatible desires can ever serve for an ultimate principle of human conduct.

23

Egoism as a Theory of Human Motives

C. D. BROAD

There seem *prima facie* to be a number of different kinds of ultimate desire which all or most men have. Plausible examples would be the desire to get pleasant experiences and to avoid unpleasant ones, the desire to get and exercise power over others, and the desire to do what is right and to avoid doing what is wrong. Very naturally philosophers have tried to reduce this plurality. They have tried to show that there is one and only one kind of ultimate desire, and that all other desires which seem at first sight to be ultimate are really subordinate to this. I shall call the view that there really are several different kinds of ultimate desire *Pluralism of Ultimate Desires*, and I shall call the view that there is really only one kind of ultimate desire *Monism of Ultimate Desires*. Even if a person were a pluralist about ultimate desires, he might hold that there are certain important features common to all the different kinds of ultimate desire.

Now much the most important theory on this subject is that all kinds of ultimate desire are *egoistic*. This is not in itself necessarily a monistic theory. For there might be several irreducibly different kinds of ultimate desire, even if they were all egoistic. Moreover, there might be several irreducibly different, though not necessarily unrelated, senses of the word "egoistic"; and some desires might be egoistic in one sense and some in another, even if all were egoistic in some sense. But the theory often takes the special form that the only kind of ultimate desire is the desire to get or to prolong pleas-

[Reprinted from C. D. Broad, *Ethics and the History of Philosophy* (Routledge & Kegan Paul, Ltd., London, 1952), by permission of Routledge & Kegan Paul, Ltd.]

ant experiences, and to avoid or to cut short unpleasant experiences, for oneself. That *is* a monistic theory. I shall call the wider theory *Psychological Egoism*, and this special form of it *Psychological Hedonism*. Psychological Egoism might be true, even though psychological hedonism were false; but, if psychological egoism be false, psychological hedonism cannot be true.

I shall now discuss Psychological Egoism. I think it is best to begin by enumerating all the kinds of desire that I can think of which might reasonably be called "egoistic" in one sense or another.

(1) Everyone has a special desire for the continued existence of himself in his present bodily life, and a special dread of his own death. This may be called *Desire for Self-preservation*. (2) Everyone desires to get and to prolong experiences of certain kinds, and to avoid and to cut short experiences of certain other kinds, because the former are pleasant to him and the latter unpleasant. This may be called *Desire for one's own Happiness*. (3) Everyone desires to acquire, keep, and develop certain mental and bodily powers and dispositions, and to avoid, get rid of, or check certain others. In general he wants to be or to become a person of a certain kind, and wants not to be or to become a person of certain other kinds. This may be called *Desire to be a Self of a certain kind*. (4) Everyone desires to feel certain kinds of emotion towards himself and his own powers and dispositions, and not to feel certain other kinds of reflexive emotion. This may be called *Desire for Self-respect*. (5) Everyone desires to get and to keep for himself the exclusive possession of certain material objects or the means of buying and keeping such objects. This may be called *Desire to get and to keep Property*. (6) Everyone desires to get and to exercise power over certain other persons, so as to make them do what he wishes, regardless of whether they wish it or not. This may be called *Desire for Self-assertion*. (7) Everyone desires that other persons shall believe certain things about him and feel certain kinds of emotion towards him. He wants to be noticed, to be respected by some, to be loved by some, to be feared by some, and so on. Under this head come the *Desire for Self-display*, for *Affection*, and so on.

Lastly, it must be noted that some desires, which are concerned primarily with other things or persons, either would not exist at all or would be very much weaker or would take a different form it if were not for the fact that those things or persons already stand in certain relations to oneself. I shall call such relations *egoistic motive-stimulants*. The following are among the most important of these. (i) The relation of ownership. If a person owns a house or a wife, e.g. he feels a much stronger desire to improve the house or to make the woman happy than if the house belongs to another or the woman is married to someone else. (ii) Blood-relationships. A person desires, e.g. the well-being of his own children much more strongly than that of other children. (iii) Relations of love and friendship. A person desires strongly, e.g. to be loved and respected by those whom he loves. He may desire only to be feared by those whom he hates. And he may desire only very mildly, if at all, to be loved and respected by those to whom he feels indifferent. (iv) The relationship of being fellow-members of an institution to which one feels loyalty and affection. Thus, e.g. an Englishman will be inclined to do services to another Englishman which he would not do for a foreigner, and an Old Etonian will be inclined to do services to another Old Etonian which he would not do for an Old Harrovian.

I think that I have now given a reasonably adequate list of motives and motive-stimulants which could fairly be called "egoistic" in some sense or other. Our next business is to try to classify them and to consider their inter-relations.

(1) Let us begin by asking ourselves the following question. Which of these motives could act on a person if he had been the only person or thing that had ever existed? The answer is that he could still have had desires for *self-preservation*, for *his own happiness*, to be a *self of a certain kind*, and for *self-respect*. But he could not, unless he were under the delusion that there were other persons or things, have desires for *property*, for *self-assertion*, or for *self-display*. Nor could he have any of those desires which are stimulated by family or other alio-relative relationships. I shall call those desires, and only those, which could be felt by a person who knew or believed himself to be the only existent in the universe, *Self-confined*.

(2) Any desire which is not self-confined may be described as *extra-verted*; for the person who has such a desire is necessarily considering, not only himself and his own qualities, dispositions, and states, but also some other thing or person. If the desire is egoistic, it will also be *intro-verted*; for the person who has such a desire will also be considering himself and his relations to that other person or thing, and this will be an essential factor conditioning his experience. Thus a self-confined desire is purely intro-verted, whilst a desire which is egoistic but not self-confined is both intro-verted and extra-verted. Now we may subdivide desires of the latter kind into two classes, according as the primary emphasis is on the former or the latter aspect. Suppose that the person is concerned primarily with himself and his own acts and experiences, and that he is concerned with the other thing or person only or mainly as an object of these acts or experiences or as the other term in a relationship to himself. Then I shall call the desire *Self-centred*. I

shall use the term *Self-regarding* to include both desires which are self-centred and those which are self-confined. Under the head of self-centred desires come the desire for *property*, for *self-assertion*, for *self-display*, and for *affection*.

(3) Lastly, we come to desires which are both intro-verted and extra-verted, but where the primary emphasis is on the other person or thing and its states. Here the relationship of the other person or thing to oneself acts as a strong egoistic motive-stimulant, but one's primary desire is that the other person or thing shall be in a certain state. I will call such desires *Other-regarding*. A desire which is other-regarding, but involves an egoistic motive-stimulant, may be described as *Self-referential*. The desire of a mother to render services to her own children which she would not be willing to render to other children is an instance of a desire which is other-regarding but self-referential. So, too, is the desire of a man to inflict suffering on one who has injured him or one whom he envies.

Having thus classified the various kinds of egoistic desire, I will now say something about their interrelations.

(1) It is obvious that self-preservation may be desired as a necessary condition of one's own happiness; since one cannot acquire or prolong pleasant experiences unless one continues to exist. So the desire for self-preservation *may* be subor-

dinate to the desire for one's own happiness. But it seems pretty clear that a person often desires to go on living even when there is no prospect that the remainder of his life will contain a balance of pleasant over unpleasant experiences. . . .

(2) It is also obvious that property and power over others may be desired as a means to self-preservation or to happiness. So the desire to get and keep property, and the desire to get and exert power over others, *may* be subordinate to the desire for self-preservation or for one's own happiness. But it seems fairly certain that the former desires are sometimes independent of the latter. Even if a person begins by desiring property or power only as a means—and it is very doubtful whether we always do begin in that way—it seems plain that he often comes to desire them for themselves, and to sacrifice happiness, security, and even life for them. Any miser, and almost any keen politician, provides an instance of this.

It is no answer to this to say that a person who desires power or property enjoys the experiences of getting and exercising power or of amassing and owning property, and then to argue that therefore his ultimate desire is to give himself those pleasant experiences. The premiss here is true, but the argument is self-stultifying. The experiences in question are pleasant to a person only in so far as he desires power or property. This kind of pleasant experience presupposes desires for something other than pleasant experiences, and therefore the latter desires cannot be derived from desire for that kind of pleasant experience.

Similar remarks apply to the desire for self-respect and the desire for self-display. If one already desires to feel certain emotions towards oneself, or to be the object of certain emotions in others, the experience of feeling those emotions or of knowing that others feel them towards one will be pleasant, because it will be the fulfilment of a pre-existing desire. But this kind of pleasure presupposes the existence of these desires, and therefore they cannot be derived from the desire for that kind of pleasure.

(3) Although the various kinds of egoistic desire cannot be reduced to a single ultimate egoistic desire, e.g. the desire for one's own happiness, they are often very much mixed up with each other. Take, e.g. the special desire which a mother feels for the health, happiness, and prosperity of her children. This is predominantly other-regarding, though it is self-referential. The mother is directly attracted by the thought of her child as surviving, as having good dispositions and pleasant experiences, and as being the object of love and respect to other persons. She is directly repelled by the thought of his dying, or having bad dispositions or unpleasant experiences, or being the object of hatred or contempt to other per-

sons. The desire is therefore other-regarding. It is self-referential, because the fact that it is *her* child and not another's acts as a powerful motive-stimulant. She would not be prepared to make the same sacrifices for the survival or the welfare of a child which was not her own. But this self-referential other-regarding motive is almost always mingled with other motives which are self-regarding. One motive which a woman has for wanting her child to be happy, healthy and popular is the desire that other women shall envy her as the mother of a happy, healthy and popular child. This motive is subordinate to the self-centred desire for self-display. Another motive, which may be present, is the desire not to be burdened with an ailing, unhappy, and unpopular child. This motive is subordinate to the self-contained desire for one's own happiness. But, although the self-referential other-regarding motive is nearly always mixed with motives which are self-centred or self-confined, we cannot plausibly explain the behaviour of many mothers on many occasions towards their children without postulating the other-regarding motive.

We can now consider the various forms which Psychological Egoism might take. The most rigid form is that all human motives are ultimately egoistic, and that all egoistic motives are ultimately of one kind. That one kind has generally been supposed to be the desire for one's own happiness, and so this form of Psychological Egoism may in practice be identified with Psychological Hedonism. This theory amounts to saying that the only ultimate motives are *self-confined,* and that the only ultimate self-confined motive is *desire for one's own happiness.*

I have already tried to show by examples that this is false. Among self-confined motives, e.g. is the desire for self-preservation, and this cannot be reduced to desire for one's own happiness. Then, again, there are self-regarding motives which are self-centred but not self-confined, such as the desire for affection, for gratitude, for power over others, and so on. And, finally, there are motives which are self-referential but predominantly other-regarding, such as a mother's desire for her children's welfare or a man's desire to injure one whom he hates.

It follows that the only form of Psychological Egoism that is worth discussing is the following. It might be alleged that all ultimate motives are *either* self-confined *or* self-centred *or* other-regarding but self-referential, some being of one kind and some of another. This is a much more modest theory than, e.g. Psychological Hedonism. I think that it covers satisfactorily an immensely wide field of human motivation, but I am not sure that it is true without exception. I shall now discuss it in the light of some examples.

Case A. Take first the case of a man who does not expect to survive the death of his present body, and who makes a will, the contents of which will be known to no one during his lifetime.

(1) The motive of such a testator cannot possibly be the expectation of any experiences which he will enjoy after death through the provisions of his will being carried out; for he believes that he will have no more experiences after the death of his body. The only way in which this motive could be ascribed to such a man is by supposing that, although he is intellectually convinced of his future extinction, yet in practice he cannot help imagining himself as surviving and witnessing events which will happen after his death. I think that this kind of mental confusion is possible, and perhaps not uncommon; but I should doubt whether it is a plausible account of such a man's motives to say that they all involve this mistake.

(2) Can we say that his motive is the desire to enjoy during his life the pleasant experience of imagining the gratitude which the beneficiaries will feel towards him after his death? The answer is that this may well be *one* of his motives, but it cannot be primary, and therefore cannot be the only one. Unless he desired to be thought about in one way rather than another after his death, the present experience of imagining himself as becoming the object of certain retrospective thoughts and emotions on the part of the beneficiaries would be neither attractive nor repulsive to him.

(3) I think it is plain, then, that the ultimate motive of such a man cannot be desire for his own happiness. But it might be desire for power over others. For he may be said to be exercising this power when he makes his will, even though the effects will not begin until after his death.

(4) Can we say that his motive in making the will is simply to ensure that certain persons will think about him and feel towards him in certain ways after his death? In that case his motive would come under the head of self-display. (This must, of course, be distinguished from the question, already discussed, whether his motive might be to give himself the pleasant experience of imagining their future feelings of gratitude towards him.) The answer is that self-display, in a wide sense, may be a motive, and a very strong one, in making a will; but it could hardly be the sole motive. A testator generally considers the relative needs of various possible beneficiaries, the question whether a certain person would appreciate and take care of a certain picture or house or book, the question whether a certain institution is doing work which he thinks important, and so on. In so far as he is influenced by these considerations, his motives are other-regarding. But they may all be self-referential. In making his will he may desire to benefit persons only in so far as they are *his* relatives or friends. He may desire to benefit institutions only in so far as *he* is or has been

a member of them. And so on. I think that it would be quite plausible to hold that the motives of such a testator are all either self-regarding or self-referential, but that it would not be in the least plausible to say that they are all self-confined or that none of them are other-regarding.

Case B. Let us next consider the case of a man who subscribes anonymously to a certain charity. His motive cannot possibly be that of self-display. Can we say that his motive is to enjoy the pleasant experience of self-approval and of seeing an institution in which he is interested flourishing? The answer is, again, that these motives may exist and may be strong, but they cannot be primary and therefore cannot be his only motives. Unless he wants the institution to flourish, there will be nothing to attract him in the experience of seeing it flourish. And, unless he subscribes from some other motive than the desire to enjoy a feeling of self-approval, he will not obtain a feeling of self-approval. So here, again, it seems to me that some of his motives must be other-regarding. But it is quite possible that his other-regarding motives may all be self-referential. An essential factor in making him want to benefit this institution may be that it is *his* old college or that a great friend of *his* is at the head of it.

The question, then, that remains is this. Are there any cases in which it is reasonable to think that a person's motive is not egoistic in any of the senses mentioned? In practice, as we now see, this comes down to the question whether there are any cases in which an other-regarding motive is not stimulated by an egoistic motive-stimulus, i.e. whether there is any other-regarding motive which is not also and essentially self-referential.

Case C. Let us consider the case of a person who deliberately chooses to devote his life to working among lepers, in the full knowledge that he will almost certainly contract leprosy and die in a particularly loathsome way. This is not an imaginary case. To give the Psychological Egoist the longest possible run for his money I will suppose that the person is a Roman Catholic priest, who believes that his action may secure for him a place in heaven in the next world and a reputation for sanctity and heroism in this, that it may be rewarded posthumously with canonization, and that it will redound to the credit of the church of which he is an ordained member.

It is difficult to see what self-regarding or self-referential motives there could be *for* the action beside desire for happiness in heaven, desire to gain a reputation for sanctity and heroism and perhaps to be canonized after death, and desire to glorify the church of which one is a priest. Obviously there are extremely strong self-confined and self-centred motives *against* choosing this kind of life. And in many cases there must have been very strong self-referential other-regarding mo-

tives *against* it. For the person who made such a choice must sometimes have been a young man of good family and brilliant prospects, whose parents were heart-broken at his decision, and whose friends thought him an obstinate fool for making it.

Now there is no doubt at all that there was an other-regarding motive, viz. a direct desire to alleviate the sufferings of the lepers. No one who was not dying in the last ditch for an oversimple theory of human nature would deny this. The only questions that are worth raising about it are these. (1) Is this other-regarding motive stimulated by an egoistic motive-stimulus and thus rendered self-referential? (2) Suppose that this motive had not been supported by the various self-regarding and self-referential motives *for* deciding to go and work among the lepers, would it have sufficed, in presence of the motives *against* doing so, to ensure the choice that was actually made?

As regards the first question, I cannot see that there was any special pre-existing relationship between a young priest in Europe and a number of unknown lepers in Asia which might plausibly be held to act as an egoistic motive-stimulus. The lepers are neither his relatives nor his friends nor his benefactors nor members of any community or institution to which he belongs.

As regards the sufficiency of the other-regarding motive, whether stimulated egoistically or not, in the absence of all self-regarding motives tending in the same direction, no conclusive answer can be given. I cannot prove that a single person in the whole course of history *would* have decided to work among lepers, if all the motives against doing so had been present, whilst the hope of heaven, the desire to gain a reputation for sanctity and heroism, and the desire to glorify and extend one's church had been wholly absent. Nor can the Psychological Egoist prove that *no* single person would have so decided under these hypothetical conditions. Factors which cannot be eliminated cannot be shown to be necessary and cannot be shown to be superfluous; and there we must leave the matter.

I suspect that a Psychological Egoist might be tempted to say that the intending medical missionary found the experience of imagining the sufferings of the lepers intensely unpleasant, and that his primary motive for deciding to spend his life working among them was to get rid of this unpleasant experience. This, I think, is what Locke, e.g. would have had to say in accordance with his theory of motivation. About this suggestion there are two remarks to be made.

(1) This motive cannot have been primary, and therefore cannot have been the only motive. Unless this person desired that the lepers should have their sufferings alleviated, there is no reason why the thought of their sufferings should be an unpleasant experience to him. A malicious man, e.g. finds the thought of the sufferings of an enemy a very pleasant experience. This kind of pleasure presupposes a desire for the well-being or the ill-being of others.

(2) If his primary motive were to rid himself of the unpleasant experience of imagining the sufferings of the lepers, he could hardly choose a less effective means than to go and work among them. For the imagination would then be replaced by actual sense-perception; whilst, if he stayed at home and devoted himself to other activities, he would have a reasonably good chance of diverting his attention from the sufferings of the lepers. In point of fact one knows that such a person would reproach himself in so far as he managed to forget about the lepers. He would *wish* to keep them and their sufferings constantly in mind, as an additional stimulus to doing what he believes he ought to do, viz. to take active steps to help and relieve them.
. . .

I will now summarize the results of this discussion.

(1) If Psychological Egoism asserts that all ultimate motives are self-confined; or that they are all either self-confined or self-centred, some being of one kind and some of the other; or that all self-confined motives can be reduced to the desire for one's own happiness; it is certainly false. It is not even a close approximation to the truth.

(2) If it asserts that all ultimate motives are either self-regarding or self-referential, some being of one kind and some of the other; and that all other-regarding motives require a self-referential stimulus, it is a close approximation to the truth. It is true, I think, that in most people and at most times other-regarding motives are very weak unless stimulated by a self-referential stimulus. . . .

(3) Nevertheless, Psychological Egoism, even in its most diluted form, is very doubtful if taken as a universal proposition. Some persons at some times are strongly influenced by other-regarding motives which cannot plausibly be held to be stimulated by a self-referential stimulus. It seems reasonable to hold that the presence of these other-regarding motives is *necessary* to account for their choice of alternatives which they do choose, and for their persistence in the course which they have adopted, though this can never be conclusively established in any particular case. Whether it is also *sufficient* cannot be decided with certainty, for self-regarding and self-referential components are always present in one's total motive for choosing such an action. . . .

I must content myself with the following remarks in conclusion. I have tried to show that Psychological Egoism, in the only form in which it could possibly fit the facts of human life, is not a monistic theory of motives. On this extended interpretation of the theory the only feature common to all motives is that every motive which can *act on* a person has one or another of a large number of different kinds of special *reference to* that person. I have tried to show that this certainly covers a very wide field, but that it is by no means certain that there is even this amount of unity among *all* human motives. I think that Psychological Egoism is much the most plausible attempt to reduce the *prima facie* plurality of ultimate kinds of desire to a unity. If it fails, I think it is most unlikely that any alternative attempt on a different basis will succeed.

For my part I am inclined to accept an irreducibly pluralistic view of human motives. This does not, of course, entail that the present irreducible plurality of ultimate motives may not have evolved, in some sense of that highly ambiguous word, out of fewer, either in the history of each individual or in that of the human race. About that I express no opinion here and now.

AFTERWORD

The issues discussed in the preceding selections are closely tied to questions raised in other chapters of this book. In particular, the issue of psychological egoism extends the discussion of determinism and moral responsibility presented in Chapter 4. After reading the selections in both chapters, it is instructive to consider whether psychological egoism is a form of determinism, or whether a libertarian could adopt some form of psychological egoism. And the discussion of ethical egoism extends a theme presented in Chapter 6, since ethical egoism is one kind of naturalistic objectivist ethical theory.

This is another point at which you may find it useful to compare your actual behavior with the theories which seem most plausible to you, to see whether your beliefs and actions are consistent. Suppose, for example, that you thought someone had acted wrongly, and you said so. If they replied to you that what they had done served their own interests more effectively than any of the alternatives, and you thought they were right about that, would you then agree that what they had done was morally acceptable, or would you think that their response was an indication of weak moral character? If you tend not to accept such appeals to self-interest as moral justifications of behavior, then is your behavior what one might expect from an egoist? (Consider Medlin's arguments carefully when you answer this question.) On the other hand, if you sometimes expect people to act in ways that serve the interests of others, but justify those expectations by pointing out how such action really is in the best interests of the agent, are you acting more like an ethical egoist or like one who is committed to the virtues of altruism?

Finally, you may find this question intriguing: If, somehow, you knew that both psychological egoism and ethical egoism were true, and you also knew that your own interests would best be served if you believed that many of your actions were unselfish, what would happen?

REVIEW QUESTIONS

Selection 19

1. Why is the claim that men are equal in physical and mental faculties important to Hobbes's argument?

2. According to Hobbes, why is the state of nature a state of war?

3. In Hobbes's view, why do men give up their liberty for the sake of peace?

4. Hobbes makes our own self-interest the basis for respecting the needs and rights of others. Explain.

Selection 20

5. Is Mill's position in this selection a version of psychological egoism or not? Explain.

6. Mill says that it doesn't matter whether our feelings of duty to others are innate or acquired. Why?

7. Explain Mill's attempt to prove that only happiness is desirable. Is his concern with what is *psychologically* desirable, or what is *ethically* desirable?

8. Mill says that in reality nothing is desired but happiness. Does he mean that each person desires his own happiness, or does he claim that we desire the happiness of others, as well as our own?

Selection 21

9. Explain Butler's argument that we pursue a variety of things for their own sake, rather than for the pleasure we get from attaining them. What is the impact of this argument on psychological egoism?

10. Why does Butler claim that happiness cannot consist of self-love alone?

11. According to Butler, is benevolence really an aspect of self-love, or is it independent of self-love? Explain.

12. Is the last sentence in this selection consistent with the arguments which precede it? Explain.

Selection 22

13. What are the differences between Universal and Individual Egoism? Categorical and Hypothetical Egoism?

14. Explain the difficulty Medlin sees in the egoist's attempting to promulgate his theory.

15. Medlin claims that the ethical egoist's principle is inconsistent. What are his arguments?

Selection 23

16. Explain what Broad means by each of the following: (*a*) egoistic desire; (*b*) egoistic motive-stimulant; (*c*) self-confined motive; (*d*) extra-verted desire; (*e*) intro-verted desire; (*f*) other-regarding desire; (*g*) self-referential desire.

17. What is Broad's argument against the view that all we desire is our own happiness? Is this the same argument that Butler used? Explain.

18. Describe the kind of psychological egoism which Broad thinks is most plausible.

19. Broad describes some situations which may serve as counterexamples to the plausible form of psychological egoism. What are they, and how effective are they?

8

The Obligation to Obey the Law

Among the moral duties we all are presumed to share is the obligation to obey the law. There are many benefits which might be expected from general public obedience to a system of well-planned laws aimed at the public good. Laws contribute to social stability, to the protection of vulnerable citizens from their malicious fellows, to finding reasonable and just means for settling serious disagreements, and to a rational distribution of goods and responsibilities.

But the relationship between law and morality is complex. Laws, or even whole systems of laws, may be instituted with vicious intent. Or well-intended laws may produce unhappy results, because of failure to understand sufficiently the problems at which the laws were aimed, or the effects the laws would have. Even laws which usually produce highly desirable results may, in certain unfortunate situations, require action which would be morally wrong. Thus, it seems clear that to obey every law, on every occasion, will be to cause some avoidable suffering or injustice. And, to cause suffering or injustice which might have been avoided clearly seems to be morally wrong.

To sum up, we seem to be inclined to believe that

331

(1)   It is a moral duty to obey the law.

(2)   Constant obedience to the law will result in some avoidable suffering, unhappiness, or injustice.

(3)   To cause avoidable suffering, unhappiness, or injustice is morally wrong.

But these three statements seem to be inconsistent, so that some of what is claimed by at least one of them must be given up.

One possible approach to this problem, of course, is to claim that the law determines what is morally right. In that case, it would not be possible for one's moral duty and one's legal duty to differ, and unswerving obedience to law would be everyone's moral obligation. Statement (1) would thus be preserved, and either (2) or (3) rejected, depending upon whether it was claimed that legally required suffering must be unavoidable, or that such suffering is avoidable but not morally wrong.

On the other extreme, it might be claimed that our only moral obligations are to moral principles, and that the law rightfully commands obedience only when it coincides with what is morally required. Such a position might be bolstered by arguments to the effect that it is wrong to compel others to act rightly, and that we all should be fully responsible for our own behavior, rather than coerced by political and social forces. Such an anarchistic position would save statements (2) and (3) at the cost of rejecting (1).

Many philosophical approaches to this problem lie somewhere in between these two extremes. In these intermediate positions it is argued that there is *some* moral obligation to obey the law simply because it is law; but also that in some kinds of circumstances other pressing moral obligations can outweigh the obligation of obedience. The focus of disagreement among different intermediate positions is on the *strength* of the obligation to obey, and the kinds of circumstances which might justify disobedience.

In the attempt to find a sound position on this issue, questions about the origin and purpose of law are of extreme importance. In the first place, it is important to decide whether law has any moral purpose to serve, or whether it is only a product of expedience and political power. Then, if it is decided (as it usually is) that law does serve some moral ends, it is important to determine just what those ends are; for it might be presumed that disobedience to law is justified only when it serves the purposes for which the law was intended more effectively than would obedience. Thus, our views about the circumstances in which disobedience is justified would follow from our views about the moral purposes which law serves.

In the following selections you should be sure to look for discussion of the origins of law, and the purposes which it serves. Additionally, you should look for discussion of the circumstances in which disobedience might serve those purposes better than would obedience. Be sure to look, also, for claims to the effect that in some cases disobedience might serve purposes *more important* than those served by the law itself.

Finally, you should be alert to two rather different approaches to the whole set of issues. You will find in many discussions that the issues are presented in very general terms. Discussion will be focused on whether there are circumstances in which large groups, or even the whole population of citizens, might be justified in mass disobedience to a law or to the whole system of laws. In these cases the interest is quite political, concentrating on the legitimacy of resisting or overthrowing part or all of the legal or political system. But there are other situations to consider. Individuals may find that they are in circumstances where they think that obedience to a law would be morally wrong, although they regard the law as acceptable in most situations. To such individuals, discussions of the overthrow of legal systems are not very useful. What they need to know is whether a person in their circumstances should or should not engage in a single act of disobedience.

24

The Address of the Laws

PLATO

[Socrates has been sentenced to death and is in prison, waiting for the sentence to be carried out. Crito has pointed out that escape would be safe and easily accomplished, and is urging Socrates not to allow his life to be taken.]

Soc. ... I proceed to argue the question whether I ought or ought not to try and escape without the consent of the Athenians: and if I am clearly right in escaping, then I will make the attempt; but if not, I will abstain. The other considerations which you mention, of money and loss of character and the duty of educating one's children, are, I fear, only the doctrines of the multitude, who would be as ready to restore people to life, if they were able, as they are to put them to death—and with as little reason. But now, since the argument has thus far prevailed, the only question which remains to be considered is, whether we shall do rightly either in escaping or in suffering others to aid in our escape and paying them in money and thanks, or whether in reality we shall not do rightly; and if the latter, then death or any other calamity which may ensue on my remaining here must not be allowed to enter into the calculation.

Cr. I think that you are right, Socrates; how then shall we proceed?

Soc. Let us consider the matter together, and do you either refute me if you can, and I will be convinced; or else cease, my dear friend, from repeating to me that I ought to escape against the wishes of the Athenians: for I highly value your attempts to persuade me to do so, but I may not be persuaded against my own better judgment. And now please

[From *Crito*, translated by Benjamin Jowett (1892). The dialogue was written sometime during the first half of the fourth century B.C.]

to consider my first position, and try how you can best answer me.

Cr. I will.

Soc. Are we to say that we are never intentionally to do wrong, or that in one way we ought and in another we ought not to do wrong, or is doing wrong always evil and dishonourable, as I was just now saying, and as has been already acknowledged by us? Are all our former admissions which were made within a few days to be thrown away? And have we, at our age, been earnestly discoursing with one another all our life long only to discover that we are no better than children? Or, in spite of the opinion of the many, and in spite of consequences whether better or worse, shall we insist on the truth of what was then said, that injustice is always an evil and dishonour to him who acts unjustly? Shall we say so or not?

Cr. Yes.

Soc. Then we must do no wrong?

Cr. Certainly not.

Soc. Nor when injured injure in return, as the many imagine; for we must injure no one at all?

Cr. Clearly not.

Soc. Again, Crito, may we do evil?

Cr. Surely not, Socrates.

Soc. And what of doing evil in return for evil, which is the morality of the many—is that just or not?

Cr. Not just.

Soc. For doing evil to another is the same as injuring him?

Cr. Very true.

Soc. Then we ought not to retaliate or render evil for evil to any one, whatever evil we may have suffered from him. But I would have you consider, Crito, whether you really mean what you are saying. For this opinion has never been held, and never will be held, by any considerable number of persons; and those who are agreed and those who are not agreed upon this point have no common ground, and can only despise one another when they see how widely they differ. Tell me, then, whether you agree with and assent to my first principle, that neither injury nor retaliation nor warding off evil by evil is ever right. And shall that be the premiss of our argument? Or do you decline and dissent from this? For so I have ever thought, and continue to think; but, if you are of another opinion, let me hear what you have to say. If, however, you remain of the same mind as formerly, I will proceed to the next step.

Cr. You may proceed, for I have not changed my mind.

Soc. Then I will go on to the next point, which may be put in the form of a question:—Ought a man to do what he admits to be right, or ought he to betray the right?

Cr. He ought to do what he thinks right.

Soc. But if this is true, what is the application? In leaving the prison against the will of the Athenians, do I wrong any? or rather do I not wrong those whom I ought least to wrong? Do I not desert the principles which were acknowledged by us to be just—what do you say?

Cr. I cannot tell, Socrates; for I do not know.

Soc. Then consider the matter in this way:—Imagine that I am about to play truant (you may call the proceeding by any name which you like), and the laws and the government come and interrogate me: "Tell us, Socrates," they say; "what are you about? are you not going by an act of yours to overturn us—the laws, and the whole state, as far as in you lies? Do you imagine that a state can subsist and not be overthrown, in which the decisions of law have no power, but are set aside and trampled upon by individuals?" What will be our answer, Crito, to these and the like words? Any one, and especially a rhetorician, will have a good deal to say on behalf of the law which requires a sentence to be carried out. He will argue that this law should not be set aside; and shall we reply, "Yes; but the state has injured us and given an unjust sentence." Suppose I say that?

Cr. Very good, Socrates.

Soc. "And was that our agreement with you?" the law would answer; "or were you to abide by the sentence of the state?" And if I were to express my astonishment at their words, the law would probably add: "Answer, Socrates, instead of opening your eyes—you are in the habit of asking and answering questions.

Tell us,—What complaint have you to make against us which justifies you in attempting to destroy us and the state? In the first place did we not bring you into existence? Your father married your mother by our aid and begat you. Say whether you have any objection to urge against those of us who regulate marriage?" None, I should reply. "Or against those of us who after birth regulate the nurture and education of children, in which you also were trained? Were not the laws, which have the charge of education, right in commanding your father to train you in music and gymnastic?" Right, I should reply. "Well then, since you were brought into the world and nurtured and educated by us, can you deny in the first place that you are our child and slave, as your fathers were before you? And if this is true you are not on equal terms with us; nor can you think that you have a right to do to us what we are doing to you. Would you have any right to strike or revile or do any other evil to your father or your master, if you had one, because you have been struck or reviled by him, or received some other evil at his hands?—you would not say this? And because we think right to destroy you, do you think that you have any right to destroy us in return, and your country as far as in you lies? Will you, O professor of true virtue, pretend that you are justified in this? Has a philosopher like you failed to discover that our country is more to be valued and higher and holier far than mother or father or any ancestor, and more to be regarded in the eyes of the gods and of men of understanding? also to be soothed, and gently and reverently entreated when angry, even more than a father, and either to be persuaded, or if not persuaded, to be obeyed? And when we are punished by her, whether with imprisonment or stripes, the punishment is to be endured in silence; and if she leads us to wounds or death in battle, thither we follow as is right; neither may any one yield or retreat or leave his rank, but whether in battle or in a court of law, or in any other place, he must do what his city and his country order him; or he must change their view of what is just: and if he may do no violence to his father or mother, much less may he do violence to his country." What answer shall we make to this, Crito? Do the laws speak truly, or do they not?

Cr. I think that they do.

Soc. Then the laws will say, "Consider, Socrates, if we are speaking truly that in your present attempt you are going to do us an injury. For, having brought you into the world, and nurtured and educated you, and given you and every other citizen a share in every good which we had to give, we further proclaim to any Athenian by the liberty which we allow him, that if he does not like us when he has become of age and has seen the ways of the city, and made our acquaintance, he may go where he pleases and take his goods with him. None of us laws will forbid him or interfere with him. Any one who does not like us and the city, and who wants to emigrate to a colony or to any other city, may go where he likes, retaining his property. But he who has experience of the manner in which we order justice and administer the state, and still remains, has entered into an implied contract that he will do as we command him. And he who disobeys us is, as we maintain, thrice wrong; first, because in disobeying us he is disobeying his parents; secondly, because we are the authors of his education; thirdly, because he has made an agreement with us that he will duly obey our commands; and he neither obeys them nor convinces us that our commands are unjust; and we do not rudely impose them, but give him the alternative of obeying or convincing us;—that is what we offer, and he does neither.

"These are the sort of accusations to which, as we were saying, you, Socrates, will be exposed if you accomplish your intentions; you, above all other Athenians." Suppose now I ask, why I rather than anybody else? they will justly retort upon me that I above all other men have acknowledged the agreement. "There is clear proof," they will say, "Socrates, that we and the city were not displeasing to you. Of all Athenians you have been the most constant resident in the city, which, as you never leave, you may be supposed to love.

For you never went out of the city either to see the games, except once when you went to the Isthmus, or to any other place unless when you were on military service; nor did you travel as other men do. Nor had you any curiosity to know other states or their laws: your affections did not go beyond us and our state; we were your special favourites, and you acquiesced in our government of you; and here in this city you begat your children, which is a proof of your satisfaction. Moreover, you might in the course of the trial, if you had liked, have fixed the penalty at banishment; the state which refuses to let you go now would have let you go then. But you pretended that you preferred death to exile, and that you were not unwilling to die. And now you have forgotten these fine sentiments, and pay no respect to us the laws, of whom you are the destroyer; and are doing what only a miserable slave would do, running away and turning your back upon the compacts and agreements which you made as a citizen. And first of all answer this very question: Are we right in saying that you agreed to be governed according to us in deed, and not in word only? Is that true or not?" How shall we answer, Crito? Must we not assent?

Cr. We cannot help it, Socrates.

Soc. Then will they not say; "You, Socrates, are breaking the covenants and agreements which you made with us at your leisure, not in any haste or under any compulsion or deception, but after you have had seventy years to think of them, during which time you were at liberty to leave the city, if we were not to your mind, or if our covenants appeared to you to be unfair. You had your choice, and might have gone either to Lacedaemon or Crete, both which states are often praised by you for their good government, or to some other Hellenic or foreign state. Whereas you, above all other Athenians, seemed to be so fond of the state, or, in other words, of us her laws (and who would care about a state which has no laws?), that you never stirred out of her; the halt, the blind, the maimed were not more stationary in her than you were. And now you run away and forsake your agreements. Not so, Socrates, if you will take our advice; do not make yourself ridiculous by escaping out of the city.

"For just consider, if you transgress and err in this sort of way, what good will you do either to yourself or to your friends? That your friends will be driven into exile and deprived of citizenship, or will lose their property, is tolerably certain; and you yourself, if you fly to one of the neighbouring cities, as, for example, Thebes or Megara, both of which are well governed, will come to them as an enemy, Socrates, and their government will be against you, and all patriotic citizens will cast an evil eye upon you as a subverter of the laws, and you will confirm in the minds of the judges the justice of their own condemnation of you. For he who is a corrupter of the laws is more than likely to be a corrupter of the young and foolish portion of mankind. Will you then flee from well-ordered cities and virtuous men? and is existence worth having on these terms? Or will you go to them without shame, and talk to them, Socrates? And what will you say to them? What you say here about virtue and justice and institutions and laws being the best things among men? Would that be decent of you? Surely not. But if you go away from well-governed states to Crito's friends in Thessaly, where there is great disorder and licence, they will be charmed to hear the tale of your escape from prison, set off with ludicrous particulars of the manner in which you were wrapped in a goatskin or some other disguise, and metamorphosed as the manner is of runaways; but will there be no one to remind you that in your old age you were not ashamed to violate the most sacred laws from a miserable desire of a little more life? Perhaps not, if you keep them in a good temper; but if they are out of temper you will hear many degrading things; you will live, but how?—as the flatterer of all men, and the servant of all men; and doing what?—eating and drinking in Thessaly, having gone abroad in order that you may get a dinner. And where will be your fine sentiments about justice and virtue? Say that you wish to live for the sake of your children—you want to bring them up and educate them— will you take them into Thessaly and deprive them of Athenian citizenship? Is this the benefit which you will confer upon them? Or are you under the impression that they will be better cared for and educated here if you are still alive, although absent from them; for your friends will take care of them? Do you fancy that if you are an inhabitant of Thessaly they will take care of them, and if you are an inhabitant of the other world that they will not take care of them? Nay; but if they who call themselves friends are good for anything, they will—to be sure they will.

"Listen, then, Socrates, to us who have brought you up. Think not of life and children first, and of justice afterwards, but of justice first, that you may be justified before the princes of the world below. For neither will you nor any that belong to you be happier or holier or juster in this life, or happier in another, if you do as Crito bids. Now you depart in innocence, a sufferer and not a doer of evil; a victim, not of the laws but of men. But if you go forth, returning evil for evil, and injury for injury, breaking the covenants and agreements which you have made with us, and wronging those whom you ought least of all to wrong, that is to say, yourself, your friends, your country, and us, we shall be angry with you while you live, and our brethren, the laws in the world below, will receive you as an enemy; for they will know that you have done your best to destroy us. Listen, then, to us and not to Crito."

This, dear Crito, is the voice which I seem to hear murmuring in my ears, like the sound of the flute in the ears of the mystic; that voice, I say, is humming in my ears, and prevents me from hearing any other. And I know that anything more which you may say will be vain. Yet speak, if you have anything to say.

Cr. I have nothing to say, Socrates.

Soc. Leave me then, Crito, to fulfil the will of God, and to follow whither he leads.

25

Natural Law and Human Law

THOMAS AQUINAS

Natural Law

... The precepts of the natural law are to the practical reason what the first principles of demonstrations are to the speculative reason, because both are self-evident principles. Now a thing is said to be self-evident in two ways: first, in itself; secondly, in relation to us. Any proposition is said to be self-evident in itself, if its predicate is contained in the notion of the subject; even though it may happen that to one who does not know the definition of the subject, such a proposition is not self-evident. For instance, this proposition, *Man is a rational being*, is, in its very nature, self-evident, since he who says *man*, says *a rational being*; and yet to one who does not know what a man is, this proposition is not self-evident. Hence it is that, as Bo-

ethius says, certain axioms or propositions are universally self-evident to all; and such are the propositions whose terms are known to all, as, *Every whole is greater than its part*, and, *Things equal to one and the same are equal to one another*. But some propositions are self-evident only to the wise, who understand the meaning of the terms of such propositions. Thus to one who understands that an angel is not a body, it is self-evident that an angel is not circumscriptively in a place. But this is not evident to the unlearned, for they cannot grasp it.

Now a certain order is to be found in those things that are apprehended by men. For that which first falls under apprehension is *being*, the understanding of which is included in all things whatsoever a man apprehends. Therefore the

[From the *Summa Theologica* (1265–1273), Q. 94, Arts. 2, 4; Q. 95, Arts. 1, 2, 4; Q. 96, Arts. 1, 2, 3, 4, 6. Reprinted from *Basic Writings of Saint Thomas Aquinas*, Vol. II, edited by Anton C. Pegis (Random House, 1945), courtesy of the Anton C. Pegis Estate.]

first indemonstrable principle is that *the same thing cannot be affirmed and denied at the same time*, which is based on the notion of *being* and *not-being*: and on this principle all others are based, as is stated in *Metaph.* iv. Now as *being* is the first thing that falls under the apprehension absolutely, so *good* is the first thing that falls under the apprehension of the practical reason, which is directed to action (since every agent acts for an end, which has the nature of good). Consequently, the first principle in the practical reason is one founded on the nature of good, viz., that *good is that which all things seek after*. Hence this is the first precept of law, that *good is to be done and promoted, and evil is to be avoided*. All other precepts of the natural law are based upon this; so that all the things which the practical reason naturally apprehends as man's good belong to the precepts of the natural law under the form of things to be done or avoided.

Since, however, good has the nature of an end, and evil, the nature of the contrary, hence it is that all those things to which man has a natural inclination are naturally apprehended by reason as being good, and consequently as objects of pursuit, and their contraries as evil, and objects of avoidance. Therefore, the order of the precepts of the natural law is according to the order of natural inclinations. For there is in man, first of all, an inclination to good in accordance with the nature which he has in common with all substances, inasmuch, namely, as every substance seeks the preservation of its own being, according to its nature; and by reason of this inclination, whatever is a means of preserving human life, and of warding off its obstacles, belongs to the natural law. Secondly, there is in man an inclination to things that pertain to him more specially, according to that nature which he has in common with other animals; and in virtue of this inclination, those things are said to belong to the natural law *which nature has taught to all animals*, such as sexual intercourse, the education of offspring and so forth. Thirdly, there is in man an inclination to good according to the nature of his reason, which nature is proper to him. Thus man has a natural inclination to know the truth about God, and to live in society; and in this respect, whatever pertains to this inclination belongs to the natural law: *e.g.*, to shun ignorance, to avoid offending those among whom one has to live, and other such things regarding the above inclination. . . .

. . . As we have stated above, to the natural law belong those things to which a man is inclined naturally; and among these it is proper to man to be inclined to act according to reason. Now it belongs to the reason to proceed from what is common to what is proper, as is stated in *Physics* i. The speculative reason, however, is differently situated, in this matter, from the practical reason. For, since the speculative reason is concerned chiefly with necessary things, which cannot be otherwise than they are, its proper conclusions, like the universal principles, contain the truth without fail. The practical reason, on the other hand, is concerned with contingent matters, which is the domain of human actions; and, consequently, although there is necessity in the common principles, the more we descend towards the particular, the more frequently we encounter defects. Accordingly, then, in speculative matters truth is the same in all men, both as to principles and as to conclusions; athough the truth is not known to all as regards the conclusions, but only as regards the principles which are called *common notions*. But in matters of action, truth or practical rectitude is not the same for all as to what is particular, but only as to the common principles; and where there is the same rectitude in relation to particulars, it is not equally known to all.

It is therefore evident that, as regards the common principles whether of speculative or of practical reason, truth or rectitude is the same for all, and is equally known by all. But as to the proper conclusions of the speculative reason, the truth is the same for all, but it is not equally known to all. Thus, it is true for all that the three angles of a triangle are together equal to two right angles, although it is not known to all. But as to the proper conclusions of the practical reason, neither is the truth or rectitude the same for all, nor, where it is the same, is it equally known by all. Thus, it is right and true for all to act according to reason, and from this principle it follows, as a proper conclusion, that goods entrusted to another should be restored to their owner. Now this is true for the majority of cases. But it may happen in a particular case that it would be injurious, and therefore unreasonable, to restore goods held in trust; for instance, if they are claimed for the purpose of fighting against one's country. And this principle will be found to fail the more, according as we descend further towards the particular, *e.g.*, if one were to say that goods held in trust should be restored with such and such a guarantee, or in such and such a way; because the greater the number of conditions added, the greater the number of ways in which the principle may fail, so that it be not right to restore or not to restore.

Consequently, we must say that the natural law, as to the first common principles, is the same for all, both as to rectitude and as to knowledge. But as to certain more particular aspects, which are conclusions, as it were, of those common principles, it is the same for all in the majority of cases, both as to rectitude and as to knowledge; and yet in some few cases it may fail, both as to rectitude, by reason of certain obstacles (just as natures subject to generation and corruption fail in some few cases because of some obstacle), and as to knowledge, since in some the reason is perverted by passion, or evil habit, or an evil disposition of nature. Thus at one time theft, although it is expressly contrary to the natural law, was not considered wrong among the Germans, as Julius Cæsar relates. . . .

The Ends of Human Law

. . . As we have stated above, man has a natural aptitude for virtue; but the perfection of virtue must be acquired by man by means of some kind of training. Thus we observe that a man is helped by diligence in his necessities, for instance, in food and clothing. Certain beginnings of these he has from nature, viz., his reason and his hands; but he has not the full complement, as other animals have, to whom nature has given sufficiently of clothing and food. Now it is difficult to see how man could suffice for himself in the matter of this training, since the perfection of virtue consists chiefly in withdrawing man from undue pleasures, to which above all man is inclined, and especially the young, who are more capable of being trained. Consequently a man needs to receive this training from another, whereby to arrive at the perfection of virtue. And as to those young people who are inclined to acts of virtue by their good natural disposition, or by custom, or rather by the gift of God, paternal training suffices, which is by admonitions. But since some are found to be dissolute and prone to vice, and not easily amenable to words, it was necessary for such to be restrained from evil by force and fear, in order that, at least, they might desist from evil-doing, and leave others in peace, and that they themselves, by being habituated in this way, might be brought to do willingly what hitherto they did from fear, and thus become virtuous. Now this kind of training, which compels through fear of punishment, is the discipline of laws. Therefore, in order that man might have peace and virtue, it was necessary for laws to be framed; for, as the Philosopher says, *as man is the most noble of animals if he be perfect in virtue, so he is the lowest of all, if he be severed from law and justice*. For man can use his reason to devise means of satisfying his lusts and evil passions, which other animals are unable to do. . . .

. . . As Augustine says, *that which is not just seems to be no law at all*. Hence the force of a law depends on the extent of its justice. Now in human affairs a thing is said to be just from being right, according to the rule of reason. But the first rule of reason is the law of nature, as is clear from what has been stated above. Consequently, every human law has just so much of the nature of law as it is derived from the law of nature. But if at any point it departs from the law of nature, it is no longer a law but a perversion of law.

But it must be noted that something may be derived from the natural law in two ways: first, as a conclusion from principles; secondly, by way of a determination of certain common notions. The first way is like to that by which, in the sciences, demonstrated conclusions are drawn from the principles; while the second is likened to that whereby, in the arts, common forms are determined to some particular. Thus, the craftsman needs to determine the common form of a house to the shape of this or that particular house. Some things are therefore derived from the common principles of the natural law by way of conclusions: *e.g.*, that *one must not kill* may be derived as a conclusion from the principle that *one should do harm to no man*; while some are derived therefrom by way of determination: *e.g.*, the law of nature has it that the evil-doer should be punished, but that he be punished in this or that way is a determination of the law of nature.

Accordingly, both modes of derivation are found in the human law. But those things which are derived in the first way are contained in human law, not as emanating therefrom exclusively, but as having some force from the natural law also. But those things which are derived in the second way have no other force than that of human law. . . .

. . . A thing can be divided essentially in respect of something contained in the notion of that thing. Thus a soul, either rational or irrational, is contained in the notion of animal; and therefore animal is divided properly and essentially in respect of its being rational or irrational, but not in the point of its being white or black, which are entirely outside the notion of animal. Now, in the notion of human law, many things are contained, in respect of any of which human law can be divided properly and essentially. For, in the first place, it belongs to the notion of human law to be derived from the law of nature, as was explained above. In this respect positive law is divided into the *law of nations* and *civil law*, according to the two ways in which something may be derived from the law of nature, as was stated above. For to the law of nations belong those things which are derived from the law of nature as conclusions from principles, *e.g.*, just buyings and sellings, and the like, without which men cannot live together; and this belongs to the law of nature, since man is by nature a social animal, as is proved in *Politics* i. But those things which are derived from the law of nature by way of particular determination belong to the civil law, according as each state decides on what is best for itself.

Secondly, it belongs to the notion of human law to be ordained to the common good of the state. In this respect, human law may be divided according to the different kinds of men who work in a special way for the common good: *e.g.*, priests, by praying to God for the people; princes, by governing the people; soldiers, by fighting for the safety of the people. Therefore certain special kinds of law are adopted to these men.

Thirdly, it belongs to the notion of human law to be framed by the one who governs the community of the state, as was shown above. In this respect, there are various human laws according to the various forms of government. Of these, according to the Philosopher, one is *monarchy, i.e.*, when the state is governed by one; and then we have *Royal Ordinances*. Another form is *aristocracy, i.e.*, government by the best men or men of highest rank; and then we have the *Authoritative legal opinions* [*Responsa Prudentum*] and *Decrees of the Senate* [*Senatus consulta*]. Another form is *oligarchy, i.e.*, government by a few rich and powerful men; and then we have *Prœtorian*, also called *Honorary*, law. Another form of government is that of the people, which is called democracy, and there we have *Decrees of the commonality* [*Plebiscita*]. There is also tyrannical government, which is altogether corrupt, which, therefore, has no corresponding law. Finally, there is a form of government made up of all these, and which is the best; and in this respect we have *law sanctioned by the Lords and Commons*, as is stated by Isidore.

Fourthly, it belongs to the notion of human law to direct human actions. In this respect, according to the various matters of which the law treats, there are various kinds of laws, which are sometimes named after their authors. Thus we have the *Lex Julia* about adultery, the *Lex Cornelia* concerning assassins, and so on, differentiated in this way, not because of the authors, but because of the matters to which they refer. . . .

. . . Whatever is for an end should be proportioned to that end. Now the end of law is the common good, because, as Isidore says, *law should be framed, not for any private benefit, but for the common good of all the citizens*. Hence human laws should be proportioned to the common good. Now the common good comprises many things. Therefore law should take account of many things, as to persons, as to matters, and as to times. For the community of the state is composed of many persons, and its good is procured by many actions; nor is it established to endure for only a short time, but to last for all time by the citizens succeeding one another, as Augustine says. . . .

. . . As was stated above, law is framed as a rule or measure of human acts. Now a measure should be homogeneous with that which it measures, as is stated in *Metaph.* x., since different things are measured by different measures. Therefore laws imposed on men should also be in keeping with their condition, for, as Isidore says, law should be *possible both according to nature, and according to the customs of the country*. Now the ability or facility of action is due to an interior habit or disposition, since the same thing is not possible to one who has not a virtuous habit, as is possible to one who has. Thus the same thing is not possible to a child as to a full-grown man, and for which reason the law for children is not the same as for adults, since many things are permitted to children, which in an adult are punished by law or at any rate are open to blame. In like manner, many things are permissible to men not perfect in virtue, which would be intolerable in a virtuous man.

Now human law is framed for the multitude of human beings, the majority of whom are not perfect in virtue. Therefore human laws do not forbid all vices, from which the virtuous abstain, but only the more grievous vices, from which it is possible for the majority to abstain; and chiefly those that are injurious to others, without the prohibition of which human society could not be maintained. Thus human law prohibits murder, theft and the like. . . .

. . . The species of virtues are distinguished by their objects, as was explained above. Now all the objects of the virtues can be referred either to the private good of an individual, or to the common good of the multitude. Thus, matters of fortitude may be achieved either for the safety of the state, or for upholding the rights of a friend; and in like manner with the other virtues. But law, as was stated above, is ordained to the common good. Therefore, there is no virtue whose acts cannot be prescribed by the law. Nevertheless, human law does not prescribe concerning all the acts of every virtue, but only in regard to those that are ordainable to the common good,— either immediately, as when certain things are done directly for the common good,—or mediately, as when a lawgiver prescribes certain things pertaining to good order, whereby the citizens are directed in the upholding of the common good of justice and peace. . . .

Unjust Laws

. . . Laws framed by man are either just or unjust. If they be just, they have the power of binding in conscience from the eternal law whence they are derived, according to *Prov.* viii. 15: *By Me kings reign, and lawgivers decree just things*. Now laws are said to be just, both from the end (when, namely, they are ordained to the common good), from their author (that is to say, when the law that is made does not exceed the power of the lawgiver), and from their form (when, namely, burdens are laid on the subjects according to an equality of proportion and with a view to the common good). For, since one man is a part of the community, each man, in all that he is and has, belongs to the community; just as a part, in all that it is, belongs to the whole. So, too, nature inflicts a loss on the part in order to save the whole; so that for this reason such laws as these, which impose proportionate burdens, are just and binding in conscience, and are legal laws.

On the other hand, laws may be unjust in two ways: first, by being contrary to human good, through being opposed to the things mentioned above:—either in respect of the end, as when an authority imposes on his subjects burdensome laws, conducive, not to the common good, but rather to his own cupidity or vainglory; or in respect of the author, as when a man makes a law that goes beyond the power committed to him; or in respect of the form, as when burdens are imposed unequally on the community, although with a view to the common good. Such are acts of violence rather than laws, because, as Augustine says, *a law that is not just seems to be no law at all.* Therefore, such laws do not bind in conscience, except perhaps in order to avoid scandal or disturbance, for which cause a man should even yield his right, according to *Matt.* v. 40, 41: *If a man*

... take away thy coat, let go thy cloak also unto him; and whosoever will force thee one mile, go with him other two.

Secondly, laws may be unjust through being opposed to the divine good. Such are the laws of tyrants inducing to idolatry, or to anything else contrary to the divine law. Laws of this kind must in no way be observed, because, as is stated in *Acts* v. 29, *we ought to obey God rather than men. ...*

... As was stated above, every law is directed to the common welfare of men, and derives the force and nature of law accordingly; but in so far as it fails of this common welfare, it is without binding power. Hence the Jurist says: *By no reason of law, or favor of equity, is it allowable for us to interpret harshly, and render burdensome, those useful measures which have been enacted for the welfare of man.* Now it often happens that the observance of some point of law conduces to the common welfare in the majority of instances, and yet, in some cases, is very injurious. Since, then, the lawgiver cannot have in view every single case, he shapes the law according to what happens most frequently, by directing his attention to the common good. Hence, if a case arise wherein the observance of that law would be injurious to the general welfare, it should not be observed. For instance, suppose that in a besieged city it be an established law that the gates of the city are to be kept closed, this is good for public welfare as a general rule; but if it were to happen that the enemy are in pursuit of certain citizens, who are defenders of the city, it would be a great calamity for the city if the gates were not opened to them; and so in that case the gates ought to be opened, contrary to the letter of the law, in order to maintain the common welfare, which the lawgiver had in view.

Nevertheless, it must be noted that if the observance of the law according to the letter does not involve any sudden risk, needing instant remedy, it is not permissible for everyone to expound what is useful and what is not useful to the state; rather those alone can do this who are in authority, and who, in the event of such cases, have the power to dispense from the laws. If, however, the peril be so sudden as not to allow the delay involved in referring the matter to authority, the necessity itself carries with it a dispensation, since necessity knows no law. . . .

Of Commonwealth and the Rights of Sovereigns

THOMAS HOBBES

Nature of a Commonwealth

The final cause, end, or design of men who naturally love liberty and dominion over others, in the introduction of that restraint upon themselves in which we see them live in commonwealths, is the foresight of their own preservation, and of a more contented life thereby; that is to say, of getting themselves out from that miserable condition of war, which is necessarily consequent, as hath been shown in Chapter XIII, to the natural passions of men, when there is no visible power to keep them in awe, and tie them by fear of punishment to the performance of their covenants and observation of those laws of nature set down in the fourteenth and fifteenth chapters.

For the laws of nature, as justice, equity, modesty, mercy, and, in sum, *doing to others as we would be done to,* of themselves, without the terror of some power to cause them to be observed, are contrary to our natural passions, that carry us to partiality, pride, revenge, and the like. And covenants, without the sword, are but words, and of no strength to secure a man at all. Therefore notwithstanding the laws of nature, which everyone hath then kept, when he has the will to keep them when he can do it safely; if there be no power erected, or not great enough for our security, every man will, and may, lawfully rely on his own strength and art, for caution against all other men. And in all places where men have lived by small families, to rob and spoil one

[From *Leviathan,* Part II, chapters 17, 18. First published in 1651.]

another has been a trade, and so far from being reputed against the law of nature, that the greater spoils they gained, the greater was their honor; and men observed no other laws therein but the laws of honor; that is, to abstain from cruelty, leaving to men their lives, and instruments of husbandry. And as small families did then; so now do cities and kingdoms, which are but greater families, for their own security enlarge their dominions, upon all pretenses of danger and fear of invasion, or assistance that may be given to invaders, and endeavor as much as they can to subdue or weaken their neighbors, by open force and secret arts, for want of other caution, justly; and are remembered for it in after ages with honor.

Nor is it the joining together of a small number of men, that gives them this security; because in small numbers, small additions on the one side or the other make the advantage of strength so great, as is sufficient to carry the victory, and therefore gives encouragement to an invasion. The multitude sufficient to confide in for our security, is not determined by any certain number, but by comparison with the enemy we fear; and is then sufficient, when the odds of the enemy is not of so visible and conspicuous moment, to determine the event of war, as to move him to attempt.

And be there never so great a multitude, yet if their actions be directed according to their particular judgments and particular appetites, they can expect thereby no defense nor protection, neither against a common enemy nor against the injuries of one another. For being distracted in opinions concerning the best use and application of their strength, they do not help but hinder one another; and reduce their strength by mutual opposition to nothing: whereby they are easily, not only subdued by a very few that agree together; but also when there is no common enemy, they make war upon each other, for their particular interests. For if we could suppose a great multitude of men to consent in the observation of justice, and other laws of nature, without a common power to keep them all in awe, we might as well suppose all mankind to do the same; and then there neither would be, nor need to be any civil government or commonwealth at all, because there would be peace without subjection. . . .

The only way to erect such a common power, as may be able to defend them from the invasion of foreigners and the injuries of one another, and thereby to secure them in such sort as that, by their own industry, and by the fruits of the earth, they may nourish themselves and live contentedly; is, to confer all their power and strength upon one man, or upon one assembly of men, that may reduce all their wills, by plurality of voices, unto one will: which is as much as to say, to appoint one man, or assembly of men, to bear their person; and everyone to own and acknowledge himself to be author of whatsoever he that so beareth their person, shall act or cause to be acted in those things which concern the common peace and safety; and therein to submit their wills, everyone to his will, and their judgments, to his judgment. This is more than consent, or concord; it is a real unity of them all in one and the same person, made by covenant of every man with every man, in such manner as if every man should say to every man, *"I authorize and give up my right of governing myself to this man, or to this assembly of men, on this condition, that thou give up thy right to him, and authorize all his actions in like manner."* This done, the multitude so united in one person, is called a *commonwealth,* in Latin *civitas.* This is the generation of that great LEVIATHAN, or rather, to speak more reverently, of that *mortal god,* to which we owe under the *immortal God,* our peace and defense. For by this authority, given him by every particular man in the commonwealth, he hath the use of so much power and strength conferred on him, that by terror thereof he is enabled to perform the wills of them all, to peace at home and mutual aid against their enemies abroad. And in him consisteth the essence of the commonwealth; which, to define it, is *one person, of whose acts a great multitude, by mutual covenants one with another, have made themselves*

every one the author, to the end he may use the strength and means of them all, as he shall think expedient, for their peace and common defense.

And he that carrieth this person, is called *sovereign,* and said to have sovereign power; and everyone besides, his *subject.* . . .

The Rights of Sovereigns

A COMMONWEALTH is said to be *instituted,* when a multitude of men do agree and covenant, everyone with everyone, that to whatsoever man, or assembly of men, shall be given by the major part the right to present the person of them all, that is to say, to be their *representative;* everyone, as well he that voted for it as he that voted against it, shall authorize all the actions and judgments of that man, or assembly of men, in the same manner as if they were his own, to the end to live peaceably amongst themselves and be protected against other men.

From this institution of a commonwealth are derived all the *rights* and *faculties* of him, or them, on whom sovereign power is conferred by the consent of the people assembled.

First, because they covenant, it is to be understood they are not obliged by former covenant to anything repugnant hereunto. And consequently they that have already instituted a commonwealth, being thereby bound by covenant to own the actions and judgments of one, cannot lawfully make a new covenant amongst themselves, to be obedient to any other, in anything whatsoever, without his permission. And therefore, they that are subject to a monarch, cannot without his leave cast off monarchy, and return to the confusion of a disunited multitude; nor transfer their person from him that beareth it, to another man, or other assembly of men: for they are bound, every man to every man, to own, and be reputed author of all, that he that already is their sovereign shall do and judge fit to be done; so that any one man dissenting, all the rest should break their covenant made to that man, which is injustice: and they have also every man given the sovereignty to him that beareth their person; and therefore if they depose him, they take from him that which is his own, and so again it is injustice. Besides, if he that attempteth to depose his sovereign, be killed or punished by him for such attempt, he is author of his own punishment, as being by the institution, author of all his sovereign shall do; and because it is injustice for a man to do anything for which he may be punished by his own authority, he is also upon that title, unjust. And whereas some men have pretended for their disobedience to their sovereign, a new covenant, made not with men but with God, this also is unjust: for there is no covenant with God, but by mediation of somebody that representeth God's person; which none doth but God's lieutenant, who hath the sovereignty under God. But this pretense of covenant with God, is so evident a lie, even in the pretenders' own consciences, that it is not only an act of an unjust, but also of a vile and unmanly disposition.

Secondly, because the right of bearing the person of them all, is given to him they make sovereign, by covenant only of one to another, and not of him to any of them; there can happen no breach of covenant on the part of the sovereign; and consequently none of his subjects, by any pretense of forfeiture, can be freed from his subjection. That he which is made sovereign maketh no covenant with his subjects beforehand, is manifest; because either he must make it with the whole multitude, as one party to the covenant, or he must make a several covenant with every man. With the whole, as one party, it is impossible, because as yet they are not one person: and if he make so many several covenants as there be men, those covenants after he hath the sovereignty are void; because what act soever can be pretended by any one of them for breach thereof, is the act both of himself and of all the rest, because done in the person, and by the right of every one of them in particular. Besides, if any one, or more of them, pretend a breach of the covenant made by the sovereign at his institution; and others, as one other of his subjects, or himself alone, pretend there was no such breach: there is in this case, no judge to decide the controversy; it returns therefore to the sword again; and every man recovereth the right of protecting himself by his own strength, contrary to the design they had in the institution. It is therefore in vain to grant sovereignty by way of precedent covenant. The opinion that any monarch receiveth his power by covenant, that is to say, on condition, proceedeth from want of understanding this easy truth, that covenants being but words and breath, have no force to oblige, contain, constrain, or protect any man, but what it has from the public sword; that is, from the untied hands of that man, or assembly of men that hath the sovereignty, and whose actions are avouched by them all, and performed by the strength of them all, in him united. ...

Thirdly, because the major part hath by consenting voices declared a sovereign, he that dissented must now consent with the rest; that is, be contented to avow all the actions he shall do, or else justly be destroyed by the rest. For if he voluntarily entered into the congregation of them that were assembled, he sufficiently declared thereby his will, and therefore tacitly covenanted to stand to what the major part should ordain; and therefore if he refuse to stand thereto, or make protestation against any of their decrees, he does contrary to his covenant, and therefore unjustly. And whether he be of the congregation or not, and whether his consent be asked or not, he must either submit to their decrees, or be left in the condition of war he was in before; wherein he might without injustice be destroyed by any man whatsoever.

Fourthly, because every subject is by this institution author of all the actions and judgments of the sovereign instituted; it follows that whatsoever he doth, it can be no injury to any of his subjects, nor ought he to be by any of them accused of injustice. For he that doth anything by authority from another, doth therein no injury to him by whose authority he acteth: but by this institution of a commonwealth, every particular man is author of all the sovereign doth: and consequently he that complaineth of injury from his sovereign, complaineth of that whereof he himself is author; and therefore ought not to accuse any man but himself; no nor himself of injury, because to do injury to one's self, is impossible. It is true that they that have sovereign power may commit iniquity, but not injustice, or injury, in the proper signification.

Fifthly, and consequently to that which was said last, no man that hath sovereign power can justly be put to death, or otherwise in any manner by his subjects punished. For seeing every subject is author of the actions of his sovereign, he punisheth another for the actions committed by himself. ...

Sixthly, it is annexed to the sovereignty, to be judge of what opinions and doctrines are averse, and what conducing to peace; and consequently, on what occasions, how far, and what men are to be trusted withal, in speaking to multitudes of people; and who shall examine the doctrines of all books before they be published. For the actions of men proceed from their opinions; and in the well-governing of opinions consisteth the well-governing of men's actions, in order to their peace and concord. And though in matter of doctrine nothing ought to be regarded but the truth, yet this is not repugnant to regulating the same by peace. For doctrine repugnant to peace can no more be true, than peace and concord can be against the law of nature. . . .

Seventhly, is annexed to the sovereignty, the whole power of prescribing the rules, whereby every man may know what goods he may enjoy, and what actions he may do, without being molested by any of his fellow-subjects; and this is it men call *propriety*. For before constitution of sovereign power, as hath already been shown, all men had right to all things; which necessarily causeth war: and therefore this propriety, being necessary to peace, and depending on sovereign power, is the act of that power, in order to the public peace. These rules of propriety, or *meum* and *tuum*, and of good, evil, lawful, and unlawful in the actions of subjects, are the civil laws; that is to say, the laws of each commonwealth in particular. . . .

Eighthly, is annexed to the sovereignty, the right of judicature; that is to say, of hearing and deciding all controversies which may arise concerning law, either civil or natural, or concerning fact. For without the decision of controversies, there is no protection of one subject against the injuries of another: the laws concerning *meum* and *tuum* are in vain; and to every man remaineth, from the natural and necessary appetite of his own conservation, the right of protecting himself by his private strength, which is the condition of war, and contrary to the end for which every commonwealth is instituted. . . .

And because they are essential and inseparable rights, it follows necessarily that in whatsoever words any of them seem to be granted away, yet if the sovereign power itself be not in direct terms renounced, and the name of sovereign no more given by the grantees to him that grants them, the grant is void: for when he has granted all he can, if we grant back the sovereignty, all is restored, as inseparably annexed thereunto.

Sovereign Power Should Not Be Resisted

This great authority being indivisible, and inseparably annexed to the sovereignty, there is little ground for the opinion of them that say of sovereign kings, though they be *singulis majores*, of greater power than every one of their subjects, yet they be *universis minores*, of less power than them all together. For if by "all together" they mean not the collective body as one person, then "all together" and "every one" signify the same, and the speech is absurd. But if by "all together" they understand them as one person, which person the sovereign bears, then the power of all together is the same with the sovereign's power, and so again the speech is absurd: which absurdity they see well enough when the sovereignty is in an assembly of the people, but in a monarch they see it not; and yet the power of sovereignty is the same in whomsoever it be placed. . . .

But a man may here object that the condition of subjects is very miserable, as being obnoxious to the lusts, and other irregular passions, of him or them that have so unlimited a power in their hands. And commonly they that live under a monarch, think it the fault of monarchy; and they that live under the government of democracy, or other sovereign assembly, attribute all the inconvenience to that form of commonwealth; whereas the power in all forms, if they be perfect enough to protect them, is the same: not considering that the state of man can never be without some incommodity or other; and that the greatest that in any form of government can possibly happen to the people in general, is scarce sensible, in respect to the miseries and horrible calamities that accompany a civil war, or that dissolute condition of masterless men, without subjection to laws and a coercive power to tie their hands from rapine and revenge: nor considering that the greatest pressure of sovereign governors, proceedeth not from any delight or profit they can expect in the damage or weakening of their subjects, in whose vigor consisteth their own strength and glory; but in the restiveness of themselves, that unwillingly contributing to their own defense, make it necessary for their governors to draw from them what they can in time of peace, that they may have means on any emergent occasion or sudden need, to resist or take advantage on their enemies. For all men are by nature provided of notable multiplying glasses, that is their passions and self-love, through which every little payment appeareth a great grievance; but are destitute of those prospective glasses, namely moral and civil science, to see afar off the miseries that hang over them, and cannot without such payment be avoided.

27

Of the Dissolution of Government

JOHN LOCKE

The Origin of Political Societies

Every man being, as has been shown, naturally free, and nothing being able to put him into subjection to any earthly power but only his own consent, it is to be considered what shall be understood to be a sufficient declaration of a man's consent to make him subject to the laws of any government. There is a common distinction of an express and a tacit consent which will concern our present case. Nobody doubts but an express consent of any man entering into any society makes him a perfect member of that society, a subject of that government. The difficulty is, what ought to be looked upon as a tacit consent, and how far it binds—i.e., how far any one shall be looked upon to have consented and thereby sub-mitted to any government, where he has made no expressions of it at all. And to this I say that every man that has any possessions or enjoyment of any part of the dominions of any government does thereby give his tacit consent and is as far forth obliged to obedience to the laws of that government, during such enjoyment, as anyone under it; whether this his possession be of land to him and his heirs for ever, or a lodging only for a week, or whether it be barely traveling freely on the highway; and, in effect, it reaches as far as the very being of anyone within the territories of that government. . . .

But since the government has a direct jurisdiction only over the land, and reaches the possessor of it—before he has actually incorporated himself in the society—only as

[From *The Second Treatise of Government*, chapters 8, 9, 19. First published in 1690.]

he dwells upon and enjoys that, the obligation anyone is under by virtue of such enjoyment, to submit to the government, begins and ends with the enjoyment; so that whenever the owner, who has given nothing but such a tacit consent to the government, will, by donation, sale, or otherwise, quit the said possession, he is at liberty to go and incorporate himself into any other commonwealth, or to agree with others to begin a new one *in vacuis locis*, in any part of the world they can find free and unpossessed. Whereas he that has once, by actual agreement and any express declaration, given his consent to be of any commonwealth is perpetually and indispensably obliged to be and remain unalterably a subject to it, and can never be again in the liberty of the state of nature, unless by any calamity the government he was under comes to be dissolved, or else, by some public act, cuts him off from being any longer a member of it.

But submitting to the laws of any country, living quietly and enjoying privileges and protection under them, makes not a man a member of that society; this is only a local protection and homage due to and from all those who, not being in a state of war, come within the territories belonging to any government, to all parts whereof the force of its laws extends. But this no more makes a man a member of that society, a perpetual subject of that commonwealth, than it would make a man a subject to another in whose family he found it convenient to abide for some time, though, while he continued in it, he were obliged to comply with the laws and submit to the government he found there. And thus we see that foreigners, by living all their lives under another government and enjoying the privileges and protection of it, though they are bound, even in conscience, to submit to its administration as far forth as any denizen, yet do not thereby come to be subjects or members of that commonwealth. Nothing can make any man so but his actually entering into it by positive engagement and express promise and compact. That is that which I think concerning the beginning of political societies and that consent which makes any one a member of any commonwealth.

If man in the state of nature be so free, as has been said, if he be absolute lord of his own person and possessions, equal to the greatest, and subject to nobody, why will he part with his freedom, why will he give up his empire and subject himself to the dominion and control of any other power? To which it is obvious to answer that though in the state of nature he has such a right, yet the enjoyment of it is very uncertain and constantly exposed to the invasion of others; for all being kings as much as he, every man his equal, and the greater part no strict observers of equity and justice, the enjoyment of the property he has in this state is very unsafe, very unsecure. This makes him willing to quit a condition which, however free, is full of fears and continual dangers; and it is not without reason that he seeks out and is willing to join in society with others who are already united, or have a mind to unite, for the mutual preservation of their lives, liberties, and estates, which I call by the general name "property."

The great and chief end, therefore, of men's uniting into commonwealths and putting themselves under government is the preservation of their property. . . .

Thus mankind, notwithstanding all the privileges of the state of nature, being but in an ill condition while they remain in it, are quickly driven into society. Hence it comes to pass that we seldom find any number of men live any time together in this state. The inconveniences that they are therein exposed to by the irregular and uncertain exercise of the power every man has of punishing the transgressions of others make them take sanctuary under the established laws of government and therein seek the preservation of their property. It is this makes them so willingly give up every one his single power of punishing, to be exercised by such alone as shall be appointed to it amongst them; and by such rules as the community, or those authorized by them to that purpose, shall agree on. And in this we have the original right of both the legislative and executive power, as well as of the governments and societies themselves. . . .

But though men when they enter into society give up the equality, liberty, and executive power they had in the state of nature into the hands of the society, to be so far disposed of by the legislative as the good of the society shall require, yet it being only with an intention in every one the better to preseve himself, his liberty and property—for no rational creature can be supposed to change his condition with an intention to be worse—the power of the society, or legislative constituted by them, can never be supposed to extend farther than the common good, but is obliged to secure every one's property by providing against those three defects above-mentioned that made the state of nature so unsafe and uneasy. And so whoever has the legislative or supreme power of any commonwealth is bound to govern by established standing laws, promulgated and known to the people, and not by extemporary decrees; by indifferent and upright judges who are to decide controversies by those laws; and to employ the force of the community at home only in the execution of such laws, or abroad to prevent or redress foreign injuries, and secure the community from inroads and invasion. And all this to be directed to no other end but the peace, safety, and public good of the people.

When Government May Be Dissolved

The reason why men enter into society is the preservation of their property; and the end why they choose and authorize a legislative is that there may be laws made and rules set as guards and fences to the properties of all the members of the society to limit the power and moderate the dominion of every part and member of the society; for since it can never be supposed to be the will of the society that the legislative should have a power to destroy that which every one designs to secure by entering into society, and for which the people submitted themselves to legislators of their own making. Whenever the legislators endeavor to take away and destroy the property of the people, or to reduce them to slavery under arbitrary power, they put themselves into a state of war with the people who are thereupon absolved from any further obedience, and are left to the common refuge which God has provided for all men against force and violence. Whensoever, therefore, the legislative shall transgress this fundamental rule of society, and either by ambition, fear, folly, or corruption, endeavor to grasp themselves, or put into the hands of any other, an absolute power over the lives, liberties, and estates of the people, by this breach of trust they forfeit the power the people had put into their hands for quite contrary ends, and it devolves to the people, who have a right to resume their original liberty and, by the establishment of a new legislative, such as they shall think fit, provide for their own safety and security, which is the end for which they are in society. What I have said here concerning the legislative in general holds true also concerning the supreme executor, who having a double trust put in him—both to have a part in the legislative and the supreme execution of the law—acts against both when he goes about to set up his own arbitrary will as the law of the society. He acts also contrary to his trust when he either employs the force, treasure, and offices of the society to corrupt the representatives and gain them to his purposes, or openly pre-engages the electors and prescribes to their choice such whom he has by solicitations, threats, promises, or otherwise won to his designs, and employs them to bring in such who have promised beforehand what to vote and what to enact. . . .

To this perhaps it will be said that, the people being ignorant and always discontented, to lay the foundation of government in the unsteady opinion and uncertain humor of the people is to expose it to certain ruin; and no government will be able long to subsist if the people may set up a new legislative whenever they take offense at the old one. To this I answer: Quite the contrary. People are not so easily got out of their old forms as some are apt to suggest. They are hardly to be prevailed with to amend the acknowledged faults in the frame they have been accustomed to. And if there be any original defects, or adventitious ones introduced by time or corruption, it is not an easy thing to get them changed, even when all the world sees there is an opportunity for it. . . .

But it will be said this hypothesis lays a ferment for frequent rebellion. To which I answer:

First, no more than any other hypothesis; for when the people are made miserable, and find themselves exposed to the ill-usage of arbitrary power, cry up their governors as much as you will for sons of Jupiter, let them be sacred or divine, descended or authorized from heaven, give them out for whom or what you please, the same will happen. The people generally ill-treated, and contrary to right, will be ready upon any occasion to ease themselves of a burden that sits heavy upon them. They will wish and seek for the opportunity, which in the change, weakness, and accidents of human affairs seldom delays long to offer itself. He must have lived but a little while in the world who has not seen examples of this in his time,

and he must have read very little who cannot produce examples of it in all sorts of governments in the world.

Secondly, I answer, such revolutions happen not upon every little mismanagement in public affairs. Great mistakes in the ruling part, many wrong and inconvenient laws, and all the slips of human frailty will be born by the people without mutiny or murmur. But if a long train of abuses, prevarications, and artifices, all tending the same way, make the design visible to the people, and they cannot but feel what they lie under and see whither they are going, it is not to be wondered that they should then rouse themselves and endeavor to put the rule into such hands which may secure to them the ends for which government was at first erected, and without which ancient names and specious forms are so far from being better that they are much worse than the state of nature or pure anarchy— the inconveniences being all as great and as near, but the remedy farther off and more difficult.

Thirdly, I answer that this doctrine of a power in the people of providing for their safety anew by a new legislative, when their legislators have acted contrary to their trust by invading their property, is the best fence against rebellion, and the probablest means to hinder it; for rebellion being an opposition, not to persons, but authority which is

founded only in the constitutions and laws of the government, those, whoever they be, who by force break through, and by force justify their violation of them, are truly and properly rebels; for when men, by entering into society and civil government, have excluded force and introduced laws for the preservation of property, peace, and unity amongst themselves, those who set up force again in opposition to the laws do *rebellare*—that is, bring back again the state of war—and are properly rebels; which they who are in power, by the pretense they have to authority, the temptation of force they have in their hands, and the flattery of those about them, being likeliest to do, the properest way to prevent the evil is to show them the danger and injustice of it who are under the greatest temptation to run into it.
. . .

The end of government is the good of mankind. And which is best for mankind? That the people should be always exposed to the boundless will of tyranny, or that the rulers should be sometimes liable to be opposed when they grow exorbitant in the use of their power and employ it for the destruction and not the preservation of the properties of their people?

Nor let any one say that mischief can arise from hence, as often as it shall please a busy head or turbulent spirit to desire the alteration of the government. It is true such men may stir whenever they please, but it will be only to their own just

ruin and perdition; for till the mischief be grown general, and the ill designs of the rulers become visible, or their attempts sensible to the greater part, the people, who are more disposed to suffer than right themselves by resistance, are not apt to stir. . . . This I am sure: whoever, either ruler or subject, by force goes about to invade the rights of either prince or people and lays the foundation for overturning the constitution and frame of any just government is highly guilty of the greatest crime I think a man is capable of—being to answer for all those mischiefs of blood, rapine, and desolation, which the breaking to pieces of governments bring on a country. And he who does it is justly to be esteemed the common enemy and pest of mankind, and is to be treated accordingly. . . .

Here, it is like, the common question will be made: Who shall be judge whether the prince or legislative act contrary to their trust? This, perhaps, ill-affected and factious men may spread amongst the people, when the prince only makes use of his due prerogative. To this I reply: The people shall be judge; for who shall be judge whether his trustee or deputy acts well and according to the trust reposed in him but he who deputes him and must, by having deputed him, have still a power to discard him when he fails in his trust? If this be reasonable in particular cases of private men, why should it be otherwise in that of the greatest moment where the welfare of millions is concerned, and also where the evil, if not prevented, is greater and the redress very difficult, dear, and dangerous? . . .

If a controversy arise betwixt a prince and some of the people in a matter where the law is silent or doubtful, and the thing be of great consequence, I should think the proper umpire in such a case should be the body of the people; for in cases where the prince has a trust reposed in him and is dispensed from the common ordinary rules of the law, there, if any men find themselves aggrieved and think the prince acts contrary to or beyond that trust, who so proper to judge as the body of the people (who, at first, lodged that trust in him) how far they meant it should extend? But if the prince, or whoever they be in the administration, decline that way of determination, the appeal then lies nowhere but to heaven; force between either persons who have no known superior on earth, or which permits no appeal to a judge on earth, being properly a state of war wherein the appeal lies only to heaven; and in that state the injured party must judge for himself when he will think fit to make use of that appeal and put himself upon it.

To conclude, the power that every individual gave the society when he entered into it can never revert to the individuals again as long as the society lasts, but will always remain in the community, because without this there can be no community, no commonwealth, which is contrary to the original agreement; so also when the society has placed the legislative in any assembly of men, to continue in them and their successors with direction and authority for providing such successors, the legislative can never revert to the people while that government lasts, because having provided a legislative with power to continue for ever, they have given up their political power to the legislative and cannot resume it. But if they have set limits to the duration of their legislative and made this supreme power in any person or assembly only temporary, or else when by the miscarriages of those in authority it is forfeited, upon the forfeiture, or at the determination of the time set, it reverts to the society, and the people have a right to act as supreme and continue the legislative in themselves, or erect a new form, or under the old form place it in new hands, as they think good.

28

Of the Measures of Allegiance

DAVID HUME

Those political writers, who have had recourse to a promise, or original contract, as the source of our allegiance to government, intended to establish a principle, which is perfectly just and reasonable; tho' the reasoning, upon which they endeavour'd to establish it, was fallacious and sophistical. They wou'd prove, that our submission to government admits of exceptions, and that an egregious tyranny in the rulers is sufficient to free the subjects from all ties of allegiance. Since men enter into society, say they, and submit themselves to government, by their free and voluntary consent, they must have in view certain advantages, which they propose to reap from it, and for which they are contented to resign their native liberty. There is, therefore, something mutual engag'd on the part of the magistrate, *viz.* protection and security; and 'tis only by the hopes he affords of these advantages, that he can ever persuade men to submit to him. But when instead of protection and security, they meet with tyranny and oppression, they are free'd from their promises, (as happens in all conditional contracts) and return to that state of liberty, which preceded the institution of government. Men wou'd never be so foolish as to enter into such engagements as shou'd turn entirely to the advantage of others, without any view of bettering their own condition. Whoever proposes to draw any profit from our submission, must engage himself, either expressly or tacitly, to make us reap some advantage from his authority; nor ought he to expect, that without the performance of his part we will ever continue in obedience.

I repeat it: This conclusion is just, tho' the principles be erroneous; and I flatter myself, that I can

[From *A Treatise of Human Nature,* Book III, Part II, section 9. First published in 1740.]

establish the same conclusion on more reasonable principles. I shall not take such a compass, in establishing our political duties, as to assert, that men perceive the advantages of government; that they institute government with a view to those advantages; that this institution requires a promise of obedience; which imposes a moral obligation to a certain degree, but being conditional, ceases to be binding, whenever the other contracting party performs not his part of the engagement. I perceive, that a promise itself arises entirely from human conventions, and is invented with a view to a certain interest. I seek, therefore, some such interest more immediately connected with government, and which may be at once the original motive to its institution, and the source of our obedience to it. This interest I find to consist in the security and protection, which we enjoy in political society, and which we can never attain, when perfectly free and independent. As interest, therefore, is the immediate sanction of government, the one can have no longer being than the other; and whenever the civil magistrate carries his oppression so far as to render his authority perfectly intolerable, we are no longer bound to submit to it. The cause ceases; the effect must cease also.

So far the conclusion is immediate and direct, concerning the *natural* obligation which we have to allegiance. As to the *moral* obliga-tion, we may observe, that the maxim wou'd here be false, that *when the cause ceases, the effect must cease also.* For there is a principle of human nature, which we have frequently taken notice of, that men are mightily addicted to *general rules,* and that we often carry our maxims beyond those reasons, which first induc'd us to establish them. Where cases are similar in many circumstances, we are apt to put them on the same footing, without considering, that they differ in the most material circumstances, and that the resemblance is more apparent than real. It may, therefore, be thought, that in the case of allegiance our moral obligation of duty will not cease, even tho' the natural obligation of interest, which is its cause, has ceas'd; and that men may be bound by *conscience* to submit to a tyrannical government against their own and the public interest. And indeed, to the force of this argument I so far submit, as to acknowledge, that general rules commonly extend beyond the principles, on which they are founded; and that we seldom make any exception to them, unless that exception have the qualities of a general rule, and be founded on very numerous and common instances. Now this I assert to be entirely the present case. When men submit to the authority of others, 'tis to procure themselves some security against the wickedness and injustice of men, who are perpetually carried, by their unruly passions, and by their present and immediate interest, to the violation of all the laws of society. But as this imperfection is inherent in human nature, we know that it must attend men in all their states and conditions; and that those, whom we chuse for rulers, do not immediately become of a superior nature to the rest of mankind, upon account of their superior power and authority. What we expect from them depends not on a change of their nature but of their situation, when they acquire a more immediate interest in the preservation of order and the execution of justice. But besides that this interest is only more immediate in the execution of justice among their subjects; besides this, I say, we may often expect, from the irregularity of human nature, that they will neglect even this immediate interest, and be transported by their passions into all the excesses of cruelty and ambition. Our general knowledge of human nature, our observation of the past history of mankind, our experience of present times; all these causes must induce us to open the door to exceptions, and must make us conclude, that we may resist the more violent effects of supreme power, without any crime or injustice.

Accordingly we may observe, that this is both the general practice and principle of mankind, and that no nation, that cou'd find any remedy, ever yet suffer'd the cruel ravages of a tyrant, or were blam'd for their resistance. Those who took up arms against *Dionysius* or *Nero,* or *Philip the second,* have the favour of every reader in the perusal of their history; and nothing but the most violent perversion of common sense can ever lead us to condemn them. 'Tis certain, therefore, that in all our notions of morals we never entertain such an absurdity as that of passive obedience, but make allowances for resistance in the more flagrant instances of tyranny and oppression. The general opinion of mankind has some authority in all cases; but in this of morals 'tis perfectly infallible. Nor is it less infallible, because men cannot distinctly explain the principles, on which it is founded. Few persons can carry on this train of reasoning: "Government is a mere human invention for the interest of society. Where the tyranny of the governor removes this interest, it also removes the natural obligation to obedience. The moral obligation is founded on the natural, and therefore must cease where *that* ceases; especially where the subject is such as makes us foresee very many occasions wherein the natural obligation may cease, and causes us to form a kind of general rule for the regulation of our conduct in such occurrences." But tho' this train of reasoning be too subtile for the vulgar, 'tis certain, that all men have an implicit notion of it, and are sensible, that they owe obedience to government merely on account of the public interest; and at the same time, that human nature is so subject to frailties and passions, as may easily pervert this institution, and change their governors into tyrants and public enemies. If the sense of common interest were not our original motive to obedience, I wou'd fain ask, what other principle is there in human nature capable of subduing the natural ambition of men, and forcing them to such a submission. Imitation and custom are not sufficient. For the question still recurs, what motive first produces those instances of submission, which we imitate, and that train of actions, which produces the custom? There evidently is no other principle than common interest; and if interest first produces obedience to government, the obligation to obedience must cease, whenever the interest ceases, in any great degree, and in a considerable number of instances.

29

The Obligation to Obey the Law

RICHARD A. WASSERSTROM

Absolute and Prima Facie Obligations to Obey

There are several different views which could be held concerning the nature of the stringency of one's obligation to obey the law. One such view, and the one which I shall be most concerned to show to be false, can be characterized as holding that one has an *absolute* obligation to obey the law. I take this to mean that a person is never justified in disobeying the law; to know that a proposed action is illegal is to know all one needs to know in order to conclude that the action ought not to be done; to cite the illegality of an action is to give a sufficient reason for not having done it. A view such as this is far from uncommon. . . .

A more moderate or weaker view would be that which holds that, while one does have an obligation to obey the law, the obligation is a prima facie rather than absolute one. If one knows that a proposed course of conduct is illegal then one has a good—but not necessarily a sufficient—reason for refraining from engaging in that course of conduct. Under this view, a person may be justified in disobeying the law, but an act which is in disobedience of the law does have to be justified, whereas an act in obedience of the law does not have to be justified.

It is important to observe that there is an ambiguity in this notion of a prima facie obligation. For the claim that one has a prima facie obligation to obey the law can come to

[Reprinted, with omissions, from *UCLA Law Review*, Vol. 10 (1963), pp. 780–807, ©1963 The Regents of the University of California. All rights reserved. Reprinted by permission of the publisher and the author.]

one of two different things. On the one hand, the claim can be this: the fact that an action is an act of disobedience is something which always does count against the performance of the action. If one has a prima facie obligation to obey the law, one always has that obligation—although, of course, it may be overridden by other obligations in any particular case. Thus the fact that an action is illegal is a relevant consideration in every case and it is a consideration which must be outweighed by other considerations before the performance of an illegal action can be justified.

On the other hand, the claim can be weaker still. The assertion of a prima facie obligation to obey the law can be nothing more than the claim that as a matter of fact it is *generally* right or obligatory to obey the law. As a rule the fact that an action is illegal is a relevant circumstance. But in any particular case, after deliberation, it might very well turn out that the illegality of the action was not truly relevant. For in any particular case the circumstances might be such that there simply was nothing in the fact of illegality which required overriding—*e.g.*, there were no bad consequences at all which would flow from disobeying the law in this case. . . .

Thus there are at least three different positions which might be taken concerning the character of the obligation to obey the law or the rightness of disobedience to the law.

They are: (1) One has an absolute obligation to obey the law; disobedience is never justified. (2) One has an obligation to obey the law but this obligation can be overriden by conflicting obligations; disobedience can be justified, but only by the presence of outweighing circumstances. (3) One does not have a special obligation to obey the law, but it is in fact usually obligatory, on other grounds, to do so; disobedience to law often does turn out to be unjustified.

It must also be made clear that when I talk about the obligation to obey the law or the possibility of actions which are both illegal and justified, I am concerned solely with *moral obligations* and *morally justified* actions. I shall be concerned solely with arguments which seek to demonstrate that there is some sort of a connection between the legality or illegality of an action and its morality or immorality. Concentration on this general topic necessarily renders a number of interesting problems irrelevant. Thus, I am not at all concerned with the question of why, in fact, so many people do obey the law. Nor, concomitantly, am I concerned with the nonmoral reasons which might and do justify obedience to law—of these, the most pertinent, is the fact that highly unpleasant consequences of one form or another are typically inflicted upon those who disobey the law. Finally there are many actions which are immoral irrespective of whether they also happen to be illegal. And I am not, except in one very special sense, concerned with this fact either. I am not concerned with the fact that the immorality of the action itself may be a sufficient reason for condemning it regardless of its possible illegality.

My last preliminary clarification relates to the fact that there is a variety of kinds of legal rules or laws and that there is a variety of ways in which actions can be related to these rules. This is an important point because many moral philosophers, in particular, have tended to assimilate all legal rules to the model of a typical law or legal order which is enforced through the direct threat of the infliction by the government of severe sanctions, and have thereby tended to assume that all laws and all legal obligations can be broken or disobeyed only in the manner in which penal laws can be broken or disobeyed. That this assimilation is a mistake can be demonstrated quite readily. There are many laws that, unlike the typical penal law, do not require or prohibit the performance of any acts at all. They cannot, therefore, be disobeyed. There are laws, for example, that make testamentary dispositions of property ineffective, unenforceable, or invalid, if the written instrument was not witnessed by the requisite number of disinterested witnesses. Yet a law of this kind obviously does not impose an obligation upon anyone to make a will. Nor, more significantly, could a person who executed a will without the requisite number of witnesses be said to have disobeyed the law. Such a person has simply failed to execute a valid will.

The foregoing observations are relevant largely because it is important to realize that to talk about disobeying the law or about one's obligation to obey the law is usually to refer to a rather special kind of activity, namely, that which is exemplified by, among other things, actions in violation or disobedience of a penal law. It is this special type of activity which alone is the concern of this article.

Conceptual Relationships Between Disobedience and Immorality

One kind of argument in support of the proposition that one cannot be justified in disobeying the law is that which asserts the existence of some sort of *logical* or conceptual relationship between disobeying the law and acting immorally. If the notion of illegality entails that of immorality then one is never justified in acting illegally just because part of the meaning of *illegal* is *immoral;* just because describing an action as illegal is—among other things—to describe it as unjustified.

A claim such as this is extremely difficult to evaluate. For one has great difficulty in knowing what is to count as truly relevant—let alone decisive—evidence of its correctness. There is, nevertheless, a supporting argument of sorts which can be made. It might go something like this:

It is a fact which is surely worth noticing that people generally justify action that *seems to be* illegal by claiming that the action *is not really* illegal. Typically an actor who is accused of having done something illegal will not defend himself by pointing out that, while illegal, his conduct was nevertheless morally justified. Instead, he will endeavor to show in one way or another that it is really inaccurate to call his conduct illegal at all. Now it looks as though this phenomenon can be readily accounted for. People try to resist the accusation of illegality, it might be argued, for the simple reason that they wish to avoid being punished. But what is interesting and persuasive is the fact that people try just as hard to evade a charge of illegality even in those situations where the threat of punishment is simply not an important or even relevant consideration. . . .

Such in brief is the argument which might be advanced and the "evidence" which might be adduced to support it. I think that such an argument is not persuasive, and I can best show this to be so in the following fashion.

Consider the case of a law that makes it a felony to perform an abortion upon a woman unless the abortion is necessary to preserve *her* life. Suppose a teenager, the daughter of a local minister, has been raped on her way home from school by an escapee from a state institution for mental defectives. Suppose further that the girl has become pregnant and has been brought to a reputable doctor who is asked to perform an abortion. And suppose, finally, that the doctor concludes after examining the girl that her life will not be endangered by giving birth to the child. An abortion under these circumstances is, it seems fair to say, illegal. Yet, we would surely find both intelligible and appealing the doctor's claim that he was nonetheless justified in disobeying the law by performing an abortion on the girl. I at least can see nothing logically odd or inconsistent about recognizing both that there is a law prohibiting this conduct and that further questions concerning the rightness of obedience would be relevant and, perhaps, decisive. Thus I can see nothing logically odd about describing this as a case in which the performance of the abortion could be both illegal and morally justified.[1] . . .

Thus an argument as strong as any of the above must fail. There is, of course, a weaker version which

---

1. I am supposing, of course, that one would regard the performance of the abortion—in the absence of the relevant penal law—as clearly morally justified. If one disagrees with this assessment of the morality of the case, then some other example ought to be substituted. One likely candidate, drawn from our own history, is that of the inherent rightness in refusing to return an escaped Negro slave to his "owner." If one believes that refusing to do so would be clearly justifiable, then consider whether the existence of the fugitive slave laws necessarily rendered a continued refusal unjustified.

may be more appealing. If it is true that there is something disturbing about justifying actions that are conceded to be illegal, then one way to account for this is to insist that there is a logical connection between the concepts involved, but it is something less than the kind of implication already discussed. Perhaps it is correct that *illegal* does not entail *immoral*; *illegal* might nevertheless entail *prima facie immoral*. The evidence adduced tends to show that among one's moral obligations is the prima facie duty to obey the law.

Once again, it is somewhat difficult to know precisely what to make of such a claim. It is hard to see how one would decide what was to count as evidence or whether the evidence was persuasive. At a minimum, it is not difficult to imagine several equally plausible alternative explanations of the disturbing character of accusations of illegal activity. In addition, to know only that one has a prima facie duty to obey the law is not to know a great deal. In particular, one does not know how or when that obligation can be overridden. And, of course, even if it is correct that acting illegally logically implies acting prima facie immorally, this in no way shows that people may not often be morally justified in acting illegally. At most, it demands that they have some good reason for acting illegally; at best, it requires what has already been hypothesized, namely, that the action in question, while illegal, be morally justified.

Thus, it is clear that if the case against ever acting illegally is to be made out, conceptual analysis alone cannot do it. Indeed, arguments of quite another sort must be forthcoming. And it is to these that I now turn.

Consequences of Disobedience: What If Everyone Did That?

One such argument, and the most common argument advanced, goes something like this: The reason why one ought never to disobey the law is simply that the consequences would be disastrous if everybody disobeyed the law. The reason why disobedience is never right becomes apparent once we ask the question "But what if everyone did that?"

Consider again the case of the doctor who has to decide whether he is justified in performing an illegal abortion. If he only has a prima facie duty to obey the law it looks as though he might justifiably decide that in this case his prima facie obligation is overridden by more stringent conflicting obligations. Or, if he is simply a utilitarian, it appears that he might rightly conclude that the consequences of disobeying the abortion law would be on the whole and in the long run less deleterious than those of obeying. But this is simply a mistake. The doctor would inevitably be neglecting the most crucial factor of all, namely, that in performing the abortion he was disobeying the law. And imagine what would happen if everyone went around disobeying the law. The alternatives are obeying the law and general disobedience. The choice is between any social order and chaos. . . .

Such an argument, while perhaps overdrawn, is by no means uncommon. Yet, as it stands, it is an essentially confused one. Its respective claims, if they are to be fairly evaluated, must be delineated with some care.

At a minimum, the foregoing attack upon the possibility of justified disobedience might be either one or both of two radically different kinds of objection. The first, which relates to the consequences of an act of disobedience, is essentially a *causal* argument. The second questions the *principle* that any proponent of justified disobedience invokes. As to the causal argument, it is always relevant to point out that any act of disobedience may have certain consequences simply because it is an act of disobedience. Once the occurrence of the act is known, for example, expenditure of the state's resources may become necessary. The time and energy of the police will probably be turned to the task of discovering who it was who did the illegal act and of gathering evidence relevant to the offense. And other resources might be expended in the prosecution and adjudication of the case against the perpetrator of the illegal act. Illustrations of this sort could be multiplied, no doubt, but I do not think either that consider-

ations of this sort are very persuasive or that they have been uppermost in the minds of those who make the argument now under examination. Indeed, if the argument is a causal one at all, it consists largely of the claim that any act of disobedience will itself cause, to some degree or other, general disobedience of all laws; it will cause or help to cause the overthrow or dissolution of the state. And while it is possible to assert that any act of disobedience will tend to further social disintegration or revolution, it is much more difficult to see why this must be so.

The most plausible argument would locate this causal efficacy in the kind of example set by any act of disobedience. But how plausible is this argument? It is undeniable, of course, that the kind of example that will be set is surely a relevant factor. Yet, there is nothing that precludes any proponent of justified disobedience from taking this into account. If, for example, others will somehow infer from the doctor's disobedience of the abortion law that they are justified in disobeying *any* law under *any* circumstances, then the doctor ought to consider this fact. This is a consequence—albeit a lamentable one—of his act of disobedience. Similarly, if others will extract the proper criterion from the act of disobedience, but will be apt to misapply it in practice, then this too ought to give the doctor pause. It, too, is a consequence of acting. But if the argument is that disobedience would be wrong even if no bad example were set and no other deleterious consequences likely, then the argument must be directed against the principle the doctor appeals to in disobeying the law, and not against the consequences of his disobedience at all.

As to the attack upon a principle of justified disobedience, as a principle, the response "But what if everyone disobeyed the law?" does appear to be a good way to point up both the inherent inconsistency of almost any principle of justified disobedience and the manifest undesirability of adopting such a principle. Even if one need not worry about what others will be led to do by one's disobedience, there is surely something amiss if one cannot consistently defend his right to do what one is claiming he is right in doing.

In large measure, such an objection is unreal. The appeal to "But what if everyone did that?" loses much, if not all, of its persuasiveness once we become clearer about what precisely the "did that" refers to. If the question "But what if everyone did that?" is simply another way of asking "But what if everyone disobeyed the law?" or "But what if people generally disobeyed the laws?" then the question is surely quasi-rhetorical. To urge general or indiscriminate disobedience to laws is to invoke a principle that, if coherent, is manifestly indefensible. It is equally plain, however, that with few exceptions such a principle has never been seriously espoused. Anyone who claims that there are actions that are both illegal and justified surely need not be thereby asserting that it is right generally to disobey all laws or even any particular law. It is surely not inconsistent to assert both that indiscriminate disobedience is indefensible and that discriminate disobedience is morally right and proper conduct. Nor, analogously, is it at all evident that a person who claims to be justified in performing an illegal action is thereby committed to or giving endorsement to the principle that the entire legal system ought to be overthrown or renounced. At a minimum, therefore, the appeal to "But what if everyone did that?" cannot by itself support the claim that one has an absolute obligation to obey the law—that disobeying the law can never be truly justified. . . .

There is one final point . . . which does appear to create something of a puzzle. Suppose that I believe that I am justified in deliberately trespassing on an atomic test site, and thereby disobeying the law, because I conclude that this is the best way to call attention to the possible consequences of continued atmospheric testing or nuclear war. I conclude that the consequences of trespassing will on the whole be more beneficial than any alternative action I can take. But suppose I also concede—what very well may be the case—that if everyone were to trespass, even for this same reason and in the same way, the consequences would be extremely deleterious. Does it follow that there is something logically incoherent about my principle of action? It looks as though there is, for it appears that I am here denying others the right to do precisely what I claim I am right in doing. I seem to be claiming, in effect, that it is right for me to trespass on government property in order to protest atomic testing only if it is the case that others, even under identical circumstances, will not trespass. Thus, it might be argued, I appear to be unwilling or unable to generalize my principle of conduct.

This argument is unsound, for there is a perfectly good sense in which I am acting on a principle which is coherent and which is open to anyone to adopt. It is simply the principle that one is justified in trespassing on government property whenever—among other things—it happens to be the case that one can say accurately that others will not in fact act on that same principle. Whether anyone else will at any given time act on any particular principle is an empirical question. It is, to repeat what has already been said, one of the possible circumstances which can be part of the description of a class of situations. There is, in short, nothing logically self-contradictory or absurd about making the likelihood of even identical action one of the relevant justifying considerations. And there is, therefore, no reason why the justifiability of any

particular act of disobedience cannot depend, among other things, upon the probable conduct of others. . . .

Consequences of Disobedience: The Chance of Error

There is one final argument which requires brief elucidation and analysis. It is in certain respects a peculiarly instructive one both in its own right and in respect to the thesis of this article.

It may be true that on some particular occasions the consequences of disobeying a law will in fact be less deleterious on the whole than those of obeying it—even in a democracy. It may even be true that on some particular occasions disobeying a law will be just whereas obeying it would be unjust. Nevertheless, the reason why a person is never justified in disobeying a law—in a democracy—is simply this: The chances are so slight that he will disobey only those laws in only those cases in which he is in fact justified in doing so, that the consequences will on the whole be less deleterious if he never disobeys any law. Furthermore, since anyone must concede the right to everyone to disobey the law when the circumstances so demand it, the situation is made still worse. For once we entrust this right to everyone we can be sure that many laws will be disobeyed in a multitude of cases in which there was no real justification for disobedience. Thus, given what we know of the possibilities of human error and the actualities of human frailty, and given the tendency of democratic societies to make illegal only those actions which would, even in the absence of a law, be unjustified, we can confidently conclude that the consequences will on the whole and in the long run be best if no one ever takes it upon himself to "second-guess" the laws and to conclude that in his case his disobedience is justified.

The argument is, in part, not very different from those previously considered. And thus, what is to be said about it is not very different either. Nonetheless, upon pain of being overly repetitive, I would insist that there is a weak sense in which the argument is quite persuasive and a strong sense in which it is not. For the argument makes, on one reading, too strong an empirical claim—the claim that the consequences will in the long run always in fact be better if no one in a democracy ever tries to decide when he is justified in disobeying the law. As it stands, there is no reason to believe that the claim is or must be true, that the consequences will always be better. Indeed, it is very hard to see why, despite the hypothesis, someone might still not be justified in some particular case in disobeying a law. Yet, viewed as a weaker claim, as a summary rule, it does embody a good deal that is

worth remembering. It can, on this level, be understood to be a persuasive reminder of much that is relevant to disobedience: that in a democracy the chances of having to live under bad laws are reduced; that in a democracy there are typically less costly means available by which to bring about changes in the law; that in a democracy—as in life in general—a justified action may always be both inaptly and ineptly emulated; and that in a democracy—as in life in general—people often do make mistakes as to which of their own actions are truly justified. These are some of the lessons of human experience which are easy to forget and painful to relearn.

But there are other lessons, and they are worth remembering too. What is especially troubling about the claim that disobedience of the law is never justified, what is even disturbing about the claim that disobedience of the law is never justified in a democratic or liberal society, is the facility with which its acceptance can lead to the neglect of important moral issues. If no one is justified in disobeying the Supreme Court's decision in *Brown v. Board of Educ.* this is so because, among other things, there is much that is wrong with segregation. If there was much that was peculiarly wrong in Mississippi this fall, this was due to the fact, among other facts, that a mob howled and a governor raged when a court held that a person whose skin was black could go to a white university. Disobeying the law is often—even usually—wrong; but this is so largely because the illegal is usually restricted to the immoral and because morally right conduct is still less often illegal. But we must always be sensitive to the fact that this has not always been the case, is not now always the case and need not always be the case in the future. And undue concentration upon what is wrong with disobeying the law rather than upon the wrong which the law seeks to prevent can seriously weaken and misdirect that awareness.

30

Legal Obligation and the Duty of Fair Play

JOHN RAWLS

The subject of law and morality suggests many different questions. In particular, it may consider the historical and sociological question as to the way and manner in which moral ideas influence and are influenced by the legal system; or it may involve the question whether moral concepts and principles enter into an adequate definition of law. Again, the topic of law and morality suggests the problem of the legal enforcement of morality and whether the fact that certain conduct is immoral by accepted precepts is sufficient to justify making that conduct a legal offense. Finally, there is the large subject of the study of the rational principles of moral criticism of legal institutions and the moral grounds of our acquiescence in them. I shall be concerned solely with a fragment of this last question: with the grounds for our moral obligation to obey the law, that is, to carry out our legal duties and to fulfill our legal obligations. My thesis is that the moral obligation to obey the law is a special case of the prima facie duty of fair play. . . .

The moral grounds of legal obligation may be brought out by considering what at first seem to be two anomalous facts: first, that sometimes we have an obligation to obey what we think, and think correctly, is an unjust law; and second, that sometimes we have an obligation to obey a law even in a situation where more good (thought of as a sum of social advantages) would seem to result from not doing so. If the moral obligation to obey the law is founded on the principle of fair play, how can one become bound to obey an unjust law, and what is there about the principle that explains the grounds for forgoing the greater good? . . .

The principle of fair play may be defined as follows. Suppose there is a mutually beneficial and just scheme of social cooperation, and that the advantages it yields can only be obtained if everyone, or nearly everyone, cooperates. Suppose further that cooperation requires a certain sacrifice from each person, or at least involves a certain restriction of his liberty. Suppose finally that the benefits produced by cooperation are, up to a certain point, free: that is, the scheme of cooperation is unstable in the sense that if any one person knows that all (or nearly all) of the others will continue to do their part, he will still be able to share a gain from the scheme even if he does not do his part. Under these conditions a person who has accepted the benefits of the scheme is bound by a duty of fair play to do his part and not to take advantage of the free benefit by not cooperating. The reason one must abstain from this attempt is that the existence of the benefit is the result of everyone's effort, and prior to some understanding as to how it is to be shared, if it can be shared at all, it belongs in fairness to no one. (I return to this question below.)

Now I want to hold that the obligation to obey the law, as enacted by a constitutional procedure, even when the law seems unjust to us, is a case of the duty of fair play as defined. It is, moreover, an obligation in the more limited sense in that it depends upon our having accepted and our intention to continue accepting the benefits of a just scheme of cooperation that the constitution defines. In this sense it depends on our own voluntary acts. Again, it is an obligation owed to our fellow citizens generally: that is, to those who cooperate with us in the working of the constitution. It is not an obligation owed to public officials, although there may be such obligations. That it is an obligation owed by citizens to one another is shown by the fact that they are entitled to be indignant with one another for failure to comply. Further, an essential condition of the obligation is the justice of the constitution and the general system of law being roughly in accordance with it. Thus the obligation to obey (or not to resist) an unjust law depends strongly on there being a just constitution. Unless one obeys the law enacted under it, the proper equilibrium, or balance, between competing claims defined by the constitution will not be maintained. Finally, while it is true enough to say that the enactment by a majority binds the minority, so that one may be bound by the acts of others, there is no question of their binding them in conscience to certain beliefs as to what is the best policy, and it is a necessary condition of the acts of others binding us that the constitution is just, that we have accepted its benefits, and so forth.

Now a few remarks about the principles of a just constitution. Here I shall have to presuppose a number of things about the principles of justice. In particular, I shall assume that there are two principles of justice that properly apply to the fundamental structure of institutions of the social system and, thus, to the constitution. The first of these principles requires that everyone have an equal right to the most extensive liberty compatible with a like liberty for all; the second is that inequalities are arbitrary unless it is reasonable to expect that they will work out for everyone's advantage and provided that the positions and offices to which they attach or from which they may be gained are open to all. I shall assume that these are the principles that can be derived by imposing the constraints of morality upon rational and mutually self-interested persons when they make conflicting claims on the basic form of their common institutions: that is, when questions of justice arise.

The principle relevant at this point is the first principle, that of equal liberty. I think it may be argued with some plausibility that it requires, where it is possible, the various equal liberties in a constitutional democracy. And once these liberties are established and constitutional procedures exist, one can view legislation as rules enacted that

must be ostensibly compatible with both principles. Each citizen must decide as best he can whether a piece of legislation, say the income tax, violates either principle; and this judgment depends on a wide body of social facts. Even in a society of impartial and rational persons, one cannot expect agreement on these matters.

Now recall that the question is this: How is it possible that a person, in accordance with his own conception of justice, should find himself bound by the acts of another to obey an unjust law (not simply a law contrary to his interests)? Put another way: Why, when I am free and still without my chains, should I accept certain a priori conditions to which any social contract must conform, a priori conditions that rule out all constitutional procedures that would decide in accordance with my judgment of justice against everyone else? To explain this (Little has remarked), we require two hypotheses: that among the very limited number of procedures that would stand any chance of being established, none would make my decision decisive in this way; and that all such procedures would determine social conditions that I judge to be better than anarchy. Granting the second hypothesis, I want to elaborate on this in the following way: the first step in the explanation is to derive the principles of justice that are to apply to the basic form of the social system and, in particular, to the constitution. Once we have these principles, we see that no just constitutional procedure would make my judgment as to the best policy decisive (would make me a dictator in Arrow's sense). It is not simply that, among the limited number of procedures actually possible as things are, no procedure would give me this authority. The point is that even if such were possible; given some extraordinary social circumstances, it would not be just. (Of course it is not possible for everyone to have this authority.) Once we see this, we see how it is possible that within the framework of a just constitutional procedure to which we are obligated, it may nevertheless happen that we are bound to obey what seems to us to be and is an unjust law. Moreover, the possibility is present even though everyone has the same sense of justice (that is, accepts the same principles of justice) and everyone regards the constitutional procedure itself as just. Even the most efficient constitution cannot prevent the enactment of unjust laws if, from the complexity of the social situation and like conditions, the majority decides to enact them. A just constitutional procedure cannot foreclose all injustice; this depends on those who carry out the procedure. A constitutional procedure is not like a market reconciling interests to an optimum result.

So far I have been discussing the first mentioned anomaly of legal obligation, namely, that though it is founded on justice, we may be required to obey an unjust law. I should now like to include the second anomaly; that we may have an obligation to obey the law even though more good (thought of as a sum of advantages) may be gained by not doing so. The thesis I wish to argue is that not only is our obligation to obey the law a special case of the principle of fair play, and so dependent upon the justice of the institutions to which we are obligated, but also the principles of justice are absolute with respect to the principle of utility (as the principle to maximize the net sum of advantages). By this I mean two things. First, unjust institutions cannot be justified by an appeal to the principle of utility. A greater balance of net advantages shared by some cannot justify the injustice suffered by others; and where unjust institutions are tolerable it is because a certain degree of injustice sometimes cannot be avoided, that social necessity requires it, that there would be greater injustice otherwise, and so on. Second, our obligation to obey the law, which is a special case of the principle of fair play, cannot be overridden by an appeal to utility, though it may be overridden by another duty of justice. These are sweeping propositions and most likely false, but I should like to examine them briefly.

I do not know how to establish these propositions. They are not established by the sort of argument used above to show that the two principles, previously mentioned, are the two principles of justice, that is, when the subject is the basic structure of the social system. What such an argument might show is that, if certain natural conditions are taken as specifying the concept of justice, then the two principles of justice are the principles logically associated with the concept when the subject is the basic structure of the social system. The argument might prove, if it is correct, that the principles of justice are incompatible with the principle of utility. The argument might establish that our intuitive notions of justice must sometimes conflict with the principle of utility. But it leaves unsettled what the more general notion of right requires when this conflict occurs. To prove that the concept of justice should have an absolute weight with respect to that of utility would require a deeper argument based on an analysis of the concept of right, at least insofar as it relates to the concepts of justice and utility. I have no idea whether such an analysis is possible. What I propose to do instead is to try out the thought that the concept of justice does have an absolute weight, and to see whether this suggestion, in view of our considered moral opinions, lead to conclusions that we cannot accept. It would seem as if to attribute to justice an absolute weight is to interpret the concept of right as requiring that a special place

be given to persons capable of a sense of justice and to the principle of their working out together, from an initial position of equality, the form of their common institutions. To the extent that this idea is attractive, the concept of justice will tend to have an absolute weight with respect to utility.

Now to consider the two anomalous cases. First: In the situation where the obligation requires obedience to an unjust law, it seems true to say that the obligation depends on the principle of fair play and, thus, on justice. Suppose it is a matter of a person being required to pay an income tax of a kind that he thinks is unjust, not simply by reference to his interests. He would not want to try to justify the tax on the ground that the net gain to certain groups in society is such as to outweigh the injustice. The natural argument to make is to his obligation to a just constitution.

But in considering a particular issue, a citizen has to make two decisions: how he will vote (and I assume that he votes for what he thinks is the best policy, morally speaking), and, in case he should be in the minority, whether his obligation to support, or not obstruct, the implementation of the law enacted is not overridden by a stronger obligation that may lead to a number of courses including civil disobedience. Now in the sort of case imagined, suppose there is a real question as to whether the tax law should be obeyed. Suppose, for example, that it is framed in such a way that it seems deliberately calculated to undermine unjustly the position of certain social or religious groups. Whether the law should be obeyed or not depends, if one wants to emphasize the notion of justice, on such matters as (1) the justice of the constitution and the real opportunity it allows for reversal; (2) the depth of the injustice of the law enacted; (3) whether the enactment is actually a matter of calculated intent by the majority and warns of further such acts; and (4) whether the political sociology of the situation is such as to allow of hope that the law may be repealed. Certainly, if a social or religious group reasonably (not irrationally) and correctly supposes that a permanent majority, or majority coalition, has deliberately set out to undercut its basis and that there is no chance of successful constitutional resistance, then the obligation to obey that particular law (and perhaps other laws more generally) ceases. In such a case a minority may no longer be obligated by the duty of fair play. There may be other reasons, of course, at least for a time, for obeying the law. One might say that disobedience will not improve the justice of their situation or of their descendants' situation; or that it will result in injury and harm to innocent persons (that is, members not belonging to the unjust majority). In this way, one might appeal to the balance of justice, if the principle of not causing injury to the innocent is a question of justice; but, in any case, the appeal is not made to the greater net balance of advantages (irrespective of the moral position of those receiving them). The thesis I want to suggest then, is that in considering whether we are obligated to obey an unjust law, one is led into no absurdity if one simply throws out the principle of utility altogether, except insofar as it is included in the general principle requiring one to establish the most efficient just institutions.

Second: Now the other sort of anomaly arises when the law is just and we have a duty of fair play to follow it, but a greater net balance of advantages could be gained from not doing so. Again, the income tax will serve to illustrate this familiar point: The social consequences of any one person (perhaps even many people) not paying his tax are unnoticeable, and let us suppose zero in value, but there is a noticeable private gain for the person himself, or for another to whom he chooses to give it (the institution of the income tax is subject to the first kind of instability). The duty of fair play binds us to pay our tax, nevertheless, since we have accepted, and intend to continue doing so, the benefits of the fiscal system to which the income tax belongs. Why is this reasonable and not a blind following of a rule, when a greater net sum of advantages is possible?—because the system of cooperation consistently followed by everyone else itself produces the advantages generally enjoyed and in the case of a practice such as the income tax there is no reason to give exemptions to anyone so that they might enjoy the possible benefit. (An analogous case is the moral obligation to vote and so to work the constitutional procedure from which one has benefited. This obligation cannot be overridden by the fact that our vote never makes a difference in the outcome of an election; it may be overridden, however, by a number of other considerations, such as a person being disenchanted with all parties, being excusably uninformed, and the like.)

There are cases, on the other hand, where a certain number of exemptions can be arranged for in a just or fair way; and if so, the practice, including the exemptions, is more efficient, and when possible it should be adopted (waiving problems of transition) in accordance with the principle of establishing the most efficient just practice. For example, in the familiar instance of the regulation to conserve water in a drought, it might be ascertained that there would be no harm in a certain extra use of water over and above the use for drinking. In this case some rotation scheme can be adopted that allots exemptions in a fair way, such as houses on opposite sides of the street being given exemptions on alternate days. The details are not significant here. The main idea is simply that if the greater sum of advantages can effectively and fairly be distributed amongst those whose cooperation makes these advantages possible, then this should be done. It would indeed be irrational to prefer a lesser to a more efficient just scheme of cooperation; but this fact is not to be confused with justifying an unjust scheme by its greater efficiency or excusing ourselves from a duty of fair play by an appeal to utility. If there is no reason to distribute the possible benefit, as in the case of the income tax, or in the case of voting, or if there is no way to do so that does not involve such problems as excessive costs, then the benefit should be foregone. One may disagree with this view, but it is not irrational, not a matter of rule worship: it is, rather, an appeal to the duty of fair play, which requires one to abstain from an advantage that cannot be distributed fairly to those whose efforts have made it possible. That those who make the efforts and undergo the restrictions of their liberty should share in the benefits produced is a consequence of the assumption of an initial position of equality, and it falls under the second principle. But the question of distributive justice is too involved to go into here. Moreover, it is unlikely that there is any substantial social benefit for the distribution of which some fair arrangement cannot be made. . . .

AFTERWORD

Thorough consideration of the moral status of the law cannot be made without drawing on some more general view of the character of morals and moral judgments. Indeed, many of the discussions of the origins and function of law in the preceding selections are based upon some general ethical theory. If you have read the selections in Chapter 6 on the objectivity of moral judgments, it would be a good idea for you to consider how various theories about the nature of moral judgments might result in theories about the functions of law.

A second question you may wish to consider is this: People frequently say that we can't legislate morality, buy *why* can't we? If the purpose of law is to promote moral behavior, then why not strive to make all forms of immorality illegal? And if the purpose of the law is not to promote moral behavior, then why should we think we have any moral obligation to obey at all? If you consider your answer to these questions carefully, you may find that it indicates something about your basic attitudes toward the function and limits of the law, and about the circumstances in which disobedience may be justified.

Yet a third question to consider is this: What should be the fate of a person who has disobeyed the law for moral reasons? Such a person does not exhibit a weak moral character, or indifference to the rights and needs of others, and thus is not like the ordinary lawbreaker (at least, not as we like to picture the ordinary lawbreaker). Should the usual punishments be handed out, then, or should some special treatment be found for such cases? And notice that the question really divides into two issues: (*a*) what should society or the state do about conscientious disobedience; and (*b*) what should the conscientious lawbreaker do about whatever punishment the state threatens to incur? In recent decades, conscientious refusal of legally required military service has provided a large number of cases in which the attempt to cope with these questions has proved difficult and painful.

Finally, you should, once again, compare your actual practices with the theories which seem most plausible to you. Do you in fact obey the law when your favorite theory says that you should—or disobey when your theory requires disobedience? And if (as with most of us) you find some discrepancy between theory and practice, are you inclined to account for it as moral deficiency in your practice, or as an indication that in practical situations you sometimes are sensitive to factors which your favorite theory has not yet taken into consideration?

REVIEW QUESTIONS

Selection 24

1. Part of the argument Socrates gives for not escaping is based on an agreement he claims to have made with the state and its laws. What is the nature of this agreement?

2. What is the role in Socrates' argument of the comparison of the laws to a parent or master?

3. Do you think Socrates would say that his arguments apply only to his situation, or are they intended to show that no one ever has the right to violate a law? Explain.

Selection 25

4. In the opening discussion of natural law, does Aquinas claim that moral principles (e.g., "Do not steal," or "Do not lie") have no exceptions? Explain.

5. According to Aquinas, what functions are performed by laws?

6. Aquinas points out several kinds of situations in which a law should be disobeyed. What are they? Why does he think disobedience is justified in each case?

Selection 26

7. What is the primary purpose of law, according to Hobbes? Why does this necessarily result in the distinction between *sovereign* and *subject?*

8. Does Hobbes recognize any limits to the power of a sovereign? Why, or why not?

9. Hobbes argues that one never is justified in breaking a law. What is the argument?

Selection 27

10. What is the primary function of law according to Locke? Do you see any significant difference between his position and that of Hobbes on this issue?

11. Locke points out circumstances under which systems of law (governments) may be disobeyed or abolished. What are these circumstances?

12. Locke replies to several objections to his position. What are the objections and the replies?

13. Does Locke's theory permit one citizen to disobey a generally just law in special circumstances where obedience would be harmful? Explain.

Selection 28

14. How does Hume's view of the formation of society differ from that of Hobbes or Locke?

15. What circumstances would justify disobedience, according to Hume? Why?

Selection 29

16. Wasserstrom describes three different positions which might be taken on the obligation to obey the law. What are they? Which of them does he prefer?

17. Why does Wasserstrom reject the view that the obligation to obey is based on a conceptual relationship between disobedience and immorality?

18. One objection to Wasserstrom's position is based on the question, "What if everyone did that?" What is the objection, and how does he reply to it?

Selection 30

19. What is the principle of fair play?

20. Rawls discusses two kinds of situations in which the duty of fair play requires obedience to laws which do not provide the greatest moral good. What are those situations, and what are his arguments regarding them?

21. Does Rawls admit that there are cases in which disobedience is morally justified? Why, or why not?

9

The Existence of God

It is widely held in the Western world that belief in the existence of God is reasonable and proper. Such belief is thought by some to provide the only basis from which a rational understanding of the world and the human condition can be derived. Others hold that moral conduct and human hopes and aspirations would make no sense without such a belief. Some have gone so far as to claim that failure to believe in the existence of a deity is a piece of perverse wickedness, deserving severe punishment.

But there is, in Western thought, another strong commitment to the view that beliefs are not reasonable unless they originate in an acceptable manner from experience or from reason. That is, we tend to regard as unacceptable beliefs which cannot be proved or shown to be probable by the evidence of our senses, or by a priori reasoning, or by some combination of both. These two tendencies would be compatible if experience and reason offered some clear proof or even strong evidence in support of the claim that God exists. But there is no clear consensus that such evidence can be found. Indeed, when pressed for such evidence, many people are likely to claim that the demand is unreasonable, that God's existence is not the sort of thing which could be proved, and that it must be taken on faith. Thus, in many people we find an inclination to accept all three of these statements:

(1) It is reasonable to believe that God exists.

(2)   Reasonable beliefs must be founded on the evidence of our senses or on reason.

(3)   Reason and our senses provide no adequate demonstration of God's existence.

Since these three statements form an inconsistent set, some revision must be made in them. But where?

It would be a serious mistake to suppose that we could neatly divide opinions about this problem into those held by believers and those held by unbelievers. There is much disagreement in both camps about the nature and sources of reasonable belief, and corresponding disagreement about what can be demonstrated. There is more disagreement in both camps about the nature of the deity whose existence is to be established, with accompanying disagreement about what would have to be demonstrated to render belief in God reasonable. And, of course, there are other camps besides these two.

Let us call those who do believe that God exists *theists* (noting that in so doing we group together many who disagree vigorously with one another, and several who would prefer to be called something else). A minority of theists do, in fact, reject statement (1). For them, it is important that religious belief should be quite unreasonable. They see such belief as necessarily the result of an act of choice, or commitment. It is (unreasonable) *faith,* not reason, which provides the basis for religious conviction for these theists. But a majority of theists will defend (1) and seek a refutation of (2) or (3).

Many theists attempt to draw upon reason or experience to provide some demonstration of God's existence—thus rejecting (3) and accepting (1) and (2). The *ontological* argument (see the selection by St. Anselm) is an attempt to prove God's existence through a priori reasoning alone. *Cosmological* arguments—arguments intended to show that God must exist as the cause or creator of the world—combine appeals to some empirical fact with a priori reasoning in the attempt to demonstrate God's existence. And even heavier reliance upon empirical observation is involved in the *teleological* argument, or argument from design, in which it is attempted to establish that the world shows evidence of having been planned or designed, so that God the Designer must exist.

Still other theists grant (3) but attempt to defend (1) by attacking the restrictions in (2) upon what constitutes a reasonable belief. One important approach of this type appeals to religious (or mystical) experience as a legitimate source of knowledge which is different from either our senses or reason. And there are other interesting attempts to show that it may be reasonable to subscribe to a belief when it is not well-supported either by reason or by sensory experience.

Those who do not believe in the existence of a deity, of course, generally agree in accepting (2) and (3) and in rejecting (1). But it is important to distinguish between those who are *atheists*—that is, those who think that reason or experience provide us with substantial evidence that no God exists—from *agnostics,* who hold that all our evidence is inadequate, so that neither belief nor disbelief is justified.

The following selections involve a complex mixture of issues. Are there special sources of religious knowledge, or must religious belief be found on the same logic and evidence as our other beliefs? Can reliable arguments be provided for theism—and what would they need to be like? And just what conception of God's nature is involved in each selection? This last question is especially important, since those who disagree very substantially about divine nature may really be arguing at cross-purposes when they seem to disagree—or, for that matter, when they seem to agree.

The Ontological Argument

ST. ANSELM

Truly There Is a God

And so, Lord, do thou, who dost give understanding to faith, give me, so far as thou knowest it to be profitable, to understand that thou art as we believe; and that thou art that which we believe. And, indeed, we believe that thou art a being than which nothing greater can be conceived. Or is there no such nature, since the fool hath said in his heart, there is no God? (Psalms 14:1). But, at any rate, this very fool, when he hears of this being of which I speak—a being than which nothing greater can be conceived—understands what he hears, and what he understands is in his understanding; although he does not understand it to exist.

For, it is one thing for an object to be in the understanding, and another to understand that the object exists. When a painter first conceives of what he will afterwards perform, he has it in his understanding, but he does not yet understand it to be, because he has not yet performed it. But after he has made the painting, he both has it in his understanding, and he understands that it exists, because he has made it.

God Cannot Be Conceived Not to Exist

And it assuredly exists so truly, that it cannot be conceived not to exist. For, it is possible to conceive of a being which cannot be conceived not to exist; and this is greater than one which can be conceived not to exist. Hence, if that, than which nothing greater can be conceived, can be conceived not to exist, it is not that, than which nothing greater can be conceived. But this is an irreconcilable contradiction. There is, then, so truly a being than which nothing

[From *Proslogium* (1077–1078), chapters II–V. Translated by Sidney Norton Deane (1903).]

greater can be conceived to exist, that it cannot even be conceived not to exist; and this being thou art, O Lord, our God.

So truly, therefore, dost thou exist, O Lord, my God, that thou canst not be conceived not to exist; and rightly. For, if a mind could conceive of a being better than thee, the creature would rise above the Creator; and this is most absurd. And, indeed, whatever else there is, except thee alone, can be conceived not to exist. To thee alone, therefore, it belongs to exist more truly than all other beings, and hence in a higher degree than all others. For, whatever else exists does not exist so truly, and hence in a less degree it belongs to it to exist. Why, then, has the fool said in his heart, there is no God (Psalms 14:1), since it is so evident, to a rational mind, that thou dost exist in the highest degree of all? Why, except that he is dull and a fool?

Hence, even the fool is convinced that something exists in the understanding, at least, than which nothing greater can be conceived. For, when he hears of this, he understands it. And whatever is understood, exists in the understanding. And assuredly that, than which nothing greater can be conceived, cannot exist in the understanding alone. For, suppose it exists in the understanding alone: then it can be conceived to exist in reality; which is greater.

Therefore, if that, than which nothing greater can be conceived, exists in the understanding alone, the very being, than which nothing greater can be conceived, is one, than which a greater can be conceived. But obviously this is impossible. Hence, there is no doubt that there exists a being, than which nothing greater can be conceived, and it exists both in the understanding and in reality.

How the Fool Has Said in His Heart What Cannot Be Conceived

But how has the fool said in his heart what he could not conceive; or how is it that he could not conceive what he said in his heart? since it is the same to say in the heart, and to conceive.

But, if really, nay, since really, he both conceived, because he said in his heart; and did not say in his heart, because he could not conceive; there is more than one way in which a thing is said in the heart or conceived. For, in one sense, an object is conceived, when the word signifying it is conceived; and in another, when the very entity, which the object is, is understood.

In the former sense, then, God can be conceived not to exist; but in the latter, not at all. For no one who understands what fire and water are can conceive fire to be water, in accordance with the nature of the facts themselves, although this is possible according to the words. So, then, no one who understands what God is can conceive that God does not exist; although he says these words in his heart, either without any, or with some foreign, signification. For, God is that than which a greater cannot be conceived. And he who thoroughly understands this, assuredly understands that this being so truly exists, that not even in concept can it be non-existent. Therefore, he who understands that God so exists, cannot conceive that he does not exist.

I thank thee, gracious Lord, I thank thee; because what I formerly believed by thy bounty, I now so understand by thine illumination, that if I were unwilling to believe that thou dost exist, I should not be able not to understand this to be true..

God Is Whatever It Is Better to Be Than Not to Be

What art thou, then, Lord God, than whom nothing greater can be conceived? But what art thou, except that which, as the highest of all beings, alone exists through itself, and creates all other things from nothing? For, whatever is not this is less than a thing which can be conceived of. But this cannot be conceived of thee. What good, therefore, does the supreme Good lack, through which every good is? Therefore, thou art just, truthful, blessed, and whatever it is better to be than not to be. For it is better to be just than not just; better to be blessed, than not blessed.

32

The Five Ways

THOMAS AQUINAS

The existence of God can be proved in five ways.

The first and more manifest way is the argument from motion. It is certain, and evident to our senses, that in the world some things are in motion. Now whatever is moved is moved by another, for nothing can be moved except it is in potentiality to that towards which it is moved; whereas a thing moves inasmuch as it is in act. For motion is nothing else than the reduction of something from potentiality to actuality. But nothing can be reduced from potentiality to actuality, except by something in a state of actuality. Thus that which is actually hot, as fire, makes wood, which is potentially hot, to be actually hot, and thereby moves and changes it. Now it is not possible that the same thing should be at once in actuality and potentiality in the same respect, but only in different respects. For what is actually hot cannot simultaneously be potentially hot; but it is simultaneously potentially cold. It is therefore impossible that in the same respect and in the same way a thing should be both mover and moved, *i.e.,* that it should move itself. Therefore, whatever is moved must be moved by another. If that by which it is moved be itself moved, then this also must needs be moved by another, and that by another again. But this cannot go on to infinity, because then there would be no first mover, and, consequently, no other mover, seeing that subsequent movers move only inasmuch as they are moved by the first mover; as the staff moves only because it is moved by the hand. Therefore it is necessary to arrive at a first mover, moved by no other;

*[From the *Summa Theologica* (1265–1273), Q. 2, Art. 3. Reprinted from *Basic Writings of Saint Thomas Aquinas,* Vol. I, edited by Anton C. Pegis (Random House, 1945), courtesy of the Anton C. Pegis Estate.]

and this everyone understands to be God.

The second way is from the nature of efficient cause. In the world of sensible things we find there is an order of efficient causes. There is no case known (neither is it, indeed, possible) in which a thing is found to be the efficient cause of itself; for so it would be prior to itself, which is impossible. Now in efficient causes it is not possible to go on to infinity, because in all efficient causes following in order, the first is the cause of the intermediate cause, and the intermediate is the cause of the ultimate cause, whether the intermediate cause be several, or one only. Now to take away the cause is to take away the effect. Therefore, if there be no first cause among efficient causes, there will be no ultimate, nor any intermediate, cause. But if in efficient causes it is possible to go on to infinity, there will be no first efficient cause, neither will there be an ultimate effect, nor any intermediate efficient causes; all of which is plainly false. Therefore it is necessary to admit a first efficient cause, to which everyone gives the name of God.

The third way is taken from possibility and necessity, and runs thus. We find in nature things that are possible to be and not to be, since they are found to be generated, and to be corrupted, and consequently, it is possible for them to be and not to be. But it is impossible for these always to exist, for that which can not-be at some time is not. Therefore, if everything can not-be, then at one time there was nothing in existence. Now if this were true, even now there would be nothing in existence, because that which does not exist begins to exist only through something already existing. Therefore, if at one time nothing was in existence, it would have been impossible for anything to have begun to exist; and thus even now nothing would be in existence—which is absurd. Therefore, not all beings are merely possible, but there must exist something the existence of which is necessary. But every necessary thing either has its necessity caused by another, or not. Now it is impossible to go on to infinity in necessary things which have their necessity caused by another, as has been already proved in regard to efficient causes. Therefore we cannot but admit the existence of some being having of itself its own necessity, and not receiving it from another, but rather causing in others their necessity. This all men speak of as God.

The fourth way is taken from the gradation to be found in things. Among beings there are some more and some less good, true, noble, and the like. But *more* and *less* are predicated of different things according as they resemble in their different ways something which is the maximum, as a thing is said to be hotter according as it more nearly resembles that which is hottest; so that there is something which is truest, something best, something noblest, and, consequently, something which is most being, for those things that are greatest in truth are greatest in being, as it is written in *Metaph*. ii. Now the maximum in any genus is the cause of all in that genus, as fire, which is the maximum of heat, is the cause of all hot things, as is said in the same book. Therefore there must also be something which is to all beings the cause of their being, goodness, and every other perfection; and this we call God.

The fifth way is taken from the governance of the world. We see that things which lack knowledge, such as natural bodies, act for an end, and this is evident from their acting always, or nearly always, in the same way, so as to obtain the best result. Hence it is plain that they achieve their end, not fortuitously, but designedly. Now whatever lacks knowledge cannot move towards an end, unless it be directed by some being endowed with knowledge and intelligence; as the arrow is directed by the archer. Therefore some intelligent being exists by whom all natural things are directed to their end; and this being we call God.

33

The Evidence for Design in Nature

WILLIAM PALEY

Proving Design in a Watch

In crossing a heath, suppose I pitched my foot against a *stone,* and were asked how the stone came to be there, I might possibly answer, that for any thing I knew to the contrary it had lain there for ever; nor would it, perhaps, be very easy to show the absurdity of this answer. But suppose I had found a *watch* upon the ground, and it should be inquired how the watch happened to be in that place, I should hardly think of the answer which I had before given, that for any thing I knew the watch might have always been there. Yet why should not this answer serve for the watch as well as for the stone; why is it not as admissible in the second case as in the first? For this reason, and for no other, namely, that when we come to inspect the watch, we perceive—what we could not discover in the stone—that its several parts are framed and put together for a purpose. . . . This mechanism being observed—it requires indeed an examination of the instrument, and perhaps some previous knowledge of the subject, to perceive and understand it; but being once, as we have said, observed and understood, the inference we think is inevitable, that the watch must have had a maker—that there must have existed, at some time and at some place or other, an artificer or artificers who formed it for the purpose which, we find it actually to answer, who comprehended its construction and designed its use.

I. Nor would it, I apprehend, weaken the conclusion, that we had

[From *Natural Theology,* chapters 1, 2, 3, 5, 6. First published in 1802.]

never seen a watch made—that we had never known an artist capable of making one—that we were altogether incapable of executing such a piece of workmanship ourselves, or of understanding in what manner it was performed; all this being no more than what is true of some exquisite remains of ancient art, of some lost arts, and, to the generality of mankind, of the more curious productions of modern manufacture. Does one man in a million know how oval frames are turned? Ignorance of this kind exalts our opinion of the unseen and unknown artist's skill, if he be unseen and unknown, but raises no doubt in our minds of the existence and agency of such an artist, at some former time and in some place or other. Nor can I perceive that it varies at all the inference, whether the question arise concerning a human agent or concerning an agent of a different species, or an agent possessing in some respects a different nature.

II. Neither, secondly, would it invalidate our conclusion, that the watch sometimes went wrong, or that it seldom went exactly right. The purpose of the machinery, the design, and the designer might be evident, and in the case supposed, would be evident, in whatever way we accounted for the irregularity of the movement, or whether we could account for it or not. It is not necessary that a machine be perfect, in order to show with what design it was made: still less necessary, where

the only question is whether it were made with any design at all.

III. Nor, thirdly, would it bring any uncertainty into the argument, if there were a few parts of the watch, concerning which we could not discover or had not yet discovered in what manner they conduced to the general effect; or even some parts, concerning which we could not ascertain whether they conduced to that effect in any manner whatever. For, as to the first branch of the case, if by the loss, or disorder, or decay of the parts in question, the movement of the watch were found in fact to be stopped, or disturbed, or retarded, no doubt would remain in our minds as to the utility or intention of these parts, although we should be unable to investigate the manner according to which, or the connection by which, the ultimate effect depended upon their action or assistance; and the more complex the machine, the more likely is this obscurity to arise. Then, as to the second thing supposed, namely, that there were parts which might be spared without prejudice to the movement of the watch, and that we had proved this by experiment, these superfluous parts, even if we were completely assured that they were such, would not vacate the reasoning which we had instituted concerning other parts. The indication of contrivance remained, with respect to them, nearly as it was before.

IV. Nor, fourthly, would any man in his senses think the existence of the watch with its various machinery accounted for, by being told that it was one out of possible combinations of material forms; that whatever he had found in the place where he found the watch, must have contained some internal configuration or other; and that this configuration might be the structure now exhibited, namely, of the works of a watch, as well as a different structure.

V. Nor, fifthly, would it yield his inquiry more satisfaction, to be answered that there existed in things a principle of order, which had disposed the parts of the watch into their present form and situation. He never knew a watch made by the principle of order; nor can he even form to himself an idea of what is meant by a principle of order, distinct from the intelligence of the watchmaker.

VI. Sixthly, he would be surprised to hear that the mechanism of the watch was no proof of contrivance, only a motive to induce the mind to think so:

VII. And not less surprised to be informed, that the watch in his hand was nothing more than the result of the laws of *metallic* nature. It is a perversion of language to assign any law as the efficient, operative cause of any thing. A law presupposes an agent; for it is only the mode according to which an agent proceeds; it implies a power; for it is the order according to which that power acts. Without this agent, without this power, which are both distinct from itself, the *law* does nothing, is nothing. The expression, "the law of metallic nature," may sound strange and harsh to a philosophic ear; but it seems quite as justifiable as some others which are more familiar to him, such as "the law of vegetable nature," "the law of animal nature," or, indeed, as "the law of nature" in general, when assigned as the cause of phenomena, in exclusion of agency and power, or when it is substituted into the place of these.

VIII. Neither, lastly, would our observer be driven out of his conclusion or from his confidence in its truth, by being told that he knew nothing at all about the matter. He knows enough for his argument; he knows the utility of the end; he knows the subserviency and adaptation of the means to the end. These points being known, his ignorance of other points, his doubts concerning other points, affect not the certainty of his reasoning. The consciousness of knowing little need not beget a distrust of that which he does know.

Suppose, in the next place, that the person who found the watch should after some time discover, that in addition to all the properies which he had hitherto observed in it, it possessed the unexpected property of producing in the course of its movement another watch like itself—the thing is conceivable; that it contained within it a mechanism, a system of parts—a mould, for instance, or a complex adjustment of lathes, files, and other tools—evidently and separately calculated for this purpose; let us inquire what effect ought such a discovery to have upon his former conclusion. . . .

The conclusion which the *first* examination of the watch, of its works, constuction, and movement, suggested, was, that it must have had, for cause and author of that construction, an artificer who understood its mechanism and designed its use. This conclusion is invincible. A *second* examination presents us with a new discovery. The watch is found, in the course of its movement, to produce another watch similar to itself; and not only so, but we perceive in it a system or organization separately calculated for that purpose. What effect would this discovery have, or ought it to have, upon our former inference? What, as hath already been said, but to increase beyond measure our admiration of the skill which had been employed in the formation of such a machine? Or shall it, instead of this, all at once turn us round to an opposite conclusion, namely, that no art or skill whatever has been concerned in the business, although all other evidences of art and skill remain as they were, and this last and supreme piece of art be now added to the rest? Can this be maintained without absurdity? Yet this is atheism.

The Argument Applied to Natural Objects

This is atheism; for every indication of contrivance, every manifestation of design which existed in the watch, exists in the works of nature, with the difference on the side of nature of being greater and more, and that in a degree which exceeds all computation. I mean, that the contrivances of nature surpass the contrivances of art, in the complexity, subtilty, and curiosity of the mechanism; and still more, if possible, do they go beyond them in number and variety; yet, in a multitude of cases, are not less evidently mechanical, not less evidently contrivances, not less evidently accommodated to their end or suited to their office, than are the most perfect productions of human ingenuity.

I know no better method of introducing so large a subject, than that of comparing a single thing with a single thing: an eye, for example, with a telescope. . . .

Every observation which was made in our first chapter concerning the watch, may be repeated with strict propriety concerning the eye; concerning animals; concerning plants; concerning, indeed, all the organized parts of the works of nature. As,

I. When we are inquiring simply after the *existence* of an intelligent Creator, imperfection, inaccuracy, liability to disorder, occasional irregularities, may subsist in a considerable degree without inducing any doubt into the question; just as a watch may frequently go wrong, seldom perhaps exactly right, may be faulty in some parts, defective in some, without the smallest ground of suspicion from thence arising that it was not a watch, not made, or not made for the purpose ascribed to it. ... So likewise it is in the works of nature. Irregularities and imperfections are of little or no weight in the consideration, when that consideration relates simply to the existence of a Creator. When the argument respects his attributes, they are of weight; but are then to be taken in conjunction—the attention is not to rest upon them, but they are to be taken in conjunction, with the unexceptionable evidences which we possess of skill, power, and benevolence displayed in other instances; which evidences may, in strength, number, and variety, be such, and may so overpower apparent blemishes, as to induce us, upon the most reasonable ground, to believe that these last ought to be referred to some cause, though we be ignorant of it, other than defect of knowledge or of benevolence in the author.

II. There may be also parts of plants and animals, as there were supposed to be of the watch, of which, in some instances the operation, in others the use, is unknown. ... But to this case, even were it fully made out, may be applied the consideration which we suggested concerning the watch, namely, that these superfluous parts do not negative the reasoning which we instituted concerning those parts which are useful, and of which we know the use; the indication of contrivance, with respect to them, remains as it was before.

III. One atheistic way of replying to our observations upon the works of nature, and to the proofs of a Deity which we think that we perceive in them is to tell us that all which we see must necessarily have had some form, and that it might as well be its present form as any other. Let us now apply this answer to the eye, as we did before to the watch. Something or other must have occupied that place in the animal's head—must have filled up, as we say, that socket: we will say, also, that it must have been of that sort of substance which we call animal substance, as flesh, bone, membrane, or cartilage, etc. But that it should have been an *eye* ...: that this fortunate conformation of parts should have been the lot, not of one individual out of many thousand individuals, like the great prize in a lottery, or like some singularity in nature, but the happy chance of a whole species; nor of one species out of many thousand species with which we are acquainted, but of by far the greatest number of all that exist, and that under varieties not causal or capricious, but bearing marks of being suited to their respective exigences: that all this should have taken place, merely because something must have occupied these points on every animal's forehead; or, that all this should be thought to be accounted for by the short answer, that "whatever was there must have had some form or other," is too absurd to be made more so by any argumentation. . . .

IV. There is another answer which has the same effect as the resolving of things into chance; which answer would persuade us to believe that the eye, the animal to which it belongs, every other animal, every plant, indeed every organized body which we see, are only so many out of the possible varieties and combinations of being which the lapse of infinite ages has brought into existence; that the present world is the relic of that variety; millions of other bodily forms and other species having perished, being, by the defect of their constitution, incapable of preservation, or of continuance by generation. Now there is no foundation whatever for this conjecture in any thing which we observe in the works of nature; no such experiments are going on at present— no such energy operates as that which is here supposed, and which should be constantly pushing into existence new varieties of beings. Nor are there any appearances to support an opinion, that every possible combination of vegetable or animal structure has formerly been tried. . . .

V. To the marks of contrivance discoverable in animal bodies, and to the argument deduced from them in proof of design and of a designing Creator, this turn is sometimes attempted to be given, namely, that the parts were not intended for the use, but that the use arose out of the parts. This distinction is intelligible. A cabinet-maker rubs his mahogany with fish-skin; yet it would be too much to assert that the skin of the dog-fish was made rough and granulated on purpose for the polishing of wood, and the use of cabinet-makers. Therefore the distinction is intelligible. But I think that there is very little place for it in the works of nature. When roundly and generally affirmed of them, as it hath sometimes been, it amounts to such another stretch of assertion as it would be to say, that all the implements of the cabinet-maker's workshop, as well as his fish-skin, were substances accidentally configurated, which he had picked up and converted to his use; that his adzes, saws, planes, and gimlets, were not made, as we suppose, to hew, cut, smooth, shape out, or bore wood with, but that, these things being made, no matter with what design, or whether with any, the cabinet-maker perceived that they were applicable to his purpose, and turned them to account. . . .

VI. Others have chosen to refer every thing to a *principle of order* in nature. A principle of order is the word; but what is meant by a principle of order as different from an intelligent Creator, has not been explained either by definition or example; and without such explanation, it should seem to be a mere substitution of words for reasons, names for causes. Order itself is only the adaptation of means to an end: a principle of order, therefore, can only signify the mind and intention which so adapts them. Or, were it capable of being explained in any other sense, is there any experience, any analogy, to sustain it? Was a watch ever produced by a principle of order; and why might not a watch be so produced as well as an eye? . . .

VII. Lastly, the confidence which we place in our observations upon the works of nature, in the marks which we discover of contrivance, choice, and design, and in our reasoning upon the proofs afforded us, ought not to be shaken, as it is sometimes attempted to be done, by bringing forward to our view our own ignorance, or rather the general imperfection of our knowledge of nature. Nor, in many cases, ought this consideration to affect us, even when it respects some parts of the subject immediately under our notice. True fortitude of understanding consists in not suffering what we know to be disturbed by what we do not know. If we perceive a useful end, and means adapted to that end, we perceive enough for our conclusion. If these things be clear, no matter what is obscure. The argument is finished. . . .

. . . The proof is not a conclusion which lies at the end of a chain of reasoning, of which chain each instance of contrivance is only a link, and of which, if one link fail, the whole falls; but it is an argument separately supplied by every separate example. An error in stating an example affects only that example. The argument is cumulative, in the fullest sense of that term. The eye proves it without the ear; the ear without the eye. The proof in each example is complete; for when the design of the part, and the conduciveness of its structure to that design is shown, the mind may set itself at rest; no future consideration can detract any thing from the force of the example.

34

The Wager

BLAISE PASCAL

... Nature presents to me nothing which is not matter of doubt and concern. If I saw nothing there which revealed a Divinity, I would come to a negative conclusion; if I saw everywhere the signs of a Creator, I would remain peacefully in faith. But, seeing too much to deny and too little to be sure, I am in a state to be pitied; wherefore I have a hundred times wished that if a God maintains nature, she should testify to Him unequivocally, and that, if the signs she gives are deceptive, she should suppress them altogether; that she should say everything or nothing, that I might see which cause I ought to follow. Whereas in my present state, ignorant of what I am or of what I ought to do, I know neither my condition nor my duty. . . .

If there is a God, He is infinitely incomprehensible, since, having neither parts nor limits, He has no affinity to us. We are then incapable of knowing either what He is or if He is. This being so, who will dare to undertake the decision of the question? Not we, who have no affinity to Him.

Who then will blame Christians for not being able to give a reason for their belief, since they profess a religion for which they cannot give a reason? They declare, in expounding it to the world, that it is a foolishness, *stultitiam*; and then you complain that they do not prove it! If they proved it, they would not keep their word; it is in lacking proofs, that they are not lacking in sense. "Yes, but although this excuses those who offer it as such, and takes away from them the blame of putting it forward without reason, it does not excuse those who receive it." Let us then examine this point, and say, "God is, or He is not." But

[From *Pensées*, translated by William Finlayson Trotter (1904). The original edition of *Pensées* appeared in 1670.]

to which side shall we incline? Reason can decide nothing here. There is an infinite chaos which separates us. A game is being played at the extremity of this infinite distance where heads or tails will turn up. What will you wager? According to reason, you can do neither the one thing nor the other; according to reason, you can defend neither of the propositions.

Do not then reprove for error those who have made a choice; for you know nothing about it. "No, but I blame them for having made, not this choice, but a choice; for again both he who chooses heads and he who chooses tails are equally at fault, they are both in the wrong. The true course is not to wager at all."

Yes; but you must wager. It is not optional. You are embarked. Which will you choose then? Let us see. Since you must choose, let us see which interests you least. You have two things to lose, the true and the good; and two things to stake, your reason and your will, your knowledge and your happiness; and your nature has two things to shun, error and misery. Your reason is no more shocked in choosing one rather than the other, since you must of necessity choose. This is one point settled. But your happiness? Let us weigh the gain and the loss in wagering that God is. Let us estimate these two chances. If you gain, you gain all; if you lose, you lose nothing. Wager, then, without hesitation that He is.—"That is very fine. Yes, I must wager; but I may perhaps wager too much."—Let us see. Since there is an equal risk of gain and of loss, if you had only to gain two lives, instead of one, you might still wager. But if there were three lives to gain, you would have to play (since you are under the necessity of playing), and you would be imprudent, when you are forced to play, not to chance your life to gain three at a game where there is an equal risk of loss and gain. But there is an eternity of life and happiness. And this being so, if there were an infinity of chances, of which one only would be for you, you would still be right in wagering one to win two, and you would act stupidly, being obliged to play, by refusing to stake one life against three at a game in which out of an infinity of chances there is one for you, if there were an infinity of an infinitely happy life to gain. But there is here an infinity of an infinitely happy life to gain, a chance of gain against a finite number of chances of loss, and what you stake is finite. It is all divided; wherever the infinite is and there is not an infinity of chances of loss against that of gain, there is no time to hesitate, you must give all. And thus, when one is forced to play, he must renounce reason to preserve his life, rather than risk it for infinite gains, as likely to happen as the loss of nothingness.

For it is no use to say it is uncertain if we will gain, and it is certain that we risk, and that the infinite distance between the *certainty* of what is staked and the *uncertainty* of what will be gained, equals the finite good which is certainly staked against the uncertain infinite. It is not so, as every player stakes a certainty to gain an uncertainty, and yet he stakes a finite certainty to gain a finite uncertainty, without transgressing against reason. There is not an infinite distance between the certainty staked and the uncertainty of the gain; that is untrue. In truth, there is an infinity between the certainty of gain and the certainty of loss. But the uncertainty of the gain is proportioned to the certainty of the stake according to the proportion of the chances of gain and loss. Hence it comes that, if there are as many risks on one side as on the other, the course is to play even; and then the certainty of the stake is equal to the uncertainty of the gain, so far is it from fact that there is an infinite distance between them. And so our proposition is of infinite force, when there is the finite to stake in a game where there are equal risks of gain and of loss, and the infinite to gain. This is demonstrable; and if men are capable of any truths, this is one.

"I confess it, I admit it. But, still, is there no means of seeing the faces of the cards?"—Yes, Scripture and the rest, etc. "Yes, but I have my hands tied and my mouth closed; I am forced to wager, and am not free. I am not released, and am so made that I cannot believe. What, then, would you have me do?"

True. But at least learn your inability to believe, since reason brings you to this, and yet you cannot believe. Endeavor then to convince yourself, not by increase of proofs of God, but by the abatement of your passions. You would like to attain faith, and do not know the way; you would like to cure yourself of unbelief, and ask the remedy for it. Learn of those who have been bound like you, and who now stake all their possessions. These are people who know the way which you would follow, and who are cured of an ill of which you would be cured. Follow the way by which they began; by acting as if they believed, taking the holy water, having masses said, etc. Even this will naturally make you believe, and deaden your acuteness.—"But this is what I am afraid of."—And why? What have you to lose?

But to show you that this leads you there, it is this which will lessen the passions, which are your stumbling-blocks.

The end of this discourse.— Now, what harm will befall you in taking this side? You will be faithful, honest, humble, grateful, generous, a sincere friend, truthful. Certainly you will not have those poisonous pleasures, glory and luxury; but will you not have others? I will tell you that you will thereby gain in this life, and that, at each step you take on this road, you will see so great certainty of gain, so much nothingness in what you risk, that you will at last recognize that you have wagered for something certain and infinite, for which you have given nothing. . . .

35

The Will to Believe

WILLIAM JAMES

I

Let us give the name of *hypothesis* to anything that may be proposed to our belief; and just as the electricians speak of live and dead wires, let us speak of any hypothesis as either *live* or *dead*. A live hypothesis is one which appeals as a real possibility to him to whom it is proposed. If I ask you to believe in the Mahdi, the notion makes no electric connection with your nature,—it refuses to scintillate with any credibility at all. As an hypothesis it is completely dead. To an Arab, however (even if he be not one of the Mahdi's followers), the hypothesis is among the mind's possibilities: it is alive. This shows that deadness and liveness in an hypothesis are not intrinsic properties, but relations to the individual thinker. They are measured by his willing-

ness to act. The maximum of liveness in an hypothesis means willingness to act irrevocably. Practically, that means belief; but there is some believing tendency wherever there is willingness to act at all.

Next, let us call the decision between two hypotheses an *option*. Options may be of several kinds. They may be—1, *living* or *dead;* 2, *forced* or *avoidable;* 3, *momentous* or *trivial;* and for our purposes we may call an option a *genuine* option when it is of the forced, living, and momentous kind.

1. A living option is one in which both hypotheses are live ones. If I say to you: "Be a theosophist or be a Mohammedan," it is probably a dead option, because for you neither hypothesis is likely to be alive. But if I say: "Be an agnostic or be a Christian," it is otherwise: trained as

[From an address to the Philosophical Clubs of Yale and Brown Universities. First published in *New World* (1896).]

you are, each hypothesis makes some appeal, however small, to your belief.

2. Next, if I say to you: "Choose between going out with your umbrella or without it," I do not offer you a genuine option, for it is not forced. You can easily avoid it by not going out at all. Similarly, if I say, "Either love me or hate me," "Either call my theory true or call it false," your option is avoidable. You may remain indifferent to me, neither loving nor hating, and you may decline to offer any judgment as to my theory. But if I say, "Either accept this truth or go without it," I put on you a forced option, for there is no standing place outside of the alternative. Every dilemma based on a complete logical disjunction, with no possibility of not choosing, is an option of this forced kind.

3. Finally, if I were Dr. Nansen and proposed to you to join my North Pole expedition, your option would be momentous; for this would probably be your only similar opportunity, and your choice now would either exclude you from the North Pole sort of immortality altogether or put at least the chance of it into your hands. He who refuses to embrace a unique opportunity loses the prize as surely as if he tried and failed. *Per contra*, the option is trivial when the opportunity is not unique, when the stake is insignificant, or when the decision is reversible if it later prove unwise. Such trivial options abound in the scientific life. A chemist finds an hypothesis live enough to spend a year in its verification: he believes in it to that extent. But if his experiments prove inconclusive either way, he is quit for his loss of time, no vital harm being done.

It will facilitate our discussion if we keep all these distinctions well in mind. . . .

II

Does it not seem preposterous on the very face of it to talk of our opinions being modifiable at will? Can our will either help or hinder our intellect in its perceptions of truth? Can we, by just willing it, believe that Abraham Lincoln's existence is a myth, and that the portraits of him in McClure's Magazine are all of some one else? Can we, by any effort of our will, or by any strength of wish that it were true, believe ourselves well and about when we are roaring with rheumatism in bed, or feel certain that the sum of the two one-dollar bills in our pocket must be a hundred dollars? We can *say* any of these things, but we are absolutely impotent to believe them; and of just such things is the whole fabric of the truths that we do believe in made up,—matters of fact, immediate or remote, as Hume said, and relations between ideas, which are either there or not there for us if we see them so, and which if not there cannot be put there by any action of our own. . . .

The talk of believing by our volition seems, then, from one point of view, simply silly. From another point of view it is worse than silly, it is vile. When one turns to the magnificent edifice of the physical sciences, and sees how it was reared; what thousands of disinterested moral lives of men lie buried in its mere foundations; what patience and postponement, what choking down of preference, what submission to the icy laws of outer fact are wrought into its very stones and mortar; how absolutely impersonal it stands in its vast augustness,—then how besotted and contemptible seems every little sentimentalist who comes blowing his voluntary smoke-wreaths, and pretending to decide things from out of his private dream! Can we wonder if those bred in the rugged and manly school of science should feel like spewing such subjectivism out of their mouths? . . .

As a rule we disbelieve all facts and theories for which we have no use. Clifford's cosmic emotions find no use for Christian feelings. Huxley belabors the bishops because there is no use for sacerdotalism in his scheme of life. Newman, on the contrary, goes over to Romanism, and finds all sorts of reasons good for staying there, because a priestly system is for him an organic need and delight. Why do so few "scientists" even look at the evidence for telepathy, so called? Because they think, as a leading biologist, now dead,

once said to me, that even if such a thing were true, scientists ought to band together to keep it suppressed and concealed. It would undo the uniformity of Nature and all sorts of other things without which scientists cannot carry on their pursuits. But if this very man had been shown something which as a scientist he might *do* with telepathy, he might not only have examined the evidence, but even have found it good enough. This very law which the logicians would impose upon us—if I may give the name of logicians to those who would rule out our willing nature here—is based on nothing but their own natural wish to exclude all elements for which they, in their professional quality of logicians, can find no use.

Evidently, then, our non-intellectual nature does influence our convictions. There are passional tendencies and volitions which run before and others which come after belief, and it is only the latter that are too late for the fair; and they are not too late when the previous passional work has been already in their own direction. . . .

III

One more point, small but important, and our preliminaries are done. There are two ways of looking at our duty in the matter of opinion,—ways entirely different, and yet ways about whose difference the theory of knowledge seems hitherto to have shown very little concern. *We must know the truth*; and *we must avoid error*,—these are our first and great commandments as would-be knowers; but they are not two ways of stating an identical commandment, they are two separable laws. Although it may indeed happen that when we believe the truth *A*, we escape as an incidental consequence from believing the falsehood *B*, it hardly ever happens that by merely disbelieving *B* we necessarily believe *A*. We may in escaping *B* fall into believing other falsehoods, *C* or *D*, just as bad as *B*; or we may escape *B* by not believing anything at all, not even *A*.

Believe truth! Shun error!—these, we see, are two materially different laws; and by choosing between them we may end by coloring differently our whole intellectual life. We may regard the chase for truth as paramount, and the avoidance of error as secondary; or we may, on the other hand, treat the avoidance of error as more imperative, and let truth take its chance. Clifford . . . exhorts us to the latter course. Believe nothing, he tells us, keep your mind in suspense forever, rather than by closing it on insufficient evidence incur the awful risk of believing lies. You, on the other hand, may think that the risk of being in error is a very small matter when compared with the blessings of real knowledge, and be ready to be duped many times in your investigation rather than postpone indefinitely the chance of guessing true.

I myself find it impossible to go with Clifford. We must remember that these feelings of our duty about either truth or error are in any case only expressions of our passional life. Biologically considered, our minds are as ready to grind out falsehood as veracity, and he who says, "Better go without belief forever than believe a lie!" merely shows his own preponderant private horror of becoming a dupe. He may be critical of many of his desires and fears, but this fear he slavishly obeys. He cannot imagine any one questioning its binding force. For my own part, I have also a horror of being duped; but I can believe that worse things than being duped may happen to a man in this world; so Clifford's exhortation has to my ears a thoroughly fantastic sound. It is like a general informing his soldiers that it is better to keep out of battle forever than to risk a single wound. Not so are victories either over enemies or over nature gained. Our errors are surely not such awfully solemn things. In a world where we are so certain to incur them in spite of all our caution, a certain lightness of heart seems healthier than this excessive nervousness on their behalf. . . .

IV

And now, after all this introduction, let us go straight at our question. I have said, and now repeat it, that not only as a matter of fact do we find our passional nature influencing us in our opinions, but that there are some options between opinions in which this influence must be regarded both as an inevitable and as a lawful determinant of our choice. . . .

. . . Wherever the option between losing truth and gaining it is not momentous, we can throw the chance of *gaining truth* away, and at any rate save ourselves from any chance of *believing falsehood*, by not making up our minds at all till objective evidence has come. In scientific questions, this is almost always the case; and even in human affairs in general, the need of acting is seldom so urgent that a false belief to act on is better than no belief at all. Law courts, indeed, have to decide on the best evidence attainable for the moment, because a judge's duty is to make law as well as to ascertain it, and (as a learned judge once said to me) few cases are worth spending much time over: the great thing is to have them decided on *any* acceptable principle, and got out of the way. But in our dealings with objective nature we obviously are recorders, not makers, of the truth; and decisions for the mere sake of deciding promptly and getting on to the next business would be wholly out of place. Throughout the breadth of physical nature facts are what they are quite independently of us, and seldom is there any such hurry about them that the risks of being duped by believing a premature the-

ory need be faced. The questions here are always trivial options, the hypotheses are hardly living (at any rate not living for us spectators), the choice between believing truth or falsehood is seldom forced. The attitude of sceptical balance is therefore the absolutely wise one if we would escape mistakes. What difference, indeed, does it make to most of us whether we have or have not a theory of the Röntgen rays, whether we believe or not in mind-stuff, or have a conviction about the causality of conscious states? It makes no difference. Such options are not forced on us. On every account it is better not to make them, but still keep weighing reasons *pro et contra* with an indifferent hand.

I speak, of course, here of the purely judging mind. For purposes of discovery such indifference is to be less highly recommended, and science would be far less advanced than she is if the passionate desires of individuals to get their own faiths confirmed had been kept out of the game. . . . On the other hand, if you want an absolute duffer in an investigation, you must, after all, take the man who has no interest whatever in its results: he is the warranted incapable, the positive fool. The most useful investigator, because the most sensitive observer, is always he whose eager interest in one side of the question is balanced by an equally keen nervousness lest he become deceived. Science has organized this nervousness into a regular *tech-*

nique, her so-called method of verification; and she has fallen so deeply in love with the method that one may even say she has ceased to care for truth by itself at all. It is only truth as technically verified that interests her. The truth of truths might come in merely affirmative form, and she would decline to touch it. Such truth as that, she might repeat with Clifford, would be stolen in defiance of her duty to mankind. Human passions, however, are stronger than technical rules. "Le cœur a ses raisons," as Pascal says, "que la raison ne connaît pas;" and however indifferent to all but the bare rules of the game the umpire, the abstract intellect, may be, the concrete players who furnish him the materials to judge of are usually, each one of them, in love with some pet "live hypothesis" of his own. Let us agree, however, that wherever there is no forced option, the dispassionately judicial intellect with no pet hypothesis, saving us, as it does, from dupery at any rate, ought to be our ideal.

The question next arises: Are there not somewhere forced options in our speculative questions, and can we (as men who may be interested at least as much in positively gaining truth as in merely escaping dupery) always wait with impunity till the coercive evidence shall have arrived? It seems *a priori* improbable that the truth should be so nicely adjusted to our needs and powers as that. In the great boarding-house of nature, the cakes and the butter and the syrup seldom come out so even and leave the plates so clean. Indeed, we should view them with scientific suspicion if they did.

V

Moral questions immediately present themselves as questions whose solution cannot wait for sensible proof. A moral question is a question not of what sensibly exists, but of what is good, or would be good if it did exist. Science can tell us what exists; but to compare the *worths*, both of what exists and of what does not exist, we must consult not science, but what Pascal calls our heart. Science herself consults her heart when she lays it down that the infinite ascertainment of fact and correction of false belief are the supreme goods for man. Challenge the statement, and science can only repeat it oracularly, or else prove it by showing that such ascertainment and correction bring man all sorts of other goods which man's heart in turn declares. The question of having moral beliefs at all or not having them is decided by our will. Are our moral preferences true or false, or are they only odd biological phenomena, making things good or bad for *us*, but in themselves indifferent? How can your pure intellect decide? If your heart does not *want* a world of moral reality, your head will assuredly never make you believe in one. Mephistophelian scepticism, indeed, will satisfy the head's play-instincts much better than any rigorous idealism can. Some men (even at the student age) are so naturally cool-hearted that the moralistic hypothesis never has for them any pungent life, and in their supercilious presence the hot young moralist always feels strangely ill at ease. The appearance of knowingness is on their side, of *naïveté* and gullibility on his. Yet, in the inarticulate heart of him, he clings to it that he is not a dupe, and that there is a realm in which (as Emerson says) all their wit and intellectual superiority is no better than the cunning of a fox. Moral scepticism can no more be refuted or proved by logic than intellectual scepticism can. When we stick to it that there *is* truth (be it of either kind), we do so with our whole nature, and resolve to stand or fall by the results. The sceptic with his whole nature adopts the doubting attitude; but which of us is the wiser, Omniscience only knows. . . .

A social organism of any sort whatever, large or small, is what it is because each member proceeds to his own duty with a trust that the other members will simultaneously do theirs. Wherever a desired result is achieved by the co-operation of many independent persons, its existence as a fact is a pure consequence of the precursive faith in one another of those immediately concerned. A government, an army, a commercial system, a ship, a college,

an athletic team, all exist on this condition, without which not only is nothing achieved, but nothing is even attempted. A whole train of passengers (individually brave enough) will be looted by a few highwaymen, simply because the latter can count on one another, while each passenger fears that if he makes a movement of resistance, he will be shot before any one else backs him up. If we believed that the whole car-full would rise at once with us, we should each severally rise, and train-robbing would never even be attempted. There are, then, cases where a fact cannot come at all unless a preliminary faith exists in its coming. *And where faith in a fact can help create the fact*, that would be an insane logic which should say that faith running ahead of scientific evidence is the "lowest kind of immorality" into which a thinking being can fall. Yet such is the logic by which our scientific absolutists pretend to regulate our lives!

VI

In truths dependent on our personal action, then, faith based on desire is certainly a lawful and possibly an indispensable thing.

But now, it will be said, these are all childish human cases, and have nothing to do with great cosmical matters, like the question of religious faith. Let us then pass on to that. Religions differ so much in their accidents that in discussing the religious question we must make it very generic and broad. What then do we now mean by the religious hypothesis? Science says things are; morality says some things are better than other things; and religion says essentially two things.

First, she says that the best things are the more eternal things, the overlapping things, the things in the universe that throw the last stone, so to speak, and say the final word. "Perfection is eternal,"—this phrase of Charles Secrétan seems a good way of putting this first affirmation of religion, an affirmation which obviously cannot yet be verified scientifically at all.

The second affirmation of religion is that we are better off even now if we believe her first affirmation to be true.

Now, let us consider what the logical elements of this situation are *in case the religious hypothesis in both its branches be really true.* (Of course, we must admit that possibility at the outset. If we are to discuss the question at all, it must involve a living option. If for any of you religion be a hypothesis that cannot, by any living possibility be true, then you need go no farther. I speak to the "saving remnant" alone.) So proceeding, we see, first, that religion offers itself as a *momentous* option. We are supposed to gain, even now, by our belief, and to lose by our nonbelief, a certain vital good. Secondly, religion is a *forced* option, so

far as that good goes. We cannot escape the issue by remaining sceptical and waiting for more light, because, although we do avoid error in that way *if religion be untrue*, we lose the good, *if it be true*, just as certainly as if we positively chose to disbelieve. It is as if a man should hesitate indefinitely to ask a certain woman to marry him because he was not perfectly sure that she would prove an angel after he brought her home. Would he not cut himself off from that particular angel-possibility as decisively as if he went and married some one else? Scepticism, then, is not avoidance of option; it is option of a certain particular kind of risk. *Better risk loss of truth than chance of error,*—that is your faith-vetoer's exact position. He is actively playing his stake as much as the believer is; he is backing the field against the religious hypothesis, just as the believer is backing the religious hypothesis against the field. To preach scepticism to us as a duty until "sufficient evidence" for religion be found, is tantamount therefore to telling us, when in presence of the religious hypothesis, that to yield to our fear of its being error is wiser and better than to yield to our hope that it may be true. It is not intellect against all passions, then; it is only intellect with one passion laying down its law. And by what, forsooth, is the supreme wisdom of this passion warranted? Dupery for dupery, what proof is there that dupery through hope is so much worse than dupery through fear? I, for one, can see no proof; and I simply refuse obedience to the scientist's command to imitate his kind of option, in a case where my own stake is important enough to give me the right to choose my own form of risk. If religion be true and the evidence for it be still insufficient, I do not wish, by putting your extinguisher upon my nature (which feels to me as if it had after all some business in this matter), to forfeit my sole chance in life of getting upon the winning side,—that chance depending, of course, on my willingness to run the risk of acting as if my passional need of taking the world religously might be prophetic and right.

All this is on the supposition that it really may be prophetic and right, and that, even to us who are discussing the matter, religion is a live hypothesis which may be true. Now, to most of us religion comes in a still further way that makes a veto on our active faith even more illogical. The more perfect and more eternal aspect of the universe is represented in our religions as having personal form. The universe is no longer a mere *It* to us, but a *Thou*, if we are religious; and any relation that may be possible from person to person might be possible here. For instance, although in one sense we are passive portions of the universe, in another we show a curious autonomy, as if we were small active centres on our own account. We feel, too, as if the appeal of religion to us were made to our own active good-will, as if evidence might be forever withheld from us unless we met the hypothesis half-way. To take a trivial illustration: just as a man who in a company of gentlemen made no advances, asked a warrant for every concession, and believed no one's word without proof, would cut himself off by such churlishness from all the social rewards that a more trusting spirit would earn,—so here, one who should shut himself up in snarling logicality and try to make the gods extort his recognition willy-nilly, or not get it at all, might cut himself off forever from his only opportunity of making the gods' acquaintance. This feeling, forced on us we know not whence, that by obstinately believing that there are gods (although not to do so would be so easy both for our logic and our life) we are doing the universe the deepest service we can, seems part of the living essence of the religious hypothesis. If the hypothesis *were* true in all its parts, including this one, then pure intellectualism, with its veto on our making willing advances, would be an absurdity; and some participation of our sympathetic nature would be logically required. I, therefore, for one, cannot see my way to accepting the agnostic rules for truth-seeking, or wilfully agree to keep my willing nature out of the game. I cannot do so for this plain reason, that *a rule of thinking which would absolutely prevent me from acknowledging certain kinds of truth if those kinds of truth were really there, would be an irrational rule.* That for me is the long and short of the formal logic of the situation, no matter what the kinds of truth might materially be. . . .

. . . If we had an infallible intellect with its objective certitudes, we might feel ourselves disloyal to such a perfect organ of knowledge in not trusting to it exclusively, in not waiting for its releasing word. But if we are empiricists, if we believe that no bell in us tolls to let us know for certain when truth is in our grasp, then it seems a piece of idle fantasticality to preach so solemnly our duty of waiting for the bell. Indeed we *may* wait if we will,—I hope you do not think that I am denying that,—but if we do so, we do so at our peril as much as if we believed. In either case we *act*, taking our life in our hands. No one of us ought to issue vetoes to the other, nor should we bandy words of abuse. We ought, on the contrary, delicately and profoundly to respect one another's mental freedom: then only shall we bring about the intellectual republic; then only shall we have that spirit of inner tolerance without which all our outer tolerance is soulless, and which is empiricism's glory; then only shall we live and let live, in speculative as well as in practical things. . . .

36

Reply to the Argument From Design

DAVID HUME

Not to lose any time in circumlocutions, said Cleanthes, addressing himself to Demea, much less in replying to the pious declamations of Philo; I shall briefly explain how I conceive this matter. Look round the world: contemplate the whole and every part of it: You will find it to be nothing but one great machine, subdivided into an infinite number of lesser machines, which again admit of subdivisions, to a degree beyond what human senses and faculties can trace and explain. All these various machines, and even their most minute parts, are adjusted to each other with an accuracy, which ravishes into admiration all men, who have ever contemplated them. The curious adapting of means to ends, throughout all nature, resembles exactly, though it much exceeds, the productions of human contrivance; of human designs, thought, wisdom, and intelligence. Since therefore the effects resemble each other, we are led to infer, by all the rules of analogy, that the causes also resemble; and that the Author of Nature is somewhat similar to the mind of man; though possessed of much larger faculties, proportioned to the grandeur of the work, which he has executed. By this argument *a posteriori*, and by this argument alone, do we prove at once the existence of a Deity, and his similarity to human mind and intelligence. . . .

What I chiefly scruple in this subject, said Philo, is not so much, that all religious arguments are by Cleanthes reduced to experience, as

[From *Dialogues Concerning Natural Religion*, Parts II, III, IV, V. First published in 1779.]

that they appear not to be even the most certain and irrefragable of that inferior kind. That a stone will fall, that fire will burn, that the earth has solidity, we have observed a thousand and a thousand times; and when any new instance of this nature is presented, we draw without hesitation the accustomed inference. The exact similarity of the cases gives us a perfect assurance of a similar event; and a stronger evidence is never desired nor sought after. But where-ever you depart, in the least, from the similarity of the cases, you diminish proportionably the evidence; and may at last bring it to a very weak *analogy*, which is confessedly liable to error and uncertainty. After having experienced the circulation of the blood in human creatures, we make no doubt that it takes place in Titius and Mævius: but from its circulation in frogs and fishes, it is only a presumption, though a strong one, from analogy, that it takes place in men and other animals. The analogical reasoning is much weaker, when we infer the circulation of the sap in vegetables from our experience, that the blood circulates in animals; and those, who hastily followed that imperfect analogy, are found, by more accurate experiments, to have been mistaken.

If we see a house, Cleanthes, we conclude, with the greatest certainty, that it had an architect or builder; because this is precisely that species of effect, which we have experienced to proceed from that species of cause. But surely you will not affirm, that the universe bears such a resemblance to a house, that we can with the same certainty infer a similar cause, or that the analogy is here entire and perfect. The dissimilitude is so striking, that the utmost you can here pretend to is a guess, a conjecture, a presumption concerning a similar cause; and how that pretension will be received in the world, I leave you to consider.

It would surely be very ill received, replied Cleanthes; and I should be deservedly blamed and detested, did I allow, that the proofs of a Deity amounted to no more than a guess or conjecture. But is the whole adjustment of means to ends in a house and in the universe so slight a resemblance? The œconomy of final causes? The order, proportion, and arrangement of every part? Steps of a stair are plainly contrived, that human legs may use them in mounting; and this inference is certain and infallible. Human legs are also contrived for walking and mounting; and this inference, I allow, is not altogether so certain, because of the dissimilarity which you remark; but does it, therefore, deserve the name only of presumption or conjecture? . . .

[Philo replies:]

Were a man to abstract from every thing which he knows or has seen, he would be altogether incapable, merely from his own ideas, to determine what kind of scene the universe must be, or to give the preference to one state or situation of things above another. For as nothing which he clearly conceives, could be esteemed impossible or implying a contradiction, every chimera of his fancy would be upon an equal footing; nor could he assign any just reason, why he adheres to one idea or system, and rejects the others, which are equally possible.

Again; after he opens his eyes, and contemplates the world, as it really is, it would be impossible for him, at first, to assign the cause of any one event; much less, of the whole of things or of the universe. He might set his Fancy a rambling; and she might bring him in an infinite variety of reports and representations. These would all be possible; but being all equally possible, he would never, of himself, give a satisfactory account for his preferring one of them to the rest. Experience alone can point out to him the true cause of any phenomenon.

Now, according to this method of reasoning, . . . it follows (and is, indeed, tacitly allowed by Cleanthes himself) that order, arrangement, or the adjustment of final causes is not, of itself, any proof of design; but only so far as it has been experienced to proceed from that principle. For aught we can know *a priori*, matter may contain the source or spring of order originally, within itself, as well as mind does; and there is no more difficulty in conceiving, that the several elements, from an internal un-

known cause, may fall into the most exquisite arrangement, than to conceive that their ideas, in the great, universal mind, from a like internal, unknown cause, fall into that arrangement. The equal possibility of both these suppositions is allowed. But by experience we find, (according to Cleanthes) that there is a difference between them. Throw several pieces of steel together, without shape or form; they will never arrange themselves so as to compose a watch: Stone, and mortar, and wood, without an architect, never erect a house. But the ideas in a human mind, we see, by an unknown, inexplicable œconomy, arrange themselves so as to form the plan of a watch or house. Experience, therefore, proves, that there is an original principle of order in mind, not in matter. From similar effects we infer similar causes. The adjustment of means to ends is alike in the universe, as in a machine of human contrivance. The causes, therefore, must be resembling. . . .

That all inferences, Cleanthes, concerning fact, are founded on experience, and that all experimental reasonings are founded on the supposition, that similar causes prove similar effects, and similar effects similar causes; I shall not, at present, much dispute with you. But observe, I entreat you, with what extreme caution all just reasoners proceed in the transferring of experiments to similar cases. Unless the cases be exactly similar, they repose no perfect confidence in applying their past observation to any particular phenomenon. Every alteration of circumstances occasions a doubt concerning the event; and it requires new experiments to prove certainly, that the new circumstances are of no moment or importance. A change in bulk, situation, arrangement, age, disposition of the air, or surrounding bodies; any of these particulars may be attended with the most unexpected consequences: And unless the objects be quite familiar to us, it is the highest temerity to expect with assurance, after any of these changes, an event similar to that which before fell under our observation. The slow and deliberate steps of philosophers, here, if any where, are distinguished from the precipitate march of the vulgar, who, hurried on by the smallest similitudes, are incapable of all discernment or consideration.

But can you think, Cleanthes, that your usual phlegm and philosophy have been preserved in so wide a step as you have taken, when you compared to the universe houses, ships, furniture, machines; and from their similarity in some circumstances inferred a similarity in their causes? Thought, design, intelligence, such as we discover in men and other animals, is no more than one of the springs and principles of the universe, as well as heat or cold, attraction or repulsion, and a hundred others, which fall under daily observation. It is an active cause, by which

some particular parts of nature, we find, produce alterations on other parts. But can a conclusion, with any propriety, be transferred from parts to the whole? Does not the great disproportion bar all comparison and inference? From observing the growth of a hair, can we learn any thing concerning the generation of a man? Would the manner of a leaf's blowing, even though perfectly known, afford us any instruction concerning the vegetation of a tree?

But allowing that we were to take the *operations* of one part of nature upon another for the foundation of our judgement concerning the *origin* of the whole (which never can be admitted) yet why select so minute, so weak, so bounded a principle as the reason and design of animals is found to be upon this planet? What peculiar privilege has this little agitation of the brain which we call *thought*, that we must thus make it the model of the whole universe? Our partiality in our own favour does indeed present it on all occasions; but sound philosophy ought carefully to guard against so natural an illusion.

So far from admitting, continued Philo, that the operations of a part can afford us any just conclusion concerning the origin of the whole, I will not allow any one part to form a rule for another part, if the latter be very remote from the former. Is there any reasonable ground to conclude, that the inhabitants of other planets possess thought, intelligence, reason, or any thing similar to these faculties in men? When Nature has so extremely diversified her manner of operation in this small globe; can we imagine, that she incessantly copies herself throughout so immense a universe? And if thought, as we may well suppose, be confined merely to this narrow corner, and has even there so limited a sphere of action; with what propriety can we assign it for the original cause of all things? The narrow views of a peasant, who makes his domestic œconomy the rule for the government of kingdoms, is in comparison a pardonable sophism. . . .

A very small part of this great system, during a very short time, is very imperfectly discovered to us: and do we then pronounce decisively concerning the origin of the whole?

Admirable conclusion! Stone, wood, brick, iron, brass, have not, at this time, in this minute globe of earth, an order or arrangement without human art and contrivance: therefore the universe could not originally attain its order and arrangement, without something similar to human art. But is a part of nature a rule for another part very wide of the former? Is it a rule for the whole? . . .

How the most absurd argument, replied Cleanthes, in the hands of a man of ingenuity and invention, may acquire an air of probability! Are you not aware, Philo, . . . that it is by no means necessary, that Theists should prove the similarity of the works of Nature to those of Art; because this similarity is self-evident and undeniable? The same matter, a like form: what more is requisite to show an analogy between their causes, and to ascertain the origin of all things from a divine purpose and intention? Your objections, I must freely tell you, are no better than the abstruse cavils of those philosophers who denied motion; and ought to be refuted in the same manner, by illustrations, examples, and instances, rather than by serious argument and philosophy.

Suppose, therefore, that an articulate voice were heard in the clouds, much louder and more melodious than any which human art could ever reach: Suppose, that this voice were extended in the same instant over all nations, and spoke to each nation in its own language and dialect: Suppose, that the words delivered not only contain a just sense and meaning, but convey some instruction altogether worthy of a benevolent being, superior to mankind: could you possibly hesitate a moment concerning the cause of this voice? and must you not instantly ascribe it to some design or purpose? Yet I cannot see but all the same objections (if they merit that appellation) which lie against the system of Theism, may also be produced against this inference.

Might you not say, that all conclusions concerning fact were founded on experience: that when we hear an articulate voice in the dark, and thence infer a man, it is only the resemblance of the effects, which leads us to conclude that there is a like resemblance in the cause: but that this extraordinary voice, by its loudness, extent, and flexibility to all languages, bears so little analogy to any human voice, that we have no reason to suppose any analogy in their causes: and consequently, that a rational, wise, coherent speech proceeded, you know not whence, from some accidental whistling of the winds, not from any divine reason or intelligence? You see clearly your own objections in these cavils; and I hope too, you see clearly, that they cannot possibly have more force in the one case than in the other.

But to bring the case still nearer the present one of the universe, I shall make two suppositions, which imply not any absurdity or impossibility. Suppose, that there is a natural, universal, invariable language, common to every individual of human race, and that books are natural productions, which perpetuate themselves in the same manner with animals and vegetables, by descent and propagation. Several expressions of our passions contain a universal language: all brute animals have a natural speech, which, however limited, is very intelligible to their own species. And as there are infinitely fewer parts and less contrivance in the finest composition of eloquence, than in the coarsest organized body, the propagation of an *Iliad* or *Æneid* is an easier supposition than of any plant or animal.

Suppose, therefore, that you enter into your library, thus peopled by natural volumes, containing the most refined reason and most exquisite beauty: could you possibly open one of them, and doubt, that its original cause bore the strongest analogy to mind and intelligence? When it reasons and discourses; when it expostulates, argues, and enforces its views and topics; when it applies sometimes to the pure intellect, sometimes to the affections; when it collects, disposes, and adorns every consideration suited to the subject: could you persist in asserting, that all this, at the bottom, had really no meaning, and that the first formation of this volume in the loins of its original parent proceeded not from thought and design? Your obstinacy, I know, reaches not that degree of firmness: even your sceptical play and wantonness would be abashed at so glaring an absurdity.

But if there be any difference, Philo, between this supposed case and the real one of the universe, it is all to the advantage of the latter. The anatomy of an animal affords many stronger instances of design than the perusal of Livy or Tacitus: and any objection which you start in the former case, by carrying me back to so unusual and extraordinary a scene as the first formation of worlds, the same objection has place on the supposition of our vegetating library. Chuse, then, your party, Philo, without ambiguity or evasion; assert either that a rational volume is no proof of a rational cause, or admit of a similar cause to all the works of nature.

Let me here observe too, continued Cleanthes, that this religious argument, instead of being weakened by that scepticism, so much affected by you, rather acquires force from it, and becomes more firm and undisputed. To exclude all argument or reasoning of every kind is either affectation or madness. The declared profession of every reasonable sceptic is only to reject abstruse, remote and refined arguments; to adhere to common sense and the plain instincts of nature; and to assent, where-ever any reasons strike him with so full a force, that he cannot, without the greatest violence, prevent it. Now the arguments for Natural Religion are plainly of this kind; and nothing but the most perverse, obstinate metaphysics can reject them. Consider, anatomize the eye; Survey its structure and contrivance; and tell me, from your own feeling, if the idea of a contriver does not immediately flow in upon you with a force like that of sensation. The most obvious conclusion surely is in favor of design; and it requires time, reflection and study, to summon up those frivolous, though abstruse objections, which can support Infidelity. Who can behold the male and female of each species, the correspondence of their parts and instincts, their passions and whole course of life before and after generation, but must be sensible, that the propagation of the species is intended by Nature? Millions and millions of such instances present themselves through every part of the universe; and no language can convey a more intelligible, irresistible meaning, than the curious adjustment of final causes. To what degree, therefore, of blind dogmatism must one have attained, to reject such natural and such convincing arguments? . . .

But to show you still more inconveniences, continued Philo, in your Anthropomorphism; please to take a new survey of your principles. *Like effects prove like causes.* This is the experimental argument; and this, you say too, is the sole theological argument. Now it is certain, that the liker the effects are, which are seen, and the liker the causes, which are inferred, the stronger is the argument. Every departure on either side diminishes the probability, and renders the experiment less conclusive. You cannot doubt of the principle: neither ought you to reject its consequences.

All the new discoveries in astronomy, which prove the immense grandeur and magnificence of the works of Nature, are so many additional arguments for a Deity, according to the true system of Theism; but according to your hypothesis of experimental Theism, they become so many objections, by removing the effect still farther from all resemblance to the effects of human art and contrivance. . . .

The discoveries by microscopes, as they open a new universe in miniature, are still objections, according to you; arguments, according to me. The farther we push our researches of this kind, we are still led to infer the universal cause of all to be vastly different from mankind, or from any object of human experience and observation.

And what say you to the discoveries in anatomy, chymistry, botany? . . . These surely are no objections, replied Cleanthes: they only discover new instances of art and contrivance. It is still the image of mind reflected on us from innumerable objects. Add, a mind *like the human*, said Philo. I know of no other, replied Cleanthes. And the liker the better, insisted Philo. To be sure, said Cleanthes.

Now, Cleanthes, said Philo, with an air of alacrity and triumph, mark the consequences. *First*, By this method of reasoning, you renounce all claim to infinity in any of the attributes of the Deity. For as the cause ought only to be proportioned to the effect, and the effect, so far as it falls under our cognisance, is not infinite; what pretensions have we, upon your suppositions, to ascribe that attribute to the divine Being? You will still insist, that, by removing him so much from all similarity to human creatures, we give in to the most arbitrary hypothesis, and at the same time weaken all proofs of his existence.

Secondly, You have no reason, on your theory, for ascribing perfection to the Deity, even in his finite capacity; or for supposing him free from every error, mistake, or incoherence in his undertakings. There are many inexplicable difficulties in the works of Nature, which, if we allow a perfect author to be proved *a priori*, are easily solved, and become only seeming difficulties, from the narrow capacity of man, who cannot trace infinite relations. But according to your method of reasoning, these difficulties become all real; and perhaps will be insisted on, as new instances of likeness to human art and contrivance. At least, you must acknowledge, that it is impossible for us to tell, from our limited views, whether this system contains any great faults, or deserves any considerable praise, if compared to other possible, and even real systems. Could a peasant, if the Æneid were read to him, pronounce that poem to be absolutely faultless, or even assign to it its proper rank among the productions of human wit; he, who had never seen any other production?

But were this world ever so perfect a production, it must still remain uncertain, whether all the excellences of the work can justly be ascribed to the workman. If we survey a ship, what an exalted idea must we form of the ingenuity of the carpenter, who framed so complicated, useful, and beautiful a machine? And what surprise must we feel, when we find him a stupid mechanic, who imitated others, and copied an art, which, through a long succession of ages, after multiplied trials, mistakes, corrections, deliberations, and controversies, had been gradually improving? Many worlds might have been botched and bungled, throughout an eternity, ere this system was struck out: much labour lost: many fruitless trials made: and a slow, but continued improvement carried on during infinite ages in the art of world-making. In such subjects, who can determine, where the truth; nay, who can conjecture where the probability, lies; amidst a great number of hypotheses which may be proposed, and a still greater number which may be imagined?

And what shadow of an argument, continued Philo, can you produce, from your hypothesis, to prove the unity of the Deity? A great number of men join in building a house or ship, in rearing a city, in framing a commonwealth: why may not several deities combine in contriving and framing a world? This is only so much greater similarity to human affairs. By sharing the work among several, we may so much further limit the attributes of each, and get rid of that extensive power and knowledge, which must be supposed in one deity, and which, according to you, can only serve to weaken the proof of his existence.

And if such foolish, such vicious creatures as man can yet often unite in framing and executing one plan; how much more those deities or dæmons, whom we may suppose several degrees more perfect?

To multiply causes, without necessity, is indeed contrary to true philosophy: but this principle applies not to the present case. Were one deity antecedently proved by your theory, who were possessed of every attribute, requisite to the production of the universe; it would be needless, I own (though not absurd) to suppose any other deity existent. But while it is still a question, Whether all these attributes are united in one subject, or dispersed among several independent beings: by what phenomena in nature can we pretend to decide the controversy? Where we see a body raised in a scale, we are sure that there is in the opposite scale, however concealed from sight, some counterpoising weight equal to it: but it is still allowed to doubt, whether that weight be an aggregate of several distinct bodies, or one uniform united mass. And if the weight requisite very much exceeds any thing which we have ever seen conjoined in any single body, the former supposition becomes still more probable and natural. An intelligent being of such vast power and capacity, as is necessary to produce the universe, or, to speak in the language of ancient philosophy, so prodigious an animal, exceeds all analogy, and even comprehension.

But farther, Cleanthes; men are mortal, and renew their species by generation; and this is common to all living creatures. The two great sexes of male and female, says Milton, animate the world. Why must this circumstance, so universal, so essential, be excluded from those numerous and limited deities? Behold then the theogony of ancient times brought back upon us.

And why not become a perfect Anthropomorphite? Why not assert the deity or deities to be corporeal, and to have eyes, a nose, mouth, ears, etc.? Epicurus maintained, that no man had ever seen reason but in a human figure; therefore the gods must have a human figure. And this argument, which is deservedly so much ridiculed by Cicero, becomes, according to you, solid and philosophical.

In a word, Cleanthes, a man, who follows your hypothesis, is able, perhaps, to assert, or conjecture, that the universe, sometime, arose from something like design: but beyond that position he cannot ascertain one single circumstance, and is left afterwards to fix every point of his theology, by the utmost license of fancy and hypothesis. This world, for aught he knows, is very faulty and imperfect, compared to a superior standard; and was only the first rude essay of some infant deity, who afterwards abandoned it, ashamed of his lame performance: it is the work only of some dependent, inferior deity; and is the object of derision to his superiors: it is the production of old age and dotage in some superannuated deity; and ever since his death, has run on at adventures, from the first impulse and active force, which it received from him. You justly give signs of horror, Demea, at these strange suppositions: but these, and a thousand more of the same kind, are Cleanthes's suppositions, not mine. From the moment the attributes of the Deity are supposed finite, all these have place. And I cannot, for my part, think, that so wild and unsettled a system of theology is, in any respect, preferable to none at all.

These suppositions I absolutely disown, cried Cleanthes: they strike me, however, with no horror; especially, when proposed in that rambling way in which they drop from you. On the contrary, they give me pleasure, when I see, that, by the utmost indulgence of your imagination, you never get rid of the hypothesis of design in the universe; but are obliged, at every turn, to have recourse to it. To this concession I adhere steadily; and this I regard as a sufficient foundation for religion.

37

Agnosticism and the Duty of Faith

THOMAS H. HUXLEY

When I reached intellectual maturity and began to ask myself whether I was an atheist, a theist, or a pantheist; a materialist or an idealist; a Christian or a freethinker; I found that the more I learned and reflected, the less ready was the answer; until, at last, I came to the conclusion that I had neither art nor part with any of these denominations, except the last. The one thing in which most of these good people were agreed was the one thing in which I differed from them. They were quite sure they had attained a certain "gnosis,"—had, more or less successfully, solved the problem of existence; while I was quite sure I had not, and had a pretty strong conviction that the problem was insoluble. And, with Hume and Kant on my side, I could not think myself presumptuous in holding fast by that opinion. . . .

This was my situation when I had the good fortune to find a place among the members of that remarkable confraternity of antagonists, long since deceased, but of green and pious memory, the Metaphysical Society. Every variety of philosophical and theological opinion was represented there, and expressed itself with entire openness; most of my colleagues were -*ists* of one sort or another; and, however kind and friendly they might be, I, the man without a rag of a label to cover himself with, could not fail to have some of the uneasy feelings which must have beset the historical fox when, after leaving the trap in which his tail remained, he presented himself

[From *Science and Christian Tradition* (New York: D. Appleton & Company, Inc., 1898), chapters VII, IX.]

to his normally elongated companions. So I took thought, and invented what I conceived to be the appropriate title of "agnostic." It came into my head as suggestive antithetic to the "gnostic" of Church history, who professed to know so much about the very things of which I was ignorant; and I took the earliest opportunity of parading it at our Society, to show that I, too, had a tail, like the other foxes. To my great satisfaction, the term took; and when the *Spectator* had stood godfather to it, any suspicion in the minds of respectable people, that a knowledge of its parentage might have awakened was, of course, completely lulled.

That is the history of the origin of the terms "agnostic" and "agnosticism;" and it will be observed that it does not quite agree with the confident assertion of the reverend Principal of King's College, that "the adoption of the term agnostic is only an attempt to shift the issue, and that it involves a mere evasion" in relation to the Church and Christianity.

The last objection . . . which I have to take to Dr. Wace's deliverance before the Church Congress arises, I am sorry to say, on a question of morality.

"It is, and it ought to be," authoritatively declares this official representative of Christian ethics, "an unpleasant thing for a man to have to say plainly that he does not believe in Jesus Christ." . . .

Whether it is so depends, I imagine, a good deal on whether the man was brought up in a Christian household or not. I do not see why it should be "unpleasant" for a Mohammedan or Buddhist to say so. But that "it ought to be" unpleasant for any man to say anything which he sincerely, and after due deliberation, believes, is, to my mind, a proposition of the most profoundly immoral character. I verily believe that the great good which has been effected in the world by Christianity has been largely counteracted by the pestilent doctrine on which all the Churches have insisted, that honest disbelief in their more or less astonishing creeds is a moral offence, indeed a sin of the deepest dye, deserving and involving the same future retribution as murder and robbery. If we could only see, in one view, the torrents of hypocrisy and cruelty, the lies, the slaughter, the violations of every obligation of humanity, which have flowed from this source along the course of the history of Christian nations, our worst imaginations of Hell would pale beside the vision.

A thousand times, no! It ought *not* to be unpleasant to say that which one honestly believes or disbelieves. That it so constantly is painful to do so, is quite enough obstacle to the progress of mankind in that most valuable of all qualities, honesty of word or of deed, without erecting a sad concomitant of human weakness into something to be admired and cherished. . . .

I am very well aware, as I suppose most thoughtful people are in these times, that the process of breaking away from old beliefs is extremely unpleasant; and I am much disposed to think that the encouragement, the consolation, and the peace afforded to earnest believers in even the worst forms of Christianity are of great practical advantage to them. What deductions must be made from this gain on the score of the harm done to the citizen by the ascetic other-worldliness of logical Christianity; to the ruler, by the hatred, malice, and all uncharitableness of sectarian bigotry; to the legislator, by the spirit of exclusiveness and domination of those that count themselves pillars of orthodoxy; to the philosopher, by the restraints on the freedom of learning and teaching which every Church exercises, when it is strong enough; to the conscientious soul, by the introspective hunting after sins of the mint and cummin types, the fear of theological error, and the overpowering terror of possible damnation, which have accompanied the Churches like their shadow, I need not now consider; but they are assuredly not small. If agnostics lose heavily on the one side, they gain a good deal on the other. People who talk about the comforts of belief appear to forget its discomforts; they ignore the fact that the Christianity of the Churches is something more than faith in the ideal personality of Jesus, which they create for themselves, *plus* so much

as can be carried into practice, without disorganising civil society, of the maxims of the Sermon on the Mount. Trip in morals or in doctrine (especially in doctrine), without due repentance or retractation, or fail to get properly baptized before you die, and a *plébiscite* of the Christians of Europe, if they were true to their creeds, would affirm your everlasting damnation by an immense majority.

Preachers, orthodox and heterodox, din into our ears that the world cannot get on without faith of some sort. There is a sense in which that is as eminently as obviously true; there is another, in which, in my judgment, it is as eminently as obviously false, and it seems to me that the hortatory, or pulpit, mind is apt to oscillate between the false and the true meanings, without being aware of the fact.

It is quite true that the ground of every one of our actions, and the validity of all our reasonings, rest upon the great act of faith, which leads us to take the experience of the past as a safe guide in our dealings with the present and the future. From the nature of ratiocination, it is obvious that the axioms, on which it is based, cannot be demonstrated by ratiocination. It is also a trite observation that, in the business of life, we constantly take the most serious action upon evidence of an utterly insufficient character. But it is surely plain that faith is not necessarily entitled to dispense with ratiocination because ratiocination cannot dispense with faith as a starting-point; and that because we are often obliged, by the pressure of events, to act on very bad evidence, it does not follow that it is proper to act on such evidence when the pressure is absent. . . .

. . . Agnosticism, in fact, is not a creed, but a method, the essence of which lies in the rigorous application of a single principle. That principle is of great antiquity; it is as old as Socrates; as old as the writer who said, "Try all things, hold fast by that which is good;" it is the foundation of the Reformation, which simply illustrated the axiom that every man should be able to give a reason for the faith that is in him; it is the great principle of Descartes; it is the fundamental axiom of modern science. Positively the principle may be expressed: In matters of the intellect, follow your reason as far as it will take you, without regard to any other consideration. And negatively: In matters of the intellect do not pretend that conclusions are certain which are not demonstrated or demonstrable. That I take to be the agnostic faith, which if a man keep whole and undefiled, he shall not be ashamed to look the universe in the face, whatever the future may have in store for him. . . .

The present discussion has arisen out of the use, which has become general in the last few years, of the terms "Agnostic" and "Agnosticism."

The people who call themselves "Agnostics" have been charged with doing so because they have not the courage to declare themselves "Infidels." It has been insinuated that they have adopted a new name in order to escape the unpleasantness which attaches to their proper denomination. To this wholly erroneous imputation, I have replied by showing that the term "Agnostic" did, as a matter of fact, arise in a manner which negatives it; and my statement has not been, and cannot be, refuted. Moreover, speaking for myself, and without impugning the right of any other person to use the term in another sense, I further say that Agnosticism is not properly described as a "negative" creed, nor indeed as a creed of any kind, except in so far as it expresses absolute faith in the validity of a principle, which is as much ethical as intellectual. This principle may be stated in various ways, but they all amount to this: that it is wrong for a man to say that he is certain of the objective truth of any proposition unless he can produce evidence which logically justifies that certainty. This is what Agnosticism asserts; and, in my opinion, it is all that is essential to Agnosticism. That which Agnostics deny and repudiate, as immoral, is the contrary doctrine, that there are propositions which men ought to believe, without logically satisfactory evidence; and that reprobation ought to attach to the profession of disbelief in such inadequately supported propositions. The justification of the Agnostic principle lies in the success which follows upon its application, whether in the field of natural, or in that of civil, history; and in the fact that, so far as these topics are concerned, no sane man thinks of denying its validity. . . .

The extent of the region of the uncertain, the number of the problems the investigation of which ends in a verdict of not proven, will vary according to the knowledge and the intellectual habits of the individual Agnostic. I do not very much care to speak of anything as "unknowable." What I am sure about is that there are many topics about which I know nothing; and which, so far as I can see, are out of reach of my faculties. But whether these things are knowable by any one else is exactly one of those matters which is beyond my knowledge, though I may have a tolerably strong opinion as to the probabilities of the case. . . .

It was inevitable that a conflict should arise between Agnosticism and Theology; or rather, I ought to say, between Agnosticism and Ecclesiasticism. For Theology, the science, is one thing; and Ecclesiasticism, the championship of a foregone conclusion as to the truth of a particular form of Theology, is another. With scientific Theology, Agnosticism has no quarrel. On the contrary, the Agnostic, knowing too well the influence of prejudice and idiosyncrasy, even on those who desire most earnestly to be impartial, can wish for

nothing more urgently than that the scientific theologian should not only be at perfect liberty to thresh out the matter in his own fashion; but that he should, if he can, find flaws in the Agnostic position; and, even if demonstration is not to be had, that he should put, in their full force, the grounds of the conclusions he thinks probable. The scientific theologian admits the Agnostic principle, however widely his results may differ from those reached by the majority of Agnostics.

But, as between Agnosticism and Ecclesiasticism, or, as our neighbours across the Channel call it, Clericalism, there can be neither peace nor truce. The Cleric asserts that it is morally wrong not to believe certain propositions, whatever the results of a strict scientific investigation of the evidence of these propositions. He tells us "that religious error is, in itself, of an immoral nature." He declares that he has prejudged certain conclusions, and looks upon those who show cause for arrest of judgment as emissaries of Satan. It necessarily follows that, for him, the attainment of faith, not the ascertainment of truth, is the highest aim of mental life. And, on careful analysis of the nature of this faith, it will too often be found to be, not the mystic process of unity with the Divine, understood by the religious enthusiast; but that which the candid simplicity of a Sunday scholar once defined it to be. "Faith," said this unconscious plagiarist of Tertullian, "is the power of saying you believe things which are incredible."

Now I, and many other Agnostics, believe that faith, in this sense, is an abomination; and though we do not indulge in the luxury of self-righteousness so far as to call those who are not of our way of thinking hard names, we do feel that the disagreement between ourselves and those who hold this doctrine is even more moral than intellectual. . . .

I trust that I have now made amends for any ambiguity, or want of fulness, in my previous exposition of that which I hold to be the essence of the Agnostic doctrine. Henceforward, I might hope to hear no more of the assertion that we are necessarily Materialists, Idealists, Atheists, Theists, or any other *ists*, if experience had led me to think that the proved falsity of a statement was any guarantee against its repetition. And those who appreciate the nature of our position will see, at once, that when Ecclesiasticism declares that we ought to believe this, that, and the other, and are very wicked if we don't, it is impossible for us to give any answer but this: We have not the slightest objection to believe anything you like, if you will give us good grounds for belief; but, if you cannot, we must respectfully refuse, even if that refusal should wreck morality and insure our own damnation several times over. We are quite content to leave that to the decision of the future. The course of the past has impressed us with the firm conviction that no good ever comes of falsehood, and we feel warranted in refusing even to experiment in that direction.

38

The Essence of Religion

LUDWIG FEUERBACH

In the perceptions of the senses consciousness of the object is distinguishable from consciousness of self; but in religion, consciousness of the object and self-consciousness coincide. The object of the senses is out of man, the religious object is within him, and therefore as little forsakes him as his self-consciousness or his conscience; it is the intimate, the closest object. "God," says Augustine, for example, "is nearer, more related to us, and therefore more easily known by us, than sensible, corporeal things." The object of the senses is in itself indifferent—independent of the disposition or of the judgment; but the object of religion is a selected object; the most excellent, the first, the supreme being; it essentially presupposes a critical judgment, a discrimination between the divine and the non-divine, between that which is worthy of adoration and that which is not worthy. And here may be applied, without any limitation, the proposition: the object of any subject is nothing else than the subject's own nature taken objectively. Such as are a man's thoughts and dispositions, such is his God; so much worth as a man has, so much and no more has his God. Consciousness of God is self-consciousness, knowledge of God is self-knowledge. By his God thou knowest the man, and by the man his God; the two are identical. Whatever is God to a man, that is his heart and soul; and conversely, God is the manifested inward nature, the expressed self of a man,—religion the solemn unveiling of a man's hidden treasures, the revelation of his intimate thoughts, the open confession of his love-secrets.

But when religion—consciousness of God—is designated as the

[From *The Essence of Christianity,* chapter 1, section 2. First published in 1843. English translation by George Eliot (Marian Evans) first published in 1854.]

self-consciousness of man, this is not to be understood as affirming that the religious man is directly aware of this identity; for, on the contrary, ignorance of it is fundamental to the peculiar nature of religion. To preclude this misconception, it is better to say, religion is man's earliest and also indirect form of self-knowledge. Hence, religion everywhere precedes philosophy, as in the history of the race, so also in that of the individual. Man first of all sees his nature as if *out of* himself, before he finds it in himself. His own nature is in the first instance contemplated by him as that of another being. Religion is the childlike condition of humanity; but the child sees his nature—man—out of himself; in childhood a man is an object to himself, under the form of another man. Hence the historical progress of religion consists in this: that what by an earlier religion was regarded as objective, is now recognised as subjective; that is, what was formerly contemplated and worshipped as God is now perceived to be something *human*. What was at first religion becomes at a later period idolatry; man is seen to have adored his own nature. Man has given objectivity to himself, but has not recognised the object as his own nature: a later religion takes this forward step; every advance in religion is therefore a deeper self-knowledge. But every particular religion, while it pronounces its predecessors idolatrous, excepts itself—and necessarily so, otherwise it would no longer be religion—from the fate, the common nature of all religions: it imputes only to other religions what is the fault, if fault it be, of religion in general. Because it has a different object, a different tenor, because it has transcended the ideas of preceding religions, it erroneously supposes itself exalted above the necessary eternal laws which constitute the essence of religion—it fancies its object, its ideas, to be superhuman. But the essence of religion, thus hidden from the religious, is evident to the thinker, by whom religion is viewed objectively, which it cannot be by its votaries. And it is our task to show that the antithesis of divine and human is altogether illusory, that it is nothing else than the antithesis between the human nature in general and the human individual; that, consequently the object and contents of the Christian religion are altogether human.

Religion, at least the Christian, is the relation of man to himself, or more correctly to his own nature (*i.e.,* his subjective nature); but a relation to it, viewed as a nature apart from his own. The divine being is nothing else than the human being, or, rather, the human nature purified, freed from the limits of the individual man, made objective—*i.e.,* contemplated and revered as another, a distinct being. All the attributes of the divine nature are, therefore, attributes of the human nature.

In relation to the attributes, the predicates, of the Divine Being, this is admitted without hesitation, but by no means in relation to the subject of these predicates. The negation of the subject is held to be ir-religion, nay, atheism; though not so the negation of the predicates. But that which has no predicates or qual-ities, has no effect upon me; that which has no effect upon me has no existence for me. To deny all the qualities of a being is equivalent to denying the being himself. A being without qualities is one which can-not become an object to the mind, and such a being is virtually non-ex-istent. Where man deprives God of all qualities, God is no longer any-thing more to him than a negative being. To the truly religious man, God is not a being without qualities, because to him he is a positive, real being. The theory that God cannot be defined, and consequently can-not be known by man, is therefore the offspring of recent times, a prod-uct of modern unbelief. . . .

That which is to man the self-existent, the highest being, to which he can conceive nothing higher—that is to him the Divine Being. How then should he inquire concerning this being, what he is in himself? If God were an object to the bird, he would be a winged being: the bird knows nothing higher, nothing more blissful, than the winged condition. How ludicrous would it be if this bird pronounced: To me God ap-pears as a bird, but what he is in himself I know not. To the bird the highest nature is the bird-nature; take from him the conception of this, and you take from him the concep-tion of the highest being. How, then, could he ask whether God in himself were winged? To ask whether God is in himself what he is for me, is to ask whether God is God, is to lift oneself above one's God, to rise up against him.

Wherever, therefore, this idea, that the religious predicates are only anthropomorphisms, has taken pos-session of a man, there has doubt, has unbelief, obtained the mastery of faith. And it is only the inconse-quence of faint-heartedness and in-tellectual imbecility which does not proceed from this idea to the formal negation of the predicates, and from thence to the negation of the subject to which they relate. If thou doubtest the objective truth of the predicates, thou must also doubt the objective truth of the subject whose predicates they are. If thy predicates are an-thropomorphisms, the subject of them is an anthropomorphism too. If love, goodness, personality, etc., are human attributes, so also is the subject which thou presupposest, the existence of God, the belief that there is a God, an anthropomorph-ism—a presupposition purely hu-man. Whence knowest thou that the belief in a God at all is not a limi-tation of man's mode of conception? Higher beings—and thou supposest such—are perhaps so blest in them-selves, so at unity with themselves, that they are not hung in suspense between themselves and a yet higher being. To know God and not oneself to be God, to know blessedness and not oneself to enjoy it, is a state of disunity, of unhappiness. Higher beings know nothing of this unhappiness; they have no conception of that which they are not.

Thou believest in love as a divine attribute because thou thyself lovest; thou believest that God is a wise, benevolent being because thou knowest nothing better in thyself than benevolence and wisdom; and thou believest that God exists, that therefore he is a subject—whatever exists is a subject, whether it be defined as substance, person, essence, or otherwise—because thou thyself existest, art thyself a subject. Thou knowest no higher human good than to love, than to be good and wise; and even so thou knowest no higher happiness than to exist, to be a subject; for the consciousness of all reality, of all bliss, is for thee bound up in the consciousness of being a subject, of existing. God is an existence, a subject to thee, for the same reason that he is to thee a wise, a blessed, a personal being. . . .

Whatever man conceives to be true, he immediately conceives to be real (that is, to have an objective existence), because, originally, only the real is true to him—true in opposition to what is merely conceived, dreamed, imagined. The idea of being, of existence, is the original idea of truth; or, originally, man makes truth dependent on existence, subsequently, existence dependent on truth. Now God is the nature of man regarded as absolute truth,—the truth of man; but God, or, what is the same thing, religion, is as various as are the conditions under which man conceives this his nature, regards it as the highest being. These conditions, then, under which man conceives God, are to him the truth, and for that reason they are also the highest existence, or rather they are existence itelf; for only the emphatic, the highest existence, is existence, and deserves this name. Therefore, God is an existent, real being, on the very same ground that he is a particular, definite being; for the qualities of God are nothing else than the essential qualities of man himself, and a particular man is what he is, has his existence, his reality, only in his particular conditions. Take away from the Greek the quality of being Greek, and you take away his existence. On this ground it is true that for a definite positive religion—that is, relatively—the certainty of the existence of God is *immediate;* for just as involuntarily, as necessarily, as the Greek was a Greek, so necessarily were his gods Greek beings, so necessarily were they real, existent beings. Religion is that conception of the nature of the world and of man which is essential to, *i.e.,* identical with, a man's nature. . . .

. . . So long as man is in a mere state of nature, so long is his god a mere nature-god—a personification of some natural force. Where man inhabits houses, he also encloses his gods in temples. The temple is only a manifestation of the value which man attaches to beautiful buildings. Temples in honour of religion are in truth temples in honour of architecture. With the emerging of man from a state of savagery and wildness to one of culture, with the distinction between what is fitting for man and what is not fitting, arises simultaneously the distinction between that which is fitting and that which is not fitting for God. God is the idea of majesty, of the highest dignity: the religious sentiment is the sentiment of supreme fitness. The later more cultured artists of Greece were the first to embody in the statues of the gods the ideas of dignity, of spiritual grandeur, of imperturbable repose and serenity. But why were these qualities in their view attributes, predicates of God? Because they were in themselves regarded by the Greeks as divinities. Why did those artists exclude all disgusting and low passions? Because they perceived them to be unbecoming, unworthy, unhuman, and consequently ungodlike. The Homeric gods eat and drink;—that implies eating and drinking is a divine pleasure. Physical strength is an attribute of the Homeric gods: Zeus is the strongest of the gods. Why? Because physical strength, in and by itself, was regarded as something glorious, divine. To the ancient Germans the highest virtues were those of the warrior; therefore their supreme god was the god of war, Odin,—war, "the original or oldest law." Not the attribute of the divinity, but the divineness or deity of the attribute, is the first true Divine Being. Thus what theology and philosophy have held to be God, the Absolute, the Infinite, is not God; but that which they have held not to be God is God: namely, the attribute, the quality, whatever has reality. Hence he alone is the true atheist to whom the predicates of the Divine Being,—for example, love, wisdom, justice,—are nothing; not he to whom merely the subject of these predicates is nothing. And in no wise is the negation of the subject necessarily also a negation of the predicates considered in themselves. These have an intrinsic, independent reality; they force their recognition upon man by their very nature; they are self-evident truths to him; they prove, they attest themselves. It does not follow that goodness, justice, wisdom, are chimaeras because the existence of God is a chimaera, nor truths because this is a truth. The idea of God is dependent on the idea of justice, of benevolence; a God who is not benevolent, not just, not wise, is no God; but the converse does not hold. The fact is not that a quality is divine because God has it, but that God has it because it is in itself divine: because without it God would be a defective being. Justice, wisdom, in general every quality which constitutes the divinity of God, is determined and known by itself independently, but the idea of God is determined by the qualities which have thus been previously judged to be worthy of the divine nature; only in the case in which I identify God and justice, in which I think of God immediately as the reality of the idea of justice, is the idea of God self-determined. But if God as a subject is the determined, while the quality, the predicate, is the determining, then in truth the rank of the godhead is due not to the subject, but to the predicate. . . .

Now, when it is shown that what the subject is lies entirely in the attributes of the subject; that is, that the predicate is the true subject; it is also proved that if the divine predicates are attributes of the human nature, the subject of those predicates is also of the human nature. But the divine predicates are partly general, partly personal. The general predicates are the metaphysical, but these serve only as external points of support to religion; they are not the characteristic definitions of religion. It is the personal predicates alone which constitute the essence of religion—in which the Divine Being is the object of religion. Such are, for example, that God is a Person, that he is the moral Lawgiver, the Father of mankind, the Holy One, the Just, the Good, the Merciful. It is, however, at once clear, or it will at least be clear in the sequel, with regard to these and other defini-

tions, that, especially as applied to a personality, they are purely human definitions, and that consequently, man in religion—in his relation to God—is in relation to his own nature; for to the religious sentiment these predicates are not mere conceptions, mere images, which man forms of God, to be distinguished from that which God is in himself, but truths, facts, realities. Religion knows nothing of anthropomorphisms; to it they are not anthropomorphisms. It is the very essence of religion, that to it these definitions express the nature of God. They are pronounced to be images only by the understanding, which reflects on religion, and which while defending them yet before its own tribunal denies them. But to the religious sentiment God is a real Father, real Love and Mercy; for to it he is a real, living, personal being, and therefore his attributes are also living and personal. Nay, the definitions which are the most sufficing to the religious sentiment are precisely those which give the most offence to the understanding, and which in the process of reflection on religion it denies. Religion is essentially emotion; hence, objectively also, emotion is to it necessarily of a divine nature. Even anger appears to it an emotion not unworthy of God, provided only there be a religious motive at the foundation of this anger.

But here it is also essential to observe, and this phenomenon is an extremely remarkable one, characterising the very core of religion, that in proportion as the divine subject is in reality human, the greater is the apparent difference between God and man; that is, the more, by reflection on religion, by theology, is the identity of the divine and human denied, and the human, considered as such, is depreciated. The reason of this is, that as what is positive in the conception of the divine being can only be human, the conception of man, as an object of consciousness, can only be negative. To enrich God, man must become poor; that God may be all, man must be nothing. But he desires to be nothing in himself, because what he takes from himself is not lost to him, since it is preserved in God. Man has his being in God; why then should he have it in himself? Where is the necessity of positing the same thing twice, of having it twice? What man withdraws from himself, what he renounces in himself, he only enjoys in an incomparably higher and fuller measure in God. . . .

39

Mysticism

BERTRAND RUSSELL

Ought we to admit that there is available, in support of religion, a source of knowledge which lies outside science and may properly be described as "revelation"? This is a difficult question to argue, because those who believe that truths have been revealed to them profess the same kind of certainty in regard to them that we have in regard to objects of sense. We believe the man who has seen things through the telescope that we have never seen; why, then, they ask, should we not believe them when they report things that are to them equally unquestionable?

It is, perhaps, useless to attempt an argument such as will appeal to the man who has himself enjoyed mystic illumination. But something can be said as to whether we others should accept this testimony. In the first place, it is not subject to the ordinary tests. When a man of science tells us the result of an experiment, he also tells us how the experiment was performed; others can repeat it, and if the result is not confirmed it is not accepted as true; but many men might put themselves into the situation in which the mystic's vision occurred without obtaining the same revelation. To this it may be answered that a man must use the appropriate sense: a telescope is useless to a man who keeps his eyes shut. The argument as to the credibility of the mystic's testimony may be prolonged almost indefinitely. Science should be neutral, since the argument is a scientific one, to be conducted exactly as an argument would be conducted about an uncertain experiment. Science depends upon perception and inference; its credibility is due to the fact that the perceptions are such as any observer can test. The mystic

[From *Religion and Science* by Bertrand Russell (1935), pp. 177–189. Reprinted by permission of Oxford University Press.]

himself may be certain that he *knows,* and has no need of scientific tests; but those who are asked to accept his testimony will subject it to the same kind of scientific tests as those applied to men who say they have been to the North Pole. Science, as such, should have no expectation, positive or negative, as to the result.

The chief argument in favour of the mystics is their agreement with each other. "I know nothing more remarkable," says Dean Inge, "than the unanimity of the mystics, ancient, mediaeval, and modern, Protestant, Catholic, and even Buddhist or Mohammedan, though the Christian mystics are the most trustworthy." I do not wish to underrate the force of this argument, which I acknowledged long ago in a book called *Mysticism and Logic.* The mystics vary greatly in their capacity for giving verbal expression to their experiences, but I think we may take it that those who succeeded best all maintain: (1) that all division and separateness is unreal, and that the universe is a single indivisible unity; (2) that evil is illusory, and that the illusion arises through falsely regarding a part as self-subsistent; (3) that time is unreal, and that reality is eternal, not in the sense of being everlasting, but in the sense of being wholly outside time. I do not pretend that this is a complete account of the matters on which all mystics concur, but the three propositions that I have mentioned may serve as representatives of the whole. Let us

now imagine ourselves a jury in a law-court, whose business it is to decide on the credibility of the witnesses who make these three somewhat surprising assertions.

We shall find, in the first place, that, while the witnesses agree up to a point, they disagree totally when that point is passed, although they are just as certain as when they agree. Catholics, but not Protestants, may have visions in which the Virgin appears; Christians and Mohammedans, but not Buddhists, may have great truths revealed to them by the Archangel Gabriel; the Chinese mystics of the Tao tell us, as a direct result of their central doctrine, that all government is bad, whereas most European and Mohammedan mystics, with equal confidence, urge submission to constituted authority. As regards the points where they differ, each group will argue that the other groups are untrustworthy; we might, therefore, if we were content with a mere forensic triumph, point out that most mystics think most other mystics mistaken on most points. They might, however, make this only half a triumph by agreeing on the greater importance of the matters about which they are at one, as compared with those as to which their opinions differ. We will, in any case, assume that they have composed their differences, and concentrated the defence at these three points—namely, the unity of the world, the illusory nature of evil, and the unreality of time. What test can we, as impartial outsiders, apply to their unanimous evidence?

As men of scientific temper, we shall naturally first ask whether there is any way by which we can ourselves obtain the same evidence at first hand. To this we shall receive various answers. We may be told that we are obviously not in a receptive frame of mind, and that we lack the requisite humility; or that fasting and religious meditation are necessary; or (if our witness is Indian or Chinese) that the essential prerequisite is a course of breathing exercises. I think we shall find that the weight of experimental evidence is in favour of this last view, though fasting also has been frequently found effective. As a matter of fact, there is a definite physical discipline, called yoga, which is practised in order to produce the mystic's certainty, and which is recommended with much confidence by those who have tried it. Breathing exercises are its most essential feature, and for our purposes we may ignore the rest.

In order to see how we could test the assertion that yoga gives insight, let us artificially simplify this assertion. Let us suppose that a number of people assure us that if, *for a certain time,* we breathe in a certain way, we shall become convinced that time is unreal. Let us go further, and suppose that, having tried their recipe, we have ourselves experienced a state of mind such as they describe. But now, having returned to our normal mode of respiration, we are not quite sure whether the vision was to be believed. How shall we investigate this question?

First of all, what can be meant by saying that time is unreal? If we really mean what we say, we must mean that such statements as "this is before that" are mere empty noise, like "twas brillig." If we suppose anything less than this—as, for example, that there is a relation between events which puts them in the same order as the relation of earlier and later, but that it is a different relation—we shall not have made any assertion that makes any real change in our outlook. It will be merely like supposing that the Iliad was not written by Homer, but by another man of the same name. We have to suppose that there are no "events" at all; there must be only the one vast whole of the universe, embracing whatever is real in the misleading appearance of a temporal procession. There must be nothing in reality corresponding to the apparent distinction between earlier and later events. To say that we are born, and then grow, and then die, must be just as false as to say that we die, then grow small, and finally are born. The truth of what seems an individual life is merely the illusory isolation of one element in the timeless and indivisible being of the universe. There is no distinction between improvement and deterioration, no difference between sorrows that end in happiness and happiness that ends in sorrow. If you find a corpse with a dagger in it, it makes no difference whether the man died of the wound or the dagger was plunged in after death. Such a view, if true, puts an end, not only to science, but to prudence, hope, and effort; it is incompatible with worldly wisdom, and—what is more important to religion—with morality.

Most mystics, of course, do not accept these conclusions in their entirety, but they urge doctrines from which these conclusions inevitably follow. Thus Dean Inge rejects the kind of religion that appeals to evolution, because it lays too much stress upon a temporal process. "There is no law of progress, and there is no universal progress," he says. And again: "The doctrine of automatic and universal progress, the lay religion of many Victorians, labours under the disadvantage of being almost the only philosophical theory which can be definitely disproved." On this matter, which I shall discuss at a later stage, I find myself in agreement with the Dean, for whom, on many grounds, I have a very high respect. But he naturally does not draw from his premises all the inferences which seem to me to be warranted.

It is important not to caricature the doctrine of mysticism, in which there is, I think, a core of wisdom. Let us see how it seeks to avoid the extreme consequences which seem to follow from the denial of time.

The philosophy based upon mysticism has a great tradition, from Parmenides to Hegel. Parmenides says: "What is, is uncreated and indestructible; for it is complete, immovable, and without end. Nor was it ever, nor will it be; for now *it is,* all at once, a continuous one." He introduced into metaphysics the distinction between reality and appearance, or the way of truth and the way of opinion, as he calls them. It is clear that whoever denies the reality of time must introduce some such distinction, since obviously the world *appears* to be in time. It is also clear that, if everyday experience is not to be *wholly* illusory, there must be some relation between appearance and the reality behind it. It is at this point, however, that the greatest difficulties arise: if the relation between appearance and reality is made too intimate, all the unpleasant features of appearance will have their unpleasant counterparts in reality, while if the relation is made too remote, we shall be unable to make inferences from the character of appearance to that of reality, and reality will be left a vague Unknowable, as with Herbert Spencer. For Christians, there is the related difficulty of avoiding pantheism: if the world is *only* apparent, God created nothing, and the reality corresponding to the world is a part of God; but if the world is in any degree real and distinct from God, we abandon the wholeness of everything, which is an essential doctrine of mysticism, and we are compelled to suppose that, in so far as the world is real, the evil which it contains is also real. Such difficulties make thorough-going mysticism very difficult for an orthodox Christian. As the Bishop of Birmingham says: "All forms of pantheism ... as it seems to me, must be rejected because, if man is actually a part of God, the evil in man is also in God."

All this time I have been supposing that we are a jury, listening to the testimony of the mystics, and trying to decide whether to accept or reject it. If, when they deny the reality of the world of sense, we took them to mean "reality" in the ordinary sense of the law-courts, we should have no hesitation in rejecting what they say, since we should find that it runs counter to all other testimony, and even to their own in their mundane moments. We must therefore look for some other sense. I believe that, when the mystics contrast "reality" with "appearance," the word "reality" has not a logical, but an emotional, significance: it means what is, in some sense, important. When it is said that time is "unreal," what should be said is that, in some sense and on some occasions, it is important to conceive the universe as a whole, as the Creator, if He existed, must have conceived it in deciding to create it. When so conceived, all process is within one completed whole; past, present, and future, all exist, in some sense, together, and the present does not have that pre-eminent reality which it has to our usual ways of apprehending the world. If this interpretation is accepted, mysticism expresses an emotion, not a fact; it does not assert anything, and there-

fore can be neither confirmed nor contradicted by science. The fact that mystics do make assertions is owing to their inability to separate emotional importance from scientific validity. It is, of course, not to be expected that they will accept this view, but it is the only one, so far as I can see, which, while admitting something of their claim, is not repugnant to the scientific intelligence.

The certainty and partial unanimity of mystics is no conclusive reason for accepting their testimony on a matter of fact. The man of science, when he wishes others to see what he has seen, arranges his microscope or telescope; that is to say, he makes changes in the external world, but demands of the observer only normal eyesight. The mystic, on the other hand, demands changes in the observer, by fasting, by breathing exercises, and by a careful abstention from external observation. (Some object to such discipline, and think that the mystic illumination cannot be artificially achieved; from a scientific point of view, this makes their case more difficult to test than that of those who rely on yoga. But nearly all agree that fasting and an ascetic life are helpful.) We all know that opium, hashish, and alcohol produce certain effects on the observer, but as we do not think these effects admirable we take no account of them in our theory of the universe. They may even, sometimes, reveal fragments of truth; but we do not regard them as sources of general wisdom. The drunkard who sees snakes does not imagine, afterwards, that he has had a revelation of a reality hidden from others, though some not wholly dissimilar belief must have given rise to the worship of Bacchus. In our own day, as William James related, there have been people who considered that the intoxication produced by laughing-gas revealed truths which are hidden at normal times. From a scientific point of view, we can make no distinction between the man who eats little and sees heaven and the man who drinks much and sees snakes. Each is in an abnormal physical condition, and therefore has abnormal perceptions. Normal perceptions, since they have to be useful in the struggle for life, must have some correspondence with fact; but in abnormal perceptions there is no reason to expect such correspondence, and their testimony, therefore, cannot outweigh that of normal perception.

The mystic emotion, if it is freed from unwarranted beliefs, and not so overwhelming as to remove a man wholly from the ordinary business of life, may give something of very great value—the same kind of thing, though in a heightened form, that is given by contemplation. Breadth and calm and profundity may all have their source in this emotion, in which, for the moment, all self-centred desire is dead, and the mind becomes a mirror for the vastness of the universe. Those who have had this experience, and believe it to be bound up unavoidably with assertions about the nature of the universe, naturally cling to these assertions. I believe myself that the assertions are inessential, and that there is no reason to believe them true. I cannot admit any method of arriving at truth except that of science, but in the realm of the emotions I do not deny the value of the experiences which have given rise to religion. Through association with false beliefs, they have led to much evil as well as good; freed from this association, it may be hoped that the good alone will remain.

AFTERWORD

In many of the preceding selections questions are raised about the ways in which we form our beliefs. You may find it worthwhile to extend these questions outside the context of debate about religious beliefs. Are there other sources of knowledge besides reason and experience? If the testimony of such sources were to conflict with that of reason or experience, which should be preferred, and why? Could there be a moral obligation to hold certain beliefs? What sorts of situations would produce such an obligation? Is it possible to *choose* to believe something, even when no evidence or observations give you a reason for such belief? These questions reflect a concern with a very fundamental philosophical problem—determining what constitutes a correct method for formulation of our beliefs, and what it means to say that such a method is correct.

Some aspects of the significance of these selections will become clearer if you carefully consider the importance of the conclusions of the arguments. For example, consider the argument from design. If it did prove that the universe had a designer, would that really be a sufficient foundation for religion and religious practices? Remember, religious attitudes and practices typically include features such as worship and obedience to a code of behavior, often at the cost of great sacrifice and expenditure of time and resources. Also, typically involved are attitudes of hope or confidence that divine love and charity finally will improve our lot. But such practices and attitudes would hardly seem appropriate with respect to some possible designers. What, for instance, if the world were designed experimentally by a Committee, whose members have since abandoned it as a bad idea and gone their separate ways to engage in more worthwhile things? What if it were all a joke? As Hume points out, religious institutions seem to require more for their justification than the mere existence of design. What is needed besides is some knowledge of the character of the designer. It is a good idea to ask of all the arguments presented: If this kind of being were proved to exist (or proved not to exist), what reason would that give us for taking up or abandoning various practices and attitudes?

But, as frequently happens in philosophy, this suggestion raises some further questions. Specifically, it leads one to wonder just what kinds of practices and attitudes would be appropriate for various kinds of deities, and *why* they would be appropriate. If there are significant differences among, say, love, respect and reverence, which would be appropriate toward what kinds of beings? Is blind obedience to the will of an omnipotent deity morally justified, or is it just a prudent idea? Does the kind of being which would welcome worship deserve it? Some considerations pertinent to these questions are found in the selections included in Chapter 10.

REVIEW QUESTIONS

Selection 31

1. Carefully state Anselm's argument in your own words.

2. Why is it important for Anselm to prove that we can conceive of the being he calls God? Can you conceive of the being he indicates?

3. Why is it important for Anselm to explain how the fool could believe that God does not exist?

Selection 32

4. In your own words carefully state each of Aquinas's five arguments.

5. Each of the five arguments is designed to prove the existence of a certain kind of being. Has Aquinas proved that it is the *same* being whose existence is established by each argument? Explain.

Selection 33

6. What is the purpose of paragraphs I–VIII in Paley's discussion of the watch?

7. Does Paley actually explain what features of the watch prove to us that it was designed? What features do you think are involved? Do you find these features in the eye or other organs?

8. Could Paley's arguments be employed to show that a being as complex as the Designer (God) must be designed? Why, or why not?

Selection 34

9. Does Pascal attempt to present a proof of God's existence, or something else? Explain.

10. Are there other beings besides the God in whom Pascal believes to which his argument might apply? If so, would that suggest a problem for his argument? Explain.

Selection 35

11. What does James mean by (*a*) live or dead hypotheses; (*b*) live or dead options; (*c*) forced or avoidable options; (*d*) momentous or trivial options?

12. Under what kinds of circumstances does James think it is both possible and appropriate to *choose* to believe something?

13. James describes two principles for guiding our selection of beliefs. What are they, and which of them does he prefer? Explain.

14. Does James try to prove that religious hypotheses are live, forced, momentous options? Does he need to prove it? Explain.

15. Does James present us with more than an elaborate version of Pascal's wager? Explain your answer carefully.

Selection 36

16. Philo raises several doubts about the similarity of natural organisms and artificial mechanisms. Why is this issue important for the argument from design?

17. According to Philo, if design in the natural world were proved, how much would that tell us about the characteristics of the designer? What are his arguments?

18. Cleanthes claims that the proof of design is a sufficient foundation for religion, regardless of the characteristics of the designer. Does that seem correct to you? Explain.

Selection 37

19. Do Huxley and James agree or disagree about whether it should be unpleasant for one to deny religious belief? Explain.

20. Huxley points out certain advantages of the agnostic position. What are they? If Pascal had considered them, might the outcome of the Wager have been different?

21. Huxley seems to think it more important to avoid error than to accept truth. Does he offer us arguments in favor of his preference?

Selection 38

22. What is Feuerbach's account of the origin of religious beliefs? If he is right, does that show that such beliefs are false? Explain.

23. Does Feuerbach offer any sort of proof for his account? What sort of proof, if any, does it require?

Selection 39

24. What sorts of agreement and disagreement does Russell find among mystics? Does he think the amount of agreement supports the mystical claims, counts against them, or is inconclusive?

25. What does Russell mean when he says that mysticism expresses an emotion rather than a fact?

26. What differences between scientific method and the procedures of the mystic seem most important to Russell? Explain.

10

The Problem of Evil

The problem presented in this chapter deals with several beliefs which traditionally are held by theists. Some of these beliefs concern the characteristics God is believed to have, and others concern the moral character of the world. If we add to these beliefs one quite plausible statement, a paradox can be formulated which suggests that something in the theological tradition must be given up. Thus, the problem of evil forms the heart of an argument against traditional theism. This argument, in one form or another, has been used by atheists, agnostics, and nontraditional theists for many centuries. Let us turn to an outline of the problem.

Traditional theism includes belief in the existence of a single deity, who is the creator of our world. Among the properties this deity is thought to have are goodness, wisdom, and power. The extreme view, frequently held, is that God is a *perfect* being, and that divine perfection involves perfect benevolence, omniscience, and omnipotence. That is, God is thought to be a perfect moral being, a being who knows all truths, no matter how difficult or insignificant, and a being who is absolutely unlimited in power. But, in fact, the problem of evil can be raised for somewhat less extreme views in which God is held to be merely *very* good, wise, and powerful.

Traditional theism also acknowledges that there is a substantial amount of evil in the world. Included in this evil is the suffering, unhappiness, and injustice caused by the actions of persons; and also included is the suffering caused by factors such as disease, drought, storms, and earthquakes, for which persons are not responsible. The first kind of evil is called *moral evil*, while the second kind is called *natural evil.*

But, and this is where the problem arises, why would a morally good, wise, and powerful creator allow such evil to occur in the world? A good creator would not wish the evil to occur, and a wise and powerful one would be able to prevent it. Thus, given the evil we observe around us, it seems that at least one of the traditional attributes must be missing. Is God wise and powerful? Then divine goodness is in doubt. Is God wise and good? Then evil must be the result of insufficient power to prevent it. Is God powerful and good? Then evil must result from lack of knowledge. In simplest terms, the traditional theist is confronted with the inconsistency of these three statements:

(1) God (the powerful, wise, and good creator) exists.

(2) There is a great deal of moral and natural evil in the world.

(3) God would not permit a great deal of moral and natural evil in the world.

One way to eliminate the inconsistency, of course, is to give up statement (1). This is the position adopted by the atheist. But it should be noted that one need not adopt atheism in giving up (1). All that is required is the admission of substantial limitation on the part of the creator/designer of the world. The existence of a creator limited in power, or wisdom, or benevolent moral intent, would be perfectly consistent with (2) and (3). Thus, this position has been adopted by some nontraditional theists, as well as atheists.

A second alternative would be to deny that there is any evil in the world. This would save the traditional view of God's perfection and benevolence, but it has the disadvantage of seeming to be obviously false. If the existence of evil is to be denied, it becomes extremely important to be able to explain why what seems to us to be evil really is not. Nor is this alternative a happy one for the traditional theist, for the existence of wickedness, suffering, and injustice plays an important part in the traditional view of the relationship between God and humankind.

Rather than simply rejecting (2), then, some traditional theists have argued that while there is evil in the world, there is no *unnecessary* evil. By this, they mean that if God had created the world in any alternative way, *more* evil would have resulted than we find in the actual world. Thus, the world we have might be called the best possible world. (Note that even an omnipotent being is admitted to be unable to do the impossible, here.) Thus, if there is to be a world at all, this one is held to be the one the traditional deity would choose.

This approach to the problem involves making some adjustment in both (2) and (3). That is, (3) is modified by claiming that there are certain circumstances in which the traditional God would permit some evil in the world, and then modifying (2) so that the evil which is acknowledged to exist is claimed to occur only in those circumstances. Besides claiming (as above) that God would allow some evil in order to prevent other, worse evils, traditional theists have argued that God would allow some evil if it were necessary in order to provide a much more significant good. This is the basic strategy of what has been called the "free-will defense." In the free-will defense it is argued that the moral evil in this world is the result of allowing people to have free will. On this view God *could* have prevented the evil, but only by creating us without freedom and moral responsibility. And the possession of freedom and responsibility is regarded as such a great good that it makes all the resulting moral evil worthwhile.

In the following selections you should try to keep track of several sets of issues. One of these is the question of the conception of God's nature that is involved. Is the discussion being directed only at the traditional perfect, unlimited deity, or is it intended to apply to creators with some limitations, too? A second set of issues involves the character and extent of the evil which is admitted to be in the world. Notice that the issue is not simply whether there is evil, but also how much there is, whether it is avoidable, or whether it is compensated by some other good. And notice that we cannot judge whether a greater evil has been avoided or a greater good secured unless we have some way of deciding just *how bad* the evils we have are. Finally, there are serious questions to be raised about whether we understand *perfection, omnipotence,* and *omniscience* well enough to involve them at all in this debate; or whether, perhaps, they are incoherent or contradictory notions.

40

Suffering and the Nature of God

DAVID HUME

I am indeed persuaded, said Philo, that the best and indeed the only method of bringing every one to a due sense of religion, is by just representations of the misery and wickedness of men. And for that purpose a talent of eloquence and strong imagery is more requisite than that of reasoning and argument. For is it necessary to prove, what every one feels within himself? 'Tis only necessary to make us feel it, if possible, more intimately and sensibly.

The people, indeed, replied Demea, are sufficiently convinced of this great and melancholy truth. The miseries of life, the unhappiness of man, the general corruptions of our nature, the unsatisfactory enjoyment of pleasures, riches, honours; these phrases have become almost proverbial in all languages. And who can doubt of what all men declare from their own immediate feeling and experience?

In this point, said Philo, the learned are perfectly agreed with the vulgar; and in all letters, *sacred* and *profane,* the topic of human misery has been insisted on with the most pathetic eloquence that sorrow and melancholy could inspire. The poets, who speak from sentiment, without a system, and whose testimony has therefore the more authority, abound in images of this nature. From Homer down to Dr. Young, the whole inspired tribe have ever been sensible, that no other representation of things would suit the feeling and observation of each individual.

As to authorities, replied Demea, you need not seek them. Look

[From *Dialogues Concerning Natural Religion,* Part X. First published in 1779.]

round this library of Cleanthes. I shall venture to affirm, that, except authors of particular sciences, such as chymistry or botany, who have no occasion to treat of human life, there is scarce one of those innumerable writers, from whom the sense of human misery has not, in some passage or other, extorted a complaint and confession of it. At least, the chance is entirely on that side; and no one author has ever, so far as I can recollect, been so extravagant as to deny it.

There you must excuse me, said Philo: Leibniz has denied it; and is perhaps the first, who ventured upon so bold and paradoxical an opinion; at least, the first, who made it essential to his philosophical system.

And by being the first, replied Demea, might he not have been sensible of his error? For is this a subject, in which philosophers can propose to make discoveries, especially in so late an age? And can any man hope by a simple denial (for the subject scarcely admits of reasoning) to bear down the united testimony of mankind, founded on sense and consciousness?

And why should man, added he, pretend to an exemption from the lot of all other animals? The whole earth, believe me, Philo, is cursed and polluted. A perpetual war is kindled amongst all living creatures. Necessity, hunger, want, stimulate the strong and courageous: Fear, anxiety, terror, agitate the weak and infirm. The first entrance into life gives anguish to the new-born infant and to its wretched parent: Weakness, impotence, distress, attend each stage of that life: and 'tis at last finished in agony and horror.

Observe too, says Philo, the curious artifices of Nature, in order to imbitter the life of every living being. The stronger prey upon the weaker, and keep them in perpetual terror and anxiety. The weaker too, in their turn, often prey upon the stronger, and vex and molest them without relaxation. Consider that innumerable race of insects, which either are bred on the body of each animal, or flying about infix their stings in him. These insects have others still less than themselves, which torment them. And thus on each hand, before and behind, above and below, every animal is surrounded with enemies, which incessantly seek his misery and distruction.

Man alone, said Demea, seems to be, in part, an exception to this rule. For by combination in society, he can easily master lions, tygers, and bears, whose greater strength and agility naturally enable them to prey upon him.

On the contrary, it is here chiefly, cried Philo, that the uniform and equal maxims of Nature are most apparent. Man, it is true, can, by combination, surmount all his *real* enemies, and become master of the whole animal creation: but does he not immediately raise up to himself *imaginary* enemies, the dæmons of his fancy, who haunt him with superstitious terrors, and blast every enjoyment of life? His pleasure, as he imagines, becomes, in their eyes, a crime: his food and repose give them umbrage and offence: his very sleep and dreams furnish new materials to anxious fear: and even death, his refuge from every other ill, presents only the dread of endless and innumerable woes. Nor does the wolf molest more the timid flock, than superstition does the anxious breast of wretched mortals.

Besides, consider, Demea; this very society, by which we surmount those wild beasts, our natural enemies; what new enemies does it not raise to us? What woe and misery does it not occasion? Man is the greatest enemy of man. Oppression, injustice, contempt, contumely, violence, sedition, war, calumny, treachery, fraud; by these they mutually torment each other: and they would soon dissolve that society which they had formed, were it not for the dread of still greater ills, which must attend their separation.

But though these external insults, said Demea, from animals, from men, from all the elements, which assault us, form a frightful catalogue of woes, they are nothing in comparison of those, which arise within ourselves, from the distempered condition of our mind and body. How many lie under the lingering torment of diseases? Hear the pathetic enumeration of the great poet.

Intestine stone and ulcer, colic-pangs,
Demoniac frenzy, moping melancholy,
And moon-struck madness, pining atrophy,
Marasmus and wide-wasting pestilence.
Dire was the tossing, deep the groans: DESPAIR
Tended the sick, busiest from couch to couch.
And over them triumphant DEATH his dart
Shook, but delay'd to strike, tho' oft invok'd
With vows, as their chief good and final hope.

The disorders of the mind, continued Demea, though more secret, are not perhaps less dismal and vexatious. Remorse, shame, anguish, rage, disappointment, anxiety, fear, dejection, despair; who has ever passed through life without cruel inroads from these tormentors? How many have scarcely ever felt any better sensations? Labour and poverty, so abhorred by every one, are the certain lot of the far greater number; and those few privileged persons, who enjoy ease and opulence, never reach contentment or true felicity. All the goods of life united would not make a very happy man: but all the ills united would make a wretch indeed; and any one of them almost (and who can be free from every one) nay often the absence of one good (and who can possess all) is sufficient to render life ineligible.

Were a stranger to drop, on a sudden, into this world, I would show him, as a specimen of its ills, an hospital full of diseases, a prison crowded with malefactors and debtors, a field of battle strewed with carcases, a fleet floundering in the ocean, a nation languishing under tyranny, famine, or pestilence. To turn the gay side of life to him, and give him a notion of its pleasures; whither should I conduct him? to a ball, to an opera, to court? He might justly think, that I was only showing him a diversity of distress and sorrow.

There is no evading such striking instances, said Philo, but by apologies, which still farther aggravate the charge. Why have all men, I ask, in all ages, complained incessantly of the miseries of life? . . . They have no just reason, says one: these complaints proceed only from their discontented, repining, anxious disposition. . . . And can there possibly, I reply, be a more certain foundation of misery, than such a wretched temper?

But if they were really as unhappy as they pretend, says my antagonist, why do they remain in life? . . .

Not satisfied with life, afraid of death.

This is the secret chain, say I, that holds us. We are terrified, not bribed to the continuance of our existence.

It is only a false delicacy, he may insist, which a few refined spirits indulge, and which has spread these complaints among the whole race of mankind. . . . And what is this delicacy, I ask, which you blame? Is it any thing but a greater sensibility to all the pleasures and pains of life? and if the man of a delicate, refined temper, by being so much more alive than the rest of the world, is only so much more unhappy; what judgment must we form in general of human life?

Let men remain at rest, says our adversary; and they will be easy. They are willing artificers of their own misery . . . No! reply I; an anxious languor follows their repose: disappointment, vexation, trouble, their activity and ambition.

I can observe something like what you mention in some others, replied Cleanthes: but I confess, I feel little or nothing of it in myself, and hope that it is not so common as you represent it.

If you feel not human misery yourself, cried Demea, I congratulate you on so happy a singularity. Others, seemingly the most prosperous, have not been ashamed to vent their complaints in the most melancholy strains. Let us attend to the great, the fortunate Emperor, Charles V, when, tired with human grandeur, he resigned all his extensive dominions into the hands of his son. In the last harangue, which he made on that memorable occasion, he publicly avowed, *that the greatest prosperities which he had ever enjoyed, had been mixed with so many adversities, that he might truly say he had never enjoyed any satisfaction or contentment.* But did the retired life, in which he sought for shelter, afford him any greater happiness? If we may credit his son's account, his repentance commenced the very day of his resignation.

Cicero's fortune, from small beginnings, rose to the greatest lustre and renown; yet what pathetic complaints of the ills of life do his familiar letters, as well as philosophical discourses, contain? And suitably to his own experience, he introduces Cato, the great, the fortunate Cato, protesting in his old age, that, had he a new life in his offer, he would reject the present.

Ask yourself, ask any of your acquaintance, whether they would live over again the last ten or twenty years of their lives. No! but the next twenty, they say, will be better:

And from the dregs of life, hope to receive
What the first sprightly running could not give.

Thus at last they find (such is the greatness of human misery; it reconciles even contradictions) that they complain, at once, of the shortness of life, and of its vanity and sorrow.

And is it possible, Cleanthes, said Philo, that after all these reflections, and infinitely more, which might be suggested, you can still persevere in your Anthropomorphism, and assert the moral attributes of the Deity, his justice, benevolence, mercy, and rectitude, to be of the same nature with these virtues in human creatures? His power we allow infinite: whatever he wills is executed: but neither man nor any other animal are happy: therefore he does not will their happiness. His wisdom is infinite: he is never mistaken in chusing the means to any end: but the course of nature tends not to human or animal felicity: therefore it is not established for that purpose. Through the whole compass of human knowledge, there are no inferences more certain and infallible than these. In what respect, then, do his benevolence and mercy resemble the benevolence and mercy of men?

Epicurus's old questions are yet unanswered.

Is he willing to prevent evil, but not able? then is he impotent. Is he able, but not willing? then is he malevolent. Is he both able and willing? whence then is evil?

You ascribe, Cleanthes, (and I believe justly) a purpose and intention to Nature. But what, I beseech you, is the object of that curious artifice and machinery, which she has displayed in all animals? The preservation alone of individuals and propagation of the species. It seems enough for her purpose, if such a rank be barely upheld in the universe, without any care or concern for the happiness of the members that compose it. No resource for this purpose: no machinery, in order merely to give pleasure or ease: no fund of pure joy and contentment: no indulgence without some want or necessity accompanying it. At least, the few phenomena of this nature are overbalanced by opposite phenomena of still greater importance.

Our sense of music, harmony, and indeed beauty of all kinds gives satisfaction, without being absolutely necessary to the preservation and propagation of the species. But what racking pains, on the other hand, arise from gouts, gravels, megrims, tooth-aches, rheumatisms; where the injury to the animal-machinery is either small or incurable? Mirth, laughter, play, frolic, seems gratuitous satisfactions, which have no farther tendency: spleen, melancholy, discontent, superstition, are pains of the same nature. How then does the divine benevolence display itself, in the sense of you Anthropomorphites? None but we Mystics, as you were pleased to call us, can account for this strange mixture of phenomena, by deriving it from attributes, infinitely perfect, but incomprehensible.

And have you at last, said Cleanthes smiling, betrayed your intentions, Philo? Your long agreement with Demea did indeed a little surprise me; but I find you were all the while erecting a concealed battery against me. And I must confess, that you have now fallen upon a subject, worthy of your noble spirit of opposition and controversy. If you can make out the present point, and prove mankind to be unhappy or corrupted, there is an end at once of all religion. For to what purpose establish the natural attributes of the Deity, while the moral are still doubtful and uncertain?

You take umbrage very easily, replied Demea, at opinions the most innocent, and the most generally received even amongst the religious and devout themselves: and nothing can be more surprising than to find a topic like this, concerning the wickedness and misery of man, charged with no less than Atheism and profaneness. Have not all pious divines and preachers, who have indulged their rhetoric on so fertile a subject; have they not easily, I say, given a solution of any difficulties, which may attend it? This world is but a point in comparison of the universe: this life but a moment in comparison of eternity. The present evil phenomena, therefore, are rectified in other regions, and in some future period of existence. And the eyes of men, being then opened to larger views of things, see the whole connection of general laws; and trace, with adoration, the benevolence and rectitude of the Deity, through all the mazes and intricacies of his providence.

No! replied Cleanthes, No! These arbitrary suppositions can never be admitted, contrary to matter of fact, visible and uncontroverted. Whence can any cause be known but from its known effects? Whence can any hypothesis be proved but from the apparent phenomena? To establish one hypothesis upon another, is building entirely in the air; and the utmost we ever attain, by these conjectures and fictions, is to ascertain the bare possibility of our opinion; but never can we, upon such terms, establish its reality.

The only method of supporting divine benevolence (and it is what I willingly embrace) is to deny absolutely the misery and wickedness of man. Your representations are exaggerated: Your melancholy views mostly fictitious: Your inferences contrary to fact and experience. Health is more common than sickness: Pleasure than pain: Happiness than misery. And for one vexation, which we meet with, we attain, upon computation, a hundred enjoyments.

Admitting your position, replied Philo, which yet is extremely doubtful, you must, at the same time, allow, that, if pain be less frequent than pleasure, it is infinitely more violent and durable. One hour of it is often able to outweigh a day, a week, a month of our common insipid enjoyments: And how many days, weeks, and months are passed by several in the most acute torments? Pleasure, scarcely in one instance, is ever able to reach ecstacy and rapture: And in no one instance can it continue for any time at its highest pitch and altitude. The spirits evaporate; the nerves relax; the fabric is disordered; and the enjoyment quickly degenerates into fatigue and uneasiness. But pain often, good God, how often! rises to torture and agony; and the longer it continues, it becomes still more geniune agony and torture. Patience is exhausted; courage languishes; melancholy seizes us; and nothing terminates our misery but the removal of its cause, or another event, which is the sole cure of all evil, but which, from our natural folly, we regard with still greater horror and consternation.

But not to insist upon these topics, continued Philo, though most obvious, certain, and important; I must use the freedom to admonish you, Cleanthes, that you have put the controversy upon a most dangerous issue, and are unawares introducing a total Scepticism, into the most essential articles of natural and revealed theology. What! no method of fixing a just foundation for religion, unless we allow the happiness of human life, and maintain a continued existence even in this world, with all our present pains, infirmities, vexations, and follies, to be eligible and desireable! But this is contrary to every one's feeling and experience: It is contrary to an authority so established as nothing can subvert: No decisive proofs can ever be produced against this authority; nor is it possible for you to compute, estimate, and compare all the pains and all the pleasures in the lives of all men and of all animals: And thus by your resting the whole system of religion on a point, which, from its very nature, must for ever be uncertain, you tacitly confess, that that system is equally uncertain.

But allowing you, what never will be believed; at least, what you never possibly can prove, that animal, or at least, human happiness, in this life, exceeds its misery; you have yet done nothing: For this is not, by any means, what we expect from infinite power, infinite wisdom, and infinite goodness. Why is there any misery at all in the world? Not by chance surely. From some cause then. Is it from the intention of the Deity? But he is perfectly benevolent. Is it contrary to his intention? But he is almighty. Nothing can shake the solidity of this reasoning, so short, so clear, so decisive; except we assert, that these subjects exceed all human capacity, and that our common measures of truth and falsehood are not applicable to them; a topic, which I have all along insisted on, but which you have, from the beginning, rejected with scorn and indignation.

But I will be contented to retire still from this intrenchment: For I deny that you can ever force me in it: I will allow, that pain or misery in man is *compatible* with infinite power and goodness in the Deity, even in your sense of these attributes: What are you advanced by all these concessions? A mere possible compatibility is not sufficient. You must *prove* these pure, unmixt, and uncontrollable attributes from the present mixed and confused phenomena, and from these alone. A hopeful undertaking! Were the phenomena ever so pure and unmixt, yet being finite, they would be insufficient for that purpose. How much more, where they are also so jarring and discordant!

Here, Cleanthes, I find myself at ease in my argument. Here I triumph. Formerly, when we argued concerning the natural attributes of intelligence and design, I needed all my sceptical and metaphysical subtilty to elude your grasp. In many views of the universe, and of its parts, particularly the latter, the beauty and fitness of final causes strike us with such irresistible force, that all objections appear (what I believe they really are) mere cavils and sophisms; nor can we then imagine how it was ever possible for us to repose any weight on them. But there is no view of human life or of the condition of mankind, from which, without the greatest violence, we can infer the moral attributes, or learn that infinite benevolence, conjoined with infinite power and infinite wisdom, which we must discover by the eyes of faith alone. It is your turn now to tug the labouring oar, and to support your philosophical subtilties against the dictates of plain reason and experience.

41

The Cause of Evil

THOMAS AQUINAS

We next inquire into the cause of evil. Concerning this there are three points of inquiry: (1) Whether good can be the cause of evil? (2) Whether the supreme good, God, is the cause of evil? (3) Whether there be any supreme evil, which is the first cause of all evils?

Whether Good Can Be the Cause of Evil?

... It must be said that every evil in some way has a cause. For evil is the absence of the good which is natural and due to a thing. But that anything fall short of its natural and due disposition can come only from some cause drawing it out of its proper disposition. For a heavy thing is not moved upwards except by some impelling force; nor does an agent fail in its action except from some impediment. But only good can be a cause; because nothing can be a cause except inasmuch as it is a being, and every being, as such, is good. And if we consider the special kinds of causes, we see that the agent, the form and the end imply some kind of perfection which belongs to the notion of good. Even matter, as a potentiality to good, has the nature of good.

Now that good is the cause of evil by way of the material cause was shown above. For it was shown that good is the subject of evil. But evil has no formal cause, but is rather a privation of form. So, too, neither has it a final cause, but is rather a privation of order to the proper end; since it is not only the end which has the nature of good, but also the useful, which is ordered to the end.

[From the *Summa Theologica* (1265–1273), Q. 49, Arts. 1–3. Reprinted from *Basic Writings of Saint Thomas Aquinas*, Vol. I, edited by Anton C. Pegis (Random House, 1945), courtesy of the Anton C. Pegis Estate.]

Evil, however, has a cause by way of an agent, not directly, but accidentally.

In proof of this, we must know that evil is caused in action otherwise than in the effect. In action, evil is caused by reason of the defect of some principle of action, either of the principal or the instrumental agent. Thus, the defect in the movement of an animal may happen by reason of the weakness of the motive power, as in the case of children, or by reason only of the ineptitude of the instrument, as in the lame. On the other hand, evil is caused in a thing, but not in the proper effect of the agent, sometimes by the power of the agent, sometimes by reason of a defect, either of the agent or of the matter. It is caused by reason of the power or perfection of the agent when there necessarily follows on the form intended by the agent the privation of another form; as, for instance, when on the form of fire there follows the privation of the form of air or of water. Therefore, as the more perfect the fire is in strength, so much the more perfectly does it impress its own form, so also the more perfectly does it corrupt the contrary. Hence that evil and corruption befall air and water comes from the perfection of the fire, but accidentally; because fire does not aim at the privation of the form of water, but at the introduction of its own form, though by doing this it also accidentally causes the other. But if there is a defect in the proper effect of the fire—as, for instance, that it fails to heat—this comes either by defect of the action, which implies the defect of some principle, as was said above, or by the indisposition of the matter, which does not receive the action of the fire acting on it. But the fact itself that it is a deficient being is accidental to good to which it belongs essentially to act. Hence it is true that evil in no way has any but an accidental cause. Thus good is the cause of evil. . . .

Whether the Highest Good, God, Is the Cause of Evil?

. . . As appears from what was said, the evil which consists in the defect of action is always caused by the defect of the agent. But in God there is no defect, but the highest perfection, as was shown above. Hence, the evil which consists in defect of action, or which is caused by defect of the agent, is not reduced to God as to its cause.

But the evil which consists in the corruption of some things is reduced to God as the cause. And this appears as regards both natural things and voluntary things. For it was said that some agent, inasmuch as it produces by its power a form which is followed by corruption and defect, causes by its power that corruption and defect. But it is manifest that the form which God chiefly intends in created things is the good of the order of the universe. Now, the order of the universe requires, as was said above, that there should be some things that can, and sometimes do, fail. And thus God, by causing in things the good of the order of the universe, consequently and, as it were by accident, causes the corruptions of things, according to 1 Kings 2:6—*The Lord killeth and maketh alive*. But when we read that *God hath not made death* (Wis. 1:13), the sense is that God does not will death for its own sake. Nevertheless, the order of justice belongs to the order of the universe; and this requires that penalty should be dealt out to sinners. And so God is the author of the evil which is penalty, but not of the evil which is fault, by reason of what is said above. . . .

Whether There Be One Highest Evil Which Is the Cause of Every Evil?

. . . It appears from what precedes that there is no one first principle of evil, as there is one first principle of good.

First, because the first principle of good is essentially good, as was shown above. But nothing can be evil in its very essence. For it was shown above that every being, as such, is good, and that evil can exist only in good as in its subject.

Secondly, because the first principle of good is the highest and perfect good which pre-contains in itself all goodness, as was shown above. But there cannot be a highest evil, for, as was shown above, although evil always lessens good, yet it never wholly consumes it; and thus, since the good always survives, nothing can be wholly and perfectly evil. Therefore, the Philosopher says that *if the wholly evil could be, it would destroy itself*. For if all good were destroyed (which is essential for something to be wholly evil), evil itself would be taken away, since its subject is good.

Thirdly, because the very nature of evil is against the idea of a first principle; both because every evil is caused by good, as was shown above, and because evil can be only an accidental cause, and thus it cannot be the first cause for the accidental cause is subsequent to an essential cause, as appears in *Physics* ii.

Those, however, who upheld two first principles, one good and the other evil, fell into this error from the same cause, whence also arose other strange notions of the ancients. For they failed to consider the universal cause of all being, and considered only the particular causes of particular effects. Hence on that account, if they found a thing injurious to something by the power of its own nature, they thought that the very nature of that thing was evil; as, for instance, if one were to say that the nature of fire was evil because it burnt the house of some poor man. The judgment, however, of the goodness of anything does not depend upon its reference to any particular thing, but rather upon what it is in itself, and on its reference to the whole universe, wherein every part has its own perfectly ordered place, as was said above. So, too, because they found two contrary particular causes of two contrary particular effects, they did not know how to reduce these contrary particular causes to a universal common cause; and therefore they extended the contrariety of causes even to the first principles. But since all contraries agree in something common, it is necessary to search for one common cause for them above their own contrary causes; just as above the contrary qualities of the elements there exists the power of the body of the heavens, and above all things that exist, no matter how, there exists one first principle of being, as was shown above. . . .

42

The Perfection of the World

GOTTFRIED WILHELM LEIBNIZ

. . . Lest any one should think that we are here confounding moral perfection or goodness with metaphysical perfection or greatness and, allowing the latter, should deny the former, it is to be observed that it follows from what has been said not only that the world is most perfect physically, or, if you prefer it, metaphysically, that is to say, that that series of things has come into existence in which the greatest amount of reality is actually manifested, but also that the world is most perfect morally because genuine moral perfection is physical perfection in minds themselves. Wherefore the world is not only the most admirable mechanism, but it is also, so far as it is made up of minds, the best commonwealth, through which there is bestowed upon minds the greatest possible happiness or joy, in which their physical perfection consists.

But, you will say, we find that the opposite of this takes place in the world, for very often the best people suffer the worst things, and those who are innocent, both animals and men, are afflicted and put to death even with torture; and indeed the world, especially if we consider the government of the human race, seems rather a confused chaos than anything directed by a supreme wisdom. So, I confess, it seems at a first glance, but when we look at it more closely the opposite conclusion manifestly follows *a priori* from those very considerations which have been adduced, the conclusion, namely, that the highest possible perfection of all things, and therefore of all minds, is brought about.

And indeed, as the lawyers say, it is not proper to judge unless we have examined the whole law. We know a very small part of eternity

[From *On the Ultimate Origination of Things*, translated by Robert Latta (1898). This paper was written in Latin in 1697, but was first published in 1840.]

which is immeasurable in its extent; for what a little thing is the record of a few thousand years, which history transmits to us! Nevertheless, from so slight an experience we rashly judge regarding the immeasureable and eternal, like men who, having been born and brought up in prison or, perhaps, in the subterranean salt-mines of the Sarmatians, should think that there is no other light in the world than that of the feeble lamp which hardly suffices to direct their steps. If you look at a very beautiful picture, having covered up the whole of it except a very small part, what will it present to your sight, however thoroughly you examine it (nay, so much the more, the more closely you inspect it), but a confused mass of colours laid on without selection and without art? Yet if you remove the covering and look at the whole picture from the right point of view, you will see that what appeared to have been carelessly daubed on the canvas was really done by the painter with very great art. The experience of the eyes in painting corresponds to that of the ears in music. Eminent composers very often mingle discords with harmonies so as to stimulate and, as it were, to prick the hearer, who becomes anxious as to what is going to happen, is so much the more pleased when presently all is restored to order; just as we take pleasure in small dangers or risks of mishap, merely from the consciousness of our power or our luck or from a desire to make a display of them; or, again, as we delight in the show of danger that is connected with performances on the tight-rope or sword-dancing, and we ourselves in jest half let go a little boy, as if about to throw him from us, like the ape which carried Christiern, King of Denmark, while still an infant in swaddling-clothes, to the top of the roof, and then, as in jest, relieved the anxiety of every one by bringing him safely back to his cradle. On the same principle sweet things become insipid if we eat nothing else; sharp, tart, and even bitter things must be combined with them, so as to stimulate the taste. He who has not tasted bitter things does not deserve sweet things and, indeed, will not appreciate them. This is the very law of enjoyment, that pleasure does not have an even tenor, for this begets loathing and makes us dull, not happy.

But as to our saying that a part may be disturbed without destroying harmony in the whole, this must not be understood as meaning that no account is taken of the parts or that it is enough for the world as a whole to be perfect, although it may be that the human race is wretched, and that there is in the universe no regard for justice and no care for us, as is the opinion of some whose judgment regarding the totality of things is not quite just. For it is to be observed that, as in a thoroughly well-constituted commonwealth care is taken, as far as may be, for the good of individuals, so the universe will not be sufficiently perfect unless the interests of individuals are attended to, while the universal harmony is preserved. And for this no better standard could be set up than the very law of justice which declares that each should participate in the perfection of the universe and in a happiness of his own in proportion to his own virtue and to the degree in which his will has regard to the common good; and by this is fulfilled that which we call charity and the love of God, in which alone, in the opinion of the wise theologians, consists the force and power even of the Christian religion. Nor ought it to appear wonderful that so great a place should be given to minds in the universe, since they most closely resemble the image of the Supreme Author; they are related to Him, not (like other things) as machines to their constructor, but as citizens to their prince; they are to last as long as the universe itself, and in a manner they express and concentrate the whole in themselves, so that it may be said that minds are whole parts.

But as to the special question of the afflictions of good men, it is to be held as certain that these afflictions have as their result the greater good of those who are afflicted, and this is true not only theologically but also naturally, as the grain cast into the earth suffers before it bears fruit. And in general it may be said that afflictions are for the time evil but in the end good, since they are short

ways to greater perfection. So in physics, liquids which ferment slowly take also a longer time to purify, while those which undergo a greater agitation throw off certain of their ingredients with greater force, and are thus more quickly rectified. And this is what you might call going back in order that you may put more force into your leap forward. Wherefore these things are to be regarded not only as agreeable and comforting, but also as most true. And in general I think there is nothing more true than happiness, and nothing more happy and pleasant than truth.

Further, to realize in its completeness the universal beauty and perfection of the works of God, we must recognize a certain perpetual and very free progress of the whole universe, such that it is always going forward to greater improvement. So even now a great part of our earth has received cultivation and will receive it more and more. And although it is true that sometimes certain parts of it grow wild again, or again suffer destruction or degeneration, yet this is to be understood in the way in which affliction was explained above, that is to say, that this very destruction and degeneration leads to some greater end, so that somehow we profit by the loss itself.

And to the possible objection that, if this were so, the world ought long ago to have become a paradise, there is a ready answer. Although many substances have already attained a great perfection, yet on account of the infinite divisibility of the continuous, there always remain in the abyss of things slumbering parts which have yet to be awakened, to grow in size and worth, and, in a word, to advance to a more perfect state. And hence no end of progress is ever reached.

43

Evil as an Element of Good

JOSIAH ROYCE

The World of Doubt

Our monism fails ... to establish itself on any ground of experience. Absolute refutation is indeed not yet thus attained, for the defender of the hypothesis of an infinite reason always has at his disposal the suggestions of the ancient theodicy, modified to suit his needs. He can say: "The partial evil is, somehow, we cannot see how, universal good." Or, again, "Evil results from the free-will of moral agents, who have to suffer for their own chosen sins." The latter answer, a very plausible one in its own sphere, is for the general problem insignificant. That there is free-will we do not dispute, and that free-will, if it exists, is a cause of much mischief is undoubted. Yet if the universe is so made that the free-will of the slave-driver, or of the murderer, or of the seducer, or of the conqueror, works untold ill to innocent victims, then the fault of the suffering of the victims rests not wholly with the evil-doer, but partly with the order of the world, which has given him so much power, such a wide freedom to do the mischief that he desires. The world in which such things happen must justify its religiously inspiring nature in some other way.

The other answer, that *partial evil is universal good*, we have to regard as a much deeper answer, shallow as have been the uses often made of it in the past. But if it is to be a valid answer, it must take a particular form. The words are usually spoken too glibly. Their meaning, if they are to have any, we must very carefully consider, ere we can dare to accept them. ...

How can a partial evil be an universal good? Only in certain cases.

[From *The Religious Aspect of Philosophy*, Book II; chapter VIII, part 4, chapter XII, part 3. First published in 1885.]

The notion plainly is that the evil in the external world of popular thought is, as known to us, only a part of the whole, and the whole, it is said, may be in character opposed to the part. This must indeed be the case, if the world as a whole is to be the work of an Infinite Reason. For if so, the evil must be, not merely a bad lesser part that is overbalanced by the goodness of the larger half of the world, but non-existent, save as a separate aspect of reality, so that it would vanish if we knew more about the truth. This is what the saying asserts: not that evil is overbalanced by good (for that would leave the irrational still real), but that evil is only a deceitful appearance, whose true nature, if seen in its entirety, would turn out to be good. One could not say of a rotting apple, however small the rotten spot as yet is, that the partial rottenness is the universal soundness of the apple. If I have but one slight disorder in but one of my organs, still you cannot say that my partial disorder must be universal health. The old optimists did not mean anything so contradictory as that. They meant that there is no real evil at all; that what seems to me to be evil, say toothaches, and broken households, and pestilences, and treasons, and wars, all that together is but a grand illusion of my partial view. As one looking over the surface of a statue with a microscope, and finding nothing but a stony surface, might say, *how ugly!* but on seeing the whole at a glance would

know its beauty; even so one seeing the world by bits fancies it evil, but would know it to be good if he saw it as a whole. And the seeming but unreal evil of the parts may be necessary in order that the real whole should be good. Such is the position of our optimists. This is the Platonic-Augustinian doctrine of the unreality of evil.

The logical possibility of all this we do not for the first either dispute or affirm. . . . But the trouble lies in the seemingly positive character of evil. Not simple lack of harmony, but horrible discord, is here. How the tortures of the wounded on a field of battle can anyhow enter into a whole in which, as seen by an absolute judge, there is actually no trace of evil at all, this is what we cannot understand. It seems very improbable. . . .

Actually, however, theodicies and kindred efforts, whether monistic or not, in trying to vindicate the rational in the world have seldom consistently maintained this high and slippery ground of the theory of Plato and of St. Augustine. Far from declaring that all physical evil is and must be apparent, the popular theodicies have often consented to accept the reality of this positive evil, and to minimize its significance by certain well-worn, and, for the purposes of this argument, contemptible devices. They have pointed out that the evil in the world, though a reality separate from the good, exists as a means to good. Or, again, they have said that evil is necessary as something outside of the good, setting it off by way of contrast. Both devices, if applied to a world in which good and evil are conceived as separate entities, are unworthy of philosophic thinkers.

For consider the first device. "Evil is a reality, not an illusion, but it is a means to good. Therefore in the world as a whole, good triumphs. Therefore reason, which desires the good, is the One Ruler." But first, to mention a lesser objection, the basis in experience for this view is surely very narrow. Much evil exists whose use as a means we cannot even faintly conceive. But grant this point. Then the real evil is a means to a separate and external good end. But if the end was good, why was it not got without the evil means? Only two answers are possible to this, in case the evil is separate from the good. Either the One Reason was driven to take just this way, and could take no less expensive one; or the One Reason, not being bound to this road, still arbitrarily chose to take it instead of a better. But either answer is fatal. Was the One Reason unable to do better? Then it is not the only power at work. The Monism fails. The Reason was bound. But he who binds the strong man is stronger than he. If, however, the One chose this way rather than a better, then the One chose evil for its own sake. The dilemma is inevitable. . . .

Even worse is the other device often suggested for explaining evil. "Evil is a reality, but it is useful as a foil to good. The two separate facts, good and evil, set each other off. By its contrast, evil increases the importance of good." When this remark is made about us personally with our limitations of body and circumstance, with our relativity of feeling and of attention, the remark has some psychological interest. Made to justify the supposed universal reason, the remark is childish. Always, indeed, it is possible that evil as a separate entity may be made out to be an illusion; and that good and evil have some higher unity that involves the perfection of the world. But if evil is real, and separate from goodness, then the talk about explaining it as a useful contrast is of no worth in the present argument. For we ask: Could not the One create a perfect good save by making good more attractive as set off against the foil evil? Shall we say that Reason could do better than to depend upon this contrast? Then why the evil? If, however, the One Reason could not do better, but had to use the contrast, then the One was less powerful in its devices than is the maker of a concert-programme, who has no need to introduce into his concert any saw-filing or tin-trumpeting or pot-scraping to set off the beauty of his songs and symphonies. But as a fact of experience, is most evil seemingly even thus useful? Are the sick needed to make the healthy joyous? . . .

The Religious Insight

... Apparently we are as far as ever from seeing *how* the partial evil can be the universal good; we only show, from the conception of the infinite itself, *that* the partial evil must be the universal good. God must see how; and we know this because we know of God. More than this we seem to be unable to suggest.

But will this do? Have we not forgotten one terrible consequence of our doctrine? The partial evil is universal good, is it? There is no evil? All apparent imperfection is an illusion of our partial view? So then *where is the chance to be in a free way and of our own choice better than we otherwise in truth should be?* Is not the arm that is raised to strike down wickedness paralyzed by the very thought that was to give it divine strength? This evil that I fight here in this finite world is a delusion. So then, why fight it? If I do good works, the world is infinitely good and perfect. If I seem to do evil works, the world is in truth no worse. Seeming good is not better than seeming evil, for if it were, then the seeming evil would be a real defect in God, in whose life is everything. If I have never loved aught but God, even so I have never hated aught but God. It is all alike. God does not need just me. Or rather I may say, in so far as he needs me to complete his infinite truth, he already has me from all eternity. I have nothing to do with the business, save to contemplate in dizzy indolence the whirling misty masses of seeming evil, and to say with a sort of amused reverence that they look very ill and opaque to me, but that of course God sees through them clearly enough somehow. The mist is in truth crystalline water, and he has so quick a sense as to look beyond the drops as easily as if they were in the calm unity of a mountain lake. And so, my religion is simply a contemplation of God's wisdom, but otherwise an idle amusement.

So says the man who sees only this superficial view of our doctrine. In so far as, standing once more outside of some evil thing, we say: "That thing yonder looks bad, but God must see it to be good," we do indeed remain indolent, and our religion simply means a sort of stoical indifference to the apparent distinction of good and evil. This is in fact the proper practical attitude of even the most earnest man in the presence of evil that he cannot understand and cannot affect. In such matters we must indeed be content with the passive knowledge. Death and the unavoidable pains of life, the downfall of cherished plans, all the cruelty of fate, we must learn to look at as things to us opaque, but to God, who knows them fully, somehow clear and rational. So regarding them, we must aim to get to the stage of stoical indifference about them. They are to us the accidents of existence.

We have no business to murmur about them, since we see that God, experiencing them, somehow must experience them as elements in an absolutely perfect life. . . .

. . . Such however is *not* the last word for us about the only evil that has any immediate moral significance, namely, the evil that we see, not as an external, shadowy mist, but as a present fact, experienced in us. Here it is that the objector just mentioned seems really formidable to us. But just here it is that we find the answer to him. For in the world of our own acts we have a wondrous experience. We realize evil, we fight it, and, at the same time, we realize our fragment of the perfect divine life in the moment itself of struggling with the evil. And in this wondrous experience lies the whole solution of the ancient problem of the existence of moral evil. For instance, I find in myself a selfish impulse, trying to destroy the moral insight. Now of this evil impulse I do not say, looking at it objectively: "It is somehow a part of the universal good;" but, in the moment of moral action I *make* it, even in the very moment of its sinfulness, a part of my good consciousness, *in overcoming it.* The moral insight condemns the evil that it experiences; *and in condemning and conquering this evil it forms and is, together with the evil, the organic total that constitutes the good will.* Only through this inner victory over the evil that is experi-

enced as a conquered tendency does the good will have its being. . . .

When I experience the victory of the moral insight over the bad will, I experience in one indivisible moment both the partial evil of the selfish impulse (which in itself as a separate fact would be wholly bad) and the universal good of the moral victory, which has its existence only in the overwhelming of the evil. So, in the good act, I experience the good as my evil lost in goodness, as a rebellion against the good conquered in the moment of its birth, as a peace that arises in the midst of this triumphant conflict, as a satisfaction that lives in this restless activity of inner warfare. This child of inner strife is the good, and the only moral good, we know.

What I here have present in me when I do a good act is an element of God's life. *I here directly experience how the partial moral evil is universal good;* for so it is a relatively universal good in me when, overcoming myself, I choose the universal will. The bad impulse is still in me, but is defeated. In the choice against evil is the very life of goodness, which would be a pale, stupid abstraction otherwise. Even so, to take another view, in the overcoming of our separateness as individuals lies, as we saw in the previous book, our sense of the worth of the universal life. And what we here experience in the single moment of time, and in the narrowness of our finite lives, God must experience, and eternally. In our single good acts we have thus the specimen of the eternal realization of goodness.

But now how simple becomes the answer to that terrible suggestion of a moment since! How simple also the solution of the problem of evil! "If I want to do evil, I cannot," said the objector; "for God the perfect one includes me with the rest, and so cannot in his perfection be hurt by me. Let me do what I will, my act can only seem bad, and cannot be bad. All evil is illusion, hence there is no moral difference in action possible."

"Right indeed," we answer, "but also wrong, because half the truth. The half kills, the whole gives life. Why canst thou not do any absolute evil? Because thy evil intent, which, in its separateness, *would be* unmixed evil, thy selfish will, thy struggle against the moral insight, this evil will of thine is no lonesome fact in the world, but is an element in the organic life of God. *In him thy evil impulse forms part of a total good will, as the evil impulse of the good man forms an element in his realization of goodness*. In God thy separateness is destroyed, and with it thy sin as evil. For good will in the infinite is what the good man finds the good will to be in himself, namely, the organic total whose truth is the *discovery of the evil*. Therefore is God's life perfect, because it includes not only the knowledge of thy finite wicked will, but the insight into its truth as a moment in the real universal will.

If then thou wert good, thou wouldst be good by including the evil impulse in a realization of its evil, and in an acceptance of the higher insight. If thou art evil, then in thyself, as separate being, thou art condemned, and just because thy separate evil is condemned, therefore is the total life of God, that includes thee with thy condemnation and with the triumph over thee, good.

This is the ground for the solution of the problem. To go more into detail: Evil is for us of two classes: the external seeming evil, such as death, pain, or weakness of character; and internal evil, namely the bad will itself. Because we know so little, therefore we can never tell whether those externally seen seeming evils are blessings in disguise, or expressions of some wicked diabolical will-power at work about us. Somehow then, we never know exactly how, these seeming great evils must be in God universal good. But with regard to the only evil that we know as an inward experience, and so as a certain reality, namely, the Evil Will, we know both the existence of that, and its true relation to universal goodness, because and only because we experience both of them first through the moral insight, and then in the good act. Goodness having its very life in the insight and in its exercise, has as its elements the evil impulse *and* its correction. The evil will as such may either be conquered in our personal experience, and then we are ourselves good; or it may be conquered not in our thought considered as a separate thought, but in the total thought to which ours is so related, as our single evil and good thoughts are related to the whole of us. The wicked man is no example of God's delight in wickedness, just as the evil impulse that is an element in the good man's goodness, and a very real element too, is no proof that the good man delights in evil. As the evil impulse is to the good man, so is the evil will of the wicked man to the life of God, in which he is an element. And just because the evil will is the only evil that we are sure of,

this explanation is enough. . . .

We do not say then that evil must exist to set the good off by way of external contrast. That view we long since justly rejected. We say only that the evil will is a conquered element *in* the good will, and is as such necessary to goodness. Our conception of the absolute unity of God's life, and that conception alone, enables us to apply this thought here. No form of dualistic Theism has any chance to apply this, the only satisfactory theodicy. If God were conceived as external to his creatures, as a power that made them beyond himself, the hopeless problems and the unworthy subterfuges of the older theodicies would come back to torment us. As it is, the solution of the problem of evil is given us in the directest and yet in the most unexpected way.

44

Evil and Omnipotence

J. L. MACKIE

The traditional arguments for the existence of God have been fairly thoroughly criticised by philosophers. But the theologian can, if he wishes, accept this criticism. He can admit that no rational proof of God's existence is possible. And he can still retain all that is essential to his position, by holding that God's existence is known in some other, non-rational way. I think, however, that a more telling criticism can be made by way of the traditional problem of evil. Here it can be shown, not that religious beliefs lack rational support, but that they are positively irrational, that the several parts of the essential theological doctrine are inconsistent with one another, so that the theologian can maintain his position as a whole only by a much more extreme rejection of reason than in the former case. He must now be prepared to believe, not merely what cannot be proved, but what can be *disproved* from other beliefs that he also holds.

The problem of evil, in the sense in which I shall be using the phrase, is a problem only for someone who believes that there is a God who is both omnipotent and wholly good. And it is a logical problem, the problem of clarifying and reconciling a number of beliefs: it is not a scientific problem that might be solved by further observations, or a practical problem that might be solved by a decision or an action. These points are obvious; I mention them only because they are sometimes ignored by theologians, who sometimes parry a statement of the problem with such remarks as "Well, can you solve the problem yourself?" or "This is a mystery which may be revealed to us later" or "Evil is something to be faced and overcome, not to be merely discussed."

[From *Mind*, Vol. 64 (1955), pp. 200–212. Reprinted by permission of *Mind*.]

In its simplest form the problem is this: God is omnipotent; God is wholly good; and yet evil exists. There seems to be some contradiction between these three propositions, so that if any two of them were true the third would be false. But at the same time all three are essential parts of most theological positions: the theologian, it seems, at once *must* adhere and *cannot consistently* adhere to all three. (The problem does not arise only for theists, but I shall discuss it in the form in which it presents itself for ordinary theism.)

However, the contradiction does not arise immediately; to show it we need some additional premises, or perhaps some quasi-logical rules connecting the terms "good," "evil," and "omnipotent." These additional principles are that good is opposed to evil, in such a way that a good thing always eliminates evil as far as it can, and that there are no limits to what an omnipotent thing can do. From these it follows that a good omnipotent thing eliminates evil completely, and then the proposition that a good omnipotent thing exists, and that evil exists, are incompatible.

A. Adequate Solutions

Now once the problem is fully stated it is clear that it can be solved, in the sense that the problem will not arise if one gives up at least one of the propositions that constitute it. If you

are prepared to say that God is not wholly good, or not quite omnipotent, or that evil does not exist, or that good is not opposed to the kind of evil that exists, or that there are limits to what an omnipotent thing can do, then the problem of evil will not arise for you.

There are, then, quite a number of adequate solutions of the problem of evil, and some of these have been adopted, or almost adopted, by various thinkers. For example, a few have been prepared to deny God's omnipotence, and rather more have been prepared to keep the term "omnipotence" but severely to restrict its meaning, recording quite a number of things that an omnipotent being cannot do. Some have said that evil is an illusion, perhaps because they held that the whole world of temporal, changing things is an illusion, and that what we call evil belongs only to this world, or perhaps because they held that although temporal things *are* much as we see them, those that we call evil are not really evil. Some have said that what we call evil is merely the privation of good, that evil in a positive sense, evil that would really be opposed to good, does not exist. Many have agreed with Pope that disorder is harmony not understood, and that partial evil is universal good. Whether any of these views is *true* is, of course, another question. But each of them gives an adequate solution of the problem of evil in the sense that if you accept it this problem does not arise for you, though you may, of course have *other* problems to face.

But often enough these adequate solutions are only *almost* adopted. The thinkers who restrict God's power, but keep the term "omnipotence," may reasonably be suspected of thinking, in other contexts, that his power is really unlimited. Those who say that evil is an illusion may also be thinking, inconsistently, that this illusion is itself an evil. Those who say that "evil" is merely privation of good may also be thinking, inconsistently, that privation of good is an evil. (The fallacy here is akin to some forms of the "naturalistic fallacy" in ethics, where some think, for example, that "good" is just what contributes to evolutionary progress, and that evolutionary progress is itself good.) If Pope meant what he said in the first line of his couplet, that "disorder" is only harmony not understood, the "partial evil" of the second line must, for consistency, mean "that which, taken in isolation, falsely appears to be evil," but it would more naturally mean "that which, in isolation, really is evil." The second line, in fact, hesitates between two views, that "partial evil" isn't really evil, since only the universal quality is real, and that "partial evil" is really an evil, but only a little one.

In addition, therefore, to adequate solutions, we must recognise unsatisfactory inconsistent solutions, in which there is only a halfhearted

or temporary rejection of one of the propositions which together constitute the problem. In these, one of the constituent propositions is explicitly rejected, but it is covertly reasserted or assumed elsewhere in the system.

B. Fallacious Solutions

Besides these half-hearted solutions, which explicitly reject but implicitly assert one of the constituent propositions, there are definitely fallacious solutions which explicitly maintain all the constituent propositions, but implicitly reject at least one of them in the course of the argument that explains away the problem of evil.

There are, in fact, many so-called solutions which purport to remove the contradiction without abandoning any of its constituent propositions. These must be fallacious, as we can see from the very statement of the problem, but it is not so easy to see in each case precisely where the fallacy lies. I suggest that in all cases the fallacy has the general form suggested above: in order to solve the problem one (or perhaps more) of its constituent propositions is given up, but in such a way that it appears to have been retained, and can therefore be asserted without qualification in other contexts. Sometimes there is a further complication: the supposed solution moves to and fro between, say, two of the constituent propositions, at one point asserting the first of these but covertly abandoning the second, at another point asserting the second but covertly abandoning the first. These fallacious solutions often turn upon some equivocation with the words "good" and "evil," or upon some vagueness about the way in which good and evil are opposed to one another, or about how much is meant by "omnipotence." I propose to examine some of these so-called solutions, and to exhibit their fallacies in detail. Incidentally, I shall also be considering whether an adequate solution could be reached by a minor modification of one or more of the constituent propositions, which would, however, still satisfy all the essential requirements of ordinary theism.

1. "Good cannot exist without evil" or "Evil is necessary as a counterpart to good."

It is sometimes suggested that evil is necessary as a counterpart to good, that if there were no evil there could be no good either, and that this solves the problem of evil. It is true that it points to an answer to the question "Why should there be evil?" But it does so only by qualifying some of the propositions that constitute the problem.

First, it sets a limit to what God can do, saying that God *cannot* create good without simultaneously creating evil, and this means either that God is not omnipotent or that there are *some* limits to what an omnipotent thing can do. It may be replied that these limits are always presupposed, that omnipotence has never meant the power to do what is logically impossible, and on the present view the existence of good without evil would be a logical impossibility. This interpretation of omnipotence may, indeed, be accepted as a modification of our original account which does not reject anything that is essential to theism, and I shall in general assume it in the subsequent discussion. It is, perhaps, the most common theistic view, but I think that some theists at least have maintained that God can do what is logically impossible. Many theists, at any rate, have held that logic itself is created or laid down by God, that logic is the way in which God arbitrarily chooses to think. (This is, of course, parallel to the ethical view that morally right actions are those which God arbitrarily chooses to command, and the two views encounter similar difficulties.) And *this* account of logic is clearly inconsistent with the view that God is bound by logical necessities—unless it is possible for an omnipotent being to bind himself, an issue which we shall consider later, when we come to the Paradox of Omnipotence. This solution of the problem of evil cannot, therefore, be consistently adopted along with the view that logic is itself created by God.

But, secondly, this solution denies that evil is opposed to good in our original sense. If good and evil are counterparts, a good thing will not "eliminate evil as far as it can." Indeed, this view suggests that good and evil are not strictly qualities of things at all. Perhaps the suggestion is that good and evil are related in much the same way as great and small. Certainly, when the term "great" is used relatively as a condensation of "greater than so-and-so," and "small" is used correspondingly, greatness and smallness are counterparts and cannot exist without each other. But in this sense greatness is not a quality, not an intrinsic feature of anything; and it would be absurd to think of a movement in favour of greatness and against smallness in this sense. Such a movement would be self-defeating, since relative greatness can be promoted only by a simultaneous promotion of relative smallness. I feel sure that no theists would be content to regard God's goodness as analogous to this—as if what he supports were not the *good* but the *better*, and as if he had the paradoxical aim that all things should be better than other things.

This point is obscured by the fact that "great" and "small" seem to have an absolute as well as a relative sense. I cannot discuss here whether there is absolute magnitude or not, but if there is, there could be an absolute sense for "great," it could mean of at least a certain size, and it would make sense to speak of all things getting bigger, of a universe that was expanding all over, and therefore it would make sense to speak of promoting greatness. But in *this* sense great and small are not logically necessary counterparts: either quality could exist without the other. There would be no logical impossibility in everything's being small or in everything's being great.

Neither in the absolute nor in the relative sense, then, of "great" and "small" do these terms provide an analogy of the sort that would be needed to support this solution of the problem of evil. In neither case are greatness and smallness *both* necessary counterparts *and* mutually opposed forces or possible objects for support and attack.

It may be replied that good and evil are necessary counterparts in the same way as any quality and its logical opposite: redness can occur, it is suggested, only if non-redness also occurs. But unless evil is merely the privation of good, they are not logical opposites, and some further argument would be needed to show that they are counterparts in the same way as genuine logical opposites. Let us assume that this could be given. There is still doubt of the correctness of the metaphysical principle that a quality must have a real opposite: I suggest that it is not really impossible that everything should be, say, red, that the truth is merely that if everything were red we should not notice redness, and so we should have no word "red;" we observe and give names to qualities only if they have real opposites. If so, the principle that a term must have an opposite would belong only to our language or to our thought, and would not be an ontological principle, and, correspondingly, the rule that good cannot exist without evil would not state a logical necessity of a sort that God would just have to put up with. God might have made everything good, though *we* should not have noticed it if he had.

But, finally, even if we concede that this *is* an ontological principle, it will provide a solution for the problem of evil only if one is prepared to say, "Evil exists, but only just enough evil to serve as the counterpart of good." I doubt whether any theist will accept this. After all, the *ontological* requirement that non-redness should occur would be satisfied even if all the universe, except for a minute speck, were red, and, if there were a corresponding requirement for evil as a counterpart to good, a minute dose of evil would presumably do. But theists are not usually willing to say, in all contexts, that all the evil that occurs is a minute and necessary dose.

2. "Evil is necessary as a means to good."

It is sometimes suggested that evil is necessary for good not as a counterpart but as a means. In its simple form this has little plausibility as a solution of the problem of evil, since

it obviously implies a severe restriction of God's power. It would be a *causal* law that you cannot have a certain end without a certain means, so that if God has to introduce evil as a means to good, he must be subject to at least some causal laws. This certainly conflicts with what a theist normally means by omnipotence. This view of God as limited by causal laws also conflicts with the view that causal laws are themselves made by God, which is more widely held than the corresponding view about the laws of logic. This conflict would, indeed, be resolved if it were possible for an omnipotent being to bind himself, and this possibility has still to be considered. Unless a favourable answer can be given to this question, the suggestion that evil is necessary as a means to good solves the problem of evil only by denying one of its constituent propositions, either that God is omnipotent or that "omnipotent" means what it says.

3. "The universe is better with some evil in it than it could be if there were no evil."

Much more important is a solution which at first seems to be a mere variant of the previous one, that evil may contribute to the goodness of a whole in which it is found, so that the universe as a whole is better as it is, with some evil in it, than it would be if there were no evil. This solution may be developed in either of two ways. It may be supported by an aesthetic analogy, by the fact that contrasts heighten beauty, that in a musical work, for example, there may occur discords which somehow add to the beauty of the work as a whole. Alternatively, it may be worked out in connexion with the notion of progress, that the best possible organisation of the universe will not be static, but progressive, that the gradual overcoming of evil by good is really a finer thing than would be the eternal unchallenged supremacy of good.

In either case, this solution usually starts from the assumption that the evil whose existence gives rise to the problem of evil is primarily what is called physical evil, that is to say, pain. In Hume's rather half-hearted presentation of the problem of evil, the evils that he stresses are pain and disease, and those who reply to him argue that the existence of pain and disease makes possible the existence of sympathy, benevolence, heroism, and the gradually successful struggle of doctors and reformers to overcome these evils. In fact, theists often seize the opportunity to accuse those who stress the problem of evil of taking a low, materialistic view of good and evil, equating these with pleasure and pain, and of ignoring the more spiritual goods which can arise in the struggle against evils.

But let us see exactly what is being done here. Let us call pain and misery "first order evil" or "evil (1)."

What contrasts with this, namely, pleasure and happiness, will be called "first order good" or "good (1)." Distinct from this is "second order good" or "good (2)" which somehow emerges in a complex situation in which evil (1) is a necessary component—logically, not merely causally, necessary. (Exactly *how* it emerges does not matter: in the crudest version of this solution good (2) is simply the heightening of happiness by the contrast with misery, in other versions it includes sympathy with suffering, heroism in facing danger, and the gradual decrease of first order evil and increase of first order good.) It is also being assumed that second order good is more important than first order good or evil, in particular that it more than outweighs the first order evil it involves.

Now this is a particularly subtle attempt to solve the problem of evil. It defends God's goodness and omnipotence on the ground that (on a sufficiently long view) this is the best of all logically possible worlds, because it includes the important second order goods, and yet it admits that real evils, namely first order evils, exist. But does it still hold that good and evil are opposed? Not, clearly, in the sense that we set out originally: good does not tend to eliminate evil in general. Instead, we have a modified, a more complex pattern. First order good (e.g., happiness) *contrasts with* first order evil (e.g., misery): these two are opposed in a fairly mechanical way; some second order goods (e.g., benevolence) try to maximise first order good and minimise first order evil; but God's goodness is not this, it is rather the will to maximise *second* order good. We might, therefore, call God's goodness an example of a third order goodness, or good (3). While this account is different from our original one, it might well be able to be an improvement on it, to give a more accurate description of the way in which good is opposed to evil, and to be consistent with the essential theist position.

There might, however, be several objections to this solution.

First, some might argue that such qualities as benevolence—and *a fortiori* the third order goodness which promotes benevolence—have a merely derivative value, that they are not higher sorts of good, but merely means to good (1), that is, to happiness, so that it would be absurd for God to keep misery in existence in order to make possible the virtues of benevolence, heroism, etc. The theist who adopts the present solution must, of course, deny this, but he can do so with some plausibility, so I should not press this objection.

Secondly, it follows from this solution that God is not in our sense benevolent or sympathetic: he is not concerned to minimise evil (1), but only to promote good (2); and this might be a disturbing conclusion for some theists.

But, thirdly, the fatal objection is this. Our analysis shows clearly the possibility of the existence of a *second* order evil, an evil (2) contrasting with good (2) as evil (1) contrasts with good (1). This would include malevolence, cruelty, callousness, cowardice, and states in which good (1) is decreasing and evil (1) increasing. And just as good (2) is held to be the important kind of good, the kind that God is concerned to promote, so evil (2) will, by analogy, be the important kind of evil, the kind which God, if he were wholly good and omnipotent, would eliminate. And yet evil (2) plainly exists, and indeed most theists (in other contexts) stress its existence more than that of evil (1). We should, therefore, state the problem of evil in terms of second order evil, and against this form of the problem the present solution is useless.

An attempt might be made to use this solution again, at a higher level, to explain the occurrence of evil (2): indeed the next main solution that we shall examine does just this, with the help of some new notions. Without any fresh notions, such a solution would have little plausibility: for example, we could hardly say that the really important good was a good (3), such as the increase of benevolence in proportion to cruelty, which logically required for its occurrence the occurrence of some second order evil. But even if evil (2) could be explained in this way, it is fairly clear that there would be third order evils contrasting with this third order good: and we should be well on the way to an infinite regress, where the solution of a problem of evil, stated in terms of evil (n), indicated the existence of an evil ($n + 1$), and a further problem to be solved.

4. "Evil is due to human freewill."

Perhaps the most important proposed solution of the problem of evil is that evil is not to be ascribed to God at all, but to the independent actions of human beings, supposed to have been endowed by God with freedom of the will. This solution may be combined with the preceding one: first order evil (e.g., pain) may be justified as a logically necessary component in second order good (e.g., sympathy) while second order evil (e.g., cruelty) is not *justified*, but is so ascribed to human beings that God cannot be held responsible for it. This combination evades my third criticism of the preceding solution.

The freewill solution also involves the preceding solution at a higher level. To explain why a wholly good God gave men freewill although it would lead to some important evils, it must be argued that it is better on the whole that men should act freely, and sometimes err, than that they should be innocent automata, acting rightly in a wholly

determined way. Freedom, that is to say, is now treated as a third order good, and as being more valuable than second order goods (such as sympathy and heroism) would be if they were deterministically produced, and it is being assumed that second order evils, such as cruelty, are logically necessary accompaniments of freedom, just as pain is a logically necessary pre-condition of sympathy.

I think that this solution is unsatisfactory primarily because of the incoherence of the notion of freedom of the will: but I cannot discuss this topic adequately here, although some of my criticisms will touch upon it.

First I should query the assumption that second order evils are logically necessary accompaniments of freedom. I should ask this: if God has made men such that in their free choices they sometimes prefer what is good and sometimes what is evil, why could he not have made men such that they always freely choose the good? If there is no logical impossibility in a man's freely choosing the good on one, or on several, occasions, there cannot be a logical impossibility in his freely choosing the good on every occasion. God was not, then, faced with a choice between making innocent automata and making beings who, in acting freely, would sometimes go wrong: there was open to him the obviously better possibility of making beings who would act freely but always go right. Clearly, his failure to avail himself of this possibility is inconsistent with his being both omnipotent and wholly good.

If it is replied that this objection is absurd, that the making of some wrong choices is logically necessary for freedom, it would seem that "freedom" must here mean complete randomness or indeterminacy, including randomness with regard to the alternatives good and evil, in other words that men's choices and consequent actions can be "free" only if they are not determined by their characters. Only on this assumption can God escape the responsibility for men's actions; for if he made them as they are, but did not determine their wrong choices, this can only be because the wrong choices are not determined by men as they are. But then if freedom is randomness, how can it be a characteristic of *will?* And, still more, how can it be the most important good? What value or merit would there be in free choices if these were random actions which were not determined by the nature of the agent?

I conclude that to make this solution plausible two different senses of "freedom" must be confused, one sense which will justify the view that freedom is a third order good, more valuable than other goods would be without it, and another sense, sheer randomness, to prevent us from ascribing to God a decision to make men such that they sometimes go wrong when he might have made them such that they would always freely go right.

This criticism is sufficient to dispose of this solution. But besides this there is a fundamental difficulty in the notion of an omnipotent God creating men with free will, for if men's wills are really free this must mean that even God cannot control them, that is, that God is no longer omnipotent. It may be objected that God's gift of freedom to men does not mean that he *cannot* control their wills, but that he always *refrains* from controlling their wills. But why, we may ask, should God refrain from controlling evil wills? Why should he not leave men free to will rightly, but intervene when he sees them beginning to will wrongly? If God could do this, but does not, and if he is wholly good, the only explanation could be that even a wrong free act of will is not really evil, that its freedom is a value which outweighs its wrongness, so that there would be a loss of value if God took away the wrongness and the freedom together. But this is utterly opposed to what theists say about sin in other contexts. The present solution of the problem of evil, then, can be maintained only in the form that God has made men so free that he *cannot* control their wills.

This leads us to what I call the Paradox of Omnipotence: can an omnipotent being make things which he cannot subsequently control? Or, what is practically equivalent to this, can an omnipotent being make rules which then bind himself? (These are practically equivalent because any such rules could be regarded as setting certain things beyond his control, and *vice versa*.) The second of these formulations is relevant to the suggestions that we have already met, that an omnipotent God creates the rules of logic or causal laws, and is then bound by them.

It is clear that this is a paradox: the questions cannot be answered satisfactorily either in the affirmative or in the negative. If we answer "Yes," it follows that if God actually makes things which he cannot control, or makes rules which bind himself, he is not omnipotent once he has made them: there are *then* things which he cannot do. But if we answer "No," we are immediately asserting that there are things which he cannot do, that is to say that he is already not omnipotent.

It cannot be replied that the question which sets this paradox is not a proper question. It would make perfectly good sense to say that a human mechanic has made a machine which he cannot control: if there is any difficulty about the question it lies in the notion of omnipotence itself.

This, incidentally, shows that although we have approached this paradox from the free will theory, it is equally a problem for a theological determinist. No one thinks that machines have free will, yet they may well be beyond the control of their makers. The determinist might reply that anyone who makes anything determines its ways of acting, and so determines its subsequent behaviour: even the human mechanic does this by his *choice* of materials and structure for his machine, though he does not know all about either of these: the mechanic thus determines, though he may not foresee, his machine's actions. And since God is omniscient, and since his creation of things is total, he both determines and foresees the ways in which his creatures will act. We may grant this, but it is beside the point. The question is not whether God *originally* determined the future actions of his creatures, but whether he can *subsequently* control their actions, or whether he was able in his original creation to put things beyond his subsequent control. Even on determinist principles the answers "Yes" and "No" are equally irreconcilable with God's omnipotence.

Before suggesting a solution of this paradox, I would point out that there is a parallel Paradox of Sovereignty. Can a legal sovereign make a law restricting its own future legislative power? For example, could the British parliament make a law forbidding any future parliament to socialise banking, and also forbidding the future repeal of this law itself? Or could the British parliament, which was legally sovereign in Australia in, say, 1899, pass a valid law, or series of laws, which made it no longer sovereign in 1933? Again, neither the affirmative nor the negative answer is really satisfactory. If we were to answer "Yes," we should be admitting the validity of a law which if it were actually made, would mean that parliament was no longer sovereign. If we were to answer "No," we should be admitting that there is a law, not logically absurd, which parliament cannot validly make, that is, that parliament is not now a legal sovereign. This paradox can be solved in the following way. We should distinguish between first order laws, that is laws governing the actions of individuals and bodies other than the legislature, and second order laws, that is laws about laws, laws governing the actions of the legislature itself. Correspondingly, we should distinguish two orders of sovereignty, first order sovereignty (sovereignty (1)) which is unlimited authority to make first order laws, and second order sovereignty (sovereignty (2)) which is unlimited authority to make second order laws. If we say that parliament is sovereign we might mean that any parliament at any time has sovereignty (1), or we might mean that parliament has both sovereignty (1) and sovereignty (2) at present, but we cannot without contradiction mean both that the present parliament has sovereignty (2) and that every parliament at every time has sovereignty (1), for if the present parliament has sovereignty (2) it may use it to take away the sovereignty (1) of later parlia-

ments. What the paradox shows is that we cannot ascribe to any continuing institution legal sovereignty in an inclusive sense.

The analogy between omnipotence and sovereignty shows that the paradox of omnipotence can be solved in a similar way. We must distinguish between first order omnipotence (omnipotence (1)), that is unlimited power to act, and second order omnipotence (omnipotence (2)), that is unlimited power to determine what powers to act things shall have. Then we could consistently say that God all the time has omnipotence (1), but if so no beings at any time have powers to act independently of God. Or we could say that God at one time had omnipotence (2), and used it to assign independent powers to act to certain things, so that God thereafter did not have omnipotence (1). But what the paradox shows is that we cannot consistently ascribe to any continuing being omnipotence in an inclusive sense.

An alternative solution of this paradox would be simply to deny that God is a continuing being, that any times can be assigned to his actions at all. But on this assumption (which also has difficulties of its own) no meaning can be given to the assertion that God made men with wills so free that he could not control them. The paradox of omnipotence can be avoided by putting God outside time, but the freewill solution of the problem of evil cannot be saved in this way, and equally it remains impossible to hold that an omnipotent God *binds himself* by causal or logical laws.

Conclusion

Of the proposed solutions of the problem of evil which we have examined, none has stood up to criticism. There may be other solutions which require examination, but this study strongly suggests that there is no valid solution of the problem which does not modify at least one of the constituent propositions in a way which would seriously affect the essential core of the theistic position.

Quite apart from the problem of evil, the paradox of omnipotence has shown that God's omnipotence must in any case be restricted in one way or another, that unqualified omnipotence cannot be ascribed to any being that continues through time. And if God and his actions are not in time, can omnipotence, or power of any sort, be meaningfully ascribed to him?

45

The Problem of Evil

JOHN HICK

To many, the most powerful positive objection to belief in God is the fact of evil. Probably for most agnostics it is the appalling depth and extent of human suffering, more than anything else, that makes the idea of a loving Creator seem so implausible and disposes them toward one or another of the various naturalistic theories of religion.

As a challenge to theism, the problem of evil has traditionally been posed in the form of a dilemma: if God is perfectly loving, he must wish to abolish evil; and if he is all-powerful, he must be able to abolish evil. But evil exists; therefore God cannot be both omnipotent and perfectly loving.

Certain solutions, which at once suggest themselves, have to be ruled out so far as the Judaic-Christian faith is concerned.

To say, for example (with con-temporary Christian Science), that evil is an illusion of the human mind, is impossible within a religion based upon the stark realism of the Bible. Its pages faithfully reflect the characteristic mixture of good and evil in human experience. They record every kind of sorrow and suffering, every mode of man's inhumanity to man and of his painfully insecure existence in the world. There is no attempt to regard evil as anything but dark, menacingly ugly, heart-rending, and crushing. In the Christian scriptures, the climax of this history of evil is the crucifixion of Jesus, which is presented not only as a case of utterly unjust suffering, but as the violent and murderous rejection of God's Messiah. There can be no doubt, then, that for biblical faith evil is unambiguously evil and stands in direct opposition to God's will.

Again, to solve the problem of

[John Hick, PHILOSOPHY OF RELIGION, 2d ed., © 1973, pp. 36–43. Reprinted by permission of Prentice-Hall, Inc., Englewood Cliffs, New Jersey] evil by means of the theory (sponsored, for example, by the Boston "Personalist" School)[1] of a finite deity who does the best he can with a material, intractable and coeternal with himself, is to have abandoned the basic premise of Hebrew-Christian monotheism; for the theory amounts to rejecting belief in the infinity and sovereignty of God.

Indeed, any theory that would avoid the problem of the origin of evil by depicting it as an ultimate constituent of the universe, co-ordinate with good, has been repudiated in advance by the classic Christian teaching, first developed by Augustine, that evil represents the going wrong of something that in itself is good.[2] Augustine holds firmly to the Hebrew-Christian conviction that the universe is *good*—that is to say, it is the creation of a good God for a good purpose. He completely rejects the ancient prejudice that matter is evil. There are, according to Augustine, higher and lower, greater and lesser goods in immense abundance and variety; but everything that has being is good in its own way and degree, except in so far as it may have become spoiled or corrupted. Evil—whether it be an evil will, an instance of pain, or some disorder or decay in nature—has not been set there by God, but represents the distortion of something that is inherently valuable. Whatever exists is, as such, and in its proper place, good; evil is essentially parasitic upon good, being disorder and perversion in a fundamentally good creation. This understanding of evil as something negative means that it is not willed and created by God; but it does not mean (as some have supposed) that evil is unreal and can be disregarded. On the contrary, the first effect of this doctrine is to accentuate even more the question of the origin of evil.

Theodicy,[3] as many modern Christian thinkers see it, is a modest enterprise, negative rather than positive in its conclusions. It does not claim to explain, nor to explain away, every instance of evil in human experience, but only to point to certain considerations that prevent the fact of evil (largely incomprehensible though it remains) from constituting a final and insuperable bar to rational belief in God.

In indicating these considerations it will be useful to follow the traditional division of the subject. There is the problem of *moral evil* or wickedness: why does an all-good and all-powerful God permit this? And there is the problem of the *non-*

---

1.   Edgar Brightman's *A Philosophy of Religion* (Englewood Cliffs, N.J.: Prentice-Hall, Inc., 1940), Chaps. 8–10, is a classic exposition of one form of this view.

2.   See Augustine's *Confessions,* Book VII, Chap. 12; *City of God,* Book XII, Chap. 3; *Enchiridion,* Chap. 4.

3.   The word "theodicy," from the Greek *theos* (God) and *dike* (righteous), means the justification of God's goodness in the face of the fact of evil.

moral evil of suffering or pain, both physical and mental: why has an all-good and all-powerful God created a world in which this occurs?

Christian thought has always considered moral evil in its relation to human freedom and responsibility. To be a person is to be a finite center of freedom, a (relatively) free and self-directing agent responsible for one's own decisions. This involves being free to act wrongly as well as to act rightly. The idea of a person who can be infallibly guaranteed always to act rightly is self-contradictory. There can be no certainty in advance that a genuinely free moral agent will never choose amiss. Consequently, the possibility of wrongdoing or sin is logically inseparable from the creation of finite persons, and to say that God should not have created beings who might sin amounts to saying that he should not have created people.

This thesis has been challenged in some recent philosophical discussions of the problem of evil, in which it is claimed that no contradiction is involved in saying that God might have made people who would be genuinely free but who could at the same time be guaranteed always to act rightly. A quote from one of these discussions follows:

If there is no logical impossibility in a man's freely choosing the good on one, or on several occasions, there cannot be a logical impossibility in his freely choosing the good on every occasion. God was not, then, faced with a choice between making innocent automata and making beings who, in acting freely, would sometimes go wrong: there was open to him the obviously better possibility of making beings who would act freely but always go right. Clearly, his failure to avail himself of this possibility is inconsistent ·with his being both omnipotent and wholly good.[4]

A reply to this argument is indirectly suggested in another recent contribution to the discussion.[5] If by a free action we mean an action that is not externally compelled but that flows from the nature of the agent as he reacts to the circumstances in which he finds himself, there is indeed no contradiction between our being free and our actions being "caused" (by our own nature) and therefore being in principle predictable. There is a contradiction, however, in saying that God is the cause of our acting as we do but that we are free beings *in relation to God*. There is, in other words, a contradiction in saying that God has

---

4. J. L. Mackie, "Evil and Omnipotence," *Mind* (April, 1955), p. 209. A similar point is made by Antony Flew in "Divine Omnipotence and Human Freedom," *New Essays in Philosophical Theology*. An important critical comment on these arguments is offered by Ninian Smart in "Omnipotence, Evil, and Supermen," *Philosophy* (April, 1961), with replies by Flew (January, 1962) and Mackie (April, 1962).

5. Flew, in *New Essays in Philosophical Theology*.

made us so that we shall of necessity act in a certain way, and that we are genuinely independent persons in relation to him. If all our thoughts and actions are divinely predestined, however free and morally responsible we may seem to be to ourselves, we cannot be free and morally responsible in the sight of God, but must instead be his helpless puppets. Such "freedom" is like that of a patient acting out a series of posthypnotic suggestions: he appears, even to himself, to be free, but his volitions have actually been predetermined by another will, that of the hypnotist, in relation to whom the patient is not a free agent.

A different objector might raise the question of whether or not we deny God's omnipotence if we admit that he is unable to create persons who are free from the risks inherent in personal freedom. The answer that has always been given is that to create such beings is logically impossible. It is no limitation upon God's power that he cannot accomplish the logically impossible, since there is nothing here to accomplish, but only a meaningless conjunction of words[6]—in this case "person who is not a person." God is able to create beings of any and every conceivable kind; but creatures who lack moral freedom, however superior they might be to human beings in other respects, would not be what we mean by persons. They would constitute a different form of life that God might have brought into existence instead of persons. When we ask why God did not create such beings in place of persons the traditional answer is that only persons could, in any meaningful sense, become "children of God," capable of entering into a personal relationship with their Creator by a free and uncompelled response to his love.

When we turn from the possibility of moral evil as a correlate of man's personal freedom to its actuality, we face something that must remain inexplicable even when it can be seen to be possible. For we can never provide a complete causal explanation of a free act; if we could, it would not be a free act. The origin of moral evil lies forever concealed within the mystery of human freedom.

The necessary connection between moral freedom and the possibility, now actualized, of sin throws light upon a great deal of the suffering that afflicts mankind. For an enormous amount of human pain arises either from the inhumanity or the culpable incompetence of mankind. This includes such major scourges as poverty, oppression and persecution, war, and all the injustice, indignity, and inequity that oc-

---

6. As Aquinas said, ". . . nothing that implies a contradiction falls under the scope of God's omnipotence." *Summa Theologica,* Part I, Question 25, Art. 4.

cur even in the most advanced societies. These evils are manifestations of human sin. Even disease is fostered to an extent, the limits of which have not yet been determined by psychosomatic medicine, by emotional and moral factors seated both in the individual and in his social environment. To the extent that all of these evils stem from human failures and wrong decisions, their possibility is inherent in the creation of free persons inhabiting a world that presents them with real choices followed by real consequences.

We may now turn more directly to the problem of suffering. Even though the major bulk of actual human pain is traceable to man's misused freedom as a sole or part cause, there remain other sources of pain that are entirely independent of the human will, for example, earthquake, hurricane, storm, flood, drought, and blight. In practice, it is often impossible to trace a boundary between the suffering that results from human wickedness and folly and that which falls upon mankind from without; both kinds of suffering are inextricably mingled together in human experience. For our present purpose, however, it is important to note that the latter category does exist and that it seems to be built into the very structure of our world. In response to it, theodicy, if it is wisely conducted, follows a negative path. It is not possible to show positively that each item of human pain serves a divine purpose of good; but, on the other hand, it does seem possible to show that the divine purpose as it is understood in Judaism and Christianity could not be forwarded in a world that was designed as a permanent hedonistic paradise.

An essential premise of this argument concerns the nature of the divine purpose in creating the world. The sceptic's assumption is that man is to be viewed as a completed creation and that God's purpose in making the world was to provide a suitable dwelling-place for this fully formed creature. Since God is good and loving, the environment that he has created for human life to inhabit will naturally be as pleasant and comfortable as possible. The problem is essentially similar to that of a man who builds a cage for some pet animal. Since our world, in fact, contains sources of hardship, inconvenience and danger of innumerable kinds, the conclusion follows that this world cannot have been created by a perfectly benevolent and all-powerful deity.[7]

Christianity, however, has never supposed that God's purpose in the creation of the world was to construct a paradise whose inhabitants would experience a maximum of pleasure and a minimum of pain. The world is seen, instead, as a place

7. This is essentially David Hume's argument in his discussion of the problem of evil in his *Dialogues,* Part XI.

of "soul making" or person making in which free beings, grappling with the tasks and challenges of their existence in a common environment, may become "children of God" and "heirs of eternal life." A way of thinking theologically of God's continuing creative purpose for man was suggested by some of the early Hellenistic Fathers of the Christian Church, especially Irenaeus. Following hints from Saint Paul, Irenaeus taught that man has been made as a person in the image of God but has not yet been brought as a free and responsible agent into the finite likeness of God, which is revealed in Christ.[8] Our world, with all its rough edges, is the sphere in which this second and harder stage of the creative process is taking place.

This conception of the world (whether or not set in Irenaeus's theological framework) can be supported by the method of negative theodicy. Suppose, contrary to fact, that this world were a paradise from which all possibility of pain and suffering were excluded. The consequences would be very far-reaching. For example, no one could ever injure anyone else: the murderer's knife would turn to paper or his bullets to thin air; the bank safe, robbed of a million dollars, would miraculously become filled with another million dollars (without this device, on however large a scale, proving inflationary); fraud, deceit, conspir-

acy, and treason would somehow always leave the fabric of society undamaged. Again, no one would ever be injured by accident: the mountain climber, steeplejack, or playing child falling from a height would float unharmed to the ground; the reckless driver would never meet with disaster. There would be no need to work, since no harm could result from avoiding work; there would be no call to be concerned for others in time of need or danger, for in such a world there could be no real needs or dangers.

To make possible this continual series of individual adjustments, nature would have to work by "special providences" instead of running according to general laws that men must learn to respect on penalty of pain or death. The laws of nature would have to be extremely flexible: sometimes gravity would operate, sometimes not; sometimes an object would be hard and solid, sometimes soft. There could be no sciences, for there would be no enduring world structure to investigate. In eliminating the problems and hardships of an objective environment, with its own laws, life would become like a dream in which, delightfully but aimlessly, we would float and drift at ease.

One can at least begin to imagine such a world. It is evident that our present ethical concepts would have no meaning in it. If, for ex-

---

8.   See Irenaeus's *Against Heresies,* Book IV, Chaps. 37 and 38.

ample, the notion of harming someone is an essential element in the concept of a wrong action, in our hedonistic paradise there could be no wrong actions—nor any right actions in distinction from wrong. Courage and fortitude would have no point in an environment in which there is, by definition, no danger or difficulty. Generosity, kindness, the *agape* aspect of love, prudence, unselfishness, and all other ethical notions which presuppose life in an objective environment could not even be formed. Consequently, such a world, however well it might promote pleasure, would be very ill adapted for the development of the moral qualities of human personality. In relation to this purpose it might be the worst of all possible worlds!

It would seem, then, that an environment intended to make possible the growth in free beings of the finest characteristics of personal life must have a good deal in common with our present world. It must operate according to general and dependable laws; and it must involve real dangers, difficulties, problems, obstacles, and possibilities of pain, failure, sorrow, frustration, and defeat. If it did not contain the particular trials and perils that—subtracting man's own very considerable contribution—our world contains, it would have to contain others instead.

To realize this is not, by any means, to be in possession of a detailed theodicy. It is to understand that this world, with all its "heartaches and the thousand natural shocks that flesh is heir to," an environment so manifestly not designed for the maximization of human pleasure and the minimization of human pain, may nevertheless be rather well adapted to the quite different purpose of "soul making."[9]

These considerations are related to theism as such. Specifically Christian theism goes further in the light of the death of Christ, which is seen paradoxically both (as the murder of the divine Son) as the worst thing that has ever happened and (as the occasion of man's salvation) as the best thing that has ever happened. As the supreme evil turned to supreme good, it provides the paradigm for the distinctively Christian reaction to evil. Viewed from the standpoint of Christian faith, evils do not cease to be evils; and certainly, in view of Christ's healing work, they cannot be said to have been sent by God. Yet, it has been the persistent claim of those seriously and wholeheartedly committed to Christian discipleship that tragedy, though truly tragic, may nevertheless be turned, through a man's reaction to

---

9. This brief discussion has been confined to the problem of human suffering. The large and intractable problem of animal pain is not taken up here. For a discussion of it see, for example, Austin Farrer, *Love Almighty and Ills Unlimited* (Garden City, N.Y.: Doubleday & Company, Inc., 1961), Chap. 5, and John Hick, *Evil and the God of Love* (London: Collins, The Fontana Library, 1968), pp. 345–53.

it, from a cause of despair and alienation from God to a stage in the fulfillment of God's loving purpose for that individual. As the greatest of all evils, the crucifixion of Christ, was made the occasion of man's redemption, so good can be won from other evils. As Jesus saw his execution by the Romans as an experience which God desired him to accept, an experience which was to be brought within the sphere of the divine purpose and made to serve the divine ends, so the Christian response to calamity is to accept the adversities, pains, and afflictions which life brings, in order that they can be turned to a positive spiritual use.[10]

At this point, theodicy points forward in two ways to the subject of life after death, which is to be discussed in later chapters.

First, although there are many striking instances of good being triumphantly brought out of evil through a man's or a woman's reaction to it, there are many other cases in which the opposite has happened. Sometimes obstacles breed strength of character, dangers evoke courage and unselfishness, and calamities produce patience and moral steadfastness. But sometimes they lead, instead, to resentment, fear, grasping selfishness, and disintegration of character. Therefore, it would seem that any divine purpose of soul making that is at work in earthly history must continue beyond this life if it is ever to achieve more than a very partial and fragmentary success.[11]

Second, if we ask whether the business of soul making is worth all the toil and sorrow of human life, the Christian answer must be in terms of a future good great enough to justify all that has happened on the way to it.

AFTERWORD

The most frequently employed defenses of traditional theism against the problem of evil all seem to involve the admission that there is some evil, coupled with the claim that it is unavoidable if some much more important good is to be obtained. In particular, it is common to explain the permission of moral evil in terms of the vast importance of human free agency. Notice that this argument requires a stand on rather difficult issues which have been raised in other chapters. Specifically, it seems to require a position on the issue of determinism, freedom, and responsibility (Chapter 4). A hard determinist seems an unlikely subscriber to the free-will defense, and a libertarian might find it plausible. But what would a soft determinist say? Notice, too, that the

10.   This conception of providence is stated more fully in John Hick, *Faith and Knowledge,* 2nd ed. (Ithaca, N.Y.: Cornell University Press, 1966), Chap. 10, some sentences from which are incorporated in this paragraph.

11.   The position presented above is developed more fully in the author's *Evil and the God of Love.*

free-will defense takes a stand on one of those typical confrontations between deontological and teleological values mentioned in the Afterword to Chapter 6. That is, it involves taking the deontological value of freedom to outweigh vast amounts of teleological disvalue in the form of pain and unhappiness.

In this connection it is worth considering carefully whether you would accept arguments similar to the free-will defense in other contexts. For example, should the state or society attempt to *prevent* harmful (criminal) activity by its citizens, even if this means restricting their freedom? Or is the proper role of the state only punitive—letting people act freely, but then punishing those who choose to act wrongly? Would not a free-will defense here amount to claiming that we should not restrain people from wrong-doing—though we may justly punish them for it afterward? But does it seem plausible to claim that human freedom is so important that we should not take a weapon away from someone attempting to commit murder with it? Note that, since murders do occur, God has not seen fit to prevent them by such simple means as, say, spoiling the aim of the murderer.

It is important here not to stop with a single example. So, consider, also, that there is a strong tendency in medical ethics to allow a patient to refuse treatment even when the physician knows that such refusal will be harmful, or even fatal, and that the available treatment would be likely to result in complete recovery. And the basis for this tendency is largely respect for the importance of human freedom. In this case, of course, the patient harms himself rather than others, and that does make a significant difference. It is much more difficult to decide whether parents may be allowed to refuse vital treatment for their children.

Considering such nontheological applications of the free-will defense may have useful effects in several ways. You may have a firm stand on the value of the theological argument, and come to a position on these other cases on the basis of that stand. Or, you may have firm convictions about the nontheological cases, and find that you can make your evaluation of the theological arguments on the basis of those convictions. Or you may find that comparing the different applications of the free-will defense improves your understanding of both theological and nontheological issues.

REVIEW QUESTIONS

Selection 40

1. Hume devotes a large part of this selection to showing us *how much* evil there is in the world. Why didn't he content himself with simply showing that there is some?

2. Is it plausible to regard Philo's acceptance of the teleological argument (Selection 35, Chapter 9) as laying the groundwork for the argument in this selection? Explain.

3. Demea suggests that present evils "are rectified in other regions, and in some future period of existence." Explain this suggestion, and explain why Cleanthes rejects it.

4. What is the point Philo makes in the next-to-last paragraph in this selection?

Selection 41

5. What does Aquinas think evil is? Can you give some examples of evil and explain how his conception of evil would apply to them?

6. Aquinas argues that God is not the cause of evil. Try to put the argument clearly in your own words.

Selection 42

7. Leibniz is arguing that the universe is perfect. What is his response to those who claim that it doesn't *seem* perfect?

8. How does Leibniz deal with human suffering? or with the suffering of innocent, or very good persons?

9. To how much of this selection does Hume's discussion reply? What are the replies?

Selection 43.

10. Why does Royce think we cannot solve the problem of evil by (*a*) claiming that evil results from free-will; (*b*) claiming that evil is a means to good; (*c*) claiming that evil is a foil to good?

11. Royce claims that evil is *part* of the good. What is the objection he anticipates will be given to this claim?

12. What is the distinction Royce makes between two classes of evil, and how does it provide the basis for Royce's response to the objection mentioned in question 11?

Selection 44

13. What does Mackie mean when he says certain solutions to the problem of evil are *adequate*? Why don't many theologians accept such "adequate" solutions?

14. Mackie discusses four fallacious solutions. What are they, and what does he think is wrong with each one?

15. What is the Paradox of Omnipotence? What solution to it does Mackie suggest? Can you think of an alternative solution?

16. Which, if any, of Mackie's arguments apply to the views of Leibniz, Aquinas, or Royce?

Selection 45

17. Hick claims that certain solutions to the problem of evil are incompatible with Judaic-Christian faith. What are they, and why are they incompatible?

18. Why is it important to distinguish between moral evil and natural evil?

19. How does Hick explain the compatibility of moral evil with the existence of an omnipotent and benevolent God?

20. How does Hick employ the concept of soul making to deal with the problem of natural evil?

21. Why does the idea of soul making lead to the question of life after death? Does this mean the problem of evil cannot be solved unless there is personal survival after death? Could we take the solution of the problem of evil to *prove* such survival? Explain.

11

Perception and Knowledge of the Physical World

There is much that we do not know about the physical world, but it would seem preposterous to claim that none of us knows anything at all about it. What could be more obvious than that we know many things about our physical surroundings—things such as the locations and characteristics of local geographical features (mountains, lakes, rivers, parks, streets, etc.); more about the flora and fauna inhabiting them; and still more about those physical objects involved in our daily lives, such as our personal possessions, food, and clothing?

Some of this knowledge we obtain second-hand, hearing it from others or reading it. But much of it is based upon our own experience and observation. We know the ordinary objects and events in our immediate physical surroundings because our senses inform us about them—we *perceive* them. And most second-hand information actually amounts to reports based upon the experience and observations of others. Even very complex theories about the nature of the physical world (e.g., theories about the chemical or atomic properties of various materials) are thought by most people to be based upon perception, for, among other things, such theories must explain to us why we perceive what we do, and they are tested for correctness by observing whether or not perception occurs as the theories predict. Many would claim that *everything* we know about the physical world is known, directly or indirectly, as a result of perception.

But perception has its problems. Things do not always appear to us as they really are. We all have mistaken one object for another, misjudged the speed at which things were moving, or their direction. We fail to identify colors, shapes, or sizes simply because things sometimes really are not as they appear to be. Further, if we consider scientific accounts of the physiological processes involved in perception, and the nature of the physical world, then we may begin to wonder if things *ever* appear to us as they really are. Objects, for example, which appear to us to be solid, with smooth surfaces, and undergoing no change, really are enormously complex structures of particles which are constantly in motion, exchanging positions, being lost from the object, or becoming incorporated into it. And all that is needed for us to seem to perceive physical objects is neurological stimulation of certain sorts. If that stimulation is provided, no matter by what means, the pertinent sensations will occur. Stimulate the brain in the proper manner and one has the visual impression of a cat on a fence. The sequence of causes leading to such stimulation may, indeed, begin with light being refracted from a real cat on a real fence. But it would make no difference in our sensations if the same stimulation could be produced by some other objects, or by surgical manipulation of the optic nerve, or by direct stimulation of the brain with electrodes. In short, the science which we take to be based upon perception tells us that perception is not a reliable source of knowledge about the physical world.

To sum up this paradoxical situation, we seem to have very good reasons for believing that:

(1) We know a great deal about the physical world.

(2) All the knowledge we have about the physical world must be based upon perception.

(3) Perception is not a reliable source of knowledge about the physical world.

But these three claims cannot all be true. Some very plausible claim must be given up.

One possibility, of course, is to give up (1). A few philosophers have been so convinced of the truth of (2) and (3) that they have seen no alternative but to reject (1). Such a position is called *scepticism*. It is important to note that the sceptic does not claim that the physical world is not as it seems to be, but only that we can't be sure what it really is like.

Most philosophers interested in this set of issues regard scepticism as an unsatisfactory answer. At the same time, they find the reasons for accepting (2) and (3) very attractive. So, they tend to regard the major problem as finding some way to avoid scepticism by showing that we are not forced into it by (2) and (3). In some cases, especially in rationalistic philosophy, statement (2) has been rejected. So, some philosophers have argued that we can discover the character of the physical world without relying on the results of perception—for example, by seeking a priori knowledge of basic physical principles and then deriving our knowledge of the actual world from those. But a more promising approach is thought by many to involve rejection of (3), to show that perception, at least under some circumstances, can be a reliable source of knowledge about physical reality.

The most tempting approach to this problem may seem to be some form of *realism*. The realist is committed to the view that physical objects and their properties exist without depending in any way upon our perception of them, and that we can learn what they are like through perception. *Naive realism* is the view that perception directly reveals things to us as they really are. Thus all shapes, colors, sounds, smells, etc., are regarded as real properties of the physical world and its objects. In such a view, of course, perception is a highly reliable source of knowledge—in fact, it may be too reliable. For it is hard to see, in the naive realist account, how it is possible for us ever to make mistakes. If we always perceive things as they really are, how could error be possible? Yet, errors do occur.

Representative realism holds that what we are aware of in perception are *sensations* (also called *ideas, impressions, percepts,* or *sense-data*) which are caused in us by the action of the physical world upon our sensory systems. In this view, we judge the nature of physical reality by inferring it from the character of our sensations. The possibility of error then can be explained in terms of our making mistaken inferences about the physical reality causing our sensations. But when we take proper precautions to assure the correctness of our inferences, knowledge of physical reality can be based securely upon our perceptions. One challenge for representative realism is to explain what these proper precautions are—to decide under what circumstances it is safe to accept what our senses seem to tell us, and under what circumstances we should withhold judgment. A second challenge is to explain how our sensations could tell us anything at all about physical reality; for if the sensations are all we *ever* are directly aware of, how could we come to know what kinds of reality are their causes?

Thus, realism confronts a serious dilemma. Either we perceive nature directly, in which case error seems impossible to explain; or we perceive sensations caused by nature and make inferences about nature on the basis of those sensations, in which case it seems impossible that we should ever have a sufficient foundation for the inferences. In response to these difficulties nonrealist theories have been offered which suggest that we abandon the notion of an independently existing physical reality which causes our sensations, and that, instead, we regard the physical world and its objects as complex structures of the very sensations themselves. Here we can deal with both sides of the realistic dilemma. Since the physical world is made up of sensations, then we do perceive it directly and can have knowledge of it. On the other hand, since a physical object is a complex structure of many sensations, error is possible because we may infer mistakenly that a particular sensation belongs to one complex rather than another. For such theories the problem remains of explaining under what circumstances our inferences are reliable; and a new problem arises in the form of a need to show that abandoning belief in a physical reality independent of our minds and experience is not unreasonable.

As you read these selections, look for accounts of the nature of perception. In particular, what is it that we are thought to perceive, and what, if anything, do we infer from it? Additionally, look for accounts of the character of physical reality, and the extent to which its existence is thought to be independent of our minds or experience. From these two kinds of account will be drawn the explanations of whether perception provides us with knowledge, and the circumstances, if any, under which it does so.

46

Sceptical Doubts about Our Knowledge of the Physical World

RENÉ DESCARTES

Things Which We May Doubt

All that I have, up to this moment, accepted as possessed of the highest truth and certainty, I received either from or through the senses. I observed, however, that these sometimes misled us; and it is the part of prudence not to place absolute confidence in that by which we have even once been deceived.

But it may be said, perhaps, that, although the senses occasionally mislead us respecting minute objects, and such as are so far removed from us as to be beyond the reach of close observation, there are yet many other of their informations (presentations), of the truth of which it is manifestly impossible to doubt; as for example, that I am in this place, seated by the fire, clothed in a winter dressing-gown, that I hold in my hands this piece of paper, with other intimations of the same nature. But how could I deny that I possess these hands and this body, and withal escape being classed with persons in a state of insanity, whose brains are so disordered and clouded by dark bilious vapours as to cause them pertinaciously to assert that they are monarchs when they are in the greatest poverty; or clothed [in gold] and purple when destitute of any covering; or that their head is

[From *Meditations on First Philosophy* (1641), Meditations I, II. Translated by John Veitch (1853).]

made of clay, their body of glass, or that they are gourds? I should certainly be not less insane than they, were I to regulate my procedure according to examples so extravagant.

Though this be true, I must nevertheless here consider that I am a man, and that, consequently, I am in the habit of sleeping, and representing to myself in dreams those same things, or even sometimes others less probable, which the insane think are presented to them in their waking moments. How often have I dreamt that I was in these familiar circumstances—that I was dressed, and occupied this place by the fire, when I was lying undressed in bed? At the present moment, however, I certainly look upon this paper with eyes wide awake; the head which I now move is not asleep; I extend this hand consciously and with express purpose, and I perceive it; the occurrences in sleep are not so distinct as all this. But I cannot forget that, at other times, I have been deceived in sleep by similar illusions; and, attentively considering those cases, I perceive so clearly that there exist no certain marks by which the state of waking can ever be distinguished from sleep, that I feel greatly astonished; and in amazement I almost persuade myself that I am now dreaming.

Let us suppose, then, that we are dreaming, and that all these particulars—namely, the opening of the eyes, the motion of the head, the forth-putting of the hands—are merely illusions; and even that we really possess neither an entire body nor hands such as we see. Nevertheless, it must be admitted at least that the objects which appear to us in sleep are, as it were, painted representations which could not have been formed unless in the likeness of realities; and, therefore, that those general objects, at all events—namely, eyes, a head, hands, and an entire body—are not simply imaginary, but really existent. For, in truth, painters themselves, even when they study to represent sirens and satyrs by forms the most fantastic and extraordinary, cannot bestow upon them natures absolutely new, but can only make a certain medley of the members of different animals; or if they chance to imagine something so novel that nothing at all similar has ever been seen before, and such as is, therefore, purely fictitious and absolutely false, it is at least certain that the colours of which this is composed are real.

And on the same principle, although these general objects, viz. [a body], eyes, a head, hands, and the like, be imaginary, we are nevertheless absolutely necessitated to admit the reality at least of some other objects still more simple and universal than these, of which, just as of certain real colours, all those images of things, whether true and real, or false and fantastic, that are found in our consciousness (cogitatio), are formed.

To this class of objects seem to belong corporeal nature in general and its extension; the figure of extended things, their quantity or magnitude, and their number, as also the place in, and the time during, which they exist, and other things of the same sort. We will not, therefore, perhaps reason illegitimately if we conclude from this that physics, astronomy, medicine, and all the other sciences that have for their end the consideration of composite objects, are indeed of a doubtful character; but that arithmetic, geometry, and the other sciences of the same class, which regard merely the simplest and most general objects, and scarcely inquire whether or not these are really existent, contain somewhat that is certain and indubitable: for whether I am awake or dreaming, it remains true that two and three make five, and that a square has but four sides; nor does it seem possible that truths so apparent can ever fall under a suspicion of falsity [or incertitude].

Nevertheless, the belief that there is a God who is all-powerful, and who created me, such as I am, has for a long time, obtained steady possession of my mind. How, then, do I know that he has not arranged that there should be neither earth, nor sky, nor any extended thing, nor figure, nor magnitude, nor place, providing at the same time, however, for [the rise in me of the perceptions of all these objects, and] the persuasion that these do not exist otherwise than as I perceive them? And further, as I sometimes think that others are in error respecting matters of which they believe themselves to possess a perfect knowledge, how do I know that I am not also deceived each time I add together two and three, or number the sides of a square, or form some judgment still more simple, if more simple indeed can be imagined? But perhaps Deity has not been willing that I should be thus deceived, for he is said to be supremely good. If, however, it were repugnant to the goodness of Deity to have created me subject to constant deception, it would seem likewise to be contrary to his goodness to allow me to be occasionally deceived; and yet it is clear that this is permitted. Some, indeed, might perhaps be found who would be disposed rather to deny the existence of a being so powerful than to believe that there is nothing certain. But let us for the present refrain from opposing this opinion, and grant that all which is here said of a Deity is fabulous: nevertheless, in whatever way it be supposed that I reached the state in which I exist, whether by fate, or chance, or by an endless series of antecedents and consequents, or by any other means, it is clear (since to be deceived and to err is a certain defect) that the probability of my being so imperfect as to be the constant victim of deception, will be increased exactly in proportion as the power possessed by the cause, to which they assign my origin, is lessened. To these reasonings I have assuredly nothing to reply, but am constrained at last to avow that there is nothing at all that I formerly believed to be true of which it is impossible to doubt, and that not through thoughtlessness or levity, but from cogent and maturely considered reasons; so that henceforward, if I desire to discover anything certain, I ought not the less carefully to refrain from assenting to those same opinions than to what might be shown to be manifestly false. . . .

I will suppose, then, not that Deity, who is sovereignly good and the fountain of truth, but that some malignant demon, who is at once exceedingly potent and deceitful, has employed all his artifice to deceive me; I will suppose that the sky, the air, the earth, colours, figures, sounds, and all external things, are nothing better than the illusions of dreams, by means of which this being has laid snares for my credulity; I will consider myself as without hands, eyes, flesh, blood, or any of the senses, and as falsely believing that I am possessed of these; I will continue resolutely fixed in this belief, and if indeed by this means it be not in my power to arrive at the knowledge of truth, I shall at least do what is in my power, viz. [suspend my judgment], and guard with settled purpose against giving my assent to what is false, and being imposed upon by this deceiver, whatever be his power and artifice. . . .

Mind More Easily
Known Than Body

I suppose, accordingly, that all the things which I see are false (fictitious); I believe that none of those objects which my fallacious memory represents ever existed; I suppose that I possess no senses; I believe that body, figure, extension, motion, and place are merely fictions of my mind. What is there, then, that can be esteemed true? Perhaps this only, that there is absolutely nothing certain.

But how do I know that there is not something different altogether from the objects I have now enumerated, of which it is impossible to entertain the slightest doubt? Is there not a God, or some being, by whatever name I may designate him, who causes these thoughts to arise in my mind? But why suppose such a being, for it may be I myself am capable of producing them? Am I, then, at least not something? But I before denied that I possessed senses or a body; I hesitate, however, for what follows from that? Am I so dependent on the body and the senses that without these I cannot exist? But I had the persuasion that there was absolutely nothing in the world, that there was no sky and no earth, neither minds nor bodies; was I not, therefore, at the same time, persuaded that I did not exist? Far from it; I assuredly existed, since I was persuaded. But there is I know not what being, who is possessed at once of the highest power and the deepest cunning, who is constantly employing all his ingenuity in deceiving me. Doubtless, then, I exist, since I am deceived; and, let him deceive me as he may, he can never bring it about that I am nothing, so long as I shall be conscious that I am something. So that it must, in fine, be maintained, all things being maturely and carefully considered, that this proposition (*pronunciatum*) I am, I exist, is necessarily true each time it is expressed by me, or conceived in my mind. ... (Caution 162)

Let us now accordingly consider the objects that are commonly thought to be [the most easily, and likewise] the most distinctly known, viz., the bodies we touch and see; not, indeed, bodies in general, for these general notions are usually somewhat more confused, but one body in particular. Take, for example, this piece of wax; it is quite fresh, having been but recently taken from the beehive; it has not yet lost the sweetness of the honey it contained; it still retains somewhat of the odour of the flowers from which it was gathered; its colour, figure, size, are apparent (to the sight); it is hard, cold, easily handled; and sounds when struck upon with the finger. In fine, all that contributes to make a body as distinctly known as possible, is found in the one before us. But, while I am speaking, let it be placed near the fire—what remained of the taste exhales, the smell evaporates, the colour changes, its figure is destroyed, its size increases, it becomes liquid, it grows hot, it can hardly be handled, and, although struck upon, it emits no sound. Does the same wax still remain after this change? It must be admitted that it does remain; no one

doubts it, or judges otherwise. What, then, was it I knew with so much distinctness in the piece of wax? Assuredly, it could be nothing of all that I observed by means of the senses, since all the things that fell under taste, smell, sight, touch, and hearing are changed, and yet the same wax remains. It was perhaps what I now think, viz., that this wax was neither the sweetness of honey, the pleasant odour of flowers, the whiteness, the figure, nor the sound, but only a body that a little before appeared to me conspicuous under these forms, and which is now perceived under others. But, to speak precisely, what is it that I imagine when I think of it in this way? Let it be attentively considered, and, retrenching all that does not belong to the wax, let us see what remains. There certainly remains nothing, except something extended, flexible, and movable. But what is meant by flexible and movable? Is it not that I imagine that the piece of wax, being round, is capable of becoming square, or of passing from a square into a triangular figure? Assuredly such is not the case, because I conceive that it admits of an infinity of similar changes; and I am, moreover, unable to compass this infinity by imagination, and consequently this conception which I have of the wax is not the product of the faculty of imagination. But what now is this extension? Is it not also unknown? for it becomes greater when the wax is melted, greater when it is boiled, and greater still when the heat increases; and I should not conceive [clearly and] according to truth, the wax as it is, if I did not suppose that the piece we are considering admitted even of a wider variety of extension than I ever imagined. I must, therefore, admit that I cannot even comprehend by imagination what the piece of wax is, and that it is the mind alone (*mens,* Lat.; *entendement,* F.) which perceives it. I speak of one piece in particular; for, as to wax in general, this is still more evident. But what is the piece of wax that can be perceived only by the [understanding of] mind? It is certainly the same which I see, touch, imagine; and, in fine, it is the same which, from the beginning, I believed it to be. But (and this it is of moment to observe) the perception of it is neither an act of sight, of touch, nor of imagination, and never was either of these, though it might formerly seem so, but is simply an intuition *(inspectio)* of the mind, which may be imperfect and confused, as it formerly was, or very clear and distinct, as it is at present, according as the attention is more or less directed to the elements which it contains, and of which it is composed.

But, meanwhile, I feel greatly astonished when I observe [the weakness of my mind, and] its proneness to error. For although, without at all giving expression to what I think, I consider all this in my own mind, words yet occasionally impede my progress, and I am almost led into error by the terms of ordinary language. We say, for example, that we see the same wax when it is before us, and not that we judge it to be the same from its retaining the same colour and figure: whence I should forthwith be disposed to conclude that the wax is known by the act of sight, and not by the intuition of the mind alone, were it not for the analogous instance of human beings passing on in the street below, as observed from a window. In this case I do not fail to say that I see the men themselves, just as I say that I see the wax; and yet what do I see from the window beyond hats and cloaks that might cover artificial machines, whose motions might be determined by springs? But I judge that there are human beings from these appearances, and thus I comprehend, by the faculty of judgment alone which is in the mind, what I believed I saw with my eyes.

The man who makes it his aim to rise to knowledge superior to the common, ought to be ashamed to seek occasions of doubting from the vulgar forms of speech: instead, therefore, of doing this, I shall proceed with the matter in hand, and inquire whether I had a clearer and more perfect perception of the piece of wax when I first saw it, and when I thought I knew it by means of the external sense itself, or, at all events, by the common sense (*sensus communis*), as it is called, that is, by the imaginative faculty or whether I rather apprehend it more clearly at present, after having examined with greater care, both what it is, and in what way it can be known. It would certainly be ridiculous to entertain any doubt on this point. For what, in that first perception, was there distinct? What did I perceive which any animal might not have perceived? But when I distinguish the wax from its exterior forms, and when, as if I had stripped it of its vestments, I consider it quite naked, it is certain, although some error may still be found in my judgment, that I cannot, nevertheless, thus apprehend it without possessing a human mind.

But, finally, what shall I say of the mind itself, that is, of myself? for as yet I do not admit that I am anything but mind. What, then! I who seem to possess so distinct an apprehension of the piece of wax,—do I not know myself, both with greater truth and certitude, and also much more distinctly and clearly? For if I judge that the wax exists because I see it, it assuredly follows, much more evidently, that I myself am or exist, for the same reason: for it is possible that what I see may not in truth be wax, and that I do not even possess eyes with which to see anything; but it cannot be that when I see, or, which comes to the same thing, when I think I see, I myself who think am nothing. So likewise, if I judge that the wax exists because I touch it, it will still also follow that I am; and if I determine that my imagination, or any other cause, whatever it be, persuades me of the existence of the wax, I will still draw the same conclusion. And what is here remarked of the piece of wax is applicable to all the other things that are external to me. And further, if the [notion or] perception of wax appeared to me more precise and distinct, after that not only sight and touch, but many other causes besides, rendered it manifest to my apprehension, with how much greater distinctness must I now know myself, since all the reasons that contribute to the knowledge of the nature of wax, or of any body whatever, manifest still better the nature of my mind? And there are besides so many other things in the mind itself that contribute to the illustration of its nature, that those dependent on the body, to which I have here referred, scarcely merit to be taken into account.

But, in conclusion, I find I have insensibly reverted to the point I desired; for, since it is now manifest to me that bodies themselves are not properly perceived by the senses nor by the faculty of imagination, but by the intellect alone; and since they are not perceived because they are seen and touched, but only because they are understood [or rightly comprehended by thought], I readily discover that there is nothing more easily or clearly apprehended than my own mind. . . .

47

Concerning Our Simple Ideas of Sensation

JOHN LOCKE

How Bodies Produce Ideas in Us

To discover the nature of our *ideas* the better, and to discourse of them intelligibly, it will be convenient to distinguish them *as they are ideas or perceptions in our minds; and as they are modifications of matter in the bodies that cause such perceptions in us:* that so we may not think (as perhaps usually is done) that they are exactly the images and resemblances of something inherent in the subject; most of those of sensation being in the mind no more the likeness of something existing without us, than the names that stand for them are the likeness of our ideas, which yet upon hearing they are apt to excite in us.

Whatsoever the mind perceives *in itself,* or is the immediate object of perception, thought, or understanding, that I call *idea;* and the power to produce any idea in our mind, I call *quality* of the subject wherein that power is. Thus a snowball having the power to produce in us the ideas of white, cold, and round,—the power to produce those ideas in us, as they are in the snowball, I call qualities; and as they are sensations or perceptions in our understandings, I call them ideas; which *ideas,* if I speak of sometimes as in the things themselves, I would be understood to mean those qualities in the objects which produce them in us.

Qualities thus considered in bodies are,

First, such as are utterly inseparable from the body, in what state soever it be; and such as in all the

[From *An Essay Concerning Human Understanding* (fourth ed.), Book II, chapters VIII, XXIII. First published in 1690.]

alterations and changes it suffers, all the force can be used upon it, it constantly keeps; and such as sense constantly finds in every particle of matter which has bulk enough to be perceived; and the mind finds inseparable from every particle of matter though less than to make itself singly be perceived by our senses: v.g. Take a grain of wheat, divide it into two parts; each part has still solidity, extension, figure, and mobility: divide it again, and it retains still the same qualities; and so divide it on, till the parts become insensible; they must retain still each of them all those qualities. For division (which is all that a mill, or pestle, or any other body, does upon another, in reducing it to insensible parts) can never take away either solidity, extension, figure, or mobility from any body, but only makes two or more distinct separate masses of matter, of that which was but one before; all which distinct masses, reckoned as so many distinct bodies, after division, make a certain number. These I call *original* or *primary qualities* of body, which I think we may observe to produce simple ideas in us, viz. solidity, extension, figure, motion or rest, and number.

Secondly, such qualities which in truth are nothing in the objects themselves but powers to produce various sensations in us by their primary qualities, i.e. by the bulk, figure, texture, and motion of their insensible parts, as colours, sounds, tastes, etc. These I call *secondary qualities.* To these might be added a *third* sort, which are allowed to be barely powers; though they are as much real qualities in the subject as those which I, to comply with the common way of speaking, call qualities, but for distinction, secondary qualities. For the power in fire to produce a new colour, or consistency, in *wax* or *clay,*—by its primary qualities, is as much a quality in fire, as the power it has to produce in *me* a new idea or sensation of warmth or burning, which I felt not before,— by the same primary qualities, viz. the bulk, texture, and motion of its insensible parts.

The next thing to be considered is, how bodies produce ideas in us; and that is manifestly by impulse, the only way which we can conceive bodies to operate in.

If then external objects be not united to our minds when they produce ideas therein; and yet we perceive these *original* qualities in such of them as singly fall under our senses, it is evident that some motion must be thence continued by our nerves, or animal spirits, by some parts of our bodies, to the brains or the seat of sensation, there to produce in our minds the particular ideas we have of them. And since the extension, figure, number, and motion of bodies of an observable bigness, may be perceived at a distance by the sight, it is evident some singly imperceptible bodies must come from them to the eyes, and thereby convey to the brain some motion;

which produces these ideas which we have of them in us.

After the same manner that the ideas of these original qualities are produced in us, we may conceive that the ideas of *secondary* qualities are also produced, viz. by the operation of insensible particles on our senses. For, it being manifest that there are bodies and good store of bodies, each whereof are so small, that we cannot by any of our senses discover either their bulk, figure, or motion,—as is evident in the particles of the air and water, and others extremely smaller than those; perhaps as much smaller than the particles of air and water, as the particles of air and water are smaller than peas or hail-stones;—let us suppose at present that the different motions and figures, bulk and number, of such particles, affecting the several organs of our senses, produce in us those different sensations which we have from the colours and smells of bodies; v.g. that a violet, by the impulse of such insensible particles of matter, of peculiar figures and bulks, and in different degrees and modifications of their motions, causes the ideas of the blue colour, and sweet scent of that flower to be produced in our minds. It being no more impossible to conceive that God should annex such ideas to such motions, with which they have no similitude, than that he should annex the idea of pain to the motion of a piece of steel dividing our flesh, with which that idea hath no resemblance.

What I have said concerning colours and smells may be understood also of tastes and sounds, and other the like sensible qualities; which, whatever reality we by mistake attribute to them, are in truth nothing in the objects themselves, but powers to produce various sensations in us; and depend on those primary qualities, viz. bulk, figure, texture, and motion of parts as I have said.

Ideas of Primary Qualities Are Resemblances; of Secondary, Not

From whence I think it easy to draw this observation,—that the ideas of primary qualities of bodies are resemblances of them, and their patterns do really exist in the bodies themselves, but the ideas produced in us by these secondary qualities have no resemblance of them at all. There is nothing like our ideas, existing in the bodies themselves. They are, in the bodies we denominate from them, only a power to produce those sensations in us: and what is sweet, blue, or warm in idea, is but the certain bulk, figure, and motion of the insensible parts, in the bodies themselves, which we call so.

Flame is denominated hot and light; snow, white and cold; and manna, white and sweet, from the ideas they produce in us. Which qualities are commonly thought to be the same in those bodies that those ideas are in us, the one the perfect resemblance of the other, as they are in a mirror, and it would by most men be judged very extravagant if one should say otherwise. And yet he that will consider that the same fire that, at one distance produces in us the sensation of warmth, does, at a nearer approach, produce in us the far different sensation of pain, ought to bethink himself what reason he has to say—that this idea of warmth, which was produced in him by the fire, is *actually in the fire;* and his idea of pain, which the same fire produced in him the same way, is *not* in the fire. Why are whiteness and coldness in snow, and pain not, when it produces the one and the other idea in us; and can do neither, but by the bulk, figure, number, and motion of its solid parts?

The particular bulk, number, figure, and motion of the parts of fire or snow are really in them,— whether any one's senses perceive them or no: and therefore they may be called *real* qualities, because they really exist in those bodies. But light, heat, whiteness, or coldness, are no more really in them than sickness or pain is in manna. Take away the sensation of them; let not the eyes see light or colours, nor the ears hear sounds; let the palate not taste, nor the nose smell, and all colours, tastes, odours, and sounds, *as they are such particular ideas,* vanish and cease, and are reduced to their causes, i.e. bulk, figure, and motion of parts. . . .

The Three Sorts of Qualities

The qualities, then, that are in bodies, rightly considered, are of three sorts:—

First, The bulk, figure, number, situation, and motion or rest of their solid parts. Those are in them, whether we perceive them or not; and when they are of that size that we can discover them, we have by these an idea of the thing as it is in itself; as is plain in artificial things. These I call *primary qualities.*

Secondly, The power that is in any body, by reason of its insensible primary qualities, to operate after a peculiar manner on any of our senses, and thereby produce in *us* the different ideas of several colours, sounds, smells, tastes, etc. These are usually called *sensible qualities.*

Thirdly, The power that is in any body, by reason of the particular constitution of its primary qualities, to make such a change in the bulk, figure, texture, and motion of *another body,* as to make it operate on our senses differently from what it did before. Thus the sun has a power to make wax white, and fire to make lead fluid. These are usually called *powers.*

The first of these, as has been said, I think may be properly called real, original, or primary qualities; because they are in the things themselves, whether they are perceived or not: and upon their different modifications it is that the secondary qualities depend.

The other two are only powers to act differently upon other things: which powers result from the different modifications of those primary qualities.

But, though the two latter sorts of qualities are powers barely, and nothing but powers, relating to several other bodies, and resulting from the different modifications of the original qualities, yet they are generally otherwise thought of. For the *second* sort, viz. the powers to produce several ideas in us, by our senses, are looked upon as real qualities in the things thus affecting us: but the *third* sort are called and esteemed barely powers. v.g. The idea of heat or light, which we receive by our eyes, or touch, from the sun, are commonly thought real qualities existing in the sun, and something more than mere powers in it. But when we consider the sun in reference to wax, which it melts or blanches, we look on the whiteness and softness produced in the wax, not as qualities in the sun, but effects produced by powers in it. Whereas, if rightly considered, these qualities of light and warmth, which are perceptions in me when I am warmed or enlightened by the sun, are no otherwise in the sun, than the changes made in the wax, when it is blanched or melted, are in the sun. They are all of them equally *powers in the sun, depending on its primary qualities;* whereby it is able, in the one case, so to alter the bulk, figure, texture, or motion of some of the insensible

parts of my eyes or hands, as thereby to produce in me the idea of light or heat; and in the other, it is able so to alter the bulk, figure, texture, or motion of the insensible parts of the wax, as to make them fit to produce in me the distinct ideas of white and fluid.

The reason why the one are ordinarily taken for real qualities, and the other only for bare powers, seems to be, because the ideas we have of distinct colours, sounds, etc., containing nothing at all in them of bulk, figure, or motion, we are not apt to think them the effects of these primary qualities; which appear not, to our senses, to operate in their production, and with which they have not any apparent congruity or conceivable connexion. Hence it is that we are so forward to imagine, that those ideas are the resemblances of something really existing in the objects themselves: since sensation discovers nothing of bulk, figure, or motion of parts in their production; nor can reason show how bodies, *by their bulk, figure, and motion,* should produce in the mind the ideas of blue or yellow, etc. But, in the other case, in the operations of bodies changing the qualities one of another, we plainly discover that the quality produced hath commonly no resemblance with anything in the thing producing it; wherefore we look on it as a bare effect of power. For, through receiving the idea of heat or light from the sun, we are apt to think *it* is a perception and resemblance of such a quality in the sun; yet when we see wax, or a fair face, receive change of colour from the sun, we cannot imagine *that* to be the reception or resemblance of anything in the sun, because we find not those different colours in the sun itself. For, our senses being able to observe a likeness or unlikeness of sensible qualities in two different external objects, we forwardly enough conclude the production of any sensible quality in any subject to be an effect of bare power, and not the communication of any quality which was really in the efficient, when we find no such sensible quality in the thing that produced it. But our senses, not being able to discover any unlikeness between the idea produced in us, and the quality of the object producing it, we are apt to imagine that our ideas are resemblances of something in the objects, and not the effects of certain powers placed in the modification of their primary qualities, with which primary qualities the ideas produced in us have no resemblance.

To conclude. Beside those before-mentioned primary qualities in bodies, viz. bulk, figure, extension, number, and motion of their solid parts; all the rest, whereby we take notice of bodies, and distinguish them one from another, are nothing else but several powers in them, depending on those primary qualities; whereby they are fitted, either by immediately operating on our bodies to produce several different ideas in us; or else, by operating on other bodies, so to change their primary qualities as to render them capable of producing ideas in us different from what before they did. The former of these, I think, may be called secondary qualities *immediately perceivable:* the latter, secondary qualities, *mediately perceivable. . . .*

The Idea of Substance

The mind being, as I have declared, furnished with a great number of the simple ideas, conveyed in by the senses as they are found in exterior things, or by reflection on its own operations, takes notice also that a certain number of these simple ideas go constantly together; which being presumed to belong to one thing, and words being suited to common apprehensions, and made use of for quick dispatch, are called, so united in one subject, by one name; which, by inadvertency, we are apt afterward to talk of and consider as one simple idea, which indeed is a complication of many ideas together: because, as I have said, not imagining how these simple ideas *can* subsist by themselves, we accustom ourselves to suppose some *substratum* wherein they do subsist, and from which they do result, which therefore we call *substance.*

So that if any one will examine himself concerning his notion of pure substance in general, he will find he has no other idea of it at all, but only a supposition of he knows not what *support* of such qualities which are capable of producing simple ideas in us; which qualities are commonly called accidents. If any one should be asked, what is the subject wherein colour or weight inheres, he would have nothing to say, but the solid extended parts; and if he were demanded, what is it that solidity and extension adhere in, he would not be in a much better case than the Indian before mentioned who, saying that the world was supported by a great elephant, was asked what the elephant rested on; to which his answer was—a great tortoise: but being again pressed to know what gave support to the broad-backed tortoise, replied—*something, he knew not what*. And thus here, as in all other cases where we use words without having clear and distinct ideas, we talk like children: who, being questioned what such a thing is, which they know not, readily give this satisfactory answer, that it is *something:* which in truth signifies no more, when so used, either by children or men, but that they know not what; and that the thing they pretend to know, and talk of, is what they have no distinct idea of at all, and so are perfectly ignorant of it, and in the dark. The idea then we have, to which we give the *general* name substance, being nothing but the supposed, but unknown, support of those qualities we find existing, which we imagine cannot subsist *sine re substante,* without something to support them, we call that support *substantia;* which, according to the true import of the word, is, in plain English, standing under or upholding. . . .

48

Our Knowledge of Sensible Things

GEORGE BERKELEY

It is evident to anyone who takes a survey of the objects of human knowledge, that they are either ideas (1) actually imprinted on the senses, or else such as are (2) perceived by attending to the passions and operations of the mind, or lastly (3) ideas formed by help of memory and imagination, either compounding, dividing, or barely representing those originally perceived in the aforesaid ways. By sight I have the ideas of lights and colors, with their several degrees and variations. By touch I perceive hard and soft, heat and cold, motion and resistance, and of all these more and less either as to quantity or degree. Smelling furnishes me with odors, the palate with tastes, and hearing conveys sounds to the mind in all their variety of tone and composition. And as several of these are observed to accompany each other, they come to be marked by one name, and so to be reputed as one thing. Thus, for example, a certain color, taste, smell, figure, and consistence, having been observed to go together, are accounted one distinct thing, signified by the name "apple." Other collections of ideas constitute a stone, a tree, a book, and the like sensible things; which, as they are pleasing or disagreeable, excite the passions of love, hatred, joy, grief, and so forth.

2. But besides all that endless variety of ideas or objects of knowledge, there is likewise something which knows or perceives them, and exercises divers operations, as willing, imagining, remembering, about them. This perceiving, active being

[From *Of the Principles of Human Knowledge*. First published in 1710.]

is what I call *mind, spirit, soul,* or *myself.* By which words I do not denote any one of my ideas, but a thing entirely distinct from them wherein they exist, or, which is the same thing, whereby they are perceived; for the existence of an idea consists in being perceived.

3. That neither our thoughts, nor passions, nor ideas formed by the imagination, exist without the mind, is what everybody will allow. And it seems no less evident that the various sensations or ideas imprinted on the sense, however blended or combined together (that is, whatever objects they compose), cannot exist otherwise than in a mind perceiving them. I think an intuitive knowledge may be obtained of this by anyone that shall attend to what is meant by the term "exist" when applied to sensible things. The table I write on I say exists—that is, I see and feel it; and if I were out of my study I should say it existed— meaning thereby that if I was in my study I might perceive it, or that some other spirit actually does perceive it. There was an odor, that is, it was smelt; there was a sound, that is, it was heard; a color or figure, and it was perceived by sight or touch. This is all that I can understand by these and the like expressions. For as to what is said of the absolute existence of unthinking things without any relation to their being perceived, that seems perfectly unintelligible. Their *esse* is *percipi,* nor is it possible they should have any existence out of the minds or thinking things which perceive them.

4. It is indeed an opinion strangely prevailing amongst men, that houses, mountains, rivers, and in a word all sensible objects, have an existence, natural or real, distinct from their being perceived by the understanding. But with how great an assurance and acquiescence soever this principle may be entertained in the world, yet whoever shall find in his heart to call it in question may, if I mistake not, perceive it to involve a manifest contradiction. For what are the forementioned objects but the things we perceive by sense? and what do we perceive *besides our own ideas or sensations?* and is it not plainly repugnant that any one of these, or any combination of them, should exist unperceived?

5. . . . Light and colors, heat and cold, extension and figures—in a word the things we see and feel— what are they but so many sensations, notions, ideas, or impressions on the sense? And is it possible to separate, even in thought, any of these from perception? For my part, I might as easily divide a thing from itself. I may, indeed, divide in my thoughts, or conceive apart from each other, those things which perhaps I never perceived by sense so divided. Thus I imagine the trunk of a human body without the limbs, or conceive the smell of a rose without thinking of the rose itself. So far, I will not deny, I can abstract, if that

may properly be called abstraction which extends only to the conceiving separately such objects as it is possible may really exist or be actually perceived asunder. But my conceiving or imagining power does not extend beyond the possibility of real existence or perception. Hence, as it is impossible for me to see or feel anything without an actual sensation of that thing, so it is impossible for me to conceive in my thoughts any sensible thing or object distinct from the sensation or perception of it.

6. Some truths there are so near and obvious to the mind that a man need only open his eyes to see them. Such I take this important one to be, to wit, that all the choir of heaven and furniture of the earth, in a word all those bodies which compose the mighty frame of the world, have not any subsistence without a mind, that their *being* is to be perceived or known; that consequently so long as they are not actually perceived by me, or do not exist in my mind or that of any other created spirit, they must either have no existence at all, or else subsist in the mind of some Eternal Spirit; it being perfectly unintelligible, and involving all the absurdity of abstraction, to attribute to any single part of them an existence independent of a spirit. To be convinced of which, the reader need only reflect and try to separate in his own thoughts the *being* of a sensible thing from its *being perceived.*

7. From what has been said it follows there is not any other substance than *spirit,* or that which perceives. But for the fuller proof of this point, let it be considered the sensible qualities are color, figure, motion, smell, taste, etc.—that is, the ideas perceived by sense. Now, for an idea to exist in an unperceiving thing is a manifest contradiction, for to have an idea is all one as to perceive; that therefore wherein color, figure, and the like qualities exist must perceive them; hence it is clear there can be no unthinking substance or *substratum* of those ideas.

8. But, say you, though the ideas themselves do not exist without the mind, yet there may be things *like* them, whereof they are copies or resemblances, which things exist without the mind in an unthinking substance. I answer, an idea can be like nothing but an idea; a color or figure can be like nothing but another color or figure. If we look but never so little into our thoughts, we shall find it impossible for us to conceive a likeness except only between our ideas. Again, I ask whether those supposed originals or external things, of which our ideas are the pictures or representations, be themselves perceivable or no? If they are, then they are ideas and we have gained our point; but if you say they are not, I appeal to anyone whether it be sense to assert a color is like something which is invisible; hard or soft, like something which is intangible; and so of the rest.

9. Some there are who make a distinction betwixt *primary* and *secondary* qualities. By the former they mean extension, figure, motion, rest, solidity or impenetrability, and number; by the latter they denote all other sensible qualities, as colors, sounds, tastes, and so forth. The ideas we have of these they acknowledge not to be the resemblances of anything existing without the mind, or unperceived, but they will have our ideas of the primary qualities to be patterns or images of things which exist without the mind, in an unthinking substance which they call *matter*. By *matter,* therefore, we are to understand an inert, senseless substance, in which extension, figure, and motion do actually subsist. But it is evident from what we have already shown, that extension, figure, and motion are only ideas existing in the mind, and that an idea can be like nothing but another idea, and that consequently neither they nor their archetypes can exist in an unperceiving substance. Hence, it is plain that the very notion of what is called *matter,* or *corporeal substance,* involves a contradiction in it.

10. They who assert that figure, motion, and the rest of the primary or original qualities do exist without the mind in unthinking substances, do at the same time acknowledge that color, sounds, heat, cold, and suchlike secondary qualities, do not; which they tell us are sensations existing in the mind alone, that depend on and are occasioned by the different size, texture, and motion of the minute particles of matter. This they take for an undoubted truth, which they can demonstrate beyond all exception. Now, if it be certain that those original qualities are inseparably united with the other sensible qualities, and not, even in thought, capable of being abstracted from them, it plainly follows that they exist only in the mind. But I desire anyone to reflect and try whether he can, by any abstraction of thought, conceive the extension and motion of a body without all other sensible qualities. For my own part, I see evidently that it is not in my power to frame an idea of a body extended and moving, but I must withal give it some color or other sensible quality which is acknowledged to exist only in the mind. In short, extension, figure, and motion, abstracted from all other qualities, are inconceivable. Where therefore the other sensible qualities are, there must these be also, to wit, in the mind and nowhere else.

11. Again, *great* and *small, swift* and *slow,* are allowed to exist nowhere without the mind, being entirely relative, and changing as the frame or position of the organs of sense varies. The extension therefore which exists without the mind is neither great nor small, the motion neither swift nor slow, that is, they are nothing at all. ... Without extension solidity cannot be conceived; since therefore it has been

shewn that extension exists not in an unthinking substance, the same must also be true of solidity.

12. That *number* is entirely the creature of the mind, even though the other qualities be allowed to exist without, will be evident to whoever considers that the same thing bears a different denomination of number as the mind views it with different respects. Thus, the same extension is one, or three, or thirty-six, according as the mind considers it with reference to a yard, a foot, or an inch. Number is so visibly relative, and dependent on men's understanding, that it is strange to think how anyone should give it an absolute existence without the mind. We say one book, one page, one line; all these are equally units, though some contain several of the others. And in each instance, it is plain, the unit relates to some particular combination of ideas arbitrarily put together by the mind. . . .

14. I shall farther add that, after the same manner as modern philosophers prove certain sensible qualities to have no existence in matter, or without the mind, the same thing may be likewise proved of all other sensible qualities whatsoever. Thus, for instance, it is said that heat and cold are affections only of the mind, and not at all patterns of real beings, existing in the corporeal substances which excite them, for that the same body which appears cold to one hand seems warm to another. Now, why may we not as well argue that figure and extension are not patterns or resemblances of qualities existing in matter, because to the same eye at different stations, or eyes of a different texture at the same station, they appear various, and cannot therefore be the images of anything settled and determinate without the mind? Again, it is proved that sweetness is not really in the sapid thing, because the thing remaining unaltered the sweetness is changed into bitter, as in case of a fever or otherwise vitiated palate. Is it not as reasonable to say that motion is not without the mind, since if the succession of ideas in the mind become swifter, the motion, it is acknowledged, shall appear slower without any alteration in any external object?

15. In short, let anyone consider those arguments which are thought manifestly to prove that colors and tastes exist only in the mind, and he shall find they may with equal force be brought to prove the same thing of extension, figure, and motion—though it must be confessed this method of arguing does not so much prove that there is no extension or color in an outward object, as that we do not know by sense which is the true extension or color of the object. But the arguments foregoing plainly show it to be impossible that any color or extension at all, or other sensible quality whatsoever, should exist in an unthinking subject without the mind,

or in truth, that there should be any such thing as an outward object.

16. But let us examine a little the received opinion. It is said extension is a mode or accident of matter, and that matter is the *substratum* that supports it. Now I desire that you would explain to me what is meant by matter's *supporting* extension. Say you, I have no' idea of matter and therefore cannot explain it. I answer, though you have no positive, yet, if you have any meaning at all, you must at least have a relative idea of matter; though you know not what it is, yet you must be supposed to know what relation it bears to accidents, and what is meant by its supporting them. It is evident "support" cannot here be taken in its usual or literal sense—as when we say that pillars support a building; in what sense therefore must it be taken?

17. If we inquire into what the most accurate philosophers declare themselves to mean by *material substance,* we shall find them acknowledge they have no other meaning annexed to those sounds but the idea of *Being in general,* together with the relative notion of its supporting accidents. The general idea of Being appeareth to me the most abstract and incomprehensible of all other; and as for its supporting accidents, this, as we have just now observed, cannot be understood in the common sense of those words; it must therefore be taken in some other sense, but what that is they do not explain. So that when I consider the two parts or branches which make the signification of the words *material substance,* I am convinced there is no distinct meaning annexed to them. But why should we trouble ourselves any farther, in discussing this material *substratum* or support of figure and motion, and other sensible qualities? Does it not suppose they have an existence without the mind? And is not this a direct repugnancy, and altogether inconceivable?

18. But though it were possible that solid, figured, movable substances may exist without the mind, corresponding to the ideas we have of bodies, yet how is it possible for us to know this? Either we must know it by sense or by reason. As for our senses, by them we have the knowledge only of our sensations, ideas, or those things that are immediately perceived by sense, call them what you will; but they do not inform us that things exist without the mind, or unperceived, like to those which are perceived. This the materialists themselves acknowledge. It remains therefore that if we have any knowledge at all of external things, it must be by reason, inferring their existence from what is immediately perceived by sense. But what reason can induce us to believe the existence of bodies without the mind, from what we perceive, since the very patrons of matter themselves do not pretend there is any necessary connection betwixt them

and our ideas? I say it is granted on all hands (and what happens in dreams, frenzies, and the like, puts it beyond dispute) that *it is possible we might be affected with all the ideas we have now, though there were no bodies existing without, resembling them.* Hence, it is evident the supposition of external bodies is not necessary for the producing our ideas; since it is granted they are produced sometimes, and might possibly be produced always in the same order we see them in at present, without their concurrence.

19. But, though we might possibly have all our sensations without them, yet perhaps it may be thought easier to conceive and explain the manner of their production by supposing external bodies in their likeness rather than otherwise; and so it might be at least probable there are such things as bodies that excite their ideas in our minds. But neither can this be said; for though we give the materialists their external bodies, they by their own confession are never the nearer knowing how our ideas are produced, since they own themselves unable to comprehend in what manner body can act upon spirit, or how it is possible it should imprint any idea in the mind. Hence it is evident the production of ideas or sensations in our minds can be no reason why we should suppose matter or corporeal substances, since that is acknowledged to remain equally inexplicable with or without this supposition. If therefore it were

possible for bodies to exist without the mind, yet to hold they do so, must needs be a very precarious opinion; since it is to suppose, without any reason at all, that God has created innumerable beings that are entirely useless, and serve to no manner of purpose.

20. In short, if there were external bodies, it is impossible we should ever come to know it; and if there were not, we might have the very same reasons to think there were that we have now. Suppose (what no one can deny possible) an intelligence without the help of external bodies, to be affected with the same train of sensations or ideas that you are, imprinted in the same order and with like vividness in his mind. I ask whether that intelligence hath not all the reason to believe the existence of corporeal substances, represented by his ideas, and exciting them in his mind, that you can possibly have for believing the same thing? Of this there can be no question; which one consideration were enough to make any reasonable person suspect the strength of whatever arguments he may think himself to have for the existence of bodies without the mind. . . .

25. All our ideas, sensations, notions, or the things which we perceive, by whatsoever names they may be distinguished, are visibly inactive: there is nothing of power or agency included in them. So that one idea or object of thought cannot produce or make any alteration in an-

other. To be satisfied of the truth of this, there is nothing else requisite but a bare observation of our ideas. For, since they and every part of them exist only in the mind, it follows that there is nothing in them but what is perceived: but whoever shall attend to his ideas, whether of sense or reflection, will not perceive in them any power or activity; there is, therefore, no such thing contained in them. A little attention will discover to us that the very being of an idea implies passiveness and inertness in it, insomuch that it is impossible for an idea to do anything, or, strictly speaking, to be the cause of anything: neither can it be the resemblance or pattern of any active being, as is evident from Sec. 8. Whence it plainly follows that extension, figure, and motion cannot be the cause of our sensations. To say, therefore, that these are the effects of powers resulting from the configuration, number, motion, and size of corpuscles, must certainly be false.

26. We perceive a continual succession of ideas, some are anew excited, others are changed or totally disappear. There is therefore some cause of these ideas, whereon they depend, and which produces and changes them. That this cause cannot be any quality or idea or combination of ideas, is clear from the preceding section. It must therefore be a substance; but it has been shewn that there is no corporeal or material substance: it remains therefore that the cause of ideas is an incorporeal active substance or Spirit.

27. A spirit is one simple, undivided, active being: as it perceives ideas it is called the *understanding,* and as it produces or otherwise operates about them it is called the *will.* Hence there can be no *idea* formed of a soul or spirit; for all ideas whatever, being passive and inert (*vide* Sec. 25), they cannot represent unto us, by way of image or likeness, that which acts. A little attention will make it plain to anyone, that to have an idea which shall be like that active principle of motion and change of ideas is absolutely impossible. Such is the nature of *spirit,* or that which acts, that it cannot be of itself perceived, but only by the effects which it produceth. If any man shall doubt of the truth of what is here delivered, let him but reflect and try if he can frame the idea of any power or active being, and whether he hath ideas of two principal powers, marked by the names *will* and *understanding,* distinct from each other as well as from a third idea of substance or being in general, with a relative notion of its supporting or being the subject of the aforesaid powers—which is signified by the name *soul* or *spirit.* This is what some hold; but, so far as I can see, the words *will, soul, spirit,* do not stand for different ideas, or, in truth, for any idea at all, but for something which is very different from ideas, and which, being an agent, cannot be like unto, or represented by, any idea whatsoever.

Though it must be owned at the same time that we have some *notion* of soul, spirit, and the operations of the mind such as willing, loving, hating; inasmuch as we know or understand the meaning of these words.

28. I find I can excite ideas in my mind at pleasure, and vary and shift the scene as oft as I think fit. It is no more than willing, and straightway this or that idea arises in my fancy; and by the same power it is obliterated and makes way for another. This making and unmaking of ideas doth very properly denominate the mind active. Thus much is certain and grounded on experience; but when we think of unthinking agents or of exciting ideas exclusive of volition, we only amuse ourselves with words.

29. But, whatever power I may have over my own thoughts, I find the ideas actually perceived by sense have not a like dependence on my will. When in broad daylight I open my eyes, it is not in my power to choose whether I shall see or no, or to determine what particular objects shall present themselves to my view; and so likewise as to the hearing and other senses, the ideas imprinted on them are not creatures of my will. There is therefore some other will or spirit that produces them.

30. The ideas of sense are more strong, lively, and distinct than those of the imagination; they have likewise a steadiness, order, and coherence, and are not excited at random, as those which are the effects of human wills often are, but in a regular train or series, the admirable connection whereof sufficiently testifies the wisdom and benevolence of its Author. Now the set rules or established methods wherein the mind we depend on excites in us the ideas of sense, are called the *laws of nature;* and these we learn by experience, which teaches us that such and such ideas are attended with such and such other ideas, in the ordinary course of things.

31. This gives us a sort of foresight which enables us to regulate our actions for the benefit of life. And without this we should be eternally at a loss: we could not know how to act anything that might procure us the least pleasure, or remove the least pain of sense. That food nourishes, sleep refreshes, and fire warms us; that to sow in the seedtime is the way to reap in the harvest; and, in general, that to obtain such or such ends, such or such means are conducive—all this we know, not by discovering any necessary connection between our ideas, but only by the observation of the settled laws of nature, without which we should be all in uncertainty and confusion, and a grown man no more know how to manage himself in the affairs of life than an infant just born.

32. And yet this insistent uniform working, which so evidently displays the goodness and wisdom of that governing Spirit whose will constitutes the laws of nature, is so far from leading our thoughts to

Him, that it rather sends them wandering after second causes. For, when we perceive certain ideas of sense constantly followed by other ideas and we know this is not of our own doing, we forthwith attribute power and agency to the ideas themselves, and make one the cause of another, than which nothing can be more absurd and unintelligible. Thus, for example, having observed that when we perceive by sight a certain round luminous figure we at the same time perceive by touch the idea or sensation called heat, we do from thence conclude the sun to be the cause of heat. And in like manner perceiving the motion and collision of bodies to be attended with sound, we are inclined to think the latter the effect of the former.

33. The ideas imprinted on the senses by the Author of nature are called *real things;* and those excited in the imagination, being less regular, vivid, and constant, are more properly termed *ideas,* or *images* of *things,* which they copy and represent. But then our sensations, be they never so vivid and distinct, are nevertheless ideas, that is, they exist in the mind, or are perceived by it, as truly as the ideas of its own framing. The ideas of sense are allowed to have more reality in them, that is, to be more strong, orderly, and coherent than the creatures of the mind; but this is no argument that they exist without the mind. They are also less dependent on the spirit, or thinking substance which perceives them, in that they are excited by the will of another and more powerful spirit; yet still they are *ideas,* and certainly no idea, whether faint or strong, can exist otherwise than in a mind perceiving it.

34. Before we proceed any farther it is necessary we spend some time in answering objections which may probably be made against the principles we have hitherto laid down. In doing of which, if I seem too prolix to those of quick apprehensions, I hope it may be pardoned, since all men do not equally apprehend things of this nature, and I am willing to be understood by everyone.

First, then, it will be objected that by the foregoing principles all that is real and substantial in nature is banished out of the world, and instead thereof a chimerical scheme of *ideas* takes place. All things that exist, exist only in the mind, that is, they are purely notional. What therefore becomes of the sun, moon, and stars? What must we think of houses, rivers, mountains, trees, stones; nay, even of our own bodies? Are all these but so many chimeras and illusions on the fancy? To all which, and whatever else of the same sort may be objected, I answer that by the principles premised we are not deprived of any one thing in nature. Whatever we see, feel, hear, or anywise conceive or understand remains as secure as ever, and is as real as ever. There is a *rerum natura,* and the distinction between realities and chimeras retains its full force. This is evident from Sec. 29, 30, and 33, where we have shewn what is meant by *real things* in opposition to *chimeras* or ideas of our own framing; but then they both equally exist in the mind, and in that sense they are alike *ideas*.

35. I do not argue against the existence of any one thing that we can apprehend either by sense or reflection. That the things I see with my eyes and touch with my hands do exist, really exist, I make not the least question. The only thing whose existence we deny is that which *philosophers* call matter or corporeal substance. And in doing of this there is no damage done to the rest of mankind, who, I dare say, will never miss it. The atheist indeed will want the color of an empty name to support his impiety; and the philosophers may possibly find they have lost a great handle for trifling and disputation.

36. If any man thinks this detracts from the existence or reality of things, he is very far from understanding what hath been premised in the plainest terms I could think of. Take here an abstract of what has been said. There are spiritual substances, minds, or human souls, which will or excite ideas in themselves at pleasure; but these are faint, weak, and unsteady in respect of others they perceive by sense—which, being impressed upon them according to certain rules or laws of nature, speak themselves the effects of a mind more powerful and wise than human spirits. These latter are said to have more *reality* in them than the former; by which is meant that they are more affecting, orderly, and distinct, and that they are not fictions of the mind perceiving them. And in this sense the sun that I see by day is the real sun, and that which I imagine by night is the idea of the former. In the sense here given of "reality" it is evident that every vegetable, star, mineral, and in general each part of the mundane system, is as much as a real being by our principles as by any other. Whether others mean anything by the term "reality" different from what I do, I entreat them to look into their own thoughts and see.

37. It will be urged that thus much at least is true, to wit, that we take away all corporeal substances. To this my answer is that if the word "substance" be taken in the vulgar sense—for a combination of sensible qualities, such as extension, solidity, weight, and the like—this we cannot be accused of taking away. But if it be taken in a philosophic sense—for the support of accidents or qualities without the mind—then indeed I acknowledge that we take it away, if one may be said to take away that which never had any existence, not even in the imagination.

38. But after all, say you, it sounds very harsh to say we eat and drink ideas, and are clothed with ideas. I acknowledge it does so; the word "idea" not being used in com-

mon discourse to signify the several combinations of sensible qualities which are called "things"; and it is certain that any expression which varies from the familiar use of language will seem harsh and ridiculous. But this doth not concern the truth of the proposition, which in other words is no more than to say, we are fed and clothed with those things which we perceive immediately by our senses. The hardness or softness, the color, taste, warmth, figure, or suchlike qualities, which combined together constitute the several sorts of victuals and apparel, have been shewn to exist only in the mind that perceives them; and this is all that is meant by calling them "ideas"; which word if it was as ordinarily used as "things," would sound no harsher nor more ridiculous than it. I am not for disputing about the propriety, but the truth of the expression. If therefore you agree with me that we eat and drink and are clad with the immediate objects of sense, which cannot exist unperceived or without the mind, I shall readily grant it is more proper or conformable to custom that they should be called things rather than ideas.

39. If it be demanded why I make use of the word "idea," and do not rather in compliance with custom call them "thing"; I answer, I do it for two reasons:—first, because the term "thing" in contradistinction to "idea," is generally supposed to denote somewhat existing without the mind; secondly, because "thing" hath a more comprehensive signification than "idea," including spirit or thinking things as well as ideas. Since therefore the objects of sense exist only in the mind, and are withal thoughtless and inactive, I chose to mark them by the word "idea," which implies those properties.

40. But, say what we can, someone perhaps may be apt to reply, he will still believe his senses, and never suffer any arguments, how plausible soever, to prevail over the certainty of them. Be it so; assert the evidence of sense as high as you please, we are willing to do the same. That what I see, hear, and feel doth exist, that is to say, is perceived by me, I no more doubt than I do of my own being. But I do not see how the testimony of sense can be alleged as a proof for the existence of anything which is not perceived by sense. We are not for having any man turn sceptic and disbelieve his senses; on the contrary, we give them all the stress and assurance imaginable; nor are there any principles more opposite to scepticism than those we have laid down, as shall be hereafter clearly shewn. . . .

45. . . . It will be objected that from the foregoing principles it follows things are every moment annihilated and created anew. The objects of sense exist only when they are perceived; the trees therefore are in the garden, or the chairs in the parlor, no longer than while

there is somebody by to perceive them. Upon shutting my eyes all the furniture in the room is reduced to nothing, and barely upon opening them it is again created. In answer to all which, I refer the reader to what has been said in Sec. 3, 4, etc., and desire he will consider whether he means anything by the actual existence of an idea distinct from its being perceived. For my part, after the nicest inquiry I could make, I am not able to discover that anything else is meant by those words; and I once more entreat the reader to sound his own thoughts, and not suffer himself to be imposed on by words. If he can conceive it possible either for his ideas or their archetypes to exist without being perceived, then I give up the cause; but if he cannot, he will acknowledge it is unreasonable for him to stand up in defense of he knows not what, and pretend to charge on me as an absurdity the not assenting to those propositions which at bottom have no meaning in them. . . .

48. If we consider it, the objection proposed in Sec. 45 will not be found reasonably charged on the principles we have premised, so as in truth to make any objection at all against our notions. For, though we hold indeed the objects of sense to be nothing else but ideas which cannot exist unperceived; yet we may not hence conclude they have no existence except only while they are perceived by us, since there may be some other spirit that perceives them though we do not. Wherever bodies are said to have no existence without the mind, I would not be understood to mean this or that particular mind, but all minds whatsoever. It does not therefore follow from the foregoing principles that bodies are annihilated and created every moment, or exist not at all during the intervals between our perception of them. . . .

60. . . . It will be demanded to what purpose serves that curious organization of plants, and the animal mechanism in the parts of animals: might not vegetables grow, and shoot forth leaves of blossoms, and animals perform all their motions as well without as with all that variety of internal parts so elegantly contrived and put together, which, being ideas, have nothing powerful or operative in them, nor have any necessary connection with the effects ascribed to them? If it be a Spirit that immediately produces every effect by a *fiat* or act of His will, we must think all that is fine and artificial in the works, whether of man or nature, to be made in vain. By this doctrine, though an artist hath made the spring and wheels, and every movement of a watch, and adjusted them in such a manner as he knew would produce the motions he designed, yet he must think all this done to no purpose, and that it is an Intelligence which directs the index, and points to the hour of the day. If so, why may not the Intelligence do it, without his being at the pains of

making the movements and putting them together? Why does not an empty case serve as well as another? And how comes it to pass that whenever there is any fault in the going of a watch, there is some corresponding disorder to be found in the movements, which being mended by a skillful hand all is right again? The like may be said of all the clockwork of nature, great part whereof is so wonderfully fine and subtle as scarce to be discerned by the best microscope. In short, it will be asked, how, upon our principles, any tolerable account can be given, or any final cause assigned of an innumerable multitude of bodies and machines, framed with the most exquisite art, which in the common philosophy have very apposite uses assigned them, and serve to explain abundance of phenomena? . . .

64. To set this matter in a yet clearer light, I shall observe that what has been objected in Sec. 60 amounts in reality to no more than this:—ideas are not anyhow and at random produced, there being a certain order and connection between them, like to that of cause and effect; there are also several combinations of them made in a very regular and artificial manner, which seem like so many instruments in the hand of nature that, being hid as it were behind the scenes, have a secret operation in producing those appearances which are seen on the theater of the world, being themselves discernible only to the curi-ous eye of the philosopher. But, since one idea cannot be the cause of another, to what purpose is that connection? And, since those instruments, being barely *inefficacious perceptions* in the mind, are not subservient to the production of natural effects, it is demanded why they are made; or, in other words, what reason can be assigned why God should make us, upon a close inspection into His works, behold so great variety of ideas so artfully laid together, and so much according to rule; it not being credible that He would be at the expense (if one may so speak) of all that art and regularity to no purpose.

65. To all which my answer is, first, that the connection of ideas does not imply the relation of *cause and effect,* but only of a mark or *sign* with the thing *signified.* The fire which I see is not the cause of the pain I suffer upon my approaching it, but the mark that forewarns me of it. In like manner the noise that I hear is not the effect of this or that motion or collision of the ambient bodies, but the sign thereof. Secondly, the reason why ideas are formed into machines, that is, artificial and regular combinations, is the same with that for combining letters into words. That a few original ideas may be made to signify a great number of effects and actions, it is necessary they be variously combined together. And, to the end their use be permanent and universal, these combinations must be made

by *rule,* and with *wise contrivance.* By this means abundance of information is conveyed unto us, concerning what we are to expect from such and such actions, and what methods are proper to be taken for the exciting such and such ideas; which in effect is all that I conceive to be distinctly meant when it is said that, by discerning a figure, texture, and mechanism of the inward parts of bodies, whether natural or artificial, we may attain to know the several uses and properties depending thereon, or the nature of the thing.

66. Hence, it is evident that those things which, under the notion of a cause co-operating or concurring to the production of effects, are altogether inexplicable, and run us into great absurdities, may be very naturally explained, and have a proper and obvious use assigned to them, when they are considered only as marks or signs for our information. And it is the searching after and endeavoring to understand those signs instituted by the Author of Nature, that ought to be the employment of the natural philosopher; and not the pretending to explain things by corporeal causes, which doctrine seems to have too much estranged the minds of men from that active principle, that supreme and wise Spirit "in whom we live, move, and have our being." . . .

49

The Bases of Empirical Knowledge

C. I. LEWIS

Empirical truth cannot be known except, finally, through presentations of sense. Most affirmations of empirical knowledge are to be justified, proximately, by others already accepted or believed: such justification involves a step or steps depending on logical truth. The classification as empirical will still be correct, however, if amongst such statements required to support the one in question, either deductively or inductively, there are some which cannot be assured by logic or analysis of meaning but only by reference to the content of given experience. Our empirical knowledge rises as a structure of enormous complexity, most parts of which are stabilized in measure by their mutual support, but all of which rest, at bottom, on direct findings of sense. Unless there should be some statements, or rather something apprehensible and statable, whose truth is determined by given experience and is not determinable in any other way, there would be no non-analytic affirmation whose truth could be determined at all, and no such thing as empirical knowledge. . . .

Let us turn to the simplest kind of empirical cognition; knowledge by direct perception. And let us take two examples.

I am descending the steps of Emerson Hall, and using my eyes to guide my feet. This is a habitual and ordinarily automatic action. But for this occasion, and in order that it

[Reprinted from *An Analysis of Knowledge and Valuation,* by C. I. Lewis, by permission of The Open Court Publishing Company, La Salle, Illinois. Copyright, 1946, The Open Court Publishing Company.]

may clearly constitute an instance of perceptual cognition instead of unconsidered behavior, I put enough attention on the process to bring the major features of it to clear consciousness. There is a certain visual pattern presented to me, a feeling of pressure on the soles of my feet, and certain muscle-sensations and feelings of balance and motion. And these items mentioned are fused together with others in one moving whole of presentation, within which they can be genuinely elicited but in which they do not exist as separate. Much of this presented content, I should find it difficult to put in words. I should find it difficult because, for one reason, if I tried to express it precisely in objectively intelligible fashion, I should have to specify such items as particular muscles which are involved and the behavior of them, and other things of this kind; and I do not in fact know which muscles I am using and just how. But one does not have to study physiology in order to walk down stairs. I know by my feelings when I am walking erect—or I think I do. And you, by putting yourself in my place, know how I feel—or think you do. That is all that is necessary, because we are here speaking of direct experience. You will follow me through the example by using your imagination, and understand what I mean—or what *you* would mean by the same language—in terms of your own experience. . . .

This given presentation—what looks like a flight of granite steps before me—leads to a prediction: "If I step forward and down, I shall come safely to rest on the step below." Ordinarily this prediction is unexpressed and would not even be explicitly thought. When so formulated, it is altogether too pedantic and portentous to fit the simple forward-looking quality of my conscious attitude. But unless I were prepared to assent to it, in case my attention were drawn to the matter, I should not now proceed as I do. Here again, the language I use would ordinarily be meant to express an objective process involving my body and a physical environment. But for the present occasion, I am trying to express the direct and indubitable content of my experience only, and, particularly, to elicit exemplary items which mark this conscious procedure as cognitive. As I stand momentarily poised and looking before me, the presented visual pattern leads me to predict that acting in a certain manner—stepping forward and down—will be followed by a further empirical content, equally specific and recognizable but equally difficult to express without suggesting more than I now mean—the felt experience of coming to balance on the step below.

I adopt the mode of action envisaged; and the expected empirical sequent actually follows. My prediction is verified. The cognitive significance of the visual presentation which operated as cue, is found valid. This functioning of it was a genuine case of perceptual knowledge.

Let us take another and different example; different not in any important character of the situation involved, but different in the manner in which we shall consider it.

I believe there is a piece of white paper now before me. The reason that I believe this is that I see it: a certain visual presentation is given. But my belief includes the expectation that so long as I continue to look in the same direction, this presentation, with its qualitative character essentially unchanged, will persist; that if I move my eyes right, it will be displaced to the left in the visual field; that if I close them, it will disappear; and so on. If any of these predictions should, upon trial, be disproved, I should abandon my present belief in a real piece of paper before me, in favor of belief in some extraordinary after-image or some puzzling reflection or some disconcerting hallucination.

I do look in the same direction for a time; then turn my eyes; and after that try closing them: all with the expected results. My belief is so far corroborated. And these corroborations give me even greater assurance in any further predictions based upon it. But theoretically and ideally it is not completely verified, because the belief in a real piece of white paper now before me has further implications not yet tested: that what I see could be folded without crack-ing, as a piece of celluloid could not; that it would tear easily, as architect's drawing-cloth would not; that this experience will not be followed by waking in quite different surroundings; and others too numerous to mention. If it is a real piece of paper before me now, then I shall expect to find it here tomorrow with the number I just put on the corner: its reality and the real character I attribute in my belief imply innumerable possible verifications, or partial verifications, tomorrow and later on.

But looking back over what I have just written, I observe that I have succumbed to precisely those difficulties of formulation which have been mentioned. I have here spoken of predictable results of further tests I am not now making; of folding the paper and trying to tear it, and so on. Finding these predictions borne out would, in each case, be only a partial test, theoretically, of my belief in a real piece of paper. But it was my intention to mention predictions which, though only partial verification of the objective fact I believe in, could themselves be decisively tested. And there I have failed. That the paper, upon trial, would really be torn, will no more be evidenced with perfect certainty than is the presence of real paper before me now. It—provided it take place—will be a real objective event about which, theoretically, my momentary experience could deceive me. What I meant to speak of was certain expected experiences—of the *appearance and feeling* of paper being folded; of its *seeming* to be torn. These predictions of *experience,* would be decisively and indubitably borne out or disproved if I make trial of them. But on this point, the reader will most likely have caught my intent and improved upon my statement as made.

Let us return to the point we were discussing. We had just noted that even if the mentioned tests of the empirical belief about the paper should have been made, the result would not be a theoretically complete verification of it because there would be further and similar implications of the belief which would still not have been tested. In the case of an important piece of paper like a deed or a will, or an important issue like the question whether "Midsummer Night's Dream" was written by Shakspere or by Bacon, such implications might be subject to test years or even centuries afterward. And a negative result might then rationally lead to doubt that a particular piece of paper lay on a certain desk at a certain time. My present example is no different except in importance: what I now believe has consequences which will be determinable indefinitely in the future.

Further, my belief must extend to any predictions such that I should accept the failure of them as disproof of the belief, however far in the future the time may be which they concern. And my belief must imply as probable, anything the failure of

which I should accept as tending to discredit this belief.

Also it is the case that such future contingencies, implied by the belief, are not such that failure of them can be absolutely precluded in the light of prior empirical corroborations of what is believed. However improbable, it remains thinkable that such later tests could have a negative result. Though truth of the belief itself implies a positive result of such later tests, the evidence to date does not imply this as more than probable, even though the difference of this probability from theoretical certainty should be so slight that practically it would be foolish to hesitate over it. Indeed we could be too deprecatory about this difference: if we interrogate experience we shall find plenty of occasions when we have felt quite sure of an objective fact perceived but later circumstance has shocked us out of our assurance and obliged us to retract or modify our belief.

If now we ask ourselves how extensive such implied consequences of the belief are, it seems clear that in so simple a case as the white paper supposedly now before me, the number of them is inexhaustible. For one thing, they presumably will never come to an end in point of time: there will never be a time when the fact—or non-fact— of this piece of paper now lying on my desk will not make some trivial difference. If that were not the case, then it must be that at some future date it will become not only practically but theoretically impossible that there should be a scintilla of evidence either for or against this supposed present fact. It would not be possible for anyone even to think of something which, if it should then occur, would be such evidence. That even the least important of real events will thus make no conceivable difference after a certain time, is not plausible. If that should be so, then what belongs to the past, beyond a certain stretch, could be something worse than an unknowable thing in itself; it could be such that the very supposition of it could make no conceivable difference to anyone's rational behavior; and any alleged interest in its truth or falsity could be shown to be fictitious or pointless, or to be confined to having others assert or assent to a certain form of words. In that sense, this belief would then become meaningless, having no conceivable consequence of its truth or falsity which would be testable or bear upon any rational interest.

It will be well for the reader to come to his own clear decision on this question; whether it is or is not the case that the truth of an objective empirical belief has consequences which are inexhaustible and are such that there is no limited number of them whose determination theoretically and absolutely precludes a negative result of further tests and hence *deductively* implies all further and as yet untested consequences.

It will be well to become thus clear because this point has decisive consequences for the nature of empirical knowledge. . . .

As we considered this first example, the attempt was to portray it as a case in which a directly apprehensible presentation of a recognizable sort functioned as cue to a single prediction; the prediction that a certain directly recognizable act would lead to a particular and directly recognizable result. If we are to describe this cognitive situation truly, all three of these elements—the presentation, the envisaged action, and the expected consequence—must be described in language which will denote immediately presented or directly presentable contents of experience. We attempted to make clear this intent of the language used by locutions such as "looks like," "feels like"; thus restricting it to what would fall completely within the passage of experience in question and what this passage of experience could completely and directly determine as true. For example, if I should say, "There is a flight of granite steps before me," I should not merely report my experience but assert what it would require a great deal of further experience to corroborate fully. Indeed, it is questionable whether any amount of further experience could put this assertion theoretically beyond all possibility of a rational doubt. But when I say, "I see what *looks like* granite steps before me,"

I restrict myself to what is given; and what I intend by this language is something of which I can have no possible doubt. And the only possible doubt *you* could have of it—since it concerns a present experience of mine—is a doubt whether you grasp correctly what I intend to report, or a doubt whether I am telling the truth or a lie.

This use of language to formulate a directly presented or presentable content of experience, may be called its *expressive* use. This is in contrast to that more common intent of language, exemplified by, "I see (what in fact *is*) a flight of granite steps before me," which may be called its *objective* use. The distinctive character of expressive language, or the expressive use of language, is that such language signifies *appearances*. And in thus referring to appearances, or affirming what appears, such expressive language *neither asserts any objective reality of what appears nor denies any*. It is confined to description of the content of presentation itself.

In such expressive language, the cognitive judgment, "If I act in manner *A*, the empirical eventuality will include *E*," is one which can be verified by putting it to the test—supposing I can in fact put it to the test; can act in manner *A*. When the hypothesis of this hypothetical judgment is made true by my volition, the consequent is found true or found false by what follows; and this verification is decisive and complete,

because nothing beyond the content of this passage of experience was implied in the judgment.

In the second example, as we considered it, what was judged was an *objective fact*: "A piece of white paper is now before me." This judgment will be false if the presentation is illusory; it will be false if what I see is not really paper; false if it is not really white but only looks white. This objective judgment also is one capable of corroboration. As in the other example, so here too, any test of the judgment would pretty surely involve some way of acting—*making* the test, as by continuing to look, or turning my eyes, or grasping to tear, etc.—and would be determined by finding or failing to find some expected result in experience. But in this example, if the result of any single test is as expected, it constitutes a partial verification of the judgment only; never one which is absolutely decisive and theoretically complete. This is so because, while the judgment, so far as it is significant, contains nothing which could not be tested, still it has a significance which outruns what any single test, or any limited set of tests, could exhaust. No matter how fully I may have investigated this objective fact, there will remain some theoretical possibility of mistake; there will be further consequences which must be thus and so if the judgment is true, and not all of these will have been determined. The possibility that such further tests, if made, might have a negative result, cannot be altogether precluded; and this possibility marks the judgment as, at the time in question, not fully verified and less than absolutely certain. To quibble about such possible doubts will not, in most cases, be common sense. But we are not trying to weigh the degree of theoretical dubiety which common sense practicality should take account of, but to arrive at an accurate analysis of knowledge. This character of being further testable and less than theoretically certain characterizes every judgment of objective fact at all times; every judgment that such and such a real thing exists or has a certain objectively factual property, or that a certain objective event actually occurs, or that any objective state of affairs actually is the case.

A judgment of the type of the first example—prediction of a particular passage of experience, describable in expressive language—may be called *terminating*. It admits of decisive and complete verification or falsification. One of the type of the second example—judgment of objective fact which is always further verifiable and never completely verified—may be called *non-terminating*. . . .

The conception is, thus, that there are three classes of empirical statements. First, there are formulations of what is presently given in experience. Only infrequently are such statements of the given actually made: there is seldom need to formulate what is directly and indubitably presented. They are also difficult or—it might plausibly be said—impossible to state in ordinary language, which, as usually understood, carries implications of something more and further verifiable which *ipso facto* is not given. . . .

Second, there are terminating judgments, and statements of them. These represent some prediction of further possible experience. They find their cue in what is given: but what they state is something taken to be verifiable by some test which involves a way of acting. Thus terminating judgments are, in general, of the form, "If A then E," or "S being given, if A then E," where "A" represents some mode of action taken to be possible, "E" some expected consequent in experience, and "S" the sensory cue. The hypothesis "A" must here express something which, if made true by adopted action, will be *indubitably* true, and not, like a condition of my musculature in relation to the environment, an objective state of affairs only partially verified and not completely certain at the time. And the consequent "E" represents an eventuality of *experience*, directly and certainly recognizable in case it accrues; not a resultant objective event, whose factuality could have, and would call for, further verification. Thus both antecedent and consequent of this judgment, "If A then E," require to be formulated in expressive language; though we shall not call it an expressive statement, reserving that phrase for formulations of the given. Also, unlike statements of the given, what such terminating judgments express is to be classed as knowledge: the prediction in question calls for verification, and is subject to possible error.

Third, there are non-terminating judgments which assert objective reality; some state of affairs as actual. These are so named because, while there is nothing in the import of such objective statements which is intrinsically unverifiable, and hence nothing included in them which is not expressible by some terminating judgment, nevertheless no limited set of particular predictions of empirical eventualities can completely exhaust the significance of such an objective statement. This is true of the simplest and most trivial, as much as of the most important. The statement that something is blue, for example, or is square—as contrasted with merely looking blue or appearing to be square—has, always, implications of further possible experience, beyond what should, at any particular time, have been found true. Theoretically complete and absolute verification of any objective judgment would be a never-ending task: any actual verification of them is no more than partial; and our assurance of them is always, theoretically, less than certain.

Non-terminating judgments represent an enormous class; they include, in fact, pretty much all the empirical statements we habitually make. They range in type from the simplest assertion of perceived fact— "There is a piece of white paper now before me"—to the most impressive of scientific generalizations—"The universe is expanding." In general, the more important an assertion of empirical objective fact, the more remote it is from its eventual grounds. The laws of science, for example, are arrived at by induction from inductions from inductions _____. But objective judgments are all alike in being non-terminating, and in having no other eventual foundation than data of given experience. ...

Perceptual knowledge has two aspects or phases; the givenness of something given, and the interpretation which, in the light of past experience, we put upon it. In the case of perceiving the white paper, what is given is a certain complex of sensa or qualia—what Santayana calls an "essence." This is describable in expressive language by the use of adjectives of color, shape, size, and so on. If our apprehension ended with this, however, there would be no knowledge here; the presentation would *mean* nothing to us. A mind without past experience would have no knowledge by means of it: for such a mind the apprehension would be exhausted in mere receptivity of presentation, because no interpretation would be suggested or imposed.

If anyone choose to extend the word "knowledge" to such immediate apprehension of sense—and many do, in fact—there is no fault to be found with that usage. Such apprehensions of the given are characterized by certainty, even though what it is that we are thus certain of, is something difficult of clear and precise expression when separated from the interpretation put upon it. And without such sense-certainties, there could be no perceptual knowledge, nor any empirical knowledge at all. We have chosen not to use the word "knowledge" in this way: and if it be given this broader meaning which would include apprehension of the immediate, it must then be remembered that one cannot, at the same time, require that knowledge in general shall possess a signification of something beyond the cognitive experience itself or that it should stand in contrast with some possible kind of error or mistake. Apprehension of the given, by itself, will meet neither of these requirements.

It is the interpretation put upon this presentation which constitutes belief in or assertion of some objective fact. This interpretation is imposed in the light of past experience. Because I have dealt with writing paper before, this presently given white oblong something leads me to believe there is a sheet of white paper before me. This interpretation is, in some measure, verified by the fact of the presentation itself: my belief has some degree of credibility merely because this presentation is given—a degree of credibility commensurate with the *im*probability of exactly such presentation as this if there were *not* a piece of white paper before me. For the rest, my belief is significant of other experience, taken to be in some sense possible, but not now given. This significance ascribed to the fact of the presentation and expressed by statement of the belief aroused, is equivalent to what *would be* accepted as complete verification of it. The *practical* possibility of such envisaged verification, or of any part of it, would not be here in point: it is the meaning which is here in question. When I entertain this interpretation of the given experience, this belief in objective fact, I must know what I thus mean in terms of experience I can envisage, if the meaning is genuine. Otherwise the truth of it would not be even theoretically determinable.

To construe this interpretation of the given experience—this belief in objective fact which it arouses—as verifiable and as something whose significance can be envisaged in terms of possible confirmations of it, is what dictates that the statement of this objective belief must be translatable into terms of passages of possible experience, each of which would constitute some partial verification of it; that is, it must be translatable into the predictive statements of terminating judgments. If we include the whole scope of the objective statement believed, endlessly many such predictions will be contained in its significance. This is correlative to the fact that, no matter to what extent the objective belief should have been, at any time, already verified, the truth of it will still make some difference to further possible experience; and correlative to the further fact that, at any moment, the truth of this objective assertion is something which I might now proceed to confirm in more than one way. That test of it which I choose to make, does not negate or extrude from the objective intent of the belief, what has reference to *other* possible confirmations which I choose *not* to put to the test. Thus it is not possible to make all possible confirmations of an objective belief or statement, and complete the verification of it. . . .

50

Naïve Realism vs. Presentative Realism

JOHN DEWEY

I

In spite of the elucidations of contemporary realists, a number of idealists continue to adduce in behalf of idealism certain facts having an obvious physical nature and explanation. The visible convergence of the railway tracks, for example, is cited as evidence that what is seen is a mental "content." Yet this convergence follows from the physical properties of light and a lens, and is physically demonstrated in a camera. Is the photograph, then, to be conceived as a psychical somewhat? That the time of the visibility of a light does not coincide with the time at which a distant body emitted the light is employed to support a simmilar idealistic conclusion, in spite of the fact that the exact difference in time may be deduced from a physical property of light—its rate. The dislocation in space of the light seen and the astronomical star is used as evidence of the mental nature of the former, though the exact angular difference is a matter of simple computation from purely physical data. The doubling of images of, say, the finger when the eyeball is pressed, is frequently proffered as a clincher. Yet it is a simple matter to take any body that reflects light, and by a suitable arrangement of lenses to produce not only two but many images, projected into space. If the fact that under definite *physical* conditions (misplacement of lenses), a finger yields two images proves the psychical character of the latter, then the fact that under certain conditions a sounding body yields one or more echoes is, by parity of reasoning, proof that the echo is made of mental stuff.

If, once more, the differences in form and color of a table to different observers, occupying different physical positions, is proof that what each sees is a psychical, private, isolated somewhat, then the fact that one and the same physical body has different effects upon, or relations with, different physical media is proof of the mental nature of these effects. Take a lump of wax and subject it to the same heat, located at different positions; now the wax is solid, now liquid—it might even be gaseous. How "psychical" these phenomena! It almost seems as if the transformation of the physical into the mental in the cases cited exemplifies an interesting psychological phenomenon. In each case the beginning is with a real and physical existence. Taking "the real object," the astronomical star, on the basis of its physical reality, the idealist concludes to a psychical object, radically different! Taking the *single* object, the finger, from the premise of its real singleness, he concludes to a double mental content, which then takes the place of the original single thing! Taking one-and-the-same-object, the table, presenting *its* different surfaces and reflections of light to different real organisms, he eliminates the one-table-in-its-different-relations in behalf of a multiplicity

of totally separate psychical tables! The logic reminds us of the story of the countryman who, after gazing at the giraffe, remarked, "There ain't no such animal." It almost seems, I repeat, as if this self-contradiction in the argument creates in some minds the impression that the object—not the argument—is undergoing the extraordinary reversal of form.

However this may be, the problem indicated in the foregoing cases is simply the good old problem of the many in one, or, less cryptically, the problem of the maintenance of a continuity of process throughout differences. I do not pretend that this situation, though the most familiar thing in life, is wholly without difficulties. But its difficulty is not one of epistemology, that is, of the relation of known to a knower; to take it as such, and then to use it as proof of the psychical nature of a final term, is also to prove that the trail the rocket stick leaves behind is psychical, or that the flower which comes in a continuity of process from a seed is mental.

II

Contemporary realists have so frequently and clearly expounded the physical explanation of such cases as have been cited that one is at a loss as to why idealists go on repeating the cases without even alluding to the realistic explanation. One is moved to wonder whether this neglect is just one of those circumstances which persistently dog philosophical discussions, or whether something in the realistic position gives ground (from at least an *ad hominem* point of view) for the neglect. There is a reason for adopting the latter alternative. Many realists, in offering the type of explanation adduced above, have treated the cases of seen light, doubled imagery, as perception in a way that ascribes to perception an inherent cognitive status. They have treated the perceptions as *cases of knowledge*, instead of as simply natural events having, in themselves (apart from a *use* that may be made of them), no more knowledge status or worth than, say, a shower or a fever. What I intend to show is that if "perceptions" are regarded as cases of knowledge, the gate is opened to the idealistic interpretation. The physical explanation holds of them as long as they are regarded simply as natural events—a doctrine I shall call naïve realism; it does not hold of them considered as cases of knowledge—the view I call presentative realism.

The idealists attribute to the realists the doctrine that "the perceived object is the real object." Please note the wording; it assumes that there is *the* real object, something which stands in a contrasting relation with objects not real or else less real. Since it is easily demonstrable that there is a numerical duplicity between the astronomical star and its effect of visible light, between the single finger and the doubled

images, the latter evidently, when the former is dubbed "*the*" real object, stands in disparaging contrast to its reality. *If* it is a case of knowledge, the knowledge refers to the star; and yet not the star, but something more or less unreal (that is, if the star be "the" real object), is known.

Consider how simply the matter stands in what I have called naïve realism. The astronomical star is *a* real object, but not "the" real object; the visible light is another real object, found, when knowledge supervenes, to be an occurrence standing in a process continuous with the star. Since the seen light is an event within a continuous process, there is no point of view from which its "reality" contrasts with that of the star.

But suppose that the realist accepts the traditionary psychology according to which every event in the way of a perception is also a case of knowing something. Is the way out now so simple? In the case of the doubled fingers or the seen light, the thing known in perception contrasts with the physical source and cause of the knowledge. There *is* a numerical duplicity. Moreover the thing known by perception is by this hypothesis in relation to a knower, while the physical cause is not. Is not the most plausible account of the difference between the physical cause of the perceptive knowledge and what the latter presents precisely this latter difference—namely, presentation to a knower? If perception is a case of knowing, it must be a case of knowing the star; but since the "real" star is not known in the perception, the knowledge relation must somehow have changed the "object" into a "content." Thus when the realist conceives the perceptual occurrence as an intrinsic case of knowledge or of presentation to a mind or knower, he lets the nose of the idealist camel into the tent. He has then no great cause for surprise when the camel comes in—and devours the tent.

Perhaps it will seem as if in this last paragraph, I had gone back on what I said earlier regarding the physical explanation of the difference between the visible light and the astronomical star. On the contrary, my point is that this explanation, though wholly adequate as long as we conceive the perception to be itself simply a natural event, is not at all available when we conceive it to be an attempt at knowing its cause. In the former case, we are dealing with a relation between natural events. In the latter case, we are dealing with the difference between an object as a cause of knowledge and an object as known, and hence in relation to mind. By the "method of difference" the sole explanation of the difference between the two objects is then the absence or presence of relation to a knower.

In the case of the seen light,[1] reference to the velocity of light is quite adequate to account for its time and space differences from the star. But viewed as a case of what is known (on the supposition that perception is knowing), reference to it only increases the contrast between the real object and the object known in perception. For, being just as much a part of the object that causes the perception as is the star itself, it (the velocity of light) *ought* logically to be part of what is known in the perception, while it is not. Since the velocity of light is a constituent element in the star, it should be known in the perception; since it is not so known, reference to it only increases the discrepancy between the object of the perception—the seen light—and the real, astronomical star. The same is true of any physical condition that might be referred to: *The very things that, from the standpoint of perception as a natural event, are conditions that account for its happening are, from the standpoint of perception as a case of knowledge, part of the object which, if knowledge is to be valid, ought to be known, but is not.*

In this fact we have, perhaps, the ground of the idealist's disregard of the oft-proffered physical explanation of the difference between the perceptual event and *the* (so-called)

---

1.   It is impossible, in this brief treatment, to forestall every misapprehension and objection. Yet to many the use of the term "seen" will appear to be an admission that a case of knowledge is involved. But is smelling a case of knowledge? Or (if the superstition persists as to smell) is gnawing or poking a case of knowledge? My point, of course, is that "seen" involves a relation to organic activity, not to a knower, or mind.

real object. And it is quite possible that some realists who read these lines will feel that in my last paragraphs I have been making a covert argument for idealism. Not so, I repeat; they are an argument for a truly naïve realism. The presentative realist, in his appeal to "common-sense" and the "plain man," first sophisticates the umpire and then appeals. He stops a good way short of a genuine naïveté. The plain man, for a surety, does not regard noises heard, lights seen, etc., as mental existences; but neither does he regard them as things *known*. That they are just things is good enough for him. That they are in relation to mind, or in relation to mind as their "knower," no more occurs to him than that they are mental. By this I mean much more than that the formulae of epistemology are foreign to him; I mean that his attitude to these things *as* things involves their *not* being in relation to him as a mind or a knower. He is in the attitude of a liker or hater, a doer or an appreciator. When he takes the attitude of a knower he begins to inquire. Once depart from thorough naïveté, and substitute for it the psychological theory that perception is a cognitive presentation to a mind of a causal object, and the first step is taken on the road which ends in an idealistic system.

III

For simplicity's sake, I have written as if my main problem were to show how, in the face of a supposed difficulty, a strictly realistic theory of the perceptual event may be maintained. But my interest is primarily in the facts, and in the theory only because of the facts it formulates. The significance of the facts of the case may, perhaps, be indicated by a consideration which has thus far been ignored. In regarding a perception as a case of knowledge, the presentative realist does more than shove into it a relation to mind which then, naturally and inevitably, becomes the explanation of any differences that exist between its subject-matter and some causal object with which it contrasts. In many cases—very important cases, too, in the physical sciences—the contrasting "real object" becomes known by a logical process, by inference—as the contemporary position of the star is determined by calculations from data, not by perception. This, then, is the situation of the presentative realist: If perception is knowledge of its cause, it stands in unfavorable contrast with another indirect mode of knowledge; *its* object is less valid than the object of inference. I do not adduce these considerations as showing that the case is hopeless for the presentative realist; I am willing to concede he can find a satisfactory way out. But the difficulty exists; and in existing it calls emphatic attention to a case which is certainly and indisputably a case of knowledge—namely, propositions arrived at through inference, judgments as logical assertions.

With relation to the unquestionable case of knowledge, the logical or inferential case, perceptions occupy a unique status, one which readily accounts for their being regarded as cases of knowledge, although in themselves they are natural events. (1) They are the sole ultimate data, the sole media, of inference to all natural objects and processes. While we do not, in any intelligible or verifiable sense, know *them*, we know all things that we do know *with* or *by* them. They furnish the only ultimate evidence of the existence and nature of the objects which we infer, and they are the sole ultimate checks and tests of the inferences. The visible light is a necessary part of the evidence on the basis of which we infer the existence, place, and structure of the astronomical star, and some other perception is the verifying check on the value of the inference. Because of this characteristic use of perceptions, the perceptions themselves acquire, by "second intention," a knowledge status. They *become* objects of minute, accurate, and experimental scrutiny. Since the body of propositions that forms natural science hangs upon them, *for scientific purposes* their nature *as* evidence, *as* signs, entirely overshadows their natural status, that of being simply natural events. The scientific man, as scientific, cares for perceptions not in themselves, but as they throw light upon the nature of some object reached by evidence. And since every such inference tries to terminate in a further perception (as its test of validity), the value of inferential knowing depends on perception. (2) Independently of science, daily life uses perceptions as signs of other perceptions. When a perception of a certain kind frequently recurs and is constantly used as evidence of some other impending perceptual event, the function of habit (a natural function, be it noted, not a psychical or epistemological function) often brings it about that the perception loses its original quality in acquiring a sign-value. Language is, of course, the typical case. Noises, in themselves mere natural events, through habitual use as signs of other natural events become integrated with what they mean. What they stand for is telescoped, as it were, into what they are. This happens also with other natural events, colors, tastes, etc. Thus, *for practical purposes*, many perceptual events are cases of knowledge; that is, they have been *used* as such so often that the habit of so using them is established or automatic.

In this brief reference to facts that are perfectly familiar, I have tried to suggest three points of crucial importance for a naïve realism: first, that inferential or evidential knowledge (that involving logical relation) is in the field as an obvious and undisputed case of knowledge; second, that this function, although embodying the logical relation, is itself a natural and specifically detectable process among natural things—it is not a non-natural or epistemological relation; third, that the *use*, practical and scientific, of perceptual events in the evidential or inferential function is such as to make them *become* objects of inquiry and limits of knowledge, and to such a degree that this acquired characteristic quite overshadows, in many cases, their primary nature.

If we add to what has been said the fact that, like every natural function, the inferential function turns out better in some cases and worse in others, we get a naturalistic or naïvely realistic conception of the "*problem* of knowledge": Control of the conditions of inference—the only type of knowledge detectable in direct existence—so as to guide it toward better conclusions.

IV

I do not flatter myself that I will receive much gratitude from realists for attempting to rescue them from that error of fact which exposes their doctrine to an idealistic interpretation. The superstition, growing up in a false physics and physiology and perpetuated by psychology, that sensations-perceptions are cases of knowledge, is too ingrained. But— *crede experto*—let them try the experiment of conceiving perceptions as pure natural events, not as cases of awareness or apprehension, and

they will be surprised to see how little they miss—save the burden of carrying traditionary problems. Meantime, while philosophic argument, such as this, will do little to change the state of belief regarding perceptions, the development of biology and the refinement of physiology will, in due season, do the work.

In concluding my article, I ought to refer, in order to guard against misapprehension, to a reply that the presentative realist might make to my objection. He might say that while the seen light is a case of knowledge or presentative awareness, it is not a case of knowledge of the star, but simply of the seen light, just as it is. In this case the appeal to the physical explanations of the difference of the seen light from its objective source is quite legitimate. At first sight, such a position seems innocent and tenable. Even if innocent, it would, however, be ungrounded, since there is no evidence of the existence of a knower, and of its relation to the seen light. But further consideration will reveal that there is a most fundamental objection. If the notion of perception as a case of adequate knowledge of its own object-matter be accepted, the knowledge relation is absolutely ubiquitous; it is an all-inclusive net. The "egocentric predicament" is inevitable. . . .

AFTERWORD

Sceptics, realists, and idealists are very hard to tell apart when they are not talking about philosophy. That is, as far as their everyday practical lives are concerned, their views on the knowledge which may be obtained from perception have very little impact. This problem is a highly theoretical issue, in which we try to blend together our most basic beliefs about perception, physical reality, and knowledge to form a single, consistent theory. The immediate goal of such efforts is an improved theoretical understanding of the character of human knowledge, and of physical reality.

But such theories do have significant impact on other philosophical problems. For example, if idealism or phenomenalism is correct, then the problem of mind-body interaction is provided with a monistic answer. And Berkeley employed his idealistic position as the foundation for an attempt at proving God's existence. More generally, belief based on perception is so common, and so important to us, that careful scrutiny will reveal many arguments in the selections included in other chapters whose usefulness and correctness depends upon the position one takes about this problem.

Now, consider two questions. First, what is it reasonable to require of a reliable source of knowledge? If you go through the preceding selections carefully, you will find a strong tendency to suppose that if it is *possible* (not likely, but just possible) for us to make a mistake in arriving at a belief in a certain way, then that method of belief-formation should be rejected as unreliable. Is this a reasonable requirement on sources of knowledge? Is it a requirement which *any* method of belief-selection could meet?

Second, what happens if we raise the question, How do we know that other minds and their experiences actually exist? Usually, the answer would be that while we do not directly observe other minds or their experiences, we can observe the behavior of the bodies associated with them, and we can infer from such bodily behavior that there are other minds, and that they are having certain kinds of experiences. But, now, if we think that bodies are really constructions out of our own experience, *and the experiences of others*, are we not involved in a problem of circularity? We do not know that there are bodies, or how they behave, unless we know that other persons' experience agrees with ours, regarding those bodies. But we cannot know what experiences other persons are having unless we know what their bodies are doing. How, then, can we know either? We could, perhaps, avoid this problem by trying to explain our knowledge of physical reality and other minds in terms of our own experience alone. But this raises serious questions about the distinction between knowledge and sheer delusion or fantasy.

REVIEW QUESTIONS

Selection 46

1. What is the discussion of dreaming intended to establish?

2. What is the point of the discussion of deception by God or an evil demon? What does this argument establish which is not established by the argument about dreaming?

3. Why can't the evil deceiver fool Descartes about his own existence?

4. Carefully explain the conclusions Descartes reaches about our knowledge of physical objects as he discusses the piece of wax.

Selection 47

5. How does Locke characterize each of the following? (*a*) ideas; (*b*) qualities; (*c*) primary qualities; (*d*) secondary qualities; (*e*) powers; (*f*) immediately perceived secondary qualities; (*g*) mediately perceived secondary qualities; (*h*) substance.

6. According to Locke, do the three kinds of qualities differ as they exist in objects or only in the kinds of ideas they produce? Explain.

7. In Locke's account, why do we believe there is physical substance?

8. Sum up Locke's discussion by explaining what kinds of knowledge of the physical world he thinks we can gain through perception.

Selection 48

9. Berkeley says (paragraph 4) that there is a "manifest contradiction" in the belief that sensible objects have existence apart from their being perceived. Why does he think so, and what is the nature of this contradiction?

10. How does Berkeley deal with Locke's distinction between primary and secondary qualities?

11. According to Berkeley, what do philosophers mean by *material substance*, and what is wrong with that concept?

12. How does Berkeley attempt to prove the existence of spirits?

13. What is a real physical thing, according to Berkeley? How does it differ from an illusion or hallucination?

14. In paragraphs 36–40, 45, 48, 60, 64, 65, Berkeley responds to several objections he expects to be raised against his view. What are the objections, and his responses to them?

Selection 49

15. Lewis discusses two examples of perceptual knowledge (the granite steps, and the piece of white paper). What are the roles of sensation and prediction in these examples, according to him?

16. Lewis says that the implied consequences of even very simple beliefs about physical objects are inexhaustible. Explain.

17. Lewis distinguishes three classes of empirical statements. What are they, and what are their differences?

18. Explain how the three classes of empirical statements are involved in the belief that there is a piece of white paper before you. In Lewis's account, is this something you could ever know for certain?

Selection 50

19. In Part I Dewey suggests that several familiar "idealist" arguments are self-contradictory. What is the nature of the contradiction?

20. Dewey distinguishes between regarding perceptions as cases of knowledge and regarding them as natural events. Explain the distinction.

21. Use the distinction you explained in response to the previous question to explain how regarding perception as a case of knowledge opens the door to the idealist's arguments.

22. Under what circumstances does Dewey say that the egocentric predicament is inevitable? What does he mean?

12

The Rationality of Induction

We can divide a posteriori knowledge into two classes. First, there are the things we know because we directly observe them to be the case. Second, there are things we know which are not directly observed to be the case, but which still are based in some way upon experience. (The reliability of any observation is questioned in Chapter 11, but here let us assume that observation is reliable.) We will focus on this second kind of a posteriori knowledge in this chapter. Examples are plentiful. If we observe rubbish littered throughout our favorite wilderness, we know that other people have been there before us, although we have not observed them there. We know that hitting a finger with a hammer would be painful, though we have never observed that finger being hit with that hammer. We know how a dish will taste as we prepare it, though we have not tasted it yet. We expect pressure on a brake pedal to slow the car, turning the knob to unlatch the door, etc., before the event has taken place.

How is it possible to know such things when they have not been observed to happen? The answer most likely to be given is that we have observed other events of the same kind, and their consequences, and on the basis of those observations we know what to expect as new situations of that kind arise. We have observed rubbish being strewed before, or fingers being hit. We have tasted other batches of the dish in question, applied brakes before, dealt with many doors and doorknobs, etc. And thus, as new instances of familiar situations arise, we know what to expect. In short, we make inferences about the cases we have not observed on the basis of the ones we have observed. This is what it is to reason inductively, and it is a kind of reasoning which we all use and trust.

But if this is a reliable way to think, shouldn't we be able to explain *why* it is reliable, or offer some proof of its reliability? It is tempting to suppose so, but such explanations or proofs have turned out to be very difficult to provide. We cannot *observe* that unobserved cases are like observed ones (because we cannot observe unobserved cases). And it would seem dangerously circular to claim that since observed uses of induction have turned out to be correct, the unobserved ones will also. Finally, since the outcome of inductive reasoning is a posteriori knowledge (if it is knowledge at all), it seems implausible that any a priori reasoning could establish its reliability. But what other sort of explanation or demonstration could be possible?

Once again we are drawn into the position of maintaining an inconsistent triad of beliefs:

(1) Inductive reasoning is a reliable source of knowledge.

(2) The reliability of a reliable source of knowledge can be explained and/or demonstrated.

(3) There is no explanation or demonstration of the reliability of inductive reasoning.

And, once again, something plausible must be given up.

The position of the *sceptic* on this problem is that the evidence for (2) and (3) is conclusive, and that we must give up the pretense that induction is a reliable method for selecting our beliefs. The sceptic does not deny that our use of induction has worked out pretty well so far, nor does he deny that it may continue to do so. What he does deny is that we are entitled to be *sure* that inductive reasoning will be fruitful for us in future applications.

Of course, the sceptical position undercuts a vast amount of what we ordinarily suppose we know, and there is a great deal of interest in refuting scepticism. But if (1) is to be saved, then either (2) or (3) must be defeated. A number of philosophers have directed their efforts toward refuting (3) by attempting to provide some explanation or demonstration of induction's reliability. A smaller number of philosophers have offered reasons for rejecting (2), attempting to convince us that not every reliable pattern of inference can be *shown* to be reliable, and suggesting that inductive reasoning is one of those patterns for which the demand for demonstration or explanation is inappropriate.

You will find that there is some variation in what different authors select as the significant features of inductive reasoning. Such variation accounts for some of the differences in opinion on the reliability of inductive reasoning. But the list of objections to attempts to prove the reliability of induction is fairly short and is recognized by nearly everyone. Arguments in defense of induction are carefully designed to avoid all those objections, and you should be careful to examine each argument critically to see if it succeeds in avoiding all the objections on the list. Finally, there is the question whether inductive reasoning requires some explanation or proof if it is to be counted as reliable. See if you can discover what reasons some philosophers have for thinking that such things are required, and what reasons others have for thinking that they are not.

51

Sceptical Doubts about Human Understanding

DAVID HUME

Part I

All the objects of human reason or enquiry may naturally be divided into two kinds, to wit, *Relations of Ideas,* and *Matters of Fact.* Of the first kind are the sciences of Geometry, Algebra, and Arithmetic; and in short, every affirmation which is either intuitively or demonstratively certain. *That the square of the hypothenuse is equal to the squares of the two sides,* is a proposition which expresses a relation between these figures. *That three times five is equal to the half of thirty,* expresses a relation between these numbers. Propositions of this kind are discoverable by the mere operation of thought, without dependence on what is anywhere existent in the universe. Though there never were

a circle or triangle in nature, the truths demonstrated by Euclid would for ever retain their certainty and evidence.

Matters of fact, which are the second objects of human reason, are not ascertained in the same manner; nor is our evidence of their truth, however great, of a like nature with the foregoing. The contrary of every matter of fact is still possible; because it can never imply a contradiction, and is conceived by the mind with the same facility and distinctness, as if ever so conformable to reality. *That the sun will not rise to-morrow* is no less intelligible a proposition, and implies no more contradiction than the affirmation, *that it will rise*. We should in vain, therefore, attempt to demonstrate its falsehood. Were it demonstratively false, it would imply a contradiction,

[From *An Inquiry Concerning Human Understanding*, Section IV. First published in 1748.]

and could never be distinctly conceived by the mind.

It may, therefore, be a subject worthy of curiosity, to enquire what is the nature of that evidence which assures us of any real existence and matter of fact, beyond the present testimony of our senses, or the records of our memory. This part of philosophy, it is observable, has been little cultivated, either by the ancients or moderns; and therefore our doubts and errors, in the prosecution of so important an enquiry, may be the more excusable; while we march through such difficult paths without any guide or direction. They may even prove useful, by exciting curiosity, and destroying that implicit faith and security, which is the bane of all reasoning and free enquiry. The discovery of defects in the common philosophy, if any such there be, will not, I presume, be a discouragement, but rather an incitement, as is usual, to attempt something more full and satisfactory than has yet been proposed to the public.

All reasonings concerning matter of fact seem to be founded on the relation of *Cause and Effect*. By means of that relation alone we can go beyond the evidence of our memory and senses. If you were to ask a man, why he believes any matter of fact, which is absent; for instance, that his friend is in the country, or in France; he would give you a reason; and this reason would be some other fact; as a letter received from him, or the knowledge of his former resolutions and promises. A man finding a watch or any other machine in a desert island, would conclude that there had once been men in that island. All our reasonings concerning fact are of the same nature. And here it is constantly supposed that there is a connexion between the present fact and that which is inferred from it. Were there nothing to bind them together, the inference would be entirely precarious. The hearing of an articulate voice and rational discourse in the dark assures us of the presence of some person: Why? because these are the effects of the human make and fabric, and closely connected with it. If we anatomize all the other reasonings of this nature, we shall find that they are founded on the relation of cause and effect, and that this relation is either near or remote, direct or collateral. Heat and light are collateral effects of fire, and the one effect may justly be inferred from the other.

If we would satisfy ourselves, therefore, concerning the nature of that evidence, which assures us of matters of fact, we must enquire how we arrive at the knowledge of cause and effect.

I shall venture to affirm, as a general proposition, which admits of no exception, that the knowledge of this relation is not, in any instance, attained by reasonings *a priori;* but arises entirely from experience, when we find that any particular objects are constantly conjoined with each other. Let an object be presented to a man of ever so strong natural reason and abilities; if that object be entirely new to him, he will not be able, by the most accurate examination of its sensible qualities, to discover any of its causes or effects. Adam, though his rational faculties be supposed, at the very first, entirely perfect, could not have inferred from the fluidity and transparency of water that it would suffocate him, or from the light and warmth of fire that it would consume him. No object ever discovers, by the qualities which appear to the senses, either the causes which produced it, or the effects which will arise from it; nor can our reason, unassisted by experience, ever draw any inference concerning real existence and matter of fact.

This proposition, that *causes and effects are discoverable, not by reason but by experience,* will readily be admitted with regard to such objects, as we remember to have once been altogether unknown to us; since we must be conscious of the utter inability, which we then lay under, of foretelling what would arise from them. Present two smooth pieces of marble to a man who has no tincture of natural philosophy; he will never discover that they will adhere together in such a manner as to require great force to separate them in a direct line, while they make so small a resistance to a lateral pressure. Such events, as bear little analogy to the common course of nature, are also readily confessed to be known only by experience; nor does any man imagine that the explosion of gunpowder, or the attraction of a loadstone, could ever be discovered by arguments *a priori*. In like manner, when an effect is supposed to depend upon an intricate machinery or secret structure of parts, we make no difficulty in attributing all our knowledge of it to experience. Who will assert that he can give the ultimate reason, why milk or bread is proper nourishment for a man, not for a lion or a tiger?

But the same truth may not appear, at first sight, to have the same evidence with regard to events, which have become familiar to us from our first appearance in the world, which bear a close analogy to the whole course of nature, and which are supposed to depend on the simple qualities of objects, without any secret structure of parts. We are apt to imagine that we could discover these effects by the mere operation of our reason, without experience. We fancy, that were we brought on a sudden into this world, we could at first have inferred that one Billiard-ball would communicate motion to another upon impulse; and that we needed not to have waited for the event, in order to pronounce with certainty concerning it. Such is the influence of custom, that, where it is strongest, it not only covers our natural ignorance, but even conceals itself, and seems not to take place, merely because it is found in the highest degree.

But to convince us that all the laws of nature, and all the operations of bodies without exception, are known only by experience, the following reflections may, perhaps, suffice. Were any object presented to us, and were we required to pronounce concerning the effect, which will result from it, without consulting past observation; after what manner, I beseech you, must the mind proceed in this operation? It must invent or imagine some event, which it ascribes to the object as its effect; and it is plain that this invention must be entirely arbitrary. The mind can never possibly find the effect in the supposed cause, by the most accurate scrutiny and examination. For the effect is totally different from the cause, and consequently can never be discovered in it. Motion in the second Billiard-ball is a quite distinct event from motion in the first: nor is there anything in the one to suggest the smallest hint of the other. A stone or piece of metal raised into the air, and left without any support, immediately falls; but to consider the matter *a priori,* is there anything we discover in this situation which can beget the idea of a downward, rather than an upward, or any other motion, in the stone or metal?

And as the first imagination or invention of a particular effect, in all natural operations, is arbitrary, where we consult not experience; so must we also esteem the supposed tie or connexion between the cause and effect, which binds them together, and renders it impossible that any other effect could result from the operation of that cause. When I see, for instance, a Billiard-ball moving in a straight line towards another; even suppose motion in the second ball should by accident be suggested to me, as the result of their contact or impulse; may I not conceive, that a hundred different events might as well follow from that cause? May not both these balls remain at absolute rest? May not the first ball return in a straight line, or leap off from the second in any line or direction? All these suppositions are consistent and conceivable. Why then should we give the preference to one, which is no more consistent or conceivable than the rest? All our reasonings *a priori* will never be able to show us any foundation for this preference.

In a word, then, every effect is a distinct event from its cause. It could not, therefore, be discovered in the cause, and the first invention or conception of it, *a priori,* must be entirely arbitrary. And even after it is suggested, the conjunction of it with the cause must appear equally arbitrary; since there are always many other effects, which, to reason, must seem fully as consistent and natural. In vain, therefore, should we pretend to determine any single event, or infer any cause or effect, without the assistance of observation and experience.

Hence we may discover the reason why no philosopher, who is rational and modest, has ever pretended to assign the ultimate cause of any natural operation, or to show distinctly the action of that power, which produces any single effect in the universe. It is confessed, that the utmost effort of human reason is to reduce the principles, productive of natural phenomena, to a greater simplicity, and to resolve the many particular effects into a few general causes, by means of reasonings from analogy, experience, and observation. But as to the causes of these general causes, we should in vain attempt their discovery; nor shall we ever be able to satisfy ourselves, by any particular explication of them. These ultimate springs and principles are totally shut up from human curiosity and enquiry. Elasticity, gravity, cohesion of parts, communication of motion by impulse; these are probably the ultimate causes and principles which we ever discover in nature; and we may esteem ourselves sufficiently happy, if, by accurate inquiry and reasoning, we can trace up the particular phenomena to, or near to, these general principles. The most perfect philosophy of the natural kind only staves off our ignorance a little longer: as perhaps the most perfect philosophy of the moral or metaphysical kind serves only to discover larger portions of it. Thus the observation of human blindness and weakness is the result of all philosophy, and meets us at every turn, in spite of our endeavours to elude or avoid it.

Nor is geometry, when taken into the assistance of natural philosophy, ever able to remedy this defect, or lead us into the knowledge of ultimate causes, by all that accuracy of reasoning for which it is so justly celebrated. Every part of mixed mathematics proceeds upon the supposition that certain laws are established by nature in her operations; and abstract reasonings are employed, either to assist experience in the discovery of these laws, or to determine their influence in particular instances, where it depends upon any precise degree of distance and quantity. Thus, it is a law of motion, discovered by experience, that the moment or force of any body in motion is in the compound ratio or proportion of its solid contents and its velocity; and consequently, that a small force may remove the greatest obstacle or raise the greatest weight, if, by any contrivance or machinery, we can increase the velocity of that force, so as to make it an overmatch for its antagonist. Geometry assists us in the application of this law, by giving us the just dimensions of all the parts and figures which can enter into any species of machine; but still the discovery of the law itself is owing merely to experience, and all the abstract reasonings in the world could never lead us one step towards the knowledge of it. When we reason *a priori,* and consider merely any object or cause, as it appears to the mind, independent of all observation, it never could suggest to us the notion of any distinct object, such as its effect; much less, show us the inseparable and inviolable connexion between them. A man must be very sagacious who could discover by reasoning that crystal is the effect of heat, and ice of cold, without being previously acquainted with the operation of these qualities.

Part II

But we have not yet attained any tolerable satisfaction with regard to the question first proposed. Each solution still gives rise to a new question as difficult as the foregoing, and leads us on to farther enquiries. When it is asked, *What is the nature of all our reasonings concerning matter of fact?* the proper answer seems to be, that they are founded on the relation of cause and effect. When again it is asked, *What is the foundation of all our reasonings and conclusions concerning that relation?* it may be replied in one word, Experience. But if we still carry on our sifting humour, and ask, *What is the foundation of all conclusions from experience?* this implies a new question, which may be of more difficult solution and explication. Philosophers, that give them-

selves airs of superior wisdom and sufficiency, have a hard task when they encounter persons of inquisitive dispositions, who push them from every corner to which they retreat, and who are sure at last to bring them to some dangerous dilemma. The best expedient to prevent this confusion, is to be modest in our pretensions; and even to discover the difficulty ourselves before it is objected to us. By this means, we may make a kind of merit of our very ignorance.

I shall content myself, in this section, with an easy task, and shall pretend only to give a negative answer to the question here proposed. I say then, that, even after we have experience of the operations of cause and effect, our conclusions from that experience are *not* founded on reasoning, or any process of the understanding. This answer we must endeavour both to explain and to defend.

It must certainly be allowed, that nature has kept us at a great distance from all her secrets, and has afforded us only the knowledge of a few superficial qualities of objects; while she conceals from us those powers and principles on which the influence of those objects entirely depends. Our senses inform us of the colour, weight, and consistence of bread; but neither sense nor reason can ever inform us of those qualities which fit it for the nourishment and support of a human body. Sight or feeling conveys an idea of the actual motion of bodies; but as to that wonderful force or power, which would carry on a moving body for ever in a continued change of place, and which bodies never lose but by communicating it to others; of this we cannot form the most distant conception. But notwithstanding this ignorance of natural powers and principles, we always presume, when we see like sensible qualities, that they have like secret powers, and expect that effects, similar to those which we have experienced, will follow from them. If a body of like colour and consistence with that bread, which we have formerly eat, be presented to us, we make no scruple of repeating the experiment, and foresee, with certainty, like nourishment and support. Now this is a process of the mind or thought, of which I would willingly know the foundation. It is allowed on all hands that there is no known connexion between the sensible qualities and the secret powers; and consequently, that the mind is not led to form such a conclusion concerning their constant and regular conjunction, by anything which it knows of their nature. As to past *Experience,* it can be allowed to give *direct* and *certain* information of those precise objects only, and that precise period of time, which fell under its cognizance: but why this experience should be extended to future times, and to other objects, which, for aught we know, may be only in appearance similar; this is the main question on which

I would insist. The bread, which I formerly eat, nourished me; that is, a body of such sensible qualities was, at that time, endued with such secret powers: but does it follow, that other bread must also nourish me at another time, and that like sensible qualities must always be attended with like secret powers? The consequence seems nowise necessary. At least, it must be acknowledged that there is here a consequence drawn by the mind; that there is a certain step taken; a process of thought, and an inference, which wants to be explained. These two propositions are far from being the same, *I have found that such an object has always been attended with such an effect,* and *I foresee, that other objects, which are, in appearance, similar, will be attended with similar effects.* I shall allow, if you please, that the one proposition may justly be inferred from the other; I know, in fact, that it always is inferred. But if you insist that the inference is made by a chain of reasoning, I desire you to produce that reasoning. The connexion between these propositions is not intuitive. There is required a medium, which may enable the mind to draw such an inference, if indeed it be drawn by reasoning and argument. What that medium is, I must confess, passes my comprehension; and it is incumbent on those to produce it, who assert that it really exists, and is the origin of all our conclusions concerning matter of fact.

This negative argument must certainly, in process of time, become altogether convincing, if many penetrating and able philosophers shall turn their enquiries this way and no one be ever able to discover any connecting proposition or intermediate step, which supports the understanding in this conclusion. But as the question is yet new, every reader may not trust so far to his own penetration, as to conclude, because an argument escapes his enquiry, that therefore it does not really exist. For this reason it may be requisite to venture upon a more difficult task; and enumerating all the branches of human knowledge, endeavour to show that none of them can afford such an argument.

All reasonings may be divided into two kinds, namely demonstrative reasoning, or that concerning relations of ideas, and moral reasoning, or that concerning matter of fact and existence. That there are no demonstrative arguments in the case seems evident; since it implies no contradiction that the course of nature may change, and that an object, seemingly like those which we have experienced, may be attended with different or contrary effects. May I not clearly and distinctly conceive that a body, falling from the clouds, and which, in all other respects, resembles snow, has yet the taste of salt or feeling of fire? Is there any more intelligible proposition than to affirm, that all the trees will flourish in December and January, and decay in May and June? Now whatever is intelligible, and can be distinctly conceived, implies no contradiction, and can never be proved false by any demonstrative argument or abstract reasoning *a priori*.

If we be, therefore, engaged by arguments to put trust in past experience, and make it the standard of our future judgement, these arguments must be probable only, or such as regard matter of fact and real existence, according to the division above mentioned. But that there is no argument of this kind, must appear, if our explication of that species of reasoning be admitted as solid and satisfactory. We have said that all arguments concerning existence are founded on the relation of cause and effect; that our knowledge of that relation is derived entirely from experience; and that all our experimental conclusions proceed upon the supposition that the future will be conformable to the past. To endeavour, therefore, the proof of this last supposition by probable arguments, or arguments regarding existence, must be evidently going in a circle, and taking that for granted, which is the very point in question.

In reality, all arguments from experience are founded on the similarity which we discover among natural objects, and by which we are induced to expect effects similar to those which we have found to follow from such objects. And though none but a fool or madman will ever pretend to dispute the authority of experience, or to reject that great guide of human life, it may surely be allowed a philosopher to have so much curiosity at least as to examine the principle of human nature, which gives this mighty authority to experience, and makes us draw advantage from that similarity which nature has placed among different objects. From causes which appear *similar* we expect similar effects. This is the sum of all our experimental conclusions. Now it seems evident that, if this conclusion were formed by reason, it would be as perfect at first, and upon one instance, as after ever so long a course of experience. But the case is far otherwise. Nothing so like as eggs; yet no one, on account of this appearing similarity, expects the same taste and relish in all of them. It is only after a long course of uniform experiments in any kind, that we attain a firm reliance and security with regard to a particular event. Now where is that process of reasoning which, from one instance, draws a conclusion, so different from that which it infers from a hundred instances that are nowise different from that single one? This question I propose as much for the sake of information, as with an intention of raising difficulties. I cannot find, I cannot imagine any such reasoning. But I keep my mind still open to instruction, if any one will vouchsafe to bestow it on me.

Should it be said that, from a number of uniform experiments, we *infer* a connexion between the sensible qualities and the secret powers; this, I must confess, seems the same difficulty, couched in different terms. The question still recurs, on what process of argument this *inference* is founded? Where is the medium, the interposing ideas, which join propositions so very wide of each other? It is confessed that the colour, consistence, and other sensible qualities of bread appear not, of themselves, to have any connexion with the secret powers of nourishment and support. For otherwise we could infer these secret powers from the first appearance of these sensible qualities, without the aid of experience; contrary to the sentiment of all philosophers, and contrary to plain matter of fact. Here, then, is our natural state of ignorance with regard to the powers and influence of all objects. How is this remedied by experience? It only shows us a number of uniform effects, resulting from certain objects, and teaches us that those particular objects, at that particular time, were endowed with such powers and forces. When a new object, endowed with similar sensible qualities, is produced, we expect similar powers and forces, and look for a like effect. From a body of like colour and consistence with bread we expect like nourishment and support. But this surely is a step or progress of the mind, which wants to be explained. When a man says, *I have found, in all past instances, such sensible qualities conjoined with such secret powers:* And when he says, *Similar sensible qualities will always be conjoined with similar secret powers,* he is not guilty of a tautology, nor are these propositions in any respect the same. You say that the one proposition is an inference from the other. But you must confess that the inference is not intuitive; neither is it demonstrative: Of what nature is it, then? To say it is experimental, is begging the question. For all inferences from experience suppose, as their foundation, that the future will resemble the past, and that similar powers will be conjoined with similar sensible qualities. If there be any suspicion that the course of nature may change, and that the past may be no rule for the future, all experience becomes useless, and can give rise to no inference or conclusion. It is impossible, therefore, that any arguments from experience can prove this resemblance of the past to the future; since all these arguments are founded on the supposition of that resemblance. Let the course of things be allowed hitherto ever so regular; that alone, without some new argument or inference, proves not that, for the future, it will continue so. In vain do you pretend to have learned the nature of bodies from your past experience. Their secret nature, and consequently all their effects and influence, may change, without any change in their sensible qualities. This happens sometimes, and with regard to some objects: Why may it

not happen always, and with regard to all objects? What logic, what process of argument secures you against this supposition? My practice, you say, refutes my doubts. But you mistake the purport of my question. As an agent, I am quite satisfied in the point; but as a philosopher, who has some share of curiosity, I will not say scepticism, I want to learn the foundation of this inference. No reading, no enquiry has yet been able to remove my difficulty, or give me satisfaction in a matter of such importance. Can I do better than propose the difficulty to the public, even though, perhaps, I have small hopes of obtaining a solution? We shall, at least, by this means, be sensible of our ignorance, if we do not augment our knowledge.

I must confess that a man is guilty of unpardonable arrogance who concludes, because an argument has escaped his own investigation, that therefore it does not really exist. I must also confess that, though all the learned, for several ages, should have employed themselves in fruitless search upon any subject, it may still, perhaps, be rash to conclude positively that the subject must, therefore, pass all human comprehension. Even though we examine all the sources of our knowledge, and conclude them unfit for such a subject, there may still remain a suspicion, that the enumeration is not complete, or the examination not accurate. But with regard to the present subject, there are some considerations which seem to remove all this accusation of arrogance or suspicion of mistake.

It is certain that the most ignorant and stupid peasants—nay infants, nay even brute beasts—improve by experience, and learn the qualities of natural objects, by observing the effects which result from them. When a child has felt the sensation of pain from touching the flame of a candle, he will be careful not to put his hand near any candle; but will expect a similar effect from a cause which is similar in its sensible qualities and appearance. If you assert, therefore, that the understanding of the child is led into this conclusion by any process of argument or ratiocination, I may justly require you to produce that argument; nor have you any pretense to refuse so equitable a demand. You cannot say that the argument is abtruse, and may possibly escape your enquiry; since you confess that it is obvious to the capacity of a mere infant. If you hesitate, therefore, a moment, or if, after reflection, you produce any intricate or profound argument, you, in a manner, give up the question, and confess that it is not reasoning which engages us to suppose the past resembling the future, and to expect similar effects from causes which are, to appearance, similar. This is the proposition which I intended to enforce in the present section. If I be right, I pretend not to have made any mighty discovery. And if I be wrong, I must acknowledge myself to be indeed a very backward scholar; since I cannot now discover an argument which, it seems, was perfectly familiar to me long before I was out of my cradle.

52

On Induction

BERTRAND RUSSELL

In almost all our previous discussions we have been concerned in the attempt to get clear as to our data in the way of knowledge of existence. What things are there in the universe whose existence is known to us owing to our being acquainted with them? So far, our answer has been that we are acquainted with our sense-data, and, probably, with ourselves. These we know to exist. And past sense-data which are remembered are known to have existed in the past. This knowledge supplies our data.

But if we are to be able to draw inferences from these data—if we are to know of the existence of matter, of other people, of the past before our individual memory begins, or of the future, we must know general principles of some kind by means of which such inferences can be drawn. It must be known to us that the existence of some one sort of thing, A, is a sign of the existence of some other sort of thing, B, either at the same time as A or at some earlier or later time, as, for example, thunder is a sign of the earlier existence of lightning. If this were not known to us, we could never extend our knowledge beyond the sphere of our private experience; and this sphere, as we have seen, is exceedingly limited. The question we have now to consider is whether such an extension is possible, and if so, how it is effected.

Let us take as an illustration a matter about which none of us, in fact, feel the slightest doubt. We are all convinced that the sun will rise to-morrow. Why? Is this belief a mere blind outcome of past experience, or can it be justified as a reasonable belief? It is not easy to find a test by which to judge whether a

[From *The Problems of Philosophy* by Bertrand Russell (1912), pp. 60–69. Reprinted by permission of Oxford University Press.]

belief of this kind is reasonable or not, but we can at least ascertain what sort of general beliefs would suffice, if true, to justify the judgement that the sun will rise to-morrow, and the many other similar judgements upon which our actions are based.

It is obvious that if we are asked why we believe that the sun will rise to-morrow, we shall naturally answer, "Because it always has risen every day." We have a firm belief that it will rise in the future, because it has risen in the past. If we are challenged as to why we believe that it will continue to rise as heretofore, we may appeal to the laws of motion: the earth, we shall say, is a freely rotating body, and such bodies do not cease to rotate unless something interferes from outside, and there is nothing outside to interfere with the earth between now and to-morrow. Of course it might be doubted whether we are quite certain that there is nothing outside to interfere, but this is not the interesting doubt. The interesting doubt is as to whether the laws of motion will remain in operation until to-morrow. If this doubt is raised, we find ourselves in the same position as when the doubt about the sunrise was first raised.

The *only* reason for believing that the laws of motion will remain in operation is that they have operated hitherto, so far as our knowledge of the past enables us to judge. It is true that we have a greater body of evidence from the past in favour of the laws of motion than we have in favour of the sunrise, because the sunrise is merely a particular case of fulfilment of the laws of motion, and there are countless other particular cases. But the real question is: Do *any* number of cases of a law being fulfilled in the past afford evidence that it will be fulfilled in the future? If not, it becomes plain that we have no ground whatever for expecting the sun to rise to-morrow, or for expecting the bread we shall eat at our next meal not to poison us, or for any of the other scarcely conscious expectations that control our daily lives. It is to be observed that all such expectations are only *probable*; thus we have not to seek for a proof that they *must* be fulfilled, but only for some reason in favour of the view that they are *likely* to be fulfilled.

Now in dealing with this question we must, to begin with, make an important distinction, without which we should soon become involved in hopeless confusions. Experience has shown us that, hitherto, the frequent repetition of some uniform succession or coexistence has been a *cause* of our expecting the same succession or coexistence on the next occasion. Food that has a certain appearance generally has a certain taste, and it is a severe shock to our expectations when the familiar appearance is found to be associated with an unusual taste. Things which we see become associated, by habit, with certain tactile sensations which we expect if we touch them; one of the horrors of a ghost (in many ghost-stories) is that it fails to give us any sensations of touch. Uneducated people who go abroad for the first time are so surprised as to be incredulous when they find their native language not understood.

And this kind of association is not confined to men; in animals also it is very strong. A horse which has been often driven along a certain road resists the attempt to drive him in a different direction. Domestic animals expect food when they see the person who usually feeds them. We know that all these rather crude expectations of uniformity are liable to be misleading. The man who has fed the chicken every day throughout its life at last wrings its neck instead, showing that more refined views as to the uniformity of nature would have been useful to the chicken.

But in spite of the misleadingness of such expectations, they nevertheless exist. The mere fact that something has happened a certain number of times causes animals and men to expect that it will happen again. Thus our instincts certainly cause us to believe that the sun will rise to-morrow, but we may be in no better a position than the chicken which unexpectedly has its neck wrung. We have therefore to distinguish the fact that past uniformities *cause* expectations as to the future, from the question whether there is any reasonable ground for giving weight to such expectations after the question of their validity has been raised.

The problem we have to discuss is whether there is any reason for believing in what is called "the uniformity of nature." The belief in the uniformity of nature is the belief that everything that has happened or will happen is an instance of some general law to which there are *no* exceptions. The crude expectations which we have been considering are all subject to exceptions, and therefore liable to disappoint those who entertain them. But science habitually assumes, at least as a working hypothesis, that general rules which have exceptions can be replaced by general rules which have no exceptions. "Unsupported bodies in air fall" is a general rule to which balloons and aeroplanes are exceptions. But the laws of motion and the law of gravitation, which account for the fact that most bodies fall, also account for the fact that balloons and aeroplanes can rise; thus the laws of motion and the law of gravitation are not subject to these exceptions.

The belief that the sun will rise to-morrow might be falsified if the earth came suddenly into contact with a large body which destroyed its rotation; but the laws of motion and the law of gravitation would not be infringed by such an event. The business of science is to find uniformities, such as the laws of motion and the law of gravitation, to which, so far as our experience extends, there are no exceptions. In this search science has been remarkably successful, and it may be conceded that such uniformities have held hitherto. This brings us back to the question: Have we any reason, assuming that they have always held in the past, to suppose that they will hold in the future?

It has been argued that we have reason to know that the future will resemble the past, because what was the future has constantly become the past, and has always been found to resemble the past, so that we really have experience of the future, namely of times which were formerly future, which we may call past futures. But such an argument really begs the very question at issue. We have experience of past futures, but not of future futures, and the question is: Will future futures resemble past futures? This question is not to be answered by an argument which starts from past futures alone. We have therefore still to seek for some principle which shall enable us to know that the future will follow the same laws as the past.

The reference to the future in this question is not essential. The same question arises when we apply the laws that work in our experience to past things of which we have no experience—as, for example, in geology, or in theories as to the origin of the Solar System. The question we really have to ask is: "When two things have been found to be often associated, and no instance is known of the one occurring without the other, does the occurrence of one of the two, in a fresh instance, give any good ground for expecting the other?" On our answer to this question must depend the validity of the whole of our expectations as to the future, the whole of the results obtained by induction, and in fact practically all the beliefs upon which our daily life is based.

It must be conceded, to begin with, that the fact that two things have been found often together and never apart does not, by itself, suffice to *prove* demonstratively that they will be found together in the next case we examine. The most we can hope is that the oftener things are found together, the more probable it becomes that they will be found together another time, and that, if they have been found together often enough, the probability will amount *almost* to certainty. It can never quite reach certainty, because we know that in spite of frequent repetitions there sometimes is a failure at the last, as in the case of the chicken whose neck is wrung. Thus probability is all we ought to seek.

It might be urged, as against the view we are advocating, that we know all natural phenomena to be subject to the reign of law, and that sometimes, on the basis of observation, we can see that only one law can possibly fit the facts of the case. Now to this view there are two answers. The first is that, even if *some* law which has no exceptions applies to our case, we can never, in practice, be sure that we have discovered that law and not one to which there are exceptions. The second is that the reign of law would seem to be itself only probable, and that our belief that it will hold in the future, or in unexamined cases in the past, is itself based upon the very principle we are examining.

The principle we are examining may be called the *principle of induction*, and its two parts may be stated as follows:

(*a*) When a thing of a certain sort A has been found to be associated with a thing of a certain other sort B, and has never been found dissociated from a thing of the sort B, the greater the number of cases in which A and B have been associated, the greater is the probability that they will be associated in a fresh case in which one of them is known to be present;

(*b*) Under the same circumstances, a sufficient number of cases of association will make the probability of a fresh association nearly a certainty, and will make it approach certainty without limit.

As just stated, the principle applies only to the verification of our expectation in a single fresh instance. But we want also to know that there is a probability in favour of the general law that things of the sort A are *always* associated with things of the sort B, provided a sufficient number of cases of association are known, and no cases of failure of association are known. The probability of the general law is obviously less than the probability of the particular case, since if the general law is true, the particular case must also be true, whereas the particular case may be true without the general law being true. Nevertheless the probability of the general law is increased by repetitions, just as the probability of the particular case is. We may therefore repeat the two parts of our principle as regards the general law, thus:

(*a*) The greater the number of cases in which a thing of the sort A has been found associated with a thing of the sort B, the more probable it is (if no cases of failure of association are known) that A is always associated with B;

(*b*) Under the same circumstances, a sufficient number of cases of the association of A with B will make it nearly certain that A is always associated with B, and will make this general law approach certainty without limit.

It should be noted that probability is always relative to certain data. In our case, the data are merely the known cases of coexistence of A and B. There may be other data, which *might* be taken into account, which would gravely alter the probability. For example, a man who had seen a great many white swans might argue, by our principle, that on the data it was *probable* that all swans were white, and this might be a perfectly sound argument. The argument is not disproved by the fact that some swans are black, because a thing may very well happen in spite of the fact that some data render it improbable. In the case of the swans, a man might know that colour is a very variable characteristic in many species of animals, and that, therefore, an induction as to colour is peculiarly liable to error. But this knowledge would be a fresh datum, by no means proving that the probability relatively to our previous data had been wrongly estimated. The fact, therefore, that things often fail to fulfil our expectations is no evidence that our expectations will not *probably* be fulfilled in a given case or a given class of cases. Thus our inductive principle is at any rate not capable of being *disproved* by an appeal to experience.

The inductive principle, however, is equally incapable of being *proved* by an appeal to experience. Experience might conceivably confirm the inductive principle as regards the cases that have been already examined; but as regards unexamined cases, it is the inductive principle alone that can justify any inference from what has been examined to what has not been examined. All arguments which, on the basis of experience, argue as to the future or the unexperienced parts of the past or present, assume the inductive principle; hence we can never use experience to prove the inductive principle without begging the question. Thus we must either accept the inductive principle on the ground of its intrinsic evidence, or forgo all justification of our expectations about the future. If the principle is unsound, we have no reason to expect the sun to rise to-morrow, to expect bread to be more nourishing than a stone, or to expect that if we throw ourselves off the roof we shall fall. When we see what looks like our best friend approaching us, we shall have no reason to suppose that his body is not inhabited by the mind of our worst enemy or of some total stranger. All our conduct is based upon associations which have worked in the past, and which we therefore regard as likely to work in the future; and this likelihood is dependent for its validity upon the inductive principle.

The general principles of science, such as the belief in the reign of law, and the belief that every event must have a cause, are as completely dependent upon the inductive principle as are the beliefs of daily life. All such general principles are believed because mankind have found innumerable instances of their truth and no instances of their falsehood. But this affords no evidence for their truth in the future, unless the inductive principle is assumed.

Thus all knowledge which, on a basis of experience tells us something about what is not experienced, is based upon a belief which experience can neither confirm nor confute, yet which, at least in its more concrete applications, appears to be as firmly rooted in us as many of the facts of experience. The existence and justification of such beliefs—for the inductive principle, as we shall see, is not the only example—raises some of the most difficult and most debated problems of philosophy. . . .

53

Of the Ground of Induction

JOHN STUART MILL

Axiom of the Uniformity of Nature

Induction properly so called, as distinguished from those mental operations, sometimes though improperly designated by the name, which I have attempted in the preceding chapter to characterize, may, then, be summarily defined as Generalization from Experience. It consists in inferring from some individual instances in which a phenomenon is observed to occur, that it occurs in all instances of a certain class; namely, in all which *resemble* the former, in what are regarded as the material circumstances.

In what way the material circumstances are to be distinguished from those which are immaterial, or why some of the circumstances are material and others not so, we are not yet ready to point out. We must first observe, that there is a principle implied in the very statement of what

Induction is; an assumption with regard to the course of nature and the order of the universe; namely, that there are such things in nature as parallel cases; that what happens once, will, under a sufficient degree of similarity of circumstances, happen again, and not only again, but as often as the same circumstances recur. This, I say, is an assumption, involved in every case of induction. And, if we consult the actual course of nature, we find that the assumption is warranted. The universe, so far as known to us, is so constituted, that whatever is true in any one case, is true in all cases of a certain description; the only difficulty is, to find what description.

This universal fact, which is our warrant for all inferences from experience, has been described by different philosophers in different forms of language: that the course of nature is uniform; that the universe is gov-

[From *A System of Logic*, Book III, chapters iii, xxi. First published in 1843.]

erned by general laws; and the like. One of the most usual of these modes of expression, but also one of the most inadequate, is that which has been brought into familiar use by the metaphysicians of the school of Reid and Stewart. The disposition of the human mind to generalize from experience,—a propensity considered by these philosophers as an instinct of our nature,—they usually describe under some such name as "our intuitive conviction that the future will resemble the past." Now it has been well pointed out by Mr. Bailey, that (whether the tendency be or not an original and ultimate element of our nature), Time, in its modifications of past, present, and future, has no concern either with the belief itself, or with the grounds of it. We believe that fire will burn to-morrow, because it burned to-day and yesterday; but we believe, on precisely the same grounds, that it burned before we were born, and that it burns this very day in Cochin-China. It is not from the past to the future, as past and future, that we infer, but from the known to the unknown; from facts observed to facts unobserved; from what we have perceived, or been directly conscious of, to what has not come within our experience. In this last predicament is the whole region of the future; but also the vastly greater portion of the present and of the past.

Whatever be the most proper mode of expressing it, the proposition that the course of nature is uniform, is the fundamental principle, or general axiom, of Induction. It would yet be a great error to offer this large generalization as any explanation of the inductive process. On the contrary, I hold it to be itself an instance of induction, and induction by no means of the most obvious kind. Far from being the first induction we make, it is one of the last, or at all events one of those which are latest in attaining strict philosophical accuracy. As a general maxim, indeed, it has scarcely entered into the minds of any but philosophers; nor even by them, as we shall have many opportunities of remarking, have its extent and limits been always very justly conceived. The truth is, that this great generalization is itself founded on prior generalizations. The obscurer laws of nature were discovered by means of it, but the more obvious ones must have been understood and assented to as general truths before it was ever heard of. We should never have thought of affirming that all phenomena take place according to general laws, if we had not first arrived, in the case of a great multitude of phenomena, at some knowledge of the laws themselves; which could be done no otherwise than by induction. In what sense, then, can a principle, which is so far from being our earliest induction, be regarded as our warrant for all the others? In the only sense, in which (as we have already seen) the general propositions which we place at the head of our reasonings when we throw them into syllogisms, ever really contribute to their validity. As Archbishop Whately remarks, every induction is a syllogism with the major premise suppressed; or (as I prefer expressing it) every induction may be thrown into the form of a syllogism, by supplying a major premise. If this be actually done, the principle which we are now considering, that of the uniformity of the course of nature, will appear as the ultimate major premise of all inductions, and will, therefore, stand to all inductions in the relation in which, as has been shown at so much length, the major proposition of a syllogism always stands to the conclusion; not contributing at all to prove it, but being a necessary condition of its being proved; since no conclusion is proved, for which there cannot be found a true major premise.

The statement, that the uniformity of the course of nature is the ultimate major premise in all cases of induction, may be thought to require some explanation. The immediate major premise in every inductive argument, it certainly is not. Of that, Archbishop Whately's must be held to be the correct account. The induction, "John, Peter, etc. are mortal, therefore all mankind are mortal," may, as he justly says, be thrown into a syllogism by prefixing as a major premise (what is at any rate a necessary condition of the validity of the argument) namely, that what is true of John, Peter, etc. is true of all mankind. But how came we by

this major premise? It is not self-evident; nay, in all cases of unwarranted generalization, it is not true. How, then, is it arrived at? Necessarily either by induction or ratiocination; and if by induction, the process, like all other inductive arguments, may be thrown into the form of a syllogism. This previous syllogism it is, therefore, necessary to construct. There is, in the long run, only one possible construction. The real proof that what is true of John, Peter, etc. is true of all mankind, can only be, that a different supposition would be inconsistent with the uniformity which we know to exist in the course of nature. Whether there would be this inconsistency or not, may be a matter of long and delicate inquiry; but unless there would, we have no sufficient ground for the major of the inductive syllogism. It hence appears, that if we throw the whole course of any inductive argument into a series of syllogisms, we shall arrive by more or fewer steps at an ultimate syllogism, which will have for its major premise the principle, or axiom, of the uniformity of the course of nature.

It was not to be expected that in the case of this axiom, any more than of other axioms, there should be unanimity among thinkers with respect to the grounds on which it is to be received as true. I have already stated that I regard it as itself a generalization from experience. Others hold it to be a principle which, antecedently to any verification by experience, we are compelled by the constitution of our thinking faculty to assume as true. Having so recently, and at so much length, combated a similar doctrine as applied to the axioms of mathematics, by arguments which are in a great measure applicable to the present case, I shall defer the more particular discussion of this controverted point in regard to the fundamental axiom of induction, until a more advanced period of our inquiry. At present it is of more importance to understand thoroughly the import of the axiom itself. For the proposition, that the course of nature is uniform, possesses rather the brevity suitable to popular, than the precision requisite in philosophical language: its terms require to be explained, and a stricter than their ordinary signification given to them, before the truth of the assertion can be admitted.

The Axiom Not True in Every Sense

Every person's consciousness assures him that he does not always expect uniformity in the course of events; he does not always believe that the unknown will be similar to the known, that the future will resemble the past. Nobody believes that the succession of rain and fine weather will be the same in every future year as in the present. Nobody expects to have the same dreams repeated every night. On the contrary, everybody mentions it as something

extraordinary, if the course of nature is constant, and resembles itself, in these particulars. To look for constancy where constancy is not to be expected, as for instance that a day which has once brought good fortune will always be a fortunate day, is justly accounted superstition.

The course of nature, in truth, is not only uniform, it is also infinitely various. Some phenomena are always seen to recur in the very same combinations in which we met with them at first; others seem altogether capricious; while some, which we had been accustomed to regard as bound down exclusively to a particular set of combinations, we unexpectedly find detached from some of the elements with which we had hitherto found them conjoined, and united to others of quite a contrary description. To an inhabitant of Central Africa, fifty years ago, no fact probably appeared to rest on more uniform experience than this, that all human beings are black. To Europeans, not many years ago, the proposition, All swans are white, appeared an equally unequivocal instance of uniformity in the course of nature. Further experience has proved to both that they were mistaken; but they had to wait fifty centuries for this experience. During that long time, mankind believed in an uniformity of the course of nature where no such uniformity really existed.

According to the notion which the ancients entertained of induction, the foregoing were cases of as legitimate inference as any inductions whatever. In these two instances, in which, the conclusion being false, the ground of inference must have been insufficient, there was, nevertheless, as much ground for it as this conception of induction admitted of. The induction of the ancients has been well described by Bacon, under the name of "Inductio per enumerationem simplicem, ubi non reperitur instantia contradictoria." It consists in ascribing the character of general truths to all propositions which are true in every instance that we happen to know of. This is the kind of induction which is natural to the mind when unaccustomed to scientific methods. The tendency, which some call an instinct, and which others account for by association, to infer the future from the past, the known from the unknown, is simply a habit of expecting that what has been found true once or several times, and never yet found false, will be found true again. Whether the instances are few or many, conclusive or inconclusive, does not much affect the matter: these are considerations which occur only on reflection; the unprompted tendency of the mind is to generalize its experience, provided this points all in one direction; provided no other experience of a conflicting character comes unsought. The notion of seeking it, of experimenting for it, of *interrogating* nature (to use Bacon's expression) is of much later growth. The observation of nature, by uncultivated intellects, is purely passive: they accept the facts which present themselves, without taking the trouble of searching for more: it is a superior mind only which asks itself what facts are needed to enable it to come to a safe conclusion, and then looks out for these.

But though we have always a propensity to generalize from unvarying experience, we are not always warranted in doing so. Before we can be at liberty to conclude that something is universally true because we have never known an instance to the contrary, we must have reason to believe that if there were in nature any instances to the contrary, we should have known of them. This assurance, in the great majority of cases, we cannot have, or can have only in a very moderate degree. The possibility of having it, is the foundation on which we shall see hereafter that induction by simple enumeration may in some remarkable cases amount practically to proof. No such assurance, however, can be had, on any of the ordinary subjects of scientific inquiry. Popular notions are usually founded on induction by simple enumeration; in science it carries us but a little way. We are forced to begin with it; we must often rely on it provisionally, in the absence of means of more searching investigation. But, for the accurate study of nature, we require a surer and a more potent instrument. . . .

The Question of
Inductive Logic Stated

In order to a better understanding of the problem which the logician must solve if he would establish a scientific theory of Induction, let us compare a few cases of incorrect inductions with others which are acknowledged to be legitimate. Some, we know, which were believed for centuries to be correct, were nevertheless incorrect. That all swans are white, cannot have been a good induction, since the conclusion has turned out erroneous. The experience, however, on which the conclusion rested, was genuine. From the earliest records, the testimony of the inhabitants of the known world was unanimous on the point. The uniform experience, therefore, of the inhabitants of the known world, agreeing in a common result, without one known instance of deviation from that result, is not always sufficient to establish a general conclusion.

But let us now turn to an instance apparently not very dissimilar to this. Mankind were wrong, it seems, in concluding that all swans were white: are we also wrong, when we conclude that all men's heads grow above their shoulders, and never below, in spite of the conflicting testimony of the naturalist Pliny? As there were black swans, though civilized people had existed for three thousand years on the earth without meeting with them, may there not also be "men whose heads do grow beneath their shoulders," notwithstanding a rather less perfect unanimity of negative testimony from observers? Most persons would answer No; it was more credible that a bird should vary in its colour, than that men should vary in the relative position of their principal organs. And there is no doubt that in so saying they would be right: but to say why they are right, would be impossible, without entering more deeply than is usually done, into the true theory of Induction.

Again, there are cases in which we reckon with the most unfailing confidence upon uniformity, and other cases in which we do not count upon it at all. In some we feel complete assurance that the future will resemble the past, the unknown be precisely similar to the known. In others, however invariable may be the result obtained from the instances which have been observed, we draw from them no more than a very feeble presumption that the like result will hold in all other cases. That a straight line is the shortest distance between two points, we do not doubt to be true even in the region of the fixed stars. When a chemist announces the existence and properties of a newly-discovered substance, if we confide in his accuracy, we feel assured that the conclusions he has arrived at will hold universally, though the induction be founded but on a single instance. We do not withhold our assent, waiting for a repetition of the experiment; or if we do, it is from a doubt whether the one experiment was properly made, not whether if properly made it would be conclusive. Here, then, is a general law of nature, inferred without hesitation from a single instance; an universal proposition from a singular one. Now mark another case, and contrast it with this. Not all the instances which have been observed since the beginning of the world, in support of the general proposition that all crows are black, would be deemed a sufficient presumption of the truth of the proposition, to outweigh the testimony of one unexceptionable witness who should affirm that in some region of the earth not fully explored, he had caught and examined a crow, and had found it to be grey.

Why is a single instance, in some cases, sufficient for a complete induction, while in others, myriads of concurring instances, without a single exception known or presumed, go such a very little way towards establishing an universal proposition? Whoever can answer this question knows more of the philosophy of logic than the wisest of the ancients, and has solved the problem of induction. . . .

The Law of Causality Rests on an Induction by Simple Enumeration

. . . The belief we entertain in the universality, throughout nature, of the law of cause and effect, is itself an instance of induction; and by no means one of the earliest which any of us, or which mankind in general, can have made. We arrive at this universal law, by generalization from many laws of inferior generality. We should never have had the notion of causation (in the philosophical meaning of the term) as a condition of all phenomena, unless many cases of causation, or in other words, many partial uniformities of sequence, had previously become familiar. The more obvious of the particular uniformities suggest, and give evidence of, the general uniformity, and the general uniformity, once established, enables us to prove the remainder of the particular uniformities of which it is made up. As, however, all rigorous processes of induction presuppose the general uniformity, our knowledge of the particular uniformities from which it was first inferred was not, of course, derived from rigorous induction, but from the loose and uncertain mode of induction *per enumerationem simplicem*; and the law of universal causation, being collected from results so obtained, cannot itself rest on any better foundation.

It would seem, therefore, that induction *per enumerationem simplicem* not only is not necessarily an illicit logical process, but is in reality the only kind of induction possible; since the more elaborate process depends for its validity on a law, itself obtained in that inartificial mode. Is there not then an inconsistency in contrasting the looseness of one method with the rigidity of another, when that other is indebted to the looser method for its own foundation?

The inconsistency, however, is only apparent. Assuredly, if induction by simple enumeration were an invalid process, no process grounded on it could be valid; just as no reliance could be placed on telescopes, if we could not trust our eyes. But though a valid process, it is a fallible one, and fallible in very different degrees: if therefore we can substitute for the more fallible forms of the process, an operation grounded on the same process in a less fallible form, we shall have effected a very material improvement. And this is what scientific induction does.

A mode of concluding from experience must be pronounced untrustworthy, when subsequent experience refuses to confirm it. According to this criterion, induction by simple enumeration—in other words, generalization of an observed fact from the mere absence of any known instance to the contrary—affords in general a precarious and unsafe ground of assurance; for such generalizations are incessantly discovered, on further experience, to be false. Still, however, it affords some assurance, sufficient, in many cases, for the ordinary guidance of conduct. It would be absurd to say, that the general-

izations arrived at by mankind in the outset of their experience, such as these, Food nourishes, Fire burns, Water drowns, were unworthy of reliance. There is a scale of trustworthiness in the results of the original unscientific Induction; and on this diversity (as observed in the fourth chapter of the present book) depend the rules for the improvement of the process. The improvement consists in correcting one of these inartificial generalizations by means of another. As has been already pointed out, this is all that art can do. To test a generalization, by showing that it either follows from, or conflicts with, some stronger induction, some generalization resting on a broader foundation of experience, is the beginning and end of the logic of Induction.

Now the precariousness of the method of simple enumeration is in an inverse ratio to the largeness of the generalization. The process is delusive and insufficient, exactly in proportion as the subject-matter of the observation is special and limited in extent. As the sphere widens, this unscientific method becomes less and less liable to mislead; and the most universal class of truths, the law of causation for instance, and the principles of number and of geometry, are duly and satisfactorily proved by that method alone, nor are they susceptible of any other proof. . . .

Now, the most extensive in its subject-matter of all generalizations which experience warrants, respecting the sequences and coexistences of phenomena, is the law of causation. It stands at the head of all observed uniformities, in point of universality, and therefore (if the preceding observations are correct) in point of certainty. And if we consider, not what mankind would have been justified in believing in the infancy of their knowledge, but what may rationally be believed in its present more advanced state, we shall find ourselves warranted in considering this fundamental law, though itself obtained by induction from particular laws of causation, as not less certain, but on the contrary, more so, than any of those from which it was drawn. It adds to them as much proof as it receives from them. For there is probably no one even of the best established laws of causation which is not sometimes counteracted, and to which, therefore, apparent exceptions do not present themselves, which would have necessarily and justly shaken the confidence of mankind in the universality of those laws, if inductive processes founded on the universal law had not enabled us to refer those exceptions to the agency of counteracting causes, and thereby reconcile them with the law with which they apparently conflict. Errors, moreover, may have slipped into the statement of any one of the special laws, through inattention to some material circumstance: and instead of the true proposition, another may have been enunciated, false as an universal law, though leading, in all cases hitherto observed, to the same result. To the law of causation, on the contrary, we not only do not know of any exception, but the exceptions which limit or apparently invalidate the special laws, are so far from contradicting the universal one, that they confirm it; since in all cases which are sufficiently open to our observation, we are able to trace the difference of result, either to the absence of a cause which had been present in ordinary cases, or to the presence of one which had been absent.

The law of cause and effect, being thus certain, is capable of imparting its certainty to all other inductive propositions which can be deduced from it; and the narrower inductions may be regarded as receiving their ultimate sanction from that law, since there is no one of them which is not rendered more certain than it was before, when we are able to connect it with that larger induction, and to show that it cannot be denied, consistently with the law that everything which begins to exist has a cause. And hence we are justified in the seeming inconsistency, of holding induction by simple enumeration to be good for proving this general truth, the foundation of scientific induction, and yet refusing to rely on it for any of the narrower inductions. . . .

54

Self-Supporting Inductive Arguments

MAX BLACK

The use of inductive rules has often led to true conclusions about matters of fact. Common sense regards this as a good reason for trusting inductive rules in the future, if due precautions are taken against error. Yet an argument from success in the past to probable success in the future itself uses an inductive rule, and therefore seems circular. Nothing would be accomplished by any argument that needed to assume the reliability of an inductive rule in order to establish that rule's reliability.

Suppose that inferences governed by some inductive rule have usually resulted in true conclusions; and let an inference from this fact to the probable reliability of the rule in the future be called a *second-order* inference. So long as the rule by which the second-order inference is governed differs from the rule whose reliability is to be affirmed, there will be no appearance of circularity. But if the second-order inference is governed by the very same rule of inference whose reliability is affirmed in the conclusion, the vicious circularity seems blatant.

Must we, then, reject forthwith every second-order inductive argument purporting to support the very rule of inference by which the argument itself is governed? Contrary to general opinion, a plausible case can be made for saying, "No."[1] Properly constructed and interpreted,

[*Journal of Philosophy*, Vol. 55, No. 17 (Aug. 14, 1958); pp. 718–725. Reprinted by permission of the author and *Journal of Philosophy*.]

1. See Max Black, *Problems of Analysis* (Ithaca, N.Y., 1954), chapter 11, and R. B. Braithwaite, *Scientific Explanation* (Cambridge, 1953), chap. 8.

such "self-supporting" inferences, as I shall continue to call them, can satisfy all the conditions for legitimate inductive inference: when an inductive rule has been reliable (has generated true conclusions from true premises more often than not) in the past, a second-order inductive inference governed by the same rule can show that the rule deserves to be trusted in its next application.

The reasons I have given for this contention have recently been sharply criticized by Professor Wesley C. Salmon.[2] In trying to answer his precisely worded objections, I hope to make clearer the view I have been defending and to dispel some lingering misapprehensions.

My original example of a legitimate self-supporting inductive argument was the following:

> (a): In most instances of the use of R in arguments with true premises examined in a wide variety of conditions, R has been successful.
> *Hence (probably):*
> In the next instance to be encountered of the use of R in an argument with a true premise, R will be successful.

The rule of inductive inference mentioned in the premise and the conclusion of the argument above is:

R: To argue from *Most instances of A's examined in a wide variety of conditions have been B* to (probably) *The next A to be encountered will be B.*

Thus the second-order argument (*a*) uses the rule R in showing that the same rule will be "successful" (will generate a true conclusion from a true premise[3]) in the next encountered instance of its use.

The rule, R, stated above is not intended to be a "supreme rule" of induction, from which all other inductive rules can be derived; nor is it claimed that R, as it stands, is a wholly acceptable rule for inductive inference. The unsolved problem of a satisfactory formulation of canons of inductive inference will arise only incidentally in the present discussion. The rule R and the associated argument (*a*) are to serve merely to illustrate the logical problems that arise in connection with self-supporting arguments: the considerations to be adduced in defense of (*a*) could be adapted to fit many other self-supporting arguments.

The proposed exculpation of the self-supporting argument (*a*) from the charge of vicious circularity is linked to a feature of the corresponding rule R that must be carefully noted. Inductive arguments governed by R vary in "strength" ac-

---

2. See Wesley C. Salmon, "Should We Attempt to Justify Induction?" *Philosophical Studies,* Volume VIII, No. 3 (April, 1957), pp. 45–47.

3. Here and throughout this discussion, I assume for simplicity that all the premises of any argument or inference considered have been conjoined into a single statement.

cording to the number and variety of the favorable instances reported in the premise. So, although *R* permits us to assert a certain conclusion categorically, it is to be understood throughout that the strength of the assertion fluctuates with the character of the evidence. If only a small number of instances have been examined and the relative frequency of favorable instances (*A*'s that are *B*) is little better than a half, the strength of the argument may be close to zero; while a vast predominance of favorable instances in a very large sample of observations justifies a conclusion affirmed with nearly maximal strength. The presence of the word "probably" in the original formulation of *R* indicates the variability of strength of the corresponding argument; in more refined substitutes for *R,* provision might be made for some precise measure of the associated degree of strength.

Variability in strength is an important respect in which inductive arguments differ sharply from deductive ones. If a deductive argument is not valid, it must be *in*valid, no intermediate cases being conceivable; but a legitimate inductive argument, whose conclusion may properly be affirmed on the evidence supplied, may still be very weak. Appraisal of an inductive argument admits of degrees.

Similar remarks apply to inductive rules, as contrasted with deductive ones. A deductive rule is either valid or invalid—*tertium non datur;* but at any time in the history of the employment of an inductive rule, it has what may be called a *degree of reliability* depending upon its ratio of successes in previous applications. A legitimate or correct inductive rule may still be a weak one: appraisal of an inductive rule admits of degrees.

Now in claiming that the second-order argument (*a*) *supports* the rule *R,* I am claiming that the argument raises the degree of reliability of the rule, and hence the strength of the arguments in which it will be used; I have no intention of claiming that the self-supporting argument can definitively establish or demonstrate that the rule is correct. Indeed, I do not know what an outright demonstration of the correctness or legitimacy of an inductive rule would be like. My attempted rebuttal of Salmon's objections will turn upon the possibility of raising the degree of reliability of an inductive rule, as already explained.

The contribution made by the second-order argument (*a*) to strengthening the rule *R* by which it is governed can be made plain by a hypothetical illustration. Suppose evidence is available that ⅘ of the *A*'s so far examined have been *B,* and it is proposed, by an application of the rule *R,* to draw the inference that the next *A* to be encountered will be *B.* For the sake of simplicity the proposed argument may be taken to have a strength of $4/5$. Before accepting the conclusion about the next A, we may wish to consider the available evidence about past successes of the rule R. Suppose, for the sake of argument, that we know R to have been successful in $9/10$ of the cases in which it has been previously used. If so, the second-order argument affirms with strength $9/10$ that R will be successful in the next instance of its use. But the "next instance" is before us, as the argument whose premise is that $4/5$ of the A's have been B. For R to be "successful" in this instance is for the conclusion of the first-order argument to be true; the strength of the second-order argument is therefore immediately transferred to the first-order argument. Before invoking the second-order argument, we were entitled to affirm the conclusion of the first-order argument with a strength of no better than $4/5$, but we are now able to raise the strength to $9/10$. Conversely, if the second-order argument had shown R to have been unsuccessful in less than $4/5$ of its previous uses, our confidence in the proposed conclusion of the first-order argument would have been diminished.

There is no mystery about the transfer of strength from the second-order argument to the first-order argument: the evidence cited in the former amplifies the evidence immediately relevant to the latter. Evidence concerning the proportion of A's found to have been B permits the direct inference, with strength $4/5$, that the next A to be encountered will be B. It is, however, permissible to view the situation in another aspect as concerned with the extrapolation of an already observed statistical association between true premises of a certain sort and a corresponding conclusion. The evidence takes the form: In 9 cases out of 10, the truth of a statement of the form "m/n X's have been found to be Y's" has been found associated in a wide variety of cases with the truth of the statement "The next X to be encountered was Y."[4] This is better evidence than that cited in the premise of the original first-order argument: it is therefore to be expected that the strength of the conclusion shall be raised.

It should be noticed that the evidence cited in the second-order argument is not merely greater in amount than the evidence cited in the first-order argument. If R has been successfully used for drawing conclusions about fish, neutrons, planets, and so on (the "wide variety of conditions" mentioned in the premise of the second-order argument), it would be illegitimate to coalesce such heterogeneous kinds of objects into a single class for the sake of a more extensive *first-order*

---

4. We might wish to restrict the second-order argument to cases in which the ratio m/n was close to 4/5. Other refinements readily suggest themselves.

argument. Proceeding to "second-order" considerations allows us to combine the results of previous inductive inquiries in a way which would not otherwise be possible.

Nothing in this conception of inductive method requires us to remain satisfied with the second-order argument. If circumstances warrant, and suitable evidence can be found, we might be led to formulate third- or even higher-order arguments. These might conceivably result in lowering the measures of strength we at present attach to certain arguments in which R is used. But if this were to happen, we would not have been shown to have been mistaken in previously attaching these measures of strength. Nor is it required that a first-order argument be checked against a corresponding second-order argument before the former can properly be used. If we have no reason to think that R is unsuccessful most of the time, or is objectionable on some logical grounds, that is enough to make our employment of it so far reasonable. The function of higher-order arguments in the tangled web of inductive method is to permit us to progress from relatively imprecise and uncritical methods to methods whose degrees of reliability and limits of applicability have themselves been checked by inductive investigations. It is in this way that inductive method becomes self-regulating and, if all goes well, self-supporting.

Salmon's objections to the foregoing conception are summarized by him as follows:

The so-called self-supporting arguments are . . . circular in the following precise sense: the conclusiveness of the argument cannot be established without assuming the truth of the conclusion. It happens, in this case, that the assumption of the truth of the conclusion is required to establish the correctness of the rules of inference used rather than the truth of the premises, but that makes the argument no less viciously circular. The circularity lies in regarding the facts stated in the premises as evidence *for the conclusion, rather than as evidence against the conclusion or as no evidence either positive or negative. To regard the facts in the premises as evidence for the conclusion is to assume that the rule of inference used in the argument is a correct one. And this is precisely what is to be proved. If the conclusion is denied, then the facts stated in the premises are no longer evidence for the conclusion.*[5]

I shall reply by making three points. (1) Salmon's reference to "conclusiveness" smacks too much of the appraisal of deductive argument. An inductive argument is not

5.   Salmon, *loc. cit.,* p. 47.

required to be "conclusive" if that means that its conclusion is entailed or logically implied by its premises; it is, of course, required to be correct or legitimate, but that means only that the rule of inductive inference shall be reliable—shall usually lead from true premises to true conclusions. The correctness of an inductive argument could only depend upon the truth of its conclusion if the latter asserted the reliability of the rule by which the argument was governed. But this was not the case in our argument (*a*). The conclusion there was that *R* would be successful in the next instance of its use: this might very well prove to be false without impugning the reliability of *R*. Salmon was plainly mistaken if he thought that the falsity of (*a*)'s conclusion entails the incorrectness of the rule by which (*a*) is governed.

(2) Can the *correctness* of argument (*a*) be "established without assuming the truth of the conclusion" of (*a*)? Well, if "established" means the same as "proved by a deductive argument," the answer must be that the correctness of (*a*) cannot be established at all. But again, a correct inductive argument in support of the rule governing (*a*) can certainly be constructed without assuming (*a*)'s conclusion. We do not have to assume that *R* will be successful in the next instance in order to argue correctly that the available evidence supports the reliability of *R*.

(3) Salmon says: "To regard the facts in the premises as evidence for the conclusion is to assume that the rule of inference used in the argument is a correct one." In using the rule of inference we certainly *treat* it as correct: we would not use it if we had good reasons for suspecting it to be unreliable. If this is what Salmon means, what he says is right, but not damaging to the correctness of (*a*). But he would be plainly wrong if he maintained that an assertion of the correctness of (*a*) was an additional premise required by (*a*), or that an argument to the effect that (*a*) was correct must precede the legitimate use of (*a*). For if this last demand were pressed, it would render deductive inference no less than inductive inference logically impossible. If we were never entitled to *use* a correct rule of inference before we had formally argued in support of that rule, the process of inference could never get started.

I shall end by considering an ingenious counterexample provided by Salmon. He asks us to consider the following argument:

> (*a'*): In most instances of the use of *R'* in arguments with true premises in a wide variety of conditions, *R'* has been *un*successful.
>
> *Hence (probably):*
> In the next instance to be encountered of the use of *R'* in an argument with a true premise, *R'* will be successful.

The relevant rule is the "counterinductive" one.

R': To argue from *Most instances of A's examined in a wide variety of conditions have not been B* to (probably) *The next A to be encountered will be B*.

Salmon says that while (*a'*) must be regarded as a self-supporting argument by my criteria, the rule here supported, *R'*, is in conflict with *R*. From the same premises the two rules "will almost always produce contrary conclusions."[6] This must be granted. But Salmon apparently overlooks an important respect in which the "counterinductive" rule *R'* must be regarded as illegitimate.

In calling an inductive rule "correct," so that it meets the canons of legitimacy of *inductive* rules of inference, we claim at least that the rule is reliable, in the sense of usually leading from true premises to true conclusions. That is part of what we *mean* by a "correct inductive rule." It can easily be shown that *R'* must fail to meet this condition.

Suppose we were using *R'* to predict the terms of a series of 1's and 0's, of which the first three terms were known to be 1's. Then our first two predictions might be as follows (shown by underlining):

1 1 1 <u>0</u> <u>0</u>

At this point, suppose *R'* has been used successfully in each of the two predictions, so that the series is in fact now observed to be 1 1 1 0 0. Since 1's still predominate, direct application of the rule calls for 0 to be predicted next. On the other hand, the second-order argument shows that *R'* has been successful each time and therefore demands that it not be trusted next time, i.e., calls for the prediction of 1. So the very definition of *R'* renders it impossible for the rule to be successful without being *incoherent*.[7] The suggested second-order argument in support of *R'* could be formulated only if *R'* were known to be unreliable, and would therefore be worthless. So we have an a priori reason for preferring *R* to its competitor *R'*. But it is easy to produce any number of alternative rules of inductive inference, none of which suffers from the fatal defect of *R'*. The choice between such rules, I suggest, has to be made in the light of experience of their use. I have tried to show in outline how such experience can properly be invoked without logical circularity.

---

6. Salmon, *loc. cit.,* p. 46.

7. A parallel situation would arise in the use of *R* in predicting the members of the 1–0 series only if *R* were to be predominantly *un*successful. But then we would have the best of reasons for assigning *R* zero strength, and the second-order argument would be pointless.

55

The "Justification" of Induction

P. F. STRAWSON

1

... What reason have we to place reliance on inductive procedures? Why should we suppose that the accumulation of instances of *A*s which are *B*s, however various the conditions in which they are observed, gives any good reason for expecting the next *A* we encounter to be a *B*? It is our habit to form expectations in this way; but can the habit be rationally justified? When this doubt has entered our minds it may be difficult to free ourselves from it. For the doubt has its source in a confusion; and some attempts to resolve the doubt preserve the confusion; and other attempts to show that the doubt is senseless seem altogether too facile. The root-confusion is easily described; but simply to describe it seems an inadequate remedy against it. So the doubt must be examined again and again, in the light of different attempts to remove it.

If someone asked what grounds there were for supposing that deductive reasoning was valid, we might answer that there were in fact no grounds for supposing that deductive reasoning was always valid; sometimes people made valid inferences, and sometimes they were guilty of logical fallacies. If he said that we had misunderstood his question, and that what he wanted to know was what grounds there were for regarding deduction *in general* as a valid method of argument, we should have to answer that his question was without sense, for to say

[From *Introduction to Logical Theory*, by P. F. Strawson (Methuen & Co. Ltd., 1952), pp. 249–263. Reprinted by permission of Methuen & Co. Ltd.]

that an argument, or a form or method of argument, was valid or invalid would *imply* that it was deductive; the concepts of validity and invalidity had application only to individual deductive arguments or forms of deductive argument. Similarly, if a man asked what grounds there were for thinking it reasonable to hold beliefs arrived at inductively, one might at first answer that there were good and bad inductive arguments, that sometimes it was reasonable to hold a belief arrived at inductively and sometimes it was not. If he, too, said that his question had been misunderstood, that he wanted to know whether induction in general was a reasonable method of inference, then we might well think his question senseless in the same way as the question whether deduction is in general valid; for to call a particular belief reasonable or unreasonable is to apply inductive standards, just as to call a particular argument valid or invalid is to apply deductive standards. The parallel is not wholly convincing; for words like "reasonable" and "rational" have not so precise and technical a sense as the word "valid." Yet it is sufficiently powerful to make us wonder how the second question could be raised at all, to wonder why, in contrast with the corresponding question about deduction, it should have seemed to constitute a genuine problem.

Suppose that a man is brought up to regard formal logic as the study of the science and art of reasoning. He observes that all inductive processes are, by deductive standards, invalid: the premises never entail the conclusions. Now inductive processes are notoriously important in the formation of beliefs and expectations about everything which lies beyond the observation of available witnesses. But an *invalid* argument is an *unsound* argument; an *unsound* argument is one in which *no good reason* is produced for accepting the conclusion. So if inductive processes are invalid, if all the arguments we should produce, if challenged, in support of our beliefs about what lies beyond the observation of available witnesses are unsound, then we have no good reason for any of these beliefs. This conclusion is repugnant. So there arises the demand for a justification, not of this or that particular belief which goes beyond what is entailed by our evidence, but a justification of induction in general. And when the demand arises in this way it is, in effect, the demand that induction shall be shown to be really a kind of deduction; for nothing less will satisfy the doubter when this is the route to his doubts.

Tracing this, the most common route to the general doubt about the reasonableness of induction, shows how the doubt seems to escape the absurdity of a demand that induction in general shall be justified by inductive standards. The demand is that induction should be shown to be a rational process; and this turns out to be the demand that one kind of reasoning should be shown to be another and different kind. Put thus crudely, the demand seems to escape one absurdity only to fall into another. Of course, inductive arguments are not deductively valid; if they were, they would be deductive arguments. Inductive reasoning must be assessed, for soundness, by inductive standards. Nevertheless, fantastic as the wish for induction to be deduction may seem, it is only in terms of it that we can understand some of the attempts that have been made to justify induction.

2

The first kind of attempt I shall consider might be called the search for the supreme premise of inductions. In its primitive form it is quite a crude attempt; and I shall make it cruder by caricature. We have already seen that for a particular inductive step, such as "The kettle has been on the fire for ten minutes, so it will be boiling by now," we can substitute a deductive argument by introducing a generalization (e.g., "A kettle always boils within ten minutes of being put on the fire") as an additional premise. This manœuvre shifted the emphasis of the problem of inductive support on to the question of how we established such generalizations as these, which rested on grounds by which they were not entailed. But suppose the manœuvre

could be repeated. Suppose we could find one supremely general proposition, which taken in conjunction with the evidence for any accepted generalization of science or daily life (or at least of science) would entail that generalization. Then, so long as the status of the supreme generalization could be satisfactorily explained, we could regard all sound inductions to unqualified general conclusions as, at bottom, valid deductions. The justification would be found, for at least these cases. The most obvious difficulty in this suggestion is that of formulating the supreme general proposition in such a way that it shall be precise enough to yield the desired entailments, and yet not obviously false or arbitrary. Consider, for example, the formula: "For all f, g, wherever n cases of $f \cdot g$, and no cases of $f \cdot \sim g$, are observed, then all cases of f are cases of g." To turn it into a sentence, we have only to replace "n" by some number. But what number? If we take the value of "n" to be 1 or 20 or 500, the resulting statement is obviously false. Moreover, the choice of any number would seem quite arbitrary; there is no privileged number of favourable instances which we take as decisive in establishing a generalization. If, on the other hand, we phrase the proposition vaguely enough to escape these objections—if, for example, we phrase it as "Nature is uniform"—then it becomes too vague to provide the desired entailments. It should be noticed that the impossibility of framing a general proposition of the kind required is really a special case of the impossibility of framing precise rules for the assessment of evidence. If we could frame a rule which would tell us precisely when we had *conclusive* evidence for a generalization, then it would yield just the proposition required as the supreme premise.

Even if these difficulties could be met, the question of the status of the supreme premise would remain. How, if a non-necessary proposition, could it be established? The appeal to experience, to inductive support, is clearly barred on pain of circularity. If, on the other hand, it were a necessary truth and possessed, in conjunction with the evidence for a generalization, the required logical power to entail the generalization (e.g., if the latter were the conclusion of a hypothetical syllogism, of which the hypothetical premise was the necessary truth in question), then the evidence would entail the generalization independently, and the problem would not arise: a conclusion unbearably paradoxical. In practice, the extreme vagueness with which candidates for the role of supreme premise are expressed prevents their acquiring such logical power, and at the same time renders it very difficult to classify them as analytic or synthetic: under pressure they may tend to tautology; and, when the pressure is removed, assume an expansively synthetic air.

In theories of the kind which I have here caricatured the ideal of deduction is not usually so blatantly manifest as I have made it. One finds the "Law of the Uniformity of Nature" presented less as the suppressed premise of crypto-deductive inferences than as, say, the "presupposition of the validity of inductive reasoning." I shall have more to say about this in my last section.

3

I shall next consider a more sophisticated kind of attempt to justify induction: more sophisticated both in its interpretation of this aim and in the method adopted to achieve it. The aim envisaged is that of proving that the probability of a generalization, whether universal or proportional, increases with the number of instances for which it is found to hold. This clearly is a realistic aim: for the proposition to be proved does state, as we have already seen, a fundamental feature of our criteria for assessing the strength of evidence. The method of proof proposed is mathematical. Use is to be made of the arithmetical calculation of chances. This, however, seems less realistic: for we have already seen that the prospect of analysing the notion of support in these terms seems poor.

I state the argument as simply as possible; but, even so, it will be necessary to introduce and explain some new terms. Suppose we had a collection of objects of different kinds, some with some characteristics and some with others. Suppose, for example, we had a bag containing 100 balls, of which 70 were white and 30 black. Let us call such a collection of objects a *population;* and let us call the way it is made up (e.g., in the case imagined, of 70 white and 30 black balls) the *constitution* of the population. From such a population it would be possible to take *samples* of various sizes. For example, we might take from our bag a sample of 30 balls. Suppose each ball in the bag had an individual number. Then the collection of balls numbered 10 to 39 inclusive would be one sample of the given size; the collection of balls numbered 11 to 40 inclusive would be another and different sample of the same size; the collection of balls numbered 2, 4, 6, 8 ... 58, 60 would be another such sample; and so on. Each possible collection of 30 balls is a different sample of the same size. Some different samples of the same size will have the same constitutions as one another; others will have different constitutions. Thus there will be only one sample made up of 30 black balls. There will be many different samples which share the constitution: 20 white and 10 black. It would be a simple matter of mathematics to work out the number of possible samples of the given size which had any one possible constitution. Let us say that a sample *matches* the population if, allowing for the difference between them in size, the constitution of the sample corresponds, within certain limits, to that of the population. For example, we might say that any possible sample consisting of, say, 21 white and 9 black balls matched the constitution (70 white and 30 black) of the population, whereas a sample consisting of 20 white and 10 black balls did not. Now it is a proposition of pure mathematics that, given any population, the proportion of possible samples, all of the same size, which match the population, increases with the size of the sample.

We have seen that conclusions about the ratio of a subset of equally possible chances to the whole set of those chances may be expressed by the use of the word "probability." Thus of the 52 possible samples of one card from a population constituted like an orthodox pack, 16 are court-cards or aces. This fact we allow ourselves to express (under the conditions, inductively established, of equipossibility of draws) by saying that the probability of drawing a court-card or an ace was 4/13. If we express the proposition referred to at the end of the last paragraph by means of this use of "probability" we shall obtain the result: The probability of a sample matching a given population increases with the size of the sample. It is tempting to try to derive from this result a general justification of the inductive procedure: which will not, indeed, show that any given inductive conclusion is entailed by the evidence for it, taken in conjunction with some universal premise, but will show that the multiplication of favourable instances of a generalization entails a proportionate increase in its probability. For, since *matching* is a symmetrical relation, it might seem a simple deductive step to move from

> I. The probability of a sample matching a given population increases with the size of the sample

to

> II. The probability of a population matching a given sample increases with the size of the sample.

II might seem to provide a guarantee that the greater the number of cases for which a generalization is observed to hold, the greater is its probability; since in increasing the number of cases we increase the size of the sample from whatever population forms the subject of our generalization. Thus pure mathematics might seem to provide the sought-for proof that the evidence for a generalization really does get stronger, the more favourable instances of it we find.

The argument is ingenious enough to be worthy of respect; but it fails of its purpose, and misrepresents the inductive situation. Our situation is not in the least like that of a man drawing a sample from a given, i.e., fixed and limited, population from which the drawing of any mathematically possible sample is equiprobable with that of any other. Our only datum is the sample. No limit is fixed beforehand to the diversity, and the possibilities of change, of the "population" from which it is drawn: or, better, to the multiplicity and variousness of different populations, each with different constitutions, any one of which might replace the present one before we make the next draw. Nor is there any *a priori* guarantee that different mathematically possible samples are equally likely to be drawn. If we have or can obtain any assurance on these points, then it is assurance derived inductively from our data, and cannot therefore be assumed at the outset of an argument designed to justify induction. So II, regarded as a justification of induction founded on purely mathematical considerations, is a fraud. The important shift of "given" from qualifying "population" in I to qualifying "sample" in II is illegitimate. Moreover, "probability," which means one thing in II (interpreted as giving the required guarantee) means something quite different in I (interpreted as a proposition of pure mathematics). In I probability is simply the measure of the ratio of one set of mathematically possible chances to another; in II it is the measure of the inductive acceptability of a generalization. As a mathematical proposition, I is certainly independent of the soundness of inductive procedures; and as a statement of one of the criteria we use in assessing the strength of evidence of a generalization, II is as certainly independent of mathematics. . . .

4

Let us turn from attempts to justify induction to attempts to show that the demand for a justification is mistaken. We have seen already that what lies behind such a demand is often the absurd wish that induction should be shown to be some kind of deduction—and this wish is clearly traceable in the two attempts at justification which we have examined. What other sense could we give to the demand? Sometimes it is expressed in the form of a request for proof that induction is a *reasonable* or *rational* procedure, that we have *good grounds* for placing reliance upon it. Consider the uses of the phrases "good grounds," "justification," "reasonable," etc. Often we say such things as "He has *every justification* for believing that p"; "I have *very good reasons* for believing it"; "There are *good grounds* for the view that q"; "There is *good evidence* that r." We often talk, in such ways as these, of justification, good grounds or reasons or evidence for certain beliefs. Suppose such a belief were one expressible in the form "Every case of f is a case of g." And suppose someone were asked what he meant by saying that he had good grounds or reasons for holding it. I think it would be felt to be a satisfactory an-

swer if he replied: "Well, in all my wide and varied experience I've come across innumerable cases of f and never a case of f which wasn't a case of g." In saying this, he is clearly claiming to have *inductive* support, *inductive* evidence, of a certain kind, for his belief; and he is also giving a perfectly proper answer to the question, what he meant by saying that he had ample justification, good grounds, good reasons for his belief. It is an analytic proposition that it is reasonable to have a degree of belief in a statement which is proportional to the strength of the evidence in its favour; and it is an analytic proposition, though not a proposition of mathematics, that, other things being equal, the evidence for a generalization is strong in proportion as the number of favourable instances, and the variety of circumstances in which they have been found, is great. So to ask whether it is reasonable to place reliance on inductive procedures is like asking whether it is reasonable to proportion the degree of one's convictions to the strength of the evidence. Doing this is what "being reasonable" *means* in such a context.

As for the other form in which the doubt may be expressed, viz., "Is induction a justified, or justifiable, procedure?", it emerges in a still less favourable light. No sense has been given to it, though it is easy to see why it seems to have a sense. For it is generally proper to inquire *of a particular belief,* whether its adoption is justified; and, in asking this, we are asking whether there is good, bad, or any, evidence for it. In applying or withholding the epithets "justified," "well founded," etc., in the case of specific beliefs, we are appealing to, and applying, inductive standards. But to what standards are we appealing when we ask whether the application of inductive standards is justified or well grounded? If we cannot answer, then no sense has been given to the question. Compare it with the question: Is the law legal? It makes perfectly good sense to inquire of a particular action, of an administrative regulation, or even, in the case of some states, of a particular enactment of the legislature, whether or not it is legal. The question is answered by an appeal to a legal system, by the application of a set of legal (or constitutional) rules or standards. But it makes no sense to inquire in general whether the law of the land, the legal system as a whole, is or is not legal. For to what legal standards are we appealing?

The only way in which a sense might be given to the question, whether induction is in general a justified or justifiable procedure, is a trivial one which we have already noticed. We might interpret it to mean "Are all conclusions, arrived at inductively, justified?", i.e., "Do people always have adequate evidence for the conclusions they draw?" The answer to this question is easy, but uninteresting: it is that sometimes people have adequate evidence, and sometimes they do not.

5

It seems, however, that this way of showing the request for a general justification of induction to be absurd is sometimes insufficient to allay the worry that produces it. And, to point out that "forming rational opinions about the unobserved on the evidence available" and "assessing the evidence by inductive standards" are phrases which describe the same thing, is more apt to produce irritation than relief. The point is felt to be "merely a verbal" one; and though the point of this protest is itself hard to see, it is clear that something more is required. So the question must be pursued further. First, I want to point out that there is something a little odd about talking of "the inductive method," or even "the inductive policy," as if it were just one possible method among others of arguing from the observed to the unobserved, from the available evidence to the facts in question. If one asked a meteorologist what method or methods he used to forecast the weather, one would be surprised if he answered: "Oh, just the inductive method." If one asked a doctor by what means he diagnosed a certain disease, the answer "By induction" would be felt as an impatient evasion, a joke, or a rebuke. The answer one hopes for is an account of the tests made, the signs taken account of, the rules and recipes and general laws applied. When such a specific method of prediction or diagnosis is in question, one can ask whether the method is justified in practice; and here again one is asking whether its employment is inductively justified, whether it commonly gives correct results. This question would normally seem an admissible one. One might be tempted to conclude that, while there are many different specific methods of prediction, diagnosis, etc., appropriate to different subjects of inquiry, all such methods could properly be called "inductive" in the sense that their employment rested on inductive support; and that, hence, the phrase "non-inductive method of finding out about what lies deductively beyond the evidence" was a description without meaning, a phrase to which no sense had been given; so that there could be no question of justifying our selection of one method, called "the inductive," of doing this.

However, someone might object: "Surely it is possible, though it might be foolish, to use methods utterly different from accredited scientific ones. Suppose a man, whenever he wanted to form an opinion about what lay beyond his observation or the observation of available witnesses, simply shut his eyes, asked himself the appropriate question, and accepted the first answer that came into his head. Wouldn't this be a non-inductive method?" Well, let us suppose this. The man is asked: "Do you usually get the right answer by your method?" He might answer: "You've mentioned one of its drawbacks; I never do get the right answer; but it's an extremely easy method." One might then be inclined to think that it was not a method of finding things out at all. But suppose he answered: Yes, it's usually (always) the right answer. Then we might be willing to call it a method of finding out, though a strange one. But, then, by the very fact of its success, it would be an inductively supported method. For each application of the method would be an application of the general rule, "The first answer that comes into my head is generally (always) the right one"; and for the truth of this generalization there would be the inductive evidence of a long run of favourable instances with no unfavourable ones (if it were "always"), or of a sustained high proportion of successes to trials (if it were "generally").

So every successful method or recipe for finding out about the unobserved must be one which has inductive support; for to say that a recipe is successful is to say that it has been repeatedly applied with success; and repeated successful application of a recipe constitutes just what we mean by inductive evidence in its favour. Pointing out this fact must not be confused with saying that "the inductive method" is justified by its success, justified because it works. This is a mistake, and an important one. I am not seeking to "justify the inductive method," for no meaning has been given to this phrase. *A fortiori,* I am not saying that induction is justified by its success in finding out about the unobserved. I am saying, rather, that any successful method of finding out about the unobserved is necessarily justified by induction. This is an analytic proposition. The phrase "successful method of finding things out which has no inductive support" is self-contradictory. Having, or acquiring, inductive support is a necessary condition of the success of a method.

Why point this out at all? First, it may have a certain therapeutic force, a power to reassure. Second, it may counteract the tendency to think of "the inductive method" as something on a par with specific methods of diagnosis or prediction and therefore, like them, standing in need of (inductive) justification.

6

There is one further confusion, perhaps the most powerful of all in producing the doubts, questions, and spurious solutions discussed in this Part. We may approach it by considering the claim that induction is justified by its success in practice. The phrase "success of induction" is by no means clear and perhaps embodies the confusion of induction with some specific method of prediction, etc., appropriate to some particular line of inquiry. But, whatever the phrase may mean, the claim has an obviously circular look. Presumably the suggestion is that we should argue from the past "successes of induction" to the continuance of those successes in the future; from the fact that it has worked hitherto to the conclusion that it will continue to work. Since an argument of this kind is plainly inductive, it will not serve as a justification of induction. One cannot establish a principle of argument by an argument which uses that principle. But let us go a little deeper. The argument rests the justification of induction on a matter of fact (its "past successes"). This is characteristic of nearly all attempts to find a justification. The desired premise of Section 2 was to be some fact about the constitution of the universe which, even if it could not be used as a suppressed premise to give inductive arguments a deductive turn, was at any rate a "presupposition of the validity of induction." Even the mathematical argument of Section 3 required buttressing with some large assumption about the makeup of the world. I think the source of this general desire to find out some fact about the constitution of the universe which will "justify induction" or "show it to be a rational policy" is the confusion, the running together, of two fundamentally different questions:

to one of which the answer is a matter of nonlinguistic fact, while to the other it is a matter of meanings.

There is nothing self-contradictory in supposing that all the uniformities in the course of things that we have hitherto observed and come to count on should cease to operate to-morrow; that all our familiar recipes should let us down, and that we should be unable to frame new ones because such regularities as there were were too complex for us to make out. (We may assume that even the expectation that all of us, in such circumstances, would perish, were falsified by someone surviving to observe the new chaos in which, roughly speaking, nothing foreseeable happens.) Of course, we do not believe that this will happen. We believe, on the contrary, that our inductively supported expectation-rules, though some of them will have, no doubt, to be dropped or modified, will continue, on the whole, to serve us fairly well; and that we shall generally be able to replace the rules we abandon with others similarly arrived at. We might give a sense to the phrase "success of induction" by calling this vague belief the belief that induction will continue to be successful. It is certainly a factual belief, not a necessary truth; a belief, one may say, about the constitution of the universe. We might express it as follows, choosing a phraseology which will serve the better to expose the confusion I wish to expose:

I. (The universe is such that) induction will continue to be successful.

I is very vague: it amounts to saying that there are, and will continue to be, natural uniformities and regularities which exhibit a humanly manageable degree of simplicity. But, though it is vague, certain definite things can be said about it. (1) It is not a necessary, but a contingent, statement; for chaos is not a self-contradictory concept. (2) We have good inductive reasons for believing it, good inductive evidence for it. We believe that some of our recipes will continue to hold good because they have held good for so long. We believe that we shall be able to frame new and useful ones, because we have been able to do so repeatedly in the past. Of course, it would be absurd to try to use I to "justify induction," to show that it is a reasonable policy; because I is a conclusion inductively supported.

Consider now the fundamentally different statement:

II. Induction is rational (reasonable).

We have already seen that the rationality of induction, unlike its "successfulness," is not a fact about the constitution of the world. It is a matter of what we mean by the word "rational" in its application to any procedure for forming opinions about what lies outside our observations or that of available witnesses. For to have good reasons for any such opinion is to have good inductive support for it. The chaotic universe just envisaged, therefore, is not one in which induction would cease to be rational; it is simply one in which it would be impossible to form rational expectations to the effect that specific things would happen. It might be said that in such a universe it would at least be rational to refrain from forming specific expectations, to expect nothing but irregularities. Just so. But this is itself a higher-order induction: where irregularity is the rule, expect further irregularities. Learning not to count on things is as much learning an inductive lesson as learning what things to count on.

So it is a contingent, factual matter that it is sometimes possible to form rational opinions concerning what specifically happened or will happen in given circumstances (I); it is a non-contingent, *a priori* matter that the only ways of doing this must be inductive ways (II). What people have done is to run together, to conflate, the question to which I is answer and the quite different question to which II is an answer; producing the muddled and senseless questions: "Is the universe such that inductive procedures are rational?" or "What must the universe be like in order for inductive procedures to be rational?" It is the attempt to answer these confused questions which leads to statements like "The uniformity of nature is a presupposition of the validity of induction." The statement that nature is uniform might be taken to be a vague way of expressing what we expressed by I; and certainly this fact is a condition of, for it is identical with, the likewise contingent fact that we are, and shall continue to be, able to form rational opinions, of the kind we are most anxious to form, about the unobserved. But neither this fact about the world, nor any other, is a condition of the necessary truth that, if it is possible to form rational opinions of this kind, these will be inductively supported opinions. The discordance of the conflated questions manifests itself in an uncertainty about the status to be accorded to the alleged presupposition of the "validity" of induction. For it was dimly, and correctly, felt that the reasonableness of inductive procedures was not merely a contingent, but a necessary, matter; so any necessary condition of their reasonableness had likewise to be a necessary matter. On the other hand, it was uncomfortably clear that chaos is not a self-contradictory concept; that the fact that some phenomena do exhibit a tolerable degree of simplicity and repetitiveness is not guaranteed by logic, but is a contingent affair. So the presupposition of induction had to be both contingent and necessary: which is absurd. And the absurdity is only lightly veiled by the use of the phrase "synthetic *a priori*" instead of "contingent necessary."

AFTERWORD

Inductive reasoning is so fundamental that we tend not to consider it as an aspect of any philosophical position which it is employed to support. For example, without inductive reasoning the arguments in favor of determinism would collapse into incoherence, the problem of mind-body interaction would assume a radically different character, and the teleological argument for God's existence would be severely weakened. But it would not normally occur to us to say of philosophical positions about determinism, interaction, or divine character, "Of course, before this position can be accepted, one must establish that induction is reliable." Normally, we simply presume that induction is reliable, and we employ it as one of many logical tools with which our arguments can be constructed. But if the sceptical position on induction were correct, the damage to positions on other philosophical issues would be extensive.

Perhaps this fundamental character of inductive reasoning should be regarded as evidence for a position such as Strawson's, in which it is held that there is nothing more fundamental than inductive reasoning itself, in terms of which a justification of induction could be constructed. But it should be noted that, unlike deductive principles of inference, induction can go wrong. There are cases in which our application of inductive methods is faultless, and our conclusion is nonetheless in error. Once again, we must consider the question raised in the Afterword to Chapter 11—is it too demanding to expect reliable sources of knowledge to be infallible? If not, then it is hard to see how induction can be saved. But if so, then may it not be appropriate at least to ask for an explanation of the significant difference between an acceptable fallible source of belief and an unacceptable one? But that would be to ask for one kind of justification of induction.

Finally, you may find it worthwhile to consider this question: If you decided that induction was not reliable, would it make any practical difference to you? Hume's response was that it should not. After all, the sceptical position on induction does not claim that we *will* make mistakes when we reason inductively, nor does it offer any more reliable alternative method of reasoning. It tells us that we naturally tend to reason inductively, and that induction is no worse than non-inductive alternatives, although perhaps no better. Why not, then, go ahead and reason inductively, but, perhaps, in our more reflective moments remind ourselves that the outcome is not as secure as we would like to think?

This argument has appeal, but before we accept it we should consider the wide variety of activities and institutions in which induction plays some part. For example, consider the ways in which we attribute moral responsibility to people for their actions. In particular, notice that we tend to excuse people from responsibility for the bad consequences of their actions if it is clear that they could not have known that those consequences would occur. Does that mean that if inductive reasoning is unreliable, and people could not be said to know what the consequences of most of their actions would be, that they would hardly ever be held responsible? (Try to imagine examples in which one could plead to be excused on the grounds that induction is unreliable.) Or are there other reasons for attributing responsibility which would apply even if the sceptic is correct about induction?

REVIEW QUESTIONS

Selection 51

1. Explain the distinction between Relations of Ideas and Matters of Fact. Why is this distinction important to Hume's argument?

2. What considerations does Hume take to show that we do not discover relations of cause and effect *a priori?* What significance does this have for the question whether we can rely on past experience?

3. Why can't we appeal to experience to establish the reliability of inductive reasoning, according to Hume?

4. Is Hume arguing that induction is unreliable, or does he have a different conclusion in mind? Explain.

Selection 52

5. Russell distinguishes between the claim that past uniformities cause expectations about the future and the claim that past uniformities give us good reason to have expectations about the future. What is the distinction, and why does he make it?

6. Why does Russell think we can never *prove* that we have discovered a law of nature?

7. State Russell's probabilistic version of the principle of induction. What does he mean when he says that probability is always relative to certain data?

8. Why does Russell claim that the inductive principle can neither be proved nor disproved?

Selection 53

9. What, exactly, does Mill mean by the claim that the course of nature is uniform?

10. What is induction by simple enumeration? How does it differ from scientific induction? What is the relationship of these questions to Mill's statement of "The Question of Inductive Logic"?

11. Mill says that induction by simple enumeration is a *valid process, though fallible*. What does he mean by that? Would Hume or Russell agree?

12. Explain how Mill thinks the law of cause and effect both supports and is supported by individual inductions by simple enumeration. Is Mill's position circular?

Selection 54

13. What is a *self-supporting* inductive inference, according to Black's account?

14. Explain carefully the way in which Black thinks a second-order argument may raise the degree of reliability of the rule it employs.

15. What are Salmon's objections to Black's position, and how does Black reply to them?

Selection 55

16. Strawson says that in some cases the demand for a justification of induction really is a demand to show that inductive arguments are deductively valid. Explain.

17. What is the "search for the supreme premise," and what are Strawson's criticisms of it?

18. What attempt to justify induction mathematically does Strawson discuss, and what are his criticisms of it?

19. What is wrong with the question, "Is the law legal?" How does Strawson compare this question to "Is induction justified?"

20. Strawson argues that induction is not a method of reasoning. What does he mean, and why is it important?

21. Strawson says that the desire to justify induction may rest in part on the confusion of two questions. What are the questions and how does he propose to deal with each of them?

I

Writing a Paper about Philosophy

Instructors in beginning philosophy courses often require their students to write one or more papers. While some students have no difficulty with such assignments, many are unsure about how to write a paper on a philsophical topic and find the writing of an assigned paper difficult and frustrating. The ability to write well is a skill based upon experience, hard work, and lots of practice. No set of rules about paper writing is a substitute for experience and practice. Consequently, the following remarks are not offered as a formula which, if followed, guarantees a high quality paper. Instead, they are simply some suggestions and tips about writing papers. A student who does everything suggested here will do a lot of hard work, and one must decide for oneself how much effort it is worthwhile to put into writing a paper. But each of the suggestions here has been helpful to some students, and if you are seriously concerned about improving the quality of your writing you should give all of them at least a little consideration.

The Purpose of the Assignment

A surprising number of students accept and complete writing assignments without having any clear idea what the assignment is supposed to achieve. But the chance of doing a good job is better if one knows why the instructor is assigning the paper. Here are some possibilities to consider:

1 The paper may be intended to measure achievement in the course. In this case, the instructor's purpose is to find out what the student has learned about a particular problem, or about the positions held by some philosophers. Or, the paper might be intended to measure what the student has learned about critical thinking—that is, about how to attack or defend a philosophical viewpoint.

2   The paper may be an instructional device, intended to get the student to learn details about some problem or viewpoint; or, it may be a kind of exercise designed to give the student practice in critical thinking.

3   The paper may be intended to promote self-knowledge. That is, the instructor may intend that as work on the paper progresses, the writer will become clearer about his or her own philosophical views, and the reasons the writer has for holding them.

Typical paper assignments are made with a combination of the above purposes in mind, but different instructors will emphasize different purposes. A careful writer will try to determine the major objectives the instructor has in making an assignment and then see that the paper offers clear evidence that those objectives have been achieved. Thus, for example, if an instructor wants to determine how much students have learned about critical thinking, it would be a serious error to write a paper which explained some philosophical viewpoint, but did not raise objections or offer supporting arguments for that viewpoint. An equally serious error would be committed in a paper presenting and defending the writer's own views when the intent of the assignment was to see how carefully some philosophical work had been read, and how well the writer had understood it.

Kinds of Papers

Let us distinguish four kinds of papers: (1)   the expository paper;   (2) the critical paper;   (3)   the developmental paper; and   (4)   the scholarly paper. An expository paper will deal with one or more philosophical works, and its major task will be to interpret and explain the claims and arguments presented in those works. Critical discussion and argument will be limited, or left out altogether. A critical paper, on the other hand, has argument and discussion of some philosopher's viewpoint as its major objective and employs only enough exposition to make clear what that viewpoint is, before the critical work begins. A developmental paper attacks some philosophical problem, attempting to work out a solution or to show why some kind of solution cannot succeed. Thus, it is least dependent upon exposition of existing philosophical works. Finally, the scholarly paper strives to trace the history and development of some problem, or of some philosophical position, as it has been presented in a body of works.

Of course, a paper may combine two or more of these objectives. But since the kinds of preparation, and even some of the skills required, vary from one kind of paper to another, a writer needs to be clear about which kind of job each part of the paper is supposed to do. Depending upon the purpose the instructor has in making a paper assignment, the assignment may specify the kind of paper the student should write. Or the instructor may indicate a preference for one type of paper rather than the others, without absolutely forbidding the other kinds. And many students will find that they are more successful with some kinds of papers than with others. All these factors should be kept in mind in deciding what kind of paper to write.

Choosing a Topic

Unless the instructor simply dictates the topic of an assigned paper, the student's first difficult decision is choosing an appropriate subject for the paper. A poorly chosen topic may leave the student with an impossibly difficult writing job. A well-chosen topic sometimes can make it seem as if the paper is writing itself.

Several factors must be considered carefully in choosing a topic. First, of course, one should take careful note of any requirements or restrictions in the paper assignment itself. Second, the student should seek a topic which will serve the purpose the instructor had in making the assignment, and about which the student will be able to write the kind of paper desired. Third, students should try to find topics which interest them. It is possible to grind out a paper of high quality about a topic which is totally uninteresting to the writer, but it is much easier to write well about something the writer finds personally interesting. A note of caution should be sounded here, however. Students sometimes find that they are so personally involved with a topic that they cannot think objectively and critically about it. It may be best to avoid such topics unless one is a very experienced and disciplined writer. Finally, if you can tell that the instructor is likely to be interested in some topics and bored by others, it makes good sense, other things being equal, to prefer a topic that will stimulate his or her interest.

It is a good idea to put together a list of possible topics. Questions may be raised in class, or as you read, which suggest good topics. The review questions or afterwords in the chapters of this book may suggest some topics. Still others may be suggested by looking over tables of contents for books on philosophy. Once there are half a dozen or more topics on the list, they can be compared to see which seems best to fit the requirements and purposes of the assignment. If there is doubt about whether a topic is acceptable or a good idea, it is worth asking the instructor about it. It frequently is not a good idea to ask other faculty members, graduate students, or advanced undergraduates, because they may not be familiar with the instructor's purposes in assigning the paper.

Do not be surprised or alarmed if the topic undergoes some change as you write the paper. Beginning students typically choose topics which are too big or too complicated. Then, as their papers develop, they realize the need to confine their remarks to some smaller set of issues. There is nothing wrong with reducing the scope of a paper, as long as the result is properly organized. A thorough treatment of a modest problem is usually preferable to incomplete and disconnected thoughts about a larger problem.

Following a Schedule

It is important to organize a writing schedule and to try hard to follow it. As soon as a paper has been assigned, deadlines should be chosen by which topic should be selected, reading and note taking completed, a first draft written, and a finished draft completed. The amount of time allotted to each job will vary according to the length and kind of paper, and according to the amount of time available for completing the assignment. But it is important to start early and, if possible, to allow more time for the completion of each job than it would normally require. Then, if problems or unplanned interruptions come up, there will be time to make adjustments and complete the paper on schedule.

A competent writer who works well under pressure often can write an acceptable short paper overnight. But it is risky to wait until the last moment, and the quality of writing can be improved considerably if several "cool-down" periods are allowed between different parts of the job. It is especially important to let at least a day or two pass between completing a first draft and beginning a final draft, and between completing a final draft and proofreading it before submission. Writers who have just finished a draft of a paper know too well what each sentence was intended to say. On reading over something just written one is likely to think that it says what one meant it to say, even if it is very badly written. After a cool-down period, one is better able to approach a draft as other readers would, and thus more efficiently detect incoherent sentences, vagueness or ambiguity, grammatical errors, and even simple mistakes in typing or spelling.

Reading and Notes

Unless you are planning a purely developmental paper, some reading will need to be done before writing can begin. And even for a developmental paper it is usually a good idea to read some related materials first. Sometimes instructors will suggest appropriate readings when a paper assignment is made. For students who need to locate readings without the instructor's guidance, *The Encyclopedia of Philosophy,* edited by Paul Edwards, is a good place to begin. It contains many excellent articles on philosophical issues and most of these contain some useful bibliographical information. Articles in philosophical journals can be located through use of *The Philosopher's Index,* which is published quarterly, and should be available in most good libraries. Such journal articles, however, are often too technical and specialized to be of much use to the beginning student.

It is important to keep the notes for the paper organized. The larger the paper, and the more notes there are, the more important this becomes. Date and number each page of the notes to provide a record of the order in which ideas occurred to you, and to make it easier to find each note when it is wanted. Follow the approach to reading and taking notes described in Chapter 3, and be sure to identify in each note the part of the text to which it pertains (it is frustrating to have to stop writing and reread several pages just to find a passage you wanted to write about). One simple way to correlate notes and text is to enter in the margin beside each note the page number(s) of the passage discussed in that note.

If a paper is to be a combination of basic types, for instance a combination of exposition and criticism, then it may be useful to devise a method for distinguishing kinds of notes. One simple procedure is to use different colors of ink when taking notes. Notes which are purely expository—that is, only about the content of the reading, can be written in one color, while critical comments, or questions can be put down in another color. For lengthy papers it may even be worthwhile to enter developmental remarks in still a third color, and so on. Then, as you plan the paper, and write it, you can quickly find the kind of notes wanted by looking only at those written in the appropriate color.

Writing the Paper

The physical facilities involved in writing are important. They should cause as little distraction as possible and contribute to efficient concentration of effort. Find a comfortable place to work without interruption or distraction. Have all the equipment and supplies gathered together ahead of time. Find writing tools which do not intrude on your thoughts and the paper. For example, one should not compose on a typewriter if that means too much attention must be given to the act of typing itself. If a draft is to be handwritten, one should not use a pen which is uncomfortable to hold, or likely to skip or smear. What is written should be easy to read. Avoid having to stop work to go out for more paper or other supplies.

Before beginning a draft of the paper, it is advisable to go over all notes and to construct a list of the topics to be discussed, points to be raised, arguments to be presented, and so forth. The result of arranging this list in the order of presentation in the paper will be an outline which can be followed in writing the first draft. A good outline is helpful, but it should not be overrated in importance. It is a waste of time to try to include in the outline every statement to be made in the paper. Nor should the outline be regarded as unalterable. As you write, it may become clear that adding or dropping some items, or changing the order of presentation, will make the paper more complete or easier to read, or more logical. Such improvements always justify departing from the outline. But when a complete draft of the paper is written, it is useful to see if an outline of the result can be drawn up. If it seems very hard to make an outline of a draft, that is a reliable indication that the draft is not well organized, and that a reader is likely to have trouble understanding how some parts of it are related to other parts.

The first draft of a paper should simply say whatever the writer wants to say, without undue attention to form, length, or style. The object at this time is to get the right content down in roughly the right order. In a second draft the writer can concentrate on how to say things clearly and effectively. Often, one's thoughts only become clear in the actual attempt to write them down. The first draft is the place to get thoughts organized, and get all of them on paper. When it is finished, let it alone for a day or two, and then look it over and note any problems in organization, gaps in the discussion, errors, or serious problems in communication. With these problems in mind, construct an outline for the finished draft of the paper.

The goal of a second or later draft should be communication with one's reader. This is the place to concentrate upon organization of paragraphs, grammatical structure, and choice of words. Remember that you are trying to argue rationally and convey information. Don't sacrifice clarity for the sake of elegant language or entertaining style. Avoid words or expressions you don't understand. Avoid irrelevant comments. Do use a dictionary. And remember at all times what kind of paper is to be written and why it was assigned. If you have difficulty writing clearly, find a copy of a simple guide to writing style (such as *The Elements of Style,* by Strunk and White), read it carefully, and make use of the advice to be found there.

When a second or later draft of a paper is completed, let a day or two pass and then read it over to see if the draft really says what you meant it to say. If it does not, make the required changes or start another draft.

Quotation, Paraphrase, and Plagiarism

Inexperienced writers frequently use quotations or paraphrases excessively. In many cases, this is an indication of failure to understand the purpose of a paper assignment. Direct quotation is appropriate where it is important to establish another author's choice of words. For example, it may be necessary to prove that an author really did say what you claim was said; or, to show that your interpretation of some passage is reasonable by pointing out the use of certain key words or expressions. Paraphrase may be appropriate if the intent is to express the gist of some passage before beginning to criticize it. But, if part of the purpose of an assigned paper is to induce the student to demonstrate that some philosophical work has been read and understood, quotation should be used very sparingly. The fact that a passage is copied does *not* show that its meaning is understood, why it was written, or what consequences it has for any philosophical issues. On the other hand, to explain in your own words, no matter how inelegantly, what a philosopher was saying, and why, will show the reader whether you have been successful in trying to master the work discussed. And the attempt to provide such an explanation will help in mastering the content of the work. Remember, the instructor is not usually looking for new insights into the works of some other philosopher in your paper but, instead, for information about *you* and your progress.

If the temptation to quote heavily occurs, try studying the work carefully and then writing about it without looking at it. Check it afterward to see if what is written is correct. Imagine that you are trying to explain it to someone who, for some reason, is unable to understand the original passage. If it is absolutely necessary to quote a few lines, then go ahead and do so. But, if it is impossible to proceed without quoting heavily, it must be asked whether you really do understand the work under discussion.

When quoting or paraphrasing, always give some citation—that is, indicate what work is being quoted, who wrote it, and where the quoted passage is to be found in the work. Complete citations may be required, or the instructor may approve some abbreviated form of citation, but do not quote or paraphrase without indicating the source in some fashion.

To use the words of some other writer in a way that suggests that they are the product of your own composition is to plagiarize. Plagiarism is illegal, against the rules of academic institutions, and a dishonest attempt to deceive the instructor about your progress. The purpose of an assigned paper certainly is not achieved by plagiarism, since copied portions of the paper are unlikley to have taught the writer anything, do not reflect the writer's accomplishments, represent no development of the writer's ideas, and generally waste everyone's time. If you are under pressure and find it impossible to complete an assignment when it is due, do *not* attempt to escape your problem by plagiarizing. Instead, talk frankly with the instructor and see if some satisfactory arrangement can be worked out. Most instructors would much prefer to discuss such a problem and try to find a way for the assignment to be completed, rather than to go through the effort involved in proving that a submitted paper is plagiarized and bringing action against the student.

The Paper as a Physical Object

When students in a beginning class turn in papers for an assignment, the instructor will be confronted with a large number of items to be handled, read, and returned after comments are made. It is to any student's benefit to submit a paper in a form which will be easily handled and which will not disrupt the instructor's attention as it is being read. Carelessly written and assembled papers offer their readers many distractions, but so do papers which are unnecessarily embellished in the attempt to make them appear attractive. Once you have taken the trouble to write a paper with all possible skill, you want the reader to focus completely on what has been said, with no distractions.

Choose the paper stock carefully. It should be standard size (8½ × 11 inches) and white. It should not be extremely thin, since thin paper is hard to handle, and lines from the page underneath usually show through the page on top. Most pages which are easily erased are also hard to write comments upon. If corrections are required, use a correcting fluid or correction tape.

If possible, type the paper, or have it typed. Avoid colored ribbons and exotic type faces. Double spacing the text will make the paper easier to read, and leave room for comments. If you must submit a handwritten paper, take pains to write clearly, with dark ink, and without smears.

Do use a title page on the paper, and be sure to identify the course, the assignment, the instructor, and yourself. Instructors often have papers to read from more than one course, and it is a distraction to spend time trying to find out what assignment a paper is intended to fulfill. It is also a good idea to number your pages and put your name next to the number on each page so that if a page becomes separated from the body of the paper it can be found and returned easily. A blank sheet at the back of the paper will protect the last page of the work and provide a place for the instructor to write any extensive comments.

Be sure to attach all pages securely. When mixed into a pile of other papers, pages bound with paper clips or folded corners tend to come apart quickly. A single staple in the upper left corner is usually adequate for short papers. Larger papers may require some kind of cover or binding. If the instructor indicates any preferences about such things, try to respect them. They probably are based on a carefully developed system for handling papers with a maximum of efficiency and protection for the student's work. In such systems, irregular papers tend to irritate, and to get set aside, And once set aside, chances are greater that a paper may get lost or be returned more slowly.

Some students include materials which are not required, such as illustrations, charts, or biographical sketches. They may even have their papers bound with spiral or post bindings. Generally, such unnecessary embellishments are not a good idea. Instructors will not confuse attractive appearance with high quality content, and unnecessary decoration of a paper will be ignored at best, or be a source of distraction or irritation to the reader at worst.

II

Biographical Notes on the Authors

Anselm, Saint (1033–1109) is regarded as the most significant theologian of the eleventh century. He belonged to the Benedictine Order, and was appointed Archbishop of Canterbury in 1093. His works include the *Monologion* (1076) in which he developed forms of the cosmological and teleological arguments, and the *Proslogion* (1077–78) in which the ontological argument is presented. Anselm was canonized in 1494.

Thomas Aquinas, Saint (c. 1226–1274) joined the Dominican Order at an early age and served for the rest of his life. The most important works of this prolific writer are the *Summa Theologica* and the *Summa Contra Gentiles*. His synthesis of Aristotelian philosophy with christian theology became the foundation of Roman Catholic doctrine. Generally regarded as the most important of medieval philosophers, Aquinas was canonized in 1323.

George Berkeley (1685–1753) was born in Ireland and studied at Trinity College in Dublin. At the age of twenty-eight he had published his three most important works: *An Essay Towards a New Theory of Vision, The Principles of Human Knowledge,* and *Three Dialogues Between Hylas and Philonous.* Berkeley worked enthusiastically but unsuccessfully to found a college in the Bermudas which would train clergymen. In 1734 he became a bishop in the Church of England

Max Black (1909–) studied at the Universities of Cambridge, Göttingen, and London. Now an emeritus professor of philosophy at Cornell University, he has written many articles and books, concentrating especially on problems in philosophy of language, and topics dealing with probability and induction.

Richard Booker Brandt (1910–) was born in Wilmington, Ohio, and educated at Cambridge and Yale University. He has taught at Swarthmore and the University of Michigan. Brandt is well known for his articles and books on ethics. Among his major works are: *Ethical Theory, Value and Obligation,* and *A Theory of the Good and the Right.*

Charlie Dunbar Broad (1887–1971) was one of the most important British philosophers of this century. He was educated at Cambridge, where he taught for many years. Broad's interest in a wide variety of philosophical issues was reflected in numerous publications, including *The Mind and Its Place in Nature, Five Types of Ethical Theory,* and *An Examination of McTaggart's Philosophy.*

Joseph Butler (1692–1752) was an important Anglican theologian of the eighteenth century. Born to a Presbyterian family, he joined the Church of England as a young man. After completing his studies at Oxford, he was ordained a priest and later became Bishop of Bristol, then Bishop of Durham. His major works are *Fifteen Sermons Preached at the Rolls Chapel* and *The Analogy of Religion.*

C. A. Campbell (1897–1974) taught for many years at the University of Glasgow. His philosophical position, a kind of idealism is presented in many articles and three books, *Scepticism and Construction, Of Selfhood and Godhood,* and *In Defense of Free Will.*

René Descartes (1596–1650) is regarded by many as the founder of modern Western philosophy. His philosophical interests were complimented by great interest in science and mathematics. Descartes invented analytic geometry and was impressed with the importance of the work of Galileo and Harvey. He refused to publish his major scientific work, *Le Monde,* during his lifetime because it contained some heretical doctrines. His best known philosophical works include *The Discourse on Method, The Meditations,* and *The Principles of Philosophy.*

John Dewey (1859–1952) is considered one of the most important American philosophers. He was born in Vermont and began his studies there. After completing his doctoral work at Johns Hopkins, he accepted a position at the University of Michigan. Later he held positions at the University of Chicago and Columbia University. Dewey was a prolific writer and an influential lecturer. Among his major works are *Ethics, Democracy and Education, Reconstruction in Philosophy, Human Nature and Conduct,* and *The Theory of Valuation.*

Ludwig Andreas Feuerbach (1804–1872) was born in Bavaria. He studied theology at Heidelberg and theology and philosophy at Berlin, where he taught for four years. When it was discovered that he had written a book, *Thoughts on Death and Immortality,* which was unsympathetic to Christianity he was dismissed from the university. From 1836 until his death he lived on a small government pension, income from his writings and his wife's interest in a pottery factory, and the charity of friends. Feuerbach's most important works include the *Critique of Hegelian Philosophy, The Essence of Christianity,* and *The Essence of Religion.*

Richard Mervyn Hare (1919–) is White's Professor of Moral Philosophy at Oxford University. His articles and books on ethics have been widely discussed in the postwar period. The most important of his works are *The Language of Morals* and *Reason and Freedom.*

John Harwood Hick (1922–   ) was born in Edinburgh and educated at Edinburgh and Oxford Universities. He served as a Presbyterian minister in England before beginning his teaching career. He has taught at Cornell, Princeton, Cambridge, and Claremont College, and is now at the University of Birmingham. Among Hick's most important works are *Faith and Knowledge, Philosophy of Religion,* and *Evil and the God of Love.*

Thomas Hobbes (1588–1679) entered Oxford University when he was fourteen. At twenty he became tutor and companion to the son of Lord Cavendish in which capacity he traveled extensively and met many leading thinkers of his time, as well as a variety of influential people. Hobbes's interests included the classics, mathematics, and the sciences, but his work on psychology, ethics, and politics has been most influential. Some of his most significant works are *The Elements of Law, Leviathan,* and *Human Nature.*

Baron d'Holbach, Paul Henri Thiry (1723–1789) was an outspoken materialist and atheist during the French Enlightenment. He traced a great deal of human misery to religious beliefs and practices. Among his works which produced the greatest controversy are *The System of Nature* and *Good Sense.*

John Hospers (1918–   ) has taught at Brooklyn College, Columbia University, the University of Minnesota, and the University of Southern California. He has written extensively on ethics, politics, and aesthetics. In 1972 Hospers was the Libertarian Party's candidate for President of the United States.

David Hume (1711–1776) was born in Edinburgh and began preparation for a career in law at Edinburgh University. But at age fifteen he left the university to follow his own course of studies. The outcome was the philosophical system presented in *A Treatise of Human Nature* (1739). Hume's important later works include *An Enquiry Concerning Human Understanding. An Enquiry Concerning the Principles of Morals,* and *Dialogues Concerning Natural Religion.* Hume is thought by many to be one of the most important Western philosophers.

Thomas Henry Huxley (1825–1895) was self-educated. He made many important biological discoveries, and is probably best known as the defender of Darwin's theories about evolution. Huxley's interest in philosophy resulted in many papers and lectures on topics in metaphysics, epistemology, ethics, and religion. Among his most important works are *Man's Place in Nature* and *Evolution and Ethics.*

William James (1842–1910) was born in New York City. His early education was irregular but enriching. After an unsuccessful year studying painting, James entered Harvard in 1861, studying chemistry, anatomy and physiology, and medicine. At Harvard he taught physiology, psychology, and philosophy. James was one of America's most original thinkers who made significant contributions to both philosophy and psychology. Among his most important works are *The Will to Believe and Other Essays, The Varieties of Religious Experience, Pragmatism,* and *The Meaning of Truth.*

Immanuel Kant (1726–1806) was born in Königsberg, East Prussia, where he received his education and served on the faculty of the university. His philosophical work produced a system of profoundly important views on epistemology, metaphysics, and ethics which changed the course of Western philosophy. Some of the most important of his numerous works are *Critique of Pure Reason, Prolegomena to All Future Metaphysics, The Foundations of the Metaphysics of Morals,* and *Critique of Practical Reason.*

Gottfried Wilhelm Leibniz (1646–1716) was born in Leipzig, where he entered the university at the age of fifteen. He studied mathematics and law, and received a doctorate of law in 1667. His most significant contribution to mathematics was the invention of the infinitesimal calculus. His philosophical efforts were devoted to developing a systematic account of the universe in which the principles of physics could be seen to depend upon principles of theology. Among his major works are *New System of Nature, Monodology, Essays in Theodicy,* and *New Essays on Human Understanding.*

Clarence Irving Lewis (1883–1964) was born in Massachusetts and educated at Harvard University. He taught philosophy at the University of California and at Harvard. Lewis worked in the areas of logic, epistemology, and ethics. His major works include *Mind and the World Order, Symbolic Logic* (with C. H. Langford), *An Analysis of Knowledge and Valuation,* and *The Ground and Nature of the Right.*

John Locke (1632–1706) was born to an English Puritan family. He studied at Oxford and became acquainted with a number of intellectually and politically significant individuals. Locke was concerned primarily with epistemology, ethics, and politics. His epistemological writings were very influential in European philosophy, and his moral and political ideas had great impact on the founders of the American Republic. The most significant of Locke's works include the *Essay Concerning Human Understanding, Two Treatises on Government,* and *Letters on Toleration.*

John L. Mackie (1917–   ) was born in Australia and studied at Sydney University and Oxford. After serving in the army during the Second World War he taught at Otego University, Sydney University, and the University of York. He is now a Fellow at Oxford University. Mackie has written several important articles and books on ethics, philosophy of science, and philosophy of religion.

Norman Malcolm (1911–   ) studied at the University of Nebraska, Harvard University, and Cambridge University. During the Second World War he served in the Navy. He has taught at Princeton University and is currently Professor Emeritus at Cornell University. Malcolm has written several important articles and books on epistemology and philosophy of mind including *Dreaming, Knowledge and Certainty, Thought and Knowledge,* and *Memory and Mind.*

Brian Herbert Medlin (1927–   ) was born in Adelaide, Australia, and educated at the University of Adelaide and Oxford University. He has taught at Oxford, Ghana, Swarthmore, and is now at Flinders University of South Australia. Medlin has contributed articles to several professional journals.

John Stuart Mill (1806–1873) was born in London and educated rigorously by his father. He was active for many social and political causes. Mill's work in epistemology and ethics has been extremely influential, and he is one of the most important British Empericists. Among his major works are the *System of Logic, An Examination of Sir William Hamilton's Philosophy, On Liberty, Utilitarianism,* and *Three Essays on Religion.*

George Edward Moore (1873–1958) was born in London and educated at Cambridge. He taught at Cambridge until his retirement, and his whole life was devoted to his intellectual activities. An extremely important philosophical figure, Moore's work in ethics and his defenses of common sense against extravagant metaphysical and epistemological theories have been very influential in British and American philosophy. His major works include *Principia Ethica, Ethics, Philosophical Studies,* and *Some Main Problems of Philosophy.*

William Paley (1743–1805) studied mathematics at Cambridge and taught philosophy there for nine years before becoming a minister in the Church of England. His liberal views in politics and religion prevented him from reaching high office in the church. Paley's works include three books which were widely read and employed as textbooks: *A View of the Evidences of Christianity, The Principles of Moral and Political Philosophy,* and *Natural Theology.*

Blaise Pascal (1623–1662) was born in Auvergne and educated by his father. He showed early genius for mathematics and science, writing his first major work on mathematics at the age of sixteen. In 1654 Pascal had a religious experience which effected his conversion and led to the development of the views expressed in his *Pensées.* While his scientific and mathematical discoveries were notable, Pascal is remembered today primarily because of his thoughts about human nature, religion, and faith.

Plato (427–347 B.C.) was born into a wealthy Athenian family and became a devoted student of Socrates. Upon the death of Socrates, Planto left Athens and settled in Megara. There he began to write his dialogues, of which we have over thirty today. At the age of forty, Plato returned to Athens and founded his Academy where students were taught mathematics, political science, and philosophy. Plato and his student, Aristotle, were among the most influential figures in the history of Western civilization.

John Bordley Rawls (1921–   ) was born in Baltimore and studied at Princeton University. He has taught at Princeton, Cornell University, and the Massachusetts Institute of Technology. He is now Professor of Philosophy at Harvard University. Rawls has written several widely discussed articles on ethics and social philosophy, and his *A Theory of Justice* is a major contribution to the literature.

Josiah Royce (1855–1916) was born in Grass Valley, California, and studied at the University of California, Johns Hopkins University, and in Germany. He taught at Harvard University. Royce developed a form of metaphysical idealism which he vigorously defended against his colleague, William James, but he was a prolific writer and made some contributions to nearly every branch of philosophy. Among his most significant works are *The Religious Aspect of Philosophy, The World and the Individual,* and *Philosophy of Loyalty.*

Bertrand Arthur William Russell (1872–1970) is undoubtedly one of the most significant and influential thinkers of the twentieth century. Russell studied mathematics and philosophy at Cambridge and taught there until he was dismissed in 1916 because of his activities as a pacifist. He supported himself with his writing, public lecturing, and a few brief teaching appointments until he returned to Cambridge in 1944. Russell was extremely active politically, and he wrote copiously about philosophy and the social issues which concerned him. It is hard to imagine treatment more mixed than that received by Russell. He was denounced, fined., imprisoned, and prevented from working. He also was awarded some of the highest honors, including the Order of Merit and the Nobel Prize for Literature. Particularly important among his hundreds of philosophical works are *The Principle of Mathematics, Principia Mathematica* (with A. N. Whitehead), *Our Knowledge of the External World, The Analysis of Mind, The Analysis of Matter,* and *An Inquiry into Meaning and Truth.*

Moritz Schlick (1882–1936) was born in Berlin and studied at the University of Berlin. After teaching for two years at the University of Rostock and another year at Kiel, he accepted a chair in philosophy at the University of Vienna, where he found the Vienna Circle and became one of the major proponents of logical positivism. His career ended when he was killed by a deranged student. Among his works are *Space and Time in Contemporary Physics* and *Problems of Ethics.*

J. J. C. Smart (1920–   ) was born in Cambridge and educated at the Universities of Glasgow and Oxford. He served with the British Army in India and Burma during World War II. Smart has taught at Princeton, Harvard, Yale, and the University of Adelaide. He is now at the Australian National University. Smart is well known as an advocate of materialism and for his writings on ethics. As well as numerous articles he has written *Philosophy and Scientific Realism* and *An Outline of a System of Utilitarian Ethics.*

Peter Frederick Strawson (1919–   ) was educated at Christ's College, Finchley and at Oxford University. He presently teaches at Oxford. Strawson has written several articles and is well known for his views on logic, philosophy of language, and metaphysics. His books, *Introduction to Logical Theory* and *Individuals,* have been influential in English and American philosophical thought.

Richard Wasserstrom (1936–   ) was born in New York City and studied philosophy and law at the University of Michigan and Stanford University. He has taught at Stanford, Tuskegee Institute, and UCLA, and is presently at the University of California at Santa Cruz. Wasserstrom is actively involved with issues concerning legal rights. He has written several articles and books on ethics and philosophy of law, including *The Judicial Decision* and *Philosophical and Social Issues: Five Studies.*

The terms included here are terms which a beginning student in philosophy might encounter but find unfamiliar or employed in a special way. Although it is long, this glossary is not complete, nor are the entries detailed. The aim has been to provide just enough information to help a reader get through a philosophical selection which contains some technical philosophical language. For terms not listed here, or for more extended discussions and explanations, one should consult a good unabridged dictionary, or the *Dictionary of Philosophy,* edited by Dagobert D. Runes (Littlefield, Adams and Company). Many of these terms are explained at length in the *Encyclopedia of Philosophy,* edited by Paul Edwards (Macmillan, 1967).

Accident See Essence.

Ad hoc Made up for the particular purpose at hand.

Ad hominem Critical comments directed at the character of a person, rather than at that person's claims or arguments.

A fortiori Said of a conclusion which is more certain than one to which it is compared.

Agent One who performs an action.

Agnosticism The view that certain kinds of fundamental claims cannot be known to be true or known to be false, especially that we cannot know whether God exists.

Altruism The pursuit of the good of others.

Amoral Neither moral nor immoral. Outside the moral realm.

Analysis Reduction to simpler component parts.

Analytic truth A statement in which the subject concept includes the predicate concept. A definitional truth. A statement whose denial involves a contradiction.

Anarchism The view that government with the power to coerce individual obedience should be abolished.

Antecedent See Conditional statement.

Antecedent cause An event which immediately precedes and necessitates the occurrence of another event.

Anthropomorphism A view that attributes human characteristics to nonhuman individuals.

Apodictic, apodeictic Absolutely certain. Necessarily true.

A posteriori An idea or belief which has its origins in experience and which could not be acquired or known without experience.

A priori An idea or belief which could be acquired or known independently of experience or observation.

Argument A group of statements in which one statement, called the *conclusion,* is supported by the others, called *premises.* The premises are intended to provide evidence or proof of the truth of the conclusion.

Assertoric A statement which asserts something as true, rather then merely possible.

Atheism The view that there is no God.

Atomism The view that there are fundamental, irreducible units (atoms) and that all things are composed of these units.

621

Attribute A quality, property, or characteristic of a thing.

Automatism The view that human and animal organisms are automata—that is, mechanisms governed by the physical laws of nature.

Autonomy Freedom. Self-determination and absence of external coercion or compulsion. An autonomous will is not subject to causal determination.

Axiology The study of the nature of values.

Axiom A basic statement or principle which cannot be deduced from other principles but which can be used as a starting point from which to deduce other statements.

Behaviorism The view that all human activity and behavior can be explained in terms of physical nature, without reference to concepts of mind, spirit, soul, or consciousness.

Cartesian Having to do with the views of Descartes.

Casuistry 1. The study of cases of conscience and methods for resolving conflicts of duty. 2. Specious or sophistical reasoning.

Categorical imperative According to Kant, the supreme moral law for all rational, autonomous beings. It admits of no exceptions and is to be contrasted with hypothetical imperatives.

Certain 1. What could not possibly be false. A necessary statement. 2. What could not be doubted. 3. An event which is inevitable or unavoidable.

Chance event 1. An event which occurs at random, or is uncaused. 2. An event which is unpredictable.

Cognition A broad term for experiences such as knowing, believing, thinking, wondering, observing, etc.

Cognitivism The view that moral judgments are assertions—that is, capable of being true or false. Opposed to noncognitivism, which is the view that moral judgments are not assertions but expressions of feelings, or commands, recommendations, etc.

Coherence theory of truth A theory which says that the truth of any statement consists in that statement's being consistent (cohering) with all the other statements in an accepted system of beliefs.

Compatibilism The view that causal determinism is consistent with human freedom and moral responsibility.

Concept An idea of the fundamental character or nature of something.

Conceivable Capable of being thought or imagined.

Conclusion See Argument.

Conditional statement A statement which asserts that if one set of conditions (the antecedent) is the case, then another set of conditions (the consequent) will be the case also. Schematically: *If (antecedent), then (consequent).*

Consequent See Conditional statement.

Consistent Two or more states of affairs are said to be consistent if it is possible for them to occur together. Two or more statements are said to be consistent if they could be true simultaneously. A single statement sometimes is said to be consistent if it is possible for it to be true—that is, if it is not self-contradictory.

Contiguous Immediately next to.

Contingent Capable of occurring, and capable of not occurring, said of states of affairs. Capable of being true, and capable of being false, said of statements.

Contradiction The denial of a statement. Two statements are contradictory when each must be false if the other is true, and each must be true if the other is false. One statement may be called a contradiction if it has contradictory parts.

Contrary statements Two or more statements related so that if one is true the other(s) must be false, but the falsehood of one does not imply the truth of the others.

Correspondence theory of truth The view that truth of a statement consists in agreement or fidelity to the actual situation.

Cosmological argument The attempt to base a proof of God's existence on the fact that natural objects exist. The "first-cause" argument.

Cosmology The study of the origin and structure of the universe.

Deduction Inferring a conclusion from premises such that, if they are true, the conclusion also must be true. Deductive arguments and deductive reasoning proceed by such inferences. Compare: Induction.

De facto Actually. Really. In fact.

Deism The view that God, although creator of the world, has no direct dealings with the world.

Demonstration A deductive proof of a statement.

Deontological ethics Any ethical view which does not make obligation depend entirely upon goodness.

Determinism The view that every event in the universe is totally a product of preceding causes and could not have occurred differently in any way unless the causes had been different.

Deus ex machina Any person, thing, concept, or process invented and introduced to solve some difficulty.

Dialectic The process of considering the merits and defects of opposing viewpoints, with the aim of developing a new position with all the merits and none of the defects of the original ones.

Dichotomy A division into two groups.

Disjunction A statement which asserts that one of two or more alternative conditions is the case but does not specify which one. Schematically: *A or B.*

Disvalue Negative value.

Dogma A belief or set of beliefs accepted without rational support, usually on the basis of authority or tradition.

Dualism See Monism.

Efficient cause The agent, action, or force which produces an effect. Compare: Formal cause, Final cause, Material cause.

Egoism The view that each person should pursue his or her own self-interest.

Emotivism The theory that moral utterances are expressions of feeling, rather than statements of objective fact. A noncognitivist ethical theory.

Empirical Based upon experience.

Empiricism In epistemology, the view that all knowledge of reality is a posteriori. Compare: Rationalism.

Entailment A logical relationship between two statements. If one statement entails another, then it is absolutely impossible for the second statement to be false when the first is true. The premises in a valid deductive argument entail the conclusion of that argument.

Epiphenomenalism The view that consciousness is a by-product of neural processes and can have no effect upon the course of those processes.

Epistemology The philosophical study of the sources and limits of human knowledge.

Equivocation Fallacious reasoning due to the ambiguity of a word or phrase.

Essence The attributes, properties, or characteristics a thing must have in order to be the thing it is. Other attributes are said to be *accidents.*

Ethics The philosophical study of moral conduct and values.

Excluded middle, law of The rule one or the other of two contradictory statements must be true, and that there is no third possibility.

Faculty An ability, power, or function. For example, the faculty of sight, or the faculty of reason.

Fallacy Strictly, an error in inference or reasoning. More broadly, a mistaken belief.

Final cause The goal, pursuit of which explains the occurrence of an event. Compare: Efficient cause, Formal cause, Material cause.

Form A pattern of reasoning in an argument, or a pattern of grammatical structure in a statement, which can be identified independently of subject matter. Formal logic studies methods for determining the validity or invalidity of arguments on the basis of their form, rather than their content.

Formal cause The pattern, or structure, or essence which determines the nature of something. Compare: Efficient cause, Final cause, Material cause.

Free will 1. The capacity to choose for oneself. 2. A will not determined by external influences. 3. A will not causally determined.

Generalization A statement which says something about all or some members of a class, as opposed to a statement about a single individual. "All rabbits are warm blooded" and "Some holidays occur in the summer" are generalizations.

Given, the Whatever is immediately present in experience, before it is interpreted or analyzed by the mind.

Hedonism In psychology, the view that pursuit of pleasure and avoidance of pain are the only motives for human action. In ethics, the view that pleasure and pain are the only bases for value and obligation.

Heteronomy of will The will's being determined by external or nonrational factors, such as desire or fear.

Heuristic Serving to find out, or to help stimulate investigation.

Hypothesis An assumption, conjecture, speculation, or theory not yet established by demonstration or observation.

Hypothetical imperative A conditional command of the form, "If you desire such and such, you should do so and so." Compare: Categorical imperative.

Hypothetical statement A conditional statement.

Idealism Any doctrine to the effect that reality is basically mental, and that what is called the physical world is actually a set of ideas or sensations which depend upon minds for their being.

Identity theory The view that all so-called mental events are identical with physical processes in the brain.

Ignoratio elenchi The fallacy of supposing that the point at issue is either proved or disproved by an argument which actually establishes something else.

Implication A relationship between statements. If A implies B, then the truth of B follows from the truth of A, and the inference from A to B will be valid.

Incompatibilism The denial of compatibilism.

Incontinence The condition of a person who is unable to overcome bodily or other desires by moral principles. Moral weakness of will.

Indeterminism The view that at least some events are not the inevitable products of preceding causes.

Induction A type of argument in which the conclusion follows from the premises with some degree of probability but not with certainty. Especially, inferring a generalization about a class of things on the basis of observation of some members of the class. Compare: Deduction.

Inference The process of judging a statement to be true on the basis of other statements accepted as true. Or, an argument whose premises and conclusion have been connected by such a process.

Innate idea An idea which is present in, or available to, the mind at birth and cannot be reduced to any combination of ideas derived from experience. The ideas of God or immortality are thought by some to be innate.

Instrumental good Good as a means to achieve or produce some desired end, but not good for its own sake.

Interactionism The view that mental events can have a causal influence on physical events, and that physical events also can have a causal influence on mental events.

Intrinsic good Good in itself, rather than as a means to some other goal.

Intuition The act or process by which one knows some truth immediately with no dependence upon inference or sense experience.

Ipso facto By the very nature of the case.

Law of nature A rule or principle which states that certain events are always preceded, accompanied, or followed by certain other events in some systematic way.

Libertarianism The view that the will is not causally determined.

Logic The study of correct inference and argument.

Logically false False in virture of logical considerations alone. Incapable of being true, thus not contingent.

Logically true True in virtue of logical considerations alone. Incapable of being false, thus not contingent. Logical truths are known a priori.

Material cause The matter, substance, or other stuff out of something arises or is formed. Compare: Efficient cause, Final cause, Formal cause.

Materialism The view that only matter exists, and that all events, processes, and entities are physical.

Matter That which takes up space, has mass, and is capable of motion or rest.

Maxim A rule of conduct.

Metaethics The study of the meaning of fundamental ethical terms ("good," "bad," "right," "wrong," "ought," etc.) and of the logical character of ethical reasoning.

Metaphilosophy The philosophical study of the goals and methods of philosophy itself.

Metaphysics The philosophical study of the nature of being (ontology) and of the origin and structure of the universe (cosmology).

Miracle An event which violates the laws of nature and which is explainable only by reference to forces outside nature.

Modus operandi The method or manner of proceeding.

Monism In metaphysics, the view that only one basic substance exists. Materialism is a kind of monism, as is idealism. Monism is to be contrasted with *dualism,* which holds that there are two basic kinds of substance (mind and matter), and with *pluralism,* which holds that there are many substances. In ethics, monism holds that there is only one intrinsic value, while pluralism admits many kinds of intrinsic value.

Motion 1. Change in physical location. 2. Any sort of change in shape, size, or place.

Mysticism The view that the basic nature of reality cannot be grasped or expressed rationally but may be grasped in an experience in which one becomes directly aware of one's relationship with the universe.

Naturalism 1. The metaphysical view that nature is all that exists. The denial of supernatural entities or forces. 2. The ethical view that moral values are to be found in nature, and thus have an objective status.

Naturalistic fallacy A mistake some critics allege is committed by naturalistic ethical theorists in thinking that moral judgments can be translated completely into factual statements.

Natural theology The attempt to base one's theory about the existence and character of God upon evidence to be found in nature.

Necessary condition What must be the case in order for some situation to occur, or for some statement to be true. Compare: Sufficient condition.

Necessary truth What could not be false under any circumstances. All logical truths are necessary truths. Necessary truth is known a priori.

Nomological Relating to laws.

Noncognitivism See Cognitivism.

Nonnaturalism The rejection of ethical naturalism.

Non sequitur An inference in which the conclusion does not follow from the premises.

Occasionalism The dualistic theory that mind and body are distinct and do not interact but appear to interact because God keeps them perfectly synchronized.

Omnipotent All-powerful. Unlimited in power and ability.

Omniscient All-knowing. Aware of all past, present, and future beings and events and of all possibilities as well as of reality.

Ontological argument The argument first devised by St. Anselm to show that the denial of God's existence is self-contradictory.

Ontology The study of the nature of being.

Panpsychism The view that all things are alive and participate in some form of consciousness.

Pantheism The view that God is all of reality, rather than distinct from some portions of it.

Paradox One or more statements which appear to involve some inconsistency but which all appear to be true.

Percept What is immediately before the mind in perception or sensation. The given in perception.

Perception Awareness of aspects of the world through the senses.

Phenomenalism The view that human knowledge of physical reality is limited to what can be learned from perception, and that all statements about physical reality can be translated into perceptual terms.

Phenomenology The attempt to describe experience without assuming any theoretical or conceptual frameworks, with the aim of discovering the underlying structure of experience.

Phenomenon Any object or event which appears to the senses.

Pluralism See Monism.

Posit To assert or entertain a statement, either because it is a self-evident truth or because it is arbitrarily assumed.

Potency The capacity to be or become something.

Premise See Argument.

Prima facie 1. Based upon immediate appearances. 2. Self-evident.

Primary quality A perceivable quality which actually exists in the object perceived, as opposed to a quality *caused* by the perceived object but existing only in the mind of the perceiver (a secondary quality). Spatial extension, shape, and motion are some commonly recognized primary qualities, while color and sound are examples of secondary qualities.

Proposition An assertion which may be true or false. A statement.

Pro tanto To a certain extent.

Rationalism The epistemological view that knowledge of reality can be obtained a priori. Compare: Empiricism.

Realism 1. The metaphysical view that reality exists independently of mind or conscious activity. The rejection of idealism. 2. In epistemology, the view that what is perceived exists independently of the act of perception. *Naive realism* maintains that things are just as they appear to be. *Representative realism* claims that in perception we are immediately aware of percepts which, with some interpretation, represent to us the condition of the perceived object.

Reductio ad absurdum The method of disproving a statement by assuming that it is true and then deriving a contradiction or obvious falsehood from it.

Reductionism The view that phenomena of one kind can all be viewed as complex structures of phenomena of some other kind. For example, that biological phenomena really are complex events of physics, or that "mental" phenomena all are really neurophysiological events.

Relativism The ethical view that the correctness of one's moral behavior must be judged in terms of principles accepted in one's own culture or society.

Scepticism See Skepticism.

Secondary quality See Primary quality.

Self-contradiction A statement with contradictory elements. Any logical falsehood.

Self-evident Known to be true without appeal to evidence or inference.

Sensation Perception.

Sensum A percept.

Sense datum A percept.

Skepticism The view that a kind of knowledge is impossible.

Solipsism The view that the solipsist is the

only reality, and that all other persons, things, and events are products of the conscious activity of the solipsist.

Sound argument A valid argument with true premises. The conclusion of a sound argument must be true.

Substance That which can exist by itself and in which the properties or qualities exist. Metaphysical dualism regards mind and matter as separate kinds of substance.

Substratum Substance.

Sufficient condition That which by itself guarantees that some situation occurs, or that some statement is true. Compare: Necessary condition.

Sui generis Unique, alone of its kind.

Summum bonum The supreme good. The ultimate end to which all human activity is directed.

Syllogism A deductive argument consisting of two premises and a conclusion, all of which are generalizations.

Synthetic truth A true statement in which the subject concept does not include the predicate concept and the denial of which is not self-contradictory.

Tautology 1. A true analytic statement. 2. A true analytic statement which is so obvious it is trivial and uninformative.

Teleological arugment The attempt to prove God's existence by appealing to evidence of design or purpose in nature.

Theism Any view which asserts the existence of a personal God separate from the physical world.

Theodicy The attempt to account for the existence of evil, given the supposition that God is a morally good creator.

Theology The study of God and God's relation to the world.

Utilitarianism The ethical theory which directs all action to aim at maximizing human happiness.

Valid A characteristic of correct deductive arguments, such that it is impossible for the conclusion to be false if all the premises are true.

Will The faculty by which one decides or chooses among alternatives.

†